William Belsham

Memoirs of the kings of Great Britain of the house of Brunswick-Lunenburg

William Belsham

Memoirs of the kings of Great Britain of the house of Brunswick-Lunenburg

ISBN/EAN: 9783742827012

Manufactured in Europe, USA, Canada, Australia, Japa

Cover: Foto ©ninafisch / pixelio.de

Manufactured and distributed by brebook publishing software (www.brebook.com)

William Belsham

Memoirs of the kings of Great Britain of the house of Brunswick-Lunenburg

MEMOIRS

OF THE

KINGS OF GREAT BRITAIN

OF THE HOUSE OF

BRUNSWIC-LUNENBURG.

BY W. BELSHAM.

VOL. I. AND II.

THIRD EDITION.

Ac mihi quidem videntur huc omnia effe referenda ab iis qui præfunt aliis, ut ii qui eorum in imperio erunt, fint quàm beatiffimi. CICERO.

DUBLIN:

PRINTED FOR J. MILLIKEN, NO. 32, GRAFTON-STREET.

M DCC XCVI.

INTRODUCTION.

At the æra of the Revolution, the grand fabric of liberty, which it had been the labor of ages to erect in this island, was at length completed; and in one of the principal nations of the earth, a system of government was by general assent established, which had for its basis the unalienable rights of man, and professing as its grand end and object, the happiness of the people. The design of the following Memoirs is to shew, by an impartial delineation of the interesting events of the succeeding reigns, how far this end has been kept in view, how far it has been deviated from, and in what respects the general system of freedom is still susceptible of enlargement and security. In consequence of the happy emancipation of these realms, by the expulsion of a wretched and merciless bigot, we were necessarily involved in a war with France, then in the zenith of prosperity, and governed by a monarch of the most aspiring ambition, supported by a degree of power truly formidable. After a long and bloody conflict, however, France was compelled to relinquish her projects in favor of the abdicated House of Stuart; and to acknowledge, by a formal and solemn treaty, WILLIAM prince of Orange as king of Great Britain. From this period, a new scene opens to our view; and England, confirmed and established in the possession of her own liberty, appears in the high and exalted character of the defender of the liberties of Europe. And it is chiefly through the efforts of this country, in which the sacred flame of freedom was happily preserved, that Europe was able to withstand, and at length effectually to baffle and defeat, the vast hopes and projects of LOUIS XIV. who seemed to extend his views to no less than universal dominion. Scarcely was the treaty of Ryswick signed *, when intrigues and negociations were revived and prosecuted by all the European courts, with unintermitted and almost unprecedented ardor and activity. The declining health of the king of Spain was the cause of this mighty internal agitation; at whose decease it became a matter of great and anxious doubt, upon whom the succession of that vast monarchy would devolve. The two most potent claimants were the emperor Leopold as head and heir-general of the House of Austria, and the dauphin of France, who was descended from Isabella eldest daughter of Philip IV. whose marriage, however, was accompanied by a formal renunciation of her eventual pretensions to the Spanish crown, which would otherwise, according to the rules of succession established in Spain, have indubitably superseded all other claims. The grand object of the ambition, both of the king and kingdom of Spain, was to secure, and to which of all the different claimants was apparently a very subordinate consideration, the entire and undivided devolution of the

* A. D. 1697.

Spanish monarchy; which included not only Spain and the Indies, but the two Sicilies, Milan, Sardinia, and the Low Countries; and which had long been in a state of extreme political debility, bending, as it were, beneath the pressure of its own enormous weight.

King William, however, who had no other end in view than to maintain the balance of power, and to preserve the general tranquillity of Europe, paid little attention to national prejudices originating in pride and folly, or even, as it must be acknowledged, to national rights and privileges, in the measures which he scrupled not to adopt, for the accomplishment of purposes so desirable and important. He concluded, therefore, with Louis, a secret treaty of partition, by which, at the decease of the king of Spain, the two Sicilies, and all the possessions of Spain eastward of the Pyrenées, were to be for ever united to the French monarchy; the Duchy of Milan was allotted to the emperor; and it was agreed, that the kingdom of Spain, and its remaining appendages, should revert to the electoral prince of Bavaria, who was descended from the second daughter of Philip IV. father of the reigning monarch. This plan, however, being rendered abortive by the death of the young prince, another treaty was concerted without the knowledge or participation of the court of Madrid, by which, in addition to her former allotment, France obtained the important Duchies of Lorraine and Bar, the Duchy of Milan being ceded to the duke of Lorraine by way of equivalent; and the arch-duke Charles II. son to the emperor was substituted as heir to the monarchy of Spain, in the room of the electoral prince. The king of Spain, from whom this treaty could not long remain concealed, exasperated at the conduct of king William, and softened by the attentive and adulatory court paid to him by Louis, who dexterously contrived to throw the whole odium of this transaction upon the king of England, was at length prevailed upon, notwithstanding his former predilection for the emperor, to make a will, by which he nominated as his sole heir the duke of Anjou, second son to the dauphin; who, supported by the power of France, would, as the Catholic king was incessantly and flatteringly told, be able to prevent what he so much dreaded, the dismemberment of the Spanish monarchy.

The death of that monarch taking place after a short interval, the Court of Versailles declared its determination of accepting the will, notwithstanding the formal renunciation of the infanta Isabella, and the actual existence of the treaty of partition; alleging, " that as the object of that treaty was the preservation of the general tranquillity, and that object could not, in present circumstances, be obtained by a strict adherence to this engagement, a departure from the letter of the treaty was clearly justifiable, if it arose solely from a desire of acting in more perfect conformity to the spirit of it."

At the meeting of parliament, in which the tory interest now predominated, the partition treaty was reprobated without any reserve, as a measure unjust in its origin, and disgraceful in its issue. It was styled, in the vehemence of debate, " a felonious treaty;" and so high did the resentment and indignation of the commons arise, that the lords Somers, Halifax, Orford, and Portland were actually impeached at the bar of the house of Peers, as the principal advisers and promoters of this treaty, which was in reality the sole project of the king himself, whose conduct on this occasion, notwithstanding the rectitude of his motives, must be acknowledged not easily reconcilable to the dictates either of justice or policy.

The

The nation in general, however, entertained the most alarming apprehensions at this vast and unexpected addition to the power of the house of Bourbon; and their fears and jealousies were kindled into rage by the impolitic conduct of Louis, who, on the death of king James, which happened about this time, formally recognized the pretended prince of Wales as true and lawful sovereign of Great Britain. The king, encouraged by the prevailing disposition of the nation, entered into an alliance with the emperor and the united provinces, in which all kings, princes and states were invited to join, in order to obtain satisfaction for the house of Austria, and ample and permanent security for the preservation of the common liberties of Europe. The parliament being dissolved, another was summoned to meet in December 1701, in which the Whigs again recovered their ascendency; and the royal speech at the opening of the session, recommending, in very animated and energetic language, unanimity in the prosecution of the most vigorous and decisive measures, was received with enthusiastic and unbounded applause. "I promise myself," said the king, "you are met together full of that just sense of the common danger of Europe, and that resentment of the late proceedings of the French king, which has been so fully and universally expressed in the loyal and seasonable addresses of my people. The eyes of all Europe are upon this parliament. All matters are at a stand, till your resolutions are known. Let me conjure you to disappoint the only hopes of our enemies by your unanimity. I have shewn, and will always shew, how desirous I am to be the common father of all my people. Do you, in like manner, lay aside parties and divisions. Let there be no other distinction heard of among us for the future, but of those who are for the protestant religion and the present establishment, and of those who

mean

mean a popish prince and a French government.—If you do in good earnest defire to fee England hold the balance of Europe, and to be indeed at the head of the proteftant intereft, it will appear by your right improving the prefent opportunity." The king, the parliament, and the nation feemed now animated with the fame fpirit, and in no period of his reign had William attained to fo great a height of popularity as at the prefent crifis; and all Europe, fixing their attention upon this monarch, and regarding him with grateful and affectionate veneration, as the great affertor of its liberties—as the head, heart, and hand of the confederacy—was eager with the expectation of feeing him once more in the field, leading on to battle the armies of that grand alliance, originally projected by him, and now revived with frefh fpirit and vigour; and which, in the prefent exhaufted ftate of France, it was prefumed, could fcarcely fail to be attended with the moft fignal and glorious fuccefs. The king, however, perceived his health and ftrength rapidly declining; and he declared to the earl of Portland, that he fhould not live to fee another fummer. On the 21ft of February, in riding to Hampton-court from Kenfington, his horfe fell under him, and his collar-bone was fractured by the violence of the fhock. Though no immediate fymptoms of danger appeared, this accident haftened his diffolution, which took place *March* 8, 1702, in the 52d year of his age. The recital of the actions of this monarch forms his beft and higheft eulogium. His character was diftinguifhed by virtues rarely found amongft princes—moderation, integrity, fimplicity, beneficence, magnanimity. Time, which has caft a veil over his imperfections, has added luftre to his many great and admirable qualities. His political views were in the higheft degree laudable and upright. He had true ideas

of

of the nature and ends of government: and the beneficial effects of his noble and heroic exertions will probably defcend to the lateft generations; rendering his name juftly dear to the friends of civil and religious liberty, and his memory ever glorious and immortal.

Never did the death of any monarch, that of Guftavus Adolphus in the midft of his career of victories againft the houfe of Auftria perhaps excepted, excite throughout the kingdoms of Europe more general grief and confternation than that of king WILLIAM. Though the grand alliance againft France was now completed, the different powers, of which this vaft body was compofed, deprived by this unexpected ftroke of the hero in whofe wifdom and rectitude they confided, and under whofe banners they had been accuftomed to engage, no longer exhibited any fymptoms of animation or vigor. Such was the prevailing dread of the power of France, which from the commencement of the adminiftration of Cardinal Richelieu had been elevated to the prefent alarming height by an almoft uninterrupted feries of military triumphs, that the alliance now formed was confidered as by no means adequate to the accomplifhment of its object in cafe of the defection of England; and how far Anne of Denmark, who now fwayed the fceptre of that powerful kingdom, was difpofed to adopt the counfels or to purfue the mighty projects formed by her illuftrious predeceffor, was confidered as a queftion highly problematical. The doubt, however, was quickly refolved; for the queen, who was laudably ambitious of popularity, finding the nation and parliament ftrongly inclined to war, and influenced by the reprefentations of the earls of Marlborough and Godolphin, who demonftrated the imminent danger to which the liberties of Europe would be expofed, were England to act with indifference or indecifion in the prefent crifis, declared

her

her refolution to fulfil, in their utmoſt extent, all the political engagements of the late king. To give efficacy to this refolution, the earl of Godolphin was placed at the head of the treafury, and the earl of Marlborough advanced to the rank of captain general of all her majefty's forces, to the extreme fatisfaction of the allies, who had, from his paſt fervices, already formed very high ideas of his military talents. This nobleman was alfo invefted with the character of ambaffador extraordinary and plenipotentiary from her majefty; and fent into Holland, in order to concert meafures with the ftates, and to affure them, as well as the other powers of the alliance, whofe ambaffadors were affembled at the Hague, of the queen's favorable fentiments and zealous attachment to the common caufe and intereft. In purfuance of the fpirited exertions of this able negociator, war was declared againſt France on the very fame day at Vienna, London, and the Hague, to the furprife and chagrin of the court of Verfailles, which had entertained the flattering hope that the projects of the allies would be entirely difconcerted by the death of the king of England, and had received the intelligence of that event with the moſt indecent marks of exultation. The war commenced with the fieges of Keiferfwart and Landau, both which fortreffes furrendered to the arms of the allies, after a very long and vigorous refiftance. The earl of Marlborough arriving at the camp in June, immediately took upon him the command of the allied army; the earl of Athlone, who had pretenfions in quality of Veldt-Marefchal of the Dutch forces to divide the command, and whofe military fame was not inconfiderable, being obliged by the ftates to relinquiſh his claim. The French army under Marechal Boufflers, precipitately retiring before the allies, the earl of Marlborough fucceffively invefted and captured the towns of Venlo, Ruremond,

mond, Stevenſwart, and Liege; and, by the judgment and ſkill with which he conducted all his meaſures, confirmed the confidence of the public, and fully eſtabliſhed his reputation as an able and enterpriſing general. Very ſplendid ſucceſs alſo attended the naval operations of the preſent ſummer: for though the duke of Ormond and Sir George Rooke failed in their attempt on Cadiz, they received intelligence, on their return to England, that the Spaniſh flota had put into the port of Vigo; and, attacking that place with reſiſtleſs intrepidity, broke the immenſe boom which extended acroſs the entrance of the harbor, reduced the forts by which it was defended, and deſtroyed or captured the whole fleet of men of war and galleons which had retreated thither for ſecurity.

When the new parliament met, an addreſs was preſented to the queen by the commons, congratulating the ſucceſs of her majeſty's arms, which had, as they choſe to expreſs it, ſignally *retrieved* the ancient honor and glory of the Engliſh nation. This was univerſally underſtood as an oblique reflection upon the memory of the late king; and it ſtrongly indicated the predominance of the Tories, who were now the favored and governing party. Of this, however, a much more important and deciſive proof was afforded, by the introduction of a bill againſt occaſional conformity—a practice by which the church was declared to be expoſed to the moſt imminent danger. This bill, which was carried through the houſe of commons by a prodigious majority, was, after long and vehement debate, thrown out by the lords.

Early in the ſpring, A. D. 1703, the earl, now duke of Marlborough, paſſed the ſea, and, at the head of the allies, opened the campaign with the ſiege of Bonne; after

ter the reduction of which, he marched towards the French army commanded by Marechal Villeroy, with an intention to give them battle: but at his approach, that general thought proper to retire within his lines, after setting fire to his camp; and the duke was obliged to satisfy himself with the conquest of the towns of Huy, Limburg, and Gueldres. In the course of this year, the king of Prussia and duke of Savoy joined the grand alliance; and the arch-duke Charles, second son to the emperor, who now assumed the title of king of Spain, was convoyed to Lisbon by an English squadron, as the claimant of a kingdom in which he did not as yet possess a single foot of land.

In the ensuing session of parliament, the occasional conformity bill was again revived by the high-church faction; the most violent partisans of which attempted, though in vain, to secure the success of it by annexing it as a tack to the land-tax bill. This was absolutely discountenanced by the ministers of the crown, and the bill itself but faintly supported by the court party, the great leaders of which, Godolphin and Marlborough, now began, from political motives, to connect themselves with the Whigs: and though the bill passed by a majority of fifty voices, it was again rejected by the lords, who would not even deign to give it a second reading. This parliament is distinguished in the English annals by the perpetual misunderstandings which prevailed between the two houses; and this winter a very remarkable dispute arose, which originated in an accidental and apparently inconsiderable cause. The shameless and scandalous manner in which the commons were wont to decide upon all petitions relative to contested elections in favor of the predominant party, was at this time perhaps more than usually notorious: and the returning officers, who happened to be in that interest, were emboldened

boldened by it to exercife the groffeft partiality in admitting or rejecting votes, knowing it might be done with perfect eafe and impunity. At the laft general election, however, the vote of one Afhby, an inhabitant of the borough of Aylefbury, being rejected by White the returning officer, he had the fpirit and refolution to commence an action at common law againft White for illegally depriving him of his franchife; and obtained a verdict for damages, at the enfuing affizes for the county of Bucks. The court of queen's bench, however, being moved to quafh all proceedings in this matter, as contrary to the privileges of the houfe of commons, the three puifne judges were of opinion, that the verdict could not be fuftained. But that great and upright magiftrate, lord chief juftice Holt, at this time prefiding in the court, declared in the moft decifive terms, " that the verdict in queftion was both legal and juft;—that though the houfe of commons poffeffed a feparate and independent jurifdiction, agreeably to the conftitution of parliament, fo far as to determine, in cafe of appeal, which of the different candidates were duly elected; yet that their authority did not fuperfede the common courfe of judicial proceedings in the courts fitting at Weftminfter, which founded their decifions on the known laws of the land, and the evidence which came regularly and properly before them; and which neither could nor would take cognizance of the proceedings of the houfe of commons, nor of the grounds of their proceedings. Where a legal right exifted, and fuch, faid this able magiftrate, is the franchife of an elector; the law, of which the courts of juftice are the fole difpenfers, will protect him in the enjoyment of that right.—That the houfe of commons were not competent to decide judicially, though they might be occafionally compelled to exercife their difcretion, in cafes of this nature, evidently ly appeared from their utter inability to grant redress, whatever might be the magnitude of the injury sustained: that if this exorbitant claim were once established, the subject might be deprived of his dearest rights, by the mere arbitrary will and pleasure of the house of commons—the most flagrant abuses of power might be committed with impunity, nay with applause and triumph, by men holding public offices, who were thus placed beyond the reach of the arm of public justice; and by a monstrous solecism in legislation and jurisprudence, an acknowledged and invaluable right might be grossly and openly violated, and the injured party remain wholly destitute of any legal or regular means of reparation or redress." The verdict, notwithstanding these cogent reasonings, was however reversed; but the cause was, by writ of error, immediately brought before the house of lords; who after requiring the opinions of the twelve judges, and debating the matter at great length, and with great ability, determined almost unanimously to supersede the judgment pronounced in the queen's bench, and to affirm the verdict originally given at the county assizes. The house of commons, enraged at these proceedings, declared by a vote of the house, " that Matthew Ashby having, in contempt of the jurisdiction of that house, commenced and prosecuted an action at common law against William White for not receiving his vote at an election for burgesses to serve in parliament for the borough of Aylesbury, was guilty of a high breach of the privileges of that house; and that all attornies, solicitors, counsellors, and serjeants at law, soliciting, prosecuting, or pleading in any such cause, were guilty of a high breach of the privileges of that house." And they ordered these resolutions, signed by the clerk of the house, to be affixed to Westminster Hall gate. So far, however, was the intrepid magistrate at the head of the

law

law from being intimidated by this imperious language, that he is said publicly to have declared, that if any messenger of the house of commons presumed to enter that hall, in order to seize the person of any attorney or pleader by virtue of his warrant, he would immediately commit him to Newgate. The house of lords, on their part, passed votes justificatory of their own conduct; copies of which were transmitted to all sheriffs and borough-reeves throughout the kingdom. The commons, finding the general voice of the people declare strongly in favor of their antagonists, seemed disposed to let it rest in its present state, and the judgment of the lords was duly and regularly executed; upon which, five other inhabitants of the borough of Aylesbury brought their several actions for damages, upon the same grounds. This threw the house of commons into a new ferment; and by their own authority they committed these five men to prison, where they lay three months, without however offering to make any submission. After the money bills were passed by the commons, and not till then, a motion being made in the queen's bench in behalf of the prisoners, for a *habeas corpus*; the three puisne judges declared themselves of opinion, as before, that the court could take no cognizance of the matter. But the chief justice, a man inflexible to ill, and obstinately just, maintained, that a general warrant of commitment for breach of privilege was of the nature of an execution: and as it appeared upon the face of the warrant itself, that the prisoners had been guilty of no legal offence, unless to claim the benefit of the law in opposition to a vote of the house of commons was such, it was his opinion that they ought instantly to be discharged. This opinion however not availing in opposition to that of the majority of the bench, the prisoners were remanded; in consequence of which, they moved for a writ of error, to bring the

matter

matter before the Lords. As this, agreeably to the forms of law, could only be obtained by a petition to the crown, the commons presented an address to the queen, humbly requesting her majesty that the writ of error might not be granted; and they also took upon them to affirm, that, in this case, no writ of error could lie. To this address the queen with great moderation and prudence replied, that she hoped never to give her faithful commons any just ground of complaint; but to obstruct the course of judicial proceedings was a matter of such high importance, that she thought it necessary to weigh and consider carefully what it might be proper for her to do. The commons received this answer in sullen silence; and immediately ordered the prisoners to be removed from Newgate into the custody of their sergeant at arms, lest they should be discharged in consequence of the queen's granting a writ of error. They likewise resolved, that the lawyers who had pleaded on behalf of the prisoners, on the return of the *habeas corpus*, were guilty of a breach of privilege; and ordered them to be taken into custody. The lords upon this voted, " that, for subjects to claim their just rights in a course of law, was no breach of privilege—that the imprisonment of the men of Aylesbury was contrary to law—and that the writ of error could not be refused, without a violation of MAGNA CHARTA." This was followed by an address to the queen, humbly beseeching her majesty to give immediate orders for issuing the writ of error. The judges, moreover, now happily recovering from their terrors, ventured to decide, that a petition for a writ of error was a petition of right, and not of grace. And the queen was pleased, in the most condescending terms, to reply to this address, " that she would certainly have complied with their lordships' request in regard to the writ of error, but that, as it now became necessary to put an end to the

session,

session, she knew it could produce no effect." The lords, considering this as a decided victory, immediately returned their humble thanks to her majesty, for this instance of her majesty's regard for the legal and impartial administration of public justice. The queen, that very day, March 14, put an end to the session; and on the 5th of April 1705 the parliament was dissolved by proclamation. "It was no small blessing," says bishop Burnet, with his accustomed solemnity, "to the queen, and to the nation, that they got well out of such hands." And it must indeed be acknowledged, that the violence and malignity manifested in their general conduct, were productive of much less evil than might reasonably be apprehended.

As, in order to exhibit a connected view of this memorable controversy, the order of events has been somewhat anticipated; it is now necessary to advert to various preceding transactions of great moment and importance. Though it must be allowed that nothing can be more uninteresting or uninstructive, in general, than the detail of military operations; yet, as the campaign of the year 1704 is one of the most remarkable in modern history, and displays the unrivalled talents of the duke of Marlborough in the most brilliant and striking point of view, it cannot but excite such emotions of curiosity as demand more than ordinary attention. In the month of January, count Wrattislau, the imperial ambassador, presented a memorial to the British court, in which he represented the alarming and dangerous situation to which the emperor and the empire were reduced, in consequence of the rapid success of the French arms in Germany, and the defection of the Elector of Bavaria, who had entered into a strict confederacy with France; had joined the armies of that monarchy with all his forces; had seized the cities of Augsburg, Ulm, and Passau, and threatened to attack even the imperial capital of Vienna itself. The emperor, therefore, implored the aid and protection of the queen and people of ENGLAND to save the ROMAN EMPIRE from impending ruin. This application, so glorious to the English nation, was not made in vain. The duke of Marlborough received orders from the queen, to concert with the states the most eligible means of accomplishing this great object. On his arrival at the Hague, he represented to their high mightinesses the necessity of making a powerful effort for the relief of the empire; and proposed that, as the frontiers of Holland were now perfectly secure, he should be permitted to march with the grand confederate army to the banks of the Moselle, there to fix the seat of the war. And as the French court would, in consequence of this diversion, be led to entertain serious apprehensions for the safety of their own territories, they would be compelled to desist from any farther prosecution of their vast and ambitious projects in Germany. Under this veil did that great commander conceal his real design, which he communicated only to the pensionary Heinsius, and two or three other leading persons, whose influence might obtain a sanction to the measure whenever a public avowal of it should be deemed necessary. The consent of the States being with some difficulty procured, and the campaign at length opened, the proposed march to the Moselle accordingly took place. Marechal Tallard, who commanded the French army, apprehending Traerbach to be in danger, and that the duke's intentions were to penetrate into France on that side, took steps to obstruct his Grace's farther progress to to the east. To the amazement, however, not only of the French general, to whom the Duke's movements were wholly incomprehensible, but to all Europe, whose attention was now fixed on this interesting scene, the allied army passed the Rhine May 26,

and,

INTRODUCTION.

and, in a few days after, the Maine and the Neckar. On his arrival at Ladenburg, June 3, the Duke thought proper to throw off the mafque; and he wrote from thence a letter to the States, acquainting their High Mightineffes, that he had received orders from his fovereign the Queen of England, to adopt the moft vigorous meafure to deliver the Empire from the oppreffion of France—that, for this purpofe, he wasproceeding on his march to the Danube, and he hoped their High Mightineffes would not hefitate to allow their troops to fhare in the glory of this enterprife. The States, finding it impracticable to recede, thought it advifable to comply with a good grace, and immediately difpatched a courier to inform the duke that his defign met with their unanimous approbation—that they entrufted their troops entirely to his difpofal, placing the moft perfect reliance on his Grace's fkill, experience and difcretion. This difficulty being thus happily furmounted, the duke proceeded on his expedition; and at Mildenheim he had an interview with prince Eugene, in which thefe two confummate generals agreed upon their future plan of operations. The prince expreffing his admiration of the fine appearance of the troops after fo long and fatiguing a march, and particularly of the uncommon fpirit apparent in their countenances, the duke of Marlborough politely replied, that this might be eafily accounted for, by the animation which the prefence of his highnefs could never fail to excite. On the firft of July, the duke, being previoufly joined by the imperial army, came in fight of the lines of Schellenburg, in which the flower of the Bavarian troops lay ftrongly entrenched, near the town of Donavert, fituated on the banks of the Danube. Early the next morning, his grace refolved upon the attack; and after a very gallant refiftance the lines were forced with great flaughter, and Donavert immediately furrendered at difcretion. But this

Vol. I.   C   fuccefs

success, though brilliant, was lost in the splendor of the subsequent victory. The elector of Bavaria obstinately refusing to listen to terms of accommodation, and being at length joined by marechal Tallard, who had with great danger and difficulty traversed the immense forests of Suabia with a view to his relief; it was resolved by the duke of Marlborough and prince Eugene, August 13, to engage the combined army of French and Bavarians, then posted near the village of BLEINHEIM, a name ever memorable in the annals of British and Gallic history. The enemy were very advantageously encamped on a rising ground. Their right flank was covered by the Danube, and the village of Bleinheim, into which the marechal had thrown a great body of his best troops: their left wing, commanded by marechal Marsin, and the elector in person, was protected by the village of Lutzingen and the adjoining woods; and they had in front of the camp a rivulet, whose banks were steep, and the bottom marshy. It being determined that the duke of Marlborough should command the attack against marechal Tallard; about noon, the left wing of the allied army passed the rivulet without molestation, and drew up in order of battle on the other side. So unaccountably supine were the French commanders on this occasion, that they suffered even the second line of cavalry to form, without descending from the heights, of which they were in possession, into the meadows which occupied the interval between the camp and the rivulet. The allies now ascending the hill in a firm compacted body, the enemy advanced with great spirit and resolution, and a furious and bloody contest ensued. The French at length giving way on all sides, marechal Tallard made an effort to gain the bridge thrown over the Danube between Bleinheim and Hochsted; but, being closely pursued, vast numbers were either killed or forced

ed into the river, and the marechal himself was made a prisoner. The troops inclosed in the village of Bleinheim, being now left destitute of support, were obliged to surrender at discretion. On the right, where prince Eugene commanded, though the success was not so decisive, the elector, and marechal Marsin, were compelled, after a severe conflict, to retreat in confusion, and with very great loss; and, upon the whole, this was one of the most complete and important victories ever gained. The French force in Germany was in effect annihilated. Exclusive of the prodigious carnage during the heat of the action, seventy entire squadrons and battalions were either captured at Bleinheim, or drowned in the Danube; and the shattered remains of their army, after the loss of forty thousand veteran troops, were utterly incapable of making head against the victors. This day entirely changed the aspect of affairs in Europe. France was no longer formidable. After her long succession of triumphs, she now experienced a fatal and sudden reverse of fortune, by which she was overwhelmed with amazement and consternation. Nor has she ever been able to regain that high ascendency in the scale of power which she possessed previously to that great event. The elector of Bavaria, at the head of a small body of troops, effected a retreat, or rather made his escape, and joined marechal Villeroy in Flanders, leaving the electorate at the mercy of the conquerors, who, after reducing Ingoldstadt, and the other fortresses of the duchy, gloriously concluded the campaign with the sieges of Landau, Triers, and Traerbach. And in the month of December the duke of Marlborough returned in triumph to England, where he was received with unbounded transports of joy. During the course of the present summer, admiral Sir George Rooke, by a very brilliant coup-de-main, surprised the fortress of Gibraltar, which, notwithstanding the repeated efforts of the Spaniards, still remains in the possession of the English. It is, however, a most expensive, invidious, and useless conquest; and while it is, by an ungenerous and pernicious policy, detained from the rightful owners, it is scarcely possible that a cordial and sincere friendship can long subsist between the two kingdoms of Great Britain and Spain.

In April 1705, the duke of Marlborough again passed into Holland. He had now formed a real intention to execute the project, respecting which the French were so needlessly apprehensive the preceding year—to penetrate into France on the side of the Moselle. For which purpose he passed that river in the beginning of June, expecting a powerful co-operation from prince Louis of Baden, who commanded the imperial army on the Rhine. But that general, who was universally believed to regard the duke of Marlborough with malignant and envious eyes, failing in every part of his engagements, his grace was compelled to retreat with some precipitation into Flanders, where marechal Villeroy had taken advantage of the duke's absence, to capture the town of Huy, and to invest the city of Liege. The duke, however, not only raised the siege of that city, and recaptured Huy, but obliged the French general to retire within his lines, which he immediately attacked with his wonted success; but the marechal retreating to the strong camp of Parcke, near Louvaine, no farther impression could be made on that frontier during the remainder of this campaign.

On the 5th of May died the emperor Leopold, who had experienced, during his long reign, very wonderful and frequent vicissitudes of fortune. He was succeeded by his son, Joseph king of the Romans. If, from the disappointments sustained by the allies during this summer, the French court derived any hope of recovering their former superiority, the ensuing campaign proved them

to

to be wholly fallacious. For the English general assembling the confederate forces early in the spring of 1706, marched against the French army, commanded by the Marechals Villeroy and Marsin, and the elector of Bavaria, who had received orders from the French Court to risque a general engagement; and on Whitsunday the two armies joined battle near the village of Ramilies. M. Villeroy, the French commander in chief, is said to have made a most injudicious disposition; and the troops, who placed little confidence in his ability, displayed no marks of spirit or courage. In a short time, all was rout and consternation; and a most complete victory was obtained, with inconsiderable loss. The almost entire conquest of the Spanish Netherlands was the immediate consequence of it. Louvaine, Mechlin, Brussels, Antwerp, Ghent, and Bruges, submitted without resistance. Ostend, Menin, Dendermond, and Aeth, surrendered almost as soon as they were summoned. And during this fortunate campaign, the success of the allied arms in Spain and Italy was scarcely inferior to this uninterrupted series of triumphs in Flanders. The duke of Savoy, who had acceded to the grand alliance in the hope of being powerfully supported by the Emperor, seemed to be abandoned to his fate. He defended himself, however, with undaunted resolution, against the efforts of the duc de Vendome, the French general: but, overpowered by the superior force and great military talents of his antagonist, he was at length reduced to take refuge in his capital of Turin, where he was closely besieged by the French army under marechal Marsin; the duc de Vendome, after the disaster of Ramilies, being recalled in order to take the command of the army in Flanders. The imperial court, determining to make one grand effort in order to relieve the duke of Savoy in this extremity, directed prince Eugene, at the head of a

powerful

powerful army, to march to the relief of Turin. With such ability, and such success, did that celebrated commander execute this important commission, that, after surmounting all the numerous difficulties which obstructed his junction with the duke, he attacked the French army in their entrenchments before Turin, and gained a most glorious and decisive victory; the unfortunate marechal Marsin falling in the action. And this event was quickly followed by the final expulsion of the French from Lombardy. A loan, as M. Voltaire relates, being negotiated by the imperial court amongst the merchants of London, in order to defray the expence of this expedition; after the battle of Turin, prince Eugene wrote to the subscribers in the following terms:—" Gentlemen, I have received your remittances, and flatter myself I have laid out the money to your entire satisfaction." The fortune of the war was not less favorable to the allies in the scene of action southward of the Pyrenées. The arch-duke Charles, recognized as king of Spain by the powers of the alliance, after vainly attempting, by the aid of the king of Portugal, in conjunction with the English and German auxiliaries, to penetrate into that kingdom on the western side, took a sudden resolution, in the course of the preceding summer, to accompany the earl of Peterborough on board the fleet commanded by sir Cloudesley Shovel, on his intended expedition to the eastern coast of that kingdom: and landing in the province of Catalonia, this monarch was received by the inhabitants with every demonstration of joy and affection. Barcelona surrendered in the month of October; and the kingdom of Valencia, with its capital, vanquished with surprising rapidity by the heroic exertions and romantic valor of the earl of Peterborough, also recognized the authority of king Charles. The reigning monarch,

seriously

seriously alarmed at the progress of his competitor, made mighty preparations early in the ensuing spring for the siege of Barcelona, which being defended by king Charles in person, made a very vigorous resistance. The earl of Peterborough, who flew from Valencia to its relief, made incredible efforts to save this capital; which, however, must inevitably have fallen into the hands of the Spaniards, had it not been for the critical arrival of the English fleet; on the appearance of which, marechal de Tessé raised the siege with great precipitation, and retired with the broken remains of his army beyond the mountains. The earl of Peterborough now urged the necessity of immediately proceeding to Madrid, in order to form a junction with the Portuguese, who, finding few obstacles in their way, had marched to that capital, of which, on the 24th of June, they took quiet and peaceable possession. The decisive counsels of the English general, happily for Spain, were disregarded by the new king. For reasons which doubtless appeared to him very important, though it is now difficult to ascertain them with precision, Charles lingered near three months in Catalonia and Arragon—thus allowing his rival full time to recruit his shattered forces, and to receive additional succours from France: and on his re-approach to the capital, the Portuguese army, dispirited by inaction, suspense, and disappointment, retreated to their own frontier. The earl of Peterborough, enraged to perceive his expostulations fruitless, and the golden opportunity lost, resigned his commission in high disgust, and immediately withdrew from the kingdom. It is related, that when it was once alleged by some of king Charles's courtiers, as a reason for delaying his march to Madrid, that his majesty's equipage and retinue were not such as were requisite for the magnificence of his public entry into that capital; general Stanhope with warmth replied, "That king William,

liam, when he made his defcent upon England, went to London attended only by a few dragoons; otherwife he had loft his crown." The fuccefs of the campaign however, upon the whole, was fplendid. At the commencement of it king Charles was clofely befieged in Barcelona, and in imminent danger of being made a prifoner; but it terminated in the recovery of Catalonia, the fecurity of Valencia, and the reduction of Arragon.

But it is now proper to turn our attention to tranfactions of a civil and domeftic nature. The new parliament, which met the beginning of the preceding winter *, foon difcovered themfelves to be actuated by a difpofition very different from their predeceffors, by paffing a folemn and almoft unanimous vote, "That whoever prefumed to affert the church to be in danger under her majefty's aufpicious adminiftration, was an enemy to the queen, the church, and the kingdom." And the two houfes joined in an addrefs to the queen, befeeching her majefty to take effective meafures for difcovering and punifhing the authors and publifhers of this feditious and fcandalous report. That unanimity which had been fo long interrupted between the two legiflative affemblies was perfectly reftored under an adminiftration and parliament, in both of which the principles of whiggifm had now gained a complete afcendency, and which enjoyed the entire confidence of the nation. Public meafures were concerted with wifdom, and executed with vigor and fuccefs; and the general afpect of the times feemed peculiarly favorable to the accomplifhment of that great defign which the late king had recommended to parliament, almoft with his dying breath, and in which every true patriot moft ardently concurred—an UNION between the two kingdoms of England and Scotland. This was

* October 1705.

at present an object of greater consequence than ever; for by an act passed by the parliament of Scotland since the accession of the queen, styled the act of Security, that assembly was empowered, in case of her majesty's demise without issue, to declare a successor to the crown of Scotland. And very serious apprehensions were entertained, that a fatal and final separation of the two British crowns might be the result of this dangerous concession *. The lord treasurer Godolphin, who had, in a moment of intimidation, advised the queen to give the royal assent to this act, which was indeed urged by the Scottish parliament with a vehemence and pertinacity not so much the result of patriotism as of faction, now exerted himself to the utmost, in order to surmount a series of obstacles, which, to a minister of less resolution and perseverance, would have appeared absolutely insuperable. And commissioners being nominated, and conferences held, after very ample discussion, and a negotiation protracted to the space of many months, the memorable Treaty of Union was at length concluded; which, after being ratified by both parliaments, received the royal assent. And from the 1st of May, A. D. 1707, the two kingdoms of England and Scotland became indissolubly incorporated, and a proclamation was issued to convoke the first parliament of Great Britain in the month of

* Such was the alarm excited in the parliament of England by this act, that a bill was immediately introduced and passed, declaring the subjects of Scotland ALIENS so long as it remained in force, prohibiting the importation of cattle into England, or the exportation of wool into Scotland, and empowering the queen's ships to seize such Scottish vessels as they should find trading to France. And the queen was addressed to put the towns of Newcastle, Carlisle, and Hull, in a state of defence, and to order the militia of the northern counties to be disciplined and armed; and Lord Godolphin's zeal for the accomplishment of the union was certainly invigorated, if not inspired, by the terrors of an impeachment.

of October. On this occasion, congratulatory addresses were sent up from all parts of England; but the Scots observed a sullen and expressive silence. Indeed it cannot be denied that this truly wise and salutary measure was reprobated by the whole Scottish nation, and at last effected by means which could be justified only by the importance and beneficial tendency of the end proposed by them. The whole weight of regal influence was exerted, every species of artifice and intrigue was employed, honours and rewards were lavished, even bribery itself was undoubtedly practised, in order to induce the Scottish nobles and demagogues to concur in a transaction in the highest degree conducive to the public welfare and happiness. It must however be acknowledged, that the honor and dignity of that ancient kingdom suffered, in consequence of this union, some degree of diminution. Nor is it possible to condemn with much severity the high-spirited language of the celebrated Fletcher of Saltoun, who scrupled not to affirm in parliament, " that the interest and honor of the nation were betrayed by the commissioners." And when called upon for an explanation, he persisted in his charge, alleging " that he could find no other word than *treachery*, to express his ideas of their conduct. It was harsh indeed, but it was truth; and if the house thought him guilty of any offence in making use of this expression, he declared himself willing to submit to their censure." A vote of censure, however, no one dared to move. And who can avoid admiring, if not approving, the noble and elevated sentiments of the earl of Belhaven, who, in the highest strain of eloquence, depictured Caledonia as sitting in the midst of the senate, looking indignantly around her, and covering herself with her royal robe, attending the fatal blow, breathing out with tender and passionate emotion the exclamation,

" Et

" Et tu quoque, mi fili!"—" I fee," fays this animated orator, " a free and independent kingdom tamely refigning that which has ever been confidered amongft nations as the prize moft worthy of contention—a power to manage and conduct their own affairs, without any foreign interference or control. We are the fucceffors of thofe who founded our monarchy, framed our laws, and who, during the fpace of two thoufand years, have handed them down to us with the hazard of their lives and fortunes. Shall we not then zealoufly plead for thofe rights which our renowned progenitors fo dearly purchafed? Shall we hold our peace, when our country is in danger? God forbid! ENGLAND is a great and glorious nation. Her armies are numerous, powerful and victorious, her trophies fplendid and memorable. She difpofes of the fate of kingdoms. Her navy is the terror of Europe. Her trade and commerce encircle the globe: and her capital is the emporium of the univerfe. But we are a poor and obfcure people, in a remote corner of the world, without name, without alliances and without treafures. What hinders us then to lay afide our divifions, to unite cordially and heartily, when that liberty which is alone our boaft, when our all, our very exiftence as a nation, is at ftake? The enemy is at our gates. Soon will he fubvert this ancient and royal throne, and feize thefe regalia, the facred fymbols of our liberty and independence. Where are our peers, and our chieftains? Where are the Hamiltons, the Douglaffes, the Murrays, and the Campbells? Will pofterity believe that fuch names yet exifted when the nation was reduced to this laft extremity of degradation, and that they were not eager in fuch a caufe to devote themfelves for their country, and die in the bed of honor? My heart," faid this noble patriot, " is full of grief and indignation, when I confider the triumph obtained

tained by England, who has, at length, brought this fierce and warlike people under subjection, who, for so many ages, shed the best blood of the nation to establish their independency. It is superfluous," added he, " to enter into a formal examination of the articles of this treaty; for though we should even receive a *carte blanche* from England, what is this in exchange for our sovereignty! But does not, in fact, this pretended union amount to a political annihilation? I see the English constitution remaining firm. The same two houses of parliament, the same municipal laws, the same commercial companies, the same courts of judicature—while we make an ignominious and entire surrender of our national polity, our rights, our liberties, our honor, and our safety!"—These were the sentiments by which the Scottish nation was almost universally actuated, and by which a generous and high-spirited people could not fail of being at such a crisis very powerfully impressed. The speech of lord Belhaven drew tears of anger and disdain from his auditors. And it was in vain that a few disinterested and dispassionate patriots, who from principle acted in conjunction with the numerous band of courtiers, placemen, and pensioners, who composed a majority of the parliament, forcibly urged the great and solid advantages which must result from this union. " That the actual situation of Scotland, in a political view," said one of the lords commissioners, who addressed the house upon this occasion *, " is disadvantageous and ineligible, no one will venture to deny. Two kingdoms subject to one sovereign, and having separate interests, must be liable to endless emulations and jealousies: and the monarch will, whenever these interests come, or are supposed to come, in competition, be obliged to decide in favor of

---

* Mr. Seaton of Pitmedden.

the

the more powerful kingdom. And the greater the difparity of power and riches, the greater and more manifest will be the partiality; as the experience of a whole century has too fatally evinced. But, to aim at an abfolute feparation of the Britifh crowns, would be a rafh and romantic project. If, in former ages, the Scots were fcarcely able, with the moft heroic exertions, to maintain their independency, how could it be imagined poffible, now, that England had acquired fuch an immenfe preponderance in the fcale of power? Were they to feek for refuge or fecurity in the revival of the ancient league with France? This would itfelf be a virtual declaration of hoftility againft England, and probably accelerate that cataftrophe which it was its profeffed object to avert. The policy of Europe would undoubtedly prevent any effectual interference of France in their behalf, in oppofition to England, the great bulwark of the liberties of Chriftendom. By an entire feparation from England, the internal tranquillity and domeftic order of the ftate would be alfo imminently endangered. Is the nation prepared for the reception of a new fyftem of laws and jurifprudence? or fhall we revert to that Gothic conftitution of government, adapted to the rude and barbarous manners of our anceftors, and productive of perpetual feuds and implacable animofities—of devaftation—outrage and anarchy—and which, previous to the union of the two crowns, we know the executive power did not poffefs energy fufficient to reprefs? If, then, the connection with England cannot be fafely diffolved, and if the political relation in which we now ftand as to that country, is the fubject of juft and grievous complaint; what remains but to form a permanent union of the two kingdoms, as well as of the two crowns, on terms of reciprocal amity and advantage? Of the neceffity and expediency of a firm and durable union, we profefs indeed

deed an almost unanimous conviction—but then it is a federal, and not an incorporative union, for which many of our countrymen entertain a zealous and invincible predilection. But this is not the union which England offers to our acceptance, or which she will herself accept. A federal union would be productive of no advantage, would remedy no evil. And where is the guarantee for the observance of the articles of a federal compact between two nations, one of which is so much superior to the other in riches, power, and number? History demonstrates, that incorporative unions, such as the kingdoms included in the Spanish monarchy afford an example of, are solid and permanent: but that a federal union is a weak and precarious bond of connection, easily dissolved by interest or ambition. Sweden and Denmark were once united by a federal compact—But were peace and concord the result of this compact? no—It was the parent of strife, of enmity and oppression; and it terminated in scenes of blood and slaughter, and in everlasting separation. Let us not then amuse ourselves with words, instead of things. By an union of kingdoms, I acknowledge, I comprehend nothing short of an union of power, of government, and of interest. Till both nations are thus incorporated into one, England will neither extend to us the benefits of her commerce, nor the protection of her arms. By this union, Scotland will be put into the immediate possession of advantages to which she could never otherwise attain. The sources of prosperity will be opened to her view, and placed within her reach. We shall have ample scope for the exercise of our national industry, in all its various branches. To the vain ambition of independence—to the mere delusive phantom of royalty, will succeed the flourishing arts of peace; and Scotland will, by a policy founded on true wisdom, acquire that security and happiness which form

the

the great and genuine end of government. We shall, with a just increase of confidence, see our liberty, property, and religion, placed under the guardian care and protection of one Sovereign, and one legislature: and every branch of the empire, every part of the body-politic, be it ever so remote from the seat of government, will participate in the universal prosperity, under the beneficial influence of the same equitable and liberal system of polity, and in the enjoyment of the same civil rights and commercial advantages, in proportion to the value of its natural products, and the vigor and perseverance of its own laudable and voluntary exertions."

Notwithstanding the good sense and political rectitude of these reasonings, such was the violence with which the treaty of union was opposed in the Scottish parliament, and such the commotions which it excited in the kingdom, that the duke of Queensberry, at this time high commissioner, absolutely despaired of success, and was desirous of adjourning the parliament, till, by time and management, he should be able to obviate those formidable difficulties. But the lord treasurer Godolphin, who saw that the measure would be lost by delay, urged him to persist in his exertions, which were at length crowned with success. The rage of opposition *suddenly* subsided; and the treaty, as originally framed, received, without any material alteration, the solemn sanction of the Scottish parliament. And the act of union being now completed on the part of Scotland, passed through both houses in the English parliament, by a very singular effort of political dexterity, almost without opposition, or even debate or discussion. For it was so contrived that the articles of the treaty, as approved and ratified by the parliament of Scotland, should be recited in the preamble of the act, and that the whole should be converted into a law by a single enacting clause. This was a mode of
conducting

conducting the business which the tories were by no means prepared to encounter, as it totally precluded them from taking the articles separately into consideration; and they could not, with the least prospect of success, oppose the general enacting clause. The bill, therefore, passed through both houses with uncommon rapidity, and by great majorities. And nothing can more strikingly demonstrate the eagerness and ardor with which this measure was prosecuted by the whigs, than their adopting this unprecedented, and, in other circumstances, unjustifiable mode of ensuring the success of it.

Encouraged by the daring spirit of faction which at this period prevailed in Scotland, the French court equipped a powerful armament at Dunkirk, with the view of making a descent in that kingdom; on board of which embarked the Chevalier de St. George, son of the late king James. Immediately on sailing from Dunkirk, they were closely pursued by an English squadron, commanded by Sir George Byng, who captured one of their flag ships; and the whole armament was so scattered and dispersed in their retreat from the action, that they could not even effect a landing, which might, at the present crisis, have been attended with very serious consequences. And after being tossed for more than a month in a stormy and tempestuous sea, they at last found their way back, in a shattered and distressed condition, to the port of Dunkirk. On this occasion, the most firm and vigorous measures were taken by the government; such, however, as sufficiently demonstrated the sense it entertained of the magnitude of the danger. The habeas corpus act was suspended—The abjuration-oath was tendered to all persons; and those who refused it were declared to be in the condition of convict recusants.—A vote of credit passed the house of commons, and twelve battalions

battalions of troops were ordered immediately from Flanders. The queen herself, in a speech to both houses, informed them of this alarming attempt to invade the kingdom, and to subvert the government; and declared for the *first* and the *last* time, as many failed not to remark, " That her firmest reliance was placed on those who were chiefly concerned in effecting the glorious revolution." In this popular speech, the chevalier de St. George was, by a new designation, styled *The Pretender*; which term was re-echoed in the numerous addresses presented to the queen from every part of the kingdom; and by this appellation he was in future usually distinguished. Soon after the termination of this business, the parliament, which had now sat three years with the highest reputation to itself, and advantage to the public, was dissolved, and a new parliament summoned to meet in November 1708, in which the whig interest still maintained its ascendency. A few weeks previous to its assembling, died his royal highness prince George of Denmark, who had been twenty-five years married to the queen. His total want of talents, his unaspiring disposition, and mildness of temper, very happily combined to qualify him for the peculiarly critical station in which his high fortune had placed him, and in which a man of more shining abilities, and more daring ambition, might have proved singularly troublesome and dangerous.

The military transactions of the present reign are of such importance, and form so interesting a part of its general history, that a regular recital, however concise, of the principal events of the war cannot be with propriety dispensed with. After the successful campaign of 1706, the most sanguine expectations were entertained, that France, whose pride was now humbled in the dust, would no longer be able to make any effectual resistance;

Vol. I.			D			and

and that the allies, as victors, might in a short time dictate the terms of peace with the point of the sword The operations of the ensuing summer, did not, however, in any degree tend to confirm these lofty ideas. The Duc de Vendôme, who had been recalled from Italy in order to take the command of the army in Flanders, chose his posts with so much skill and judgment, that the duke of Marlborough could not, without manifest rashness, venture upon an attack. This was the only campaign during the war, in which that great commander did not obtain some signal advantage over the enemy: and the French general, whose policy it was to act upon the defensive, fully sustained his high reputation, by thus putting, after his Grace's long career of victories, a sudden and total stop to the progress of his arms. If in Flanders the wishes and expectations of the confederates were not satisfactorily answered, in Spain they suffered a fatal reverse: for, a general engagement taking place at Almanza, the Spanish army commanded by the duke of Berwick, gained a most complete victory. The loss sustained by the allies was estimated at no less than 10,000 men; and they were constrained, in consequence of this disaster, to abandon the kingdoms of Arragon and Valencia, and to retire once more to the remote province of Catalonia, which still continued faithful in its attachment to the house of Austria. The projects of the allies in Italy also proved unhappily abortive. In the month of July, prince Eugene and the duke of Savoy passed the Var, at the head of 30,000 men, and marched directly towards Toulon, to which they laid close siege. As the principal naval magazines of France, and the greater part of the fleet, were inclosed within its walls, or its harbor, this enterprise excited a general consternation. The place was however defended with the most heroic valor; and troops being assembled from all parts,

in

in great force, for its relief, the duke of Savoy, who feared left his retreat to Italy should be intercepted, thought proper to raise the siege with precipitation, and to repass the Var, without any acquisition of honor or profit from this undertaking, into his own dominions. Great blame was upon this occasion imputed to the emperor, who detached a large body of troops, destined for this expedition, to the kingdom of Naples, of which he effected a complete conquest: and this was the only advantage gained by the allies during this unfortunate campaign; which, however, did not prevent the house of peers from passing a resolution, much applauded by the zealous whigs, " That no peace could be safe and honorable for her majesty and her allies, if Spain and the Indies were suffered to continue in the possession of the house of Bourbon."

The king of France, emboldened by the success of the last campaign, and confiding in the talents of his general, was inclined to act more upon the offensive; and early in the spring 1708, the Duc de Vendôme surprised the cities of Ghent and Bruges, and laid siege to the town of Oudenard. The duke of Marlborough, however, being now joined by prince Eugene, compelled the enemy to raise the siege of Oudenard; and following them in their retreat, forced them to a general engagement in the vicinity of that place. Though the Duc de Vendôme, whose measures were, during the whole of this campaign, much embarrassed by the presence of the duke of Burgundy, acted the part of a great general upon this occasion, rallying, in person, the broken battalions, calling the officers by name, and conjuring them to maintain the honor of their country; the French army was, in the end, entirely defeated. Night however saved them from total ruin; and the Duc de Vendôme, seeing all hope of retrieval lost, formed his best troops

into

into a rear-guard, with which he secured a tolerable retreat. In consequence of this important victory, the generals of the allies determined to undertake the siege of Lisle, the capital of French Flanders—a town, on the fortifications of which Vauban had exhausted his utmost skill, and which was defended by a garrison so numerous that the success of the enterprise was adjudged extremely doubtful. After happily surmounting the numerous obstacles which the ability and vigilance of the Duc de Vendôme, still more than the unrivalled art of the engineer, continually created; and in some of which the superior fortune, rather than skill, of the duke of Marlborough, was apparent; this important town, together with its citadel, surrendered to the allied army, to the inexpressible chagrin of the French court, who saw the frontier of France, by this conquest, exposed to the most dangerous future attacks. Ghent and Bruges were also recovered before the end of this campaign, which terminated only with the year.

In Spain and Italy the war seemed for the present to slumber. But, during the course of the summer, Sir John Leake made a complete conquest of the island of Sardinia; and, in concert with general Stanhope, also of Minorca. And the POPE was menaced by the British admiral with the bombardment of Civita-Vecchia, in return for the assistance he had publicly afforded the Pretender in his late expedition into Scotland. From this affront, however, the holy Pontiff was saved by the seasonable interposition of the imperial court in his favour.

The campaign in Flanders was opened in June 1709, by the siege of Tournay, which surrendered at discretion, after a long and obstinate resistance. The allies next prepared to attack the city of Mons. But the French army, now commanded by mareschal Villars, posting

ing themselves behind the woods of La-Merte and Taniers, in the neighborhood of Malplaquet, in order to obstruct this design, the duke of Marlborough and prince Eugene formed a resolution to attack the French General in his camp, which, naturally strong, he had fortified with redoubts, and intrenchments behind intrenchments, with such diligence and skill as to make it apparently inaccessible. After an obstinate, fierce, and bloody engagement, however, the lines were forced, but not till marechal Villars had been wounded and carried off the field. And it was not without some appearance of reason the marechal was accustomed to boast, that had it not been for this accident, the allies would certainly have been defeated. Marechal Boufflers, second in command, made an excellent retreat; and the loss of the victors was little less than that of the vanquished. The victory, however, was crowned by the capture of Mons; after which, both armies went into winter quarters. In Spain, count Staremberg, the Austrian general, maintained his ground with reputation to the imperial arms. The duke of Savoy, since the failure of his great enterprise, contented himself with operations merely defensive, wisely shunning those risques which might have reduced him once more to that extremity of distress from which he had so lately been almost miraculously rescued.

Prince Eugene and the duke of Marlborough again took the field together in Flanders, April 1710; and the success of the campaign was equal to the expectations excited by the junction of such extraordinary talents. Notwithstanding the utmost exertions of marechal Villars, who directed the operations of the French army with great ability, the allies successively reduced the towns of Douay, Bethune, St. Venant, and Aire, passing in the prosecution of these sieges one hundred and fifty

fifty days in open trenches. The most interesting events of the present summer passed however in Spain. The monarch, eager to put a final termination to the hopes and claims of his competitor, advanced at the head of a powerful army into Arragon, in order to bring matters to a decisive issue. General Stanhope notwithstanding, with a force very inferior, attacked and totally routed the Spanish cavalry at Almanara. And count Staremberg following the motions of the king, who found it necessary, in consequence of this check, to retire towards Saragossa, discovered the Spanish army drawn up in order of battle, near that place; and an engagement ensuing, the enemy were entirely defeated. King Charles entered Saragossa in triumph, while Philip retired with the wreck of his army to Madrid. The good fortune of Charles, however, was of short duration; proceeding without delay, to Madrid, in pursuit of his competitor, he had the mortification to find that city entirely deserted by all the Spanish grandees, and to receive the most convincing proofs of the fidelity and attachment of the Castilians to his rival. Great efforts being made by Philip to collect another army, he soon appeared again in force; and count Staremberg, being wholly unsupported, and apprehending his retreat to Catalonia might be intercepted, thought it expedient to retrace his footsteps; and in the beginning of November, his army marched back to Saragossa: but the greater part of the British forces, under General Stanhope, imprudently halting at Brihuega, were suddenly surprised and surrounded by the Spanish army, and reduced to the fatal necessity of surrendering themselves prisoners of war. And in a few days afterwards, Staremberg himself was attacked at Villa Viciosa with great valor, but doubtful success: He was, however, compelled, victor as he styled himself, to abandon Arragon, and retire to Catalonia; and being closely pursued

sued by the Duc de Vendôme, now at the head of the Spanish forces, he was at last driven to take shelter under the walls of Barcelona. Thus the flattering successes of the allies at the commencement of this campaign, proved wholly delusive; and, during the remaining years of the war, Charles was never able to regain even a temporary superiority.

In the month of May in the succeeding year, 1711, the duke of Marlborough appeared, for the last time, at the head of the grand army in Flanders—prince Eugene commanding a separate body of forces on the Rhine. This campaign was not distinguished, on the part of his grace, by brilliant success; but it attracted uncommon attention, as exhibiting the most consummate proofs of military skill and conduct. Marechal Villars had, with great labor and perseverance, drawn lines from Bouchaine on the Scheldt along the Sanset and Scarpe, to Arras and Canché, which he had fortified by redoubts, batteries, and other military works, in such a manner that he scrupled not publicly to boast that they were impregnable, and that the English general had at length arrived at his *ne plus ultra*. The duke, however, boldly advanced within two leagues of the French lines, making every preparation in order to a vigorous attack the next morning; and Villars drew, with all possible diligence, his whole force on that side, in full expectation of an immediate and furious engagement. This being foreseen by the duke, he had given previous orders to generals Cadogan and Hompesch, with a strong detachment, secretly drawn from the neighbouring garrisons, to take possession of the passes on the river Sanset, at Arleux. At nine in the evening the duke silently decamped, and by eight the next morning he arrived at Arleux with his whole army, after a march of ten leagues, without halting. Villars, on being certified of the duke's motions,

within

within a few hours of his departure, marched all night with such expedition, that at eleven next morning, he was in sight of the duke of Marlborough, who, to his unspeakable mortification, had, as he now found, entered those lines which he had himself vauntingly pronounced impregnable, without the loss of a man. His grace immediately invested the important fortress of Bouchaine, which surrendered after twenty days open trenches only. And this admired and hazardous military achievement closed the long glories of this celebrated commander; who, at the critical moment in which he had almost penetrated the French barrier, and when another Ramilies might have removed all obstacles in his march to Paris, was, by the mandate of that sovereign whom he had served with such unparalleled ability and success, divested of all his civil and military employments. The gradation of causes which led to this event, at which all Europe stood in astonishment, it will now be necessary concisely to develope.

Of the favorable opinion universally entertained by the English nation, respecting the general purity and rectitude of the queen's intentions, the epithet of the *good* queen Anne, so commonly applied to this princess, is itself a sufficient proof. This good queen, however, had imbibed, in a very great degree, the hereditary prejudices of her family respecting the nature and extent of the sovereign authority. And there is reason to believe that the successful resistance of the nation to the late king James, was, in her eyes, justified only by the attempts made to establish popery upon the ruins of the protestant religion; to which, in the form exhibiting itself to her perception, as inculcated and professed by the church of England, she entertained a zealous attachment, or rather a blind and bigoted devotion. As her prejudices, political

political and religious, precisely coincided with those of the Tories, she cherished a strong predilection for that powerful and dangerous faction, in opposition to the Whigs, who were considered as for the most part latitudinarians in religion, or at best as cool and luke-warm friends of the church; and who certainly regarded the particular mode in which the protestant religion was professed, as of little importance, when put in competition with the preservation, enlargement, or security of the civil and religious liberties of the kingdom. The political views of the sectaries, who were very numerous and active, entirely corresponded with those of the Whig party; and their whole weight was invariably thrown into this scale. In return, the Whigs were the strenuous and constant advocates of the dissenters, whenever they were threatened with any species of persecution or oppression. It has been already remarked, that the passions of all the zealous adherents of liberty were, at the period of queen's accession, extremely inflamed against the French monarch—that imperious and restless despot —on account of the open and avowed protection which he granted to the son of the late king James. When England, therefore, acceded to the grand alliance, the Whigs rejoiced in the prospect of humbling the pride, and reducing the power, of that haughty tyrant. Previous to the death of king William, the idea of a war with France had become exceedingly popular; and after the accession of the queen, the leaders of the Tories, Rochester, Nottingham, &c. who opposed a declaration of war on the part of England as unnecessary and impolitic, were over-ruled in the council, chiefly through the all-powerful influence of the earl of Marlborough, who, though himself attached to the Tories, was impatient to give full scope to his talents; and in whose breast an ardent thirst for glory, that " infirmity of noble minds,"

superseded

superseded every other consideration. This influence was obtained chiefly through the medium of the countess of Marlborough, who had been long employed in stations near the queen's person, and who had gradually acquired a complete ascendency over her. In process of time, Marlborough, and Godolphin his friend and coadjutor, finding that the war received a faint and feeble support only from the Tories, began to connect themselves with the Whigs, who were zealous and sanguine in the prosecution of it. And the queen, under the direction and government of these two noblemen, suffered the Tories to be gradually displaced, an administration composed entirely of Whigs to be formed, and two successive parliaments to be chosen under the influence of the court, in which that party maintained a decided superiority. While affairs continued in this state, a trivial and fortuitous incident eventually occasioned a total change in the face of Europe. The duchess of Marlborough had introduced a female relation and dependant at the court, who so artfully and rapidly insinuated herself into the queen's affection and favor, that the duchess found herself absolutely supplanted, almost before she was apprised of the danger. The new favorite, Mrs. Masham, soon discovering the queen's secret predilection for the Tories, combined with Mr. Harley, at this time secretary of state, but who aspired to nothing less than the station of prime minister, to prepossess the mind of the queen against the duke of Marlborough, and the earl of Godolphin; who, as they said, and truly said, made her majesty a mere cypher in the government, and engrossed all power, influence, and patronage, into their own hands—omitting, however, to inform the queen of another truth, not less palpable; *viz.* that such was the imbecility of her majesty's understanding and capacity, that she must necessarily remain a cypher, in whatever hands

hands her affairs were placed. And the voice, not of England only, but of Europe, declared, that the public interests could not be entrusted to more faithful or more able directors than the present ministers. The intrigues of Harley with the Tories soon transpiring, he was compelled immediately to relinquish his employments, though with manifest tokens of resentment and alienation from the Whigs, on the part of the queen. The entire management of affairs nevertheless still remained with that party; and so little force and vigor of mind did the queen possess, that if subsequent circumstances had not in a remarkable and unexpected manner favored a revolution in politics, it is very doubtful whether it would ever have been effected. Notwithstanding the wonderful successes of the present war, the heavy burdens which in consequence of its long continuance it became necessary to impose, considerably damped the ardor of the public, and by degrees had much abated its original popularity. And the overtures for a general accommodation made by Louis from time to time, and the great concessions offered by that monarch, led the generality of intelligent and dispassionate people to consider the grand object of the war as now sufficiently attained. At the conferences held first at the Hague, and in the following year at Gertruytenberg, A. D. 1710, so low were the mighty fallen, that the king of France, through the medium of the marquis de Torcy, his prime minister, who upon this occasion took upon him the office of negotiator in person, condescended to acknowledge the arch-duke Charles as true and rightful sovereign of the Spanish monarchy; and made in all other respects such ample concessions as the dire necessity of his affairs demanded; such indeed as amply secured the interests, and ought to have satisfied the utmost ambition, of the allies. With all the insolence of prosperity, however, they insisted

sisted that Louis should absolutely engage for the entire restitution of the Spanish monarchy to the house of Austria, in the space of two months. It was in vain that he urged " this was a promise not in his power to perform; and that he could not at his pleasure depose a king of Spain, or impose a monarch upon the Spanish nation contrary to their own inclination." The plea was treated as idle and frivolous. And even the offer which he ultimately made, to surrender three fortresses in Flanders into the hands of the allies as pledges for the restitution of Spain, and to furnish his quota in money or troops for the reduction of that kingdom, should Spain refuse to accede to the treaty, was rejected with disdain; to the extreme dissatisfaction of all moderate and reasonable persons, who saw that the war was in future to be continued, merely to gratify the immeasurable ambition of the house of Austria, and that, exclusive of the flagrant injustice of forcing a sovereign on the Spaniards, who was the object of the national abhorrence, the policy of the measure was in present circumstances extremely doubtful. For the power of France being so greatly reduced, while the grandeur of the imperial family was elevated in the same proportion, not less danger was to be apprehended by transferring Spain and the Indies to the house of Austria, than by leaving them in the possession of a prince of the house of Bourbon. The parliament, notwithstanding, highly approved the conduct of the British plenipotentiaries, and returned the duke of Marlborough their unanimous thanks for his public services, when it became every day more apparent, that he was actuated chiefly by private considerations, and that he invariably opposed all overtures of conciliation, prompted by the suggestions of ambition and of interest. In order however effectually to check and intimidate

that

that rising spirit of discontent, evident symptoms of which began now to appear in the nation, and to display the firmness of their attachment to those principles in which this once popular war had originated, the parliament determined to give full scope to their vengeance, on an occasion which certainly called for no such extraordinary violence of exertion.

On the 5th November 1709, an obscure clergyman of the name of Sacheverel, of the high-church faction, preaching at St. Paul's cathedral upon the words of St. Paul, "Perils from false brethren," indulged himself in the most virulent defamation and abuse of the present administration, and of their measures. The lord treasurer in particular was scurrilously attacked, under the name of VOLPONE; and divers of the right reverend bench were also inveighed against with much scorn and malignity, as "perfidious prelates and false sons of the church," on account of their moderation respecting the dissenters, and their avowed approbation of the toleration. He asserted, in terms the most unqualified, the doctrines of passive obedience and non-resistance; and pretended, that to say the revolution was inconsistent with those doctrines, was to cast black and odious imputations upon it. He affirmed that the church was violently assailed by her enemies, and faintly defended by those who professed themselves her friends. He vehemently urged the necessity of standing up in defence of the church; for which he declared that he sounded the trumpet, and exhorted the people to put on "*the whole armour of GOD.*" This inflammatory and libellous harangue being published at the request of the lord mayor, was extravagantly extolled and applauded by the Tories, and circulated by them with great industry throughout the kingdom. At the very height of the popular ferment and clamor excited by this extraordinary invective, and which would doubtless have

soon

soon died away, had no public notice been taken of it, a complaint was formally preferred to the house of commons, by one of the members of that house, of this sermon, as containing positions contrary to revolution principles, to the present government, and to the protestant succession. As it was by this means obtruded upon the notice of the house, it was impossible not to express in some mode their disapprobation of these nefarious and seditious tenets. The wiser members thought it sufficient to order the sermon to be burnt by the common hangman, and to commit the writer to Newgate during the remainder of the session. This, however, was by no means satisfactory to the majority, who determined to raise this contemptible libeller to the rank of a political delinquent of great consequence and dignity, by a solemn parliamentary impeachment at the bar of the house of lords. No sooner was this absurd and unaccountable resolution made public, than every possible artifice was put in practice, by the Tory faction, to inflame the minds of the public; and to represent Sacheverel as the champion and martyr of the church, which the Whigs had, as they affirmed, a fixed intent to subvert: and of which project the impeachment of Sacheverel was only the prelude. These calumnies however gross and palpable, were swallowed by the populace with amazing avidity. During the trial, which lasted three weeks, his coach, in passing between Westminster Hall and the Temple, where he then lodged, was constantly attended by vast multitudes with shouts and acclamations of applause. And great tumults prevailed in the metropolis, where several places of worship licensed under the act of toleration were pulled down; the houses of many of the most eminent dissenters were plundered; and those of the lord chancellor, lord Wharton, the bishop of Sarum, &c. were threatened with demolition. The managers of the house of commons,

mons, amongſt whom were the celebrated names of KING, STANHOPE, and WALPOLE, neverthelefs exerted themſelves with great courage and ability in ſupport of the proſecution *. And divers of the lords ſpiritual as well

---

* As the ſentiments of the Whig managers of this impeachment, and of the revolution Whigs in general, have of late been grofsly and daringly miſrepreſented, it cannot be improper to make a few extracts from the ſpeeches delivered at this celebrated trial; from which a competent judgment may be formed of the general ſtrain and ſpirit of the proceedings on this occaſion, in behalf of the commons of Great Britain.

Lord Coningſby.—" The doctor, by reflecting on the neceſſary means to bring about the revolution—the foundation on which our preſent happy eſtabliſhment is built—*by aſſerting that her majeſty ought to depend on no other title to her throne, than her hereditary one*, deſigned by ſuch deſtructive poſitions to bring back the pretender, with popery and French tyranny attending him, to govern the ſtate."—As long therefore as a pretender to the throne exiſted, it was true that the political claims and rights of the kings of England reſted, like thoſe of magiſtrates of every other denomination, upon the general conſent and will of the people, or community at large, as the only proper and rational baſis. But the very ſhadow of competition being at length vaniſhed, they are now adviſed by ſome who preſume to ſtyle themſelves WHIGS, to revert for the future to the old ground of inviolable hereditary right.

Mr. Dolben.—" This gentleman, Dr. S. muſt be allowed the infamy to have ſtretched and improved this pernicious tenet to the exalted height of making all our laws, liberties, religion, and lives, to be held only at the precarious pleaſure of any bold invader, when it is taught that no oppreſſion, no violence, can juſtify an oppoſition to it. My lords, the commons have brought this offender before you, with a view not only to detect and puniſh his offence, but to obtain an occaſion in the moſt public and authentic manner to avow the principles and juſtify the means upon which the preſent government and the proteſtant ſucceſſion are founded and eſtabliſhed; and this more out of a generous concern for poſterity, than for our own preſent ſecurity. We hope the record of this proceeding will remain a laſting monument to deter a ſucceſſor that may inherit the crown, but not the virtues of her majeſty, from attempting to invade the laws or the people's rights; and if not, that it will be a noble precedent to excite our poſterity to *wreſtle and tug*

for

well as temporal, diftinguifhed themfelves by the fpirit and liberality of their remarks on this interefting occafion. The earl of Wharton, knowing at the time the queen to be in the houfe *incognita,* took the opportunity to obferve, that if the revolution was not lawful, many in that houfe, and vaft numbers out of it, were guilty of bloodfhed and treafon; and that the queen herfelf was no legal fovereign, fince the beft title fhe had to the crown was her parliamentary title, founded on the revolution. Dr. Wake, bifhop of Lincoln, remarked, that by falfe and injurious reprefentations men had been made to believe the church to be in danger, when in reality it enjoyed the moft perfect fecurity; but that fuch invectives, if not timely corrected, might kindle fuch heat and animofities as would truly endanger both church and ftate. And Burnet, bifhop of Sarum, juftified the principle of refiftance

for liberty as we have done."—Could it poffibly have entered into the imagination of this patriotic fpeaker, to accufe any one of fedition for teaching that the people *have* a right, while in the fame breath he accufed Dr. S. of a high offence for teaching that the people have *not* a right, to depofe their governors for mifconduct?—And will it be pretended by thofe who have the audacity to bring forward fuch prepofterous charges, that they agree in *all* points of political theory and practice with the Whigs of the revolution!

"If," fays Sir Jofeph Jekyl, " this doctrine of unlimited non-refiftance prevail, we muft give up our right to the laws and liberties of the kingdom, and hold them only during pleafure.—Hath not this principle of unlimited non-refiftance been revived by the profeffed and undifguifed friends of the pretender? The law is the only meafure of the prince's authority and the people's fubjection, and it derives its being and efficacy from COMMON CONSENT; though patriarchal or other fantaftical fchemes have been framed to reft the authority of the law upon."—It is plain therefore, that as the general theory of this juftly applauded manager perfectly accords with that which it is now the fafhion to explode, the theories which effentially vary from it, on whatever grounds the ingenuity of their inventors may place them, muft be ranked amongft the number of thofe *fantaftical fchemes,* which Sir Jofeph Jekyl rejects with indignation and contempt.

fiftance without referve. He mentioned the conduct of queen Elizabeth, who had affifted the French, the Scots, and the Hollanders, in refifting their refpective fovereigns, and who was fupported in this practice both by her parliaments and her convocations. He obferved that king Charles I. had affifted the city of Rochelle; and that Mainwaring had incurred the fevereft cenfure of parliament, for broaching the doctrine of the divine right of kings:—that though this became afterwards a fafhionable doctrine, yet its moft zealous affertors were the firft to refift, when actually fuffering under oppreffion. He faid that by inveighing againft the revolution, the toleration, and the union, the delinquent at their lordfhips' bar had arraigned and attacked the queen herfelf; fince her majefty had a diftinguifhed fhare in the firft, had often declared fhe would maintain the fecond, and that fhe looked upon the third as the moft glorious event of her reign. He affirmed, that this audacious libeller had likewife caft the moft fcandalous reflections upon her majefty's minifters; and that he had, in particular, drawn the portrait of a noble peer then prefent, in colors fo lively, and had fo plainly pointed him out by a vile and fcurrilous epithet, which he would not repeat, that it was impoffible to miftake in making the application.— This unintentional farcafm on the lord treafurer fomewhat difcompofed the gravity of the houfe; and in violation of dignity and decorum, the bifhop was called upon to name him; which, in the fervor of his zeal, and in the wanderings of that mental abfence for which he was remarkable, he might perhaps have done, had not the lord chancellor interpofed, and declared that no peer was obliged to fay more than he himfelf fhould deem proper. In conclufion, Sacheverel was, after high debates, found guilty of a mifdemeanor, by a majority of feventeen voices only*; and he was adjudged to be suspended from preaching for the space of three years, and his sermon ordered to be publicly burnt. And to the same flames was also somewhat whimsically, though deservedly, committed the famous decree of the university of Oxford, passed near thirty years before, asserting the absolute authority and indefeasible right of princes. This mild sentence, which cast an air of ridicule over the whole proceedings, was considered as equivalent to an acquittal by the Tory faction, who celebrated their triumph by bonfires and illuminations, not only in London, but over the whole kingdom. These rejoicings were succeeded by numerous addresses expressive of a zealous attachment to the church, and an utter detestation of all anti-monarchical and republican principles. And in a progress which Sacheverel afterwards made into a remote part of the country, he was sumptuously entertained by the university of Oxford, invited to the palaces of different noblemen, received in many towns by the magistrates in their formalities, and generally attended by a numerous escort of horse. In other places the hedges were ornamented with garlands of flowers, the steeples were covered with streamers and flags, and the air every-where resounded with the cry of " The Church and Sacheverel!" The enthusiasm spread like a contagion through all ranks and orders of the people. Men seemed to suffer a temporary dereliction of sense and understanding, and the mob and the nation were for a time terms of the same import. No martyr suffering in the glorious cause of civil and religious liberty was ever perhaps so much the object of public applause and veneration, as this wretched and fanatical preacher of nonsense, impiety, and sedition.

Encouraged by the disposition now universally prevalent, the queen gave the first public indication of her total change of system, by dismissing the marquis of Kent,

Kent, April 1710, and giving the office of chamberlain to the duke of Shrewſbury. In June, the ſeals were taken from the earl of Sunderland, and given to the earl of Dartmouth: and in Auguſt, the lord high treaſurer Godolphin was ordered to break his ſtaff; and the treaſury was put into commiſſion, earl Paulet being appointed firſt commiſſioner. But this appointment was conſidered as merely nominal; Mr. Harley who was conſtituted chancellor of the exchequer, being regarded as chief, or rather ſole miniſter. In October, the queen came in perſon to the council, and ordered a proclamation to be iſſued for diſſolving the parliament; upon which the lord chancellor roſe to ſpeak; but the queen declared that ſhe would admit of no debate, for that SUCH WAS HER PLEASURE. At the ſame time ſhe diſmiſſed the lord Somers, and made the earl of Rocheſter lord preſident of the council. The duke of Buckingham was declared lord ſteward, in the room of the duke of Devonſhire. The ſeals in the poſſeſſion of Mr. Boyle were given to Mr. St. John. The lord high chancellor Cowper was ſucceeded by Sir Simon Harcourt. The earl of Wharton reſigned the government of Ireland; and the earl of Orford, his ſeat at the head of the admiralty. The duke of Marlborough alone was ſtill ſuffered to retain his employments, which he was deterred from reſigning by the preſſing entreaties of the emperor and the States-General, who conceived the fortune of the war to be in a great meaſure attached to his perſon. On his return from the enſuing campaign, he was however, as mention has already been made, diveſted of his command, which was immediately conferred upon the duke of Ormond.

The parliament, which met in November, was compoſed almoſt wholly of Tories, who eagerly ſought occaſion to diſplay their hatred to the principles and perſons of their predecessors. An enquiry was set on foot in the house of peers into the conduct of the war in Spain: and the earl of Galway and general Stanhope, being Whigs, were censured for resolving to adopt offensive measures, at the opening of the campaign in 1707, contrary to the advice of the earl of Peterborough; which resolution was with singular sagacity voted to be the cause of the loss of the battle of Almanza, with all its fatal consequences: and the earl of Peterborough, a zealous Tory, was thanked for his great and eminent services. Though the earl of Godolphin had been one of the most incorrupt of ministers, a vote of censure also passed upon him, on pretence that his accounts were not regularly audited. For the sake of offering an indignity to the memory of king William, the house of commons ordered in a bill, empowering commissioners to examine all grants made by that monarch, and to report the value of them, and the considerations upon which they were bestowed. This, however, was rejected by the lords. Great pains were taken to fix a stigma upon the character of the duke of Marlborough; and the customary perquisites which he received in the capacity of commander in chief were voted to be unwarrantable and illegal; and it was resolved by the house, that the sums so received ought to be accounted for as public property; and the queen ordered the attorney general to commence a prosecution against the duke for money actually received by virtue of her own warrant.

Early in the year 1711, Harley was raised to the dignity of lord high treasurer, and created earl of Oxford and earl Mortimer. About this period died Joseph, emperor of the Romans. His brother, the arch-duke Charles, nominal king of Spain, was elected emperor without opposition. This event afforded a fair opening to renew the overtures for a general peace, which was

now

now not less the object of the eager wishes of the court of London than that of Versailles. After a secret, or, as it was styled by the Whigs, a clandestine negotiation with the agents of the French court, protracted for many months, it was at last agreed, that Utrecht should be the place of congress, and that the conferences should be opened the first of January 1712. The new emperor, who was previously informed that Spain and the Indies were, by the consent of England, to remain in the possession of Philip, vehemently opposed the project of a treaty, by which he considered his interests as sacrificed: and the States-General themselves acceded to it with much reluctance, and after long and repeated delays.— The Whigs exclaimed with all the violence of party rage against a plan of accommodation founded on this basis, which they represented as fraught with treachery to our allies, and ruin to ourselves. The ideas inculcated by the leaders, and swallowed by the dupes of the faction, are strongly, though undesignedly, depictured by bishop Burnet; who gravely informs us, that when the queen condescended to ask of him his sentiments respecting peace, upon obtaining permission to speak his mind plainly, he told her Majesty, " That it was his opinion, that any treaty by which Spain and the Indies were left to king Philip, must in a little while deliver up all Europe into the hands of France. And if any such peace should be made, she was betrayed, and we were all ruined. In less than three years time, she would be murdered, and the fires would be again kindled in Smithfield."

The parliament being now convened, the earl of Nottingham, after copiously expatiating on the dangers to be apprehended from leaving a prince of the house of Bourbon in possession of the monarchy of Spain, moved, that a clause might be added to the address in answer

swer to the speech from the throne, representing to her majesty, "that in the opinion of that house, no peace could be safe or honorable to Great Britain or Europe, if Spain and the Indies were allotted to any branch of the house of Bourbon." The previous question being put upon this motion, it was carried in the affirmative by a single vote; and the main question by three voices, against the utmost efforts of the court. The earl of Nottingham was himself, one of the most distinguished leaders of the Tory party; but he was at this period, extremely discontented at the ascendency acquired by the earl of Oxford, under whom he would not deign to act a subordinate part. The reward for the service thus rendered to the Whigs was their support, or rather acquiescence, in a bill which the same nobleman now moved for leave to bring in against occasional conformity; without which, as he said, he was only an individual; but with it, an host. As there was little doubt, from the present temper of the times, that this famous bill, so often and so strongly agitated, would be revived, the Whigs made no scruple to permit the earl of Nottingham to conciliate the confidence of his party, by being himself the mover of it, especially as the penalties of the proposed bill were much milder than they would probably have been if introduced under the auspices of the court. In consequence of this previous agreement, the bill passed through both houses with silence and rapidity. The dissenters, however, who did not perfectly comprehend these political and courtly manœuvres, loudly complained that they were deserted by their friends, who endeavored in vain to persuade them that they consulted their interest in consenting to their oppression.

At this period prince Eugene arrived in England, being charged with instructions from the emperor, to represent to the queen, in terms the most urgent, the fatal conse-

consequences which would attend the defection of England from the alliance, and to propose a new plan for the future conduct of the war, in which his imperial majesty would take upon himself a larger proportion of the burden than had been required from his predecessors Leopold and Joseph. The remonstrances of his highness, however, produced no effect; and during his residence in London he had even the mortification to see twelve peers created in one day, in order to secure a majority in favor of the court in the house of lords. When the time arrived for opening the campaign, prince Eugene nevertheless received positive assurances from the new general, that he would concur with him in a vigorous prosecution of the war; and when the prince invested Quesnoy, the duke of Ormond undertook to cover the siege: but when the place was on the point of surrender, his highness was informed by the British commander, that an armistice was agreed upon between the two crowns of England and France; and that he was obliged, by his instructions, immediately to begin his march towards Dunkirk, in order to embark his forces for England. The prince in vain expostulated with the duke on the unparalleled baseness of this violation of national faith and honor, and the danger and ruin which might ensue upon this desertion. The duke was immoveable, and ordered the suspension of hostilities to be proclaimed by sound of trumpet: but the foreign troops in the pay of Great Britain unanimously refused to obey his grace's orders. Notwithstanding the departure of Ormond, prince Eugene immediately on the surrender of Quesnoy invested Landreci; but the history of this campaign, after the separation of the British forces, is the recital of a continued series of losses and disasters. Marechal Villars, after defeating a part of the allied army at Denain,

proceeded

proceeded to Marchiennes, which contained the prince's grand *depôt* of military stores. After the reduction of Marchiennes, he undertook the siege of Douay, which compelled the prince to raise that of Landreci, without however being able to save Douay. And before the end of the campaign, the French also retook Quesnoy and Bouchaine. So that the triumph of Villars was complete, and the allies were overwhelmed with shame and consternation. In the beginning of August, Mr. Secretary St. John, now created viscount Bolingbroke, went *incognito* to the court of Versailles, in order, by his presence, to obviate all obstacles to the treaty between France and England. And a total suspension of hostilities by sea and land, for the space of four months, was quickly agreed upon; but the treaty was not signed in form till the April succeeding. All the powers of the alliance, the emperor excepted, at length acceded to the terms prescribed by England, which were much less advantageous than those voluntarily offered by France two years before. Louis saw the impolitic ardor with which the British minister pursued and even courted peace, and wisely improved it to his own benefit. M. Mesnager, the original negociator of the treaty, informs us, that when setting out from Paris, the king of France said to him, " I am of opinion that Harley and his new party may stand in as much need of peace as of victory; and that they may want me as much as I want them *."

And

---

* The innate goodness of the queen's disposition, and her artless simplicity, are strongly marked by a circumstance related by M. Mesnager, who tells us, that on being introduced by a certain nobleman privately to the queen at Kensington, her majesty said, " My lord * * * here has given me an account of what steps you have taken—You may let him hear what you have to say." M. Mesnager bowed, but was prevented replying by the queen's addressing herself to the nobleman;

after

And he adds, that it was impoffible to defcribe the tranfports of joy the king was in at the news of the diffolution of the Whig parliament. A feparate peace was at laft concluded November 1713, at Al-Raftadt, between the emperor and France; by which the former acknowledged the title of the king of Spain; and Naples, Milan, Sardinia, and the Low Countries were ceded to the houfe of Auftria.

A new parliament being convened in December, debates ran, if poffible, higher than ever between the two ftate factions. Thefe were occafioned chiefly by the fears and jealoufies entertained by the Whigs, that the proteftant fucceffion was in danger, from the fecret defigns of the minifters of the crown in favor of the Pretender; though it muft be acknowledged, no very clear proof has yet been adduced that any fuch defigns were ferioufly harbored. "It was eafy to fee," fays M. Mefnager, "that feveral who were near the queen had inclinations favorable to the court of St. Germains; but they could not make it practicable, as they all faid, to take any fteps in that intereft, without hazard to *their own:* and I never found they had a true zeal for any thing elfe." OXFORD and BOLINGBROKE, the two principal leaders of adminiftration, had long been at variance, and the diffenfion between them now became open and public. Oxford was a man not remarkable for capacity, but long and intimately converfant in bufinefs; clofe, plaufible, fubtle, jealous, intriguing, and ambitious. He aimed at engroffing the entire confidence of the

---

after which fhe again turned to M. Mefnager, and faid, " 'Tis a good work; I pray God fucceed you in it: I am fure I long for peace; I hate this dreadful work of blood:"—and fhook her head two or three times as fhe retired, adding fome words, which M. Mefnager tells us he was extremely forry he was not able to overhear. Vide Mefnager's Memoirs.

the queen, and the sole management of affairs: and instead of admitting Bolingbroke to the rank of a coadjutor, he viewed him with meanness of fear and suspicion; as a competitor, by whom he dreaded to be eclipsed and perhaps supplanted. On the other hand, Bolingbroke finding himself regarded in the light of a rival, made no scruple to become so. This celebrated nobleman, exclusive of the exterior and personal advantages by which he was distinguished, was possessed of abilities of the first order, of manners the most captivating, of eloquence the most commanding. In almost every thing, the reverse of the earl of Oxford; his temper was open and generous; his conduct, both in public and private life, high-spirited and magnanimous; and his measures bold and decisive. Equally with Oxford the slave of ambition, and less scrupulous in the means of gratifying it, there was good reason to fear lest a minister of this description, in order to secure the favor of the sovereign, who cherished a secret but inveterate dislike to the house of Hanover, would engage with ardor in the prosecution of projects, which the phlegmatic caution of Oxford would deem romantic and impracticable, and which were also abhorrent from his feelings and principles. While Oxford entirely lost the confidence of the Tories, which indeed he never perfectly possessed, by his slowness, duplicity, and indecision; Bolingbroke gained ground, both with the queen and the faction, by the superiority of his talents, his firmness and vigor. Resolute and daring, from that consciousness of genius which led him to place an entire reliance upon the resources of his own mind, he very early acquired, and ever after maintained, in a degree which no political leader since the death of Shaftesbury had been able to attain, the most surprising ascendency over the opinions of all his political associates.

I:

It is difficult to conjecture, however, under what pretence or color any attempt could have been made to subvert the protestant succession, for which both parties publicly and uniformly professed the most zealous attachment. In the beginning of March, the queen, whose health was much affected by the violence of those parties which she found herself unable to control, and the still more distressing animosities and contentions of her own ministers, went in person to the house of lords; and after magnifying the advantages secured to England by the late treaty of peace, she observed, "That some persons had been so malicious as to insinuate, that the protestant succession in the house of Hanover was in danger under her government; but that those who endeavored to distract the minds of men with imaginary dangers, could only mean to disturb the public tranquillity." This declaration was much better received by the commons than in the house of peers, where the Whigs were very numerous and powerful. The question being proposed by the earl of Wharton, Whether the protestant succession was in danger under the present administration? a very warm debate ensued; and the lord treasurer Oxford, laying his hand upon his heart, declared, that he had on so many occasions given such signal proofs of affection to the protestant succession, that he was confident no member of that august assembly could ever mean to call it in question. The protestant succession was at length voted out of danger by a small majority*. The earl of Wharton

---

* Upon this occasion the earl of Anglesea, who had the reputation of being at the head of the *Trimmers*, divided with the Whigs. And it has been shrewdly suggested, that the reason why so many of this class voted the protestant succession to be in danger, was their firm persuasion that it was perfectly safe. "The art of the Whigs," says lord Bolingbroke,

Wharton then moved, that an address should be presented to the queen, to issue a proclamation, promising a reward to any person who should apprehend the Pretender, dead or alive; to which lord Trevor very humanely and properly proposed to add, " in case of his landing, or attempting to land, in Great Britain or Ireland." To the motion, thus mitigated and modified, the house agreed; and on its being presented to the queen, she replied in the following terms: " My lords, it would be a real strengthening to the succession in the house of Hanover, as well as a support to my government, that an end were put to those groundless fears and jealousies which have been so industriously propagated. I do not, at this time, see any occasion for such a proclamation: whenever I judge it to be necessary, I shall give my orders for having it issued." The next step which the never-ceasing jealousy of the Whigs led them to adopt, was, to persuade the court of Herenhausen to order baron Schutz, the Hanoverian envoy, to demand of the chancellor a writ for the electoral prince as duke of Cambridge, with a view to his residence in England. Of this design the queen, however, expressed her disapprobation to the princess Sophia, in terms so strong, that it was thought expedient to lay it aside. The death of the electress taking place at this period, the elector of Brunswic was, by an order of the court, prayed for by name in all churches and chapels throughout England, as presumptive heir to the English crown. In May, a

---

Bolingbroke, " was to blend as undistinguishably as they could, all their party interests with those of the succession, and they made just the same factious use of the *supposed* danger of it, as the Tories had endeavored to make some time before of the *supposed* danger of the church."

bill

bill to prevent the growth of Schism was introduced: by which dissenters were prohibited from all interference in the business of education. For though the evil effect was acknowledged to be without remedy, and therefore entitled to some indulgence, the evil cause, it was said, ought to be prevented, and was therefore entitled to none. Notwithstanding the utmost efforts of the Whigs, who were enflamed with a just indignation at this atrocious invasion of the natural rights of mankind, this detestable bill passed through both houses, and received the royal assent. This was however the last triumph of the Tory party, many of whom were undoubtedly disposed to have gone far greater lengths. But the queen's constitution was now so entirely broken, that it was evident she approached towards the conclusion of her life: and the ministers of the crown, in the alarming prospect of her dissolution, thought of little else than their private interests and personal safety. Oxford and Bolingbroke were now so exasperated against each other, that they could not abstain from the most indecent and bitter altercation, even in the presence of the queen. Not a single measure, however, was adopted at this critical period, by which it could be inferred that the ministry entertained designs hostile to the protestant succession. On the contrary, attempts having been made to enlist men for the service of the Pretender, a proclamation was immediately issued, promising a reward of 5000l. for apprehending the Pretender, whenever he should land, or attempt to land, in Great Britain or Ireland. Both houses voted an address of thanks for this proclamation; and lord Bolingbroke himself brought in a bill, denouncing the penalties of high treason against those who should enlist, or be enlisted, in the Pretender's service. On the 9th of July the session was terminated by a speech from the throne, in which the queen affirmed, that her chief concern was to preserve the proteſtant religion, the liberty of her ſubjects, and the tranquillity of the kingdom. On the 27th of July the earl of Oxford was unexpectedly diveſted of the ſtaff of treaſurer; and Bolingbroke found himſelf elevated to the ſummit of power, by the ſudden and total fall of his rival. This ſplendid pre-eminence, however, he enjoyed only for a moment. The queen, who was perceived to be extremely agitated from the time of the difmiſſion of lord Oxford, never recovered her compoſure of mind; but, as if altogether exhauſted by inceſſant fatigue, chagrin, and vexation, ſhe gradually ſunk into a kind of lethargy, in which ſtate ſhe remained till Sunday morning Auguſt 1 (1714), when ſhe expired, in the 50th year of her age, and the 13th of her reign.

Whatever projects Bolingbroke might have in contemplation, they were entirely diſconcerted by the firmneſs and ſpirit with which the leaders of the Whig party acted upon this occaſion. A meeting of the privy council being convened when the queen was on the verge of departure, they took their places at the council-board without any regular ſummons, and immediately proceeded, by the moſt vigorous meaſures, to provide for the ſecurity of the kingdom. Orders were diſpatched to ſeveral regiments of horſe and dragoons to march towards the metropolis. Directions were given for equipping a fleet with all expedition. An expreſs was ſent off to the elector of Hanover, ſignifying, that the queen's life was deſpaired of, and deſiring that he would without delay repair to Holland, where he would find a Britiſh ſquadron ready to convoy him to England. Inſtructions were at the ſame time diſpatched to the earl of Strafford, ambaſſador at the Hague, to demand from the ſtates the performance of their engagements, as guarantees of the proteſtant ſucceſſion; and the heralds at arms

were

were kept in waiting, in order to proclaim the new king the inſtant the throne ſhould become vacant. No ſymptoms of popular tumult or diſcontent however, much leſs of oppoſition, appeared on this great occaſion; and whatever might be intended, it is certain nothing was effected by the late queen and her miniſters in favor of the Pretender.

The death of that princeſs muſt notwithſtanding, upon the whole, be regarded as a very ſeaſonable and fortunate event. For, had Bolingbroke been fully eſtabliſhed in the poſt of prime miniſter, it is impoſſible to aſcertain the extent of the miſchief which might eventually have reſulted from the union of ſuch uncommon talents with ſuch a total want or diſregard of principle. The queen, however, merits our pity at leaſt as much as our cenſure. Her partiality for her own family, and her diſlike of the houſe of Hanover, were natural and pardonable. The queen's own political conduct, notwithſtanding her high theoretical principles of government, was uniformly regulated by the ſtricteſt regard to the laws and liberties of the kingdom, for the welfare of which ſhe entertained even a maternal ſolicitude: and, if ever ſhe indulged the idea of cauſing the crown, at her deceaſe, to revert to the hereditary, and, doubtleſs, as ſhe imagined, the true and rightful claimant, it was certainly only on conditions, which, in her opinion, would have effectually ſecured both the proteſtant religion and the Engliſh conſtitution from the hazard of future violation.

K. GEORGE I.

GEORGE-LOUIS, elector of Hanover, and head of the house of BRUNSWIC-LUNENBURG, derived his descent from the blood-royal of England by his mother Sophia, daughter of Frederic, elector palatine and king of Bohemia; who married Elizabeth of England, only daughter of James I. It is evident therefore, that the title of this prince was founded solely on the choice of the parliament, *i. e.* of the people or nation; and that the usual order of succession was entirely superseded. For, *admitting* the male line of the house of Stuart to have been extinguished in the person of James II., the right of blood rested in the house of Savoy, descended from Henrietta Duchess of Orleans, daughter of Charles I. And the princess Sophia herself being the youngest daughter of the unfortunate Palatine, more than fifty descendants of that prince prior in the order of succession were passed over in the act of William, which settled the crown of England on the house of Hanover. So that the rights of the people were not only asserted, but exercised in their full extent: and the family upon the throne is indisputably *an elected family*, though the general law or rule of succession remains unaltered. The new monarch was, at the period of his accession,

accession, in the 55th year of his age, being born the day before the restoration of K. Charles II. The uniform prudence with which this prince had conducted himself throughout the conflicts of the late reign, the general respectability of his character, and the auspicious circumstances which attended his elevation, seemed to augur calm and prosperous days. The embers of civil discord and animosity were extinguished however only in appearance, and the violent measures which the King was unhappily persuaded to adopt, soon rekindled not only the torch of sedition but the flames of war. The kingdom might at this time be considered as divided with great nearness of equality into the two adverse factions of Whigs and Tories; the latter of which, from the egregious indiscretion of the Whigs in the fatal business of Sacheverel, had recently acquired a great addition of strength and vigor. But it must not be imagined that all who were included in the appellation of Tories, who detested the principles, civil and religious, maintained by the Whigs, as destructive of the ancient constitution and orthodox faith, and who hated still more the persons of the Whigs than their principles, as their perpetual and implacable rivals for power, distinction, and popularity, were therefore attached as a party to the exiled family. Doubtless a great majority of them would have been seriously alarmed at any attempt to restore the son of the late king James to the throne, at least while he remained a papist; and his notorious bigotry precluded almost every hope or expectation of his conversion to protestantism. Previous to the æra of the revolution, the speculative line of discrimination between the two grand factions of the state, now gradually fading into obscurity, was clearly and strongly marked. The WHIGS maintained civil government to be an institution of human origin and appointment, consonant indeed to the divine will,

will, as essential to the order and happiness of the moral creation. The powers vested in the civil magistrate they regarded therefore as a delegation or trust from the people: and it was a necessary consequence of this doctrine, that the individuals entrusted with these powers were ultimately responsible to the people for the exercise of them, and liable to be degraded and punished for the abuse of them. They asserted that there were unalienable rights inherent in human nature, for the preservation of which, government was originally instituted; amongst the chiefest and most important of which they accounted the right which every man possesses of worshipping GOD, not according to a decree of the state, but to the dictates of his own conscience. In other words, they maintained the principle of TOLERATION, not as a matter of favor, but of justice. And this principle was considered by them as violated, not only by laws professedly penal, but by any exclusion from the common rights and privileges of citizenship, founded not on any species of civil delinquency, but the mere unavoidable diversity of religious opinions. The TORIES, on the other hand, rejected these doctrines with vehement indignation and abhorrence, as subversive of the welfare, and even of the existence, of civil society. They asserted that government was expressly ordained of GOD, from whom alone princes derive their authority, and to whom alone they were responsible for their actions—that to resist the will of the Sovereign, was in effect to resist the will of GOD—and that although, when the commands of the sovereign were directly opposed to the commands of GOD, an active obedience could not be lawfully yielded; yet even in these extreme cases it was the duty of the subject quietly to submit to all the consequences of his non-compliance: and that passive obedience and non-resistance were at all times and in all cases right and obligatory,

gatory, where active obedience became either criminal or impracticable. They were far from denying that it was the duty of the prince to confult and provide for the welfare and happinefs of the people, as the great end of his government; but for any neglect or contempt of this duty, there was, as they afferted, no lawful remedy but humble petition and remonftrance. That the people had rights, they admitted; but thefe rights were not to be defended by force. In the number of thefe rights, however, they did not include the right of private judgment in religion. They conceived it to be the duty of individuals to acquiefce in that *formula* of doctrines, and to conform to that mode of worfhip, which the wifdom of the ftate had provided; that to oppofe private to public opinion was in all cafes prefumptuous and unwarrantable; and in matters of religion more efpecially dangerous, and doubly culpable, as a contemptuous defiance of the united authority of church and ftate*. Subfequent to the revolution, however, in which great tranfaction the Tories had taken a very laudable and decided part, they appear to have been much embarraffed to maintain the credit and confiftency of their fyftem. At the trial of Sacheverel, the duke of Leeds, fo famous under his former title of earl of Danby, and who had himfelf given a noble proof of his patriotifm by figning the invitation to the

---

* That this delineation of the principles by which the two great parties in the ftate were diftinguifhed is accurate and juft, may be demonftrated by an appeal to that perfect ftandard of Toryifm and Highchurchifm, the ever-memorable decree of the univerfity of Oxford, paffed in full convocation, July 21, 1683, and prefented to the King (Charles II.), July 24. " The VICE-CHANCELLOR, doctors, proctors, and mafters, regent and not regent, met in convocation, decree, judge, and declare, to the honor of the holy and undivided Trinity, the prefervation of the catholic truth in the church, and that the king's majefty may be fecured from the machinations of treacherous heretics and fchifmatics

the prince of Orange, scrupled not to declare the revolution to be an event, however urgent the political necessity of it, utterly irreconcileable with any just principles of government; that those who examined it least therefore were its best friends; and that a veil ought to be thrown over that transaction, instead of quoting it as a precedent fit and proper for imitation*. Many of this party

schismatics—all and every of the following propositions (cum multis aliis) to be false, seditious, and impious, and destructive of all government in church and state.

* * * * * *

" All civil government is derived originally from the people.

* * * * * *

" That there is a mutual compact, tacit or express, between a prince and his subjects, and that if he perform not his duty, they are discharged from theirs.

* * * * * *

" That if lawful governors become tyrants, or govern otherwise than by the law of God and Man they ought to do, they forfeit the right they had unto their government.

* * * * * *

" The sovereignty of England is in three estates—viz. king, lords, and commons; the king having but a co-ordinate or subordinate power.

* * * * * *

" Self-preservation is the fundamental law of nature, and supersedes all others whensoever they stand in competition with it.

* * * * * *

" There is no obligation upon christians to passive obedience, when the prince commands any thing contrary to the laws.

* * * * * *

" It is not lawful for superiors to impose any thing in the worship of God that is not antecedently necessary.

* * * * * *

" Wicked kings and tyrants ought to be put to death; and if the judges and inferior magistrates will not do their office, the power of the sword devolves to the people."

* Nothing is more common or easy than for persons who are far removed from the embarrassments and temptations incident to those who occupy distinguished stations in public life, to censure the least deviation

from

party satisfied themselves with the notion of an abdication on the part of the monarch, and asserted with Sacheverel himself, in defiance of facts, that the nation did not resist. The generality of the Tories, however, including almost the whole body of the clergy, highly offended with the unexpected advancement of the prince of Orange to the throne, adopted the famous distinction of a king *de facto*, and a king *de jure*: and by yielding a passive obedience to the monarch in possession, they flattered themselves that they consulted their interest without abandoning their principle. After the death of the duke of Gloucester, the MARCELLUS of England, the national detestation of popery, which equally pervaded all parties, induced the Tories to acquiesce in the parliamentary settlement of the crown on the house of Hanover, as the least of two great evils, without appearing very solicitous, after the lapse of so many years, to reconcile their practice with a theory the original uncontaminated dignity of which it was no longer possible for them to maintain. The Whigs, on the contrary, had ever distinguished themselves by the ardor of their zeal for the Hanover succession. Nor would the strength of their attachment to that house have been shaken or impaired by

from the rigid line of rectitude, in terms of harsh and indiscriminate severity; thus indirectly asserting their own claim to the praise of immaculate and incorruptible integrity, beyond the possibility of *confutation*; though there may perhaps arise a *suspicion* that, in the hour of trial and danger, the patriotism and public spirit of the accused might be found beyond all comparison to surpass that of their dogmatical and virulent accusers, who would fain persuade us that there is no virtue in men whose conduct indicates any mixture of human weakness and infirmity.—These observations are particularly applicable to the earl of Danby, who more than redeemed his political errors and delinquencies by the glorious ardor with which, at the extreme hazard of his life and fortune, he concurred in the original formation, and subsequent happy and successful accomplishment, of the ever-memorable revolution.

by any recantations or proteſtations, however frequent or ſolemn, on the part of the Pretender. Under the banners of this party, the diſſenters of all denominations ranged themſelves with eagerneſs; and in a political view they might be conſidered as directly oppoſed to the Jacobites, who regarded the Sectaries with peculiar malignity, and who, under the general denomination of Tories, ſought for occaſions of ſubverting the preſent eſtabliſhment, with anxiety as inceſſant as the diſſenters to fortify and ſecure it. Under theſe circumſtances, it is no wonder that the king ſhould entertain a ſtrong predilection for the Whigs; and being educated in the principles of Lutheraniſm, which bear a nearer analogy to preſbyterianiſm than to epiſcopacy, he regarded the diſſenters with favor, as men whoſe political and religious opinions rendered them his firmeſt and moſt unalterable friends; and it is ſaid that, the unfortunate fate of king Charles I. being once mentioned in his preſence, as a proof of their implacable animoſity to kings, he replied with a pleaſant indifference, "that he had nothing to fear, for that the king-killers were all on his ſide." Convinced that no danger was to be apprehended on the death of the queen, either from foreign or domeſtic enemies, he appeared in no haſte to leave Herenhauſen; and it was not till the middle of September that he arrived in England, which exhibited every where the appearance of ſatisfaction and tranquillity. The king of France, of whom alone any jealouſy could be entertained, ordered, on the firſt intelligence of the demiſe of the queen, M. D'Ibberville, his envoy extraordinary at the court of London, to declare, in the moſt explicit terms, his reſolution to adhere to the terms of the late treaty, and his ſincere deſire to maintain the moſt perfect amity and good underſtanding with the new ſovereign: and count Konigſeg, the

the imperial ambaſſador, offered, in the name of the emperor his maſter, any number of troops that might be wanted at this criſis, to ſupport the authority of government. Previous to the departure of the king from Hanover, notwithſtanding the preſent fair and flattering appearances, he had tranſmitted orders to the regency*, conſiſting of the ſeven great officers of ſtate, and certain other perſons appointed in virtue of an act paſſed in the late reign, to remove lord Bolingbroke from his poſt of ſecretary of ſtate, and to ſeal up the doors of his office. This was ominous of the change of miniſtry, which took place immediately on his aſſumption of the regal power. And it was no leſs abſolute and deciſive than that which preceded it, A. D. 1710. The earl of Halifax was made firſt commiſſioner of the treaſury, the king refuſing to create a lord high treaſurer; not chooſing, as he ſaid, that there ſhould be any greater man in the kingdom than himſelf.

---

* For the mere purpoſe of embarraſſing the Whigs, a motion had been made in parliament by the Tories, A. D. 1705, for an addreſs to the queen, beſeeching her majeſty to invite the princeſs Sophia, preſumptive heireſs to the crown, to reſide within the realm. The Whigs raiſed their credit extremely with the queen, to whom this motion was very offenſive, by the ſtrenuous oppoſition which they heſitated not to give to it; and in order to preſerve their credit with the nation, a bill was brought in, under the ſanction of the Whig miniſtry, for ſecuring the proteſtant ſucceſſion; by which, in caſe of the queen's demiſe, the executive power of government was veſted in the perſons holding the offices of archbiſhop of Canterbury, lord Chancellor, lord Treaſurer, lord Preſident, lord Privy Seal, lord High Admiral, and lord Chief Juſtice of the queen's bench, in conjunction with certain other perſons, nominated as regents by the ſucceſſor in three liſts to be ſealed up and depoſited with the archbiſhop of Canterbury, the lord Chancellor, and the miniſter reſidentiary of Hanover. This bill the Tories in their turn oppoſed with violence; but it paſſed by a great majority, and with the general approbation of the nation; and the Tories, by their injudicious conduct in the whole of this tranſaction, afforded their rivals a great and deciſive advantage.

himself. Lord Townshend and general Stanhope were nominated secretaries of state, and to them was chiefly committed the direction of foreign affairs. The earl of Nottingham, the only Tory admitted into the new administration, was declared president of the council, the former council being previously dissolved. Lord Cowper was reinstated in the high office of chancellor; the command of the army restored to the duke of Marlborough; the privy seal given to the earl of Wharton, and lord Sunderland appointed to the government of Ireland.—Hitherto no more was done than might have been with certainty expected: no more than the attachments and even the interests of the new government might reasonably perhaps be thought to require. But it quickly appeared that measures of great severity, amounting to almost a general proscription of the Tory party, were determined upon by the Whigs, who were now in full and exclusive possession of the government; and whose power seemed established on a basis so firm, as might, if the spirit of equity and moderation had influenced their councils, have inclined them to a milder and more temperate system of policy. The parliament, which assembled in March 1715, was composed almost entirely of Whigs, who were well disposed to second the most vindictive measures which could be suggested by the administration: " For the ministers," says lord Bolingbroke, " whose true interest it must always be to calm the minds of men, were upon this occasion the tribunes of the people."

The royal proclamation convoking this assembly contained in it the following indiscreet expressions: " It having pleased Almighty GOD, by most remarkable steps of his providence, to bring us safe to the crown of this kingdom, notwithstanding the designs of evil men, we do not doubt that our loving subjects will, in the ensuing elections,

elections, have particular regard to such as shewed a firmness to the proteftant fucceffion *when it was in danger.*" This was ftyled by fir William Wyndham, a member confpicuous for his parliamentary talents, no lefs than his zealous attachment to the Tory intereft, " an unprecedented and unwarrantable exertion of the prerogative, and of dangerous confequence to the very being of parliaments," for which, having refufed to apologize, he was, by order of the houfe, reprimanded by the fpeaker, who intimated that it was owing to the extraordinary lenity of the houfe, that he was not committed to the tower. Sir William Wyndham in reply declared, " that he was neither confcious of offering any indignity to his majefty, nor of violating the privileges of that houfe ; and that he had therefore no thanks to give thofe gentlemen, who, under pretence of lenity, had brought this cenfure upon him." This incident fufficiently indicated the temper of the houfe, the attention of which was however quickly engaged by far greater objects, in confequence of official information from general Stanhope and Mr. Walpole, a man of diftinguifhed ability, and who had in the late reign fuffered feverely for his attachment to the Whig intereft, under the recollection of which he yet fmarted[*], that the papers found in the office of the late lord Bolingbroke would afford ample ground for impeaching various of the members of the former adminiftration, which they affirmed to be the moft wicked and corrupt that had ever fat at the helm

[*] In the feffion of parliament 1711, Mr. Walpole, on pretence of a *douceur* of 1000 guineas faid to have been received by him, or with his confent, from the profits of a certain government contract made by him when fecretary at war, was voted guilty of an high breach of truft and notorious corruption, was committed prifoner to the tower, and expelled the houfe, and a profecution ordered to be inftituted againft him.

helm of affairs in this country. This nobleman, who had hitherto preserved the appearance of great serenity; attending and even taking a part, as usual, in the debates of the house of lords; now withdrew with great precipitation to the continent. In the beginning of April general Stanhope laid before the house of commons all the papers relating to the negociations of the late ministry with France, which were immediately referred to a select committee of twenty-one persons; and in June Mr. Walpole, as chairman, made the report, in which the secret preliminaries signed with M. Mesnager, the suspension of arms, the seizure of Ghent and Bruges by the duke of Ormond, lord Bolingbroke's journey to Paris, and separate conferences with the French ministry; in a word, all the measures which preceded or facilitated the conclusion of the peace of Utrecht, were stated as highly criminal. And Mr. Walpole, boldly asserting that to vindicate these measures was in a manner to share the guilt of them, terminated the report by impeaching Henry lord viscount Bolingbroke of HIGH TREASON; and lord Coningsby immediately standing up, exclaimed, "The worthy chairman has impeached the hand, but I impeach the head—I impeach Robert earl of Oxford and earl Mortimer of high treason." On the 21st of June general Stanhope impeached the duke of Ormond of high treason; and the day following Mr. Aiflabie impeached the earl of Strafford of high crimes and misdemeanors. And such was the temper of the house, that these impeachments were for the most part carried without difficulty, and almost without a division. It is notwithstanding very hard to discover upon what constitutional grounds any of these impeachments could be voted, and much less how the charges contained in them could amount to the crime of high treason. The measures adopted by the late Tory ministry were, it must be allowed, disgraceful

graceful to the reputation, incompatible with the engagements, and in some points injurious to the interests, of the kingdom. But as nothing was done without the sanction and concurrence of parliament, on what pretence of justice ministers could be punished for carrying into effect measures of state policy which had received either the previous or subsequent approbation of the legislature, it seems difficult or rather impossible to devise. To mislead or delude the parliament into a mistaken approbation of any specific measures of government by defective or erroneous information, is indeed an high offence : But to execute measures approved by the legislature, in consequence of full and sufficient information, cannot be criminal in individuals holding offices of responsibility, because it is their duty to conform to the public will; and to the legislature itself it would be solecism and absurdity to impute criminality. Of the impeachment of the duke of Ormond in particular, a nobleman of unblemished integrity, of honor without a stain, equally distinguished by courtesy and courage; no less the ornament of his country than its defence; the injustice appears gross and manifest. Of all the charges adduced against the late ministry, the suspension of arms, which was productive of consequences so disastrous and fatal, was one of the most, or rather was incomparably the most serious, and of the greatest magnitude. But it cannot be pretended that the duke of Ormond could or ought to exercise any discretion in this case : His orders were peremptory and positive. And for any military commander to assume, under such circumstances, a dispensing power, and to presume to act in open contradiction to the authority from which he derives his commission, would indeed call for and justify a parliamentary impeachment. The duke seeing the spirit of faction and revenge so strongly predominate in the proceedings

against

against him, followed lord Bolingbroke to the continent; and both these noblemen, irritated by persecution, and destitute of resource, entered into the service of the court at St. Germaine's, now removed to Commerci in Lorraine, which received by this means a dangerous addition of talents and strength*. On his arrival in France lord Bolingbroke apologized in a letter to his friend lord Lansdowne for his sudden and abrupt departure: " You will," said he, " excuse me when you know that I had certain and repeated information, from some who are in the secret of affairs, that a resolution was taken by those who have power to execute it, to pursue me to the scaffold."

* Though lord Bolingbroke suffered himself to be engaged by earnest solicitation in the service of the pretender, and even accepted the seals as secretary of state to that shadow of a king, while, as he expresses it, " the smart of a bill of attainder tingled in every vein;" on perceiving the hopeless condition of his affairs, and the weakness and distraction of his counsels, he willingly received, in about six months, his dismission from this unenviable pre-eminence. It is a curious circumstance, that on leaving the pretender's service this nobleman had articles of impeachment formally exhibited against him, branched out into the several heads of treachery, incapacity, and neglect: To which he made an elaborate reply, expressing, at the close of it, his obligation to the pretender, for " cutting by this means that Gordian knot asunder, by which he had conceived himself for ever bound to his interests, and which would have effectually precluded every idea of making his peace at home;" an event which from this time became the object of his incessant intrigues and solicitations. The duke of Ormond, who was much more in earnest in his attachment to the exiled family, and who disdained to court a reconciliation with that country by which he considered himself as treated with the highest injustice and ingratitude, retained, during the remainder of his life, his station in the pretender's court, around the cheerless and contracted circle of which he alone reflected some scattered rays of lustre. Previous to his departure from London he visited, for the last time, the earl of Oxford, who dissuaded him from flying with as much earnestness as he intreated Oxford to make his escape. He at length parted from the earl with these words: " Farewell, Oxford, without a head." To which Oxford replied, " Farewell, duke, without a duchy."

fold. Had there been the least reason to hope for a fair and open trial, after having been already prejudged unheard by two houses of parliament, I should not have declined the strictest examination. I challenge the most inveterate of my enemies to produce one instance of a criminal correspondence, or the least corruption of any part of the administration in which I was concerned."— The earl of Oxford, however, conscious of the steadiness of his attachment to the house of Hanover, of the king's real obligation to him, and of his knowledge of that obligation, determined to abide the fury of this political tempest; and the impeachment preferred by the commons being followed by a motion in the house of peers for his commitment, he rose to speak in his defence, observing " that the whole charge might be reduced to the negotiation and conclusion of the peace. That the nation wanted a peace," he said, " no one would deny; and he averred, that the conditions upon which it was made were as good as the obstinate and perverse reluctance of the allies to concur in the queen's measures would admit: That it had been approved by two successive parliaments: That he had acted by the express commands of his sovereign, without offending against any known law; and being justified in his conscience, was unconcerned for the life of an insignificant old man." The earl was attended to the tower by a prodigious concourse of people, shouting, " High Church, Ormond and Oxford for ever!" And the riots and tumults which ensued in various parts of the kingdom, fully justified and verified the expression of the earl of Anglesey, in the debate of this day, " that it was to be feared such violent measures would make the sceptre shake in the king's hands;" for which the house in its wisdom insisted upon his making an apology. When the articles of impeachment were exhibited against the earl of Strafford, that nobleman complained

complained of the arbitrary and illegal seizure of his papers, and defired a competent time to prepare for his defence; requiring for this purpofe duplicates both of fuch as had been laid before the committee of fecrefy, and of thofe remaining in the hands of government.— This requeft, to the difgrace of the ruling party, was vehemently oppofed, until the earl of Ilay reprefented, "that in all civilized nations, all courts of judicature, *the inquifition excepted,* allowed the perfons arraigned all that was neceffary to their juftification; and that the houfe of peers of Great Britain would not, he was perfuaded, in a cafe of this nature, do any thing contrary to that honor and equity, for which they were fo juftly renowned through Europe." The houfe, thus fuddenly and powerfully awakened to a fenfe of their own dignity, refolved that the earl fhould be allowed copies of fuch papers as he might have occafion to ufe in his defence.— Bills of attainder, in default of perfonal appearance, paffed againft the duke of Ormond and lord vifcount Bolingbroke. Their names and armorial bearings were erazed from the rolls of the peerage, by order of the houfe; and the duke's atchievements as knight of the garter taken down from St. George's chapel at Windfor: And from the addrefs of the fpeaker to the king at the clofe of the feffion, which was protracted to the end of the fummer, it does not appear that the anger of the houfe had fuffered any abatement. "Your commons," faid the fpeaker, Sir Spencer Compton*, "could net fee without the utmoft indignation the glories of her late majefty's reign tarnifhed by a treacherous ceffation of arms—the faith of treaties violated—that ancient probity for which the Englifh nation had been juftly renowned throughout all ages, expofed to fcorn and contempt.—

Such

---

* Afterwards created Earl of Wilmington.

Such was the condition of the kingdom, when it pleased the divine Providence to call your majesty to the throne of your anceſtors, under whoſe auſpicious reign, your commons behold with pleaſure the glory of the Plantagenets, your majeſty's royal anceſtors, revive, and have an unbounded proſpect of the continuance of this happineſs to the lateſt poſterity." A very great part of the nation being much inflamed with the late extraordinary proceedings, the partizans of the pretender were incited to exert themſelves with redoubled vigor and activity; and it was determined at one and the ſame time to take up arms in both kingdoms againſt the government. In the month of September 1715, the earl of Mar ſet up the ſtandard of rebellion, and proclaimed the pretender, under the ſtyle and title of king James III. at Caſtletown in Scotland, and ſoon collected an army of ten thouſand men. The vigilance of the government in a great meaſure rendered abortive the deſigns concerted by the adherents of the houſe of Stuart on the ſouth of the Tweed. The Habeas Corpus Act being ſuſpended, ſeveral noblemen were committed to the tower, amongſt whom were Lord Lanſdowne and the earl of Jerſey, who had engaged to join the duke of Ormond on his intended landing in the weſt. By previous conſent of the lower houſe of parliament, Sir William Wyndham, Mr. Harvey, and various other members of that houſe, were ſeized and committed to cloſe cuſtody, the bail of the duke of Somerſet, father-in-law to Sir William Wyndham, being peremptorily refuſed, and the duke himſelf, for ſome indiſcreet expreſſions of reſentment, removed from his place of maſter of the Horſe. Notwithſtanding, however, theſe ſpirited and reſolute meaſures of prevention, the earl of Derwentwater and Mr. Foſter appeared at the head of an armed force in Northumberland, and proclaimed the pretender at Warkworth, Penrith, Lancaſter, easter, and other places, in their progress to the southward. At their arrival at Preston, November 12, they were attacked by the king's forces under the generals Willes and Carpenter, who investing the town on all sides, compelled them to surrender at discretion: And the very same day a bloody battle was fought, between the earl of Mar and the duke of Argyle, at Sheriffmoor, near Dumblaine in Scotland. The duke, apprized of the intention of the earl of Mar to cross the Forth, in order to join the insurgents in the Lowlands, hastened to secure the passes of that river, which he himself crossed at Stirling, and immediately took possession, with a force not exceeding 4000 men, of the heights of Dumblaine. The earl of Mar now advanced to the attack; and the Clans of Glengary and Clanronald, which formed part of the enemy's right wing, rushed down upon the royalists, sword in hand, with such determined and irresistible impetuosity, that the left wing of the king's army was in a short time entirely broke, and general Whetham, who commanded it, carried the news of his own defeat with incredible expedition to Stirling—declaring the ruin of the whole army to be inevitable. In the mean time, the duke of Argyle, who commanded the right wing in person, charged the enemy with the most heroic ardor, and drove them before him, about two miles, as far as the Loch of Allen, though they repeatedly attempted to rally. On his return from this pursuit, he was unexpectedly confronted by the victorious rebels on their return from the pursuit of Whetham: and each army found itself possessed of the station occupied, in the early part of the engagement, by the adversary. In this posture they remained till evening, when the rebels returned to Ardoch, and the duke to Dumblaine; and next day marching back to the field of battle, he carried off the wounded, and several pieces of cannon

cannon left by the enemy. Though the engagement was thus indecisive, all the honor, as well as advantage, of the fight, rested with the duke of Argyle, who, with a force so inferior, had entirely disconcerted the schemes of his antagonist by the most intrepid personal exertions.— Various successes were obtained also by the royalists in the northern parts of Scotland, where the loss of Inverness was very severely felt by the rebels; and Argyle being now joined by large reinforcements, it was with difficulty Mar kept the field till the arrival of the pretender in person, who landed at Peter-head Dec. 26th, and immediately issued various proclamations: One of which was for summoning a convention of the Estates; a second ordering all fencible men to repair to his standard; and a third fixing a day for his coronation. He cherished, however, no sanguine hope of success; "For me," said he, in a speech addressed to his friends convened in council, "it will be no new thing if I am unfortunate: My whole life, even from my cradle, has shewn a constant series of misfortunes, and I am prepared, if so it please God, to suffer the threats of my enemies and yours." In a very short time the folly and rashness of the enterprise became so apparent, that on receiving intelligence of the approach of the duke of Argyle, he resolved to embark on board a French ship lying in the harbor of Montrose, accompanied by the earls of Mar and Melfort, which stretching over to Norway, in order to avoid pursuit, and coasting along the shores of Germany and Holland, arrived in five days at Graveline: The rebel army retiring northward, quietly dispersed without making any farther effort, or receiving the slightest molestation. The extreme misconduct and want of capacity apparent in the whole of this enterprise, was decisive of the personal disposition and character of the claimant of the British crown; and the impolitic violence,

which

which had hitherto predominated in the counfels of the new monarch, was happily compenfated by the wretched imbecility of his rival. "Should the pretender ever be reftored, it was eafy," Lord Bolingbroke tells us, "to fee that the court of St. James's would be conftituted in the fame manner as that of St. Germain's." On being prefented with the draft of a declaration to be difperfed in England, he took exception againft feveral paffages, and particularly thofe by which a direct promife of fecuring the churches of England and Scotland was made.— He was *told*," he faid, "that he could not, in confcience, make fuch a promife;" and, on being farther urged to compliance, afked with warmth, why the Tories were fo defirous to have him, if they expected thofe things from him which his religion did not allow?" And after confulting his confidents and cafuifts, the papers were at length printed, with amendments which exhibited the extreme of Jefuitical prevarication, infomuch that lord Bolingbroke abfolutely refufed to counterfign them. Intoxicated with fuperftition and enthufiaftic zeal, all efforts were quickly perceived to be loft on a man whofe obftinacy and prejudice were fortified by the native narrownefs of his underftanding. "His religion," fays the nobleman juft mentioned, "is not founded on the love of virtue, and the deteftation of vice, on a fenfe of that obedience which is due to the will of the Supreme Being, or of thofe obligations which creatures formed to live in a mutual dependence on one another lie under. The fpring of his whole conduct is *fear*; he has all the fuperftition of a Capuchin, but I found in him no tincture of the religion of a prince; and I converfed with very few among the Roman Catholics themfelves, who did not think him too much a papift." Although the rebellion in both kingdoms was thus happily and fpeedily fuppreffed, the clemency of the king did not appear fo confpicuous as might have been wifhed, and reafonably expected. The lords Derwentwater, Nithifdale, and Nairne, with divers other noblemen, being tried in Weftminfter-hall, received fentence of death, earl Cowper prefiding as lord high fteward. And notwithftanding the affecting and urgent fupplications of the countefles of Derwentwater and Nithifdale, and lady Nairne, who threw themfelves at the king's feet, and implored his mercy, no mitigation of the fentence could be obtained; and very many of the lower claſſes of the people fell a facrifice to the fatal delufion of thofe miftaken principles which led them to engage in this revolt*, which might, in all human probability, have been eafily prevented by the adoption of a more equitable and generous policy.—" Certain it is," fays lord Bolingbroke, " if milder meafures had been purfued, that the Tories would never have univerfally embraced Jacobitifm: the violence of the Whigs forced them into the arms of the pretender, and dyed the royal ermines in blood." The king was, notwithftanding of a difpofition by no means harfh or implacable. On the contrary, it was with extreme hefitation and reluctance that he concurred in the meafures which he was aſſured were neceſſary to his fafety. And we are told, that when lord Somers, who in a ftate of

great

---

* For the following curious anecdote we are indebted to the Rev. Mr. Macaulay's ingenious topographical hiftory of the parifh of Claybroke in Leicefterfhire: One Paul, a clergyman, and vicar of Orton upon the Hill in that county, was tried and convicted, A. D. 1715, of high treafon, he having joined the rebels at Prefton in Lancafhire, and fuffered, with the moft undaunted refolution, the utmoft rigor of the law. On the Sunday previous to his departure he preached a fermon at his own parifh church, from Ezek. xxi. 26, 27. " Thus faith the Lord God, remove the diadem, and take off the crown. Exalt him that is low, and abafe him that is high. I will overturn, overturn, overturn, and it fhall be no more, until he come whofe right it is, and I will give it unto him."

great corporeal infirmity still retained his wonted powers of mind, was informed by lord Townshend, with much exultation, that the king had at length consented to all that was required of him, this aged and venerable patriot asked him with great emotion, and shedding many tears, whether they meant to revive the proscriptions of Marius and Sylla*. The ministry, perceiving and probably resenting the general discontent and disaffection of the

people

---

* " All the traditional accounts of this nobleman," says Mr. Walpole, now lord Orford, who has delineated his character with great felicity, " the historians of the last age, and its best authors, represent him as the most incorrupt lawyer and the honestest statesman ; as a master-orator, a genius of the finest taste, and as a patriot of the noblest and most extensive views ; as a man who dispensed blessings by his life, and planned them for posterity. Mr. Addison, who has drawn a labored but diffuse and feeble character of him in the Freeholder, tells us that he gained great esteem with queen Anne, who had conceived many unreasonable prejudices against him. Mr. Addison might as well have said that the queen had at first disbelieved, and was afterwards converted to Sir Isaac Newton's system of comets. Her majesty was full as good a judge of astronomy as of lord Somers's merits. The momentous times in which he lived gave lord Somers opportunities of displaying the extent of his capacity, and the patriotism of his heart.—The excellent balance of our constitution never appeared in a clearer light than with relation to this lord, who, though impeached by a misguided house of commons, with all the intemperate folly that at times disgraced the free states of Greece, yet had full liberty to vindicate his innocence, and manifest an integrity which could never have shone so bright unless it had been juridically aspersed. In this country happily the factious and the envious have not a power of condemning by a shell which many of them cannot sign." To these excellent observations it may be permitted to add, that when we reflect on the firm and undaunted stand made by the house of lords on this and other interesting occasions against the democratic fury of the commons, we shall not be forward to applaud the wisdom of those by whom that house was once voted, or of those who are now ready to pronounce it, useless. That there should exist one sovereign will only in a state, is certain ; but the legislative body in which this will resides may, by a just and wise organization, contain within itself a principle of vigorous

collision

people to a government which willingly concealed even from itself the defire of vengeance by which it was actuated, under the veil of loyalty and patriotifm, now found or imagined the neceffity of adopting a meafure for the prefervation of the public fafety, which has been ever confidered as the higheft and moft unconftitutional exertion of parliamentary authority attempted fince the æra of the revolution; and if we except the act of Henry VIII. declaring the proclamations of the crown equal in validity to acts of parliament, and the perpetuity act of Charles I., it may not be too much to affirm, fince the exiftence of parliaments. This was no other than the introduction of the famous *Septennial Bill*, in the feffion of 1716, by which the parliament not only affumed a power of prolonging the duration of future parliaments, but even its own: and being elected by the nation for three years, they elected themfelves for four years more. As the difcretion vefted in parliament has however no precife

collifion and controul. But we have lately heard much from certain prefumptuous fpeculatifts on the fcience of government, of the ridiculous folly and abfurdity of permitting, under a free conftitution, any portion of hereditary authority—or, to adopt their own phrafeology "hereditary nonfenfe," to exift, however limited or modified; though it is remarkable, that previous to thefe recent difcoveries in politics, wifdom was ever accounted the grand characteriftic feature of ariftocracy, as power of monarchy, and public fpirit of democracy. And of the juftnefs of this political axiom, not to appeal to ancient times, the celebrated republics of Venice and Berne exhibit at this day ftriking and obvious examples. Nor are the reafons,—the permanent caufes of this permanent effect,—difficult to develop; but at prefent, in politics, as at no very diftant period in philofophy, a pretended *common fenfe*, made up of audacity of affertion, and infolence of abufe, is to fuperfede all inductions of reafon, knowledge, and experience. The harfhnefs of this cenfure muft however be qualified with the acknowledgment that in the writings now alluded to are to be found many important and interefting truths, expreffed in language peculiarly ftriking and energetic.

precife limits, no one has ventured formally or judicially to impeach the validity of this act; and it has been truly urged in its favor, that it was in fact agreeable to the fentiments of a great and refpectable part of the nation, who had long feen and deplored the evils attending the frequent recurrence of parliamentary elections under the prefent miferably corrupt, though long-eftablifhed, modes of election; and who were convinced of the danger which muft eventually have arifen from the diffolution of the prefent parliament at a juncture fo critical. The bill, which originated in the houfe of peers, was oppofed with great ability by divers noblemen, and in particular by the earl of Nottingham, who, difgufted and provoked by the intemperate conduct of the adminiftration, had now quitted his connections with the Whigs. This nobleman obferved, " that frequent parliaments were of the effence of the Englifh conftitution, and were fanctioned by the practice of ages; that the members of the lower houfe were delegated by the body of the nation for a certain term of years, at the expiration of which they were no longer the reprefentatives of the people: that by thus lengthening, at their own pleafure, the duration of their own authority, they deprived the people of the only remedy which the wifdom of our anceftors had provided againft the ignorance and corruption of thofe who might be tempted to betray the truft repofed in them: that as to the pretence of adding energy or ftability to the foreign tranfactions or projected alliances of government, what prince or ftate could rationally entruft us with the care of their interefts, when we appeared fo ready to abandon our own? that the preamble of the bill itfelf might fuffice to deter them from entering into engagements with our government, when they underftood by it that the popifh and jacobite faction was fo powerful as to threaten deftruction to the prefent eftablifhment; and that the government

vernment acknowledged its weakness to be such, as to make so extraordinary a provision necessary for its safety; when it appeared that the nation was not to be trusted, and that the affections of the king's subjects were restricted within the limits of the house of commons. He affirmed that a long parliament would encourage every species of corruption in every class of the community; that the value of a seat would bear a determinate proportion to the legal duration of parliaments, and the purchase would rise accordingly; that a long parliament would both enhance the temptations, and multiply the opportunities, of a vicious ministry, to undermine the integrity and independency of parliaments far beyond what could occur if they were short and frequent; that the reasons urged for prolonging the duration of this parliament to seven years, would probably be as strong, and by perseverance in the same impolitic conduct, might be made much stronger before the end of that term, for continuing and even perpetuating their legislative power."

When this bill was transmitted to the commons, it had to encounter an opposition still more vehement and formidable. No sooner was it announced to the house, by two judges sent from the peers, that their lordships had passed a bill for enlarging the time of the continuance of parliaments, to which they desired their concurrence, than lord Guernsey moved to reject the bill without reading it. The house, however, determined by a great majority to receive it; and the bill being a first and second time read, Mr. Shippen arose to oppose the commitment of it. He commenced his observations with remarking, "that he too well knew the hazard attached to every unguarded expression in that house, to venture to say, that by any measures already taken—alluding to the late great augmentation of the land forces—we have paved

paved the way to a despotic and military government.—
Such reflections, indeed, might be pardoned from persons without doors, who are not able to enter into the
depth and wisdom of our counsels, and who presume to
censure what they cannot comprehend. But the present
bill is yet unpassed, and we have as yet a right to investi-
gate its merits with freedom. It has been urged, that the
disaffection of the people is so great, and the enemies of
the government both at home and abroad are so powerful,
that a new election, at this period, may be destructive of
its peace, and even of its safety. If this argument be
applied to the ministry, it is enough to reply, that it is
no concern of ours, whether they have rendered themselves odious to the people or not—They may be destroyed, and the government subsist and flourish. But if it
be applied to his majesty, no argument could be offered
so injurious to his honor. How is it that, in the infancy
of his reign, he hath deprived himself of the love and
affection of a people who so lately received him with
every expression of joy? But, admitting the fact, is this
the way to extinguish the discontents already existing, or
will it not rather increase and create fresh discontents?
Agreeably to the law as it now stands, a dissolution will
not be necessary for a year and a half; and can national
discontents be imagined to exist so long under so wise,
so excellent, and so indulgent an administration as we
now enjoy? Another reason for passing this bill is, that
it may encourage our ancient allies to enter into new
treaties, which, under the actual constitution of things,
they may hesitate or refuse to do. In order therefore to
obtain the favor and friendship of those nations in whose
support we have on so many occasions lavished our treasure and our blood, we must, it seems, alter the present
frame of our constitution! What emotions of indignation must not the insolence of this demand excite—especially

cially if it happen to be urged by a state which owes its very being to England, and which continues to subsist as a sovereign power by our aid and protection! Sir, his majesty, as king of Great Britain, is the arbiter of Europe, and may dictate to other nations, who will for their own sakes court his friendship, and who have always found their account in the alliance of the crown which he now wears. The expence attending frequent elections has been also mentioned. But this is an argument which merits no attention. Every gentleman is a judge of his own circumstances, and knows how far they are competent to the necessary expences of an election; for I will not suppose that the advocates of this bill can mean to extend this argument to *corrupt expences*, when the incorrupt, unbiassed and constitutional mode in which the elections of the present parliament was conducted is so *notorious*. The manner in which this bill has been introduced into the house, is itself a sufficient reason for its rejection. It is sent from the Lords; and as it relates merely to ourselves, I apprehend it to be inconsistent with our honor to receive it. Our predecessors have shewn a determination to resist all attempts to innovate on their privileges; and shall this glorious house of commons be content humbly to model themselves at the pleasure of the lords? Shall we tamely and meanly acquiesce in an attack that strikes at the very foundation of our authority? But however unlimited our complaisance, I humbly conceive we have it not in our power to consent to this bill; for I cannot discover by what rule of reason or law we, who are only representatives, can enlarge, to our own advantage, the authority delegated to us—or that by virtue of such delegated authority we can destroy the fundamental rights of our constitution. This house has no legislative authority, but what it derives from the people. The members of this assembly were chosen
under

under the triennial act. Our truft is therefore a triennial truft; and if we extend it beyond the ftrict legal duration, we ceafe from that inftant to be the truftees of the people, and are our own electors. From that inftant, we act by an unwarrantable affumption of power, and take upon us to create a new conftitution. For though it is a received maxim in civil fcience, that the fupreme legiflature cannot be bound, yet an exception is neceffarily implied, that it is reftrained from fubverting the foundation on which it ftands. The triennial act, which reftored the freedom and frequency of Parliaments, was a conceffion made to the people by king William, in the midft of his difficulties; and the policy of thofe minifters who may advife his majefty to give his royal affent to the repealing of it, is of a nature too refined for my underftanding. And as his majefty has been pleafed to propofe that prince as a model to himfelf, and is emulous to imbibe his fpirit and to equal his glory, it is a matter of aftonifhment to thofe who are not in the fecret of affairs, to fee the falutary meafures adopted on the moft mature deliberation, with a view to the public good, in the reign of the former monarch, fo eagerly and rafhly refcinded in the very commencement of that of the latter. There muft certainly be fome latent caufe for the precipitation with which this bill has been urged; there muft be fome fecret meafure in contemplation, which the minifters of the crown fufpect will not ftand the teft of a new parliament. It muft be fomething, I repeat, hereafter to be done by them; for I will do them the juftice to believe, that for all the manifold mifchiefs that have been done, they feel entirely at their eafe—perfectly callous to the emotions of fenfibility or remorfe. A ftanding parliament, which it is the object of this bill to eftablifh, has been faid to refemble a ftanding pool, the waters of which grow, for want of frefh and free current, offenfive and fetid.

fetid. But the present parliament may more justly be compared to a torrent, which, in its furious and foaming course, desolates the land, bearing down all the landmarks and ancient mounds which have been raised to confine it within its regular and accustomed banks."

After a variety of able speeches from the most distinguished members on both sides of the house, Sir Robert Raymond, afterwards lord Raymond, and chief justice of England, concluded the debate with a comprehensive reply to the arguments in favor of the bill, and a masterly recapitulation of the objections urged against it, of which the multifarious particulars that demand a place in general history will suffer only a concise and cursory mention.— " The arguments for the bill were, according to the enumeration of this able speaker, I. The expences attending frequent elections ; II. The divisions and animosities excited by them ; III. The advantages to be derived by our enemies from these domestic feuds ; IV. The encouragement which this bill holds out to our allies to form with us more strict and permanent connections. As to the expences of election, they were, he acknowledged, of late years, most alarmingly increased, and were become very grievous and burdensome. They have increased, however, not from the contests of neighboring gentlemen with each other, but from the intrusion of strangers, who have no natural interest to support them, and coming no one could tell from whence, have recourse to the scandalous arts of bribery and corruption, which have imposed a necessity upon gentlemen to enlarge their expences, in order to preserve their ancient and established interests in their respective counties ; and the impunity which the practice of bribery and corruption had too often met with in that house, he was compelled to add, had greatly enhanced the evil. But would any one assert that septennial parliaments were competent to remedy

medy this evil? Would they not rather increase it? For those that will give money to obtain a seat in parliament for three years, will give proportionably more for seven. No—not septennial, but annual parliaments are the true constitutional remedy for this grievance: this was our ancient constitution, and every departure from it has been attended with inconvenience and injury. With respect to the animosities and divisions attending frequent elections, they are chiefly of a private nature, and little affect the public: such as they are, however, this bill is more calculated to inflame than to extinguish them. But our most alarming and pernicious animosities proceed certainly from a very different source—from the resentment and ambition of some, from the folly and prejudice of others. That our enemies will take advantage of our divisions whenever it is in their power cannot be doubted; but since the triennial act passed, ten successive parliaments have sat, two long and bloody wars have been waged, our factions ran high, and our enemies were vigilant; yet no such inconveniences were felt as are now apprehended or alleged: nor were any attempts made by them, as far as I have heard, to our prejudice during the temporary ferments of those elections. The last argument is deduced from the encouragement this will give to your allies to enter into treaties with you. Sorry should I be to suppose we had any allies who refused to treat with us because we refused to relinquish our constitution: were such a requisition to be made to them on our part, would it not be rejected on theirs with contempt and indignation? But the measure now proposed is calculated not to strengthen the hands of the executive power, but to lessen its influence with foreign nations. Is it not to proclaim to the world that the king *dare* not to call a new parliament? that he *dare* not trust the people in a new choice? And is not this a supposition dishonorable alike to the monarch

monarch and to the parliament now existing? It presumes that another house of commons would act differently from the present, which implies that this house does not truly represent the people. Frequent parliaments are coeval with the constitution. In the reign of Edward III. it was enacted, that parliaments should be holden every year once, and oftener if need be. This must be understood of new parliaments; for prorogations and long adjournments were not then known. Every long interruption of parliaments has been attended with mischief and inconvenience to the public: and in the declaration of rights at the revolution it is asserted, as the undoubted right of the subject, that parliaments should be held frequently; and the preamble of the bill, which we are now called upon to repeal, declares, 'that by the ancient laws and statutes of the realm frequent parliaments ought to be held, and that frequent NEW parliaments tend very much to the happy union and the good agreement of the king and his people.' Before this repeal takes place, I hope it will be shewn in what consists the error of those assertions. Would the king establish his throne in the hearts of his people, this is the most sure and effectual way; for such frequent appeals to the people generate confidence, and confidence is a great advance towards agreement and affection. Will not the people say with reason, if this bill should pass, that when the original term of delegation is elapsed, you are no longer their representatives? In my opinion, with great submission I speak it, king, lords, and commons, can no more continue a parliament beyond its natural duration than they can make a parliament. The wisest governments, it is well known, have ever been the most cautious in continuing these persons in authority to whom they have entrusted the supreme power. A standing parliament and a standing army are convertible, and fit instruments to support

support each other's powers. For thefe reafons, and becaufe no ftate neceflity can be alleged or pretended for the paffing of fuch an act, at a time when the prefent parliament may be convened for two fucceeding feffions, I fhall give my vote againft the commitment of the bill." On a divifion, the queftion of commitment was carried in the affirmative by a majority of 284 againft 162 voices.

While this memorable bill was pending in the houfe, various petitions were prefented againft it: one, in particular, from the borough of Horfham, ftating, ' that they looked upon this bill as an overturning of the conftitution, and an infringement of their liberties,' gave fuch an offence, that the houfe refufed to receive it; and the general queftion, *that this bill do now pafs*, was carried in the affirmative by a triumphant majority of 264 votes againft 121; and on the 26th of June 1716, it received the royal affent, the king expreffing in his fpeech the fatisfaction he felt at the profpect of a *fettled government*, fupported by a parliament which had fhewn fuch zeal for the profperity of their country, and the proteftant intereft of Europe. And his majefty now deeming himfelf in a ftate of perfect fecurity, and being, by an act paffed in the laft feffion, relieved from the difagreeable embarraffment of a claufe in the act of fettlement, reftraining him from leaving the kingdom without the confent of parliament, determined to revifit his dominions in Germany, the ftate of affairs on the Continent demanding his moft ferious attention.—LOUIS XIV. king of France, had terminated his long career, in the courfe of the preceding fummer, September 1, 1715. For more than half a century, this monarch had reigned the dread and envy of Europe, and at no period fince the foundation of the monarchy had France difplayed

fuch

such power or splendor. During the continuance of the feudal system, the authority of the monarch and the collective force of the monarchy were restrained and diminished by the independent authority vested in the nobles. When the regal authority was at length fully restored, and established, by the insidious and profound policy of Louis XI. the power of France was for a series of years eclipsed by the superior greatness of the house of Austria. But at the accession of Louis XIV. the pride of that haughty family had been signally humbled by the genius of Richelieu and the arms of Gustavus. Thus, by the dangerous policy of the last century, France was left without a rival, and Louis XIV. soon shewed himself of a disposition to improve and extend that superiority to its utmost limits. Vain, unfeeling, unprincipled, haughty, ambitious, the ruling passion of his life was the thirst of GLORY *. For this he scrupled not to sacrifice the repose of nations, and to deluge Europe in blood. A prospect of the internal state and condition of France under his government discovers an amazing contrast of magnificence and wretchedness. In religion, a malignant and merciless bigot, he forced from their native homes, by the violence of his persecution, myriads of the most industrious and virtuous of his subjects, the loss of whom France yet feels and laments. From the impression made, nevertheless, by the first rapid glances of history, his character appears in a variety of dazzling and

---

* In a letter written by Louis to the count D'Estrades, ambassador at the court of London, January 1662, he declares that the king of England, and his minister Clarendon, do not as yet sufficiently know him—that he aims at GLORY, preferable to any other consideration—that all motives of interest are as nothing to him in comparison of a point of honor—and that he shall always be ready to hazard all, rather than tarnish that GLORY at which he aims, as the principal object of all his actions.

and impoſing points of view. He was poſſeſſed of ſtrong natural powers of mind, and of great perſonal accompliſhments. He was generous, affable, condeſcending, a munificent patron, and rewarder of merit. Under his reign, great characters were formed, great public works both of ornament and utility conſtructed. Science and the arts flouriſhed under his auſpices, and a new Auguſtan age appeared. He ſuſtained the adverſe fortune of his later years with firmneſs and magnanimity. His heart, ſoftened by diſtreſs, ſeemed at length to feel for the diſtreſſes of his people: and he acknowledged, when too late to rectify his error, that he had formed miſtaken opinions reſpecting that *glory* which he had been ſo anxiouſly ſolicitous to acquire. His death took place at a critical moment, and the projects formed in favor of the houſe of Stuart, which were by its ableſt adherents, before that event, deemed " wild and uncertain," became, in conſequence of it, mad and deſperate. He was ſucceeded by Louis XV. an infant only five years of age, and the government of the kingdom was now veſted in the hands of the duke of Orleans, regent of France. This prince, who, in caſe of the death of the infant monarch, had juſt pretenſions, founded on the arrangements of the treaty of Utrecht, to the throne of France, dreaded with reaſon, notwithſtanding the act of renunciation, the competition of the king of Spain. And the ſituation of the king of England, who had alſo the deſigns of a reſtleſs rival to oppoſe, being analogous to that of the Regent, they concluded with an emulation of eagerneſs—all political difficulties being previouſly obviated by the ability and addreſs of the earl of Stair, now ambaſſador at Paris—a treaty of friendſhip and alliance for their mutual aſſiſtance and ſupport, to which the ſtates-general readily acceded. But in England, where diſtruſt and hatred of France were univerſally prevalent, it ex-

cited much murmur and surprise; nor would the nation easily be persuaded to believe that the protestant succession in England could derive any additional security from the officious or insidious guarantee of France. The affair, however, which principally engaged the king's solicitude at this period, and which forms, indeed, the grand key to almost all the numerous and intricate negotiations, conventions, and alliances of the present reign, was the recent cession of the Duchies of Bremen and Verden by Denmark, who had conquered them from the Swedes; and for which Denmark was to receive a certain equivalent in money from Hanover. Exclusive, however, of this pretended equivalent, the king of England, as elector of Hanover, undertook to guarantee to Denmark the Duchy of Slefwic, conquered by that power from the duke of Holstein, the ally of Sweden; his Danish majesty thus wisely parting with one half of his conquests, in order to establish a permanent property in the other. This whole transaction the king of Sweden regarded as a most flagrant injury and insult. And little regarding, in the vehemence of his anger, the distinction arising from the twofold character sustained by his adversary, as king of England and elector of Hanover, and well knowing that, in the mere capacity of elector, he would not have ventured to gratify his ambition so much at the risque of his safety, he directed all the efforts of his vengeance against the English nation, who appeared to him to countenance this usurpation, and whom he therefore considered as his determined and mortal enemies. In the summer of the preceding year, 1715, Sir John Norris sailed with a strong squadron to the Baltic, for the protection of the national commerce, which had suffered extremely from the hostile resentment of the Swedes. The king of Sweden
was

was at this time deeply engaged in negotiations and intrigues with the English malcontents; and a project was formed for the invasion of the kingdom, by that heroic and romantic monarch, at the head of a large body of forces, which would doubtless have been joined by great numbers of the disaffected, who waited only a favorable moment for revolt. The king of England, who had received information from various quarters of this dangerous conspiracy, on his return from the Continent, January 1717, caused the Swedish ambassador count Gyllenburg to be arrested. At the same time, baron Goertz, the Swedish resident in Holland, was also, by an excess of complaisance for which it would not be easy to find a precedent, arrested at the requisition of the king by order of the states: and in the papers of these two noblemen, which by a bold and irregular exertion of power were seized and searched, was found ample proof of their secret machinations. The foreign ministers were not a little alarmed at this extraordinary procedure. And the marquis de Monteleone, the Spanish ambassador, in particular, expressed his astonishment and regret, that no other mode of preserving the peace of the kingdom could be devised, than by arresting the persons of ambassadors, and seizing their papers—the sacred repositories of their masters' secrets. The secretary of state, Mr. Methuen, stated the urgent necessity which had impelled the king his master to adopt a measure so contrary to his inclinations: and Baron Goertz openly avowed the whole project of the invasion, of which he acknowledged himself the author, and which he said " was amply justified by the conduct of the king of Great-Britain, who had joined the confederacy against the king of Sweden, without having received the least provocation—who had assisted the king of Denmark in subduing the Duchies of Bremen and Verden, and then purchased them of the usurper—and who had, in the course of this summer, sent a strong squadron of ships to the Baltic, where it joined the Danes and Russians against the Swedes." The states of Holland not venturing to detain the baron long in confinement, he prosecuted his designs with increase of zeal and earnestness. Soon after the meeting of Parliament, February 1717, the king informed the house of commons, by a royal message delivered by general Stanhope, of the danger which impended over the nation from the designs of Sweden, and demanded an extraordinary supply, to enable him to make good such engagements as it might be necessary for him to contract with other powers, in order effectually to avert it. A supply of 250,000l. was accordingly voted, but by a perilous majority of *four voices* only, and not without vehement debate and opposition, chiefly in consequence of an alarming division in the administration, and the eventual secession of various of its members, distinguished equally by eminence of station and ability—amongst whom, lord Townshend, some time secretary of state, and lately appointed lord lieutenant of Ireland, and Mr. Walpole, who had succeeded the earl of Halifax as first commissioner of the treasury, appeared most conspicuous. The leaders of the secession, by the faint and languid support which those who took any part in the debate gave to this motion, and the obstinate silence of the rest, sufficiently shewed their disapproval of the conduct of the court, which, for the sake of an useless acquisition of territory in Germany, scrupled not to involve Great Britain in an expensive, dangerous, and destructive war. And it was now clearly perceived, though unfortunately at a period too late, that the separation of the kingdom from the electorate ought to have constituted the basis of the settlement of the crown upon the house of Hanover. The message was

was declared, by Mr. Shippen, to be unparliamentary and unprecedented; penned, he supposed, by some foreigner, totally unacquainted with their accustomed forms of procedure, and their invariable usage of granting money only on estimate, and for certain specified services. And he asked, what glorious advantages were to be obtained for England, which made it necessary to incur this expence, and to encounter this danger? Mr. Hungerford ridiculed the idea of courting, and much more of purchasing, foreign alliances; and said, that a nation so lately the terror of France and Spain was surely able to defend itself in any cause, which called for national exertion, from the attack of so inconsiderable an enemy as Sweden. General Stanhope, in the warmth of debate, asserting, "that none could refuse compliance with this message, but such as were not *the king's friends*;" much offence was taken at this expression by many members, far removed from the suspicion of disaffection: and Mr. Lawson, member of Cumberland, observed, " that he was surprised to hear such unguarded expressions fall from so respectable a person; and that if every member of the house who used freedom of speech must be accounted an enemy to the king whenever he happened to disapprove of the measures of his ministers, he knew no service they could render to their country in that house, and it were better at once to retire to their country-seats, and leave the king and his ministers to act entirely at their discretion."

On the commitment of the bill, Mr. Pulteney, who had now resigned his office of Secretary at war, protested that he could not persuade himself that any Englishman had dared to advise his majesty to send such a message; but he hoped that the house would not be swayed by German counsels; and that such resolutions would be adopted as would make a German miniftry tremble *. It was again urged, that no occafion did or could exift for entering into foreign alliances with a view of defending Great Britain from this danger; that we had an army and a fleet far fuperior to any force that Sweden could in her prefent ftate bring into action againft us; that we were in actual alliance with France, from whofe former connection with Sweden apprehenfions might otherwife have been entertained. But if the court perfifted in afferting the neceffity of new and foreign engagements againft Sweden, it was doubtlefs requifite to ftate, fince no one could pretend to conjecture, what thofe engagements were. And the fpeaker, who took part in the debate, declared, that no additional burdens on the public appeared at this time neceffary. It was his opinion, therefore, that if the fum now demanded were expended for our fafety abroad, fuch proportion of the national troops as equalled the amount of the expenditure ought to be difbanded at home. Lord Finch, eldeft fon of the earl of Nottingham, reprobated in ftrong terms this novel fyftem of politics. It appeared, as he alfo faid, from the memorial recently prefented by the Ruffian minifter, and by the anfwer which had been returned to the fame, that fuch meafures were purfued as were likely to engage us in a quarrel with the Czar. To which general Stanhope replied, "that as for the inftances which his majefty has caufed to be made with the Czar, and the meafures he may have concerted to get the Ruffian troops out

---

* Lord Townfhend was difmiffed from his office of lord lieutenant of Ireland on the evening of the day (April 9, 1717) on which the firft debate and divifion on this motion had taken place. And Mr. Walpole, Mr. Methuen fecretary of ftate, and Mr. Pulteney, delivered in their refignations the next morning. Lord Cowper alfo relinquifhed the great feal, and was fucceeded by the earl of Macclesfield.

out of the Duchy of Mecklenburg, his majesty has acted in all this as elector and prince of the empire; and he was persuaded all the gentlemen here would agree with him, that the king's dignity, as king of Great Britain, was never understood to tie up his hands with respect to his interests in Germany, and as prince of the empire*." The fact itself nevertheless remained indisputable, that the Germanic politics of the king had embroiled the kingdom of Great Britain in a dangerous contest, not only with Sweden but Russia; for the Czar, passionately resenting the conduct of king George, who vehemently opposed

* Early in the month of March 1717, the minister of the Czar presented a memorial to the court of London, setting forth the solicitude of the Czar to conclude a treaty of amity with his majesty, and to guarantee the Hanover succession; and says, " And it was not the fault of his Czarish majesty that the said negotiation was not brought to a happy conclusion. Although his Czarish majesty has lately observed, that several contrary steps have been taken by your majesty's ministers in many foreign courts, particularly at the court of Vienna and those of Denmark and Prussia, as well as at the Diet of Ratisbon, though his Czarish majesty had given no cause for such measures, notwithstanding that he had sufficient reasons to be upon his guard, and to provide for his own security, considering the general reports and the particular advices he had from many places that your majesty is negotiating a separate peace with Sweden, in which you promise your assistance against his Czarish majesty upon the condition of the cession of Bremen and Verden, as it plainly appears by the letters lately published by the Swedish minister." An answer was delivered to this memorial, dated April 2, 1717, which says, " As to the complaints contained in that memorial of the steps which his majesty may have taken at several courts in Germany with regard to the Russian troops in the empire; granting it to be true, that the British ministers had acted with vigor at the said courts, in order to procure the evacuation of the said troops, his Czarish majesty ought not to be in the least surprised at it, considering the strict union which has so long subsisted between Great Britain, the emperor, and the empire, which union has been confirmed and strengthened the last year by a new treaty of alliance and guarantee between the emperor and the king."

opposed his favorite and invidious project of a settlement in Germany as a prince of the empire, and being at open variance with the king respecting the affairs of the Duchy of Mecklenburg, which in the view of his Britannic majesty were inferior in importance only to those of Bremen and Verden, now hastily acceded to the preliminaries of a convention, which a short time would probably have ripened into a definitive peace, through the dextrous intervention of baron Goerz, with his inveterate rival the king of Sweden, with whom he had been near twenty years at war; and assented to the project of elevating the Pretender to the throne of Great Britain. But the good fortune of the king of England, which throughout the whole course of his life was ever remarkable, delivered him from all apprehensions, by the death of the king of Sweden, who was killed by a cannon-ball in the trenches before the fortress of Frederickshall in Norway, November 30, 1718, O. S. an event which produced great political convulsions in Sweden, in the first shock of which baron Goertz lost his head on the scaffold. This monarch was one of the most remarkable characters which the present or indeed any age has produced. Attacked in early youth, without pretence or provocation, by an ambitious and unprincipled confederacy of kings, he defended himself with heroic valor and glorious success. But, intoxicated by a long and uninterrupted course of prosperity, inflamed with an eager desire of revenge, and indulging wild and extravagant ideas of conquest, he refused with disdain all terms of accommodation, and at length experienced a fatal reverse of fortune, the calamitous consequences of which Sweden still most sensibly feels. Nevertheless the memory of this romantic monarch is held in high veneration by the Swedes, who yet celebrate the anniversary of

his

his birth with an enthusiasm due only to that of the great restorer of Swedish liberty and independency, the illustrious GUSTAVUS VASA—a name profaned and insulted by this commemoration: for a tyranny more oppressive than that of Charles XII. was never exercised, nor a submission more abject ever exacted by any monarch from any people *. The Czar, in consequence of this unexpected

* The following portrait of this extraordinary man, drawn by the pen of genius, cannot but prove interesting and acceptable:

On what foundation stands the warrior's pride,
How just his hopes, let Swedish CHARLES decide:
A frame of adamant, a soul of fire,
No dangers fright him, and no labors tire;
O'er love, o'er fear, extends his wide domain,
Unconquer'd lord of pleasure and of pain.
No joys to him pacific sceptres yield:
War sounds the trump—he rushes to the field;
Behold surrounding kings their force combine,
And one capitulate, and one resign.
Peace courts his hand, but spreads her charms in vain.
" Think nothing gain'd," he cries, " till nought remain,
On Moscow's walls till Gothic standards fly,
And all be mine beneath the polar sky!"
The march begins in military state,
And nations on his eye suspended wait;
Stern famine guards the solitary coast,
And winter barricades the realm of frost.
He comes—not want or cold his course delay;
Hide, blushing glory! hide Pultowa's day.
The vanquish'd hero leaves his broken bands,
And shews his miseries in distant lands;
Condemn'd a needy supplicant to wait,
While ladies interpose and slaves debate.
—But did not chance at length her error mend?
Did no subverted empire mark his end?
Did rival monarchs give the fatal wound?
Or hostile millions press him to the ground?

pected event, though it prudent to desist from the farther prosecution of his hostile designs; and Bremen and Verden were left in the possession of Hanover, though the investiture of those Duchies by the emperor was still wanting to complete the validity of the purchase. This, therefore, now became the grand object of the attention and solicitude of the English court; and as the emperor, notwithstanding the recent renewal of treaties, affected delay and reluctance to comply with the eager applications of the English monarch, means were to be devised to obviate his objections, or at least to convince his imperial majesty how much it concerned the interests of the court of Vienna not to insist too strongly or pertinaciously on them. By the treaty of Utrecht the kingdoms of Naples and Sardinia were ceded to the house of Austria, together with Milan and the Low Countries; and the island of Sicily, with the title of king, to the duke of Savoy. The pride of Spain was, however, deeply wounded by this forcible dismemberment of her monarchy, though the experience of almost a century had shewn how little accession of strength she really derived from the possession of these detached and remote provinces, or rather how great an increase of weakness. Cardinal Alberoni, prime minister of Philip V. a man of a lofty and aspiring genius, which delighted to form bold and dangerous projects, at this time entertained the chimerical hope of re-uniting to the monarchy of Spain the kingdoms and provinces of which she had been divested. And the emperor being actually engaged in a

war

His fall was destin'd to a barren strand,
A petty fortress, and a dubious hand :
He left that name at which the world grew pale,
To point a moral or adorn a tale.

Johnson's Im. of Juv. Sat. 1o.

war with Turkey *, the Cardinal embraced the opportunity to equip a formidable armament, which sailed from Barcelona July 1717, and landing at Cagliari, the capital of Sardinia, soon made an entire conquest of the island; pretending, as a reason for this invasion, the previous violation of the most positive engagements on the part of the emperor, or, to adopt the haughty language of the court of Madrid, of the ARCH DUKE †.

The

---

* In this war the imperial arms, under the auspicious conduct of prince Eugene, triumphed gloriously over the Ottoman power. Servia and Croatia were added to the Austrian dominions; and "the Turkish moons wandered in disarray" over the impurpled fields of Peterwaradin and Belgrade.

† It must be remarked, that no definitive treaty had taken place between Spain and the emperor since the war of the succession, nor had the respective titles of these rival potentates been as yet reciprocally and formally acknowledged. "Greatness of soul," (says the Marquis de Grimaldi in his circular letter addressed to the ministers of the several foreign courts) made his majesty bear the dismemberment of his dominions, which the plenipotentiaries would sacrifice to the tranquillity of Europe: After which he persuaded himself, that these stipulated sacrifices would at least have secured to him the rest of this nation as glorious as afflicted. But no sooner had he complied with the surrender of Sicily, in favor of the repose of Spain, upon the condition of the evacuation of Catalonia and the island of Majorca, than he found that the orders received for that purpose were concealed; and when at last it came to the knowledge of his allies, it was pretended that the treaty should be executed, by virtue whereof his majesty demanded the evacuation of the places. Nothing was more easy for that purpose than for the garrisons of the *Arch-duke* to have surrendered to the king's troops the gates of the places they possessed, in the same manner as was reciprocally practised among the potentates of Europe. But quite on the contrary, the generals of the *Archduke*, violating the public faith of treaties and the reciprocal engagements, abandoned the places to the Catalans, making them, at the same time, believe that they would soon return; and thereby fomented their disquiet and rebellious spirit, so far as to induce them to think of a furious and obstinate resistance."

The emperor loudly complaining of this hostile, and, as he termed it, sacrilegious attack, while his armies were combating the common enemy of the christian faith; and the king of Spain professing a willingness to submit the justice of his quarrel to equitable arbitration, the king of England and the regent of France, in concert with the states general, undertook the accommodation of these differences. And conferences being opened with the court of Vienna, the famous QUADRUPLE ALLIANCE was at length concluded, by which it was determined that Sardinia, now actually in the possession of Spain, should be transferred to the house of Savoy; and Sicily, a far more valuable possession, ceded in exchange to the emperor. The claims of Spain were altogether disregarded; only it was stipulated that the succession to the Duchies of Tuscany, Parma, and Placentia, claimed by the queen of Spain as heiress of the houses of Medicis and Farnese, should devolve upon her eldest son in case of a failure of male issue: and three months only were allowed to the parties interested in these cessions to declare their acceptance or rejection *. Spain, as may be im-

---

* Although the regent of France, from his eager desire to secure the friendship of England, and from personal animosity to the king of Spain, entered entirely into the views of the English monarch upon this occasion, he retained at the bottom all the Bourbon prejudices against the house of Austria. The principal obstacle to the alliance concluded in 1716 between the two kingdoms, was the willingness of the Regent to assent to the expulsion of the Swedes, the ancient enemies of that house, from Germany. "I have," says the ambassador, lord Stair, in a dispatch addressed to secretary Craggs, "all along endeavored to persuade the Regent that, in the present state of the kingdom of Sweden, it can be of no great use to France that that crown should preserve a foot in the empire; and that the true and solid balance against the emperor, and for preserving the liberty of Germany, must be by making a close conjunction among the Princes of the north of Germany. This thought, in general, pleases the Regent very well; but he does

imagined, was little difposed to acquiefce in this fettlement. And the propofitions of general Stanhope, the Englifh fecretary of ftate, who was himfelf invefted with the character of ambaffador extraordinary to the court of Madrid on this occafion, were refufed with difdain. A ftill more formidable armament than the former was now fitted out by the indefatigable exertions of the Cardinal, deftined for the invafion of Sicily; his Sicilian majefty having concerted his own meafures by a feparate negotiation with the court of Vienna; wifely refolving to fubmit to terms, however difadvantageous, which he found himfelf unable to oppofe with effect. The Spaniards having landed their forces, confifting of 30,000 men, flattered themfelves with the fpeedy reduction of this rich and beautiful ifland. But the king of England, in order to counteract the defigns of Spain, had, with the con-

does by no means like the particular part of it, to deprive the crown of Sweden of their dominions in Germany." When affairs, after this, took a different turn; when jealoufies and diffenfions arofe between the emperor and the king of England, and hopes were entertained that England might be effectually detached from the Auftrian intereft; the court of Verfailles entered with more fincerity, and even with apparent eagernefs, into the projects of Hanoverian aggrandizement; fenfible that the facrifice made by France was trivial in comparifon of the advantage gained. Lord Stair, at this period, had the generofity zealoufly to intercede with the court of London for the pardon of the earl of Mar. After being, however, a confiderable time amufed with the hope of obtaining it, he met with a final and harfh repulfe. " Lord Mar," fays the ambaffador to Mr. Craggs, " is *outré* at the ufage he has met with. He fays, our miniftry may be great and able men, but that they are not fkilful in making profelytes, or keeping friends when they have them. I am pretty much of his mind. He was certainly determined to leave the Pretender's intereft. He is now full of refentment, and in moft violent agitations." How ftriking the contraft between the policy of the Englifh court in this reign, and that of Henry IV. of France, after his triumphs over the faction of the League! But every king is not a hero.

concurrence of parliament, though England had no
imaginable motive to interfere in the diftant fcenes of
contention, caufed a formidable fleet to fail for the Mediterranean, under the command of Sir George Byng,
with peremptory orders to attack the Spanifh fleet if engaged in any hoftile enterprife againft Naples or Sicily.
The Britifh admiral, on his arrival off Cadiz, tranfmitted by his Secretary a copy of his inftructions to the
Cardinal, who perufed them with great emotion, and after fome deliberation returned for anfwer, " that the
chevalier Byng might execute the orders he had received
from the king his mafter *." The admiral proceeding,
therefore, on his voyage, caft anchor with his whole
fleet in the bay of Naples, where the magnificence of the
fpectacle drew immenfe multitudes of people to the fur-
rounding fhores, which refounded with loud acclamations.

On

* The inftructions of the admiral were as follow— " You are to
make inftances with both parties to ceafe from ufing any farther acts of
hoftility; but in cafe the Spaniards do ftill infift with their fhips of war
and forces to attack the kingdom of Naples, or other the territories of
the emperor in Italy, or to land in any part of Italy, which can only
be with a defign to invade the emperor's dominions, againft whom
only they have declared war by invading Sardinia; or if they fhould
endeavor to make themfelves mafters of the kingdom of Sicily, which
muft be with a defign to invade the kingdom of Naples; in fuch cafe
you are with all your power to hinder and obftruct the fame. If it
fhould fo happen, that at your arrival with our fleet under your command in the Mediterranean, the Spaniards fhould already have landed
any troops in Italy, in order to invade the emperor's territories, you
fhall endeavor amicably to diffuade them from perfevering in fuch an
attempt; and offer them your affiftance to help them to withdraw
their troops and put an end to farther acts of hoftility. But in cafe
thefe your friendly endeavors fhould prove ineffectual, you fhall, by
keeping company with or intercepting their fhips or convoys, or if it be
neceffary, by openly oppofing them, defend the emperor's territories
from any farther attempt."

On receiving intelligence from count Daun, the viceroy, that Messina, the capital of Sicily, was reduced to the last extremity; he again weighed anchor, and on the 9th of August 1718 he came in sight of the Faro of Messina, and dispatched his own captain with a message to the marquis de Lede, commander of the Spanish forces, proposing a cessation of arms in Sicily for two months, that the powers of Europe might have opportunity to concert measures for restoring a lasting peace; declaring, at the same time, that should this proposal be rejected, he should, in pursuance of his instructions, use all his force to prevent farther attempts to disturb the dominions the king his master had engaged to defend. The Spanish general answered, " that he had no power to treat of an armistice, but should obey his orders, which were, to reduce Sicily to the dominion of his master the king of Spain." On the 11th of August the Spanish fleet, consisting of twenty-seven sail of the line, was descried off the coast of Calabria, lying-to in the order of battle; and though on the approach of the British squadron they bore away apparently with the view of maintaining a running fight, the superior manœuvres of the English commander soon brought on a close action, which before sunset terminated in the almost total destruction of the Spanish fleet; Don Castanita the commander in chief, and three other admirals, being captured. Captain Walton being detached by Sir George Byng, with five ships of the line, in pursuit of a division of the Spaniards much superior in force, acquainted the English admiral with the event of his undertaking, in the following memorable letter:—" Sir, We have destroyed all the Spanish ships and vessels which were upon the coast, the number as per margin." Upon inspecting the margin of this laconic epistle, no less than

thirteen

thirteen ships of war of different descriptions were found comprised in it. It is said that rear-admiral Cammock, a native of Ireland, who commanded one of the divisions of the Spanish fleet, proposed to the commander in chief to remain in the road of Paradise, where the coast is bold and the anchorage good, with their broadsides towards the sea, in order of battle: a position in which the British fleet might have been greatly annoyed from the batteries erected on shore; and the various and rapid currents would have prevented a close and regular approach. But the evil genius of Spain predominated, and this proposal was rejected. In reward of this great victory, Sir George Byng was raised to the dignity of the peerage by the style and title of viscount Torrington, and received other distinguished marks of the royal favor. But the court of Madrid exclaimed in the most passionate language against the conduct of England, as contrary to the law of nations, and a flagrant violation of the most solemn engagements; and orders were issued at all the ports of Spain and the Indies, for making reprisals upon the English; in consequence of which, war was formally declared by England against Spain, which was soon followed by a like declaration on the part of the Regent of France.

These transactions, however, did not pass abroad without severe notice and animadversion at home. In the session of parliament which commenced Nov. 1717, the king had in his speech assured the two houses that his endeavors to preserve the public tranquillity had not been unsuccessful; and that he had reason to believe they would in the end produce their full effect. A considerable reduction of the army was in consequence proposed on the part of the ministers, who contented themselves with moving for 18,000 men only for the service of the ensuing

ensuing year. Even this force was deemed by the opposition very unnecessary, and an effort was in vain made to limit the number to 12,000. Mr. Walpole, in particular, declaimed with much energy on the danger of a standing army in a free country; and he affirmed, that though a considerable proportion of the privates had been disbanded, the officers had been retained; and the soldiers wanting to complete the several companies and regiments might be raised with beat of drum in twenty-four hours; so that a force double to what was intended by parliament was virtually vested in the crown. And Mr. Shippen, in the course of a very able speech, declared the expence attending the army to be the smallest objection to it. The chief argument against it was, that the civil and military power would not long subsist together. Far from being necessary to our protection, he apprehended so great a force to be inconsistent with our safety. In certain circumstances an army might be necessary, but in such circumstances it was only to be chosen as the lesser evil; for that, abstractedly considered, it was an evil, every lover of liberty must acknowledge. " I know (said this inflexible patriot that these assertions interfere with some paragraphs of his majesty's speech. But we are to consider that speech as the composition of the ministers and advisers of the crown, and we are therefore at liberty to controvert every proposition in it, *particularly those which seem calculated rather for the* MERIDIAN *of* GERMANY *than of* GREAT BRITAIN. *But it is the infelicity of his majesty's reign, that he is unacquainted with our language and* CONSTITUTION; and it is therefore the more incumbent upon his British ministers to inform him, that our government does not stand upon the same foundation with that which is established in his German dominions. If we recur to the history of Europe, we shall find that the nations once free have lost their liberties by allowing, on some plausible pretence of exigence, their princes to maintain an armed force during peace. They perceived, too late, that they had erected a power superior to themselves, and they now wear the chains which they forged for their own necks. The consent of parliament is indeed alleged in favor of the army entrusted to the crown in this country. But the consent of parliament cannot alter the nature of things, or prevent the same causes from producing the same effects. No art can disguise from an army, however denominated, the knowledge of its own strength ; and the experience of the last century has taught us, that a parliament army may give as deep a wound to the constitution as an army of the crown. So long as the army, therefore, is continued, so long is the constitution suspended ; so long is it at the mercy of those who command it."—During this speech, Mr. Lechmere had taken down in writing those marked expressions which seemed pointed not so much against the ministers as the king : and when Mr. Shippen had sat down, Mr. Lechmere immediately rose and stated to the house that these words were a scandalous invective against his majesty's person and government—such as merited the highest resentment of that house; and he therefore moved, that the member who had spoken them be committed to the tower. This motion was immediately seconded by Mr. Spencer Cowper, supported by Sir Joseph Jekyl and various others ; on which Mr. Walpole desired that the member might be permitted to explain these rash words, spoken in the heat of debate. But Mr. Shippen declared that he desired no such indulgence, and that the words needed neither explanation nor apology. The house in a flame immediately resolved that the chairman leave the chair; and the speaker resuming his place, Mr. Farrer, member for Bedford, reported

ported from the committee the words spoken by Mr. Shippen; upon which Mr. Shippen withdrew. And the question being put, " that the words spoken by William Shippen, Esq. a member of this house, are highly dishonorable to, and unjustly reflecting on, his majesty's person and government," it was carried in the affirmative by 175 voices against 81, and the speaker was ordered to issue his warrant for the immediate commitment of Mr. Shippen to the tower.

The session closed in March; a few days previous to which, the king by a royal message informed the house " that he had reason to judge from the information he had lately received from abroad, that an additional naval force would be necessary;" and an address was moved and presented, assuring his majesty, " that the house would make good such exceedings as his majesty in his royal wisdom should deem necessary for the purpose of giving effect to his unwearied endeavors to preserve *the peace of Europe.*" No division on this motion took place —Mr. Walpole alone observing, " that this *pacific address* had violently the air of a DECLARATION OF WAR." The parliament again meeting Nov. 1718, the king, in his speech, declared that the court of Spain had rejected all his amicable proposals, and had broke through their most solemn engagements for the security of the British commerce. To vindicate therefore the faith of his former treaties, as well as to maintain those he had lately made, and to protect and defend the trade of his subjects, which had been violently and unjustly oppressed, it became necessary for his naval forces to check their progress; that notwithstanding the success of his arms, that court had lately given orders at all the ports of Spain, and the West-Indies, to fit out privateers against the English. He said, that he was persuaded a British parliament would enable him to resent such treatment; and he assured them that his good brother the Regent of France was ready to concur with him in the most vigorous measures. An address of thanks and congratulation being proposed, it was forcibly urged, that such address might be attended with the most serious consequences, as stamping with the sanction of parliament, measures which, upon examination, might appear equally contrary to the law of nations and the interests of Great Britain. And it was moved in the house of peers by lord Strafford, that the instructions of admiral Byng might be laid before the house. General (now created earl) Stanhope replied, that there was no occasion to submit the admiral's instructions to public discussion, as the treaties, of which the late sea-fight was a necessary consequence, had already received the approbation of parliament. He accused the court of Spain of a violation of the treaty of Utrecht and of public faith, in attacking the emperor while he was engaged in a war against the common enemies of Christendom. He added likewise, that it was high time to check the growth of the naval power of Spain, in order effectually to protect the British commerce, which had been violently oppressed by the Spaniards. In the lower house, Mr. Walpole declaimed with much vehemence and energy against the late measures; and affirmed, that to sanction them by the proposed address would answer no other purpose than to screen from punishment the ministers of the crown, who had dared to plunge the nation into a war with Spain, of which they now wished to relieve themselves from the responsibility. He declared that, instead of the entire *satisfaction* which they were called upon to express, he would substitute an entire *dissatisfaction*; for the conduct of administration had been both faithless and pernicious. And on a subsequent resumption of the question, Mr. Shippen, with unbroken

unbroken spirit, observed, "that there existed no necessity for involving this nation in a war, on account of any mercantile grievances, as there was every reason to believe they might be amicably redressed; and added, that the war seemed to be calculated for another MERIDIAN." The expression, though amounting to a sort of defiance, passed unnoticed; and Mr. Methuen, who had recently resigned the seals, accounted and apologized for the dilatoriness of the court of Spain, in respect to the mercantile grievances complained of from the multiplicity and diversity of regulations which prevailed in the several provinces and ports of that kingdom*. An expression in the answer of the English court to a memorial of the marquis de Monteleone, the Spanish ambassador, was animadverted upon as very extraordinary—it being therein stated, "That his majesty the king of Great Britain did not seek to aggrandize himself by any new acquisition, but was rather inclined to sacrifice something of his own to procure the general quiet and tranquillity of Europe." This was said to be a very uncommon stretch of condescension. The king of Spain was to be tempted by an offer from England—which offer was suspected to be the cession of Gibraltar, or Minorca—to accede to the terms of the quadruple alliance, by which nothing was gained by England, and the great object of which was plainly the security of the king's German acquisitions, and the aggrandizement of Hanover. The address however was at length carried; but the commons thought proper to vote no more than 26,000 men for the entire amount of the sea and land service of the year.

Wholly

---

* Mr. Methuen, afterwards Sir Paul Methuen, had resided several years in the quality of ambassador at the court of Lisbon, where he negotiated the famous treaty with Portugal known by the name of the METHUEN TREATY.

Wholly actuated by the blind and furious spirit of revenge, Cardinal Alberoni had by this time formed a rash and romantic project for the elevation of the pretender, now received and acknowledged as king of England at Madrid, to the throne of Great Britain. And a new armament was equipped at Cadiz, on board of which 6000 regular troops, with arms for a much larger number, were embarked under the command of the duke of Ormond. Scarcely, however, had they reached Cape Finisterre, but they were dispersed and shattered by a violent tempest, which totally disabled them from prosecuting their voyage. Two frigates only, with the earls Mareschal and Seaforth and the marquis of Tullibardine, with 300 Spanish soldiers on board, arrived in Scotland, where they were joined by some clans of highlanders.— But on the approach of the king's forces the highlanders, after a vain though vigorous attempt to defend the pass of Glenshiel, dispersed, and the Spaniards surrendered themselves prisoners of war. Meantime the efforts of the English arms abroad were attended with brilliant success. In consequence chiefly of the able and unintermitted exertions of Sir George Byng, and the powerful assistance which the Imperialists derived from the British fleet, the Spaniards were reduced to the humiliating necessity of evacuating the island of Sicily and Sardinia.— For though the marquis de Lede, notwithstanding the decisive victory obtained by Sir George Byng, had compelled the city of Messina to surrender, the Spanish army was effectually precluded, by the vigilance of the British admiral, from receiving any reinforcements or supplies by sea. And on the other hand, a numerous body of Imperialists, commanded by the Count de Merci, was landed on the island under convoy of the British fleet; by the vigorous co-operation of which the city of Messina was recovered. On the approach of spring, Palermo was

was invested, the Count de Merci marching across the mountains, while the British fleet coasted along the shore. The Marquis de Lede, who had retreated under the cannon of Palermo, now prepared to give battle to the Imperialists, although in his circumstances a defeat must have proved fatal; when a felucca arrived with dispatches from the court of Madrid, empowering the marquis to sign a convention, by which Spain agreed to relinquish her pretensions to Sicily; and the shattered remains of her troops were immediately embarked at Tauromini for Barcelona. Such was the just confidence placed by the king of England in the zeal and ability of the gallant officer invested with the high and arduous commission thus prosperously terminated, that in reply to an application for instructions, his majesty declared, " he would send him none, for that he well knew how to act without any." And the uniform success attending all his enterprises, vulgarly ascribed to fortune, a more just and accurate discernment, tracing the concatenation of events, perceived to be the natural consequence of the wisdom and vigor with which his measures were invariably planned and executed. During these transactions in Sicily, lord Cobham, with a considerable force, made a descent on Spain and took Vigo. Preparations also were making for an expedition against Spanish America; and an army of French, which had penetrated into Spain, under the duke of Berwick, reduced the towns of Fontarabia and St. Sebastian. So that the court of Madrid found itself attacked on all sides, its schemes completely disconcerted, and no resource left but to accede, however reluctantly, to the terms of the quadruple alliance—the remaining differences between the emperor and the king of Spain being referred to a congress at Cambray, which, however, after a very long and tedious discussion, was at last dissolved without coming to any terms of agreement

A treaty

A treaty of peace was now likewife concluded (November 1719), through the mediation of France, by the king of England, with Ulrica Queen of Sweden, fifter and fucceffor to Charles XII.; by which Bremen and Verden were fecured to Hanover at the expence of a million of rix-dollars—a far more confiderable fum than the revenues of that electorate were generally deemed competent to difcharge. This peace, entitled a peace between Sweden and Great Britain, was negociated and figned by a Hanoverian minifter, one Adolph-Frederic Van Baffawitz, who had the prefumption to engage, " in the name of his Britannic majefty, both as king and elector, immediately to renew the ancient alliances and friendfhips, &c. &c. as alfo *the guaranties upon the foundation of the treaty of peace concluded amongft the allies of the North, or which may be concluded or applied to the profit of the ducal houfe of Holftein Gottorph*,"—or, in plain terms, he undertakes to guarantee Slefwic to Denmark, Bremen and Verden to Hanover, and the eventual equivalent for Slefwic to the duke of Holftein. Early in the following year (1720) a treaty of alliance was concluded between the crowns of Great Britain and Sweden, by which his Britannic majefty ftipulated not only to furnifh the powerful fuccors therein fpecified, but to engage his friends and allies to contribute by fubfidies and auxiliary troops " *ad coercendum Czarum Ruffiæ*"—the exprefs words of the treaty. In both thefe treaties the loffes fuftained by the Englifh commerce in confequence of the depredations of the Swedes, which formed the only plaufible pretext for involving Britain in this quarrel, were paffed over unnoticed. And while the petition from the merchants was lying neglected and forgotten on the table of the houfe of commons, the fum of 72,000l. in confequence of a meffage from his majefty, was voted as a fubfidy to Sweden. After all the indefatigable exertions and expenfive pensive sacrifices of the king of England to procure from the court of Stockholm the absolute cession of Bremen and Verden, and which was at length so happily and unexpectedly accomplished, the investiture of those duchies, of which he had been so long and eager an expectant, notwithstanding the mighty services rendered to the house of Austria, was not yet obtainable from the gratitude or condescension of the court of Vienna. On the contrary, the emperor seemed to think those services amply compensated by the *protectorial commission* with which that monarch had been recently invested by his imperial majesty for the administration of the duchy of Mecklenburg—the duke of Mecklenburg being suspended from his government, by a sentence of the aulic council, for tyranny and mal-administration. And it is even asserted upon good authority, that this commission was actually and formally exchanged at the court of Vienna, for the "INSTRUCTIONS of Sir George Byng." The affairs of Mecklenburg had long occupied a large share of the attention of the king of England, who was strongly suspected of a design to add that Duchy to his other acquisitions in Germany. And the duke of Mecklenburg, in his several memorials to the diet at Ratisbon, openly charges the house of Lunenburg with aspiring to the absolute sovereignty of LOWER SAXONY; and affirms that the troubles in his dominions have been continually fomented and inflamed by the court of Herenhausen expressly with that view. But though the emperor was at little pains to conceal his dislike and jealousy of these designs, the necessity of his affairs compelled him to this concession, which was apparently considered only as a prelude to a more firm and permanent possession. The king of England, in pursuance of his engagements with Sweden, sending in the summer of this year, 1720, a powerful squadron into the Baltic, the Russians—

knowing

knowing that the commander Sir John Norris had instructions similar to those under which Sir George Byng had lately acted—retired into their ports; and a peace was soon afterwards concluded between the crowns of Sweden and Russia; not, however, without strong marks of resentment on the part of the Czar, at what he styled "The insolent interposition of Great Britain."

It will now be proper to revert to those domestic occurrences, the relation of which has been interrupted by this recital of foreign transactions. The riots and tumults which were the natural consequence of the measures adopted by the present ministry, broke out afresh from time to time in various parts of the kingdom with alarming symptoms of disaffection and violence. But the spirit of disloyalty and sedition seemed to display itself at this period with more conspicuous malignity at the city of Oxford than perhaps any other place; insomuch that it was necessary by the government to station there a considerable military force, between whom and the youth of the university frequent occasions of quarrel arose, some of which were of magnitude to come under judicial cognizance; and that ancient and venerable seat of the muses seemed by a deplorable fatality to be converted into the temple of civil discord. On the return of the king from the continent numerous addresses of congratulation were presented; amongst which one from the university of Cambridge, particularly noticing the suppression of the late rebellion, was most graciously received. At a meeting of the vice-chancellor and heads of the houses in Oxford, a motion being made for that purpose, it was rejected with marked indignation. Dr. Smalridge, bishop of Bristol and dean of Christ Church, had the preceding year been removed from his post of lord Almoner for refusing, with Atterbury bishop of Rochester, to sign the protestation of the episcopal bench against the claims

of

of the pretender: this prelate now gratified his resentment by declaring " that the rebellion had been long suppressed, and that there would be no end of addresses should one be presented every time his majesty returned from Hanover—that any marks of royal favor they had received were more than counterbalanced by the troops now quartered upon them—and that the history of this country afforded no precedent for addressing a king on his return from his GERMAN DOMINIONS." As a decisive proof of their alienation from the court, or rather the government, Sir Constantine Phipps, who on a strong presumption of disaffection had been removed from his office as one of the lords justices of Ireland, had an honorary degree conferred upon him with marks of peculiar distinction: and the earl of Arran, on the attainder of his brother the duke of Ormond, was chosen to succeed him as chancellor of the university*. The cry of " the

CHURCH

---

* So marked at this period was that opposition of politics by which the two universities were long distinguished, and all symptoms of which are not at this day entirely obliterated, that we cannot wonder the court should embrace with eagerness every opportunity to display its resentment against the one, and its approbation of the other. A royal present of books having been sent to Cambridge soon after the commencement of the tumults at Oxford, the celebrated Dr. Trapp took occasion from this circumstance to pen the following well-known Epigram:

> Our royal master saw with heedful eyes
> The wants of his two Universities:
> Troops he to Oxford sent, as knowing why
> That learned body wanted loyalty,
> But books to Cambridge gave, as well discerning
> That that right loyal body wanted learning.

This Epigram received a very happy and decisive retort from the late Sir William Brown, as it is said, *impromptu:*

> The king to Oxford sent a troop of horse,
> For Tories know no argument but force.
> With equal care to Cambridge books he sent,
> For Whigs allow no force but argument.

Church and Sacheverel" seemed still to retain its full efficacy and influence over the multitude; and the dwelling-houses and meeting-houses of the sectaries were the favorite objects of the popular vengeance. In consequence of these outrages the house of commons presented an address to the king, in which they state, " that great numbers of his Majesty's deluded subjects had assembled in a tumultuous and rebellious manner, had committed great disorders, and done great injuries to others of their fellow-subjects and fellow-protestants—and they declare it to be their indispensable duty to express their utmost abhorrence of all such traitorous proceedings, and their highest resentment against the authors and promoters of them; and beseech his majesty, that the laws now in force may be put in speedy and vigorous execution against them. And they farther desire, that in justice to those who for their zeal and firm adherence to his majesty's government have been sufferers in the said tumultuous and traitorous disorders, his majesty would be graciously pleased to direct an exact account to be taken of the losses and damages sustained by such sufferers, in order that full compensation may be made; and assuring his majesty that all expences so incurred shall be made good out of the first aids granted by parliament." To which the king replied, " that he would give immediate directions for putting in execution the several matters so justly recommended to him." This was followed by a very loyal and proper address from the dissenters themselves, acknowledging the seasonable protection granted them by government, and expressing " a grateful sense of his majesty's gracious answer to the address of his faithful commons in favour of those whose sufferings they so justly impute to the zeal displayed by them for his majesty's person and government. We desire," say they, " nothing more than to enjoy our civil rights, with a full liberty

liberty to profess our own religious sentiments, which we take to be a privilege due to all men. Nor know we any reason why we have now suffered from the outrages of disaffected persons, but because we were known to be a body of men fixed in our duty to your majesty." To this address his majesty replied in the most gracious terms, "expressing his deep concern at the unchristian and barbarous treatment which they had met with, and assuring them of his royal protection and a full compensation for all their sufferings." At this period the RIOT ACT passed for the prevention of similar disorders, declaring it to be felony for more than twelve persons to remain assembled more than one hour after its being publicly read by the magistrate: and by the salutary operation of this law, the internal tranquillity of the kingdom was in a great degree restored and established.

Notice has been already taken of the resignation of Mr. Walpole, who had succeeded, on the decease of the earl of Halifax*, to the high and important post of first lord commissioner of the treasury. During his short continuance in office he had exhibited a signal proof of his financial ability, in the introduction of the memorable

---

* The earl of HALIFAX survived a very short time only, his appointment as first lord commissioner of the treasury, which office he had before sustained with high reputation, during the latter years of the reign of king WILLIAM—dying after a few days illness, in the vigor of his age, May 19, 1715. It is believed that he aspired to the post of lord high treasurer, and was little pleased with the king's determination to put the treasury into commission. Though the abilities of this nobleman as a financier and a statesman were unquestionably great, he is chiefly known to posterity as a munificent patron of literature; maintaining in this respect an illustrious rivalship with the earl of Oxford, the head of the opposite faction; and in the space of eighty intervening years, these noblemen have had, it is not enough to say, no equals, but no successors. When, on the great and memorable change of administration, A. D. 1710, the earl of Halifax interceded with the earl of Oxford

ble bill which enacted, that all the public funds redeemable by law, and bearing higher interest than five per cent. be redeemed according to their respective provisoes or clauses of redemption, or, with consent of the proprietors, be converted into an interest or annuity not exceeding five per cent. per annum, redeemable by parliament. And by this bill the joint surplusses arising, as well from the proposed reduction of interest from six to five per cent. as from the excesses of the several taxes appropriated to the payment of the interest, were solemnly declared to be solely and unalienably applicable, under

Oxford in favour of the English Menander, Congreve, who, through the favor of Halifax, enjoyed a lucrative place under the government; Oxford, with great dignity and elegance, replied,

"Non obtusa adeo gestamus pectora Pœni,
Nec tam aversus equos Tyriâ sol jungit ab urbe."

A very invidious caricature portrait of the earl of Halifax is to be found in the satires of Pope, under the name of Bufo:

"Proud as Apollo on his forked hill
Sat full-blown Bufo, puff'd by every quill;
Fed with soft dedication all day long,
Horace and he went hand in hand in song;
His library, where busts of Poets dead,
And a true Pindar stood without a head,
Receiv'd of wits an undistinguish'd race,
Who first his judgment ask'd—and then a place;
Dryden alone—what wonder! came not nigh,
Dryden alone escap'd this judging eye:
But still the Great have kindness in reserve—
He help'd to bury whom he help'd to starve."

Pope has elsewhere taken pains to impress the idea, that this nobleman was a mere sciolist in literature; and having matters of much more importance than poetry to engage his attention, it may easily be supposed that his criticisms were often hasty and superficial. The poetical remains of lord Halifax, it must be confessed, do little honor to his memory, except as they afford a proof of his early and devoted attachment

under the denomination of a SINKING FUND, to the discharge of the principal of the public debt contracted previous to the 25th of December of the preceding year 1716. Had this plan been as steadily prosecuted as it was wisely concerted, the nation would have been soon relieved from her pecuniary difficulties. For, as in consequence of the progressive redemption of the debt the surplusses must increase with accelerated rapidity, its internal energy, without strict attention to the regular though complex mode of its operation, is wholly inconceivable. Of this plan of redemption it may with peculiar and striking propriety be said.

"Mobilitate viget, viresque acquirit eundo."
"—— —— Every moment brings
New vigor to its flight, new pinions to its wings."

The immediate cause of the secession of Mr. Walpole, whose example was followed by his friends, Mr. Methuen secretary of state, and Mr. Pulteney secretary at war, afterwards so famous and so formidable as his antagonist, has been already intimated, and was now unreservedly avowed to be his total disapprobation of the continental politics of the court, which he perhaps deemed not merely injurious to the nation, but eventually hazardous
to

ment to the muses. There is however one beautiful passage, which well deserves to be rescued from oblivion, in his epistle to the earl of Dorset, on the victory gained by king WILLIAM on the banks of the Boyne, in which that monarch received a slight contusion from a musquet ball, which grazed on his shoulder:

" O, if in France this hero had been born,
What glittering tinsel would his acts adorn!
Their plays, their songs, would dwell upon his wound,
And operas repeat no other sound:
Boyne would for ages be the painter's theme,
The Gobelins' labor, and the poet's dream;
The wounded arm would furnish all their rooms,
And BLEED for ever PURPLE in their looms."

to the safety of the minister who should venture publicly to justify or support them. For it did not at this time clearly appear how far the complaisance of parliament would in time extend. Nor was it previously very credible that the interests of three powerful kingdoms should be made entirely subservient, by men chosen to guard and protect them, to the aspiring views of a German electorate. But experience and observation taught this minister very different and much juster notions of things. Mr. Walpole was succeeded in the treasury at first by general Stanhope, who finding and ingenuously acknowledging his incompetency for that station, soon resigned to the earl of Sunderland, who had long aspired to the possession of it. Under this nobleman Mr Aislabie acted as chancellor of the exchequer; and the celebrated Addison was advanced in the room of Mr. Methuen to the post of secretary: but being found essentially deficient in the requisite qualifications of a minister of state, he resigned, on the pretence of ill health and the fatigues of office, to Mr. Craggs. And General Stanhope, being created an earl, resumed the seals of the foreign department, leaving Aislabie and Craggs to conduct the affairs of government in the house of commons; who, though men of good parliamentary talents, were considered only as secondary ministers to the great efficient leaders, Sunderland and Stanhope. The earl of Oxford, who had now remained two years in the tower, was encouraged, by the defection of his most powerful adversary, to petition the house of lords that his imprisonment might not be indefinite; and the house appointed an early day for his trial in Westminster hall, for which the most solemn and magnificent preparations were made, earl Cowper presiding, as on former occasions, in the capacity of lord high steward. The articles of the impeachment being read, and Sir Joseph Jekyl standing up as one of the committee

committee of managers in the name of the house of commons of England to make good the first charge, lord Harcourt arose and observed, "that the articles of the impeachment being numerous, and two of them only extending to the charge of high treason, it was superfluous to enter into the investigation of the rest till these had been decided upon; for, supposing him guilty of all, the utmost their lordships could inflict, or the earl could suffer, would amount to no more than the forfeiture of life and estate." The commons affected to resent what they styled an encroachment upon their privileges, and peremptorily refused to proceed in the order prescribed by the lords. The lords, on their part, haughtily refused a *free conference* on this subject, as demanded by the commons: and on their non-appearance at the subsequent adjournment of the court, the earl was acquitted; not, as was generally believed, without the secret approbation and concurrence of the crown. The commons, however, presented an address to the king, desiring that he might be excepted out of the intended act of grace; by which they expressed at once their sense of the earl's demerit, and their contempt of their lordships' sentence of acquittal. The act of grace accordingly passed with this and some other exceptions: and Oxford, to preserve appearances, was forbidden to present himself at court, but no attempt was at any time made to revive the proceedings against him. By virtue of this act the lords Carnwath, Widrington, and Nairne, with many other persons of distinction concerned in the late rebellion, were discharged. Lord Nithisdale had previously effected his escape; the earl of Derwentwater and lord viscount Kenmuir only suffering the utmost rigor of the law.

In the course of this year (1718) the attention of the public was excited in a most uncommon degree by a sermon preached before the king at the chapel-royal, and

Vol. I. K published

published at his express command, by Dr. Benjamin Hoadley, lord bishop of Bangor, " On the nature of the kingdom of CHRIST." As the foundation of this memorable discourse, the bishop selected the famous declaration of Christ to Pilate, the Roman procurator; " MY KINGDOM IS NOT OF THIS WORLD." And the direct and undisguised object of it was, to prove " that the kingdom of Christ, and the sanctions by which it is supported were of a nature wholly intellectual and spiritual—that the CHURCH, taking the term in its utmost latitude of signification, did not, and could not, possess the slightest degree of AUTHORITY under any commission, or pretended commission, derived from him: that the church of England, and all other national churches, were merely civil or human institutions, established for the purposes of diffusing and perpetuating the knowledge and belief of christianity; which contained a system of truths, not in their nature differing from other truths, excepting by their superior weight and importance; and which were to be inculcated in a manner analogous to other truths, demanding only, from their more interesting import, proportionably higher degrees of care, attention, and assiduity in the promulgation of them." It is scarcely to be imagined in these times, with what degree of furious and malignant rancor these plain, simple, and rational principles were attacked by the zealots and champions of the church. On the meeting of the convocation, a committee was appointed to examine this famous publication; and a representation was quickly drawn up, in which a most heavy censure was passed upon it, as tending to subvert all government and discipline in the church of Christ, to reduce his kingdom to a state of anarchy and confusion, to impugn and impeach the royal supremacy in matters ecclesiastical, and the authority of the legislature

to

to enforce obedience in matters of religion by civil sanctions. A sudden stop however was put to these disgraceful proceedings, by a royal prorogation; and from this period the convocation has never been convened but as a mere matter of form, and for the purpose of being again prorogued. Perhaps, however, in these more enlightened times, this assembly might be again permitted to resume its deliberative and legislative powers, with advantage to the community—and in no other assembly could propositions of ecclesiastical reform originate with so much effect or propriety. The controversy which thus commenced, was carried on for several years with great ability and animation on the part of the bishop, aided by various excellent pens, though opposed by men whose learning and talents gave an artificial lustre to bigotry and absurdity. No controversy, however, upon the whole, ever more fully and completely answered the purpose intended by it. The obscurity in which this subject had been long involved, was dissipated. The public mind was enlightened and convinced. CHURCH AUTHORITY, *the chimæra vomiting flames*, was destroyed; and the name of HOADLEY will be transmitted from generation to generation, with increase of honor, of esteem, and grateful veneration. It would be injustice also to deny to the king himself his share of praise for countenancing and supporting opinions so opposite to those which have usually constituted a part of the policy of princes; and which reflect equal credit upon his understanding and integrity. As a far more important proof, however, of the liberal and benignant disposition of this monarch, earl Stanhope, his favorite and confidential minister, presented to the house of lords, December 1718, a bill for the repeal of the occasional conformity and schism acts, passed under the late administration; and likewise such clauses of the test and corporation acts as operated to the

K 2 exclusion

exclusion of proteſtant diſſenters from civil offices. The latter part of the bill had an unexpected and formidable obſtacle to encounter in the oppoſition of the lord Cowper, who joined the Tory lords in founding the alarm of DANGER *to the* CHURCH, ſhould the diſſenters be admitted to the common rights and privileges of citizens in the ſtate. Dr. Wake, archbiſhop of Canterbury, a prelate eminent for learning and general reſpectability of character, but who, ſince his elevation to the primacy, ſeemed to have loſt ſight in a great meaſure of thoſe principles to which he owed his advancement, employed upon this occaſion ſome arguments againſt the diſſenters, which were conſidered by his former friends as not a little extraordinary. He affirmed, " That the acts this bill propoſed to repeal were the main bulwarks of the Engliſh church; and though he had *all imaginable tenderneſs for well-meaning and conſcientious diſſenters,* he was compelled to ſay, that many of that perſuaſion had made a wrong uſe of the *favor and indulgence* ſhewn them at the revolution; it was therefore deemed neceſſary for the legiſlature to interpoſe, in order to put a ſtop to the ſcandalous practice of occaſional conformity. As to the act againſt ſchiſm—the proteſt of the lords againſt which, reprobating, in the moſt indignant terms, that deteſtable ſtatute, he had himſelf ſigned—his Grace added, that the repeal of it was SUPERFLUOUS, as no advantage had been taken of the act to the prejudice of the diſſenters*."

In

---

* It might be imagined, from that " tenderneſs to well-meaning diſſenters," which this prelate ſo oſtentatiouſly profeſſes, and which they no doubt are bound with ſuitable humility and gratitude to acknowledge, that the diſſenters are a weak and ignorant people, entertaining abſurd notions on ſubjects of high and general concern, and wholly deſtitute of learning and ability to defend their own principles. But of this, not the preſent times only, but " the centuries to come," will

In opposition to these *novel sentiments* of his grace, the bishop of Bangor demonstrated "that the acts styled by the archbishop the bulwarks of the church, under whatever false colors they might be disguised, were acts of real persecution: that if the *mere pretext* of self-preservation, or self-defence, was once admitted as a sufficient ground for passing laws of this nature, all the heathen persecutions against christians, and all the popish persecutions against protestants, would be justified: that the church of England as by law established stood not, and he trusted would never stand, in need of such miserable supports; that toleration was not a *favor*, or *indulgence*, but a natural right; and that the safety of the church was secured by no means so effectually, as by a regard to the just and equitable claims of their fellow-citizens. He added, "that the ardent and intemperate zeal which many displayed for the interests of the church, was, he feared, principally incited by a regard to their own interests, and by a secret and fond attachment to the power, the honors, and the emoluments which appertain to it.—

The will judge. As an amusing contrast to these sentiments of archbishop Wake, it may not be improper to oppose those of his venerable predecessor archbishop Tennison, who in the debate on the occasional conformity bill, A. D. 1704, declared this decided disapprobation of the measure. Far from considering occasional conformity as "a scandalous practice," or "dangerous to the church," he affirmed, that it ought to be encouraged by all good churchmen, as having an evident tendency to conciliate the affections, and to moderate the prejudices, of the dissenters; being in itself a laudable exercise of Christian charity, and nowise incompatible with the strictest integrity. "The employing of persons," said this excellent prelate, "of a religion different from the established in civil offices, has been practised in all countries where liberty of conscience has been allowed. We have already gone farther in excluding dissenters than any other country has done. Whatever reasons there were to apprehend our religion in danger from papists, when the test act was passed, cannot be applicable to the dissenters at present. On the contrary, manifest inconveniences result from this exclusion."

The defire of power and riches was, he owned, natural to all; but reafon and religion ought to reftrain men from indulging it, to the injury or prejudice of others; or in any manner inconfiftent with the general rights and liberties of mankind." Thefe fentiments of the bifhop of Bangor were ftrongly enforced by Dr. Kennet bifhop of Peterborough, who declared his opinion, that the repeal of the acts in queftion would not be detrimental to the church, but would redound to her advantage and fecurity. He affirmed that the evidence of hiftory proved the church to be moft fafe and flourifhing when the clergy did not affect more power than appertains to their fhare, and were tender of the rights and liberties of their fellow-fubjects: but that arbitrary meafures and perfecutions firft brought, as the experience of the laft century fufficiently evinced, fcandal and contempt upon the clergy, and, at laft, ruin both upon church and ftate. The CHURCH, faid this prelate, is, I admit, a term of facred and venerable import, and therefore it is, that in the mouths of bigots, or of malicious and defigning men, it has produced fuch fatal effects. ' The TEMPLE of the LORD— the TEMPLE of the LORD are WE,' was of old the boaft of the feditious and abandoned among the Jews, and was ufed as a color and incentive to every evil purpofe. The bifhop faid, that the diffenters, though the moft zealous promoters of the revolution, had hitherto been no gainers by it; for it was well known that they enjoyed the full benefits of toleration under king James. And he ftated as a grofs political abfurdity, that they were incapacitated by the teft from ferving that government of which they were allowed to be the firmeft friends; and alluding to what had paffed in the courfe of the debate, he declared, that he hoped it would not be thought fufficient, in oppofition to the plaineft dictates of juftice and

equity,

equity, which called aloud for the repeal of these acts, to say, "that the example of SWEDEN was otherwise."

In this memorable debate, no one diftinguifhed himfelf more than lord Lanfdowne, who had imbibed in all their virulence the antient principles of Toryifm; who had been a fteady and inveterate enemy to the Hanoverian fucceffion; and who was happy to embrace this occafion of pronouncing an invective againft the diffenters, replete with malignant and farcaftic wit, and breathing a fpirit which, unreftrained by external caufes, would doubtlefs have difplayed itfelf in all the terrors of the moft fanguinary perfecution. This nobleman declared, "That he always underftood the act of toleration to be meant as an indulgence for tender confciences, not a licenfe for hardened ones—and that the act to prevent occafional conformity was defigned only to correct a particular crime of particular men, in which none were included but thofe followers of Judas who came to the Lord's fupper for no other end but to fell and betray him. It is to me (faid his lordfhip) a matter of aftonifhment, to hear the merit of diffenters fo highly extolled and magnified within thefe walls. Who is there among us, but can tell of fome anceftor either fequeftered or murdered by them? Who voted the lords ufelefs? The diffenters.—Who abolifhed epifcopacy? The diffenters.—Who deftroyed freedom of parliament? The diffenters.—Who introduced government by ftanding armies? The diffenters.—Who wafhed their hands in the blood of their martyred fovereign? The diffenters.—Have they repented? No.—they glory in their wickednefs at this day. That they have remained not only quiet, but have appeared zealous in the fupport of the prefent eftablifhment, is no wonder: for who but themfelves, or their favorers, have been thought worthy of countenance? If univerfal difcontent pervades at this time all ranks of people throughout the nation,

nation, the reason is plain, flagrant, and notorious. It arises from the insolence and the presumption of the dissenters—from their open insults of the clergy—from their public vindication of the murder of king Charles I. and their vile reflections upon the memory of queen Anne, ever dear to the people of England; besides other indecent and arrogant provocations, too many to enumerate, too grievous to endure. And if all this is done, not only with impunity, but with authority and reward, is there not more than sufficient reason for jealousy? a jealousy, which this new attempt to break down all the fences and boundaries of the church at once, will certainly have no tendency to extinguish. If indeed (concluded his lordship) there are individuals amongst them who pretend to peculiar merit, let them stand forth, and clearly and explicitly state their claims—for GOD forbid but that all of them should have their deserts!"—If at this distance of time, and on a cool and impartial review of facts, we are compelled severely to censure the conduct of the whigs, now exercising the entire powers of government, as exhibiting plain indications of the rage and hatred characteristic of a political faction, it is not difficult to conjecture, from this and similar specimens of Tory eloquence, to what far more dangerous extremes of violence the opposite faction, if triumphant, were prepared to resort. The speculative principles of the Whigs also being in their own nature just, beneficent, and generous; the spirit of their administration, after the first emotions of rancor and revenge were gratified, became insensibly mild, easy, and equitable; whereas, had the Tories gained a permanent ascendency, the certain foundation would have been laid of an internal and everlasting system of oppression, distraction, and calamity.

After long debate, the house agreed to leave out the clauses respecting the corporation and test acts; in which state it was transmitted to and passed by the commons; and in the royal speech, at the close of the session, his majesty expressed the highest satisfaction at this signal instance of legislative wisdom and moderation*.

Previous however, to the recess of parliament, a bill was unexpectedly brought in, under the sanction of the government, for limiting the peerage, by restraining the
crown

---

* Sir Robert Walpole, at this time in opposition, with a view to embarrass the measures of the court, spoke and voted against this repeal: and he is said frequently to have expressed, in the latter years of his life, his regret at having joined in the clamors of the high church party on this occasion. Lord Chesterfield, then a very young man, and in the service of the prince of Wales, who at this period countenanced the opposition, voted on the same side with more sincerity: " I thought it (says he) impossible for the honestest man in the world to be saved out of the pale of the church, not considering that matters of opinion do not depend upon the will—that it is as natural and allowable that another man should differ in opinion from me, as that I should differ from him; and that if we are both sincere, we are both blameless, and should consequently have mutual indulgence for each other." It may be transiently remarked, in answer to the virulent accusations of Lord Lansdowne, that it is the height of folly, as well as injustice, to charge the acts of Cromwell's usurpation upon the dissenters or presbyterians of the last century—when it is notorious, that they opposed them to the utmost of their power—and that 200 members of the house of commons of that denomination were secluded by military violence from the house before the ordinance passed for the trial of the king. Had the condemnation of that merciless and perfidious tyrant—for such, notwithstanding his boasted private and personal virtues, he undoubtedly was—resulted from the unbiassed will of the nation, future ages might have applauded the act, though, as perpetrated by a desperate and lawless faction, in opposition to the public will, it is indeed the subject of just abhorrence. Let the guilt of the individuals concerned in this transaction, however, be what it may; why are we, who have only an historical knowledge of the fact, and who live in another age of the world, called upon to express our penitence and contrition for it? Certainly, the service of the 30th of January is a political farce, upon which the wisdom of government ought long ago to have dropped the curtain.—There is indeed a charge omitted by lord Lansdowne, but which might
be

crown from enlarging the prefent number of peers by more than fix new creations. This was generally confidered as a meafure not fo much of policy as of refentment on the part of the crown, eagerly and intemperately defirous to excite the chagrin, and diminifh the political importance, of the prince of Wales, who had highly offended the court by the fupport he had for fome time paft given to the oppofition. The court influence, weakened by the late feceffion, and in this inftance oppofed by the general fenfe of the nation, which faw its tendency to elevate the ariftocracy, and by the *efprit du corps* of the houfe of commons, was however found, upon trial, not fufficiently powerful to carry this favorite but very exceptionable project into effect: and the bill, after being withdrawn by lord Stanhope in order to its revival with greater force the enfuing feffion, when it paffed the lords with very little difficulty, was ultimately rejected by the commons, not without evident marks of indignation; the divifion on the queftion of commitment being 269 to 177 voices.

Mr.

be properly urged againft the diffenters, as containing not fictitious, but real culpability. It is that, poffeffing the authority and confidence of the nation in the convention parliament of 1660, they had the unpardonable weaknefs to reftore king Charles II. to the crown, without any previous limitations or conditions. Let the idolizers of kings, who have hearts to feel, if not underftandings to be convinced, view the interefting and affecting portrait now in the poffeffion of lord Elliot, of his illuftrious anceftor Sir John Elliot, who, with many other diftinguifhed patriots, was, for his noble exertions in the caufe of liberty, committed to the Tower, after the diffolution of the laft of the early parliaments of Charles I. He is drawn pale, languifhing, and emaciated—but difdaining to make the abject fubmiffion required of him by the tyrant, he expired under the exceffive rigors of his confinement, leaving this portrait as a legacy and memento to his pofterity and to mankind; who, in the contemplation of fuch enormities, have reafon to rejoice

> " When vengeance in the lurid air
> Lifts her red arm expos'd and bare."

Mr. Walpole particularly diftinguifhed himfelf by the animation of his oppofition to this bill. By an allufion *happily imagined*, he compared the two houfes of parliament to the temples of Fame and Virtue, and obferved that, " among the Romans, the former was placed behind the latter, to denote that fame was no otherwife attainable than by virtue. But if the prefent bill paffed into a law, one of the moft powerful incentives to virtue would be taken away. He affirmed that this bill would not only operate as a difcouragement to merit, but would endanger the conftitution: that the peers were already poffeffed of fufficient privileges; but that the propofed limitation of their number would prodigioufly enhance their authority, and in time reduce the commons to a ftate of. fervile dependency: that he was aftonifhed their lordfhips could prefume to fend fuch a bill to that houfe, or that they could flatter themfelves it would ever receive their concurrence, or expect that they would voluntarily exclude themfelves and their pofterity from the honors of the peerage. And he thought it a very injurious and ungrateful return in one, who had himfelf been advanced to a participation of thofe honors for his public fervices, to endeavor, on his admiffion to the houfe of peers, to bar the door againft future claimants."

In allufion to this bill, the king, in his fpeech from the throne, had ufed thefe remarkable expreffions: " As I can truly affirm that no prince was ever more zealous to increafe his own authority, than I am to perpetuate the liberty of my people, I hope you will think of all proper methods to eftablifh and tranfmit to your pofterity the freedom of our happy conftitution; and particularly to fecure that part which is moft liable to abufe." And by an exprefs meffage to the lords, when the bill was pending, his majefty declared, " That he had fo much at heart the fettlement of the Britifh peerage, upon fuch a foundation

foundation as might secure the freedom and constitution of parliaments in all future ages, that he was willing his prerogative should not stand in the way of so great and necessary a work." Certainly it would be harsh and uncandid to ascribe this apparent generosity of sentiment to the exclusive influence of invidious motives; but it may well be doubted whether the remedy proposed by the ministers of the crown, for the abuse so reasonably apprehended, and which time has contributed rather to strengthen than impair, might not in its consequences be productive of political inconvenience still more serious than the evil it was intended to obviate.

In the session of 1719, also, the celebrated declaratory bill, for the better securing the dependency of Ireland upon the crown of England, was introduced and passed; in which the supremacy of the appellant jurisdiction of the English house of peers, and the right of the English parliament to make laws to bind the kingdom of Ireland in all cases whatsoever, were asserted in a high tone, in consequence of the refractory spirit which had lately displayed itself in various instances in that kingdom. Nor was it conceivable at this period, by any effort of political sagacity, that Ireland would be in a situation, before the termination of the century, to extort from England an entire and absolute renunciation of these haughty and unjust pretensions. The parliament of Ireland assembling July 1, 1719, the duke of Bolton, lord lieutenant of that kingdom, in his speech, strongly urged the necessity of guarding against the designs of the disaffected, and declared, that it would be very pleasing to his Majesty, if any method could be found, not inconsistent with the security of the church, to render the protestant dissenters more useful and capable of serving his majesty, and supporting the protestant interest, than they now are—they having upon all occasions given sufficient proofs of their being

being well affected to his majefty's perfon and government, and to the fucceffion of the crown in his royal houfe. And this his excellency declared he was exprefsly ordered to lay before the legiflature, as a thing greatly importing his majefty's fervice, and the national fecurity. In confequence of this interpofition, an act paffed to relieve the diffenters from certain penalties inflicted by the exifting laws; but the repeal of the facramental teft, to which the king plainly extended his views, could not be obtained by any effort of regal influence from the equity or complaifance of the prefent parliament*.

About

---

* Nearly at this period the earl of Stair, who had ferved his country for feveral years with diftinguifhed ability, as ambaffador at the court of Verfailles, was recalled in confequence of a political difference between him and the lords Stanhope and Sunderland, refpecting the famous Law, raifed by the regent to the comptroller-generalfhip of the finances, and whofe credit at the French court, from the knowledge of his mifchievous defigns, the ambaffador had labored to fubvert. In a letter to Mr. Secretary Craggs, dated February 14, 1720, he vindicates his public character and conduct with great fpirit, and in a manner highly characteriftic of his well known firmnefs and elevation of mind. A few fentences it may be permitted as the privilege of a note to tranfcribe.—
"If (fays he) lord Stanhope has not gained Mr. Law, I am afraid we fhall not find our account in his lordfhip's fupporting him, when he was ready to fall—in making him firft minifter, and recalling me from this court, where my long ftay fhould have enabled me to be better able to judge of their defigns, and of their ways of working, than a ftranger of greater capacity could poffibly be. After the ufage I meet with, I do not wonder to fee that our minifters have fo few friends. As to my revocation, if it was poffible I fhould have a mind to ftay in this country, you have made it impracticable—you have taken all the effectual ways to deftroy any perfonal credit I had with the regent—you have made it plain to him, that I have no credit with the king—you are under a neceffity of fending therefore another minifter to this court.— As to the matter of my revocation, I do not care to make the grimace of defiring it for falfe reafons. I expect nothing, and I fear nothing.— As to my behavior when I come home, I fhall ever be a faithful fervant to the king, and act as a man in whom the love of his country is fuperior to all other confiderations." *Hardwicke State Papers.*

About this period, the famous South-sea bill was introduced into the British house of commons, by Mr. Aiflabie, chancellor of the exchequer; the earl of Sunderland presiding at the board of treasury; and, after long and able discussion, received the royal assent, April 7th, 1720. By this bill, which proposed eventually to reduce all the different public securities into one grand aggregate fund, the South-sea company was invested with certain commercial privileges, and authorized to take in, by purchase or subscription, both the redeemable and irredeemable debts of the nation, to the amount of about thirty-three millions, at such rates and prices as should be agreed upon between the company and the respective proprietors—a clause proposed in the house of commons, for ascertaining what share of the capital stock of the company should be vested in those proprietors of government stock, who might voluntarily subscribe, being most unwisely rejected. In return, the company consented that the interest upon their original capital of 9,400,000l. as well as the interest upon the public debts, to be redeemed in the mode prescribed by the present act, should, after Midsummer-day 1727, be reduced to four per cent. redeemable by parliament; and exclusive of this reduction, the company agreed to pay into the exchequer four years and a half purchase of all the long and short annuities that should be subscribed, and one year's purchase of such long annuities as should not be subscribed; amounting, on the execution of the act, to no less than seven millions; for raising which sum, they were impowered to open books of subscription, to grant annuities redeemable by the company, and to convert the money so raised into additional stock. It is evident, from the wild and extravagant terms of this contract, that it was never meant to be seriously fulfilled. In vain did the sagacity of Walpole discern, and his eloquence display, the mighty mischiefs contained in this cafket of Pandora. In vain did he urge the acceptance of the equitable and rational propofals of the bank. The houfe was fafcinated by the dazzling and magnificent appearance of the South-Sea project; and the bill paffed with general applaufe, and by a vaft majority of votes, 55 members only dividing againft it. But in a fhort time this myftery of iniquity began to unfold itfelf. The moft artful and infidious methods were put in practice to delude the public with the notion of the vaft emoluments eventually to be derived from the commercial intercourfe which it was pretended would, with the confent of the court of Madrid, and as an equivalent for the ceffion of Gibraltar and Minorca, be eftablifhed with the empires of Mexico and Peru. The fucceffive fubfcriptions filled with amazing rapidity; and the court of directors declaring a dividend of 30 per cent. for Chriftmas 1720, and 50 per cent. for no lefs than twelve years after, the transfer price of the company's ftock advancing in proportion to the public demand, rofe from 130, which was the price it bore while the bill was depending in parliament, in a very fhort fpace of time to 1000; by which means an opportunity was offered, to thofe who were concerned in the project, or rather the plot, to make immenfe fortunes, before the burfting of this mighty bubble. And the ftock falling with the fame, or even greater rapidity, than that with which it had rifen; vaft numbers of adventurers—and fuch was the general infatuation, that upon this occafion the whole nation feemed to have become adventurers—awaking from their golden dreams of profperity, found themfelves reduced to a ftate of the moft deplorable diftrefs and ruin. On a parliamentary inveftigation of this dark and dangerous bufinefs, which was ftyled, in the report of the fecret committee, " a train of the deepest villainy and fraud Hell ever contrived for the ruin of any nation;" it appeared, that transfers of the company's stock, to a very great amount, had been made to persons high in office, to facilitate the passing of the bill—that the scandalous artifices practised by the company, and their shameless abuse of the public confidence, had received not only the connivance but the encouragement of several, at least, of the ministers: and lord Sunderland and Mr. Aislabie were compelled to a precipitate and disgraceful resignation of their offices—the latter being also expelled the house, and committed to the tower. Mr. Craggs, secretary of State, was exempted only by the stroke of death, from a similar fate: and many other persons of figure and consequence, who were found, on inquiry, more or less culpable, were variously punished; though, in the opinion of the exasperated public, not with an adequate degree of severity. Nevertheless, the house acted with a spirit and unanimity on this great occasion, which reflected upon their proceedings the highest honor; and sufficiently manifested the indignation they felt, at having been, under specious pretences, made the unintentional instruments of an injury so extensive, and a deception so dreadful.

Mr. Waller, son-in-law to Aislabie, to whom South-Sea stock to an immense amount had been transferred, had preserved no minutes of his transactions; and pretended, on his examination, that he could not recollect for what persons or purposes he had accepted it. Sir John Blount, accounted the original projector, and one of the most guilty agents in this business, refusing to answer certain interrogatories put to him in the house of lords by the duke of Wharton; and being supported somewhat too peremptorily in his refusal, by lord Stanhope; the duke maliciously observed, that the government of the best princes was sometimes rendered intolerable

rable to their subjects by bad ministers—mentioning the example of Sejanus, who had made the reign of Claudius hateful to the Romans. Conscious of the unsullied rectitude of his conduct, lord Stanhope, in a transport of anger, rose to speak in his own vindication; and in consequence of the vehemence of his exertions, was seized with a sudden illness, which compelled him to retire: and after a short interval of languishment and insensibility, he expired in the evening of the next day, extremely regretted by his sovereign, and possessing the general esteem and regard of the nation *. On the decease of this nobleman, and the compulsive resignation of Sunderland, a new arrangement of administration was formed; and Mr. Walpole, lord Townshend, lord Cowper, and Mr. Methuen, now reconciled to the court, were re-instated with great *eclat* in their former or other principal offices: and from this period, Mr. Walpole—who being in the progress of royal favor invested with the order of the Garter, assumed the title of Sir Robert Walpole—must be regarded as prime minister †.

Through

---

* The king, as the countess of Chesterfield, who was present on the occasion, related to the respectable author of the "Memoirs of the earl of Chesterfield," received the intelligence of this nobleman's death when at supper; and not being able to suppress the emotions of his grief, he rose from table, and retired—his eyes being suffused with tears. Lord Stanhope died, Feb. 1721. Sir Robert Walpole's commission, as first lord of the treasury, bore date April 2, 1721.

† Though a real and very important difference of opinion was believed to exist in the cabinet, previous to the secession, on the subject of continental politics; the animosities of the Whigs, it must be remarked, may be traced to another and much less honorable source—the insatiable ambition of the earl of Halifax, divided the court into two opposite and hostile parties. Lord Stanhope, who possessed the entire confidence of the king, and who had acquired a great ascendency over him, was much disposed to favor the views and was himself manifestly under

Through the judicious and vigorous refolutions adopted by parliament, in purfuance of his recommendations, public credit was fpeedily and effectually reftored. Knight, Cafhier of the South-Sea company, for the apprehending of whom a royal proclamation had been iffued, had efcaped at a critical moment to the Continent; carrying with him the famous *Green Book*, which was fuppofed to contain the entire fecret of the tranfaction. Being arrefted at Tirlemont, by the vigilance of the Englifh refident at Bruffels, application was made to the marquis du Prie, governor of the Low Countries, to deliver him up to juftice. But anfwer was unexpectedly made

der the influence, of the artful Sunderland. Walpole and Townfhend, finding themfelves excluded from the fecret counfels of the king, and becoming every day more infignificant, determined upon a refignation. A vehement mutual refentment and averfion from this time fubfifted between Stanhope and Walpole, which broke out on one occafion in an altercation and reciprocal crimination in the houfe of commons fo violently, that the houfe was obliged to interpofe its authority, to prevent any difaftrous confequences. And Mr. Hungerford obferved, " that it became the members of that houfe, after the Oriental fafhion, to avert their countenances, while thefe two great men, the fathers of the ftate, were thus expofing each other's nakednefs." After the difgrace of Sunderland, and the death of Stanhope, no fhadow of competition remained; and Townfhend and Walpole were invefted with the full powers of government. But no fooner had they attained the fummit of their wifhes, than a violent jealoufy arofe between thefe quondam friends; and the influence of Walpole at length prevailing, lord Townfhend, after a long-protracted ftruggle, refigned his offices, and retired to his eftates in Norfolk; where he paffed his remaining years highly refpected, amufing himfelf, and benefiting the country around him, with his agricultural experiments—to which there is an allufion in one of Pope's epiftolary imitations of Horace—" All Townfhend's turnips, and all Grofvenor's mines." But thefe court-intrigues are amongft thofe arcana of ftate, which lie too deep for " men of common minds" to difcufs. They are unfathomable myfteries, facred as thofe of the *Bona Dea*: PROCUL ESTE PROFANI.

made by the imperial court, that this could not be done, confiftently with the privileges of the ftates of Brabant—for by an article of the *Joyeufe Entrée*, no perfon, againft whom a criminal accufation is brought, can be removed for trial out of the province. It was thought that, in a cafe of this momentous nature, his imperial majefty, for whom England had conquered kingdoms, might have prevailed upon the ftates to wave their privilege: and very prefling inftances were anew made, for the furrender of Knight. But, in the interim, he effected a fecond efcape from the citadel of Antwerp—and in the fequel, he received a free pardon. Vehement fufpicions, therefore, arofe, that Knight's evidence was too decifive to be produced; and that the late minifter had ftill fufficient influence to fcreen himfelf from that punifhment, which the whole nation believed him to merit, and from which his fuperior adroitnefs of management only protected him.

Lord SUNDERLAND did not long furvive his difmiffion from his high office; but died April 1722, leaving behind him a character which bore a ftriking analogy to that of his father—bold, reftlefs, infidious, faithlefs, ambitious, excelling in all the arts of courtly addrefs, and diftinguifhed by his extent of political knowledge and fagacity, though he attained not to the dignity of true wifdom, which is infeparably connected with rectitude of heart and conduct. Nearly at the fame time expired the celebrated JOHN duke of MARLBOROUGH, to whom Sunderland was clofely allied, by marriage with his eldeft daughter. So varioufly has the character of this great man been delineated, that it is no eafy tafk clearly to afcertain the truth. With refpect to political probity, however, he feems not inferior to the generality of his cotemporaries. He has been accufed of bafe ingratitude in the defertion of his royal mafter and benefactor, king James II. But this defertion took place at a time when it was not unattended with danger: and there appears in his conduct, at that great political crifis, nothing inconfiftent with the fuppofition that his motives were laudable and patriotic. And furely no private obligation can be of force to fuperfede the duties we owe to our country. It is, indeed, far more difficult to juftify the correfpondence which he afterwards carried on with the abdicated monarch: but this guilt he appears to have fhared with fo many other diftinguifhed, and, upon the whole, refpectable perfons, that it cannot be imputed to him as a fubject of peculiar reproach. The truth is, that a fecret fufpicion and apprehenfion pervading the minds of the bulk of the nation, that the exiled family would, by fome revolution in politics, be one day reftored, as in the perfon of king Charles II. it had once before been; many, perhaps a majority of thofe who acted a confpicuous part in public life, allowed themfelves, by a too lax political morality, to entertain a clandeftine correfpondence with the court of St. Germaine's, with a view to avert the effects of its indignation in cafe the actual ftate of things fhould be reverfed, but who were far from wifhing to contribute to the acceleration of fuch a cataftrophe. And it is evident that the court of St. Germaine's was the perpetual dupe of thefe egregious artifices. The military talents of the duke of Marlborough tranfcend all praife, and may be fet with advantage in competition with thofe of any commander ancient or modern [*]. To Marlborough alone, no one has ventured

---

[*] When prince Eugene was in England, during the adminiftration of lord Oxford, being one day entertained at the table of the lord treafurer, that minifter politely remarked, that he might congratulate himfelf

ventured to impute either error or misfortune. In his political capacity, he was a moſt able and ſucceſsful negotiator: and though, in conſequence of his early initiation into the brilliant and diſſipated circles of the court, neceſſarily and groſsly illiterate; all defects of this nature were more than compenſated by the native excellence of his underſtanding, the faſcination of his manners, and his profound knowledge of mankind—the fruit, not of abſtract ſpeculation, but of actual obſervation and long experience. His perſon was eminently graceful, and his countenance noble and engaging: his diſpoſition was mild, his deportment affable, and the general tenor of his private ſocial life regular and unblemiſhed. He has been, indeed, uſually repreſented as deeply tinctured with the vice of avarice: but though he was, doubtleſs, eager in the accumulation of riches, it does not appear that he degraded the dignity of his ſtation and character, by the parſimony of his expences. And he is known to have reſiſted with firmneſs and magnanimity the immenſe offers made to him in the name of Louis XIV. by the marquis de Torcy at the conferences of Gertruydenberg. In the laſt years of his life he exhibited an affecting proof of the imbecility of human nature and the vanity of human greatneſs *—leaving upon the public mind an impreſſion of compaſſion, which the unexampled

ſelf on having for his gueſt the firſt general in Europe: to which his highneſs, in alluſion to the recent diſgrace of the duke of Marlborough, replied, That if it were ſo, it was to his lordſhip he was indebted for the pre-eminence.

* "In life's laſt ſcene what prodigies ſurpriſe!
Fears of the brave, and follies of the wiſe!
From Marlborough's eyes the ſtreams of dotage flow,
And Swift expires—a driveller and a ſhow."
Johnson's Im. of Juv. Sat. 10.

pled pomp of his funeral obsequies did not tend to weaken.

A vehement controversy having recently arisen on the subject of the TRINITY, chiefly in consequence of the learned tracts published in opposition to the established doctrine by the famous professor Whiston, the university of Oxford in full convocation resolved "that the solemn thanks of that body should be returned to the earl of Nottingham, for his most noble defence of the Catholic faith, contained in his answer to Mr. Whiston's letter concerning the eternity of the son of GOD and of the Holy Ghost." And at the instance of this theological statesman, a bill was introduced into the house of peers for the suppression of blasphemy and profaneness; which enacted, that if any one spoke or wrote against the being of a GOD, the divinity of Jesus Christ or the Holy Ghost, the doctrine of the Trinity, the truth of the Christian religion, or the divine inspiration of the scriptures, he should suffer imprisonment for an indefinite term, unless in a certain form prescribed he should publicly renounce and abjure his errors. And by a clause in this bill, the archbishops and bishops within their respective jurisdictions, and the justices of peace in their several counties at their quarter session, were authorized to summon any dissenting teacher, and to require his subscription to a declaration of faith containing the articles above enumerated; and upon his refusal, it was enacted, that he should be *ipso facto* deprived of the benefit of the act of toleration. The lords being summoned on the second reading of this bill (May 1721), Dr. WAKE, archbishop of Canterbury, sealed his apostacy from the principles of civil and religious liberty, by moving to have it committed. Upon which lord Onslow rose, and declared " that though he was himself zealously

ly attached to the doctrines of the church of England, he would never consent to support even the truth itself by persecution; and he moved that the bill might be THROWN OUT." He was seconded by the duke of Wharton, who said, that having been himself frequently accused of impiety and irreligion *, he conceived that he could not more effectually vindicate his character from these imputations, than by opposing to the utmost a measure

* This is the nobleman whose character is so happily delineated by POPE, in his Epistle to lord viscount Cobham.

—" WHARTON, the scorn and wonder of our days,
 Whose ruling passion is the lust of praise,
 Born with whate'er could win it from the wise;
 Women and fools must like him—or he dies.
 Though wondering senates hung on all he spoke,
 The club must hail him master of the joke.
 Shall parts so various aim at nothing new?
 He'll shine a TULLY and a WILMOT too.
 Thus with each gift of nature or of art,
 And wanting nothing but an honest heart,
 Grown all to all—from no one vice exempt,
 And most contemptible, to shun contempt;
 His passion still to covet general praise,
 His life to forfeit it a thousand ways—
 He dies sad outcast of each church and state;
 And, harder still—flagitious, yet not great."

There seems a remarkable resemblance between the character of this nobleman and that of the last VILLIERS duke of Buckingham, described with such masterly strokes of genius under the appellation of ZIMRI in Dryden's Absalom and Ahitophel, and like him,

" Beggar'd by fools—whom still he found too late;
 He had his jest—and they had his estate."

On leaving England with a ruined constitution and fortune, he entered into the service of the Pretender then patronized by the court of Madrid;

a measure so repugnant to the spirit of Christianity. And taking a bible from his pocket, he excited the amazement of the house by reading with much gravity many passages from the sacred volume, containing exhortations to universal charity, meekness, and mutual forbearance. The earl of Peterborough, with uncommon boldness and happiness of expression, declared, that though he was for a parliamentary king, he was not for a parliamentary GOD or a parliamentary religion; and that if this bill were to pass, he should be ambitious of a seat in the conclave of cardinals, as more honorable than that which he occupied in the British house of peers. Dr. Kennet, bishop of Peterborough, protested, that he NEVER would be concerned in the execution of such a law—and he earnestly hoped that his brethren on the bench would not concur in the establishment of a PROTESTANT INQUISITION. The lords Cowper and Townshend also spoke with much ability against this infamous and execrable bill; by which a pretended regard for the honor of religion was, as usual, made a pretext for the gratification of the most malignant passions—a bill, which openly and impudently avowed and adopted the most profligate practices of the Romish church—and the principle of which, if once admitted, would lead to all the horrors of the rack, the stake, and the wheel *. It was

drid; and receiving, when in that city, a letter from his sovereign the king of England, commanding his return home, he is said to have thrown it scornfully out of the coach window. After running a rapid and astonishing career of profligacy and extravagance, he expired—" with not a friend to close his eyes," at a convent near Terragona in Spain, A. D. 1731, when he had not completed the thirty-second year of his age.

* It has been justly observed, that every man disclaims the character and appellation of a persecutor. GARDINER and BONNER doubtless professed

was on the other hand supported by the earl of Nottingham, the lords Bathurst and Trevor, the bishops of London, Winchester, Lichfield and Conventry, and various others. But on the division, the bill was rejected by a majority of sixty voices against thirty-one.

At this period died Pope Clement XI. who had sat in the papal chair above twenty years—a man respectable for

professed themselves animated, not by a spirit of persecution, but of *holy zeal* for the preservation of the Catholic faith in its genuine purity. And if the earl of NOTTINGHAM had been left to decide upon the fate of the learned professor his antagonist, he might very possibly have had the *moderation and candor* to say, in the words of the well-known epistle of king James I. to the states of Holland, in relation to the famous Vorstius, " that he would not presume positively to pronounce what resolutions it might be proper to take respecting him; but SURELY NEVER HERETIC BETTER DESERVED THE FLAMES." On account of his temporary junction with the Whigs during the administration of Oxford, the earl of Nottingham is satirized in various *jeux d' esprit* of Swift, under the appellation of DISMAL. A humorous parody of the celebrated speech of this nobleman, in opposition to the treaty of Utrecht, thus concludes:

" Since the Tories have thus disappointed my hopes,
And will neither regard my figures nor tropes,
I'll *speech* against peace while DISMAL's my name,
And be a true Whig, while I am—NOT-IN-GAME."

In the " Windsor prophecy" he is styled, in allusion to his name and original title, baron Finch of Daventry, " the tall black Daventry bird." And in the ballad on the surrender of Dunkirk he is again complimented:

" Sunderland's run out of his wits,
 And DISMAL double-dismal looks;
Wharton can only swear by fits,
 And strutting Hal is off the hooks.
Old Godolphin, full of spleen,
Made false moves and lost his queen."

for his talents, but haughty, inflexible, and zealously devoted to the interests of the house of Stuart. He was succeeded by Benedict XIII. of the house of Conti.

Although the pernicious tendency of the continental connections of England had been the constant theme of Mr. Walpole's eloquence while in opposition to the court, one of the first measures of his administration was to move for a subsidy to Sweden, with whom an alliance offensive and defensive had been just concluded—a British squadron being also at this very time cruising in the Baltic for the protection of that kingdom against the designs of Russia. So that, as lord Molesworth observed, "We were not only required to assist the Swedes with whom we had been so long at variance, but to purchase at an enormous price the permission to assist them. His lordship affirmed, that our engagements were inconsistent and contradictory—that our politics were not only variable, but incomprehensible to every man who, knowing merely the state of Great Britain, was unapprized of the several petty interests of the electorate, which were the secret springs of our transactions abroad—that we were in turn the allies and the dupes of all nations—that if such solicitude for the restoration of the conquests made by Russia upon Sweden were reasonable, it was incumbent upon Hanover to set the example, by the restoration of Bremen and Verden, and of Prussia our ally by that of Pomerania—that, whatever might be the connections or engagements of Hanover, Great Britain had neither any interest nor any right to intermeddle in the affairs of the empire, and that the friendship or enmity of the powers of the Baltic was of little importance to England, as we procured nothing from the kingdoms of the North which we could not with more advantage import from our own colonies in America, were proper encouragement

couragement held out to them. His lordship acknowledged that the diftreffed condition to which the Swedes were reduced would be really worthy of compaffion, could we forget that they had been the authors in a great meafure of their own misfortunes, by their tame fubmiffion to a defpotic tyrannical prince, who had facrificed their fubftance in purfuit of his rafh and unjuft defigns; and that any nation which followed their example deferved the fame fate.—His lordfhip touched on the affairs of the Duchy of Mecklenburg, which he infinuated to have been the fecret caufe of the rupture with the Czar; and entered into a detail of the treaties of Rofchild and Travendahl, in order to fhow how widely we had deviated from engagements of which we were ourfelves the guarantees. His lordfhip faid he would go as far as any man to maintain and fupport the honor and dignity of the crown of Great Britain, but he would never confent to fquander, in the mode now recommended, what yet remained of the wealth and refources of the nation." The vote of fupply at length paffed, not without much angry objection and difficulty. The terms of the treaty of peace with Spain alfo, when laid before parliament (October 1721), underwent very fevere cenfure. It was faid, that as the war was undertaken without provocation, fo the peace was concluded without advantage—that the Spanifh fleet had been attacked without any declaration of war, while amicable negotiations were carrying on at Madrid: and by an article of the treaty, we now fubmitted to the reproachful condition of reftoring the fhips fo captured, or of paying the full value of thofe previoufly difpofed of: that the trade with Spain, which conftituted one of the moft valuable branches of the Britifh commerce, had been interrupted and endangered, and the interefts of England wantonly and daringly facrificed to an obftinate predilection for

that

that Germanic fyftem of politics with which we had no national concern: that the navy debt was increafed to an immenfe amount, by keeping feamen in pay in order to maintain fleets in the Mediterranean and the Baltic, not for the fervice of Great Britain, but for the prefervation of the king's acquifitions in the empire. The court however, now ftrengthened by the recent coalition of the Whigs, fet all oppofition at defiance, and the new minifter foon proved himfelf fuperior to all his predeceffors in the art of adroit and dextrous parliamentary management.

In the courfe of this feffion a fingular petition was prefented to parliament from that refpectable clafs of citizens known by the appellation of Quakers. It is a wellknown tenet of this fect, diftinguifhed by its harmlefs peculiarities, that oaths even judicially adminiftered are in their own nature unlawful; and the legiflature had long fince wifely and indulgently paffed an act to render their folemn affirmation in all matters of civil concern, equivalent to an oath. The object of the prefent application was the omiffion of the words "in the prefence of Almighty God," in the legal form of that affirmation; it being juftly alleged, that while thofe words remained, the effence of an oath was preferved. But to the penalties of perjury, fhould this affirmation be in any inftance violated, they profeffed their willing and cheerful fubmiffion. The court, ever ready under this reign to extend and eftablifh the civil and religious privileges of the fubject, countenanced and fupported this application, and a bill for this purpofe paffed the houfe of commons without difficulty. But in its paffage through the houfe of lords, the fpirit of bigotry, now awakened from its tranfient flumber, difplayed itfelf in all its malignity. Dr. Atterbury bifhop of Rochefter obferved, that

that he knew not why such a distinguishing mark of indulgence should be allowed to a set of people who were hardly christians. And a petition was presented by the archbishop of York to the house, from the London clergy, "expressing a serious concern lest the minds of good men should be grieved and wounded, and the enemies of christianity triumph, when they should see such condescension made by a christian legislature to a set of men who renounce the divine institutions of christianity, particularly that by which the faithful are initiated into this religion, and denominated christians." This petition was rejected by the house, not without symptoms of disgust and contempt: and the bill finally passed, though accompanied with a protest signed by several lords eager to record their own disgrace and folly.

The first Septennial parliament of Great Britain was dissolved March 1722, and early in the ensuing month of October the king opened the new parliament with a speech from the throne, in which he expressed his concern in being obliged to inform them, that a dangerous conspiracy had been for some time past formed, and was still carrying on, against his person and government, in favor of the Pretender. His majesty declared that the discoveries made at home, the information obtained from his ministers abroad, and the intelligence received from the various powers in alliance with him in different parts of Europe, had afforded him ample and concurrent proofs of this wicked design. Some of the conspirators were already, he added, secured, and endeavors used for apprehending others—and he referred to the wisdom of parliament the measures necessary to be taken for the safety of the kingdom—expressing at the same time his firm belief that the hopes and expectations of their common enemies were very ill founded, in suppoſing that the diſcontents occaſioned by the loſſes and misfortunes of individuals, however induſtriouſly fomented, were turned into difaffection and a ſpirit of rebellion. "Had I, ſaid this monarch in very animated and dignified language, ſince my acceſſion to the throne ever attempted any innovation in our eſtabliſhed religion; had I in any one inſtance invaded the liberty or property of my ſubjects, I ſhould leſs wonder at any endeavor to alienate the affections of my people, and draw them into meaſures that can end in nothing but their own deſtruction. But to hope to perſuade a free people, in full enjoyment of all that is dear and valuable to them, to exchange freedom for ſlavery, the proteſtant religion for popery, and to ſacrifice at once the price of ſo much blood and treaſure as have been ſpent in defence of our preſent eſtabliſhment, ſeems an infatuation not to be accounted for.—Your own intereſt and welfare call upon you to defend yourſelves.—I rely upon the divine protection, the ſupport of my parliament, and the affections of my people, which I ſhall endeavor to preſerve by continuing to make the laws of the realm the rule and meaſure of all my actions." On the communication of this intelligence, a very great and general alarm was excited in the nation. A conſiderable augmentation of the forces was immediately voted; the habeas-corpus act was ſuſpended, contrary to all precedent, for no leſs than twelve months. On the requiſition of the king, a body of troops was held by the ſtates-general in readineſs to embark from Holland, and ſix regiments were likewiſe ordered from Ireland. And both houſes joined in expreſſing the ſtrongeſt deteſtation and abhorrence of this "traitorous and unnatural conſpiracy." Mr. Walpole affirmed to the houſe, that this wicked deſign was formed

ed about christmas last: that the conspirators had made
application to certain foreign potentates for troops; but
being disappointed in their expectation from abroad, they
had resolved desperately to go on, confiding in their
own strength, and fondly depending upon the general
discontent and confusion excited by the failure of the fatal South-Sea project: that the plan was to seize upon
the tower, the bank, and the exchequer, and to secure
by violence the persons of the king and the prince: that
government had received information of this plot ever
since May last: but two terms coming at that time together, it was thought advisable to postpone the apprehending of the conspirators till the long vacation, that
no advantage might be taken of the habeas-corpus act.
An exact account of this detestable conspiracy he assured
the house would in time be laid before them." But the
plot itself seems to have been discovered while yet in
embryo, and it is probable that no regular project of invasion or insurrection had been digested or matured; nor
have the circumstances explanatory either of its nature
or extent ever been clearly developed. Various persons,
however, of high distinction, amongst whom were the
duke of Norfolk and the lords Orrery, North, and
Grey, were apprehended on a very strong presumption
of their concurrence in this conspiracy. Pains and penalties were inflicted by act of parliament on several of
the conspirators. But one only suffered capital punishment—Christopher Layer, a barrister of the Temple,
convicted of high treason in enlisting men for the Pretender. He was repeatedly reprieved, and much endeavor was used to procure from him a full confession; but
he persisted in a resolute refusal. Beyond comparison,
however, the trial which attracted most of the public attention was that of the celebrated Atterbury bishop of
Rochester,

Rochester, who was found to be a party in this conspiracy, or at least confidentially privy to it: and he was, by a bill which passed both houses by great majorities, deprived of his episcopal dignity, and sentenced to perpetual banishment. Mr. Yonge, the mover of the bill, declared this prelate to be a disgrace and dishonor to a church conspicuous for loyalty; that his holy function and elevated station, with the solemn oaths he had taken, were the most unpardonable aggravations of his crime; and he concluded with applying to him the denunciation authorized by warrant of holy writ—" Let his habitation be desolate, and let no man dwell therein, and his bishopric let another take." The declaration of the Pretender, framed for the occasion, and dated from Lucca, was by both houses voted to be a false, insolent, and traitorous libel, and ordered to be burnt at the Royal Exchange. In this declaration the Pretender, with singular modesty and all the appearance of gravity, proposed, that if king George would relinquish to him the throne of Great Britain, he would in return consent to his retaining the title of king in his native dominions, and would invite all other states to confirm it: and he likewise most graciously engaged to leave to king George his succession to the British dominions secure, whenever, in due course, his natural right should take place. An address was presented to the throne by the two houses, expressing their " astonishment at the extravagant presumption of this declaration, and repeating their assurances to support his majesty against the impotent efforts of an attainted fugitive, bred up in the maxims of tyranny and superstition." The proofs in support of the charge against the bishop of Rochester being somewhat deficient in legal precision, though sufficiently clear to induce an intire conviction of his guilt, much clamor

was

was excited by the bill of banishment passed by the commons against him; though, had not a spirit of lenity pervaded the proceedings of government on this occasion, he would scarcely have escaped a bill of attainder. When it came under the discussion of the lords, the duke of Wharton, in a speech of uncommon ability, exposed what he styled the weakness, insufficiency, and contradiction of the evidence against the bishop; and added, that such proceedings, like the stone of Sisyphus, frequently rolled back on those who were the chief promoters of them. Lord Cowper, now in opposition to the court, enlarged much on the danger and injustice of swerving from the fixed rules of evidence. He affirmed, "that the penalties inflicted by this bill were either much greater or much less than the bishop deserved; that whatever might be the nature or extent of the accusation, the law of the land and the established forms of judicial procedure ought to be strictly adhered to, not only in the courts below, but in the high court of parliament itself; that every Englishman had a right to a trial by law; that this was in a more especial manner the privilege of a peer of the realm. And the political necessity which was alleged in vindication of this measure he did not believe to exist; the government was sufficiently secured by the powers vested in the crown in consequence of the suspension of the habeas-corpus act, and the additional troops raised for its defence." And lord Bathurst, in the course of an eloquent speech on the same side, turning to the bench of bishops, sarcastically remarked, " that he could not account for the inveterate hatred and malice which some persons bore the learned and ingenious bishop of Rochester, unless they were intoxicated with the infatuation of certain tribes of savage Indians, who believed they inherited not only the spoils but even the abilities of any great enemy whom they killed

killed in battle." Notwithstanding the reasonings of lord Cowper, it seems erroneous and unsafe to deny the general position, that deviations from the established forms of judicial procedure in extraordinary cases are justifiable, and even necessary, where the public safety is concerned—provided that the executive justice of the state depart not from that *substantial justice* which is founded in the nature of things. So entirely opposite were now the politics of France from those which had prevailed in the late reign, that upon this occasion the Regent offered twenty battalions of veteran troops to the king of Great Britain, in order to defend his person and government against the attempts of that family which Louis XIV. had employed the whole force of his kingdom to protect and restore—but this offer it was judged prudent to decline.

That the vengeful and merciless spirit by which the Whigs had been actuated when first restored to power, was now, notwithstanding the pretended rigor of the late proceedings, most sensibly abated, the reversal at this period of the act of attainder passed against lord Bolingbroke is a decisive proof. The bishop of Rochester, on his arrival at Calais, hearing that lord Bolingbroke was waiting there for a passage, exclaimed, with an emotion from which much was inferred, " Then we are exchanged." This nobleman, however, though restored to his honors and paternal estate, was still excluded from a seat in the house of peers, through the inflexible opposition of the minister, who clearly discerned and dreaded the consequences which might eventually result from the irresistible force of his eloquence and talents, when exerted in that grand field of action. Fired with ambition to resume his former station in public life, and a philosopher only through necessity, he cherished a fixed and mortal

resentment

resentment against Sir Robert Walpole; and regardless of his recent obligations, in a short time joined with eagerness that opposition to his administration, so celebrated for the ability of its members, and which began now to assume a regular and systematic form. The chagrin of lord Bolingbroke was undoubtedly enhanced by seeing his former coadjutors in office, lord Oxford and lord Harcourt, in full possession of those high privileges which he vainly and incessantly pined to regain. The latter of these noblemen was even received into an high degree of favor at court; which, it is said, occasioning some severe reflections from the passionate lips of Atterbury, lord Harcourt was provoked to retaliate, by declaring that on the quee's death the bishop came to him and lord Bolingbroke, and said, nothing remained but immediately to proclaim king JAMES—offering, if they would give him a guard, to put on his lawn sleeves, and head the profession *.

Early

* This celebrated prelate, his learned friend Dr Smalridge, on presenting him, A. D. 1710, to the upper house of convocation, as the prolocutor, most elegantly styles, "Vir in nullo literarum genere hospes, in plerisque artibus et studiis diu et feliciter exercitatus—in maxime perfectis literarum disciplinis perfectissimus." His eloquence and learning, none, indeed, have presumed to dispute; and his public character has all that dignity which arises from firmness and consistency. Of the violence and virulence of his temper he gave early proofs in his reply to the famous treatise of Dr. WAKE, " On the authority of christian princes, and the rights, powers, and privileges of convocations:" " Were (says he) all that Dr. Wake affirms strictly true and justifiable; yet whether laboring the point so heartily as he does, and shewing himself to be so willing to prove the church to have no rights and privileges, be a very decent part in a clergyman, I leave his friends to consider. But when all a man advances is not only ill designed, but ill-founded, and his principles are as false as they are scandalous, there are no names and censures too bad to be bestowed on such writers and their writings." One cannot sufficiently admire the effrontery of the insinuation, that whether the AUTHORITY claimed by the church be well or ill-founded,

Early in the present session, a bill which occupied much of the attention of parliament, and was kept long depending in the house, was introduced and supported by the minister, for levying the sum of one hundred thousand pounds on the estates of all Roman Catholics, upon pretext of "the constant endeavors of the Papists to subvert the present happy establishment; though he professed that he would not take upon him to charge any particular person among

ed, it is at all events incumbent on the clergy, *as such*, to defend and support it. For this performance an honorary degree was conferred upon Atterbury by the university of Oxford. But in animadverting upon it, bishop Burnet happily remarks, "that the applause with which it was received, when the temper and spirit with which it is written are considered, forms a much stronger argument against the expediency of a convocation, than any he brings or can bring in favor of it." And Dr. Wake himself declared, "that such a spirit of wrath and uncharitableness pervaded the whole book, as he had hardly ever met with before; though, to do no injustice to his adversary, he admits that Dr. Atterbury has done all that a man of parts and zeal could do, to defend the cause he had espoused. One thing only was wanting: He had not TRUTH on his side—his work is a MERE ROMANCE." In 1703, when the principles of Whiggism began to predominate, Hooper, Dean of Canterbury, a man distinguished by the steadiness of his attachment to them, was, by an unexpected and unsolicited nomination, raised to the bishopric of St. Asaph, "with a view (as Dr. Atterbury tells his friend Trelawney bishop of Exeter), as he supposes, to take the lead in the administration of ecclesiastical affairs; in which case, says he, I am sure to be oppressed and kept under, as much as if archbishop Tillotson were alive and at the helm—a very ill return for making that *scuffle* which set him at the head of the lower clergy." But surely this was a ground of obligation, on which few persons would have thought of founding a claim of gratitude. In June 1713, the Tories being now triumphant, Dr. Atterbury was advanced to the bishopric of Rochester. His sanguine hopes of attaining to the primacy were however quickly blasted, by the death of the queen; and at the accession of King George I. he engaged, with all the fervor of party rage and disappointed ambition, in the most violent measures of the opposition; and was at length instigated by passion and revenge, to embark in a wild and ill-conducted conspiracy, which terminated in his ruin. He died at Paris, Feb. 1732.

among them, with being concerned in the prefent *horrid confpiracy*. But it was well known, that many of them had been engaged in the *late* rebellion; and the prefent plot, he averred, was contrived at Rome, and the Englifh Catholics were not only well-wifhers to it, but had contributed large fums to carry it on. And he thought it highly reafonable, that the fomenters of the public difturbances fhould themfelves bear the chief fhare of the burdens, which muft be neceffarily incurred for their fuppreffion." This propofition was hearkened to with extreme difapprobation, and incurred heavy cenfure, not only from the partifans of the Tory and Jacobite factions, but from many of the moft enlightened and intelligent members of the houfe. And it was fo ably combated by Mr. Lutwyche in particular, in a fpeech delivered on the motion of commitment, as to merit a diftinct and moft honorable tranfmiffion for the inftruction of fucceeding times.

" The gentlemen (faid this excellent citizen and fenator) who have fpoken in favor of this bill, have urged the invariable and inveterate enmity of the Catholics againft the prefent eftablifhment; and have afferted, that if they did not fhew themfelves openly againft the government in the late confpiracy, it proceeded from motives of prudence, and not for want of zeal in the Pretender's caufe. A general charge of this kind may, indeed, form a fufficient ground for *a preamble* to a bill of this nature; but the enacting part ought to be fupported by fpecific facts, clearly and plainly proved; otherwife we may involve the innocent in a punifhment due only to the guilty. Becaufe *fome* of the Roman Catholics are *fufpected* to have been concerned in this confpiracy, fhall the whole body be not only charged with the guilt, but actually fuffer the penalty? The law fuppofes every man to be accountable for his own actions, and doth not require

quire what is in no man's power to perform—that he
should be answerable for the conduct of another. As
to the disaffection of the Catholics in the present instance, I appeal to the house whether any mention is
made in the report, of any Roman Catholic of eminence,
except a noble duke, to whom a letter is supposed to
have been written, implying his knowledge and approbation of the conspiracy. How unjust then, upon so
slender a suspicion, to inflict the severities enacted by this
law, upon numerous innocent families who harbor no
dangerous designs, and wish for no political revolution!
If you abandon the ground of disaffection, and make
their religion, supposed so inimical to that established in
this country, the pretext for this measure; it is a species
of persecution odious in itself, incompatible with the honor of the legislature, and destructive of the freedom
and happiness of the subject. Let it not be said, that
his majesty's mild and gracious reign has been blemished
by an act so rigorous, of which the evident tendency is
to confirm the obstinate in their errors, and alienate the
affections of the well-disposed. There has been, indeed,
a political reason assigned for this measure, deduced from
its expediency; and it is said to be indeed to deter the
Jacobites abroad from rash enterprises, by making their
friends here pay the expence which the nation finds necessary for its security. As this is a reason founded on
mere speculation, I will venture to oppose one conjecture to another. And it is my opinion, that as the claims
of the Pretender are in themselves unfounded and unjust, his only hope of success can be derived from the
discontents of the people; the more ground, therefore,
there is for complaint, the better prospect he has of success, and the wider scope will be afforded to the Jacobites, to aggravate the errors and faults of the government.

ment. If the peaceable and quiet behavior of the Catholics does not entitle them to the protection of the law—if the principle on which this bill is founded be in future adopted as just and equitable—if the most dutiful and unreserved submission cannot exempt them from criminal imputations, and even from the penalties of open sedition and rebellion, will they not embrace any opportunity to free themselves from this intolerable tyranny, thinking that under no form of government they can receive worse treatment? It is alleged that, for many years past, the legal impositions have not been levied from the Catholics; and that a much larger sum than the present is actually due from them, if the forfeitures were rigorously exacted. The fact I will not dispute; but the question to be resolved is—Why do you now change your lenity into cruelty? The executive government, it is evident, conceived the terrors of the penal code to be intended for security, not revenge. And in consequence of the peaceable demeanor of the catholics, these acts were virtually suspended. If these statutes were, therefore, justly and wisely dispensed with before, why are they to be put in execution now? At the æra of the revolution, the Roman catholics were far more numerous and powerful than at present. It was well known that they held correspondence, and were deeply engaged in the interests of King James, who was openly supported by France. At that period, the competition for the crown was indeed of a serious nature, and greatly different from that originating from the wild and extravagant pretensions of a forlorn fugitive, expelled from all the courts of Europe, and obliged to seek for shelter and sanctuary at Rome. But king WILLIAM, though warned of the dangers of his situation, fully apprised of the severity of the laws enacted against the Papists, and repeatedly urged to carry them into strict execution,

ecution, resolutely and constantly refused compliance. That great monarch knew that no free state could long subsist in a departure from the rules of equal and impartial justice. It has been said, that the liberties of England can never be in danger, but from the Roman Catholics: the truth is, that the chief danger arises from the divisions and animosities subsisting between the various denominations of protestants in this country—animosities arising from an erroneous and contracted policy, and perpetuated by artful and ambitious leaders for their own purposes, by exciting unnecessary fears and groundless jealousies. I know, said this enlightened senator, no better rule of government, than to punish the guilty, and protect the innocent—but precipitately to treat as criminal a body of men, because you suspect them to be guilty, when farther inquiry and better information may prove them to be innocent, is no very satisfactory mode of displaying the impartiality of your proceedings. Considering the great vigilance of the ministry, and their diligence in unravelling the most subtle contrivances of the conspirators, I think it very unlikely that any considerable foreign remittances made by the Roman Catholics should have escaped their notice. To single out one set of men, therefore, and upon a mere supposition to inflict penalties upon them, which the clearest proof of guilt only could warrant, is an act impossible to reconcile to that justice and equity which ought invariably to guide and direct the proceedings of this assembly."

This iniquitous bill, which was, in its progress through the house, extended to all nonjurors, notwithstanding these irrefragable reasonings, finally passed by a majority of 217 against 168 voices, and received the royal assent; on which occasion a speech was made by Sir Spencer Compton,

Compton, the speaker, shewing, or at least endeavoring to shew, the policy and necessity of this measure, from the countenance and support given by the papists and nonjurors to the "late horrid and execrable conspiracy." As no oppression, however, of a similar nature was afterwards attempted, there is reason to believe that the generous efforts now made in the cause of justice and humanity were not wholly lost. And if the magnitude of the subject may be deemed not such as to require so particular a detail, it ought to be remarked, that the arguments of Mr. Lutwyche are not of a temporary or local kind, but comprise truths of universal and perpetual importance and obligation.

On the 27th of May 1723, an end was put to this long and interesting session by a speech from the throne; in which his majesty expressed in warm terms "his satisfaction at the proceedings of the parliament, and in particular at those exertions of legislative authority which were necessary in this crisis of danger, for the punishment of offenders, whose guilt there was no room to doubt, but whose wicked arts and practices had been brought to such perfection, that they confidently carried on their traitorous projects in defiance of the law, from an assurance of being able to elude it. Some EXTRAORDINARY AFFAIRS, his majesty added, calling him abroad this summer, he doubted not but that the wisdom and vigilance of his good subjects would prevent their common enemies from taking advantage of his absence; and that they will at length cease to flatter themselves with the vain imagination of being able to subvert our religion and present establishment."

About this period, Philip V. king of Spain, yielding himself up without reserve to vain and superstitious fervors of devotion, retired to the monastery of St. Ildefonso; whence he made a solemn renunciation of the

crowns

crowns of Castile and Arragon, in favor of his eldest son, Don Louis, Prince of Asturias—" committing him and his people to the powerful protection of the HOLY VIRGIN," under whose auspices the young prince ventured to assume the reins of government, without the usual formality of assembling the Cortez. But, dying soon after his elevation to the throne, the abdicated monarch was reluctantly prevailed upon again to encounter the cares and burdens of royalty. Devoting himself, nevertheless, entirely to monkish exercises of religion, the task of government devolved upon the queen; whose influence in the Spanish counsels had been for some time past, very conspicuous.

The public tranquillity being now perfectly restored, the king put in execution his resolution to revisit his dominions on the continent, where new and unexpected political connections and combinations were taking place, by no means favorable to the views and wishes of his Britannic Majesty. The enmity between Russia and Sweden had at length terminated by a treaty concluded at Nystad, A. D. 1721; conformably to which, the fertile and extensive provinces of Livonia, Ingria, Esthonia, and Carelia, were confirmed to Russia, and the barren deserts of Finland, only, restored to Sweden. This peace was quickly matured into an union of counsels and designs, which gave extreme umbrage and uneasiness to the king of England; who, having ground to believe the immediate object of this coalition to be the restoration of the duchy of Slefwic to the duke of Holstein, trembled for the safety of his favorite and contiguous acquisitions of Bremen and Verden—the security of all these possessions resting only on the tottering basis of the mutual guarantee of Denmark and Hanover. After a short interval of anxious suspense, it was ascertained that the treaty

of

of Stockholm, signed February 1724, contained in it a
secret article, by which the high contracting parties obliged themselves " in the most effectual manner to use
their *good offices* for the restoring the duke of Holstein—
who was nearly related to both—to the Duchy of Sleswic; and if these proved ineffectual, *other methods should
be thought of*. In particular, application should be made
to the powers who stood engaged with them to guarantee the said Duchy to the said duke, of whom England
by the treaty of Travendahl was one—leaving it more
immediately to his IMPERIAL MAJESTY, to concert such
measures as might with the greatest security for ever cut
off this source of such *infinite troubles* to the north." A
visible coldness had for some time subsisted between the
king of England and the emperor, who in every instance opposed, as far as he could venture to oppose, the
aspiring views of the house of Lunenburg; and who
persisted in his refusal to grant the investiture of the
Duchies of Bremen and Verden, but upon terms with
which the king of England persisted in his refusal to
comply—the emperor requiring, as it is said, on his part,
" a refreshing fee" to an enormous amount; and his
Britannic majesty being anxiously desirous, in contrariety to the positive constitutions of the empire, and the
peremptory declarations of the emperor, to include the
imperial city of Bremen in the new investiture. Unfortunately also, an imperial East-India company had been
recently established at Ostend, which was viewed, both
by England and Holland, with the malignant eyes of
commercial jealousy. A vote, and, in the sequel, an
act, passed in the British parliament, declaring it to be
an high crime and misdemeanor for any subject of Great
Britain in any manner to engage in or countenance this
undertaking; and repeated remonstrances, much more
urgent

urgent than reasonable, were made by the English ministry, to induce the emperor to abandon this enterprise.

During this state of things in Europe died Philip duke of Orleans, regent of France, the firm and faithful ally of the king of England*. This prince was possessed of shining talents, which were nevertheless greatly clouded and obscured by an extravagant propensity to pleasure, which he indulged without reserve or decorum. From the love of fame incident to an elevated mind, he was anxious that his conduct should appear in a favorable light to posterity, and had formed a serious resolution of convoking the estates-general of the kingdom, for the purpose of effecting a grand reformation in the state, from which he was with difficulty diverted by his confidential minister and favorite the cardinal Dubois †. The Regent frequently expressed his indignation at the wretched state of political degradation to which France was reduced; declaring that, had he been born a commoner, he would have defended the cause of liberty against the oppression of the government. But his voluptuous life and the profligacy of his morals were totally incompatible with the predominance of public virtue or public spirit in his counsels. Under the administration of the duke of Bourbon, his successor, the same good understanding seemed to subsist between the crowns of Great Britain and France; and both courts viewed with

---

* December 2, 1722.

† On this man, the abandoned high-priest and companion of the nocturnal orgies of the Regent, the following epitaph was written:

> Rome rougit d'avoir rougi
> Le maquereau qui git ici.

with equal aftonifhment and apprehenfion the fudden termination of the long and deeply-rooted animofity of the emperor and the king of Spain by a treaty concluded at Vienna, April 1725; in conformity to which, Spain became guarantee of the Auftrian fucceſſion, according to the PRAGMATIC SANCTION *. Such was the appellation given to the imperial edict, confirmed and ratified by the diet of the empire, by which the vaft dominions of that houfe were declared to be a perpetual and indivifible feoffment limited to the heirs-general of the prefent emperor. And the emperor, on his part, granted the inveftiture of the Duchies of Tufcany, Parma, and Placentia, to the eldeft fon of Philip V. by his prefent queen, in default of heirs in the actual poſſeſſors. High offence had been recently given by the court of Verfailles to the court of Madrid, by the difmiffal of the young Infanta of Spain, affianced to the king of France, but to whom that monarch had conceived a diflike approaching to averfion. The Spaniſh court not only in the firft emotions of its anger fent back to France mademoifelle de Beaujolois, daughter of the late Regent, and betrothed to Don Carlos, fecond fon of his Catholic majefty; but offered, in its eager folicitude of revenge, to adjuft all exifting differences with the emperor, under the fole mediation of Great Britain. But at this propofition, fo flattering and advantageous in various refpects, the king of England was compelled to hefitate; knowing that this mediation could not be accepted without exciting the extreme umbrage and jealoufy of France; and the treaty was fuddenly and unexpectedly

---

* The term " pragmatic," univerfally applied to this famous edict, is ufed in a fenfe fo uncommon, that it may be pardonable, *en paſſant*, to remark its derivation from the Greek πραγματικος, carrying with it the complex meaning of a public and weighty fanction.

expectedly signed without the intervention of any other power. To this treaty the court of Petersburg, after an interval of deliberation and delay, acceded: and military preparations were made by all these courts, which were supposed to indicate farther designs than it was yet thought proper to avow.

To counterbalance the weight of this confederacy, a similar treaty of alliance was signed at Hanover, Sept. 1725, between England, France, Denmark, and Prussia; to which Holland and Sweden afterwards acceded. When this treaty was communicated to the English parliament, which met January 1726, after two succeflive quiet and tranquil sessions demanding no distinct historic notice, it was strongly urged, " that the British nation would be eventually engaged by it in a war for the defence of the king's German dominions, contrary to an express provision made in the act of settlement, which, as the basis the present family rested their title to the crown upon, ought to be held sacred and inviolable. And the whole scope and tenor of it was said to be diametrically opposite to the uniform policy of Great Britain for a long succession of years. For by this treaty we had abandoned an alliance upon which the balance of power in Europe, and the preservation of its liberties, were generally and justly believed to depend; and with unexampled eagerness and assiduity of folly had solicited the friendship of a nation, whose views and interests stood in direct opposition no less to those of England than of the house of Austria." Mr. Horace Walpole, brother to the minister, and much employed, and confided in, by him in all foreign transactions, and who had been the chief negotiator of this treaty, undertook to obviate all objections to it in a studied and elaborate harangue, in which he explained to the house at great length the

different situations and interests of the principal states of Europe, from the peace of Utrecht to the present time. This minister assured the house, "that the constant care and endeavor of his majesty, since his happy accession to the throne, had been to secure the tranquillity of Christendom, to promote the honor and interest of his kingdoms, and settle the balance of power in Europe on a solid foundation. With these great and laudable views, he said, his majesty had assumed the character both of mediator and guarantee of the Barrier treaty concluded in 1715, and of the convention by which it was subsequently confirmed between the emperor and the states. Actuated by the same motives, he had in 1716 signed a defensive alliance with the emperor, and in 1717 another with the most christian king and the states-general. In order to fortify these treaties, and more effectually to secure the repose of Europe, the king had in 1718 made a convention with his most christian majesty, for proposing ultimate conditions of peace between the emperor and Spain; and also between his imperial majesty and the then king of Sicily. That this treaty was followed, after a very short interval, by a treaty of alliance between the emperor, the king of Great Britain, his most christian majesty, and the republic of Holland; whence this treaty derived its popular appellation of the quadruple alliance. That within a few months the king of Sicily was admitted as a party to this treaty; and at length the king of Spain himself was compelled to accede to the terms of it, which was chiefly owing to the generous assistance his Britannic majesty gave to the emperor in the Mediterranean; that the remaining points in dispute between their imperial and Catholic majesties were referred to the decision of a congress opened at Cambray. After an unsuccessful negotiation of three years the congress was suddenly dissolved,

ed, upon advice that the emperor and king of Spain had adjusted their differences, by a separate treaty concluded at Vienna That this unexpected event had occasioned no little surmise and alarm; and had raised jealousies which a more perfect knowledge of this transaction had fully justified. That this treaty of peace was followed by a treaty of commerce, the principal object of which was the establishment of an India company at Ostend, in violation of our rights, and to the ruin of our trade. That the remonstrances made by his majesty's ministers at the courts of Vienna and Madrid had been received by the ministers of his catholic majesty with coldness, and by those of his imperial majesty with the utmost haughtiness; insomuch that they scrupled not to insinuate that if his Britannic majesty persisted in adopting resolutions hostile to the treaty of Vienna, his imperial majesty would think himself disengaged from the guarantee of the protestant succession to the crown of Great Britain. And they had even gone so far as to affirm, that such measures might be attended with disagreeable consequences in relation to his majesty's dominions in Germany. Such however was the firmness of his majesty, that no impression could be made on him by these menaces; nor was he by any suggestions to be deterred from concerting with other powers the means of counteracting the ambitious views of this formidable alliance. And this was the more necessary, because there were just grounds to believe that this extraordinary and unexpected reconciliation was owing to the fixed and favorite purpose of the house of Austria, of rendering the imperial dignity hereditary in their family. In order to that, it might be *supposed* that the treaty of Vienna was to be cemented by a marriage between the Emperor's eldest daughter and the infant Don Carlos.— Who did not foresee the fatal consequences of this conjunction?

junction? The issue of such a marriage might in time inherit, not only the imperial crown, and the vast hereditary dominions of the Austrian family, but the entire monarchy of Spain with its appendages, which would entirely overthrow the balance of power, and render the liberties of Europe wholly precarious. If this was not within the contemplation of these two monarchs, how would any one undertake to account for the extensive privileges bestowed by the king of Spain, in contravention of the most solemn treaties with Great Britain, upon the emperor's subjects in the Netherlands; or for the emperor's so far forgetting his obligations to England and Holland, as to persist in supporting the Ostend company, established with no other view than to distress the maritime powers? or for his engaging to assist the king of Spain in the recovery of Minorca and Gibraltar? In order to put a timely stop to the progress of such alarming and dangerous designs, his majesty had, *in his great wisdom*, entered into a defensive alliance with his most christian majesty and the king of Prussia, to which several other powers, and particularly the states-general, were invited to accede: that the grand design of this alliance was to maintain the tranquillity of Christendom and the balance of power, and the respective rights and immunities of all nations, particularly those relating to commerce: and that his majesty, ever attentive to the support and protection of the protestant interest, had engaged, by a separate article of this treaty, the most christian king and the king of Prussia, who together with his majesty were guarantees of the treaty of Oliva, concluded between the crowns of Poland and Sweden, A. D. 1660, to interpose in behalf of our distressed protestant brethren in Poland; and to cause reparation to be made for what may have been done at Thorne, contrary to the stipulations of that treaty. And he concluded with passing

passing very lavish encomiums on the wisdom, vigilance, steadiness, and resolution of his majesty, in the conduct of all these weighty and important affairs."

The house, no doubt completely enlightened and convinced by the perspicuity of this statement and the force of these reasonings, and admiring the beautiful harmony with which these complicated, multifarious, and seemingly dissonant treaties, alliances, and conventions, concurred in promoting the interest of Great Britain, with a single eye to which they were so demonstrably concluded, voted by a prodigious majority, *viz.* 285 against 107, an address to the king, declaratory of the highest approbation of the treaty of Hanover; and expressive of the unfeigned gratitude of the house, for the measures so wisely concerted by his majesty for obviating and disappointing the dangerous views of the emperor and the king of Spain; and reprobating the treaty of commerce concluded between those powers, as "calculated for the entire destruction of the British trade; and assuring his majesty, that, in vindication of the honor of the British crown, the house will effectually stand by and support his majesty against all insults and attacks that any power, in resentment of the measures so wisely taken, shall make upon any of his majesty's territories, though not belonging to the crown of Great Britain." This unexpected revolution in the general politics of Europe was chiefly effected through the instrumentality of the famous M. de Ripperda, a native of Holland; who, from the condition of a private gentleman, was advanced, after the fall of Alberoni, to the rank of a Grandee of Spain, and succeeded to the post of prime minister. He was inspired by a kindred genius, and prosecuted the same projects of aggrandisement by different means. Finding the power of England the grand and perpetual obstacle to the accomplishment

complishment of his designs, he frequently indulged himself in very indiscreet and passionate expressions of resentment, and openly affirmed that the interests of Europe required the restoration of the house of Stuart. After the conclusion of the treaty of Hanover, he haughtily exclaimed, "Well, well, we shall teach these petty gentlemen (meaning the electors of Hanover and Brandenburg) to make treaties!" And he was frequently accustomed to say, that cardinal Alberoni made a false step, in sending that fleet to Sicily, which he ought to have sent to England. In a memorial addressed by colonel Stanhope *, the British minister at Madrid, to the Spanish secretary of state, the marquis de la Paz, at a subsequent period, heavy complaints are made of the insolent discourses of the Duc de Ripperda during his embassy at Vienna: "There can be no stronger proof (said the English minister) of their Catholic majesties' approbation of M. de Ripperda's behavior, than the great honors to which they promoted him, and the entire trust they conferred upon him, at his return to Madrid. And as what he had given out at Vienna, relative to Gibraltar, was verified by the peremptory demand of that fortress; so from that time measures were taken, to make good what he had likewise said there, that the king should be driven out of his dominions, and the Pretender placed upon the throne of Great Britain. It is freely left to the judgment of every impartial person, that he who declared there was a secret offensive alliance, was actually prime minister to his Catholic majesty, who honored him with his entire confidence— that it was he who had himself made the treaties of Vienna—that he never denied making such declaration, when

---

* Afterwards created earl of Harrington; and who, on his return from this embassy, succeeded lord Townshend in the post of secretary of state.

when it was publicly talked of; and that he was never disowned in it by the king his master, who continued him a long time after in his service; nor was it alleged as one of the causes of his disgrace." The Spanish minister, in reply, declares, " that the king of Spain does not consider himself as responsible for the vain and idle discourses of the Duc de Ripperda, whose extravagancies had at length induced his Catholic majesty not only to divest him of his offices, but to secure the person of a minister as culpable as dangerous. But he acknowledged, that the Duc de Ripperda was justified in declaring, that the good correspondence and friendship of England and Spain depended on the speedy restitution of Gibraltar, agreeably to the positive engagements of the king of England." This extraordinary man, after his disgrace, escaped from the tower of Segovia, where he was closely confined, and sought for refuge in England, where he resided three years in great pomp and splendor. But not finding his wild schemes and projects of revenge likely to be adopted by the British court, he took a sudden resolution to offer his services to Muley Abdalla, emperor of Morocco, by whom they were received with eagerness; and embracing the Mahommedan faith, he was created a Bassa and prime minister and Vizier of the empire. After experiencing divers vicissitudes of fortune he expired at Tetuan, October 1737, professing himself a true and sincere penitent; and being received as such into the bosom of the holy Catholic church, in the communion of which he was originally educated; though early in life he had abjured the errors of Popery, and embraced the protestant faith, which he afterwards renounced on entering into the service of Spain: on receiving absolution from a Monk of Mequinez, he became, although previously agonized with remorse, calm and

and ferene, and at laft died with cheerfulnefs and hope. —Such is the fafcination of the Roman Catholic religion. The political connection between Ruffia and Sweden, fo recently formed, was already much weakened by the unexpected death of the Czar, Peter the Great, January 1725; and the harmony between England and Sweden was, in confequence of that event, after an interval of intrigue and negotiation, completely reftored. This monarch muft be regarded as the moft extraordinary phænomenon of the age in which he lived. Previous to his acceffion to the throne of his anceftors, Ruffia was fcarcely known as an European power, except by her occafional wars with Poland, and by the commercial intercourfe which fhe maintained with England, through the medium of the remote port of Archangel, fituated at the extremity of the Frozen Ocean. PETER, who, by a rare conjunction of qualities, joined a moft daring and ardent fpirit of enterprife to a clear and folid judgment, early entertained the vaft defign of civilizing his immenfe dominions—burning with ambition to occupy a confpicuous and leading ftation amongft the powers of Europe. With what fuccefs he profecuted and accomplifhed this grand project, it is foreign to the purpofe of the prefent hiftory to relate. After furmounting, by the inceffant labor of thirty years, difficulties infuperable to any other man, he lived to fee himfelf in poffeffion of all which had engaged his wifhes and his hopes—applauded as a hero, venerated as a legiflator. By his conquefts he had fubjected various rich and populous provinces to his dominion, and in the midft of them he had built a magnificent city bearing the name of its founder, and which will atteft to future and fucceffive ages the grandeur and fublimity of his genius. He introduced difcipline into his armies; he created a powerful navy; and

and in the room of Afiatic ignorance, prejudice, and barbarifm, he fubftituted the arts, the learning, the cuftoms and manners of Europe. His fyftem of improvement and aggrandifement has been eagerly and invariably purfued by his fucceffors in the empire, and with a degree of fuccefs which may reafonably excite univerfal jealoufy and apprehenfion: for to the rapid and unexampled increafe of the power of Ruffia no other European ftate bears a juft or relative proportion. The king of England, alarmed at the great naval equipments of the emprefs Catherine, upon whom the imperial crown of the late Czar her hufband had by his will devolved, profeffed, with great oftentation of generofity, to feel an extreme apprehenfion left Sweden fhould be eventually endangered by them. And though Sweden, clearly perceiving that Slefwic was the real object of his folicitude, openly declared herfelf in perfect amity with Ruffia; a ftrong fquadron under Sir Charles Wager failed, by order of the king of England, to the Baltic, early in the year 1725, with exprefs directions not to fuffer the Ruffian fleets to leave their ports, till the emprefs had obviated all ground of fufpicion by an explicit declaration of her pacific intentions. The emprefs, though highly offended at this imperious requifition, protefted, "that nothing was farther from her thoughts, than any defign to difturb the peace of the North—expreffing at the fame time her aftonifhment, that fhe had not received his majefty's letter until his fleet was at anchor before Revel; a procedure totally inconfiftent with the amity fo long maintained between her kingdoms and the crown of Great Britain." That Ruffia, at leaft after the death of the Czar, was willing and defirous to maintain amity with Great Britain, and even with Hanover, as connected with Britain, appears from the

tenor

tenor of the negotiations carried on in the summer of 1725; when the Czarina declared her readiness to concede in all other points, provided Slefwic were restored to the duke of Holstein, or an equivalent found for it. To this idea of an equivalent the king of England professed not to object; but after much laborious discussion of this knotty point, no equivalent could be devised; though, had not Hanover been at this period the darling care of England, Bremen and Verden would probably have been deemed a very fit and commodious one. Notwithstanding the declaration of the empress, Sir Charles Wager, who had been joined at Copenhagen by a Danish squadron, continued in his station till the season was too far advanced to admit of any farther naval operations. Thus provoked, the Czarina acceded in form to the treaty of Vienna (August 1726). And the government of Sweden, perceiving Russia unable to cope with the naval power of England, and feeling sensibly the operative influence of the *golden showers* which now diffused themselves in rich profusion over that barren land, acceded, March 1727, to the treaty of Hanover*. Two other powerful squadrons were also at this period

---

* In consequence of the unlimited votes of credit passed by the commons in 1726 and 1727, it appears that the sum of 435,000l. was expended during those two years in *secret services*, necessary, to adopt the language of parliament, " to fulfil and perfect his majesty's engagements for securing the peace of Europe." In the month of June 1726, when the British fleet was actually in the Baltic, Mr. Poyntz, ambassador at the court of Stockholm, presented a MEMORIAL to that court, declaring, " That his Britannic majesty, always attentive to preserve the peace of the North, had no sooner concluded the treaty of Hanover but he had communicated it to Sweden, and desired its accession thereto—that it was with great concern he saw this negotiation lengthened out to above six months, and that in the mean time Sweden had entered

period fitted out at an immense expence, though, as far as appears, without any determinate object; and indicating only the jealous fears and restless surmises of the king of England. One of these, under the command Sir John Jennings, with a body of land-forces on board, cruized for a considerable time off the coasts of Spain, to the great consternation of the inhabitants, but attempted no act of hostility. Another fleet under rear-admiral Hosier sailed for the West-Indies, with orders to block up the galleons in the Spanish harbors; or to capture them, in case they should presume to venture out. But his instructions authorizing no farther or more direct act of hostility, and the Spaniards having reconveyed, on the first intelligence of this armament, their treasures from Porto Bello to Panama, this gallant officer was compelled to remain inactive in his station till the greater part of his men, and at length the admiral himself,

tered into engagements with other powers (alluding to the accession of the emperor, April 1726, to the treaty of Stockholm, of February 1724); notwithstanding which, his majesty, fearing these delays should endanger Sweden, to shew his exactness in fulfilling his engagements and his attention to the succor of Sweden, was willing to put that crown in possession of the good fruits of its accession, even before it had acceded, by sending a powerful squadron into the Baltic *without any requisition thereof*—that the British admiral had been presented to his Swedish majesty, to assure him, that if he thought himself in any immediate danger from the armament of his neighbors, he was in that case to concert measures with his majesty for the defence of Sweden; but that while the said admiral continued at Stockholm, his Swedish majesty had graciously answered in writing, THAT HAVING A DEFENSIVE ALLIANCE WITH RUSSIA, HE THOUGHT HIMSELF IN NO DANGER FROM THENCE.—If after the departure of the English fleet any misfortune should happen to Sweden for want of timely precautions, it is hoped such misfortune will not be imputed to his Britannic majesty. And the ambassador concludes with saying, that his majesty cannot imagine that the fear of danger ought not to be a sufficient inducement to guard against

himself, perished deplorably by the diseases of that destructive climate. The ships also were said to be ruined by the worms; and loud and general complaints were made in England of the improvident and wanton waste of lives and money, in this unaccountable and disastrous expedition.

During the session of the preceding year, 1725, the earl of Macclesfield, lord high chancellor of Great Britain, was impeached, by the house of commons, of high crimes and misdemeanors, upon the ground of his having made unusual and exorbitant profits from the sale of places—as also from the abuse of his trust, as general guardian of the persons and estates of orphans and lunatics; and, after a trial of twenty days, he was convicted by the peers, and sentenced to pay a fine of 30,000l. and to imprisonment in the tower till the same was paid.—A memorable example of the upright and impartial administration of criminal justice in Great Britain. He was succeeded in the chancellorship by Sir Peter King, created baron King of Ockham in Surry, who had acquired great and deserved reputation in his former station of lord chief justice of England. But to this new and more elevated employment his talents were

against those dangers; nor that the loose and uncertain hopes of future advantages from Russia can afford a reasonable motive to reject the friendship of those powers which have ever been the support of Sweden; nor that those imaginary and insidious promises can be balanced against a clear and net subsidy of 100,000 ducats per month, to commence from your majesty's accession to the treaty of Hanover, and with a prospect of more considerable assistance in case of need." Surely the gravest counsellor in the senate of Sweden must have found it difficult to read this memorial with a serious countenance; for who ever heard, before, of an armament sent out of pure good-will to rescue a nation from the danger of its own alliances?

not

not deemed equally adapted: and on his resignation the great seal was consigned to lord Talbot, a nobleman of the highest mental accomplishments, of profound professional knowledge, and whose private life was the mirror of every virtue. His death, which most unhappily took place soon after his advancement, in the vigor of his age, was honored with the deepest expressions of national veneration and sorrow. He was succeeded by Sir Philip Yorke, lord chief justice of England, created baron Hardwicke, who presided in the court of chancery with high reputation no less than nineteen years.

At this period the king revived the antient order of knights of the Bath—an institution which affords a cheap and honorable recompense to men who have merited of the public, so long as such distinctions retain in the public estimation their present artificial and ideal value*.

The parliament of Great Britain being convened January 1727, the king informed the two houses "that the alliance offensive and defensive concluded between Spain and the emperor had laid the foundation of a most exorbitant and formidable power—a power levelled against the dearest interests and privileges of the English nation, which must either surrender Gibraltar to Spain, and acquiesce in the emperor's usurped exercise of commerce, or resolve vigorously to defend their undoubted rights. He assured them that it was a secret article of this alliance to place the Pretender upon the throne of Great Britain; and that Russia was actuated by the same views, which she had however been prevented from taking

---

* To attempt with philosophical severity to expose the frivolousness of these distinctions, were " to reason too curiously."
  " These little things are great to little man."

any steps to accomplish by the recent operations of the British fleet in the Baltic. Two other squadrons, he said, had been equipped, the advantage and glory accruing to the nation from which sufficiently spoke their praise.—And he concluded with informing them, that the king of Spain had actually ordered his ambassador to quit the kingdom, leaving a memorial containing a formal demand for the restitution of Gibraltar." The commons, in reply to his majesty's speech, voted a most loyal and zealous address, expressing "their determination to stand by and support his majesty with their lives and fortunes against all his enemies; and engaging not only cheerfully and effectually to raise the supplies necessary for the present exigency, but to enable his majesty to make good his engagements with his allies, in order to preserve the balance of power in Europe and undoubted rights of the crown of Great Britain." In vain was it urged by the patriots in opposition, "that it was sufficient on this occasion to return thanks to his majesty for his most gracious speech, and appoint a day for taking it into consideration, without precipitately pledging themselves to support measures the rectitude and wisdom of which they had as yet been furnished with no means to ascertain; that the address implied an approbation of measures taken to prevent dangers. But could this be done with propriety without knowing of what nature those measures were, or whether the dangers alleged were imaginary or real? On this occasion they said the advice of the house might be quite as necessary as its support; that the question of peace and war was the most momentous which could fall under the cognizance of that assembly; that it was incumbent upon them not rashly to decide, but maturely to deliberate; and for this purpose it was necessary that those papers which could alone elucidate and establish the facts stated in his ma-

jesty's

jesty's speech, should be laid before them." Sir William Wyndham remarked, that of late years our counsels had been in a state of perpetual fluctuation; that, Penelope-like, we were continually weaving and unravelling the same web—now raising, now depressing the power of the house of Austria, and engaging in successive quarrels with every power of the continent, under the pretence of preserving the balance of Europe." It was asked by Mr. Hungerford, " by what fleets the Pretender was to be convoyed to England; and whether he proposed to embark on the floating island of Gulliver—a scheme which seemed not more chimerical than the other circumstances of this romantic tale. He hoped that matters were not yet carried to such desperate lengths, but that means of accommodation might be found without engaging the nation in a war, which could only prove an aggravation of misfortunes." Sir Thomas Hanmer declared, that if the dangers which this nation was now said to be threatened with, were so real and so imminent as some pretended, he would be one of the foremost in recommending speedy and vigorous resolutions. But he acknowledged his incredulity; these dangers appeared to him mere phantoms, distant and almost indiscernible. And as to the Pretender, though his name might be converted to a political use by foreign princes, in order to frighten and alarm us; his interest was never so low, nor his party so despicable, as at present; and all mention of him in this day's debate ought to be left entirely out of the question. He confessed himself extremely apprehensive that the acquisition of certain foreign dominions had sown the seeds which had now produced these divisions and disturbances, which menaced Europe with a general war; and that we had involved ourselves in our present difficulties by COMPLIANCES, unaccountable on any possible ground connected with the national interests; or which

which could be dictated by any other motive than the security of those acquisitions." These reasonings, however, were too weak to have the least influence on the decision of the house; and the address was carried on the division by a majority of 251 against 81 voices. The demand of the king of Spain, mentioned in the speech from the throne, and alluded to by Sir Thomas Hanmer, was founded upon what his Catholic majesty affected to consider as a positive engagement of the king of England himself; who, in order to facilitate the accomplishment of the purposes which were at that time the object of negotiation at the court of Madrid, had, in a letter written in his own hand to the king of Spain, flattered that monarch with the idea of this restitution; which was afterwards, in consequence of the indignation excited by the mere suggestion of this project to the house of commons, laid aside as wholly impracticable; not however without leaving an apparent stain, or at least casting a certain shade, upon the honor of the king*. Such was the umbrage given by the

---

* Of this celebrated letter from the king of England to the king of Spain, the following is a translated copy from the French original:—

"SIR, MY BROTHER,

"I have learned with great satisfaction from the report of my ambassador at your court, that your majesty is at last resolved to remove the obstacles that have for some time delayed the entire accomplishment of our union. Since, from the confidence which your majesty expresses towards me, I may look upon the treaties which have been in question between us as re-established, and that accordingly the instruments necessary for carrying on the trade of my subjects will be delivered out; I do no longer hesitate to assure your majesty of my readiness to satisfy you with regard to your demand touching the restoration of Gibraltar, promising you to make use of the first favorable opportunity to regulate this article with the consent of my parliament. And to give your majesty a further proof of my affection, I have ordered my ambassador, as soon as the negotiation with which he has been charged shall

the king's speech to the court of Vienna, that M. de Palm, the Imperial resident at London, was ordered by the emperor to present a remonstrance to the British court, framed in terms unusually bold and pointed, charging the king with " calumnious misrepresentations, and with hazarding assertions void of all foundation. He affirmed that there was no *offensive* alliance subsisting between the Imperial and Spanish crowns; that the article relating to the Pretender was an ABSOLUTE NULLITY; and that the restitution of Gibraltar, however just the claim of the king of Spain, was foreign to the purpose of the treaty." The two houses expressed, in a formal address to the throne, their indignation at the insolence of this memorial, which they style an extravagant insult upon his majesty, and a presumptuous and vain attempt to instil into the minds of his faithful subjects a distrust of his royal word." As no positive evidence has however yet been adduced to confirm the assertions of the king of England, it is probable that the intelligence received respecting this political mystery did not merit that implicit credit which, predisposed by the credulity of habitual apprehension and suspicion, the court of London appears to have given to it—although lord Townshend hesitated

not

---

shall be finished, to propose to your majesty *new engagements to be entered into in concert and jointly with France*, suitable to the present conjuncture, not only for strengthening our union, but also for securing the tranquility of Europe. Your majesty may be persuaded that I on my part will shew all facility imaginable, promising myself that you will do the same for the mutual benefit of our kingdoms—being most perfectly,

" Sir, my brother,

" Your majesty's good brother,

June 1, 1721.   GEORGE, R.

" *To the King of Spain, Monsieur my brother.*"

But

not to declare in the houfe of lords, "that if the fafety of the ftate permitted to lay the advices in poffeffion of government before the houfe, their lordfhips would no more queftion the certainty of fuch an article than if they had been prefent at the figning of it." On the other hand, count Palm in his memorial declares, " that his Imperial majefty was ftruck with the utmoft aftonifhment that the king of Great Britain could fuffer himfelf to be prevailed upon to declare from the royal throne to that moft renowned nation, as certain and undoubted facts, things abfolutely void of all foundation.—And the ambaffador declares that his Imperial majefty has exprefsly authorifed and commanded him moft folemnly to affirm in his name, and upon his Imperial word, that there exifts no fecret article or convention whatfoever which contains or can tend to prove the leaft tittle of what has been alleged." And in another part of this famous memorial

But this, though the chief, was not the fole ground upon which the king of Spain refted his claim of reftitution. Towards the conclufion of lord Stair's embaffy at Paris, lord Stanhope went over to France charged with a fecret commiffion. And the cardinal Dubois, after his departure, informed the ambaffador, " that lord Stanhope had given a verbal promife to the regent, or at leaft what the regent underftood as fuch, for the reftoration of Gibraltar—that the regent thus authorifed, had pofitively and formally affured the king of Spain that Gibraltar fhould be reftored ; and that the honor of his highnefs as well as that of the king was now engaged for its accomplifhment, and that a failure in this point might be attended with difaftrous confequences."—That lord Stanhope fhould be impowered to offer an abfolute ceffion of Gbraltar is, however, not credible; as the king of England himfelf acknowledges in his letter to the king of Spain the confent of parliament to be neceffary; and the prejudices of the kingdom with regard to Gibraltar were far too great and obvious to admit the fuppofition that this confent could be at any time believed eafily attainable. It is probable, therefore, that the offer was made by the Englifh court chiefly to amufe, though the king and his minifters were certainly not averfe to the furrender of this invidious conqueft.——*Vid. Hardwicke ftate papers.*

he protests "that there exists not even a pretence to say that this treaty can be grievous or hurtful to a nation for which his Imperial majesty has the greatest affection and esteem, and whose glorious exploits and important succors no time will efface out of his memory." The emperor was believed to be envious of the power and grandeur of the House of Lunenburg since its accession to the throne of Great Britain, to a degree which the zealous and uniform attachment of the princes of that house to the interests of the Imperial family could never soften. But that he should seriously listen to any proposals from the court of Madrid in favor of the house of Stuart, from whose gratitude he had little to expect, and from whose deeply-rooted animosity and revenge he might eventually have every thing to fear, carries with it the face of great improbability. Highly resenting nevertheless the conduct of the king of England, and considering himself as abandoned by the treaty of Hanover, he had in the course of the preceding year (April 1726) acceded to the secret article of the treaty of Stockholm; from which æra the exorbitant power of the house of Austria, and the danger to which the balance of power and the liberties of Europe were consequently exposed, had become the fashionable theme of declamation in the court and parliament of Great Britain.

With the memorial also was transmitted from Vienna a letter from the chancellor count Zinzendorf to count Palm, expressly commanding him, in the name of his imperial majesty, after presenting the memorial to the king of Great Britain, to publish it, together with the letter annexed, for the information of the British nation. The chancellor Zinzendorf affirms in this letter, "that it is easy to see that the speech was made for no other purpose but to excite the nation to a rupture and open war with the emperor and Spain; and to make the parliament approve

approve the precipitate and burthenfome meafures *which the government has taken for private ends too well known.*— That on the firſt report of thefe falſe fuppofitions, the emperor and the king of Spain, in order to filence them, propofed a formal act *de non offendendo*, into which all the contracting parties of the treaties of Vienna and Hanover might enter, till fuch time as a definitive agreement might have taken place ; but that this propofition was rejected. He fays, that the articles of the quadruple alliance are exprefsly and publicly laid down as the unalterable bafis of the treaty of Vienna, and that to affirm that by a fecret pact concluded at the fame time, engagements have been entered into by their Imperial and Catholic majefties, repugnant to the fame, is an outrageous infult to the majefty of the two contracting powers, who have a right to demand a reparation proportioned to the enormity of the affront. And that the high contracting parties had no other view than that of making peace between themfelves, without injuring any one elfe." The allegations contained in this letter and memorial feem but too well founded ; but the intemperate language of thefe papers gave high and juft offence; and Mr. Shippen, Mr. Hungerford, Sir William Wyndham, and all the leaders of oppofition in parliament, warmly concurred in the addrefs prefented to the throne *on this occafion ;* and which pafled the houfe without a diffentient vote. And an order was fent to M. de Palm, fignifying "that the faid Palm having delivered into the hands of his majefty, at his late audience, a memorial highly injurious to the honor and dignity of his crown, and having alfo publicly difperfed the fame with a letter from the count de Zinzendorf to him the faid Palm, ſtill more infolent than the memorial, his majefty looked upon him no longer as a public minifter, and required him forthwith to depart out of this kingdom." Vigorous preparations were

were now made on both sides for war; and before the end of the session, the king informed the parliament that the fortress of Gibraltar was actually besieged. The forces of Great Britain were augmented by sea and land. Thirty thousand Swedes, Danes, and Hessians, were taken into British pay. And amongst other more usual ways and means of providing the supplies called for on this occasion, the king was empowered, by a clause of appropriation in one of the revenue bills of the year, " to apply such sums as should be necessary for making good the expences and engagements which had been or should be made before the 25th of September next, for the purposes of establishing the security of commerce and restoring the tranquillity of Europe." And it was in vain urged, " that this mode of asking and granting supplies was in the highest degree unparliamentary—that such an unlimited power ought never to be given under a free government—that such confidence in the crown might be attended, through the influence of evil ministers, with the most dangerous consequences—that no provision was made for the responsibility of those entrusted with the disposal of this money—that the constitution could no otherwise be preserved, than by a strict adherence to the essential parliamentary forms of granting supplies upon estimates, and of appropriating those supplies to services and occasions publicly avowed, and judged necessary—and that such an unwarrantable delegation of authority transfers that discretion to the crown which can with safety be vested in the legislature alone." The sum of 370,000l. issued in exchequer bills, was also charged on the surplus produce of certain duties appertaining to the sinking fund, towards the expences of the war, notwithstanding the vigorous opposition of Sir Joseph Jekyl and Mr. Pulteney, who demonstrated how essentially the efficacy of the fund would, by such a practice, be impaired. The latter of these gentlemen, in particular, affirmed

firmed, "That by charging new loans upon old and appropriated furpluffes, the public were grofsly deceived; that by thefe expedients to put off the evil day, taxes would be perpetuated; and that notwithftanding the great merit affumed by the inventors of this boafted fcheme of redemption, the national debt had really increafed fince the fetting up of that pompous project." This infidious alienation of a fund hitherto regarded as facred was the more remarkable, as the houfe of commons, in reply to the fpeech from the throne, exprefsly recommending to their attention the ftate of the finking fund, had faid— "And that all who wifh well to the peace and quiet of your majefty's government, may have the fatisfaction to fee that our prefent neceffities fhall make no interruption in the progrefs of that defirable work, of gradually reducing the national debt; we will confider of the moft proper method for immediately applying the produce of the finking fund to the ufes for which it was fo wifely contrived, and to which it ftands now appropriated." The court having now carried all its meafure by great and decifive majorities, the parliament was prorogued May 15, 1727.

Sir John Norris at this time failing with a powerful fleet to the Baltic was joined by a Danifh fquadron.— But the Czarina dying at this critical juncture, and the politics of the court of Peterfburg fuftaining another unexpected change, the armament became happily ufelefs. Meantime, through the active and feafonable intervention of the court of Verfailles—reluctant to carry matters to farther extremity againft the emperor, while fupported by Spain, whofe friendfhip fhe was folicitous to recover —preliminary articles of accommodation were figned, May 1727, by the minifters of all the belligerent powers; who, though much exafperated againft each other, were actuated by no motives of fufficient weight to induce them to involve anew all Europe in the horrors of a general war. These articles imported, that hostilities should immediately cease; that the charter of the Ostend company should be suspended for seven years; and that a congress should be opened in four months, at Aix-la Chapelle, afterwards transferred to Soissons, to settle the terms of a final pacification *.

The king of England seemed at length to have surmounted all his political difficulties; and if we cannot always applaud the justice or the wisdom of his counsels, it must at least be acknowledged, that they were enforced with an extraordinary degree of vigor and success. A fair prospect of peace and tranquillity now seemed to open; and the king embraced with his usual eagerness this favorable opportunity of revisiting his electoral dominions, to which he ever retained a fond and partial attachment, and by which he was in a degree not inferior revered and beloved. Embarking at Greenwich, June 3, 1727; he landed in Holland on the 7th, and immediately set out on his journey to Hanover. On the road between Delden and Ofnaburg he was seized with a kind of lethargic paralysis; and feeling himself attacked by the stroke of death, he said to the nobleman who accompanied him in the carriage, " *C'est fait de moi.*" He appeared, however, extremely anxious to reach the capital of his dominions; but on his arrival at the palace of his brother, the bishop of Osnaburg, it was found impossible to proceed; and on Sunday the 11th of June 1727, he expired, in the 68th year of his age, and 13th of

---

* So seriously nevertheless did France enter into the views of England, or rather Hanover, at this crisis, for the abasement of the house of Austria, that she had actually engaged for the payment of an annual subsidy to Denmark of 350,000 rix-dollars, for four years; and likewise of 50,000 ducats monthly to Sweden, to commence from the period of her accession to the treaty of Hanover.

his reign—leaving iſſue by his conſort Sophia Dorothea, heireſs of the houſe of Zell, George, ſucceſſor to the crown, and a daughter, married previous to the acceſſion of the Brunſwic family to the royal dignity, to Frederic William, king of Pruſſia.

If this prince was not diſtinguiſhed for ſhining talents or heroic virtues, much leſs can we diſcern, on a general review of his character, any remarkable deficiency of underſtanding or propenſity to vice. Acceding to the crown of Great Britain when far advanced in life, he ſeemed ever to conſider himſelf rather as elector than as king: and the influence and power of Great Britain were of little eſtimation in his eyes, when directed to any other end than the aggrandizement of his native country. With reſpect to the internal government of his kingdoms, the rectitude and benevolence of his intentions were always apparent: but he was, from the nature of his ſituation, compelled to throw himſelf into the hands of a party; and from the eaſineſs of his diſpoſition he was too often perſuaded to acquieſce in meaſures which a more perfect acquaintance with the real ſtate of facts and opinions would have ſhewn to be as contrary to his intereſts, as there is reaſon to believe they frequently were to his inclination. In the view of Europe at large, he ſuſtained the character of a prudent, an able, and a fortunate prince. And if, in contemplating the hiſtory of this reign, we have juſt cauſe to lament the weakneſſes and defects of the external ſyſtem of policy by which its counſels were influenced; we have ample reaſon, on the other hand, to expreſs our ardent wiſhes, that the noble ſpeculative principles of government, and of liberty civil and religious, which this monarch was not only ready but anxious on all occaſions to avow, and by which the general tenor of his conduct was regulated, may never
ceaſe

cease to be the distinguishing and favorite characteristics of the royal and electoral house of BRUNSWIC.

With respect to the general state of literature and the arts during this reign, it may suffice to observe, that notwithstanding the total neglect of the court, and the violence of party rage, descriptive of this as well as of the former reign, they continued to flourish in a very high degree; and we view with surprise, amidst scenes of contention and turbulence, a constellation of geniuses shedding a peculiar lustre over this period of British history. Scarcely had LOCKE, TEMPLE, and DRYDEN, the departing luminaries of the former age, sunk below the western sky; when ADDISON, SWIFT, POPE, SHAFTESBURY and BOLINGBROKE arose in the east. The writings of Addison, in particular, merit a most distinguished and honorable mention. Amidst the din of hostile and malignant factions, they exhibit an almost cloudless picture of urbanity, candor, good sense, and beneficence. The advantage which the community has reaped from the wide and almost boundless diffusion of them, no power of calculation can ascertain. And exclusive of their moral and political merit, his exquisite delineations of life and manners will charm as long as our nation and language exist. In poetry, Pope rose far superior to all his contemporaries; and if inferior to any in that mode of versification which he chose to adopt, he is inferior to Dryden alone. In the province of architecture, Gibbs and Kent, with unequal steps and at almost viewless distance, followed the celebrated Sir Christopher Wren; of whom the magnificent plan for rebuilding the city of London in 1666—an effort of genius which can never be contemplated without admiration and indignant regret—would have alone sufficed to perpetuate the memory. And at this period

period the English school of painting could produce, a Thornhill excepted, no greater artist than Jervas, whose name is indeed immortalized—not by the "warmth divine" of his own performances, but of "the verse eternal which embalms the dead." During the course of this reign, Sir ISAAC NEWTON terminated his long career of life; but his career of fame and glory will be coeval only with that of the world itself, whose laws he has developed and explained, with an energy and sagacity wholly stupendous, and approaching, perhaps, the limits of supernatural intelligence.

K. GEORGE II.

ON the arrival of an exprefs from Ofnaburg with the intelligence of the death of the king, the new monarch, affembling the privy council, commanded the members to be fworn anew; and declared to them his firm purpofe to preferve inviolate the conftitution in church and ftate, and to cultivate thofe alliances which his father had made with foreign princes. All the great officers of ftate were continued in their places; and it was at once apparent that the political fyftem eftablifhed by the late king would fuffer no effential alteration. The prime minifter, Sir Robert Walpole, feemed even to poffefs an higher and more exclufive fhare of favor and confidence than before. Lord Townfhend, fecretary of ftate for foreign affairs, a nobleman not deftitute of knowledge or talents—open, generous, and fincere—was alone able for a time to preferve fome degree of independent political confequence: but finding the competition too unequal, and his power and influence rapidly on the wane, he he retired—a statesman cured of ambition—to cultivate his paternal acres *. The duke of Newcastle, his colleague, was a man illustrious by his birth, affable and popular in his address, liberal in his sentiments, and magnificent in his expences. But his capacity was very inadequate to his elevated station. With intentions disinterested and upright, his zeal and attachment to the house of Hanover too frequently prompted him to inconsiderate compliances. And to oppose the measures of the court, however contrary to the interests of the nation, argued in his estimation criminal disaffection to the king's person and government. Mr. Pelham, secretary at war, and brother to the duke, was esteemed for his probity, respected for his talents, and beloved for his candor. The earl of Chesterfield, ambassador at the Hague, and soon afterwards appointed lord Steward, who seemed ambitious to form himself upon the model of lord Bolingbroke, though he rose not to an equality with that great and unrivalled original, was at once a man of wit, of pleasure, and of business. The high polish of his manners, approaching perhaps the verge of frivolity, indicated rather the accomplished courtier than the commanding statesman; and left an impression somewhat unfavorable to the solidity of his judgment,

though

---

* A cotemporary poet of no ignoble fame has celebrated the praises of this respectable nobleman in the following elegant lines:

" ———Townshend, whom all the world admires,
From all the world illustriously retires;
And calmly wand'ring in his Raynham roves,
By lake, or spring, by thicket, lawn, or groves;
Where verdant hills, or vales, where fountains stray.
Charming each thought of idle pomp away;
Unenvied views the splendid toils of state,
In private happy, as in public great."

though his political opinions appear to have been uniformly clear and juft. As a fpeaker, his elocution was elegant, and his ftyle flowing and chafte; and his capacity, naturally excellent, was improved by diligent literary cultivation *. John duke of Argyle was diftinguifhed beyond all his cotemporaries, by an uncommon union of civil and military talents. He had fignalized himfelf in the wars of Flanders under the late duke of Marlborough, whilft yet in early youth, by a fagacity of conduct furpaffing his years, and by a fpirit of gallantry which rofe to heroifm. As commander in chief of the forces in North Britain, he was eminently inftrumental in quelling the rebellion of 1715. And the firm and hereditary attachment of his family to the principles of liberty and whiggifm rendered the name of Argyle dear to the majority of the people of Scotland, where his influence and popularity were boundlefs. His fpeeches in parliament were characterized by a vehemence and energy, which rendered him, as a political adverfary, very formidable.

---

* The character of this nobleman—" Stanhope in wifdom as in wit divine"—has been thought greatly to refemble that of his maternal grandfather, the celebrated marquis of Halifax. Amongft the " ftate maxims" of the latter, is an obfervation, which alone might ferve as a proof that he has not been applauded without reafon for his fagacity : " The prince is to take care that the greater part of the people may not be angry at the fame time—for though the firft beginning of their ill-humour fhould be againft one another, it will naturally end in anger againft him." And of his wit we have the following excellent fpecimen : After the Revolution, in which the marquis had borne a diftinguifhed part, many abfurd applications were made to him from perfons pretending great fervices, for his recommendation to pofts and places under the government, which they were for the moft part utterly unqualified to fill Being at laft wearied with their importunities, he faid " that he had frequently been told that the Roman republic had been faved by geefe, but he never heard that thofe geefe were made confuls."

formidable. He was not wanting in a very exalted idea of the importance of his services and the lustre of his talents. The high and lucrative offices which he held under the crown he seemed to regard rather as what it were injustice to with-hold, than favor to confer. He was imperious, passionate, and capricious, but honest, undisguised, and magnanimous—troublesome as a friend, but dangerous as an enemy. Lord Carteret was however, unquestionably, the only man connected with this administration, of whose abilities the Premier could entertain any reasonable jealousy or apprehension. Dignified and even stately in his deportment, the habitual superiority he appeared to assume was sustained by an extraordinary energy of genius and extent of knowledge. Deeply versed in the labyrinths of foreign politics, he at once discerned and despised all the littlenesses of that system by which the English court had been governed, from the period of her connection with Hanover. Aspiring in his views, resolute in his temper, and diverted by no inferior or collateral object from the pursuits of his ambition, he seemed by the potency of his alliance to menace the minister whom he deigned to honor with his support.

The entire produce of the civil list revenues, estimated at 800,000l. was, on the motion of Sir Robert Walpole, settled on the king for life, instead of the clear annual revenue of 700,000l. granted to the late monarch—not, however, without some debate and opposition. The incorrupt and inflexible Shippen observed, " That the sum of 700,000l. was, at the accession of his late majesty, considered by all as an ample royal revenue; and it was to be hoped that in this reign many personal expences, particularly those incurred in the frequent journeys to Hanover, would cease. He affirmed, that the civil list revenue in the reign of the late queen

did

did not in general exceed the sum of 550,000l. and that the parliament was called upon only once in a reign of thirteen years to pay the debts contracted in her civil government; and these were occasioned by the unparalleled instances of her piety and generosity—especially by her devoting 100,000l. per annum to the public service during the war. But in the late reign 500,000l. had been twice voted for the discharge of the civil list debts; and last session, he said, a sum of 125,000l. was granted for purposes not yet explained: notwithstanding which there was yet a debt of 600,000l. unaccounted for; and therefore he supposed contracted in a manner not fit to be owned, or swallowed up in the bottomless gulph of secret service. This amazing extravagance, he said, had happened under the conduct of persons pretending to surpass all their predecessors in the knowledge and care of the public revenue. But, instead of granting any addition to the civil list, he should move that the duties appropriated to this purpose should be continued to his majesty, so as to make up the clear yearly sum of 700,000l." The amendment, however, was rejected by a great majority; and in lieu of it, a resolution founded upon a royal message delivered to the house by Sir Paul Methuen, for settling the sum of 100,000l. per ann. as a jointure upon the queen, passed without difficulty.

The parliament being dissolved in August, a new parliament was convened in January 1728, of which Arthur Onslow, Esq. was chosen speaker, and which seemed to vie, in all expressions of duty and loyalty, with the most loyal of its predecessors. The king assured them, in his speech from the throne, of the absolute necessity of continuing those preparations which had hitherto *secured the nation*, the execution of the preliminaries, actually

tually signed, having been retarded by unexpected difficulties, raised chiefly by the obstinate opposition of the court of Madrid, although the ratifications had been actually exchanged with the emperor. The sum of 280,000l. was therefore voted for the maintenance of the Hessian and Swedish auxiliaries, and a subsidy of 100,000l. payable in four years to the duke of Wolfenbuttle; who, in return, took upon him to guarantee, by a formal treaty, to his Britannic majesty the possession of his three kingdoms, and to *keep in readiness* for his service a corps of 5000 men during the same term. This notable alliance occasioned, however, some severe animadversions; and Sir Joseph Jekyl, master of the Rolls, a firm and zealous Whig, but one who carried not his complaisance to the court so far as to abandon on any occasion what he conceived to be the true interest of his country, in reply to Sir Robert Walpole, who had launched out into the highest praises of the treaty of Hanover, affirmed, " That whatever gloss might be put upon such measures, they were repugnant to the maxims by which England in former times had steered, and squared its conduct with relation to its interests abroad—that the navy was the natural strength of Great Britain, its best defence and security; but if, in order to avoid a war, they should be so free hearted as to buy and maintain the forces of foreign princes, they were never like to see an end of such extravagant expences*."

The

---

* It may deserve mention, that the lord chancellor King was so struck with the inexpressible absurdity of this *provisional treaty* with the duke of Wolfenbuttle, that he absolutely refused to affix the great seal to it, till ratified by parliament, and the money actually voted. " What," says an able political writer of the last reign, " our histories may hereafter say of this transaction I know not; but the persons then at the head of the opposition *took the liberty* to declare upon that occasion,

The house was even prevailed upon, during the suspension of its good humour, to address the king for a particular and distinct account of the sum of 250,000l. charged in the general statement of national expenditure to have been issued "for preserving and restoring the peace of Europe." His majesty, nevertheless, declined to comply with their request; but informed them in general terms, that part of the money had been disbursed by his late majesty, conformably to the powers vested in him by parliament; and the remainder by himself, for carrying on necessary and important services, which required the greatest secrecy. And he hoped that the house would repose the same confidence in him, and be assured that the money had been necessarily expended, agreeably to the ends for which it was granted. This answer, the house, upon calmer consideration, thought fit to approve; Sir Robert Walpole affirming it to be "impossible that public services should be carried on, considering the great complication of interests on the Continent, if *every shilling* that was expended for the advancement of the common cause, and for maintaining the balance of Europe, was known to all the world:" though Mr. Pulteney, now in open opposition to the court, inveighed against this vague and loose mode of accounting for the expenditure of the public money, as tending to render parliaments altogether insignificant; to encourage and invite the most shameful embezzlements; and to screen corrupt and rapacious ministers from even

---

sion, "that we paid for a great many forces to be in *readiness* on account of the Hanover treaty; and last of all the GOOD WILL of his highness the duke of Wolfenbuttle was obtained, who engaged to guarantee all his majesty's dominions with a body of 5000 men, not to be moved out of Holland or Germany, at so small an expence as 25,000l. per ann. for four years."—*Case of the Hanover forces.*

the possibility of detection and punishment. No impression, however, was made by these reasonings, as too plainly appeared by the discretionary vote of credit, passed at the requisition of the court, by 237 voices against 101, previous to the close of the session.

In the course of the present year arrived in England Frederic prince of Wales, who had hitherto resided at Hanover, as if it were determined to perpetuate the Hanoverian system, by suffering no interruption of the original associations and attachments of the reigning family. About this time died Ernest Augustus, bishop of Osnaburg, only brother of the late king, and created by him duke of York, but never resident in England. He was succeeded in the bishopric by the elector of Cologne, agreeably to the *pactum* by which Osnaburg is alternately possessed by a prince of the house of Brunswic and that elector.

The congress at Soissons made little progress in the business of pacification. France and Spain were now perfectly reconciled; and the court of Madrid, confiding in the strength of her ally, though her short-lived friendship with the emperor was now at an end, became less solicitous for an accommodation with England. Loud and general exclamations were raised, and petitions presented from the great mercantile towns to the house of commons, at the meeting of parliament early in the year 1729, complaining of the losses and obstructions they had sustained in their commerce, through the depredations of the Spaniards in the West Indies. The house, in a grand committee, after an ample investigation of the subject, passed a resolution, justificatory of the instructions given to admiral Hosier to seize the flota and galleons; and another, declaring that the Spaniards had violated the treaties subsisting between the two crowns. And an address was presented to the king,

desiring

"desiring that his majesty would be graciously pleased to use his utmost endeavors to procure just and reasonable satisfaction for these injuries, and for securing to his majesty's subjects the free exercise of commerce and navigation to and from the British colonies in America;" which his majesty assured them he would not fail to do. The house of peers also resolving itself into a committee on the state of the nation, and the letter of the late king to the king of Spain, touching the restitution of Gibraltar, among other state-papers, being laid before them, a resolution was moved, " That for the honor of his majesty, and the preservation and security of the trade and commerce of the kingdom, effectual care should be taken, in the present treaty, that the king of Spain should renounce, in explicit terms, all claim and pretension to Minorca and Gibraltar." After a violent debate the motion was negatived, but not without a strong protest; and a second motion, " That the house did entirely rely upon his majesty, that he would, for maintaining the honor and securing the trade of this kingdom, take effectual care in the present treaty to preserve his undoubted right to Gibraltar and Minorca," passed in the affirmative. It is singular, that an address was again presented to the throne by the commons, desiring to be informed in what manner a large sum, stated to have been expended for restoring the peace of Europe, was disposed of; to which an answer, similar to that returned to the former address, was given, in which the house had again the complaisance to acquiesce. Previous to the recess, the king declared his intention of visiting his German dominions, leaving the queen sole regent, under whose mild and equitable administration no cause of discontent or disaffection arose. But Ireland had been for some time past convulsed with folly and faction, in consequence of a patent granted to one Wood, by the late king, for coining a certain quantity of copper for the use of that kingdom, and which was confessedly much wanted for the purposes of commercial intercourse. The coinage being found of a base and inferior quality, the famous Swift, Dean of St. Patrick's, seized with eagerness the opportunity of venting his spleen and rancor against the government, by publishing a series of tracts, in which he attempted to prove, that the ruin of the kingdom must be the inevitable consequence of this abuse. Lord Carteret, being now appointed to the government of Ireland, was compelled to issue, in his official capacity, a proclamation offering a reward for the discovery of the author of these seditious and libellous publications. Notwithstanding which, this haughty and factious priest ventured to appear at all places of public resort as usual, and had even, in the presence-chamber of the castle of Dublin, the boldness to expostulate with the lord lieutenant upon the pretended tyranny and iniquity of this proclamation, and presumed to ask, "how it was possible that his excellency could suffer it to be issued?" To which lord Carteret, indulging the sympathies of friendship and genius, with equal elegance and magnanimity replied, *Res dura, et regni novitas, me talia cogunt moliri.* Under the administration of this nobleman peace and order were restored and established, various excellent laws were enacted for the encouragement of manufactures, commerce, and agriculture, and many salutary regulations adopted in the civil departments of government. The beneficial effects of a liberal and enlightened policy were universally felt; and the parliament of that kingdom, in their unanimous approval of the measures of their present Governor, paid that homage to wisdom which it had frequently been known to refuse to power.

The congress of Soissons proving finally abortive, conferences were opened at Seville between the ministers of France, Spain, and England, to the exclusion of the emperor, who conceived much resentment at this affront; and a treaty was signed in the month of May 1729, of which his imperial majesty openly and heavily complained to the Diet assembled at Ratisbon, as contrary to the express stipulations of the quadruple alliance. In the course of this year Victor Amadeus, king of Sardinia, resigned his crown to his son Charles Emanuel, and retiring to the castle of Chamberri, espoused the countess of St. Sebastian, who refused with disdain the title, as she could not participate in the power, of royalty. In October (1729) died Peter II. Czar of Muscovy, and grandson of Peter the Great, by the unfortunate Alexiowitz. He was succeeded on the throne of Russia by the princess Anne Iwanowna, duchess of Courland, second daughter of the Czar Iwan, elder brother to Peter the Great. Early in the following year died Pope Benedict XIII. and was succeeded by cardinal Corsini, already near 80 years of age, who nevertheless filled the Papal chair ten years under the name of Clement XII.

At this eventful period also a sudden and surprising revolution, if under so despotic a government any revolution can surprise, took place at Constantinople, by the deposition of the grand seignor Achmet III. and the elevation of his nephew Mahmout or Mahomet V. From the æra of the memorable victory obtained by the illustrious Sobieski under the walls of Vienna, the Ottoman power had suffered a great and rapid decline; and Mahomet IV. who had succeeded when an infant to the throne, on the deposition of his father the sultan Ibrahim (A. D. 1648), was himself in consequence of the general rage excited by the misfortunes of that disastrous war, compelled to submit to the same fate. During the short and feeble reigns of his brothers Solyman II. and Achmet II. the triumphs of the Imperialists continued. The reign of the succeeding emperor Mustapha II. son of Mahomet IV. was distinguished by the famous battle of Zenta won by prince Eugene, and the consequent treaty of Carlowitz. After a reign of seven years, the sultan Mustapha was, by another revolution, hurled from his throne, and his brother Achmet III. raised to the same high and dangerous pre-eminence. This prince is well known by his hospitable and generous reception of the king of Sweden, after the defeat of that monarch at Pultowa. Being afterwards involved in a war with the emperor Charles VI. his armies were repeatedly defeated by prince Eugene, and the war was terminated, greatly to the disadvantage of the Turks, by a treaty concluded under the mediation of Great Britain at Passarowitz, A. D. 1718. The avarice and oppression of his subsequent government, together with the war carried on negligently and unsuccesfully against the Persians, made the reign of Achmet odious to the people. Recourse being had to a very unusual and dangerous expedient in Turkey, the imposition of a new tax called the *Bedead*, a species of excise very arbitrary in the collection, in order to defray the expence of this war, three Janisaries, named Calil, Muslu, and Ali, very obscure men, fancying themselves particularly aggrieved by it, assembled, in the absence of the grand seignor and grand vizier then at Scutari, a considerable number of their comrades in the *Atmeidan*, where they presented to them a naked sword on which they had themselves sworn, and required of all who engaged with them to swear the death of the grand vizier, the Caimacan, and the Reis Effendi. The Aga of the Janisaries repairing in haste to the Atmeidan, Calil demanded if he were come to join the brave Mussulmen who were

resolved

resolved on a reformation in the state, and the punishment of the tyrants? The Aga, being destitute of force to suppress the revolters, retired in silence. The sultan, attended by the vizier, returned with precipitation on the first intelligence of this insurrection at Constantinople, where they arrived at midnight. On the next morning, by order of the emperor, the standard of Mahomet was displayed, but without effect; and the number of revolters continually increasing, the seraglio was on the day following formally invested. Measures being now in preparation to force the gates of the palace, their astonishment was great to see the dead bodies of the proscribed ministers brought out on litters, preceded by an officer of the Bostangis, who announced the condescension of the emperor, and commanded them in his name to separate. The three leaders of the revolt, fully aware of the danger of their situation, expressed their dissatisfaction at this concession, and, declaring the sultan Achmet unworthy of the throne, boldly exclaimed, that they would have sultan Mahmoud for their sovereign. The name of Mahmoud was repeated with loud acclamations, resounding even to the inmost recesses of the seraglio. The sultan Achmet hastily assembling a divan, asked, with a faltering voice, what the rebels had yet to desire; on which an Iman replied, " my lord, thy reign is at an end—thy revolted subjects will no longer have thee for a master.—They demand with shouts thy nephew Mahhoud—it is in vain for thee to flatter thyself that they will return to their allegiance." At these words the sultan turned pale, but soon recovering himself, said, " Why was I not informed of this sooner? Follow me." Immediately he went to the prison of Mahmoud, attended by all the members of the divan; and, having taken that prince by the hand, " The wheel has turned for you as

for

for me," said he to him, conducting him to the divan chamber; "I resign to you the throne which Muſtapha my brother reſigned to me." After which he returned to the apartment from whence he had taken Mahmoud, there to end his life. Thus in the ſpace of about eighty years no leſs than four emperors had been ſucceſſively dethroned at Conſtantinople by lawleſs and popular violence. A demonſtration ſo ſtriking of the inſtability and inſecurity of military and deſpotic governments, might ſurely ſuffice to reconcile the proudeſt deſpot to the eſtabliſhment of a regular and permanent ſyſtem of liberty *.

The parliament of England aſſembling in January 1730, the king, in his ſpeech from the throne, declared the peace of Europe to be firmly eſtabliſhed by the treaty of Seville, which was built, as he aſſerted, on the foundation of the quadruple alliance. He affirmed, that Spain had agreed to an ample reſtitution and reparation for all unlawful ſeizures and depredations; that the free and uninterrupted exerciſe of Britiſh commerce was fully ſecured; and that all rights, privileges, and poſſeſſions belonging to him and his allies were confirmed and ſolemnly guaranteed. Violent oppoſition was made to the terms of this treaty when ſubmitted to the inveſtigation of parliament; though it muſt be acknowledged

---

* It is ſaid that a grand Vizier of Turkey once inquiring of Mr. Montague, the Engliſh ambaſſador at Conſtantinople, whether it were really true, as he had been informed, that the Engliſh nation had ſtruck off the head of one of their kings on a public ſcaffold? the ambaſſador anſwered, that it was: And the Vizier farther inquiring at what diſtance of time this incredible act of wickedneſs and rebellion had been committed, the ambaſſador told the Vizier, with great coolneſs, that, to the beſt of his recollection, it was in the very ſame year in which the grand ſeignor Ibrahim was depoſed, and ſtrangled by the Janiſaries.

that

that some of the objections urged by the patriots, when viewed through the long vista of years which has now intervened, appear rather minute and captious. They affirmed that the article by which the British merchants were required to make proof of their losses at the court of Madrid was injurious to them, and dishonorable to the nation; and that there was little probability of obtaining that redress by means of commissaries, which was refused to plenipotentiaries. They complained that the right of Great Britain to Gibraltar and Minorca was not acknowledged in this treaty; they disliked the guarantee of Tuscany, Parma, and Placentia, to Don Carlos and his successors, as a concession which might involve Great Britain in future quarrels about a country with which we had no concern. But the principal objection, and that which constituted the chief ground of the high offence taken by the emperor, was founded upon that article of the treaty by which England not only guaranteed the succession of these Duchies to the Infant, but engaged to convey a body of Spanish troops to Italy, in order to secure those possessions without waiting for the Imperial investiture; which was not only an open and flagrant affront offered to the Imperial dignity, but likewise a palpable deviation from the letter of the quadruple alliance, by which neutral troops only were to be admittted, till the investitures were granted. And if any obstacles arose in carrying this article of the convention of Seville into execution, the contracting parties, in conjunction with France, under whose mediation it was concluded, agreed by force of arms to obtain the accomplishment of it. So much incensed was the court of Vienna at the insult, still more perhaps than the injury offered in the treaty of Seville, that his Imperial majesty issued an edict, prohibiting the subjects of Great Britain from trading in his dominions; and made great military

military preparations and demonstrations of a determination to assert his rights by a declaration of war. In the course of this session, and while things remained in this posture, a very warm debate arose in consequence of a bill introduced by the minister to prevent any subject of Great Britain from advancing money by way of loan to foreign princes or states, without license first obtained from his majesty under his privy seal. This bill was ably opposed by Sir John Barnard, one of the representatives of the city of London, a man of strict integrity and extensive commercial knowledge, as "a measure which would render Holland the mart of money to the nations of the Continent. He said, that by this general prohibition the English were disabled from assisting their best allies; that the king of Portugal frequently borrowed money of the English merchants residing within his dominions; that the licensing power was liable to dangerous abuse; and that the clause which empowered the attorney general to compel the discovery on oath of such loans, would convert the court of Exchequer into a court of Inquisition." In consequence of these arguments the bill was modified in such a manner as to render it much less exceptionable; and it was declared, " that the object of it was merely to prevent the subjects of the state from assisting the enemies of the state. It was well known that at this very time the emperor was negotiating a loan in the metropolis, and it was manifestly impolitic and absurd to permit individuals to enrich themselves by any mode of traffic detrimental to the general interests of the kingdom." The bill at length passed; and it must be acknowledged, that the principle on which it is founded appears perfectly equitable, and that no inconvenience has, in fact, been found to result from it.

A bill

A bill passed by the commons in the course of this session "for making more effectual the laws in being for disabling persons from being chosen members of parliament, who enjoyed any pension during pleasure, or for any number of years, or any office holden in trust for them," was rejected on the second reading by the lords; and on the 15th of May 1730 the king went to the house of peers, and closed the session with a speech, in which very harsh and angry mention was made of " those *incendiaries* who, by scandalous libels, labored to alienate the affections of his people, to fill their minds with groundless jealousies and unjust complaints, in dishonor of him and his government, and in defiance of the sense of both houses of parliament *."

Early in the year 1731, the parliament was again convened, and the session opened by a remarkable speech from the throne, indicating a very extraordinary and alarming situation of affairs. The king declared, " that in consequence of the measures formerly taken, and the conclusion of the treaty of Seville, the dangerous consequences so justly apprehended from the treaty of Vienna were entirely obviated; and that union which had alarmed all Europe not only dissolved, but the treaty of Hanover strengthened by the additional power of the crown of Spain. His majesty observed, that from this situation of affairs just hopes were entertained that the

---

* The *scandalous libels* mentioned in the king's speech were supposed chiefly to allude to the periodical papers entitled "The Craftsman," supported by the ablest political writers of the age, lord Bolingbroke and Mr. Pulteney being themselves of the number, and in which the measures of the administration were attacked with equal animosity, wit, and argument. So transient, however, is the fame attached to controversial politics, that this publication, so admired and celebrated in its day, is already consigned to obscurity and almost to oblivion.

conditions of the treaty of Seville would have been complied with without the necessity of coming to extremities; but that this desirable event had been hitherto delayed: and as the treaty imposed an obligation upon all the contracting parties to prepare for the execution of it, WE must be in readiness to perform OUR part, in order to procure the satisfaction due to our allies. The resolutions of parliament were expected by foreign powers with impatience, and the great event of peace or war would be very much affected by their first decisions. He said, that *the plan of operations for the execution of the treaty of Seville by* FORCE *was now under consideration*; that their just concern for the true interest of their country would, he doubted not, induce them to grant the supplies necessary to make good his engagements, with that cheerfulness and affection which became a British house of commons tender of the honor of the crown, careful and solicitous for the glory and prosperity of the kingdom." Never was the truth more apparent than at the present moment, of the memorable observation of lord Molesworth on a former occasion, and which well deserves the repetition, " that to a man acquainted only with the situation of Great Britain, and unapprised of the several petty interests of the electorate of Hanover, the conduct of the English court would appear not only fluctuating and capricious, but absolutely unintelligible and incomprehensible." For what shadow of pretence, connected with the interest of Great Britain, could be devised to justify or palliate an outrage upon the emperor, so flagrant as the forcible introduction of foreign troops into Parma and Placentia by a British fleet, for the purpose of transferring those Duchies, which were acknowledged fiefs of the empire, to the king of Spain, previous to the investiture of his imperial majesty, and in direct contradiction to the laws

and

and constitutions of the empire; by this means wantonly and voluntarily incurring the eventual risque of a war with the house of Austria, the ancient, natural, and faithful ally of Great Britain? The key to this apparently unaccountable and extravagant conduct is, however, perfectly easy. The two imperial courts of Vienna and Petersburg had not yet relinquished their designs in favor of the duke of Holstein; and still flattered that prince with the hope of procuring, either by amicable or hostile means, the restitution of the Duchy of Slesvic, guaranteed originally by Hanover, and afterwards by England, to the king of Denmark. So long, therefore, as this project was entertained, so long did the elector-kings of England consider their favorite acquisitions of Bremen and Verden, which were the price and reward of that guarantee, as in the most imminent danger. For the sole purpose of counteracting this project was the treaty of Hanover concluded; for this purpose was the insidious policy of France countenanced and encouraged by a continued refusal, on the part of England, to assent to the edict of the pragmatic sanction; for this purpose was the ambition of Spain gratified by the forcible introduction of troops into the Parmesan. In vain was it alleged, in opposition to the proposed address of approbation and support, "that our ancestors were never so complaisant as to declare their approval of measures without full and regular information respecting them. Why was it that the house pledged itself for the support of *any measures* of the executive government? Doubtless, on the ground of their being just and reasonable. But who could pronounce the measures in contemplation just, when no one could say what they were, or what they might ultimately prove to be? Every one, indeed, knew the expence which this nation had incurred in their endeavors

vors to reduce the exorbitant power of France, which, by a fatal negligence, had been suffered to arise to a height which menaced the general liberties of Europe. But by joining the house of Bourbon in this war against the house of Austria, France might be enabled to extend her conquests beyond the Rhine, or, perhaps, to annex the low countries to her empire, and become more formidable than ever. It was affirmed, that French alliances had ever been fatal to England; that our kings, by a connection with France, had been led to imbibe the love of arbitrary power, and encouraged to entertain designs against the liberty of their subjects; and that Gallic faith was to be depended upon no farther than their interest was concerned in adhering to it; that their enmity to England was inveterate; and that we should, in the end, pay dear for any temporary favors which they may seem to confer." And an amendment to the address was offered, " that his majesty should be defired not to concur in a war against the emperor either in Flanders or upon the Rhine."

The Walpoles, and the courtiers in general who took part in the debate, maintained, in opposition to these objections, " that his majesty's prudence was so great, and had been so strikingly manifested in his whole conduct since his happy accession, that no suspicion could reasonably be entertained of the propriety of his present or future measures; that the amendment now proposed was an encroachment on his majesty's prerogative. They acknowledged that France ought not to extend the bounds of her empire, and his majesty would, *no doubt*, take proper precautions to prevent the inconveniences apprehended from the weight of the confederacy against the house of Austria; that the design of the potent alliance formed against the emperor was to convince him of the impossibility of a successful resistance; it would be grossly
impolitic,

impolitic, therefore, if the allies were restrained from attacking him in Flanders, or on the Rhine, where he was most vulnerable. By enfeebling the operations of the war, such restraint would virtually and proportionally add to the strength of the emperor, and thereby make a pacification hopeless and impracticable." Another amendment was then proposed, far more judicious and comprehensive: " that the house would support his majesty's engagements so far as they related to the interest of Great Britain;" and it was urged by Mr. Wyndham, the mover of it, " that the act of settlement, by virtue of which his majesty held the crown of these realms, expressly provided that this nation shall not be obliged to enter into a war for the defence of any dominions not belonging to the crown of Great Britain; and that the house *could not* therefore, agreeably to this act, go farther than the amendment imported." To this the minister and the courtiers replied, " that the adoption of this amendment would *seem to insinuate* that his majesty *had* entered into engagements that did not relate to the interests of Great Britain; which would be the highest disrespect and ingratitude, when those that had the honor to serve his majesty could testify that the interest of Great Britain was the sole object of his majesty's solicitude. They said that every member of the house was, they hoped, convinced that his majesty never would enter into any engagement that was not absolutely necessary for the happiness and safety of his people, and therefore it was wholly unnecessary to narrow the assurances of support in the address by any such limitation." The house seeming, however, to pause upon the validity of these arguments, more fit indeed for a Turkish divan than a British senate, Mr. Heathcote arose, and declared, " that the offering of advice to his majesty could never be regarded by him as an encroachment on the prerogative, since it

was

was the proper bufinefs of parliament, which was the king's great council, to advife the crown in all matters of importance—it was what many parliaments had done, and what they were obliged in duty to do; that to fupport any hoftile operations againft the emperor in Flanders or upon the Rhine, was abfolutely deftructive to the intereft of England, tending evidently to the total fubverfion of the balance of power; and the houfe had, therefore, good reafon to believe that no minifter would DARE to advife his majefty to concur in fuch a meafure. Upon that account only he confidered it as fuperfluous to advife his majefty againft it; that unanimity in their refolves was certainly defirable, and would undoubtedly add great weight to his majefty's endeavors to effect a general accommodation of differences; and for his part he looked upon all addreffes, containing affurances of fupport, as in their nature general, and no farther obligatory than the meafures to be fupported fhall be found conducive to the public intereft; that he, therefore, willingly concurred in the addrefs as originally moved, taking it at prefent for granted, that the engagements alluded to were fuch as the interefts of Great Britain required: but leaving himfelf at full liberty to object to any fpecific meafures which fhould be moved by the minifters of the crown in purfuance of this addrefs, if they appeared to him, in any refpect, inconfiftent with the public welfare. He was fure that his majefty could mean nothing but what was for the advantage of the nation; and if the engagements in queftion proved otherwife, he fhould confider them as the engagements of the minifter, not of the king." Sir Jofeph Jekyl and feveral other refpectable and independent members declaring, that they regarded addreffes precifely in the fame light and agreeably to the explanation now given, the oppofition acquiefced, and the queftion paffed in the affirmative without a divifion. But it could not escape the penetration of the minister, how repugnant to the feelings of the house was the idea now suggested of carrying on an offensive war against the house of Austria, in concert with the two branches of the house of Bourbon. Ever since the conclusion of the treaty of Hanover, a very large body of auxiliaries had been kept, at an immense expence, in constant pay, from the incessant apprehension of a war. But when the estimate for the charge of maintaining 12,000 Hessians came before the house, it was objected against as entirely superfluous. It was said, that if fears and apprehensions would justify the waste of money thus lavished in subsidies, we should never be free from these burdens; that it was time enough to hire troops when we were actually involved in war; and there was no doubt, from the disposition of the European princes, that men might be always had for money. These objections, however, were over-ruled, and the troops continued in pay, under the idea that to dismiss them at the present crisis, though their actual services might not be called for, would tend to encourage the emperor in his contumacy.

Notwithstanding the recent convention of Seville, complaints were renewed from all parts of the depredations and cruelties committed by the Spaniards in the West Indies: and the house of commons, satisfied of the truth of these allegations, presented an address to the king, desiring " that his majesty would be graciously pleased to continue his endeavor to prevent such depredations for the future; to procure full satisfaction for the damages already sustained; and to secure to the British subjects the full and uninterrupted exercise of their trade and navigation, to and from the British colonies in America."

A very judicious bill was at this period introduced into parliament, and passed into a law, for preventing delays of justice occasioned by the use of the Latin tongue in proceedings at law, and enacting that all the processes and pleadings should be entered in the English language. There are not wanting, however, at all times many inveterate enemies of INNOVATION, "who cherish old prejudices because they are prejudices," and who have in all ages been found equally eager and obstinate in opposing the most salutary reforms; and it was urged by this class of men, on the present occasion, that this bill would render useless the antient records, which were written in that language—and, far from expediting, would introduce confusion and delay of justice, by altering the ESTABLISHED form and method of judicial proceedings. These reasonings, however, did not prevail; and this law remains an incontrovertible proof, that INNOVATION may *possibly* be the medium of improvement.

In the debate on the pension bill, now for the second time passed by the commons and rejected by the lords, Dr. Sherlock bishop of Bangor gave high offence, by declaring "that an independent house of commons, or an independent house of lords, is as inconsistent with our constitution as an independent, that is absolute, king; and that a lover of his country will no more desire to see the one than the other." This proposition, nevertheless, understood in a sober and qualified sense, cannot be justly controverted. For a parliament absolutely independent of the crown would in a short time infallibly reduce the crown to a state of absolute and abject dependence upon itself. And, unquestionably, it is not by the perpetual conflicts of authority, but by the reciprocal dependence of the different branches of government, that the balance of the constitution, and the harmony of its movements, are most advantageously and effectually preserved. And a total annihilation of that influence, the

prodigious

prodigious and dangerous preponderance of which this bill was wisely calculated to check, would be attended with a train of new and alarming political evils. Lord Carteret, who had now joined the oppofition, defended the principle and practical operation of this bill with great eloquence and energy. In confequence of the bifhop of Bangor's invidious oppofition to it, a motion was made for leave to bring a bill into the houfe of commons, to prevent the tranflation of bifhops; which, the utmoft influence of the court being exerted againft it, paffed, on a divifion, in the negative.

On the 7th of May, 1731 the feffion was terminated by a fpeech, in which his majefty informed the two houfes " that a treaty of peace had been figned at Vienna *, and the ratifications exchanged between him and the emperor. As this treaty, he faid, principally regarded the execution of the treaty of Seville, it was communicated to the courts of France and Spain, as parties to that treaty; and it was now under the confideration of the ftates-general, who had been invited to accede to it He added, that the new engagements entered into by him on this occafion were agreeable to the neceffary concern which this nation muft always have for the fecurity and prefervation of the balance of power in Europe: and he expreffed his affurance, that all malicious infinuations to the prejudice of his meafures muft vanifh, when it fo evidently appeared that his firft and principal care had been for the intereft and honor of this kingdom." By this treaty his imperial majefty agreed that Spain fhould take poffeffion of the duchies of Parma and Placentia for the infant Don Carlos, in the mode prefcribed by the treaty of Seville; and that the Oftend company, which had given fuch umbrage to the maritime powers, fhould

* March 16, 1731.

be totally diffolved, on condition that England and the other contracting powers of the treaty of Seville fhould become guarantees of the pragmatic fanction. And the duke of Parma dying at this juncture, an Englifh fleet under Sir Charles Wager was fitted out, which having joined the Spanifh fleet at Barcelona, convoyed the Spanifh troops deftined for Italy to Leghorn, Don Carlos himfelf taking the route of France; when, the imperial forces which had marched into Parma being withdrawn, the infant took peaceable poffeffion of his new territories.

Thus at length was terminated the violent and acrimonious conteft, which for more than feven years had divided the houfe of Auftria from Great Britain, its ancient and faithful ally. And nothing can be more clear and evident, from an impartial review and fummary of facts, than that the quarrel originated folely in the unfortunate connection formed by this nation, at the acceffion of the prefent royal family, with the electorate of Hanover, whofe interefts ftood almoft conftantly and diametrically oppofed to thofe of England. Jealous of the afpiring views of the houfe of Lunenburg in the empire, the emperor could never be brought cordially to concur in the meafures concerted for the fecurity of the new acquifitions of Bremen and Verden, and ftill lefs in the infidious defigns of the court of Herenhaufen upon the duchy of Mecklenburg; although, to merit the favor of the court of Vienna, the king of England fcrupled not to engage in a war with Spain, with whom Great Britain had then no imaginable pretence of difpute, and actually effected the transfer of the ifland of Sicily from the houfe of Savoy to the houfe of Auftria. Finding the emperor ftill cold and intractable, it was thought neceffary to enter into ftricter connections with France, who readily gave her countenance and fupport to the petty fchemes of electoral aggrandizement, fo long as the house of Austria was deprived, by this artful policy, of the strength she derived from the powerful alliance of Great Britain. By the treaty signed at Madrid, therefore, A. D. 1721, a SECRET DEFENSIVE ALLIANCE was, by a SEPARATE ARTICLE, concluded between England, France, and Spain, to which the Dutch were left at liberty to accede, and all the late acquisitions of Hanover secured by an EXPLICIT GUARANTEE: and, in return, Spain was artfully and insidiously flattered with the hope of the restitution of Gibraltar. After the conclusion of this treaty, the court of London was very little solicitous to obtain for the emperor advantageous or satisfactory terms of pacification with Spain; and the congress of Cambray, which was convened under the pretended mediation of England and France, after a long and tedious negociation, broke up *re infecta*. But the court of Spain in process of time, finding her expectation of recovering Gibraltar wholly delusive, and enraged at the affront offered to the infanta by France, became anxious to establish a real and permanent amity with the emperor —not, however, without inviting the king of England to become the sole arbitrator of their differences. Though nothing, certainly, could be more favorable to the interests of Great Britain, than this happy occasion of detaching Spain for ever from her connection with France; it was rejected, from the apprehension of giving umbrage to that power, upon whom Hanover at this period relied for the support of her new acquisitions and farther schemes of aggrandizement. A treaty of peace and alliance, nevertheless, between Spain and the emperor being quickly signed at Vienna, without the intervention of any foreign power, the memorable treaty of Hanover was concluded between England and France, to which all the powers of Europe under their influence were urged to accede. In order to give a plausible color to this treaty,

treaty, so contrary to the interests of Great Britain, much was said on the necessity of reducing the exorbitant power of the house of Austria, which England had lately been at such an immense expence of blood and treasure to establish. And a violent and absurd clamor was raised against the imperial East-India company of Ostend, as creating a rivalship fatal to the commercial interests of Great Britain. But the real object of the treaty of Hanover, on the part of the king of England, was evidently no other than to counterbalance the designs of the two imperial courts, now in strict alliance with Spain, for the restoration of Slesvvic, Bremen, and Verden, the evacuation of Mecklenburg, and the final annihilation of the ambitious projects of Hanover. The views by which France was actuated were, however, of a far more elevated and comprehensive nature. For the great object of the policy of the court of Vienna, at this period, being to secure to the eldest daughter of the emperor the undivided succession of the house of Austria, France could discover no other method so certain to defeat that design, and to lay the foundation of the ruin of that house, and its own consequent unrivalled pre-eminence, by the dismemberment of its vast possessions, whenever the dissolution of the emperor, now in the decline of life, should take place, than to detach Great Britain entirely from its ancient and natural ally. The treaties of Vienna and Hanover, A. D. 1725, in which almost all the powers of Europe were parties, had nearly given rise to a general war; which, however, was with much difficulty averted by the preliminaries signed at Aix-la-Chapelle A. D. 1727. At the ensuing conferences for a final pacification at Soissons, France having found means to effect a reconciliation with Spain, the court of Vienna, which still espoused the interests of the dukes of Holstein and Mecklenburg, found itself greatly overbalanced and almost deserted. The imperial minister's demand of the guarantee of the pragmatic sanction was treated with neglect and contempt; and the English ministers, *after having conferred with those of France*, answered, that the pragmatic sanction was not the point in question; that, not being the object of the present disputes, it ought not to be a subject of the present negotiations, and that the proposition was not *traitable*. The plenipotentiaries of Holland, however, who were not under the same artificial and extrinsic bias, refused to join in this answer—declaring, on the contrary, that they thought it a point which might hereafter so highly affect the tranquillity of Europe, that it deserved consideration at least, and an inquiry what the emperor would do in exchange for it. Thus the congress of Soissons broke up, like the former congress of Cambray, to the mutual satisfaction of France and Hanover, leaving the security of the Austrian succession to the decision of chance and fortune. It was now the policy of France to accommodate the differences subsisting between the courts of Madrid and London, and to unite them both in a firm opposition to the emperor. For this purpose the treaty of Seville was concluded, under the mediation of France, and mortal offence given to the emperor, by the stipulated introduction of Spanish troops into the duchies of Parma and Placentia, previous to the granting the imperial investiture. Upon such high ground did the court of London, or rather of Herenhausen, now conceive itself to stand, that it presumed to insult the emperor by an offer, made (1730), in conjunction with her high allies, France and Spain, to guarantee the succession of the Austrian dominions—*in* ITALY *only*—to the arch-duchess Maria Theresa, eldest daughter of the emperor, on the condition that the affairs of SLESWIC and MECKLENBURG were regulated to their joint satisfaction. This proposition, however, was rejected

jected with difdain; and his imperial majesty appearing determined to rifque a war with the houfe of Bourbon, —a war in which England had with the groffeft and moft culpable inattention to her interefts and even to her fafety, and the extreme hazard of entirely fubverting the balance of power in Europe, involved herfelf as a principal,—the minifters of the crown, who had ventured to the edge of the precipice, as the crifis approached, recoiled at the view of the gulph into which they were about to plunge. Apparently alarmed at the rafhnefs and abfurdity of their own projects, they fuddenly refolved to fet on foot a negotiation at Vienna; as the bafis of which, an offer was made of the guarantee of the pragmatic fanction, including the whole Auftrian fucceffion, by Great Britain. This the emperor readily and gladly embraced. In return, the inveftitures of Bremen and Verden were conceded; Hanover was to receive a ftipulated fum in lieu of all its claims upon Mecklenburg; and, " *to preferve the peace of* LOWER SAXONY, *and to put an end to the* CAUSE *of troubles in the* NORTH," the emperor and Ruffia guaranteed SLESWIC to the king of Denmark, upon condition that one million of rix-dollars were paid to the duke of Holftein as an *equivalent*—500,000 down, and 100,000 per ann. till the whole was completed *. And however re-

---

* It is a curious circumftance, that Denmark declared itfelf under no obligation to make good this equivalent—having been long in actual poffeffion of Slefwic under the guarantee of Hanover. And though his Danifh majefty afterwards confented to the payment of this fum, it will be found, conformably to the accounts delivered in to parliament, Feb. 10 and 12, 1735, that the fums paid, or to be paid, on different pretences to Denmark within a certain fpecified time, amount to the complete fum of *one million of rix-dollars* : fo that there exifts a ftrong prefumption that the duchy of Slefwic, thus bought and fold by contract of two foreign potentates, was at laft paid for out of the pockets of the fimple and unfufpecting people of Great Britain.

luctant

luctant the duke of Holstein might be to part with Slefwic upon such terms, he was compelled to accept of this pretended equivalent, or seek elsewhere for protectors. The treaty of Vienna being concluded without the participation of France, in direct contravention of an article of the treaty of Hanover, all real amity between the two courts of London and Versailles was now at an end; and a cold exterior civility succeeded to that confidence which had subsisted without interruption for the space of fifteen years. The treaty of Hanover was considered on both sides as virtually renounced by the late treaty of Vienna, to which the states-general soon acceded, and which seemed to establish, by the guarantee of the maritime powers, the pragmatic sanction, so much the object of Gallic jealousy and aversion, on a firm and solid basis. The politics of Europe now reverted to their antient and regular order. But it is obvious that England and Holland had undertaken this guarantee, at a period far less favorable than that which had occurred at the former treaty of Vienna, six years before; and that through a preposterous predilection and attachment to the views and interests of Hanover, a most propitious opportunity of dissolving for ever the political connection of Spain and France was irretrieveably lost; and that by the re-union of those powers, France was encouraged to persist in prosecuting those schemes of ambition which she had long cherished for the future humiliation of the house of Austria, and which, in the sequel, England thought it necessary to employ such mighty efforts to oppose and defeat. "Truth," says a noble cotemporary writer, "should be made known; and it should be known to those whom it most imports to know it—those are the best friends to the king and kingdom, who, by shewing how incompatible the interests of the electorate are with those of Great Britain, may suggest the prudent and necessary

cessary measure of separating the dominions themselves, and supplying that great defect in the act of settlement, which every body now wishes had been done, and wonders was not *

On the regular return of the session, Jan. 1732, the king made an elaborate speech to both houses, containing a very high eulogium upon his own conduct. He congratulated the parliament " on the restoration of the general tranquillity; and he affirmed, that the part taken in the late transactions by the crown of Great Britain had redounded much to *the honor and interest* of the nation. By the treaty of Seville, he said, that union of the imperial and Catholic crowns, which had given such universal alarm, had been dissolved; and the execution of that treaty, supposed to be attended with insurmountable difficulties, was at length happily accomplished. Parma and Placentia were in the actual possession of Don Carlos, and the reversion of Tuscany secured by an express convention with the great duke. Parliament had seen, he said, the happy effects of their zeal and resolution—and now reaped the fruits of the confidence which they had reposed in him; and it must be a great satisfaction to them to reflect that the expence incurred had been so amply recompensed." It is observable, that in the whole series of royal speeches and messages in this and

---

* Vide a series of tracts styled, " Case of the Hanover Forces," with a first and second " vindication" of the same, ascribed to the earl of Chesterfield. The first of these tracts was answered by Mr. Horace Walpole, afterwards lord Walpole, brother to the minister, in a publication styled, " The Interests of Great Britain steadily pursued." Lord Chesterfield, in his vindication, shrewdly remarks, " that the three years in which the writer of the pamphlet declared himself so violently against Hanover-projects, ought at least to be excepted out of the British scheme of politics, which he undertakes to demonstrate hath been so *steadily pursued.*"

the

the preceding reign, not a syllable is mentioned of Bremen, Sleswic, or Mecklenburg, the secret springs of every resolution taken by the English court respecting the affairs of the continent for almost twenty years past. And with a firm reliance on the complaisance of the parliament, and the ignorance of the people, a bold —for a harsher epithet would be indecorous—a bold attempt was now made to establish the idea that the quarrel between Great Britain and the emperor respected solely the investiture of the duchies of Tuscany, Parma, and Placentia:—although, had this indeed been the fact, scarcely would it have amounted to an extenuation of the folly: For to whom these duchies should belong, was an object wholly beneath the attention of Great Britain: and admitting the necessity of preserving the equipoise of power, they could be considered as little more than dust in the balance. If king WILLIAM has incurred just censure for involving this nation too deeply in continental politics—if the blood and treasure of Great Britain were in his reign lavished with a too unsparing hand—at least it must be acknowledged, that the ends he had in view were in the highest degree noble, just, and disinterested. The *grand alliance* was not projected by that renowned monarch, in order to procure the cession of a district, to be added to his principality of Orange; but for the glorious purpose of asserting the liberty and independency of Christendom, in opposition to the aspiring aims of an haughty tyrant; and of fixing an insurmountable barrier to the farther progress of his triumphs. Absorbed in the contemplation of this great object, his ideas rose infinitely above all those miserable artifices of petty aggrandizement, which had, for so many years previous to this period, perplexed the counsels, and interrupted the repose of nations. When an

address

K. GEORGE II.

address was moved by lord Hervey*, in the usual style of courtly adulation and submission, the indignation of the patriots seemed uncommonly excited; and the incoherency and absurdity of the whole political system of the court were ably and vigorously exposed. Sir William Lawson, who first rose, observed, "that the treaties, respecting which so much had been said, were not yet before the house; therefore he was not prepared to join in the approval of them. It appeared, however, sufficiently plain, that, notwithstanding the great things we had done for Spain, very little satisfaction had as yet been received for the injuries done to us. He knew of nothing, a vague order of his Catholic majesty to the governors of his ports in the West Indies against illegal depredations excepted, upon which any construction they thought proper might be put; but this surely could not be considered as a sufficient reparation of past injuries." Mr. Shippen "confessed himself so unfashionable, that he neither pretended to judge without information, or to applaud without reason. The servile and flattering addresses now in vogue, he said, were unknown in former times;—in opposing them, he shewed his regard for the

---

* This nobleman long occupied a place in the foremost rank of courtiers, and was a frequent speaker in parliament, though with little historic notice. His endowments appear to have been very superficial, and his manners effeminately frivolous; though, by a duel with Mr. Pulteney, he sufficiently established his character for personal courage. Lord Hervey's quarrel with POPE is well known. The portrait drawn by that vindictive satirist of this nobleman under the name of Sporus, is replete with malignity and distortion; though, had it been perfectly just, the poet stands deservedly condemned by his own previous acknowledgment:

> Satire or sense, alas! can Sporus feel?
> Who breaks a butterfly upon *the* wheel?

honor

honor and dignity of that houfe; and for his reputation as a courtier, he felt little concern. He moved, therefore, to leave out the complimentary paragraphs, and to reftrain the addrefs to a general expreffion of thanks to his majefty, and of fatisfaction at the eftablifhment of general tranquillity. But the moft interefting and eloquent fpeech on this occafion was made by Mr. Pulteney, who declared, that if we were now right, he was certain that the time had long ago elapfed, when we might have been *as right*, with infinitely lefs expence and trouble. But at the period to which he alluded, the guarantee of the pragmatic fanction was reprefented as inconfiftent with the intereft and happinefs of the nation, by the very perfons who now plume themfelves, and demand the applaufe of the houfe for affenting to it. For his part, he faid, he neither confidered the pragmatic fanction in fo formidable, or in fo favorable a light, as the prefent minifters had, at different times, done. Admitting it to be agreeable to the general interefts of England, that the Auftrian fucceffion fhould be tranfmitted whole and undivided, he greatly doubted the policy of our obliging ourfelves, by an explicit and pofitive guarantee, to maintain this fucceffion at a future and indeterminate period, when England might, for reafons impoffible to forefee, find it very incompatible with her intereft to engage in a foreign war upon any account: and no alternative would be then left us, but to violate our faith, or to rifque our fafety. To violate the national faith, indeed, he obferved, was no new thing with the prefent minifters; for the treaty of Vienna itfelf was concluded in violation of the treaty of Hanover, to the conditions of which, though Pruffia had withdrawn herfelf, France and Holland had ftrictly adhered. He could not, therefore, allow, that in the late tranfactions either the *intereft* or the *honor* of the nation had been confulted.

With

With regard to the forcible introduction of Don Carlos into Italy, that prince, whose name had, for several years past, been converted to such commodious uses, and who, according to a ludicrous observation in the course of this debate, was either a *giant* or an *infant* as it suited the purpose of the court—Mr. Pulteney declared that he thought it very likely to prove the origin of fresh troubles. But if, upon the whole, our affairs abroad were now wisely adjusted, and our domestic grievances were to be, at the same time, completely redressed, the minister at the helm of government might be compared to a pilot who, though there was a clear, safe, and straight channel into harbor, took it into his head to navigate the ship through rocks, sands, and shallows, and after much danger and much damage, at last, by chance, gains the port, and triumphs in his good conduct." In reply to Mr. Pulteney, Mr. Horace Walpole, upon whom the minister willingly devolved the task of defending his system of foreign politics, undertook to demonstrate " the wisdom and rectitude of those measures of administration, so contemptuously derided and so injuriously arraigned. He wished, he said, to be informed to what period of time the observations of the last speaker were intended to refer. He knew that the guarantee of the pragmatic sanction had been proposed to us some years ago; but then it was in a style so dogmatic, that it was inconsistent with the honor of his majesty and of the nation to pay the slightest attention to it. Besides, there was just reason to fear that Don Carlos was the person fixed upon by his imperial majesty as his successor; and it was manifestly against the interests of Great Britain to contribute to the establishment of a Prince in the entire possession of the Austrian succession, who held in his own right dominions so considerable in Italy, and who was so nearly related to the crowns both of Spain and France.

France. This guarantee was again offered when the treaty of Seville was in agitation; but it was again rejected, because it was well known to be intended only to *disturb the negotiation*. But as soon as the treaty of Seville was concluded, and the emperor became reasonable in his proposals, we embraced the opportunity, and joined without reserve in the guarantee. As to any inconvenience which might arise from a supposed eventual inability to maintain our engagements, he would take upon him to assert, that were the imperial house in danger of subversion, we *must* engage in their rescue, let our circumstances be at the time what they will; for our own ruin was closely and inevitably connected with theirs. This guarantee he affirmed it would have been highly desirable to have entered into sooner, on account of the fatal consequences which might have ensued in case of the demise of the emperor. But it was impossible to agree to it, till his imperial majesty had given satisfaction to Spain respecting the Italian Duchies, and to England and Holland in regard to the Ostend company, which his majesty, by the wisdom, vigor, and *steadiness* of his measures, had at last procured. He begged leave to repeat the expression, the *steadiness* of his majesty's measures; for, he said, though the means were various, the objects of those measures were uniform— the preservation of the balance of power, and the assertion of our commercial rights. We had engaged by the quadruple alliance to see the infant Don Carlos settled in the succession of the Italian Duchies; and Spain *could not be easy* till this was effectuated, nor could we or our allies, the Dutch, *be easy*, till we saw the Ostend company absolutely demolished. As soon as these two grand points were conceded by the imperial court, we began to think seriously of establishing the future tranquillity of Europe, and the balance of power, on a solid foundation;

tion; for which purpose we had at length agreed to the formal guarantee of the pragmatic sanction. How then could it be affirmed that the honor and interest of the nation had not been consulted in our foreign negotiations, or that our engagements had not been fulfilled? France had no reason to be dissatisfied, having declared that her sole object was the preservation of the general tranquillity, agreeably to the terms of the quadruple alliance, which was accomplished by the treaty of Vienna: and the fact was, that the court of Versailles had declared itself satisfied*. As to the commercial differences between England and Spain, they were referred to the decision of commissaries, who, there was every reason to believe, would settle all points in dispute in an amicable manner." This speech was no less favorably received by the majority of the house, than the harangue formerly made by this minister in the vindication of the treaty of Hanover; and the address, as originally moved, was presented to his Majesty, who declared in reply, " that he had no doubt of the continuance of the affection and confidence of the house, and that they should ever find his views tending to the honor, interest, and security, of his crown and people."

The nation being at length allowed, and asserted on the highest authority, to be in a state of actual and perfect security, a grand effort was thought advisable by the patriots in opposition, or the *Country-party*, as they were

---

* Upon the same principle, doubtless, on which SHYLOCK, after " recording a gift of all his wealth," declares, in answer to the question, " Art thou contented, Jew?"—" I am content;" though a catastrophe not very pleasing certainly in itself, and little to be expected from the tenor of the existing BOND.

now generally styled, to effect a reduction of the standing army. This rooted and habitual grievance the courtiers endeavored to disguise and soften, by bestowing upon it the appellation of a *parliamentary army*, as voted and maintained by parliamentary authority. They pleaded, that this force was necessary to secure the interior tranquillity of the kingdom, and to overawe malcontents, though too inconsiderable to excite the jealousy of the people even under an ambitious monarch, and much less under a prince who could not be accused, or even suspected, of entertaining the remotest wish of infringing upon the liberties of his subjects. In favor of the reduction it was argued, " that a standing military force in time of peace had, previous to the æra of the Revolution, always been accounted not only superfluous, but unconstitutional and dangerous; that the internal tranquillity of the country might be secured, as heretofore it had been, by the civil power aided by the militia, which, under proper regulation, was as capable of discipline, and as active in exertion, as a standing army; that the number of malcontents was altogether contemptible; but that the most effectual means of increasing it was the obstinate perseverance in measures odious and arbitrary; that though they had all imaginable confidence in his majesty's regard for the liberty of his subjects, should a standing army be ingrafted into the constitution, another prince might arise of more dangerous talents and of deeper designs, and employ it for the worst purposes of ambition: that other nations had been enslaved by standing armies; and though the officers were at present men of honor and probity, these might be easily discarded, and the army new-modelled, in order to effect the subversion of the constitution. The expence of this great military force was also insisted upon on as extremely burdensome and oppressive to the nation; and it was asserted, that the money raised for the subsistence of 18 or 20,000 men in England would maintain 60,000 French or Germans. Previous to the Revolution it was well known that the people of England did not raise above two millions for the whole of the public charge; but now the current expence far exceeded that sum, and the civil list, the interest due to the public creditors, and the sinking fund, added together, composed a burden of six millions yearly; and though at so recent a period as the accession of the late king, the army did not exceed 6000 men, it was now augmented, on various pretences, to more than three times that number. And farther pretences would never be wanting, were parliament willing to listen to them for farther augmentations." These arguments, however, proved wholly fruitless and unavailing *, and in proportion to the frequency of their repetition, the impression seems to have been impaired and weakened; for it is unhappily, though unquestionably, certain, that, for almost a century past, the *standing army* has been *a progressive army*, and that every effort for its reduction has terminated in its increase and enlargement. Such was the offence given by Mr. Pulteney to the court by the zealous part he took in this and other political questions at this period, that the king, calling for the council-book, with his own hand struck out his name from the list of privy counsellors, which, however, on-

---

* The numbers on the division were 241 against 171 voices. Lord Hervey urging the multiplicity of seditious writings, as an argument against any reduction of the military force; Mr. Plumer replied, "that if *scribblers* gave the government uneasiness, they ought to employ *scribblers*, and not soldiers, to defend them from the danger."

ly ferved to extend his fame, and eftablifh his popularity.

Notwithftanding the indifcriminate fupport given by Sir Robert Walpole, after the example of his predeceffors, to the long-eftablifhed royal fyftem of continental politics, and without which he well knew the impoffibility of maintaining poffeffion, even for a day, of his high and precarious office, it ought not to be fuppofed that this minifter was abfolutely indifferent to the intereft and welfare of the kingdom over whofe councils he prefided. This it would be flagrant injuftice to affirm. His fituation was, in many refpects, critical and hazardous; and if juft allowance be made for the difficulties and embarraffments which he perpetually experienced from the prevalence of Hanoverian prejudices on the one fide, and Jacobite prejudices on the other, it will not perhaps be too much to affert, that a man, upon the whole, better adapted to the ftation which he occupied, or better qualified to difcharge the various and complicated duties of it, could no-where be found. To change the minifter would have availed nothing without a radical change of fyftem; and fo long as the nation at large fhall continue to approve, or acquiefce in, this corrupt and defective fyftem, where is the minifter to be found, who fhall with fincerity and earneftnefs labor to accomplifh any comprehenfive plan of political reform? Or, indeed, what right have we to expect from any man fuch an heroic and, at the fame time, ufelefs effort of virtue? The celebrated ftatefman whofe character and conduct we have now been contemplating—and whofe actions have been brought to the teft of that fiery ordeal of relentlefs truth and juftice which human frailty is fo incompetent to abide, and over whofe burning ploughfhares no man ever yet with impunity paffed—was poffeffed, fessed, nevertheless, of talents admirably calculated for public life. An understanding clear, masculine, and vigorous, was in him combined with a temper mild, equable, and dispassionate. And by the most perfect accuracy and regularity of method, the toils of government were rendered apparently easy and pleasant. He was fully sensible of the folly of that warlike spirit which had predominated in the British councils since the æra of the Revolution. The favorite object of his administration was to preserve and maintain the general tranquillity; and the treaty of Vienna, recently concluded at a moment so critical, strongly indicated his extreme solicitude for the continuance of peace. He conceived the prosperity of the nation to be most effectually advanced by the encouragement of manufactures and commerce, the true principles of which he perfectly comprehended and steadily pursued. His return to office had been distinguished by a most beneficial alteration of the commercial system of Great Britain, in the abrogation of a multiplicity of duties payable on the importation of raw materials, and the exportation of wrought goods. And it has been affirmed, that he found the English book of rates almost the worst, and left it the very best, in Europe. At this period he had formed a project, to which he appears to have been incited by the clearest conviction of its utility, for effecting a radical alteration in the national system of taxation. The principal branches of the revenue might at this time be divided into port-duties or customs—duties of excise—and taxes levied on immoveable property, such as the duties on land, houses, hearths, and windows. This latter description of duties the minister considered as of a nature highly oppressive, partial, and inequitable. And the various taxes on consumable commodities, to which every citizen contributes in an exact proportion to his confumption; and which, being included in the price of the commodity, are eafily and infenfibly paid; conftituted, in his opinion, incomparably the moft eligible mode of raifing the fupplies neceffary for the public fervice. He alfo well knew the grofs and fhamelefs frauds daily practifed in the collection of the cuftoms; and which, from the very nature of thofe frauds, and the extreme facility of committing them, he had no hope to remedy. He thought, therefore, that to convert the greater part of the cuftoms into duties of excife, would be equally advantageous to Government, and to the fair trader; and that the laws of excife might be fo ameliorated, that, notwithftanding the odium generally attached to them as oppreffive and arbitrary, no juft or real ground of complaint fhould remain. With a view, therefore, to an effential change in the firft fpecies of taxation, and to the eventual annihilation of the laft, he brought into the houfe, in the month of February 1732, a bill for the revival of the falt duties, which had been repealed fome years back, as a fubftitute for one fhilling in the pound of the land-tax—and if this propofal met the approbation of the houfe, he fignified his intention—the land-tax being at this time two fhillings only in the pound—altogether to abolifh that tax in the courfe of the enfuing feffion; in which he declared he fhould rejoice, as the annihilation of a moft grievous and intolerable burden. " The duty on falt, he faid, affected, it was true, all claffes of citizens, the poor as well as the rich; but the burden of this tax being fo equally and generally diffufed, the fum contributed by the lower claffes of the people would be found, on computation, fo trifling, as fcarcely to deferve the mention. This tax, while it exifted, was never the fubject of complaint; and when it was repealed, no one feemed to think himfelf benefited. He

knew,

knew, he said, the reproaches he had to expect on this
occasion; but he had been long accustomed to be affronted and insulted, both within the walls of that place,
and without: and while he knew his intentions to be
upright, and his only aim to serve his country to the
best of his knowledge, and the utmost of his power,
he should continue to disregard those reflections which he
was conscious he did not deserve." After very vehement
and obstinate debates, in which the minister was repeatedly charged with deep and malignant designs against
the liberties of his country, and the welfare and happiness of his fellow-citizens, which no one perhaps seriously suspected him to harbor, the bill passed by a majority of 207 voices against 135. And it must be acknowledged, that the opposition against the measures of
Sir Robert Walpole's administration was so invariable,
and at times so intemperate, that the bounds of patriotism and faction seem to have been divided by a very
slender partition. In the course of the present session,
the pension bill was a third time passed by the commons, and rejected by the lords. And on the 1st of
June 1732, the king terminated the session with a
speech, in which he informed the parliament of the formal
accession of the states general to the treaty of Vienna;
and declared his intention of visiting his electoral dominions, and of leaving the queen, as before, sole regent
during his absence. On his arrival in Germany, he had
the satisfaction at length to receive the investitures of
the Duchies of Bremen and Verden, so long solicited,
and so long delayed by the policy, pride, or resentment
of the emperor.

During this summer, Victor Amadeus, the abdicated
monarch of Sardinia, was discovered to be deeply engaged, at the instigation of his wife, the Marchioness

of St. Sebastian, in intrigues for the resumption of the crown.—upon which, his person was seized by order of his son, the reigning king, and conveyed to Rivoli; and the Marchioness committed close prisoner to the castle of Seva. And the world had a new proof, little wanted indeed, how weak are the ties of gratitude and affection, when placed in competition with the suggestions of ambition and interest.

At this period, a royal charter was granted for the settlement of a new colony to the southward of the Carolinas, to which the name of Georgia was given: and general Oglethrope, a man distinguished for the activity and ardor of his benevolence, was appointed Governor *, and embarked at Greenwich with a number of families, who founded a town called Savannah on the river of that name. This enterprise excited the jealousy and apprehension of the Spaniards; and as it was difficult, or rather impossible, to ascertain the precise limits of the English colony of Georgia and the Spanish settlement of Florida, a foundation of future dispute and contention between the two nations was unavoidably laid. Previous to the final decision of Government respecting this measure, seven chiefs of the Cherokee and other southern Indian tribes were conveyed to England; and being introduced to the king, surrendered, by a formal deed, in the name of their countrymen, all right of property and dominion in the lands now about to be occupied by the new colonists. And in amazement at the riches and magnificence of the British court, they are said to have laid their crowns and ensigns of dignity

---

* " One—driven by strong benevolence of soul—
Shall fly like OGLETHORPE, from pole to pole."   POPE.

at the king's feet, requesting to be received in the number of his subjects.

Parliament being convened as usual, early in the year 1733, a motion was framed and approved for an address to the king, to know what satisfaction had been made by Spain for the depredations committed on the British merchants—to which the king replied, " that the meetings of the commissaries of the two crowns had been delayed by unforeseen accidents, and that a perfect account of their proceedings could not as yet be laid before the house of commons." On the motion relative to the army estimates in the committee of supply, which differed not materially from those of the last year, a violent debate arose; and the arguments formerly urged were again repeated and anew enforced. Mr. Horace Walpole, in reply, hesitated not to assert, " that the number of troops then proposed was absolutely necessary to support his majesty's government, and would be necessary so long as the nation enjoyed the happiness of having the present illustrious family on the throne." Mr. Shippen remarked upon this assertion, " that the question seemed at length to have taken a new turn—for, in former debates, the continuance of the army *for one year only* had been contended for; but now the mask was thrown off, and the house was given to understand that it was intended to be PERPETUAL. This he would not believe could come from his majesty. His majesty KNEW how much the nation was loaded with debts and taxes—and how *inconsistent it was with our constitution to keep up a standing army in time of peace.*" Mr. Shippen, being called vehemently to order for these last words, declared himself " peculiarly unfortunate; for that, in a former parliament, he had incurred the severe displeasure and censure of that house, for asserting
that

that the late monarch *was unacquainted* with the conftitution; and he now gave high offence, by declaring that his prefent majefty *was not unacquainted* with the conftitution." On a divifion, the motion was carried by 239 votes againft 171.

In deliberating upon the fupplies to be granted for the enfuing year, Sir Robert Walpole moved that the fum of 500,000l. fhould be iffued out of the finking fund for the current fervices. This was the firft open and direct attack upon the finking fund *; and it produced a moft animated and indignant remonftrance from the patriotic party, who warned the minifter, though in vain, that he was drawing down the curfes of pofterity upon his head—and expatiated upon the iniquity of pillaging, in a time of profound peace, this facred depofit, and demonftrated the folly of facrificing the ineftimable advantages arifing from the undifturbed and progreffive operation of this fund, to a little temporary eafe; and conjured him not to demolifh with his own hand the faireft monument of his fame. Sir William Wyndham acknowledged, " that he had never been without apprehenfion that violence might be offered to this fund, by an enterprifing minifter, in cafe of exigency and in a time of war: but to fee attempts made upon it in a feafon of perfect tranquillity, was what he never expected. Is the public expenditure, exclaimed this patriotic fpeaker, never to be leffened? Are the people of England always to groan under the fame heavy and grievous taxes? Surely, if there is

---

* Between the years 1727 and 1732, various new loans were made, the interefts of which were charged upon different furpluffes, appertaining, conformably to the original plan of redemption, to the finking fund.

any

any intention of diminishing the present enormous debt of the nation, now is the time for doing it. What can be said in vindication of those who are thus loading posterity? Can they imagine that there will ever be less occasion for public expence—or can they imagine that our descendants will possess greater ability for discharging these incumbrances than ourselves? Surely not—unless far other and wiser measures of government should be adopted, than any which have yet originated from the present ministers." No impression, however, could be made upon the predetermined purpose of the minister; and the measure received without difficulty the sanction of the house of commons: and though in the house of lords it was again attacked, with the united powers of argument, wit, and eloquence, by the lords Bathurst, Chesterfield, and Carteret, it finally received the royal assent.

The compliant disposition of parliament now encouraged the minister to bring forward, in pursuance of the grand plan of revenue reform before mentioned, his famous bill for subjecting the duties on wine and tobacco to the laws of excise. But probably to the surprise, certainly to the chagrin, of the minister, on moving his primary resolution, " that the duties on tobacco do from the 24th of June 1733 cease and determine," no less than 205 members divided against it—the majority, in a house of 471 members, being only 61.

No man, perhaps, at this time, stood higher in public or parliamentary estimation than Sir Paul Methuen. His long experience, his extensive political and commercial knowledge, the high offices he had successively occupied, the respectability of his private with the moderation and equanimity of his public character, and the
dignified

dignified candor with which he always oppofed, when he deemed it neceffary to oppofe, the meafures of adminiftration, though long removed from power by the fuperior afcendancy of WALPOLE, all combined to give the decided part which he took on this occafion, as an opponent of the bill, the greateft weight; and his opinion was fuppofed materially to have influenced very many of the moft refpectable members who voted in this formidable minority.

A prodigious clamor, inftigated, without doubt, in a great degree by thofe perfons whofe fraudulent practices this plan was intended to counteract, was artfully and induftrioufly raifed againft the bill, which was indeed deemed dangeroufly inimical to the conftitution, by many very intelligent and impartial perfons, to whofe judgment much deference is due; though it has in our own times been carried fubftantially into effect without caufing any public alarm, or even exciting any very uncommon fhare of attention—juftifying in its operation the ideas and expectations of the minifters with whom it originated. On this occafion, however, the oppofition againft the bill might with propriety be ftyled national; and Sir Robert Walpole perfifting to urge this favorite project with a very improper, and with him a very unufual degree of heat and paffion—applying the contumelious expreffion of " fturdy beggars" to the merchants who attended in the lobby of the houfe of commons with petitions againft the bill, the public difcontent was heightened into rage. The avenues to Weftminfter Hall were occupied by immenfe crowds of people; and the perfons of thofe members who voted in favor of the bill were grofsly infulted, and even their lives endangered. At length Sir Robert Walpole thought proper to move that the fecond reading of the bill might be poftponed to a diftant day. The defeat of

the

the scheme was celebrated with general rejoicings; and the minister was burned in effigy and loaded with execrations, though his conduct appears no otherwise censurable in this business, than as it exhibits some symptoms of pride and obstinacy. It is related, nevertheless, to his praise, that, on the evening previous to the report, a meeting was convened by the minister, of the members who had supported this obnoxious measure. Their unanimous opinion was, to persevere: but Sir Robert Walpole declared, "that in the present inflamed temper of the people, the act could not be carried into execution without an armed force, and he would not be the minister to enforce any system of taxation at the expence of blood; for, if supplies were to be raised by the sword, there is an end of British liberty. He was therefore resolved to adjourn the report for six months; or, should his opinion be over-ruled, to make an immediate resignation of his office." The unfortunate pension bill, passed for the fourth time, in four successive years, by the house of commons, was for the fourth time thrown out by the house of peers; although, as a measure which solely regarded the purity and integrity of the national representation, these repeated rejections appeared particularly harsh and invidious on the part of the lords. On the 11th of June 1733, the king closed the session with a speech, in which severe notice was taken of " the wicked endeavors that had been lately used to inflame the minds of the people, by the most unjust representations."

EUROPE was now destined to be involved in fresh troubles. These were occasioned by the death of Augustus, king of Poland and elector of Saxony, January 1733. The candidates for the vacant crown were, Augustus son to the late king, and Stanislaus, whom Charles XII. in the zenith of his prosperity had elevated to the throne, and which on the decline of that monarch's fortune he
had

had been compelled to relinquish. Louis XV. king of France, having married the daughter of Staniflaus, supported the pretenfions of this prince with all his power; and the Polifh primate, and a majority of the diet, being gained over by the intrigues of the French ambaffador, proceeded to the election, and Staniflaus was unanimoufly chofen king at Warfaw, and proclaimed with loud acclamations. The imperial courts of Vienna and Peterfburg, however, between whom it is remarkable that a ftrict and almoft uninterrupted harmony had fubfifted, from the period that Ruffia affumed her proper rank as a European power, efpoufed with warmth the interefts of the houfe of Saxony: and protefting by their refpective minifters againft the election of Staniflaus as null and void, an army of Auftrians was affembled on the frontiers of Silefia; and 50,000 Ruffians under general Lafci actually entered Poland, on the fide of Lithuania. Being quickly joined by a body of Saxons and Poles of the electoral party, the elector of Saxony was proclaimed king of Poland by the bifhop of Cracow. King Staniflaus, finding himfelf wholly unable to refift fo great a force, abandoned Warfaw to his rival, and retired to Dantzic, where he was purfued and clofely befieged by the Ruffians and Saxons. This prince, however, found means to efcape, previous to the furrender of the city, which was followed by a general fubmiffion to the authority of Auguftus, and a general amnefty was in return granted to the partifans of Staniflaus. Though the court of Verfailles failed in their grand object in Poland, in order to be fully avenged upon the emperor, who had been the principal obftacle to its accomplifhment, and whofe dominions lay much more open to attack than Ruffia, the duke of Berwick received orders to pafs the Rhine at the head of a numerous army in October, and Fort Kehl was in a fhort time compelled to capitulate. The winter months having paffed passed over, he renewed his operations with great vigor. After the reduction of Traerbach, the duke invested the important town of Philipsburg; and visiting the trenches was killed on the 12th June * by a cannon-ball, leaving behind him an high reputation for valor and military skill. The French general had been opposed, during the whole of this campaign, by the celebrated prince Eugene, now far advanced into the vale of years, in a state of languishment and infirmity, and retaining little resemblance of the hero of Blenheim and Belgrade. Notwithstanding the loss sustained by the French in the death of their commander, Philipsburg was obliged, after a brave defence, to surrender, though upon the most honorable terms. During these transactions the French king had concluded a treaty with Spain and Sardinia, in conformity to which, those powers declared war against the emperor. And the marechal duc de Villars, the antient rival of Marlborough and Eugene, was prevailed upon to take the command of the French army in Italy †; which, being joined by the forces of Savoy, expelled the imperialists from the Milanese. He survived, however, but a short time the fatigues of the campaign, in which he fully sustained the glory of his name and nation, dying at Turin early in the ensuing spring, at the age of

* 1734.

† M. Voltaire tells us, that the Marechal de Villars, on being solicited to resume his military honors, and to place himself at the head of the army destined for Italy, repeated with energy and enthusiasm the following lines, from Racine's tragedy of Bajazet:

> Quoi! tu crois, cher Osmin, que ma gloire passée
> Flatte encore leur valeur & vit dans leur pensée!
> Tu crois qui'ils me suivroient encore avec plaisir,
> Et qu'ils reconnoîtroient la voix de leur Visir?

eighty.

eighty. After the death of this great man, the command devolved upon the marechal de Coigné; between whom and the imperial generals, the count de Merci and marechal Konigseg, various fierce and bloody, but indecisive encounters took place, into the particular narration of which it is not necessary to enter. Whilst the Austrians were thus driven from the Milanese, and with difficulty maintained their ground in the Mantuan, the Neapolitan nobility, irritated and oppressed under the government of the count de Visconti, the imperial Viceroy, joined in an invitation to Don Carlos, the infant duke of Parma, to attempt an invasion of that kingdom. He accordingly entered the Neapolitan territories at the head of a considerable army, and was received in the metropolis with loud acclamations, as the national deliverer. The count de Visconti, having retreated into Apulia, was followed thither by the Spanish general, the count de Montemar; who, attacking the Austrians at Bitonto, May 25, 1734, gained a most complete victory. Don Carlos, being now proclaimed and acknowledged king of Naples, immediately determined upon the reduction of Sicily: and the count de Montemar, landing in that island in the month of August, proceeded with great rapidity in his conquests, the natives displaying every where a disposition rather to assist than to oppose the progress of his arms; and on the arrival of Don Carlos in person, the imperialists were compelled finally to evacuate the island. The emperor, finding himself unable to cope with his adversaries, applied for succor in this emergency to his powerful ally, the Czarina, who immediately ordered a body of thirty thousand men to march to his assistance. But, before they could arrive at the scene of action, a general treaty of peace was concluded in the spring of 1735, nearly on the terms proposed by the maritime powers; and agreeably to which, Naples and

and Sicily were yielded to the infant Don Carlos; and Parma and Placentia, the patrimonial poſſeſſions of the infant, were ceded to the houſe of Auſtria, to whom alſo the other conqueſts of the allies in Italy and Germany were reſtored. The reverſion of the grand duchy of Tuſcany, now formally relinquiſhed by Spain, was conferred as a fief of the empire, at the demiſe of the grand duke, laſt of the illuſtrious houſe of Medicis, upon the duke of Lorraine, who was deſtined for the future huſband of the eldeſt arch-duchefs Maria Thereſa, a princeſs diſtinguiſhed for her perſonal and mental accompliſhments, and ſole heireſs, under the *pragmatic ſanction*, of the vaſt dominions of the houſe of Auſtria. The elector of Saxony was acknowledged as king of Poland, and the duchy of Lorraine was ceded to Staniſlaüs, who was permitted to retain the title of king; and after the death of the titular monarch, to be for ever united to the crown of France, which thus made, under the unambitious and pacific adminiſtration of cardinal Fleury, an acquiſition of far greater importance and value than any which had reſulted from the moſt ſplendid ſucceſſes of Richelieu, Mazarine, or Louvois. The king of Sardinia was gratified by the ceſſion of ſome ſmall diſtricts of the Milaneſe; which is ſaid to have been compared, by one of the anceſtors of this monarch, to an artichoke, which, from its magnitude not being digeſtible at once, muſt be devoured leaf by leaf.

On reverting to the regular progreſſion of domeſtic events, we find the ſeſſion of 1734 diſtinguiſhed by a very vigorous effort to repeal the act for ſeptennial parliaments—as a flagrant encroachment upon the rights of the people—as having a dangerous tendency to increaſe the influence of the crown, and as being actually productive of very pernicious effects. The miniſter having defied the oppoſition to adduce a ſingle inſtance in which

the

the interests of the nation had been injured by the operation of this bill, or by any undue exercise of the royal prerogative as connected with it, Sir William Wyndham observed, " that it was reasonable and just to argue against the continuance of a bill of this nature; not merely from what had happened, but from what might happen. Let us suppose then (said he) a man of mean fortune and obscure origin, abandoned to all notions of virtue and honor, and pursuing no object but his own aggrandizement, raised by the caprice of fortune to the station of first minister: let us suppose him palpably deficient in the knowledge of the interests of his country; and employing, in all transactions with foreign powers, men still more ignorant than himself: let us suppose the honor of the nation tarnished, her political consequence lost, her commerce insulted, her merchants plundered, her seamen perishing in the depths of dungeons—and all these circumstances palliated or overlooked, lest his administration should be endangered: suppose him possessed of immense wealth, the spoils of an impoverished nation; and suppose this wealth employed to purchase seats in the national senate for his confidential friends and favorites.—In such a parliament, suppose all attempts to inquire into his conduct constantly over-ruled by a corrupt majority, who are rewarded for their treachery to the public by a profuse distribution of pensions, posts, and places under the minister.—Let us suppose this minister insolently domineering over all men of sense, figure, and fortune, in the nation; and having no virtuous principles of his own, ridiculing it in others, and endeavoring to destroy or contaminate it in all. With such a minister, and such a parliament, let us suppose a prince upon the throne—uninformed, and unacquainted either with the interests or inclinations of his people—weak, capricious, and actuated at once by the passions of ambition

ambition and avarice. Should such a case ever occur, could any greater curse happen to a nation, than such a prince, advised by such a minister, and that minister supported by such a parliament. The existence of such a prince and such a minister, no human laws may indeed be adequate to prevent; but the existence of such a parliament may, and ought to be prevented; and the repeal of the law in question I conceive to be a most obvious, necessary and indispensable means for the accomplishment of that purpose." Notwithstanding the admiration excited by this sudden burst of eloquence, and the ability with which the motion of repeal was supported by various other speakers, it was negatived on the division, though not by the accustomed ministerial majority, the numbers being 247 against 184.

The duke of Bolton and lord Cobham being about this time arbitrarily divested of their military commissions, on account of their parliamentary opposition to the measures of the court, a very dangerous—the more dangerous indeed, because a very plausible—motion was made by lord Morpeth, eldest son of the earl of Carlisle, for leave to bring in a bill for securing the constitution, by preventing the removal of officers not above the rank of colonels, otherwise than by judgment of a court martial, or by an address of either house of parliament. The court, alarmed in the highest degree by this motion, exerted the whole force of ministerial ability and eloquence in the house of commons, in order to defeat it. It was strongly urged, " that the great danger to be guarded against in all armies, is the raising them to a state of independency. The most important of all restraints on the military in this country, is the prerogative vested in the crown, of displacing officers on suspicion, or even at pleasure. But should this power once be transferred to the army, a time may come, nor may the period be far distant, when the whole of our constitution shall be at its mercy. At prefent the army itfelf depends upon the king and parliament for its very duration and exiftence. But give the officers a permanent intereft in their commiffions, by the adoption of a meafure which would convert them as it were into freeholds, and the king and parliament would foon find themfelves dependent upon the army. By this bill a door would be opened for the uncontrolled and uncontrollable commiffion of every fpecies of military licenfe and oppreffion. And fhould a reduction of the army at any future period be determined upon, is it to be imagined that thefe military chieftains, with fwords in their hands, would contentedly lay them down, and retire to their refpective homes, at the requifition of the civil power? no: they would exclaim, where are our accufers? we are by law amenable to our own courts martial only, and to them alone will we fubmit. The minifter remarked, that the two noblemen lately removed were fucceeded by others—the duke of Argyle and lord Pembroke—in no refpect inferior. And fhould the motion pafs into a law, the government of England would have an irrefiftible tendency to a *ftratocracy*, or a military conftitution. Suppofing, faid this fagacious ftatefman, the charges fo often urged by the zealous partifans of this motion againft a late celebrated general, to be well-founded—that he cherifhed views of ambition, contrary to the fpirit of the conftitution—that he afpired to perpetuate his authority, and to rife above all control, by obtaining a commiffion conftituting him general for life, how would the exiftence of a law, fuch as is now recommended, have facilitated the fuccefs of thofe daring projects? and how would fuch a motion have been received by the gentlemen who now urge it as equitable and wife, had it been brought forward under the aufpices of the duke of Marlborough? and what fhould induce us to believe that meafure to be now beneficial, which

which would then have been univerfally reprobated as pernicious and unconftitutional?" The queftion, being put, was carried in the negative, without a divifion. A far more reafonable and moderate motion was then made by Mr. Sandys, "for prefenting an humble addrefs to his majefty, that he would be gracioufly pleafed to inform the houfe by whofe advice it was that his majefty was pleafed to difcharge his grace Charles duke of Bolton, and the right honorable lord vifcount Cobham, from the regiments lately under their command, and what offences were alleged againft them as the occafion of their difmiffion." All the arguments being now on the other fide, the minifter contented himfelf with calling for the queftion; and on a divifion the motion was negatived, by a majority of 252 againft 193.

The very fame day on which lord Morpeth made his famous motion in the houfe of commons, the duke of Marlborough prefented a bill of fimilar import to the houfe of lords. The debate which enfued was rendered memorable by the eloquent fpeeches of the lords Chefterfield and Scarborough—the former in fupport, the latter in oppofition to the bill. Thefe two noblemen, who ranked amongft the moft diftinguifhed ornaments of the Englifh court, had long maintained a mutual and inviolable friendfhip. To the accomplifhments of the courtier, lord Scarborough joined the ardor of patriotifm and the enthufiafm of virtue. He might with propriety be regarded as the FALKLAND of the age—and the great qualities he poffeffed, were unfortunately clouded by the fame dark tinge of melancholy. Such was his high fenfe of honor, that thinking it neceffary to take a decided part in oppofition to the bill in queftion, he previoufly refigned his place of mafter of the horfe, left, by an injurious imputation, he should be supposed actuated by any interested motive. Not satisfied with the negative put upon the motion for the second reading of the bill, he urged the rejection of it by the house, which was agreed to without a division *.

In the same session a very important bill, which had at various times been proposed and rejected, was revived by Mr. Sandys, entitled, " A bill for securing the freedom of parliament, by limiting the number of officers, civil and military, in the house of commons." In opposition to this bill, the minister contended, " that the constitution was already sufficiently secured, by the provision which orders a re-election when a member accepts of a place; that to disable any gentleman or citizen from sitting in parliament merely because he has the honor to serve the crown, was really taking from the people

* " When I confess there is who feels for fame,
And melts to goodness, need I SCARBOROUGH name?"
POPE.

The character of this nobleman has been delineated by lord Chesterfield, with the glowing pencil of sensibility and affection. According to this *finished portrait*—confirmed indeed by the general voice of his cotemporaries—Lord Scarborough possessed in the highest degree, the air, manners, and address of a man of quality—politeness with ease, and dignity without pride. He had the advantage of a fine person; and when cheerful, the most engaging countenance imaginable. His knowledge, classical and historical, was very extensive; and it was accompanied with a just and delicate taste. In his common expences he was liberal; but in his charities and bounties his generosity was unlimited. In parliament, though not an ambitious or florid speaker, truth and virtue, which never want and seldom wear ornaments, seemed only to borrow his voice. He was a true constitutional, and yet practicable patriot: a sincere lover and a zealous assertor of the natural, the civil, and the religious rights of his country. Though bred in camps and courts, his moral character was so unsullied, that what
a cele-

people their inherent right of choosing such representatives as they deemed best qualified to exercise the functions of their delegation; and that the state would be divided by it into factions, those acting under the executive power not coalescing with, but constituting a formidable phalanx against those who composed the legislative; and that it argued an hostile distrust of the crown not compatible with the genius of the constitution." The motion was, however, in itself plausible and popular, and it received additional weight from the near approach of a dissolution of parliament, so that on the question of commitment it was negatived by a majority of 39 voices only in a house of 426 members.

Although a very large addition to the naval force of the nation had, in the early part of the session, been unanimously voted, on the 28th of March, a prorogation being now almost daily expected, a message was delivered by Sir Robert Walpole from the crown, acknowledging the zeal and affection shewn by the parliament, and desiring that his majesty might be enabled, during the recess or interval of parliaments, to make good such engagements with foreign powers as honor, justice, and prudence may call upon him to fulfil or contract, and such augmentation of his forces by sea and land as might be necessary for the honor and defence of his kingdoms, and as the exigency of affairs may re-

---

a celebrated historian formerly said of SCIPIO, might, almost without any allowance for the imperfections of humanity, be applied to him: " Nil non laudandum aut dixit, aut fecit, aut sensit."—" This small tribute of praise, says the noble writer, I owe to the memory of the best man I ever knew, and the dearest friend I ever had. If he had any enemies—for I protest I never knew one—they could only be such as were weary of always hearing of Aristides the Just."

S 2 quire,

quire, the war on the Continent still unhappily continuing." On this occasion all the patriotic ardor was again awakened, and the impolicy, the folly, and the danger of entrusting such dictatorial powers in the hands of the monarch, were exposed with all the energy of truth and eloquence. Mr. Shippen in particular distinguished himself by a speech worthy of the English CATO. He said, "that when the address was moved in reply to his majesty's speech at the commencement of the session, he had expressed his fears and suspicions, from certain expressions in both, that a vote of credit was in contemplation; but he had then been assured that there was not the least ground even to imagine so improbable a thing, although we were now told that, from his majesty's manner of expressing himself upon that occasion, every gentleman in the house must have expected a demand of this nature—a demand for no less than a total surrender of all the rights of parliament; for we are now called upon to give the king a power of raising what money he pleases, and also what military force he pleases, which are the rights on which all other rights depend; and all this without any necessity, or even any plausible reason alleged to us. Is invasion by a foreign enemy to be apprehended? Is any dangerous domestic conspiracy discovered? No: The right honorable gentleman himself says that he believes the nation to be in safety, but does not desire that its safety should depend on his belief. GOD forbid that it should; and happy would it be for us that it did not depend upon his administration. But this unlimited delegation of power is, it seems, designed to guard against new counsels, against any *sudden alteration* of measures. Surely, Sir, this is not meant to be seriously urged: for can this plea ever be wanting? Are we not in as great danger of
sudden

sudden and alarming changes in a time of profound peace, as when the powers of Europe are engaged in a bloody war, and courting with eagerness our assistance, or at least our neutrality? If we now, therefore, agree to grant such powers, we may expect in future the demand regularly repeated, and never refused. Never can such requisitions on the part of the crown be made with less color of necessity, never can compliance on our part be yielded more unconstitutionally. When not only an expiring session, but an expiring parliament, grants such powers, how easily may they be extended, before the next parliament is suffered to meet, beyond all possibility of control! The precedents that have been adduced to justify the present demand are wholly inapplicable. In the year 1702 a vote of credit passed the house in consequence of a message from the late queen; but this message contained no such demand or requisition as the present. It simply stated the danger to which our allies, the states-general, were at that period exposed from France; and this danger was not only asserted, but proved by papers laid before the house: we were then ourselves actually engaged in a war, and it was not merely pretended that we might be eventually endangered by a change of counsels. Even in this situation the queen was far from asking such powers as are now demanded. She did not in fact ask any thing, saying only in general terms, that she doubted not but the house would adopt such measures as would most conduce to the honor of her crown, the safety of her kingdoms, and the support of her allies. On the other hand, the house were far from granting such powers as are now asked. The vote was restrained to a power of increasing the forces destined to act with those of the states-general, and limited by the condition that England should not be charged with the pay of such additional

tional troops, but from the day that all commerce and correspondence between the subjects of the states, and those of France and Spain, should be totally prohibited. As to the message in the year 1715, it was sent to the house at a time of actual rebellion and expected invasion; and it was not granted at the termination of a session, and much less at the expiration of a parliament. The message in 1719 was similarly circumstanced: the nation was in danger of being invaded, and would have been invaded, had it not been for the disasters which the Spanish fleet met with after leaving their ports. The last precedent of the year 1725, it must be allowed, approaches nearest to the present case. We then did, as we are now desired to do—grant away millions in the dark without any cause or reason assigned; but then this was a precedent of the right honorable gentleman's own making, which may be thought perhaps somewhat to diminish its authority. The right honorable gentleman has, however, improved upon his own precedent; for the nation was not, at the period alluded to, in a state of absolute tranquillity, nor did the message ask for a discretion so unlimited as the present; but merely for an indefinite power to add to the *naval* force, and to negotiate treaties. But if his majesty is invested with the powers now demanded, nothing will remain for the crown to ask but a parliamentary resolve, impowering his majesty to make, repeal, suspend, or alter, such laws, and in such manner, as he shall judge necessary for the public safety. And where indeed is the difference between granting this power at once, and putting the crown in a capacity to assume it whenever it may choose so to do? Such complaisance as this must surely render us most despicable in his majesty's eyes: He might justly say of us as the Roman emperor of the Roman

man senate, "*O homines servire paratos!*" But we are told that an account is to be rendered to the next parliament of whatever may be done in pursuance of these powers. Sir, I have been so often deceived by ministerial promises, that I am ashamed ever to have placed any degree of faith in them. How often, when I and others have called for such accounts, have we been told that matters were not ripe for laying them before parliament, or that it would be dangerous to the state to reveal the secrets of government? and the highest satisfaction we could ever obtain was to be told that the expenses incurred were necessarily incurred for foreign and secret services. Whence that necessity arose was ever kept from the knowledge of parliament: we had the word of the minister to rest our faith upon; and the same implicit resignation will be required, doubtless, from every succeeding parliament. When at the termination of the session we return to our several counties, and are requested to assign our reasons for this very extraordinary vote—a vote by which such vast additional burdens may be imposed on the nation—how satisfactory must it be to our constituents to be informed that, though we are at present in amity or actual alliance with all the powers of Europe, military preparations, by sea and land, must be made in order to guard against a *variation* of foreign counsels! Sir, in my opinion, the resolution now moved is neither necessary, nor safe, nor founded upon precedent. Precedents, indeed, there may be, which resemble it in a certain degree; but were they ever so numerous, and in all respects analogous, it would be no argument with me for agreeing to what is proposed. Whatever may have been the duration or extent of the practice, it is now high time to put a stop to it, and to establish a PRECEDENT of REFUSAL; otherwise parliaments will become wholly useless, or

serve,

serve, by a sanction so pernicious, to make ministers the more daring, and the oppressions of the people the more grievous."

In answer to this eloquent and patriotic speaker, Mr. Horace Walpole ventured to attempt a vindication of the measures thus indignantly arraigned. He said, that after all the pains taken to point out a dissimilarity between the case now under discussion and the precedents adduced in support of it, he could discern no material difference. It had been evidently the practice of parliament, in times of danger, to grant extraordinary powers to the crown, and in this particular way. For his part he acknowledged he thought the precedent of 1702 a bad one; because the parliament discovered so much diffidence and distrust; and all the ill effects of their slow and lukewarm proceedings ought to induce us to strengthen the hands of his majesty at the present juncture. It was surprising, he said, to him to hear it asserted by gentlemen, that nothing had been laid before the house to shew the necessity of granting the powers now asked for. Did not his majesty, in his speech at the opening of the session, inform us of the war then begun in Europe? Does he not by the present message acquaint us that the war still continues? And is not every gentleman convinced, by what he knows of the situation of Europe, that the balance of power in Europe entirely depends on the event of that war? Supposing either side to prevail too far, the balance of power must be overturned; and this nation will be under an obligation to interpose, in order to prevent so fatal an effect. Besides, does not every gentleman know that the French have lately fitted out a very powerful naval armament, which, with more probability, threatens Great Britain than any other place in the world, unless

unless we excepted the city of Dantzic? He believed, indeed, he said, that it was designed against Dantzic; but if that affair should blow over, can we imagine ourselves in security, while so large a squadron lies within a few hours' sail of the English coast? Our allies, the Dutch, he said, were in a very critical state: their barrier in Flanders was in a very weak and defenceless condition, and if we should sit still and do nothing, they might be tempted to throw themselves entirely into the arms of France. They had not indeed, he acknowledged, done any thing as yet themselves by way of augmentation of their forces, but then they had postponed that reduction of 10,000 men, which, previous to the war, they had meditated; and they were now desirous to go hand in hand with us. Gentlemen, he said, might, if they pleased, call this a vote of credit; but his majesty having expressly promised an account of the expenditure, it was in his opinion only a vote of confidence, which, by shewing the entire reliance we place on the wisdom of his majesty's measures, will give his influence with foreign powers that weight which is so necessary to the preservation of the balance of power in Europe, without which this nation can never be in any safety or security." The debate was unusually prolonged by a succession of very able speeches: and Sir John Barnard particularly attracted the attention of the house, by declaring "that the assertions hazarded in royal speeches or messages were not to be implicitly depended upon; for that the crown might assert, and in fact had asserted in consequence of hasty or treacherous information, what afterwards proved not to be true. Parliament had, he said, been assured by a solemn speech from the throne, that an alliance had been entered into between the emperor and Spain, in conformity to the secret articles of which, Gibraltar was to have been wrested from us, and the pretender placed by force on the throne

throne of Great Britain. Confidering the fituation and
circumftances of the contracting powers at that period,
this intelligence appeared to many at the time romantic
and incredible; and it was now known to be falfe, though
it was then reprefented as highly difrefpectful to the
crown fo much as to doubt it. We were now called upon, in a manner ftill more extraordinary, to give credit
to a furmife of danger from France, which the right
honorable gentleman himfelf does not profefs to believe;
and in confequence of this groundlefs apprehenfion, to
devolve for fix months the whole power of parliament
upon the crown—a demand which deferved to be treated
with ridicule, and rejected with indignation." Sir Robert Walpole immediately rofe, and protefted, "that
while he had the honor to ferve the crown, he could not
fit ftill and hear it fo injurioufly reflected upon. His
late majefty's affertion, relative to the fecret articles of
the treaty of Vienna, he faid, was as true and as well
founded as any that ever came from the throne. It was
indeed infolently contradicted by M. Palm, the imperial
ambaffador; but the king received his information from
thofe who could not be deceived—and the minifter declared himfelf to be as certain that there were fuch articles, as if he had been prefent at the framing of them *:
and however indifcreet this declaration might be thought
in actual circumftances—he could not, in juftice to the
memory of the late king, fay lefs." In conclufion, the
queftion being put, upon the motion for the addrefs, it
was carried in the affirmative, by 248 voices againft 147
—although Mr. Pulteney, who terminated the debate,

---

* Lord Townfhend, fecretary of ftate at the period alluded to, made
f... ir declaration in the houfe of peers; without, however, being
... remove the obftinate incredulity of a great part of his noble
... ors.

had

had given it as his opinion, that "the meſſage before the houſe was of a nature ſo extraordinary, and involved in it ſuch culpability, that if the ſpirit of liberty—that ſpirit which brought about the revolution, and eſtabliſhed the preſent family upon the throne—was not abſolutely extinguiſhed in the nation, we might expect to ſee a future parliament not only cenſure, but condemn and puniſh, thoſe who had been the chief adviſers of ſuch a meaſure." On the 16th of April the king put an end to the ſeſſion by a ſpeech, in which he declared, that " he ſhould think himſelf inexcuſable if he parted with this parliament, without doing them the juſtice to acknowledge the many ſignal proofs they had given, through the courſe of ſeven years, of their duty, fidelity, and attachment to his perſon and government, and their conſtant regard to the true intereſt of their country." The parliament having now ſat nearly the full term preſcribed by the ſeptennial act, was diſſolved on April 18, 1734, and a new parliament immediately convoked by royal proclamation.

In the ſpring of this year the marriage of the princeſs royal with the prince of Orange was celebrated with great magnificence and public rejoicings; and the parliament, as a teſtimony of their entire approbation of this alliance, voted the ſum of 80,000l. as a portion to the princeſs, and an annuity for life of 5000l. payable out of the civil liſt. His ſerene highneſs the prince is thus favorably deſcribed, in a letter to lord Townſhend, ſecretary of ſtate, from the earl of Cheſterfield, ambaſſador at the Hague: " The prince of Orange has extreme good parts; is perfectly well-bred; with an eaſe and freedom that is ſeldom acquired, but by a long knowledge of the world. The acclamations of the people are loud and univerſal. He aſſumes not the leaſt dignity, but has all the affability

and

and infinuation that is neceffary for a perfon who would raife himfelf in a popular government."

The new parliament being convened in January 1735, quickly difcovered a difpofition to fupport, with zeal not inferior to that of their predeceffors, the meafures of the prefent adminiftration. The king, in his fpeech, expreffed " his concern at the prefent commotions on the continent; and though he had hitherto refifted the preffing folicitations of the court of Vienna for aid in this war, he hoped that his good fubjects would not repine at the neceffary means of placing him in a fituation to act that part which might eventually be incumbent upon him." The houfe, in a grand committee of fupply, voted, in confequence of this fuggeftion, near 60,000 men for the fea and land-fervice of the year; though not without the vehement oppofition of the patriots, who demonftrated the folly of taking any part whatever in thefe unintelligible and everlafting broils upon the continent, upon pretence of which this alarming augmentation of our military force was founded: and Sir William Wyndham remarked, " that notwithftanding the long continuance of peace, fuch had been the exorbitant charges and expences by fubfidies and armaments, that the people had not been relieved from the burden of a fingle tax impofed during the preceding war."

A claufe being inferted in the addrefs, affuring his majefty " that this houfe will cheerfully and effectually raife fuch fupplies as fhall be neceffary for the honor and fecurity of his majefty and thefe kingdoms"—it was moved that the following words be added, " fo foon as the proper information of the ftate of public affairs fhall be communicated to this houfe, and in proportion to fuch efforts as fhall be made by fuch of the allies who are under the fame engagements as this nation, and who are not involved in the war." On a divifion the amendment

ment was rejected, by 265 votes against 185—a minority plainly indicative of the reluctance of the house to engage as parties in the present war; in which it appears that England interfered so far, as to give extreme umbrage to the courts of Versailles and Madrid, though not far enough to render any real service to the emperor, who had flattered himself with the hope of a revival of the grand alliance in his favor.

Mr. Horace Walpole was not discouraged, however, from almost immediately moving for a subsidy to Denmark, pursuant to a treaty entered into by his majesty with the king of Denmark for that purpose; and which originated, according to the allegations of the mover, in a just and proper regard to the preservation of the *balance of power* in Europe *—an expression so incessantly in the mouth of this minister, that he was commonly known under the ludicrous appellation of *balance-master*. The leaders of opposition treated the motion with indignant contempt. All the powers of Europe, it was affirmed, were as much or more interested in the preservation of this *balance* as England: and should it ever be really endangered, they would certainly engage in its defence, with-

---

* The secret history of this Danish subsidy has already been transiently alluded to. It is *a mystery of State*, involved in too much obscurity and perplexity to be fully and completely developed. By this treaty, 80 crowns were allowed for each horseman, and 30 for every foot-soldier: one half to be paid immediately on signing the treaty, and the remainder when the troops shall be *delivered*. Besides this, his majesty the king of Great Britain engages to pay to his majesty the king of Denmark the annual sum of 250,000 crowns *banco*, till such time as the said troops shall be taken into full pay, and the sum of 150,000 crowns yearly afterwards. What a happiness for Britain, that the equipoise of the political balance, whenever disordered, may be so easily re-adjusted, by the judicious application of these golden weights! No less than 178 members of the house of commons divided nevertheless against this so obviously wise and salutary measure.

out being hired to do so by British subsidies. But were England perpetually the first to take the alarm, and should this practice of subsidizing be established, every state would expect a gratification for doing what it would otherwise be obliged to do for its own preservation, and the whole charge of maintaining this balance would fall upon Great Britain. Even our allies the states-general might at last refuse to assist in trimming this balance, unless the grand pensionary of Holland were also to become the *grand pensionary* of England. The question being put, the motion was approved, and the subsidy granted by the house. The session closing in May (1735), the king thanked his faithful commons for the supplies they had granted with such cheerfulness and dispatch; and immediately after the prorogation, his majesty embarked for the continent, leaving the queen, as usual, sole regent during his absence.

For several years past, a strict amity had subsisted between the two courts of Madrid and Lisbon, which was in the year 1728 cemented by a double marriage of the royal families—the prince of Asturias espousing the eldest princess of Portugal, and the prince of Brazil the infanta of Spain, formerly affianced to Louis XV. king of France—the courts meeting in a temporary edifice erected over the bed of the Coya, which divides the two kingdoms, where the princesses were exchanged. In the course of this year, however, the good understanding between them was unhappily interrupted by a frivolous dispute, originating in a real or pretended violation of the privileges of the ambassador of Portugal resident at Madrid. The quarrel ran so high, that the ministers of the two crowns were recalled, and warlike preparations made on each side. The king of Portugal, conscious of his inability to encounter the power of Spain, nominated Don Antonio d'Alzeveda as his ambassador extraordinary to the

the court of London, to folicit the aid and protection of his ally the king of Great Britain. By the efficacious affiftance of England had the independency of Portugal and the rights of the ducal and royal houfe of Braganza been ultimately eftablifhed, after a conteft of twenty-eight years: and as a juft compenfation for this great fervice, very important commercial privileges were conceded to the Englifh nation by the crown of Portugal; and thus the interefts of that opulent but feeble kingdom became infeparably connected with thofe of Great Britain; and upon this potent alliance fhe chiefly depended, and ftill depends, for her exiftence as a diftinct and fovereign power. Don Pedro, who fucceeded to the throne on the depofition of his brother Alphonfo, died A. D. 1706, after a reign of thirty years. His fon, Don Juan, faithfully adhered to the political engagements entered into by his father as a party in the grand alliance againft the houfe of Bourbon. But after the conclufion of the treaty of Utrecht, the court of Lifbon had cautioufly avoided involving herfelf in the various contentions of the European powers. Upon the prefent occafion the court of London adopted, without hefitation, meafures the moft vigorous and decifive. A powerful fleet, under the command of Sir John Norris, failed for the Tagus, in order to protect the coafts and the commerce of Portugal; and particularly to convoy the Brazil fleet, then richly laden, in fafety to Lifbon. And Mr. Keene, the Britifh envoy at Madrid, was exprefsly commanded to communicate to his Catholic majefty, the refolution of the king of England to grant effectual fuccors to his ally. Notwithftanding fome angry complaints on the part of Spain, of the partial conduct of England, this interpofition completely anfwered the purpofe intended by it; and an accommodation took place between the courts

of

of Spain and Portugal, before the conclusion of the year.

The succeeding session of parliament was distinguished chiefly by a motion made in the house of commons, March 1736, for the repeal of those clauses in the test act, which barred or obstructed the admission of *protestant dissenters* to civil employments. This motion, though ably supported, seems to have been somewhat unadvised and unseasonable—as being brought forward, not merely without the concurrence, but contrary to the inclination of the court, and at a juncture in no respect favorable to its success. It is not, however, to be inferred, that the court was really adverse to the purport of the motion abstractedly considered; but the minister well knew the risque and obloquy which might attend his open and avowed support of this measure. He recollected, doubtless, that the utmost influence of the crown had been unavailingly exerted in the late reign to procure the repeal of these clauses, when a bill for that purpose was moved by the late earl Stanhope. His popularity had lately sustained a rude shock, in consequence of the attempt made to extend and invigorate the operation of the laws of revenue: and he dreaded lest the cry of DANGER TO THE CHURCH should produce effects still more detrimental to his credit and safety, than that which still vibrated in his ears, of LIBERTY, PROPERTY, AND NO EXCISE. Although he had, previously to the late election, flattered the dissenters with the hope of relief, he thought proper, therefore, when the motion was actually made, to oppose the repeal, as in present circumstances inexpedient, impolitic, and improper; in consequence of which it was rejected by a very great majority. The motion was, by a fruitless and injudicious perseverance, revived in a subsequent session of this parliament, when it was again negatived by the same ministerial majority. It is remarkable,

able, however, that no confiderable or lafting refentment appears to have been excited in the breafts of the diffenters in confequence of this difappointment: fo well was it underftood that the king was himfelf ftrongly difpofed to favor the repeal, and that the minifter was actuated by motives, not of animofity, but of an urgent and overruling political neceffity. It muft not be omitted, that in this feffion the parliament repealed the antient ftatutes againft conjuration and witchcraft, thereby relieving the Englifh judicial code from a fmall part of that heavy load of trumpery, abfurdity, and oppreffion, by which, in the worfe than Egyptian darknefs of paft ages, it had been fo unhappily and dreadfully difgraced.

About this time a new fect of religionifts arofe, diftinguifhed by the appellation of *methodifts*, who foon appeared to be divided into two diftinct claffes under their refpective leaders, Whitfield and Wefley—priefts of the Englifh church, regularly educated and ordained—the firft of them adopting the calviniftic, the latter the arminian dogmas in theology; correfponding in this refpect to the fects of janfenifts and molinifts, in the gallican church. Profeffing ftill to adhere to the communion of the church of England, of which they boafted themfelves to be the only true and genuine members, they yet indulged in the wildeft flights and extravagancies of fectarian fanaticifm—preaching in the fields to vaft multitudes—fuffering with patience every infult and outrage, and perfifting, at the extreme peril of their lives, in thofe fpiritual labors to which they conceived themfelves called by a fort of fupernatural impulfe*. Many refpectable perfons were

Vol. I. T of

---

* "God in the fcripture," fays one of the leaders of this fect, in very elevated language, "commands me, according to my power, to inftruct the ignorant, reform the wicked, and confirm the virtuous.

A dif-

of opinion, that the government ought in some mode to interfere in order to check these novel and dangerous ebullitions of enthusiasm. But to the honor of the government, not only was the idea of persecution in every form rejected with abhorrence, but the protection of the law was extended to them upon all occasions. And the wisdom of maintaining inviolate the grand principle of TOLERATION has rarely appeared in a more striking point of view. In a few years the fanatical fervors characteristic of a new sect, not being irritated and inflamed by the opposition of the civil powers, gradually subsided. And though the number of proselytes was prodigious—part remaining in and part seceding from the established church; no injury to the community has resulted from this diffusion of methodistic principles. On the contrary, the good effects of their moral and religious instructions, though still blended with much speculative absurdity and mysticism, are at this time apparent in the orderly and virtuous conduct of thousands in their communities, who would otherwise have sunk in the depths of ignorance, vice, and barbarism. And truth and justice require the acknowledgement, that many, both of the clergy and laity, who now pass under the vague and popular denomination of methodists, are persons of the highest worth, talents, and respectability.

The tranquillity which prevailed throughout the kingdom at this time was unhappily interrupted by a tu-

---

A dispensation of the gospel is committed to me, and woe is me if I preach not the gospel! In whatever part of the world I am, I judge it meet, right, and my bounden duty, to declare unto all that are willing to hear the glad tidings of salvation. This is the work which I *know* God hath called me unto. And if it be his pleasure to throw down the walls of Jericho, not by the engines of war, but by the blasts of rams horns; who shall say unto him, what doest thou?"——*Wesley's works*.

mult of a very fingular nature, which took place in the city of Edinburgh, during the abfence of the king. It happened that, at the execution of a man convicted under circumftances of peculiar hardfhip, by trial in the court of admiralty, as a fmuggler, the military guard which attended were grofsly infulted by the populace; in revenge of which, captain Porteous, the commandant, was provoked to order the foldiers to fire upon the people, without the previous fanction of the magiftrate. In confequence of this rafh and precipitate order, feveral innocent perfons fuffering the lofs of their lives, Porteous was tried for murder, convicted, and received fentence of death; but the queen, as regent, thought fit to grant him a reprieve. The populace of Edinburgh, neverthelefs, exafperated in the higheft degree at the conduct of this officer, who was well known to be a man of abandoned morals, determined that he fhould not efcape punifhment: and on the very evening of the day on which, according to his fentence, he was deftined to fuffer, the prifon of the Tolbooth was forced with fuch order and deliberate refolution, as afforded a ftrong prefumption that it was the refult of a plot formed by perfons far above thofe ufually concerned in fimilar outrages. Leaving the delinquent fufpended by the neck from a dyer's pole, they quickly and quietly difperfed; nor was it ever difcovered who were the perpetrators of this daring act of violence, notwithftanding a reward of 200l. was offered by proclamation for fuch detection. The government, inflamed with refentment at this atrocious violation of the laws, inftituted a parliamentary inquiry into the circumftances of this extraordinary affair; in the courfe of which three Scottifh judges in their robes were examined as witneffes at the bar of the houfe of lords. And though it did not appear that the magiftrates had been any way deficient in their duty upon this occafion, a bill was brought in for disabling the lord provost of Edinburgh from holding any office of magistracy in Great Britain—for abolishing the guard of that city, and for taking away the gates of the Nether-bow-port, which during this transaction had been shut, in order to prevent the troops quartered in the suburbs from entering the city. This bill was opposed by almost all the Scottish representatives, and many other respectable members of both houses, with great vehemence: and the duke of Argyle, in particular, arguing against the principle of it, said, that "he could not think of a measure more harsh or unprecedented than the present bill; and he believed there was no instance of the whole weight of parliamentary indignation falling upon any individual, and far less upon any community, for crimes that were within the reach of the inferior courts of justice—that should the present bill pass into a law, the lord provost and citizens of Edinburgh would suffer by a cruel, unjust, and fantastical proceeding—a proceeding of which the worst use might be made, if ever the nation should have the misfortune to fall under a vindictive, arbitrary, and tyrannical administration"—an observation which subsequent events forcibly recalled to public recollection. Notwithstanding all opposition, the bill passed, and was carried into rigorous execution, to the great and inexpressible indignation of the whole Scottish nation. And this rash and passionate attempt to vindicate the honor of the crown by insulting the majesty and wounding the feelings of the people, afforded a new proof of the truth and justice of the observation of the celebrated chancellor Oxenstierne, "that it is wonderful by how small a portion of wisdom the world is governed." In the stead of these impolitic measures of revenge and degradation, it would have given pleasure to every liberal mind, had occasion been taken from this incident, supposing it to indicate any want of energy in the executive power,

power, to restore to Scotland those distinctions of national honor and authority of which that kingdom had been unnecessarily and invidiously divested by the treaty of union. There appears no just reason why Scotland should not have its own resident great officers of state, why its privy council should be annihilated, why the high commissioner of the crown should not, as in the times preceding the union, be enabled to support his elevated rank and station in a manner suitable to the national dignity; and why the royal palace of the kings of Scotland should be suffered to exhibit a picture of melancholy and decay, scarcely to be distinguished from the ruins of BALCLUTHA. " I have seen," says the antient bard of Caledonia, " the walls of Balclutha, but they were desolate. The fire had resounded in the halls, but the voice of the people is heard no more. The stream of Clutha was removed from its place by the fall of the walls. The thistle shook there its lonely head; the moss whistled to the wind. The fox looked out from the windows; the rank grass of the wall waved round his head. Desolate is the dwelling of Moina; silence is in the house of her fathers."

In April 1736, the marriage of the prince of Wales, who was considered as the determined enemy of the minister, and the head of the opposition, with Augusta princess of Saxe-Gotha, was celebrated; and in the course of the ensuing session a motion was made by Mr. Pulteney, and seconded by Sir John Barnard, for an address to the king, that he would be pleased to settle 100,000l. per annum out of the civil list revenues upon the prince*. This was violently opposed by the courtiers,

---

* The prince of Wales highly resented, and with great apparent reason, that out of a civil list of 800,000l. a revenue of 50,000l. per ann. only should be allotted to him, although his father, when prince, had

tiers, as an encroachment upon the king's prerogative; and it was finally negatived by a majority of 30 voices, the numbers being 234 to 204, though not without producing an entire alienation between the two courts of St. James's and Leicester house; and the prince was not even permitted, in the last illness of the queen, who expired November 1737, much esteemed and lamented by the English nation, to implore her forgiveness or to receive her departing benediction.

At this period, a war broke out between the Russian and Ottoman empires, occasioned, as was pretended, by certain incursions of the Tartar tribes into the Russian territories: but in reality by the ambitious and eager desire of the court of Petersburg to regain possession of the important maritime city of Asoph, which was one of the earliest acquisitions of the emperor Peter the great, but which that monarch was afterwards compelled to sacrifice, in order to extricate himself from the perilous extremity to which, in his last war with Turkey, he found himself reduced, on the banks of the Pruth. Asoph was accordingly besieged and taken; and when satisfaction and reparation were offered by the Porte, for the injuries suf-

---

had 100,000l. out of a civil list of 700,000l.—nor does the sum required by the prince appear more than adequate to the superiority of his rank and station. As this resolution of the prince embarrassed many who held places under the government, and were at the same time desirous to keep on fair terms with the successor, he was advised by Mr. Doddington, afterwards lord Melcombe, whom he admitted into his confidence, to apply to parliament for an *additional grant* of 50,000l. per ann.; but the prince replied, with a generosity truly noble, " THAT THE NATION HAD DONE ENOUGH FOR HIS FAMILY ALREADY, AND THAT HE WOULD RATHER BEG HIS BREAD FROM DOOR TO DOOR, THAN BE A FARTHER CHARGE TO THEM." Many of the tories, regarding the motion as dangerously democratic, left the house in a body previous to the division, though Sir William Wyndham had taken upon him to answer to the prince for their concurrence.

tained

tained by Ruffia, the Czarina declared her refolution not to relinquifh her conqueft. And the emperor of Germany, being under obligation by treaty to affift the Ruffians, became in a fhort time a principal in the war, which proved to him only a feries of difafters. A peace was at length obtained at the expence of Orfova, Belgrade, and the entire province or kingdom of Servia, which were ceded by the emperor to the Turks. The Ruffians, who had, under the conduct of the famous Marefchal Munich, made great progrefs in the reduction of the provinces north of the Danube, on their part reftored Oczakow, Choczim, and Bender, and the poffeffion of Afoph was confirmed to them by the Porte.

In the feffion of parliament held A. D. 1737, a motion being made for the continuance of the fame number of land-forces as had been voted the preceding year, a vehement debate arofe. For though, in our own more courtly days, a much larger number is annually voted almoft as a matter of courfe, it was confidered as one of the moft important and moft laudable objects of patriotifm in thefe times to procure, if not an abolition, at leaft a reduction, of a military force, detefted and deprecated as ufelefs, expenfive, and dangerous. In vindication of the motion, the miniftry fcrupled not to affirm, " that if the army was difbanded, the *tory intereft* would quickly predominate—that the kingdom was filled with clamor and difcontent, which a ftanding military force only could effectually reprefs—that the fupport of the *whig intereft* demanded the maintenance of this force; and it was hoped and prefumed that the houfe would vote triple the number, if adjudged neceffary for this purpofe." The members of the oppofition replied, in their accuftomed ftrain of *vain reafoning*, " that this vindication contained in it a fentence of felf-condemnation—for to what caufe could the fpirit of clamor and difcontent be afcribed, but

to

to the misconduct of the ministry? and it was from their own acknowledgement clear, that what they were pleased to style the whig interest, was in fact an inconsiderable party which had engrossed the power of government by indirect and unconstitutional methods—which acted contrary to the sense of the nation, and which depended for support upon that very military force which was the grand source of the national discontent, which perpetuated the national taxes, and which menaced the national liberties with destruction. The claim of the ministry and their adherents in the house to the appellation of whigs, was warmly disputed; and Sir John Hynde Cotton declared, " that a genuine whig could never vote for a standing army in time of peace. Whigs, said this member, who are true to their principles, will oppose all unlimited votes of credit—will deprecate the corruption of the legislative power, as the greatest curse that can befall a nation—they will esteem the liberty of the press to be the invaluable privilege of a free people; and frequent parliaments to be the grand bulwark of their liberties. A whig administration would never suffer injuries done to the British commerce to pass unnoticed, or insults offered to the British flag to pass unrevenged." It is remarkable, that Sir John Hynde Cotton was himself educated in tory principles, and was in early life closely connected with the principal leaders of that once formidable faction. But the panegyric now pronounced upon whig principles clearly and infallibly indicated, that the proper and peculiar tenets of toryism—passive obedience, non-resistance, and the indefeasible rights of royalty—were now fallen into contempt. The tories were insensibly led, in the course of their opposition to the erroneous and unconstitutional measures of government, to adopt consistent and rational principles. The very name

of

of Tory began to be confidered as a term of reproach, and as fuch was, in this debate, refented and repelled. Still, however, in a certain fenfe, Whiggifm and Toryifm have never ceafed, and will never ceafe to fubfift. Whatever tends to enlarge the power of princes or of magiftrates beyond the precife line or limit of the general good, whatever impofes oppreffive or even fuperfluous reftraints upon the liberty of the people, or introduces any fpecies of civil inequality, not founded on the bafis of public utility, is of the effence of Toryifm. On the other hand, genuine Whiggifm is nothing more than good temper and good fenfe, or, to adopt higher and more appropriate terms of expreffion, benevolence and wifdom applied to the fcience of government.

The theatre in the metropolis of Britain having been recently, in various inftances abufed, as in ancient times at Athens, to the purpofes of perfonal and political fatire, a bill was at this period introduced for the prevention of this great and growing evil; agreeably to the provifions of which, no new dramatic pieces could be exhibited without the exprefs licenfe firft obtained of the lord Chamberlain. This bill paffed through both houfes with little oppofition, excepting that which it met with from the earl of Chefterfield, who combated the principle of it with much animation and eloquence. His lordfhip declared, " that he regarded this meafure as of a very extraordinary and dangerous nature; as a reftraint not on the licentioufnefs merely, but on the liberty of the ftage; and as tending to a ftill more dangerous reftraint on the liberty of the prefs, which was intimately and infeparably connected with the general liberty of the fubject. He affirmed the laws, as they at prefent ftood, to be fufficient for the purpofe of punifhing feditious or immoral performances. The beft, and indeed the only, mode of avoiding public ridicule and cenfure censure was, he said, to avoid ridiculous and vicious actions; for the people will neither ridicule those they love and esteem, nor suffer them to be ridiculed. An administration destitute of esteem or respect among the people will be censured and ridiculed, nor will the severest edicts be found of force to prevent it. If we agree to the bill now before us, what shadow of excuse can be suggested for refusing to proceed a step farther, and to extend the prohibition to printing and publishing those dramas which are deemed unfit for public exhibition? Still political satires will appear under the title of Novels, Secret History, Dialogues, &c.; but will you allow, my lords, a libel to be printed and dispersed only because it does not bear the title of a play? Thus, from the precedent before us, we shall be gradually prevailed upon to revive a general IMPRIMATUR, and then adieu to the liberties of Great Britain. I admit, my lords, that the stage ought not to meddle with politics, but for this very reason among others I object to the bill before us; for I fear it will be the occasion of its meddling with nothing else—it will be made subservient to the politics of the court only. This we know was actually the case in king Charles the Second's days; we know that Dryden, the poet Laureat of that reign, made his wit and genius thus subservient to the designs of the court. When the second Dutch war was in contemplation, he wrote his " Amboyna," in which he represents the people of Holland as avaricious, cruel, and ungrateful. When the exclusion bill was moved for, he wrote his " Duke of Guise," in which those who were zealous for preserving and securing the liberties and religion of their country, were exposed as a faction leagued together for the purpose of excluding a virtuous and heroic prince from that throne which was his lawful right, on account of his adopting a faith different

from

from their own. The peculiar province of the stage, my lords, is, to expose those vices and follies which the laws cannot lay hold of; but under the restraint of an arbitrary course licenfe, it will be entirely perverted from its proper use. To a man bred in the habits of a court, that may appear to be a libel against the court which is only a just and salutary satire upon its vices and follies. Courtiers, my lords, are too polite to reprove one another; the only place where they can meet with just rebuke is a free, though not a licentious stage. But by this bill, inftead of leaving it what it now is, and always ought to be —a scourge for fashionable vices—it will be converted into a channel for propagating them throughout the kingdom. Let us confider, my lords, that arbitrary power has seldom or never been introduced into any country but by flow degrees, step by step, lest the people should perceive its approach. When the preparatory steps are made, the people may then indeed see flavery and arbitrary power making huge and hideous strides over the land, when it is too late to avert the impending ruin. The bill before us I confider as a step very neceffary to this purpose; and should such design ever be formed by any ambitious king or guilty minister, he would have reafon to thank us for having so far facilitated his attempt; though such thanks, I am convinced, every one of your lordships would blush to receive, and scorn to deferve." The ill effects apprehended by this generous and patriotic nobleman have not, however, been as yet very apparent: and it must be acknowledged, that in a very few instances only does the invidious difcretion vefted by this bill in the lord Chamberlain seem to have been capriciously or improperly exercifed *.

In

---

* The GUSTAVUS VASA of Brooke, the MUSTAPHA of Mallet, and the EDWARD and ELEONORA of Thomson, were in the number

of

In the course of the same session the house of commons having resolved itself into a grand committee to take into consideration the state of the national debt, Sir John Barnard, member for the city of London, a man whose patriotism was dignified by the extent of his

of the Dramas rejected under the authority of this act. The first of these performances is animated throughout by a noble and enthusiastic spirit of liberty; but the writer protests in his prefatory remarks, "that he had nothing to fear or hope from party or preferment—his attachments were only to truth; that he was conscious of no other principles, and was far from apprehending that such could be offensive." There were, however, some passages in this tragedy which could not fail to be invidiously applied, if they could be supposed not invidiously designed. A specimen or two may suffice:

> " Are ye not mark'd, ye men of Dalecarlia,
> Are ye not mark'd by all the circling world?
> —Say, is not liberty the thirst, the food,
> The scope and bright ambition of your souls?
> Why else have you and your renown'd forefathers,
> From the proud summit of their glittering thrones,
> Cast down the mightiest of your lawful kings
> That dar'd the bold infringement? What but liberty,
> Thro' the fam'd course of thirteen hundred years,
> Aloof hath held invasion from your hills,
> And sanctified their shade? And will ye, will ye
> Shrink from the hopes of the expecting world?
> Bid your high honors stoop to FOREIGN INSULT?
> And in one hour give up to infamy
> The harvest of a thousand years of glory?

> " Where is that power whose engines are of force
> To bend the brave and virtuous man to slavery?
> Base fear, the laziness of lust, gross appetites,
> These are the ladders and the grovelling footstool
> From whence the tyrant rises on our wrongs.
> Secure, and sceptred *in the soul's servility*,
> *He has debauch'd the Genius of our country*,
> And rides triumphant, while her captive sons
> Await his nod—the silken slaves of pleasure."

knowledge,

knowledge, the foundness of his understanding, and the benevolence of his heart, moved for a bill to enable his majesty to raise money either by the sale of annuities, or by borrowing at an interest not exceeding 3 *per cent.* which sum so raised should be applied towards the redemption of the South-Sea annuities, allowing the preference of subscription to the annuitants. Sir John Barnard remarked, " that even those public securities which bore an interest of 3 *per cent.* only, were now considerably above *par*; therefore there could be no room to doubt that the subscription would immediately fill, were it a condition of the contract that the principal should be made irredeemable for the term of fourteen years. When the South-Sea annuitants were thus reduced, the same plan might be adopted for redeeming the capital of the other trading companies, and, in time, of the whole public debt, without any violation of the public faith; that, by this means, the sinking fund would be so much increased, that in a few years the parliament would be able to annihilate those taxes which lay heaviest upon the laboring and manufacturing poor; and that the remaining part of it, if faithfully applied, would, in a short time, free the nation from all incumbrances." By this motion, at once so popular, feasible, and beneficial, the minister seemed much embarrassed; and it was clearly discernible that the executive government entertained no real wish or intention that the public debt, which so materially added both to its influence and its security, should ever be liquidated. In order, therefore, to counteract the effect of a motion, which it would have been too hazardous openly and directly to oppose, Mr. Winnington, a zealous partisan of the minister, moved that all the public creditors, as well as the South-Sea annuitants, should

should be comprehended. To this Sir John Barnard objected, "that it might be easy for the government to borrow money at 3 *per cent.* sufficient for the redemption of a certain proportion of the public debt, though it might be extremely difficult, or even impracticable, to borrow money enough at once to liquidate the whole, amounting at this time to almost forty-eight millions." A bill was, however, ordered in upon the basis of Mr. Winnington's propositions, which, being in the sequel warmly attacked, and faintly defended, was finally postponed to a distant day by motion of the minister; though there is great reason to believe, from the success of a similar and more recent attempt, that the patriots in opposition formed an erroneous judgment respecting the difficulties attending its execution *.

In

---

* In the month of January (1737) died Dr. William Wake, who had filled the metropolitan See of Canterbury twenty-one years. Previous to his elevation to that high dignity, he had very honorably distinguished himself by the liberality of his sentiments, and the vigor of his exertions both in convocation and in parliament, particularly in his contest with Atterbury on the nature and extent of ecclesiastical authority; and in a most conspicuous manner at the ever-memorable trial of Sacheverel. As one of the ablest and firmest champions of the Low Church Party he was advanced, on the death of Dr. Tennison, A. D. 1716, to the Archiepiscopal chair; but he soon made it visible that "Lowliness is young ambition's ladder;" and when he had "attained the topmost round," he adopted, like his famous predecessor Becket, a totally new system of principles and conduct. By the vehemence and pertinacity of his opposition, he essentially impeded on all occasions the meritorious endeavors of the court for the advancement, and security, of the general system of civil and religious liberty. And in a more especial manner he labored to counteract the grand effort made by that generous and beneficent statesman, lord Stanhope, under the auspices of the late king, for the annihilation of those odious distinctions which divided, and which continue to divide, the nation, and to perpetuate the animosities of contending factions. Dr. Wake was

succeeded

In recording the transactions of the succeeding year (1738), it is unfortunately necessary to notice the violent misunderstanding which arose between the regency of Hanover and the king of Denmark, respecting the petty lordship of Steinhorst, the revenue of which scarcely exceeded one thousand pounds sterling *per annum*. The castle of Steinhorst, garrisoned by a slight detachment of Danish dragoons, was carried by assault, and the king of Denmark made great warlike preparation in order to revenge this affront, which most assuredly would never have been offered, had not Hanover depended upon the aid and protection of England. And the king of Denmark, conscious of his inability to cope with Hanover, *and her* ALLY, had the address to convert this incident to his own advantage, by concluding a convention with the king of England, agreeably to which he engaged to *hold in readiness* a body of 6000 men for the service of Great Britain. In return, Denmark, in addition to the stated pay of these troops, was to receive a subsidy of 250,000 crowns *per ann. and the lordship of Steinhorst was ceded to Hanover*. When the duke of Newcastle produced this treaty in the succeed-

---

succeeded by Dr. Potter, translated from the See of Oxford—a man morose in disposition, and in deportment haughty; but of extensive learning and exemplary morals. After filling the metropolitan throne ten years, this prelate was succeeded by Dr. Herring, archbishop of York, of whom it is difficult to be too profuse in the praise. Placed at the head of the national communion, he appeared scarcely less preeminent in dignity of character than of station; and the various excellencies ascribed by the poet to various contemporary ornaments of the episcopal bench were in him happily consolidated:

" Secker is decent, Rundle has a heart,
Manners with candor are to Benson given,
To Berkely every virtue under heaven."   POPE.

ing seffion for parliamentary ratification, lord Carteret earnestly requested to be informed what use was intended to be made of these troops, as it was expressly stipulated by the articles of the treaty, that they should neither be employed on board the fleet, nor be transported in whole or in part beyond sea, nor serve against France or Spain, except in Germany or Flanders. His grace, however, *not being at liberty to divulge* THE KING's SECRETS, the subsidy was granted; and at the same time, in consequence of a message from the throne, stating the exigency of public affairs, a vote of credit conformable to a similar resolution of the commons passed the house, notwithstanding the animated remonstrances of lord Carteret, who declared that nothing could be more dangerous to the constitution than this practice, which was but of modern date in England; it was never heard of before the Revolution, and but rarely till the nation was blessed with the present administration. Such a demand, he said, our ancestors would have heard with amazement, and rejected with scorn. If a general and unlimited vote of credit and confidence, his lordship affirmed, were to become a customary compliment at the end of every session, parliaments would grow despicable in the eyes of the people; and it might be depended upon as an infallible consequence, that when parliaments were once perceived to be useless and servile, they would, by a rapid gradation, become arbitrary and tyrannical.

END OF THE FIRST VOLUME.

MEMOIRS

OF THE

KINGS OF GREAT BRITAIN.

VOL. II.

MEMOIRS

OF THE

KINGS OF GREAT BRITAIN

OF THE HOUSE OF

BRUNSWIC-LUNENBURG.

BY W. BELSHAM.

VOL. II.

Ac mihi quidem videntur huc omnia esse referenda ab iis qui præsint aliis, ut ii qui eorum in imperio erunt, sint quàm beatissimi. CICERO.

DUBLIN:

PRINTED FOR J. MILLIKEN, NO. 32, GRAFTON-STREET.

MDCCXCVI.

K. GEORGE II.

CONTINUED.

Notwithstanding the Treaty of Seville, concluded so long since as the year 1729, the Spaniards had never desisted from the commission of those insults and depredations, for the prevention of which it was chiefly and professedly made. They were even emboldened by the phlegmatic indifference, or pusillanimity, of the English Minister, to proceed to still farther extremities. They now therefore disputed the right of the English traders to cut logwood in the Bay of Campeachy, and to gather salt in the island of Tortuga, though of antient and established practice, and never before called in question. On pretence of the illicit commerce carried on by the British West India Islands with the Spanish Main,—and which, however contrary to the absurd policy of Spain, was doubtless equally necessary and beneficial to both countries—armed vessels, known by the name of *Guarda-Costas,*

Coſtas, were ſtationed in the uſual track of commercial intercourſe, which, on the plea of ſearching for contraband goods, ſeized, plundered, and inſolently detained, a great number of Britiſh merchant-ſhips at their diſcretion; and, without regarding the faith of nations, impriſoning the crews, and confiſcating the cargoes. The repeated memorials preſented by the Britiſh Ambaſſador at the Court of Madrid produced no ſort of effect. Evaſive anſwers, vague promiſes of inquiry, and cedulas of inſtructions ſent to the Spaniſh Governors in America, intended merely to amuſe, were all the advances which were made towards reparation and redreſs. The nation ſeemed at length fired with a general and juſt reſentment at theſe outrages. Petitions were preſented to Parliament in the ſeſſion of 1738, from the mercantile towns and cities, ſtating the violences to which they had been expoſed, and imploring relief and protection. The Houſe, in a grand committee, proceeded to hear counſel for the merchants, and to examine evidence; in the courſe of which it appeared, that the moſt horrid and wanton acts of cruelty had in various inſtances been perpetrated by the Spaniards on the ſubjects of Great Britain. One Jenkins, who appeared on this occaſion at the bar of the Houſe, gave a ſimple and affecting narrative of the ſavage treatment he had met with from the captain of a Spaniſh guarda-coſta, who, after exhauſting his invention in various modes of torture, tore off one of his ears, and bade him carry it to his King, adding withal many contumelious and opprobrious expreſſions. Deſpairing to eſcape alive from the hands of this barbarian, he recommended, he ſaid, his ſoul to God, and the revenge of his wrongs to his country. The Houſe, ſcarcely leſs inflamed than the populace with this recital, voted an unanimous addreſs to the King, " beſeeching his Majeſty to uſe his endeavors to obtain effectual relief for his injured ſubjects, to convince the Court of Spain that his Majeſty could no longer

longer suffer such constant and repeated insults and injuries to be carried on to the dishonor of his Crown, and to the ruin of his subjects—and in case his applications proved fruitless, assuring him, that the House would effectually support his Majesty in taking such measures as honor and justice should make it necessary for him to pursue." To this address the King returned a gracious and favorable answer, and on the 20th of May 1738 the Parliament was prorogued.

Various motives concurred, nevertheless, to excite in the breast of the Minister an extreme reluctance firmly to resolve on a declaration of war. During the long course of his administration, it had been the constant and favorite object of his policy, to preserve the kingdom from that dire calamity. He perhaps doubted his talents for conducting a war with vigor and ability; and he might reasonably apprehend, that any disastrous event in the course of it might endanger his authority and safety. He was persuaded that the commercial interests affected by these depredations were in themselves too trivial, and of a nature too equivocal in point of right, to warrant the nation in having recourse to a remedy so violent. He well knew that the union of the two Crowns of France and Spain was so strongly cemented, that a war with one must inevitably involve us in a war with the other. And it was his invariable and avowed opinion, though contradicted happily by later experience, that England alone was not equal to cope with the combined force of the House of Bourbon. Possessed with these sentiments, he concluded, during the recess of Parliament, a CONVENTION with Spain, signed at the PARDO in Madrid; by which the King of Spain obliged himself to make reparation to the British subjects for their losses within a certain period; and commissioners were appointed " for regulating all those grievances and abuses which had interrupted the commerce of Great Britain in the American seas; and for settling

tling all other matters in difpute, in fuch a manner as might for the future prevent and remove all new caufes and pretences of complaint." When the terms of the Convention were communicated to the Parliament, which met February 1, 1739, it was treated with the moft poignant contempt and ridicule. It was afferted by the Oppofition, that Spain, fo far from giving up her groundlefs and unjuftifiable claim of vifiting and fearching Britifh fhips failing to and from the Britifh plantations, openly infifted upon it as a matter of right; for it was merely the differences which had arifen in the exercife of this pretended right, and not the right itfelf, which they had fubmitted to difcuffion. So that the undoubted and indifputable rights of England, and the infolent ufurpations of Spain, were referred to the mediation of plenipotentiaries, as refting upon the fame bafis of equality. It was obferved, that if the miniftry had made the refolutions taken by Parliament in the laft feffion the foundation of their demands, a decifive anfwer muft have been obtained; but this Convention, ftyled a treaty, was evidently no more than a preliminary to a treaty; and a moft injurious and difgraceful preliminary. It was an expedient illufory and ignominious, infecure though abject: and an affertion was rifqued, which eventually proved indeed ftrictly true, that the expence of the commiffion would exceed the fum ultimately granted by Spain as an indemnification to the mercantile fufferers *. It was alfo objected that the regulation of the limits of Carolina and Florida was referred to the determination of thefe plenipotentiaries, fo that the territorial right of the infant colony of Georgia, which indubitably belonged to the Crown of Great Britain, was left open to difpute, to the great and manifeft difcourage-

* The fum allowed by Spain as an indemnification, a very inadequate one indeed, to the Britifh merchants, was 95,000l.; from which, under various pretences, fuch deductions were made, as reduced the balance to lefs than 20,000l. The Convention was figned at the Pardo, January 14, 1739.

discouragement of the settlers, who must deem themselves placed in a most precarious and dangerous situation. The Minister, whose equanimity of temper was rarely ruffled by the bitterest invectives, at length arose, and in a very able speech vindicated his own conduct, and the terms of this Convention, by arguments which merit a much more impartial and dispassionate attention than at this period of national delirium they could hope to obtain. "From the military glory of this empire, we are apt, said this cautious and sagacious statesman, to flatter ourselves that our arms are invincible; and the wars between England and Spain are particularly dazzling and fascinating to the imagination. We see great navies defeated, great treasures gained, and great glory acquired; and we have no leisure to reflect that the situation of affairs is at present entirely different from what it once was. Spain indeed has long ceased by its own unassisted strength to excite the dread and terror of Europe. But the very circumstance of its internal debility has been the means of procuring the support and alliance of Powers, in conjunction with whom it would be romantic to expect that it should not be able to defend itself against the most formidable attacks of England. We know that France, who is actually connected with Spain by the closest ties of policy and of blood, has at her command vast armies, fleets, and revenues; and to venture the honor and interest of the empire against such a combination of superior forces, would, without extreme necessity, be not only rash but criminal. I do not affirm that no such necessity can arise; but I affirm that no such necessity yet exists. France and Holland have never contested those claims which we profess to regard with such indignation, and of which it is pretended we ought to insist upon an absolute renunciation on the part of Spain, without even suffering them to become the subject of discussion. But in the lowest state to which Spain has been ever reduced, this claim, which from long
prescription

prescription she no doubt thinks to be just, and perhaps essential to the preservation of her American empire, has been invariably maintained. Spain is a nation steady to her purpose, proud, fond of power, and even of the shadow of it—scrupulously attached to formal inquiries and discussions. Let gentlemen then lay their hands on their hearts, and say whether it were advisable to offer an insult so gross—or reasonable to expect compliance with a demand so imperious. No one, it is surely presumable, would have been better pleased than myself, had Spain thought fit to have given up this point by a clear and positive renunciation. But it is certain that the most successful war would scarcely have been able to extort this concession as a preliminary to a future treaty. But by this Convention a virtual renunciation at least is obtained—for Spain has consented to indemnify the subjects of Great Britain for the injuries they have sustained in consequence of her pretended rights as founded upon this claim. Surely then the administration of Great Britain must have been mad, had they desperately plunged their country into a war, while it was in their power to conclude a peace, of which this great, this decisive concession was to serve as the foundation. Was it for Great Britain to resolve to reject all concessions, and to hear of no other mode of terminating this difference than that of the sword? Could it be consistent with just policy to leave Spain in possession of a plea so plausible, so likely to interest all the Powers of Europe in her favor, as such a conduct must have inevitably furnished? Might she not have said, " I have offered satisfaction, I have offered indemnity, I have offered a firm and faithful observance of treaties; but these offers have been refused; England therefore certainly harbors some deep and dangerous design, which it is the common interest of nations to oppose and counteract." Holland doubtless depends upon her commerce for her support and political importance, as much as ourselves. But I am convinced that the government of that country would not have indulged the complaints of private traders so far as to make a public inquiry, which might have occasioned an open rupture; nor would their Ministers have insisted on immediate satisfaction. They know too well that very great abuses are daily committed in the American trade. They know too well that the result of such inquiry might and would have been very little to their advantage. It requires no great art, no great ability, in a Minister to pursue such measures as might make a war inevitable. But as events depend so much on fortune, it is the part of a wise Minister to leave as little as possible to fortune. And the success which any former Minister has met with from the favor of fortune, is no reason why a succeeding one should tread the same dangerous and uncertain paths, when the same ends can be compassed in a way more safe and certain. I well know indeed that it is impossible for a Minister, let him adopt what mode of conduct he may, to satisfy those whose invariable maxim it is, that the Minister can never be in the right, and consequently that in their uniform opposition to all his measures they can never be in the wrong. Let us suppose that a war had been precipitately declared and vigorously prosecuted. Can we not easily imagine to ourselves that we hear a systematic opposition-man violently declaiming on the benefits of peace?—telling the world that a commercial people ought ever to avoid war, as destructive to their interests even when most successful? Fair and reasonable terms, he would exclaim, have been offered. Spain has even consented to indemnify our merchants for their losses. They have proposed an amicable meeting, to adjust all points in difference—yet our ministry, far from listening to advances so reasonable and equitable, have *blundered* us into an unjust, expensive, and hazardous war. This I confess would have been *blundering*—and for the first time

time perhaps in the courfe of fuch an oppofition, the term would have been rightly applied. Future ages however, always impartial in their cenfure or praife, will, I am confident, do that juftice to the counfels which have produced the Convention under our difcuffion, which paffion and prejudice now refufe. And there is even reafon to believe that a fhort time will remove thofe mifapprehenfions refpecting it, which, in confequence of the clamors of artful and malicious traducers, fo many perfons of real fenfe, candor, and probity, have unhappily been led to entertain."—At length the queftion being put for an addrefs of approbation to the King, as moved by Mr. Horace Walpole, it was carried in the affirmative, in a Houfe confifting of 496 members, by a majority only of 28. The numbers being declared, Sir William Wyndham rofe and remarked, " that the addrefs was intended to convince mankind that the treaty under confideration was a juft and honorable treaty—but if the people refufed implicitly to refign their reafon to a vote of that Houfe, and a vote fo circumftanced, will not Parliament lofe its authority and influence with the public? Will it not be thought that the kingdom is governed by a faction, determined at all events to fupport the meafures of the Minifter? I fhall perhaps, faid he, trouble you no more, but my earneft petition to Almighty God is, that he will preferve this people—whom he has fo often wonderfully protected, from the impending danger which threatens the nation from without, and likewife FROM THAT STILL GREATER DANGER WHICH THREATENS THE CONSTITUTION FROM WITHIN. Sir Robert Walpole was upon this occafion provoked, in bitter and paffionate language, to recall to the recollection of the Houfe, " that the gentleman who was now the mouth of his opponents, was twenty-five years before deeply engaged with thofe traitors who had confpired the deftruction of their country; that the only ufe he had

made

made of the clemency of government then extended to him, was to endeavor its subversion; and he expressed his hope and confidence, that such treachery and ingratitude would produce an union of all true friends to our present happy establishment." Agreeably to the intimation previously given, a grand secession of the members in opposition took place during the remainder of this session, and the succeeding year Sir William Wyndham died, deeply regretted by the public at large, who had long forgotten his early political attachments, as one of the chief ornaments of the British senate and nation. In eloquence he had, by general acknowledgment, no rival but Mr. Pulteney. In the calm discussion of ordinary topics, he is indeed said to have been an uninteresting and ungraceful speaker; but when warmed and animated with his subject, he displayed all the fire and force of a Demosthenes. In the House of Lords the opposition of the Court was no less formidable. The Prince of Wales divided in person against the address, and his example was followed by seventy-three Peers—thirty-nine of whom afterwards signed a protest against it, framed in terms of distinguished spirit and ability. Towards the conclusion of the session the House of Commons voted the sum of five hundred thousand pounds, for augmenting the forces of Great Britain in case of emergency. A motion being made in the House of Peers by Lord Bathurst for an address to know whether Spain had paid the money stipulated by the Convention, the time limited for the payment being now expired; the Duke of Newcastle acquainted the House, that he was commanded by his Majesty to inform them that it was not paid; and that Spain had as yet given no reason for the non-payment—Upon which Lord Carteret moved, that the failure of Spain in this particular was a breach of the Convention, a high indignity to his Majesty, and an injustice to the nation. After a vehement debate the motion

motion was evaded by the previous question. And June 14, 1739, the session was closed by a speech from the throne, in which the King assured the two Houses, "that he would not be wanting in his endeavors to vindicate and maintain the undoubted rights of the nation, and to answer the just expectations of his people." Immediately on the prorogation of Parliament, letters of marque and reprisal were issued against the Spaniards. But the Minister still indulging a fond and lingering hope of averting that war, which was now become certain and inevitable, transmitted instructions to Mr. Keene, the British Envoy at Madrid, to declare that the King of Great Britain did not intend to be thereby understood to break the peace, or to deviate from the treaties subsisting between the two Crowns—and that he had it expressly in charge to assure the Court of Spain, that as soon as the Catholic King should be disposed to make the just satisfaction demanded of him, reprisals should cease, and give way to an accommodation. To which the Marquis de Villarias, the Spanish Minister, with great dignity replied in the name of his sovereign, "that the King of Spain neither acknowledged the right of the King of England to make reprisals, or to authorize others to make them—that his Catholic Majesty would regard these reprisals as a declaration of war, and that on the first intelligence of such act of hostility, Mr. Keene should have notice to leave the kingdom." Lord Waldegrave, the British Ambassador at Paris, having communicated to the Court of Versailles the resolution of the King of England, Cardinal Fleury appeared much moved—and styling it a *terrible resolution*, told the Ambassador that he sincerely deprecated the consequences which there was too much reason to believe would be found to result from it. The Cardinal however, in this crisis, offered as a last resort, through the medium of the French Ambassador in London, the mediation of France, in order to compromise

compromise the differences subsisting between the two Crowns; at the same time intimating that his Most Christian Majesty, in case of a refusal of his good offices, would be obliged to fulfil his engagements with Spain. To which it was replied by the English Court, that the union subsisting between France and Spain was too strong to permit his Most Christian Majesty to act with perfect impartiality in such a mediation, and that this must be considered as a sufficient reason for declining the acceptance of it. Upon which the Ambassador declared his presence in London to be entirely useless, and his continuance probably of very short duration. If the Minister be justly chargeable with tameness and pusillanimity in the conduct of his long and tedious negotiations with Spain, it must be acknowledged that he seemed determined, by the formidable preparations both naval and military, which were now made, to carry on that war with vigor and effect, into which he had entered with so much hesitation and reluctance, and which would have been in all probability much more effectually prevented, by the early assumption of a bolder and more resolute tone, and the actual appearance of a powerful British squadron in the West Indies, than by the numberless querulous and garrulous memorials presented for a succession of years at the Court of Madrid; which appeared to deem it sufficient condescension to suffer the incessant repetition of the same unheeded tale. In the month of October 1739, war was formally declared against Spain: and Rear-admiral Vernon, a rough and resolute seaman, having been previously appointed to the command of the British naval force on the West India station, universal joy was excited by the important intelligence which arrived early in the ensuing year, that he had taken the city of Porto-Bello on the isthmus of Darien, with six ships only. Admiral Vernon received on this occasion the thanks of the House of Commons, and became the theme of the

most

moſt extravagant panegyric. It was however remarked by ſome political *cynics*, that though the attempt was bold, the reſiſtance was feeble; and had it not been crowned with ſucceſs by the caprice of fortune, the commander would have incurred very ſevere cenſure for making a diſplay of his valor ſo much at the expence of his diſcretion. The talents of this officer were, in conſequence of the glory acquired by this brilliant *coup-de-main*, thought equal to any undertaking. And one of the moſt formidable armaments which ever ſailed from the harbors of Great Britain, deſtined for the attack of Carthagena on the Spaniſh main, was entruſted to his care and conduct, with the higheſt confidence of ſucceſs. The command of the land forces on board the fleet, on the death of Lord Cathcart, devolved upon General Wentworth; and it ſoon appeared that the leaders of this expedition were palpably deficient in the moſt eſſential requiſites of their reſpective ſtations. Ignorance, raſhneſs, and diſſenſion characterized all their operations: and after ſuſtaining immenſe loſs, not ſo much from the ill-concerted attacks made upon the town and its adjoining forts, as from the tropical diſeaſes which raged amongſt the troops, they were finally compelled to a precipitate and diſgraceful retreat. And after reinforcements had been received from England, and the health of the men reſtored, nothing was attempted by the Admiral to retrieve his own reputation, or the honor of the Britiſh arms; and the nation began to be ſenſible that they had formed much too high an idea of his character*. A ſquadron under the command of Commodore Anſon was detached into the South Seas, in order to annoy the

---

* Previous to the ſailing of this great armament for Carthagena, the Court of Verſailles again offered its mediation, declaring its willingneſs for this purpoſe to act in concert with the Courts of Vienna and Liſbon—but this offer was, probably with ſecret reluctance, rejected by the Court of London.

Spanish settlements in that quarter. But from the harm sustained in the perpetual war of storms and tempests, rather than opposition of the enemy, the primary design of the expedition proved abortive. The Commodore made however a great number of rich prizes off the coasts of Chili and Peru, which he long kept in alarm. Landing with a detachment of seamen and marines, he took and plundered the town of Paita, and the consternation excited by this enterprise extended even to the city of Lima; but his force was too inconsiderable to attempt any permanent conquest. In crossing the Pacific Ocean, he had the good fortune to meet with and capture a Spanish galleon, bound from Acapulco to the Philippines, of immense value; and returning by the Cape of Good-Hope to England, after a complete circumnavigation of the globe, was received with NATIONAL ACCLAMATION.

An event in which all Europe was deeply interested, and had some time past anxiously expected, at length took place October 20, 1740, in the demise of the Emperor CHARLES VI. the last heir-male of the House of Austria Hapsburg. And in a few days after the Emperor expired Anne Iwanowna, Empress of Russia, who bequeathed her crown to Iwan the infant grandson of her elder sister the Duchess of Mecklenburgh. But this disposition not being agreeable to the Russians, a revolution soon took place in favor of Elizabeth, youngest daughter of Peter the Great by the late Empress Catherine, who adopted the same general system of policy with her predecessors, and governed that vast empire with the same uninterrupted success and reputation. Notwithstanding the famous edict styled the Pragmatic Sanction, of which such repeated mention has been made, and by virtue of which almost all the Powers of Europe had guaranteed the possessions of the House of Austria, to the Arch-duchess Maria Theresa, now assuming the title of Queen of Hungary, the death of the Emperor seemed as a signal to set the world in arms. Frederic King of Prussia,—who had a few months only previous to this event acceded to the throne of his father,—to the astonishment of the Court of Vienna, advanced a dormant and antiquated claim to certain districts of the Duchy of Silesia; and in order to supply all deficiency of argument, he marched a formidable army into that province, and after a rapid succession of conquests made his public entry into Breslau the capital—the Queen of Hungary having rejected with disdain the offer he made to advance a large sum for her immediate accommodation, and assist her with all his forces against whatever enemies might arise in order to obtain her consent to the cession of the territory in question. Till this period it is to be remarked that Prussia had scarcely been numbered amongst the Powers of Europe; and had never been deemed of sufficient consequence to take any other than a subordinate, or secondary part, in the contentions of the Continent. It was not without long and urgent solicitation that the Emperor Leopold had consented to confer the title of KING upon the Marquisses of Brandenburg; and, as it is said, expressly against the advice and remonstrance of Prince Eugene, who warned the Emperor that he was raising up a rival to himself; and that the acquisition of the royal title would probably incite to future dangerous schemes and projects of aggrandizement*.

The

---

* The King of Prussia himself, with his characteristic frankness, says, "Frederic I. en érigeant la Prusse en Royaume, avoit par cette vaine grandeur mis un germe d'ambition dans sa postérité qui devoit fructifier tôt ou tard." The King determined, as he tells us, on a mature consideration of the forlorn situation of Austria, whose finances were miserably deranged, whose armies were ruined by the late unsuccessful war with Turkey, and which was now governed by a young Princess without experience, under the additional disadvantage of a doubtful title—to assert what he is pleased to style *incontestable rights* to Silesia. Though so chimerical did his claims appear to the

The late King of Pruffia was a man capricious, ignorant, and brutal. The relentlefs defpotifm which he exercifed over his fubjects led him to increafe the number, and to pay the clofeft attention to the difcipline of his troops; and his infatiable avarice prompted him to the conftant accumulation of treafure, gradually rifing in a long fucceffion of years to an immenfe amount, and procured by every fpecies of rapine and extortion. And thus the new Monarch, who had fought for refuge from the tyrannic jealoufy of his father in the fhades of retirement, and who had ftrongly excited the attention of Europe, by an uncommon difplay of talents even in that obfcure and fequeftered retreat, now found himfelf in a condition to undertake the boldeft defigns which intereft or ambition could fuggeft. The Elector of Bavaria refufed to acknowledge the title of the Queen of Hungary, alleging that the kingdoms of Hungary and Bohemia belonged to him, in virtue of an antient compact, as the rightful heir of the Emperor Ferdinand I. The King of Poland, as Elector of Saxony, unmindful of his obligations to the late Emperor, claimed the whole Auftrian fucceffion in right of his mother, daughter of the Emperor Jofeph. And France, refolving to embrace the favorable moment for which fhe had long and anxioufly waited, to abafe the pride and annihilate the power of her antient rival, entered into engagements with the Elector of Bavaria, with a view to elevate this Prince to the Imperial throne, and to enable him, in concert with the Houfes of Brandenburg and Saxony, to feize and divide the Germanic dominions of the Houfe of Auftria; the object of the confederacy being to confine the power of the Queen of Hungary

the Conrt of Vienna, that when, in co: fequence of the military preparations actually carrying on in the Pruffian dominions, M. Damrath, the Imperial Envoy at Berlin, warned his Court that a ftorm was gathering which might poffibly burft over that province, the Council of the Queen replied, "Nous ne voulons ni ne pouvons ajouter foi aux nouvelles que vous mandez."

Oeuvres de Frederic II.

within

within the narrow limits of that remote kingdom. Spain also, desirous of a share of the spoils, boldly advanced her pretensions to the Italian dominions of Austria: and the Queen of Spain, heiress of the House of Farnese, a woman of daring ambition, who gloried, like Catherine of Medicis, in styling herself the *Mother of Kings*, entertained the project of erecting these dominions into a Monarchy, under the title of the Kingdom of Lombardy, in favor of her youngest son the Infant Don Philip, brother to Don Carlos King of the Sicilies, who also became a willing party in this formidable confederacy against the Imperial House; in the general wreck of which, the Austrian Netherlands were allotted to France. The treaty of Nymphenburg was concluded in the spring of 1741, between France and Bavaria—a powerful army under Mareschal Maillebois marched at the same time into Westphalia, in order to over-awe the Electorate of Hanover. And the King of England, then at Hanover, thought proper to countermand the march of the Danes and Hessians in the pay of Great Britain, who had received orders to advance to the relief of the Queen of Hungary, and to sign a treaty of neutrality for that Electorate, as the purchase of which he engaged to vote for the Elector of Bavaria at the ensuing election of an Emperor; although this great concession, by which the Imperial diadem was in appearance, and probability, for ever transferred from the House of Austria to that of Bavaria, was obviously and utterly irreconcileable with the general policy of England, which had for a long series of years considered the power of the Austrian family as the only effectual counterbalance to that of the House of Bourbon.

In July 1741, the Elector of Bavaria being joined by the French forces under Mareschal Broglio, entered the Arch-duchy of Austria at the head of 70,000 men, and captured the important cities of Lintz and Passau. But understanding that Vienna was strongly fortified and garrisoned,

risoned, he determined to direct his march to Bohemia; and **Prague** surrendering after a short resistance, the Elector made his public entry into that capital, where he was proclaimed King of Bohemia, and inaugurated with the usual solemnities. Notwithstanding this success, the Elector has been accused of egregious indiscretion, in suffering his attention to be diverted from the siege of Vienna, the conquest of which, exclusive of the lustre it would have reflected upon the confederate arms, must have materially obstructed the communication between the Germanic and Hungarian territories of the Queen; and in its consequences would probably have proved decisive. Nothing however had as yet interrupted the tide of his prosperity.

The Diet of the Empire being convened at Francfort on the Maine, the Elector was unanimously chosen Emperor of the Romans, February 1742, by the name of Charles VII. and a subsidy of fifty Roman months granted him to defray the expences of the war. Reduced to the lowest external ebb of misfortune, Maria Theresa retired to the mountainous recesses of Hungary, and, assembling the States of that kingdom at Presburg, made in person an eloquent and affecting speech*, in which she declared " that she placed her sole reliance on their courage, fidelity, and attachment: and holding up to their view the infant Prince whom she bore in her arms, conjured them to protect and defend the sacred deposit which she entrusted to their care, and to shew in this crisis of danger, by the generous ardor of their loyalty, the affection and reverence which they entertained for the blood of their antient Monarchs." Moved by this uncommon spectacle of Imperial beauty in distress, and fired by the charms of her person no less than the energy of her supplication; this rude but gallant people, drawing suddenly

---

* In the Latin tongue, which is familiar to the Polish and Hungarian nobility.

their sabres, replied with loud acclamations, "Moriamur pro Rege nostro Maria Theresa!" In consequence of the powerful aid she derived from the zeal of her Hungarian subjects, affairs soon began to wear a more favorable aspect.

Early in the spring 1742, the Austrian General Count Khevenhuller, whose military talents entitle him to rank with the greatest commanders, forcing the passes of Scardingen, marched into the Electorate of Bavaria, ravaged the whole country, and made himself master of Munich the capital. Prince Charles of Lorraine, who had married the Arch-duchess Marianne, sister to the Queen of Hungary, entered Silesia at the head of 50,000 men, in order to oppose the progress of the Prussian arms. After two fierce encounters at Molwitz and Czaslaw, in both of which the Prussians had the advantage, a peace was concluded through the mediation of England at Breslau (June 1742); by which the entire province of Silesia, the most fertile, rich, and populous, in the whole extent of the Austrian dominions, was ceded to Prussia. Such was the exultation of his Prussian Majesty at the conclusion of this treaty, the advantages of which so far exceeded his most sanguine hopes and utmost demands at the commencement of the war, that he is said to have declared himself willing to sacrifice his right hand, to insure the perpetual and faithful observance of it*.

In September following an accommodation also took place with Saxony, at the expence of some inconsiderable districts ceded to the King of Poland. The Prince of

---

* The Queen of Hungary, little aware of the extent of the combination against her, had not only rejected with haughtiness the proposals of the King of Prussia, but had formed a project, as was universally believed, with the approbation of the Court of London, for a partition of his dominions; in which the Duchy of Magdeburg was allotted to the King of England—the knowledge of which induced his Prussian Majesty to conclude that alliance with France, by which the very existence of the House of Austria seemed at one time to be endangered.

Lorraine,

Lorraine, now advancing into Bohemia, found that the French forces, under the Mareschals Broglio and Belleisle, had abandoned their conquests on being themselves abandoned by their allies, and had now retired under the cannon of Prague, which was immediately invested by the Austrians: and the siege being prolonged for many months, the French garrison was reduced to difficulties, which the most invincible resolution only could have sustained. The Austrians, supposing that they must finally surrender at discretion, refused to listen to terms of capitulation: but, by an extraordinary effort of military skill and courage, the French Generals forced a passage through the Austrian army, and in the depth of winter made their retreat good to Alsace; eluding, by the secrecy and rapidity of their marches, all attempts to intercept them. The Emperor, being reduced in his turn to the extremity of distress, retired to Francfort, where he chiefly resided during the short and wretched remainder of his life, in a state of exile and indigence. In this destitute and forlorn situation, however, this Prince thought fit to issue a commissorial decree against the Queen of Hungary, couched in terms which the pride and grandeur of Aurelian in the midst of his triumphs over Zenobia scarcely had exceeded *. Referring to a former decree addressed to the Imperial Diet assembled at Francfort, and complaining of the insult and outrage offered to the whole ROMAN EMPIRE, by the *Grand Duchess of Tuscany*, in her refusal to acknowledge his dignity and the validity of his election, he says, " that he had most graciously required of that Assembly with

---

* AURELIANUS Imperator Romanæ Orbis ZENOBIÆ.

Spontè facere debuistis id quod meis literis nunc jubetur. Deditionem præcipio impunitate vitæ propositâ, ita ut illic, Zenobia, cum tuis agas vitam ubi te ex Senatûs amplissimi sententia collocavero. Gemmas, argentum, aurum, sericum, equos, camelos in ærarium Romanum conferas. Palmyrenis jus suum servabitur.

most

most resplendent moderation, how and after what manner the most high Imperial dignity might be sustained—and declaring, from the fulness of Imperial power, inadmissible and null, and utterly cancelling and rendering void the two protestations of the Court of Vienna, of September in the preceding and July in the present year, as injurious in the highest degree to the majesty and supreme dignity of the EMPEROR OF THE ROMANS and the grandeur of the whole ROMAN EMPIRE."

On the side of Italy, the Spaniards, in order to carry their magnificent projects into effect, had assembled, in conjunction with the Neapolitans, an army of 60,000 men at Rimini, A. D. 1742, under the command of the Duc de Montemar, afterwards succeeded by Count de Gages, who attempted in vain to penetrate into Tuscany. And the King of Sardinia, who dreaded with reason the aggrandizement of the House of Bourbon in Lombardy, having declared in favor of the House of Austria, and joined Count Traun the Austrian General in the Parmesan; another Spanish army, under the Infant Don Philip in person, entered Savoy *, and took possession of Chamberri; and though his Sardinian Majesty returned to the defence of his own dominions at the first notice of this attack, he could not prevent the Spaniards from taking up their winter-quarters in Savoy. In the course of this campaign, the army under Count Gages was extremely weakened by the defection of the Neapolitan troops, who were recalled by a mandate of the King of Naples, issued in consequence of the unexpected and unwelcome appearance of an English squadron in the Bay of Naples, detached by Admiral Matthews, the British Commander in the Mediterranean, with the peremptory denunciation of an immediate bombardment of the

* "Tell your master (said the Queen of Spain to the Sardinian Ambassador on his departure from Madrid) that my son shall be a King in spite of all his efforts to prevent it."

city of Naples, if his Neapolitan Majesty refused to sign an explicit declaration of neutrality. The ensuing campaign in Italy did not at all advance the progress of the Spaniards. Count Gages having, contrary to his better judgment, attacked the combined army of Austrians and Piedmontese under the command of the brave and experienced Maresehal Traun at Campo-Santo *, was obliged to retreat with considerable loss, after an engagement which commenced at sun-rise, and which continued till seven at night by the light of the moon. The Mareschal being destined to yet more urgent and important services in Germany, resigned his command, September 1743, to Prince Lobkowitz. In Savoy the Infant Don Philip, reinforced by 20,000 French auxiliaries, attacked the Piedmontese lines at Chateau Dauphine—but was repulsed in repeated attacks with much damage; upon which the French retired into Dauphiné, and the Spaniards took refuge in their winter-quarters. In order to exhibit a connected view of this Italian war, which bears a very remote relation to the history of Great Britain, and to which it will not be necessary to revert, it may be proper to relate, in a few words, the principal events of the succeeding campaigns.

The King of Naples, renouncing his compulsory profession of neutrality, re-assembled his army in the summer of 1744, and openly joined Count de Gages. Prince Lobkowitz the Austrian General, marching through the Papal territories, advanced to the frontiers of Naples; and published, though with little effect, a manifesto to exhort the Neapolitans to shake off the Spanish yoke, and return to the dominion of the House of Austria.

---

* This battle was rashly and unexpectedly fought, February 3. 1743; Count de Gages receiving positive orders from the Court of Madrid, to attack the enemy in three days after the arrival of the courier, or to resign his command to Count Mariani.

Count

Count Brown being secretly detached by the Austrian Commander to attack the town of Velletri, where the King of Naples had established his quarters in a state of perfect apparent security, so successfully executed his commission, that his Neapolitan Majesty escaped in the darkness of the night, through a postern, with great difficulty. But Count de Gages, repairing to the post in person, with great presence of mind rallied the troops, and at length compelled the Austrian General to sound a retreat. The Imperial army having suffered much from the excessive heats of the summer, and the consequent epidemical diseases of an unaccustomed climate, decamped in November, in order to take up their winter-quarters in Parma. Scarcely had the Austrian Commander passed the Tiber, and lost sight of the walls of Rome, but his antagonist Count de Gages, accompanied by his Neapolitan Majesty, entered that city—but finding the bridges broken down, they desisted from the pursuit; and the Holy Father received both these contending powers with the same external demonstrations of joy and affection.

In Savoy the Infant Don Philip, being joined by his allies the French, attacked the King of Sardinia, though strongly entrenched amidst the mountains of Villa-Franca; and after an obstinate engagement, this Monarch, being overpowered by numbers, was obliged to abandon his posts, and to embark on board the British squadron then cruizing off the coast, which transported him and his troops to Vado. Don Philip now prepared to penetrate through the territories of Genoa to the Milanese; but the British Commander, Admiral Matthews, declared that the King of England would consider the permission of the republic as a violation of their neutrality. The Spaniards therefore defiled towards Piedmont, and forced the strong post of Chateau-Dauphine, defended by the King of Sardinia in person, who now retreated to Saluces

ces in order to cover his capital, while the combined army invested the strong and important fortress of Coni. Had this enterprise succeeded, the Sardinian Monarch would have been reduced to a very critical situation: but Baron Leutrum the Governor made so gallant a defence, that the Infant and the Prince of Conti, who commanded the French army, were compelled to raise the siege at the approach of winter, and to retire with great precipitation to the frontiers of France.

The campaign of 1745 proved still more disastrous and alarming: for Count de Gages, at the head of the Spanish and Neapolitan forces, passed the Appenines, and directing his march through the territories of Genoa, which—in consequence of provocations no patience could endure—had now joined the confederacy, accomplished a junction with the army of the Infant Don Philip; and the Austrians retiring before them, the Milanese, Parma, and Placentia, submitted to the dominion of Spain. All Piedmont on both sides the Po was likewise reduced, and Turin itself menaced with a siege; yet the King of Sardinia adhered with unshaken fidelity to his engagements, and rejected with heroic firmness all proposals of a separate accommodation.

In the memorable march of Count Gages, whose passage over the Appenines was compared by the Italians to that of Hannibal over the Alps; nothing, as the historian Buonamici informs us, appeared so surprising as the plenty which the army of that General found, when sinking under the pressure of distress, at their entrance into the territories of the republic of Lucca, though in point of natural fertility far inferior to the countries they had traversed. The roads from all the surrounding villages were crowded with carriages, conveying forage and provisions into the camp, at a season of the year when it might have been imagined that the public stores were exhausted. And it was seen and felt with irresistible conviction, that the

misery

misery or happiness of the subject arises not from the nature of the soil, but of the government*.

In the ensuing year, 1746, fortune, ever capricious and inconstant, began once more to smile upon this Prince, when apparently reduced to the very verge of ruin. The Court of Vienna being no longer pressed on the side of Germany, sent powerful reinforcements into Italy, and the coffers of his Sardinian Majesty being amply replenished with British subsidies, he was enabled to take the field with redoubled force. Early in the spring Baron Leutrum, the Piedmontese General, recovered Aste, Allesandria, and Casal; Marcschal Maillebois, who now commanded the French armies, retiring into the Genoese territories. On the other side, Count de Gages and Don Philip were compelled to abandon Milan, Pavia, and Parma, and retreat to Placentia, where, in the month of June, they were joined by Mareschal Maillebois. In consequence of this junction, the Infant, finding himself at the head of 50,000 men, determined to attack the Austrians in their camp at San Lazaro, but met with a most severe repulse; and the Austrians pursuing their victory, in their turn attacked the enemy, August 10, near the town of Tortona, on the southern banks of the Po, the passage of which the combined armies of French and Spaniards effected not without great difficulty and loss. The Infant was, in consequence of this second defeat, compelled to abandon the city of Placentia, containing immense magazines of ammunition and military stores; and retreating towards Genoa, after a short interval

---

* The difference between the general state and condition of the people under despotic and republican governments, however modified, forces itself upon the observation. " I know very well," says a writer of discernment, " that the republics of Genoa and Venice are not in general allowed to be free States. M. Montesquieu has demonstrated, that they are not free. But there is undoubtedly some excellence in them which has escaped this wise man, for the contrast betwen these and the neighboring States is very remarkable."

quitted

quitted the territories of the republic, and took the route of Provence. Genoa was now compelled to furrender to the Auftrians, who exercifed the rights of conqueft with fuch mercilefs rigor, that the Genoefe flew to arms, and in a fhort time, with a courage worthy of their antient fame, totally expelled their oppreffors. Whilft the Imperial Generals kept poffeffion of Genoa, the bank of St. George was exhaufted by the enormous contributions levied by the Auftrians, who boafted that the wealth of this proud city was theirs, and that Genoa would in a fhort time be deluged in blood. And General Botta, the Auftrian Commander, is faid to have told the Genoefe deputies, who pathetically pleaded for the mitigation of their fufferings, that he would leave them nothing except their eyes, to behold the deftruction of their country, and to weep over its ruins.

In April 1747, the French, under Marefchal Belleifle, once more croffed the Var, and took poffeffion of Nice, Montalban, Villa-Franca, and Ventimiglia, almoft without refiftance, the Auftrians and Piedmontefe being employed in an attempt to recover the city of Genoa. On fummoning the citizens to furrender, they replied with that fpirit which almoft invariably animates and pervades all claffes of men living under a republican form of government, " that they would defend their liberty with the laft drop of their blood, and would rather be buried in the ruins of their capital, than fubmit to the *clemency* of the Court of Vienna." Count Schuylenburg, the Auftrian Commander, who conducted the operations of the fiege with great fkill and vigor, was at length reduced reluctantly to liften to the remonftrances of the King of Sardinia, who reprefented to him the neceffity of abandoning his enterprize in order to cover Piedmont and Lombardy from the efforts of the Marefchal de Belleifle. But the Chevalier de Belleifle, brother to the Marefchal, attempting to force the important pafs of Exiles, was

repulfed

repulsed with prodigious slaughter; and seizing a pair of colors, with a resolution, on the renewal of the attack, to plant them with his own hand upon the ramparts, he was shot dead with a musquet ball. The troops immediately gave way in the utmost confusion, and the Mareschal, informed of this disaster, retreated back to the Var, and his Sardinian Majesty menaced Dauphiné with an invasion in his turn; but excessive rains prevented the execution of his design.

The succeeding campaign (A. D. 1748), which was the last of the war, was distinguished by no very material transaction; the near prospect of peace rendering it equally unadvisable on both sides to risque any hazardous enterprize. And the Infant Don Philip was by one of the articles of the Treaty put into possession of Parma, Placentia, and Guastalla—the King of Sardinia receiving, in conformity to a previous agreement with the Queen of Hungary, and as a just remuneration for the fidelity and attachment he had discovered to the interests, and the courage he had displayed in the defence of the House of Austria, some contiguous districts of Novara and the Milanese. As soon as certain intelligence had arrived, that the treaty of Aix-la-Chapelle was signed, the British Admiral acquainted the Senate of Genoa of that event, in a message delivered by one of his captains, who had at the same time express orders to assure the republic how great was the admiration he entertained of the fortitude and valor displayed by them in the defence of their liberties. "Such, says the Italian historian, is the magnanimity of the British nation[*]."

It is now high time to advert to the situation of Great Britain, and to trace the mazes of that policy by which she became a principal in this destructive war, which, had she consulted her proper interests, would scarcely have

---

[*] Buonamici's Commentaries, Book IV.

involved

involved her as an auxiliary. The Opposition exulted much in the royal declaration of war against Spain, which they affirmed to be an echo of their reasonings and arguments against the Convention; although the truths it contained were at that time positively denied by the Minister and his adherents—and since that time not one event had happened which was not by his opponents previously foretold.

The session which commenced November 1739, closed April 29, 1740, without producing any remarkable event. The Pension Bill was, according to almost annual custom, passed by the Commons and rejected by the Lords. But the Place Bill, which was again introduced with many judicious modifications and numerous exceptions, was thrown out by a very small majority of the Commons in a very full House, the numbers being 222 to 206. As it was clearly perceived that the Court was forced into the present contest against Spain, the great popularity of the war did not at all diminish, or rather it tended to heighten, the unpopularity of the Minister. After the capture of Porto-Bello, and the ill-conducted attempt on Carthagena, the spirit of enterprize seemed no more—the fleets of Spain sailed unmolested from their harbors, though British squadrons were stationed off the Spanish coasts, for the professed purpose of intercepting them. Commerce was interrupted by the numbers of seamen pressed into the service of Government—and still more by the incredible number of prizes taken by the Spanish privateers. The discontents of the merchants were unnecessarily inflamed by the rash and passionate answer of Sir Charles Wager, who, when a memorial was presented to him as first Lord of the Admiralty, for protection and redress,—replied, "It is your own war, and you must take it for your pains." The harbor and fortifications of Dunkirk were repaired by order of the French King, in open violation of the treaty of Utrecht. A French fleet had sailed

sailed in company with the Spaniards to the West Indies, for the avowed purpose of protecting the Spanish commerce, and serious apprehensions were entertained for the safety of Jamaica.

When the Parliament was convened in November 1740, the nation, throughout all the different ranks and descriptions of citizens, exhibited evident and alarming symptoms of discontent. Eager to embrace the favorable moment, Mr. Sandys, one of the leaders of Opposition, soon after the commencement of the session, notified to Sir Robert Walpole in the House of Commons, his intention on the Friday following to bring forward a charge against him. At this unexpected intimation, the Minister seemed at first somewhat disconcerted and surprised: but recovering himself, after a short pause, replied, " that as he was conscious of no crime, he had no doubt of being able to make a proper defence—and laying his hand with emotion on his breast, he added, with Roman dignity,

———————" Hic murus aheneus esto,
Nil conscire sibi, nullâ pallescere culpâ*."

On the day appointed, Mr. Sandys accordingly, at the close of a long speech, in which he recapitulated all the political delinquencies, real or pretended, of the Minister, moved, " that an humble address should be presented to the King, beseeching his Majesty that he would be graciously pleased to remove the Right Honorable Sir Robert Walpole, first Commissioner of the Treasury, &c., from his Majesty's presence and counsels for ever." The motion was ably sustained by the members in opposition, particularly by Mr. Pulteney, who took a very severe retrospective view of the conduct of the Minister, from the commencement of his administration. " By the

---

* " Be this my brazen bulwark of defence,
Still to preserve a conscious innocence." FRANCIS.

treaty of Seville, said this eloquent speaker, we were very nearly driven to the perilous extremity of entering into a war with the Emperor, as the direct consequence of our conjunction with France and Spain. But the nation took the alarm, and the Minister was obliged to consult his safety; and this impelled him to avert the danger by a precipitate unconditional guarantee of the Pragmatic Sanction. But though, in consequence of this rash measure, and this alone, the Emperor consented to the introduction of Spanish troops into the Duchies of Parma and Placentia, Spain performed nothing on her part of what she had engaged. On the contrary, the depredations of that nation on our West India commerce daily increased; and thus affairs stood when France, in alliance with Spain and Sardinia, thought fit to attack the Emperor in 1733, with an avowed design to strip him of all his dominions in Italy. Of this attack we remained idle, though not unexpensive, spectators, till we saw on the one hand Naples, and even Sicily, procured for him by England at the price of a war with Spain, wrested from the Emperor; and on the other, the Duchy of Lorraine added to the Monarchy of France. On the first accession of the Minister to the sole direction of public affairs, there was a fair prospect, Mr. Pulteney said, of discharging, within a reasonable time, every shilling of the public debt —but this would have diminished the Minister's fund for corruption, and it was therefore by all means to be prevented; and the public charge was to be yearly increased, in order to oblige us to the alternative of applying the produce of the Sinking Fund to the current service, or of contracting a new debt, equal to that which was paid off. The expences of the civil government were also so prodigiously enhanced, that a demand of 500,000l. was made in the year 1725, to pay the debts of the Civil List, though the like sum had been granted for the same purpose but four years before. Upon his present Majesty's accession, an addition of 100,000l. was made to the Civil List, besides 115,000l. for making good a pretended deficiency in that revenue. But what furnished the most successful pretext for increasing the public burdens, was the famous TREATY of HANOVER, professedly concluded for preventing the dangers with which Europe was threatened from the overgrown power of the House of Austria. Had the danger alledged been *real*, this nation ought to have been the last, because it had certainly the least to fear. But the fact was, that the Dutch, who lay most exposed, were so little apprehensive of danger, that it was not without much solicitation, and after considerable delay, that they could be persuaded to accede to this treaty. And France, to whom the alliance of Spain and the Emperor might reasonably be supposed to appear formidable, neither chose to incur any expence, nor discovered any solicitude to assist us when actually attacked by Spain in consequence of this treaty; whereas WE took 12,000 Hessians into our pay; granted subsidies to the Kings of Sweden and Denmark, and, what was most extraordinary, to the Duke of Wolfenbuttle, six months after the preliminaries of peace with Spain and the Emperor were signed: and the Hessians were continued in pay for several years. When a scheme was afterwards offered by a patriotic Member of this House—Sir John Barnard—for reducing the interest payable upon all our public funds; it is unnecessary to say by whom, and by what means, that scheme was defeated—and considering how practicable a plan it was at that time, we must conclude that the Minister who opposed it could have no design that our debts should be ever paid, or our taxes diminished."

On this trying occasion, Sir Robert Walpole nevertheless defended himself with such vigor and ability, that the motion of Mr. Sandys was finally rejected by a very great majority. " The successive measures of his administration,

tion, the Minister alledged, were adapted to the different exigencies of the times—they had received the repeated and unequivocal sanction of successive Parliaments—the sole object of that system of policy by which his public conduct had been regulated, was to preserve the tranquillity of Europe, which was to be effected only by maintaining the balance of Europe.—The charge of corruption, so generally brought, the Minister as generally denied—and, to the amazement and confusion of his friends, he positively challenged his accuser to produce one specific instance of this nature in confirmation of his accusation. In the course of his speech he animadverted with great spirit upon the indiscriminate use of the term *patriotism*. A Patriot, Sir! said he, addressing the chair—I venerate the name. But then, it is the real, and not the pretended Patriot, who is the object of my reverence. In these times, Sir, Patriots spring up like mushrooms—I could raise twenty of them in a night—A Minister has nothing more to do, than to refuse compliance with an unjust or unreasonable demand, and up starts a Patriot. But, Sir, the unprincipled efforts of such Patriots I alike disdain and detest." After a short interval, a motion to the same purport with that of Mr. Sandys, was made in the House of Peers by Lord Carteret and supported by the Duke of Argyle, and the Lords Gower, Bathurst, and Chesterfield. It was negatived, but thirty Peers entered their protest; and the credit and authority of the Minister were sensibly impaired by these repeated attacks.

In April 1741, the King delivered in person a speech to both Houses of Parliament, informing them that the Queen of Hungary had made a requisition of assistance from England, agreeable to the tenor of the subsisting treaties—that he had ordered the Danish and Hessian auxiliaries to be in readiness to march for that purpose—that in this complicated and uncertain state of affairs, it might become necessary for him to incur extraordinary expences for maintaining inviolate the Pragmatic Sanction, for which he trusted they would provide. The Commons assured the King in their address " that they entirely approved of the measures already pursued, and that they would enable him effectually to support his engagements with the Queen of Hungary." Two hundred thousand pounds were accordingly voted upon the motion of the Minister, as a parliamentary grant or gratuity to that Princess, and 300.000l. more to his Majesty, to be employed at his discretion, in the manner most conducive to her service; seventy thousand men had been before voted for the army and navy, and the accustomed subsidies granted to Denmark and Hesse Cassel. "HONEST SHIPPEN *" only ventured to oppose this wild and wanton waste of the public money. "He protested, on this as on all other occasions, against any interposition in the affairs of Germany. He protested against that clause of the address, by which the House engaged to defend his Majesty's foreign dominions from insult, or attack, as utterly inconsistent with the Act of Settlement—declaring, that if the repeated and shameful evasions of that Act, or rather the open violations of it, could have been foreseen, they would probably have for ever precluded from the succession of that illustrious family, to which the nation owed such NUMBERLESS BLESSINGS, SUCH CONTINUED FELICITY." On the 25th of April 1741, the session closed, and the King took his leave of this Parliament in the prospect of its dissolution, with many expressions of gratitude and satisfaction.

The NEW PARLIAMENT being convened December 1, 1741, the King in his speech expressed his hope and expectation, that the two Houses would confirm the resolutions formed by their predecessors for the support of the

---

* " I love to pour out all myself, as plain
  As HONEST SHIPPEN, or downright Montagne." POPE.

Pragmatic Sanction, the preservation of the balance of power, the liberties of Europe, and the security of his dominions. An address of thanks and approbation being moved as usual, a clause was proposed to intreat his Majesty not to engage these kingdoms in a war for the preservation of his foreign dominions. In vindication of which, Mr. Shippen arose and declared, ' that he was neither afraid nor ashamed to affirm that thirty years had made no change in any of his political opinions. He said that he was grown old in the House of Commons, and had lived to see his conjectures and predictions ripened into knowledge. I may, said he, perhaps fall under the censure of the House, and be once more treated as a criminal, for asserting what they who punish me cannot deny—that Hanoverian maxims are inconsistent with the interest and happiness of this nation—that the wise policy of the Act of Settlement ought to be adhered to; and that England ought not to be endangered, in order that the King's foreign dominions may be secured."—" Are we, exclaimed with energy another Member *, in reference to the same question, to stand up single in the defence of the Pragmatic Sanction? to fight for ever the quarrels of others? and live in perpetual war, that our neighbors may enjoy the advantages of peace?" The address, as it was originally moved, was however presented to the King, the Opposition not deeming it a fit opportunity to make trial of their strength. But a petition from the Electors of Westminster coming after a short interval under the cognizance of the House, the election of the sitting Members, who were the Court candidates, was declared void by a majority of four voices; and the High Bailiff was committed to custody. Other controverted elections being likewise decided to the disadvantage of the Court, and against its utmost exertions; Sir Robert Walpole became sensible that his political career hastened to its

* Mr. Viner.

termination.

termination. Anxious however to make one effort more to retain that authority which he had so long exercised almost without control, and which he could not now relinquish without danger; he caused a royal message to be sent to the Prince of Wales, importing that if his Royal Highness would accede to terms with his Majesty, his revenue should be immediately raised to 100,000l. per annum;—200,000l. should be advanced for the payment of his debts; he and his friends should be taken into favor, and a suitable provision made for all his followers. But the Prince positively declared, "that he would accept of no such conditions, or of any conditions, while public affairs continued under the direction of Sir Robert Walpole—whom he regarded as the bar which separated his Majesty from the affections of his people—as the grand author of the national losses, disgraces, and grievances, at home and abroad." Repulsed in this attempt, the Minister, now in imminent danger of an impeachment, endeavored in vain to detach from their political connection some of the leaders of the opposite party: and finding himself on the next division again left in a minority, he declared he would never more enter the walls of that House. On the ensuing day, February 3, 1742, the King adjourned both Houses of Parliament to the 18th, and immediately upon this adjournment, Sir Robert Walpole was created Earl of Orford, and resigned all his employments. Various intrigues and negotiations were carried on during this recess; and it soon appeared that a fatal division had taken place among the Patriots, and that divers of them who had made the loudest professions of honor and virtue, who had repeatedly menaced the Minister with clamors of inquiry and denunciations of vengeance, and who had boasted that no art could dissolve the cement by which they were united, had secretly acceded to an insidious and disgraceful accommodation with the Court, of which the impunity of the late Minister

was

was understood to be a fundamental article. The Duke of Newcastle, and Mr. Pelham, with their adherents, were allowed to retain their places. The Earl of Wilmington succeeded Sir Robert Walpole, as first Lord Commissioner of the Treasury Mr. Sandys was appointed Chancellor of the Exchequer. Lord Carteret took the Seals, as Secretary of State for the foreign department, and was regarded as chief Minister; and Mr. Pulteney, who refused to accept any office of responsibility, was sworn anew of the Privy Counsel, and was soon afterwards created Earl of Bath—but though he had flattered himself with the idea of guiding unseen the reins of government, he was never admitted to the least share of royal confidence, and remained the victim of his own treachery—" a solitary monument of blasted ambition." The nation saw with astonishment and indignation, in this coalition of parties, a change, not of measures but of men; they saw the old system not only adopted, but confirmed and strengthened; they saw the same influence in Parliament exerted for the same purposes, and in the transports of their resentment the new Ministers were branded as apostates and betrayers of their country; and patriotism was ridiculed and exploded as an illusive and empty name *. Soon after the new Ministry had entered

* The Duke of Argyle, who had, on the dismission of Sir Robert Walpole, accepted the command of the royal regiment of horse, and master-generalship of the ordnance, on being apprised of the political collusion which had been practised, in a very short time, in the utmost resentment, threw up his places.

At or about this period an ODE was addressed by the celebrated AKENSIDE, the votary of Apollo in his twofold capacity—*per me concordant carmina, medicina meum est*—to Mr. Pulteney, under the name of CURIO, containing very bitter and poignant reflections on his political apostacy. The following stanzas Indignation has exalted into poetry:

" At length in view the glorious end appear'd,
We saw thy spirit through the senate reign;

upon their functions, the PENSION BILL, which had been formerly the darling object of the Patriots, was revived and passed by the Commons, but once more received sentence of condemnation from the Lords; LORD CARTERET HIMSELF GIVING HIS VOTE AGAINST IT. A motion made for leave to bring in a Bill to repeal the Septennial Act was vehemently opposed by Mr. PULTENEY and Mr. SANDYS, and the question passed in the negative. The Place Bill, now brought forward by Mr. Lyttelton, met with the same fate. The motion for an inquiry into the conduct of Robert Earl of Orford, during the twenty years of his administration, was also rejected; but the motion being renewed, and limited to the last ten years, it was with great difficulty carried against the Court: but a subsidiary Bill, for indemnifying those who should be summoned to give evidence against that Nobleman, was rejected, after it had passed the Commons, through the opposition of Lord Carteret: so that the inquiry proved, as it was no doubt intended to prove, finally abortive. Two reports, however, were actually presented by the Committee of inquiry to the House, by which,

> And Freedom's friends thy instant omen heard
> Of laws, for which their fathers bled in vain :—
> O Alfred, father of the English name,
> O valiant Edward, first in civil fame,
> O William, height of public virtue pure,
> Bend from your radiant seats a joyful eye,
> Behold the sum of all your labors nigh,
> Your plans of law complete, your ends of rule secure.
>
> " 'Twas then, O shame! O soul from faith estrang'd,
> O Albion, oft to flatt'ring vows a prey;
> 'Twas then—thy thought what sudden frenzy chang'd?
> What rushing palsy took thy strength away?
> Is this the man in Freedom's cause approv'd?
> The man so great, so honor'd, so belov'd?
> Whom the dead envied, and the living bless'd?
> This patient slave by tinsel bonds allur'd?
> This wretched suitor for a boon abjur'd?
> Whom those that fear'd him scorn, that trusted him detest?"

amongst

amongst other interesting particulars, it appears on record, that, exclusive of all the open and avowed means of influence, the enormous sum of one million four hundred and fifty-three thousand pounds had been expended during the last ten years for SECRET SERVICE. Paxton, Solicitor to the Treasury, refusing to answer interrogatories put to him by the Committee, was committed to close custody, but still persisted in his contumacy, and Scroope, Secretary to the Treasury, through whose hands vast sums had passed, declared, that he could not IN CONSCIENCE, after consulting the ablest lawyers and divines, and laying his case before his Majesty, to whom alone he thought himself responsible, discover in what manner this money had been expended, or to what purposes appropriated. And the Committee state in their reports, as a subject of most serious complaint, that the very magnitude and extent of the evil are become the means of screening it from detection and punishment. Amongst those whose eloquence enforced a reluctant adoption of the motion of inquiry, no one more distinguished himself than Mr. Pitt, a young man of extraordinary talents, who had risen during the few years he had sat in the House of Commons into very high reputation. In reply to the pretext of danger in the State from this investigation, he declared, " that he was so far from apprehending danger from this inquiry, that he firmly believed the nation could only be injured by a long neglect of such examinations. Is it, said he, unbecoming the wisdom and dignity of this assembly, to inquire to what causes and to what misconduct it is to be imputed, that we are neither able to acquire the laurels of war, nor to enjoy the blessings of peace? that, during the long continuance of the national tranquillity, our debts have not been diminished from that state to which they were raised by fighting at our own expence the general quarrel of mankind? why the sinking fund, that inviola-

ble

ble deposit, has been annually diverted from its appropriated purposes? I fear not to declare, that I expect, in consequence of such inquiry, to find, that our treasure has been exhausted, not to humble our enemies, or to obviate domestic insurrections—not to support our allies, or to suppress our factions—but for purposes which no man who loves his country can think of without indignation—the purchase of votes, the bribing of boroughs, the enriching of hirelings, the multiplying of dependents, the corruption of senates. If those to whom the administration of affairs has been for twenty years confided, have betrayed their trust—if they have invaded the public rights with the public treasure, and employed the power committed to them by their country only to enslave it, who will not acknowledge that a sacrifice to justice is called for—that they ought to be set as land-marks to posterity, to warn those who shall hereafter launch on the ocean of power, not to be too confident of an ever-prosperous gale, but to remember that there are rocks on which whoever rushes must inevitably perish *?"

In forming a just estimate of the political character of Sir Robert Walpole, who, for more than twenty years, governed these kingdoms with distinguished reputation and ability, we shall find ample ground both for applause and censure. Regarding him in the most favorable point of view, we are compelled to acknowledge that, under the auspices of this Minister, justice was equitably and impartially administered; the prerogative of the Monarch was invariably restrained within the strict limits of the law; commerce was, by many wise laws, encou-

---

* A bill appointing Commissioners, seven in number, for taking, examining, and stating, the public accounts of the kingdom, passed with little opposition; but, on the ballot, the courtiers exerted themselves so successfully, that the numbers were decidedly in favor of the court list; upon which the patriots, in sullen resentment, suffered the bill, after being reported, to be finally thrown out.

raged and extended; the riches of the nation rapidly increased; and the rights and liberties of the people were maintained inviolate. But, if we contemplate the interior policy of his administration, we perceive, it, however fair in appearance, *rotten at the core*, tainted and *sicklied o'er* with the cadaverous hue of corruption; and threatening, in its progress, to undermine all public virtue, and to extinguish every spark of public spirit. Compelled, in order to secure the favor of his Sovereign, and with the vain hope to perpetuate himself in office, to adopt measures contrary to his better judgment, and the true interests of his country, he saw that the most, or rather the only, certain method of carrying those obnoxious measures into effect, was to create an interest in Parliament separate from that of the people; by the basest and most degrading arts of political depravity, a majority of votes in both Houses was obtained and secured; and since the establishment of this system of ministerial corruption, which has descended to us in its full force, the deliberations of Parliament are become little better than the conflicts of faction, or the empty forms of freedom *. Parliament, which ought to exhibit an unclouded display of wisdom, integrity, and benevolence,

combined

---

* Foreign, as it may justly be deemed, from the purpose of history, which descends not to the contemplation of the private characters of men, any further than they may be interwoven with their public life, it may be transiently remarked that this Minister, although he cannot be applauded for the purity of his morals, possessed, in an eminent degree, all those happy social qualities which conciliate affection, if they fail to engage esteem. This striking trait of Sir Robert Walpole's general character has been touched in a masterly manner by the poetic pencil of POPE:

"Seen him I have, but in his happier hour
Of social pleasure, ill exchang'd for power;
Seen him uncumber'd with the venial tribe,
Smile without art, and win without a bribe."

combined in one illustrious assemblage is virtually degraded to a court convened only for the purpose of enregistering the royal edicts. It is not the grave and well-weighed counsels of the legislature which, under this system, direct the movements of the executive power; but it is the caprice, the pride, and the folly of the executive power which have too frequently influenced and governed the volitions of the legislative body. It is an acknowledged truth, a truth upon parliamentary record —that "THE INFLUENCE OF THE CROWN OUGHT TO BE DIMINISHED;" but no vigorous steps have yet been taken to effect that diminution. A reform of the representation, a reduction of the standing military force, a progressive redemption of the public debt, and a total abolition of all useless and superfluous places, pensions, and sinecures, upon which the monster CORRUPTION feeds and thrives, are alone adequate to accomplish the mighty task of a national regeneration. And if that energy and virtue are wanting in the community at large, which will in time incite to the adoption of such means as are necessary to effectuate this end, what remains but to await, in deep and tranquil silence, the moment in which the national liberty is fated finally to terminate in that absolute monar-

Sir Robert Walpole, in person, was tall, somewhat bulky, and his countenance is described as noble and benign. Of his attachment to the fine arts, the magnificent collection of pictures of Houghton *was* a very decisive proof; but his neglect or contempt of literature, though not himself wholly devoid of learning, exposed him to continual disgrace; for while the measures of his administration were attacked by men of the highest talents, they were vindicated only by scribblers, who were liberally paid for writing what even the most partial friends of the Minister could scarcely endure to read. A pension of three thousand livres granted by Louis XV. to the celebrated M. Crebillon, gave rise in England to the following *jeu d'esprit:*

    " At reading this, great WALPOLE shook his head;
    How! wit and genius help a man to bread!
    With better skill we pension and promote;
    None eat with us who cannot give a vote."

thy which, according to a profound and celebrated writer, forms the true *euthanasia* of the BRITISH CONSTITUTION?

The new administration was now completely formed, and the whole formidable series of patriotic motions had been successfully consigned, by their former advocates, to repose and oblivion. Affairs, therefore, now reverting to their regular and accustomed channels, the House of Commons was moved, by the Chancellor of the Exchequer, to resolve itself into a Committee of Supply; and, conformably to the estimates and resolutions brought forward, upwards of an hundred thousand seamen and landmen were voted for the service of the current year; the sum of five hundred thousand pounds was granted to the Queen of Hungary, and the subsidies to Denmark and Hesse Cassel continued *. But this was deemed by the Court a very inadequate aid; and it soon appeared that the new Minister, Lord Carteret, a man

---

* " Such, says the Gothic annalist of the times, were the exertions of the new ministers to make some *figure* with the people in support of the measures of his Majesty, that no less than five millions seven hundred and twenty-three thousand pounds had been granted this session in the Committee of Supply: all of it, he adds exultingly, except 20,000l. *voted for building Westminster bridge*, for the purposes of the war, or for supplying the deficiencies of the expence of last year's warlike preparations." Is it not worth while, however, to pause a moment, and ask whether the community has not, *according to the calm verdict of reason*, derived more real and permanent advantage from the expenditure of the 20,000l. in a work of public utility and magnificence, than of the millions so eagerly and lavishly appropriated to the purposes of devastation and destruction? Is it pity or scorn, amazement or sorrow, indignation or derision, that such national infatuation as this is calculated in a philosophic mind most strongly to excite? Or is power delegated by communities to individuals only to multiply and perpetuate their own miseries? How forcibly does history confirm the humiliating reflection of the poet:

   "———Man, proud man,
  Drest in a little brief authority,
  Plays such fantastic tricks before high Heaven
  As make the angels weep."

haughty

haughty and confident, had formed vast and dangerous projects, calculated for the sole purpose of recommending himself to the favor of the King, who was ambitious to signalize his talents, as King WILLIAM had formerly done, at the head of a grand Continental army. With this view, therefore, sixteen thousand regular troops, afterward increased to a much larger number, and which might have been employed to great advantage in different naval expeditions, were, in the month of April 1742, embarked for Flanders, and were shortly after joined by sixteen thousand Hanoverians and six thousand Hessians, in British pay, and a numerous body of Austrians. The Earl of Stair, created, on the recent resignation of the Duke of Argyle, Field-Marshal of Great Britain, a Nobleman distinguished as well for his personal accomplishments as his military and political talents, was appointed Generalissimo of this new army. Being invested with the character of Ambassador Extraordinary to the States General, he exerted in vain the whole force of his eloquence to prevail upon their High Mightinesses to concur in the projects of the King of Great Britain. Although the States had come to a previous resolution considerably to augment their forces, they declared their determination to adhere to their neutrality. And the English General, finding himself unable, without their assistance, to engage in those offensive operations he had in contemplation, which were said to be the siege of Dunkirk, to be followed, if successful, by a rapid march to the Somme, distributed his army into cantonments in the countries of Flanders, Liege, and Luxemburg.

Lord Stair's negotiation proving ineffectual, Lord Carteret was himself delegated with new propositions for the consideration and choice of their High Mightinesses: 1. That the republic should declare war against France in concert with England, &c. 2. That they should garrison the fortified towns in Flanders belonging to the
Queen

Queen of Hungary, to enable her to employ her troops in the field: 3. That Great Britain should take thirty thousand of the troops of Holland into British pay: Lastly, To enter into a new treaty of commerce very advantageous to the republic. The States General, in reply, declared their reluctance, by entering into the war, to make it more bloody; they, with a noble pride, asserted, that the troops of the republic were raised only for the defence of the republic, and THEY HAD NEVER HIRED THEM OUT. As to the last proposition, it was acknowledged to be very acceptable, but too dearly purchased at the expence of a war. These answers, however consonant to the moderation, wisdom, and dignity of the republic, gave little satisfaction to the English Minister, who returned to London much displeased and disappointed at his failure.

When the Parliament of Great Britain met in November 1742, the conduct of the new Ministry was arraigned in the bitterest terms of severity. The Earl of Chesterfield, who had not been included in the new arrangements of Office, asserted, that the assembling an army in Flanders without the concurrence of the States General, or any other power engaged by treaty, or bound by interest, to support the Queen of Hungary, was a rash and ridiculous measure; that it would inevitably involve the nation as principals in an expensive and ruinous war; and that the arms and wealth of Great Britain alone were not adequate to the purpose of raising the House of Austria to its former height of elevation; that, while England exhausted her resources to carry into effect her romantic and impracticable projects, the Electorate of Hanover, though under the same engagements, and governed by the same Prince, contributed nothing as an ally to her assistance, but was paid by Great Britain for all the forces it had sent into the field, and at a very exorbitant price. After having exalted the Elector of

Hanover

Hanover from a state of obscurity to the Crown, this nation, said his Lordship, is condemned to hire the troops of that Electorate to fight in their own cause, to hire them at a rate which was never demanded before, and to pay levy-money for them, though it is known to all Europe that they were not raised for this occasion. The Duke of Bedford also, a Nobleman of many private and public virtues, and of a family illustriously distinguished by the ardor of its attachment to the true interests of their country, affirmed, on this occasion, " that the measures of the English Ministry had long been regulated by the interest of his Majesty's Electoral territories; that these had long been considered as a gulf, into which the treasures of Great Britain had been thrown; that the state of Hanover had been changed, without any visible cause, since the accession of its Princes to the throne of England. The marks of affluence and prosperity were of late discernible in all its districts, without any discovery of mines or extension of commerce; and new dominions had been purchased, the price of which it was more than suspected was never paid from the revenues of Hanover." The motion, however, for an address to the throne, " beseeching and advising his Majesty to exonerate his subjects of the charge and burden of those mercenaries who were taken into the service last year without the knowledge or consent of Parliament," was rejected; Lord Carteret, the new Minister, with heroic effrontery, setting every appearance of consistency at defiance, and engaging with the most zealous ardor in the prosecution and defence of measures which he had himself repeatedly held up to the public scorn, indignation, and derision. In the course of the session, the Place Bill was again brought forward, and again rejected by the Commons; the numbers, on the division, being 221 against 196. Mr. Sandys declared himself indeed to be as great, if not a greater, friend than ever to

the

the bill, but that the TIME was improper; that it was
neceffary previoufly to remove certain prejudices which
had been fcattered round the throne; and that he was
againft urging the meafure at prefent, becaufe he
hoped the period would fhortly arrive when it
would be readily agreed to by every branch of
the legiflature. A motion for reviving the inquiry
into the conduct of Sir Robert Walpole for the laft ten
years, was negatived by 253 againft 186. In purfuance
of the plan of Continental warfare now adopted by the
Court of London, the Earl of Stair affembled the confederate forces early in the fpring (A. D. 1743), with a
view, as was believed, of penetrating the frontier of
France on the fide of the Mofelle; but being oppofed by
the Auftrian and Hanoverian Generals intrufted with the
fecret refolves of the Englifh Court, the whole army directed its courfe towards the Maine. On their near approach to Francfort, the Emperor, alarmed with the apprehenfion of falling as a captive into the hands of the
King of England, prepared to fly for refuge, though he
feemed fcarcely to know whither; but the Englifh commander deputed, without delay, an officer of diftinction
with a meffage to his Imperial Majefty, affuring him, in
the name of the King his mafter, that the refpect due to
the Imperial dignity fhould not be violated, nor the city
he had chofen for his perfonal refidence molefted. The
Emperor, notwithftanding, retired firft to Munich, and,
on the re-approach of the Auftrians, to Augfburg,
whence he returned, at the termination of the campaign
to his former refidence at Francfort. The Court of Verfailles, which had in vain made advances of accommodation to the Court of Vienna, now apprehending the junction of the allies commanded by Lord Stair with the Auftrians under Prince Charles of Lorraine, directed the
Marefchal de Noailles to affemble an army of 60,000
men on the Maine, while the Marefchal de Coigné was
placed

placed at the head of a yet superior army in Alsace, to oppose any attempt of the Austrian commander to penetrate into France by forcing the passage of the Rhine. The King of England, eager to gather those laurels which imagination had already woven into wreaths and garlands, accompanied by his younger son the Duke of Cumberland—now, for the first time, appearing in the field—arrived in June at the camp of Aschaffenburg. Here, however, to his unspeakable surprise and chagrin, the Monarch soon found himself and his whole army reduced to a very critical situation, by the superior skill and conduct of the Mareschal de Noailles, whose plan of military operation during this campaign, the King of Prussia tells us, would have done honor to the most renowned captain. This General had, early in the summer, taken possession of the cities of Spire, Worms, and Oppenheim, and, passing the Rhine, had encamped on the east side of the river, above Francfort, in a position which commanded the navigation of the upper Maine; at the same time occupying all the adjacent posts on the Rhine and Maine, so as effectually to bar all access with the surrounding country, and to intercept all convoys of provisions or supply. The King of England, therefore, found himself under the necessity of decamping from Aschaffenburg, and directed his march to Hanau, where he expected to meet large reinforcements. But the Mareschal, foreseeing that the Allies would not long be able to maintain their position, had taken his measures accordingly; and, on approaching the village of Dettingen, his Britannic Majesty found the French army drawn up in battle array, with a view to oppose his farther progress. To so perilous an extremity no King of England, in encountering a foreign enemy, had ever been reduced. In front were the narrow and dangerous defiles of Dettingen, occupied in force by the enemy; on the left flowed the river Maine, on the high opposite banks of which the

French

French had planted a formidable line of batteries; on the right were mountains and woods, interfected by a morafs; and all retreat was precluded by the vigilance of the French commander, who had taken poffeffion of Afchaffenburg immediately on its being evacuated by the Britifh forces. No event more favorable could be expected than that the whole army muft, in a fhort time, furrender themfelves prifoners of war; and the Marefchal de Noailles might reafonably prefume, that for him was referved the glory of avenging the fatal cataftrophe of Poictiers. But the rafh and inexperienced valor of the Duc de Grammont blafted thefe brilliant hopes; advancing through the defiles, contrary to the exprefs orders of the Marefchal, who was compelled to move with the whole army to fuftain this unfeafonable attack, he offered the enemy battle upon equal terms in the inclofed plain. The French charged with their ufual impetuofity, but were received by the Englifh with cool and determined intrepidity; the Earl of Stair making the neceffary previous difpofitions with great military fkill. The King himfelf difplayed much perfonal courage, and the French were repulfed with great flaughter, and compelled to repafs the Maine with the lofs of 6000 men; though they fuffered no moleftation in their retreat, the King of England purfuing without delay his march to Hanau, impatient to receive his expected fupplies and reinforcements. The Duke of Cumberland, who fought with great gallantry, was wounded in the action. At Hanau the King was vifited by Prince Charles of Lorraine and Count Khevenhuller; but no operations of confequence took place during the remainder of this campaign, the original or fpecific object of which it might baffle the profoundeft fagacity to devife. Towards the latter end of the fummer, the allied army paffed the Rhine at Mentz, and the King of England fixed his head-quarters at Worms. Here the advances of the Diet, who, folicitous to reftore the peace of the Empire, wrote letters to the King of England and the States General, requesting, in concert with themselves, the mediation of the maritime powers, being previously rejected, a treaty was signed with the Queen of Hungary and the King of Sardinia, who engaged to maintain 40,000 infantry and a proportionable corps of cavalry, for the service of the Queen of Hungary in Italy. The allurements held out to his Sardinian Majesty were, an English subsidy of 280.000l. *per annum*, the transfer of certain districts of the Milanese, and the prospect of gaining the Marquisate of Finale, her pretensions to which, by an article of this treaty, her Hungarian Majesty most generously assigned over to this Monarch; although an actual and unconditional cession of that territory to the republic of Genoa, to which it had antiently belonged, though wrested from her by the violence of the House of Austria, had been made by the late Emperor Charles VI. for the sum of 400,000 golden crowns, for which it had been previously mortgaged; and which sum, it is true, her Hungarian Majesty now condescended to grant her royal permission to the republic to receive from any power willing and able to repay it *. The republic remonstrated in the strongest

---

* The tenth article of the Treaty of Worms, relating to the cession of Finale, is a great historical curiosity, and exhibits the crooked and insidious policy of Lord Carteret in a very striking point of view. It is as follows : " As it is of importance to the public cause, that his Majesty the King of Sardinia should have an immediate communication of his dominions with the sea and with the maritime powers, her Majesty the Queen of Hungary and Bohemia yields to him all the rights which she may have in any manner, and upon any title whatsoever, to the town and marquisate of Finale, which rights she yields and transfers, without any restrictions, to the King, in the same manner as she does the countries described in the foregoing article ; in the just expectation that the republic of Genoa will facilitate, as far as shall be necessary, a disposition so indispensably requisite for the liberty and security of Italy, *in consideration of the sum which shall be found due to the republic, without his Majesty the King of Sardinia, or her Majesty the Queen of Hungary, being obliged to contribute to the payment of the said sum* : provided always, that the town of Finale be and remain for ever a free-port town, as is Leghorn ; and that it shall be allowable for his Majesty the King of Sardinia to re-establish there the forts which

strongest manner against a treaty so injurious to her rights; protesting also, in a memorial presented to the Imperial Diet, against this transaction, and claiming the protection of that august body; Finale being an ancient and acknowledged fief of the Empire. But Lord Carteret, who had accompanied the King of England to Germany, and negociated this affair in person, treated the embassy of the Republic with the most marked and insufferable contempt, though the Queen of Hungary herself hesitated to insist upon the validity of her claim. In consequence of this abominable injustice, the Senate of Genoa concluded a treaty of alliance, offensive and defensive, with Spain, at

which have been demolished, or to cause others to be built, according as he shall judge convenient." It is evident that Lord Carteret, conscious of the nefariousness of this attempt, dared not openly to sacrifice the faith and honour of the English nation, which had actually guaranteed, by the fourth article of the Quadruple Alliance, the possession of Finale to the Genoese, by making it a direct party in the transaction. It was no doubt the *purpose* of the English Minister to persuade the Parliament of Great Britain to pay the money in question, and to compel the Senate of Genoa to take it. But, if he found the opposition to this measure too strong, he had this evasion in reserve, that the rights of the Queen of Hungary, if invalid in themselves, gave no additional sanction to the claims of the King of Sardinia; that the republic was not obliged to consent to the redemption of the mortgage, nor was Great Britain under any obligation to offer it. Thus a flagitious scheme was formed, which might be easily abandoned if found impracticable in the execution. A negociation at the close of the summer was carried on with the Emperor, and articles of accommodation actually agreed upon, with the reluctant concurrence of the Queen of Hungary, by which the hereditary dominions of the Emperor were to be restored, on condition of a renunciation of his claims on the Austrian succession. By a separate article of the treaty, the sum of six millions of florins was, by a temporary assignment on certain lands, allotted to the Emperor for the support of the Imperial dignity, all deficiencies in the payment of which were to be made good by the King of England. Lord Carteret, however, resolving not to take upon himself the sole responsibility of this article, delayed the signing of the treaty till a messenger was dispatched to the Regency in London, requiring their assent to it. But, to the surprise and chagrin both of the King and the Emperor, the Regency sent word, " that they were of opinion, it was better, till the accomplishment of a general peace, to leave the burden of supporting his Imperial Majesty on the Court of France, who would soon be tired of the expence." The negotiation, therefore, proved ultimately abortive.

Aranjuez,

Aranjuez, the following year—provoking, by this means, the implacable resentment of the House of Austria, which appeared to deem the absolute annihilation of the republic scarcely an adequate atonement for such an act of presumption. In September, the Allies, now encamped at Spire, were joined by 20,000 Dutch auxiliaries; the States General, notwithstanding the solicitations and menaces of France, being at last prevailed upon openly to declare themselves in favor of the Queen of Hungary. Marefchal Noailles having retired into Alsace, the Allies, as if now pleased and proud to march about, made various random and fruitless incursions, and demolished the entrenchments already abandoned by the French on the banks of the Queich; after which they separated into winter-quarters *. Prince Charles of Lorraine also, being foiled in his attempts to penetrate into France on the side of Alsace, by the Marefchal de Coigné, marched back to the Palatinate; and the campaign closed with no decisive advantage on either side. But Lord Stair, the English Commander in Chief, immediately on the termination of it, threw up his commission in high disgust; determined not to lend the authority of his name to military operations, in the concerting and directing of which he had, by his own declaration, so little share. This celebrated Nobleman was one of the most remarkable, and in all respects, one of the most accomplished personages of his time. He had, early in life, distinguished himself by his zeal in support of the Revolu-

---

* " Pour se convaincre (says the King of Prussia) du peu de suite qu'il y a dans les actions des hommes, il n'y a qu'à faire l'analyse de cette campagne. On assemble une armée sur le Mein, sans pourvoir à ses subsistances: la faim et la surprise obligent les Alliés à se battre; ils sont vainqueurs des François; ils passent le Rhin, ils vont à Worms; le Speyerbach les arrête, sans qu'ils trouvent des expédiens pour en déposter les ennemis; ils avancent enfin sur le Speyerbach que M. de Noailles les abandonne, et ils ne reçoivent les secours des Hollandois que pour prendre des quartiers d'hiver dans le Brabant et dans la Westphalie.—Après quoi le Roi George prit le chemin de Londres, pour y faire à son Parlement, dans une harangue pompeuse, le recit de des exploits."—*Oeuvres de Frederic II.*

tion,

tion, to the principles of which he continued ever steadily attached. Devoting himself to a military life, his valor and conduct were conspicuously displayed in the wars of the Revolution and Succession; and his knowledge and address being no less eminent than his courage, he was employed in various political negotiations, residing several years in a diplomatic capacity at the courts of Warsaw and Versailles. During the regency of the Duke of Orleans, the Earl of Stair rose to the highest degree of favor, and was admitted to the most intimate confidence of that Prince, who, as we are told, upon some interesting political occasion, being asked what part his Royal Highness meant to take, replied, with a smile, " Whatever the English Ambassador pleases." After passing through a variety of high offices, he was at length, in consequence of his determined opposition to the measures of Sir Robert Walpole, divested of all his employments; and retiring to Scotland, lived upon his estate many years in dignified obscurity. But, on the formation of the Continental army, he was recalled in the most flattering and honorable manner, in order to be placed at the head of it; and it is by many believed that, if his plans had been adopted in their full extent, France would have found it difficult to resist the sudden and powerful impression which, in the spirit of a great commander, he is known to have meditated.

Early in the following spring, March 1744 war was formally declared by France against England; and, in a short time after, by England against France. In the declaration of France, the King of Great Britain was accused of a violation of his neutrality, and of having dissuaded the Court of Vienna from acceding to any terms of accomdation. " The war, says the King of Prussia, speaking of the situation of affairs at this period, had changed its object. The original idea of self-preservation on the part of the House of Austria had given place to projects of conquest. The success of the Court of Vienna had excited its ambition;

on; and there was no longer room to doubt that the dethronement of the Emperor was in contemplation, and that the King of England secretly labored to effect the same purpose." The mild, the equitable, and pacific Fleury, who, at the age of seventy, had assumed the reins of government in France, and had successfully directed the counsels of that great monarchy for a period of eighteen years, was now no more. And, in consequence of his demise, the Court of Versailles appeared far less solicitous to terminate the subsisting differences: and formal reciprocal declarations of war were now published by the Courts of Versailles and Vienna. In the former, his Most Christian Majesty charged the Queen of Hungary with "obstinate implacability, with a fixed determination not to listen to terms of accommodation, and with harboring projects of insatiable ambition, hatred, and revenge." On the other hand, the Queen of Hungary charged his Most Christian Majesty with "a violation of his most solemn engagements respecting the Pragmatic Sanction; with insidiously inciting different pretenders to lay claim to the succession of the late Emperor; with endeavouring to instigate the common enemy of Christendom against her; and with having acted the part of a public incendiary in the north of Europe, in order that the Czarina might be prevented from assisting the House of Austria, while the armies of France were spreading desolation throughout the Empire." And all impartial persons were compelled to acknowledge, that the criminations and recriminations of these opposite declarations were, to the misfortune of mankind—oppressed by the ceaseless contentions of these proud rival Houses—strictly and literally true. Vast preparations were now made by the Court of Versailles for the ensuing campaign in Flanders, where an army of one hundred and twenty thousand men was assembled, under the command of the famous Mareschal Comte de Saxe, who invested and reduced the towns of Menin, Ypres, and Furnes. The allied

ed army, commanded by the Duke of Cumberland, a general of almost one whole year's experience, and very inferior to that of the French in force, was unable to impede the progress of his arms; which, however, received a sudden and unexpected check from the success of Prince Charles of Lorraine, who, having found means to elude the vigilance of Marefchal Coigné, had crossed the Rhine at the head of a numerous army, had secured the passes of Lorraine, and laid the whole country under contribution. Forty thousand men being detached to reinforce the army in Alsace, the Allies ventured to approach the French commander, now acting on the defensive; but found no favorable opportunity of attack; and, after various inexplicable and inconsistent movements, they at length retired, without hazarding either siege or battle, into winter-quarters*.

In the mean time, all France was in consternation at the progress of the Austrians under the Prince of Lorraine, accompanied by the veteran Marefchal Traun. The fate of the kingdom seemed involved in the issue of a battle. But their schemes of conquest were entirely frustrated by the alarming intelligence that the King of Prussia had a second time entered the dominions of the Queen of Hungary; that the city of Prague and all Bohemia had submitted almost without resistance, being entirely unsuspicious of danger, and consequently destitute of the proper means of defence. " Kings, says one of the most respectable writers of antiquity, have no reason to blame the people for changing for interest, since in that they do but imitate their masters, who are patterns of treachery and perfidiousness, and who think those men most capable of serving them

---

* The French garrison at Lifle, we are told, displayed their wit at the expence of the inactive warriors they could see from their walls. Harlequin was introduced upon the stage, pompously exhibiting a bundle of papers under each arm. Being asked what he had under the right, he answered, *Orders*; and what under the left, with equal solemnity—*Counter-orders*.

who pay the leaft regard to honefty *." Scarcely were
the ratifications of the treaty of Breflaw exchanged, before the treaty itfelf was violated by one of the parties, in
the apprehenfion that it would *eventually* be violated by
the other: and Silefia was deftined to be once more deluged in blood, in order to determine whether it fhould be fubject to the tyranny of Auftria or Brandenburg. Prince
Charles immediately prepared to march to the relief of Bohemia, and repaffed, by the light of the full moon, the
Rhine, in the face of the French army, commanded by the
Marefchals de Coigné, Noailles, and Belleifle, who, it was
fufpected indeed, had ftill lefs inclination than ability to
prevent his departure. The King of Pruffia himfelf acknowledges, that the real motive of this invafion was his
apprehenfion that the French would be compelled to conclude fuch a peace as the Auftrian arrogance fhould pre-
fcribe; and that the whole force of the Queen of Hungary would afterwards be employed in the recovery of Silefia; relying, as he tells us, little on the guarantee of
England; and knowing that the King of England, in a
letter written in his own hand to the Queen of Hungary,
had, in allufion to the conqueft of Silefia, made ufe of this
remarkable expreffion—" Madame, ce qui eft bon à prendre eft bon à rendre." The oftenfible ground, however,
for this hoftile attack, was the reftoration of the tranquility of the Empire, and the juft rights of the Emperor; for
which purpofe a treaty had been figned at Francfort May
22, 1744, in which the Emperor, the King of Pruffia, the
King of Sweden, as Landgrave of Heffe Caffel, and the
Elector Palatine, were the " moft high, and high contracting parties:" and by which they engaged themfelves
to oblige the Queen of Hungary to reinftate his Imperial
Majefty in his Electoral dominions, to acknowledge the
validity of his election, and to deliver up the archives of
the Empire, ftill in her poffeffion; and, by an article yet

---

* Plutarch, in Vit. Pyrr.

more alarming, to compel her Hungarian Majesty to submit the various claims relative to the Austrian succession to a regular juridical decision. And the King of Prussia, in his public rescript to M. d'Andrie, his Minister at the British Court, expressed his indignation at, "the interference of Great Britain in the internal affairs of the Empire, and the unreasonableness of pretending, that such powerful and respectable Princes as those of the Empire, should be obliged to regulate their conduct according to the inclinations of those among the English who strive to make their countrymen enter into foreign quarrels, that are of no manner of concern to England *." The Prince of Lorraine, under the able direction of Mareschal Traun, proceeded from the banks of the Rhine, with rapid marches, into Bohemia, where the Austrians were reinforced by twenty thousand Saxons; the King of Poland, Elector of Saxony, having signed with her Hungarian Majesty a convention for the mutual guarantee of their dominions. This sudden return of the Austrian army entirely disconcerted the projects of the Prussian Monarch, who, having advanced with some indiscretion towards the frontiers of the Arch-Duchy, was himself in imminent danger of having his retreat intercepted by the skilful manœuvres of Mareschal Traun: and finding this wary and cautious veteran constantly encamped in inaccessible situations, he had no other resource remaining than to abandon his conquests in Bohemia, and to gain the passes of Silesia, which he effected not without great difficulty and loss, leaving his heavy

---

* By the treaty of Francfort, the Hessians, to whom such immense sums had been paid in subsidies during the years of peace, not only refused farther to co-operate with us as allies, but actually took a decided part in opposition to Great Britain, alarmed at the ambitious projects formed, with the concurrence of England, for the aggrandisement of the House of Austria.

artillery

artillery and magazines in the hands of the enemy.* Such, says the King of Prussia, was the end of a campaign, the commencement of which promised the most brilliant success; and in the conduct of which he, with a noble ingenuousness, confesses himself chargeable with a series of errors, while he applauds the skill and sagacity of his antagonist as worthy of the highest admiration. " Mareschal Traun (says he) acted the part of Sertorius, and the King that of Pompey. The conduct of that commander in this campaign was a model of perfection, which every soldier who is attached to his profession ought to study and to imitate so far as he possesses the ability." The King often mentioned this campaign as his *école de la guerre*, and Mareschal Traun as his military preceptor; and the Prince of Lorraine, on his return to Vienna, was received with acclamations of applause, to which, though on all occasions he had displayed much personal gallantry, he had only a secondary claim.

During these transactions, Count Seckendorf, the Imperial General, being liberally supplied with subsidies from

* The King of Prussia had no expectation of the re-appearance of the Austrian army in Bohemia during this campaign, and highly resented the inactivity of the French Generals, who notwithstanding the urgent remonstrances of the Prussian Minister Schmettau, made very faint and feeble efforts to impede the retreat of the Prince of Lorraine from the French territories; little impressed, as it should seem, with the arguments of the Court of Berlin, tending to shew the *impolicy* of this conduct. " Schmettau (says his Prussian Majesty) étoit désespéré de la mollesse des François. Il présentoit des memoires au Roi, il pressoit les Ministers, il écrivoit aux Maréchaux. Et quel risque couroit la France? Quand M. de Noailles auroit été battu, les troupes de la Reine étoient également obligées de quitter l'Alsace; et si les François étoient victorieux, ils détruisoient l'armée Autrichienne, qui vivement poursuivie, au lieu de repasser les ponts du Rhin, se seroit noyée dans ce fleuve. Les François emportèrent le village d'Achenheim, et s'amusèrent des formalités superflues, tandis que le Prince de Lorraine mit ce tems à profit pour repasser le Rhin sur les ponts de Bleinheim qu'il rompit avant l'aube du jour. Les François firent sonner des rodomontades; et le Prince de Lorraine continua paisiblement sa marche par la Souabe et le Haut Palatinat pour entrer en Boheme."—*Oeuvres de Frederic II.*

France,

France, had found means to assemble an army, with which he had made an irruption into Bavaria, and the Emperor once more took possession of Munich, his capital. But this faint gleam of prosperity was of short duration: knowing that the Austrians, now triumphant in Bohemia, were once more preparing to expel him from his hereditary dominions, destitute of resource, and overwhelmed with a succession of misfortunes, he expired at Munich January 18, 1745, of that most insupportable of sublunary ills—a broken heart; leaving to future ages a most striking and memorable example of the instability and vanity of human greatness *.

The Grand Seignior, Mahmout V. had observed with exemplary and inviolable fidelity, during the troubles of the Queen of Hungary, the treaty recently concluded with the Emperor Charles VI.; and at this period, from the mere spontaneous impulse of generosity, he offered his mediation, in order to effect a general accommodation amongst the contending potentates of Christendom. For this purpose the Grand Vizier delivered a rescript to the Ministers of the belligerent powers resident at the Porte,

---

* No apology can be necessary for recalling to the public recollection the beautiful lines of the late Dr. Johnson relative to this Prince, in his masterly Imitation of the tenth Satire of Juvenal:

" The bold Bavarian in a luckless hour
Tries the dread summits of Cæsarean power—
With unexpected legions bursts away,
And sees defenceless realms receive his sway.
Short sway! fair Austria spreads her mournful charms,
The Queen, the beauty, sets the world in arms;
From hill to hill the beacon's rousing blaze
Spreads wide the hope of plunder and of praise;
The fierce Croatian, and the wild hussar,
And all the sons of ravage, crowd the war.
The baffled Prince in honor's flattering bloom
Of hasty greatness finds the fatal doom;
His foes' derision, and his subjects' blame—
And steals to death from anguish and from shame."

replete

replete with sentiments of justice and humanity. "WAR is affirmed, in this memorial, to be the malady which infects Princes; but how just soever they may be in their commencement, wars cannot, with any shadow of justice, be long continued, because the consequences that attend them are worse than the evils they meant to take away. The SUBLIME PORTE hoped, for these reasons, that the Princes of Christendom would have put an end to the war, in order to prevent such calamities: but being informed by the Ambassadors, Envoys, Residents, and Agents, settled here, that they are about to take the field with very numerous armies this campaign, from whence nothing can be expected but black events, it has been thought proper to represent to all the Ministers at the Court of the most gracious, most invincible, most puissant Emperor, the shadow of God upon earth, that, 1st. This must occasion a vast effusion of human blood, and must expose a multitude of innocent families to ruin and destruction. 2. That it must give a sanction to the breach of all laws human and divine, by attributing to force what ought to belong to right, and thereby confound all order, industry, and arts. 3. That it must prove the cause of interrupting commerce even amongst the subjects of such powers as are not engaged in war, to the great loss and detriment of the human species in general. That his Sublime Highness, having a tender sense of humanity, which is natural to all great minds, has judged it proper to interpose, and to endeavour to find out the means of compromising these differences. The Grand Vifier, therefore, has thought it his duty to inform the respective powers at war of this most beneficent and laudable design in the sight of God and man of his Sublime Highness, in order to know their sentiments thereupon." It is superfluous to say, that this offer was wholly unavailable: it was doubtless regarded as a hopeless and impracticable task so to explain the complicated politics of the European courts, as to to have made this *ignorant barbarian* comprehend what it was that the Christian Princes were quarrelling about.

In a short time after the death of the Emperor, the Austrian armies entered the Electorate of Bavaria ; and the young Elector, unable to contend against such superior force, was compelled to abandon his capital, and retire to Augsburg ; and a treaty was soon afterwards concluded at Fuessen between him and the Queen of Hungary, by which an entire restitution of her conquests was made by that Princess, in consequence of a relinquishment of all claims on the Austrian succession on the part of the Elector ; and, which was of far greater importance, his voice in favor of the Grand Duke of Tuscany at the ensuing election of an Emperor of the Romans, and his acknowledgement of the validity of the electoral vote of Bohemia in the person of the Queen : and the Court of Vienna having now secured all the voices of the electoral college, those of Brandenburg and the Palatinate excepted, the Grand Duke was, on the second of September 1745, declared Emperor of the Romans at Francfort, by the name of Francis I. Although the campaign of 1744 had redounded little to the reputation of the Prussian arms, the political views of the King were in a great measure answered by it. The French regained the ascendant on the Rhine, where they captured, after an obstinate resistance, the Imperial city of Fribourg ; and they were enabled to take the field in Flanders with redoubled force and vigor. The Prussian Monarch, on his part, opened the campaign of 1745 in Silesia at the head of seventy thousand men ; and the Austrians and Saxons having penetrated into that province through the defile of Landshut, the two armies joined battle at Friedburg, and after a furious conflict, maintained from the early dawn of morning till noon, the Austrians were defeated with great loss ; and retiring into Bohemia, were followed thither by the King, whose career of victory shewed that he had no longer Mareschal
Traun

Traun for his adversary, that officer having been appointed to the command of the army of the Empire, assembled for the protection of the Diet at Francfort. The Prussian Monarch however, conceiving himself abandoned by France, whose conquests on the Maese or the Scheld were, as he affirmed to his most Christian Majesty, of no more advantage to Prussia than victories on the Scamander, would willingly have accommodated his difference with the Empress-Queen, by which appellation her Hungarian Majesty was now distinguished; but that Princess haughtily rejected his advances: and the Prince of Lorraine received positive orders from the Court of Vienna to risk another engagement. An opportunity offering itself of attacking the Prussians to advantage in their camp of Sohr, near Staudentz, a second pitched battle took place on the thirtieth of September; and though the Austrians seemed at first to have a fair prospect of success, forcing their way into the interior of the Prussian camp, and even carrying off the military chest and the King's own cabinet, they were finally repulsed. In this battle, the brother-princes Ferdinand and Louis of Brunswick were personally opposed to each other, and fought with an emulation of valor. Notwithstanding this victory, his Prussian Majesty thought proper to retire from Bohemia, which he always considered as an ineligible and hazardous scene of military operation, and entered the rich and fertile country of Lusatia. And the Saxons being defeated, December 15, by the Prince of Anhalt at Kesseldorf, his Polish Majesty was obliged to abandon the city of Dresden, of which his Prussian Majesty took immediate possession: and, in consequence of the continued successes of that Monarch, the Empress-Queen was at length induced to sign a treaty of peace at Dresden, January 1746, by which the King of Prussia acknowledged the Grand Duke of Tuscany as Emperor; the Electorate of Saxony, in consideration of the payment of one million of German Crowns, was restored

stored to his Polish Majesty, and Silesia once more guaranteed to Prussia. Vehement remonstrances were made by France against this treaty, which she affected to resent as a violation of the most solemn engagements. But it is sufficiently evident, that both France and Prussia, from the commencement to the termination of their political connection, were actuated entirely by the same motives; and that neither observed any faith with the other farther than it happened to be conformable to their own separate interest. "What is the real language," says the King of Prussia, "of these remonstrances of the Court of Versailles? Conti knows so well how to detain the principal forces of the Queen of Hungary in Germany, that he has repassed the Rhine, leaving any persons that pleased at liberty to elect an Emperor; that Traun has been enabled to detach Grune to Saxony, purposing to follow with the remainder of his troops, if the Queen of Hungary thinks fit to employ them against you. I have done great things this campaign. *Mention* also has been made of you: I regret the dangerous situation in which you are placed, for your attachment to me; but glory is to be acquired only by sacrificing yourself for France. Be firm and constant, and suffer without complaining. Imitate the example of my other allies, whom I have abandoned indeed, but to whom I have given alms when they have lost their possessions. You, without doubt, will have ability to extricate yourself from these embarrassments; but if unfortunately you should be brought to ruin, I will engage that the French Academy shall compose the funeral oration of your empire." In a letter written with his own hand to the King of France, his Prussian Majesty thus apologises for his defection: "After the letter addressed to your Majesty in November last, I thought I had a right to expect from your Majesty real and effective succors. I do not enter into the reasons which may have induced your Majesty to abandon your allies to the caprice of fortune: for this time

Vol. II. E the

the valor of my troops has extricated me from the danger in which I found myself involved. Had I been overwhelmed by the number of my enemies, your Majesty would have contented yourself with lamenting my fate, and I should have been left destitute of resource. Your Majesty advises me to counsel myself: I have done so; and I find that reason loudly proclaims the necessity of putting a speedy termination to a war which at present exists without an object, since the Austrians are no longer the invaders of Alsace, and an Emperor is actually chosen. Reason warns me to watch over my own safety; and to consider the formidable armament preparing by Russia on the one side, and the army of the Mareschal Traun advancing from the banks of the Rhine on the other. The Austrians and Saxons have sent their respective Ministers to this place to negotiate a peace, and I have no other option than to sign it. May I hope for the happiness of being employed by your Majesty to mediate a general pacification? The interests of France cannot be confided to any person more attached to your Majesty than myself; and I beseech your Majesty to believe, that the continuance of your friendship will be always dear and precious to me." France was in reality too deeply engaged in her favorite projects of conquest in the Low Countries, to entertain any serious intention of granting efficacious assistance to the King of Prussia.

Early in the year 1745, Mareschal Saxe, accompanied by the King and the Dauphin, took the field at the head of an immense army, and invested the important city of Tournay. The Allies, commanded by the Duke of Cumberland, assisted by Mareschal Konigseg and the Prince of Waldeck, though far inferior in number, determined to make an effort for the relief of the place. On the 11th of May, they advanced with great resolution to the attack of the French army, encamped under cover of the village of Fontenoy, and protected by a prodigious fire
from

from the batteries they had planted on all sides. The enterprise was considered as a singular instance of military rashness. But such was the intrepidity displayed by the English and Hanoverian infantry, that the French were driven beyond their lines, and in imminent danger of a defeat; but the Dutch failing in their attempt on the village of Fontenoy, and the English General not making, as it is said, the proper use of his first success, by dividing the column of attack after he had broke the centre of the French, Mareschal Saxe had time to bring up his *corps de reserve*, and the English found themselves inclosed as it were within a circle of fire, from the redoubts which they had already passed, the masked batteries planted on each side, and the artillery, which, under the direction of Mareschal Saxe himself, played upon them with dreadful execution in front. In this situation, the most heroic efforts were totally unavailing, and the Allies were compelled to retreat with the loss of more than ten thousand men, to which that of the French was supposed nearly equal; but the extent of the misfortune could be known only by the consequences. Tournay surrendered, after a gallant defence, by an honourable capitulation. Ghent and Bruges were captured by a *coup de main:* Ostend, Dendermond, Newport, and Aeth, were successively reduced; and the Allies retired for safety beyond the canal of Antwerp: and, at the end of the campaign, the King of France entered the city of Paris in triumph.

Towards the latter end of the summer, the French Court, desirous of causing an effectual diversion to the English army in Flanders, incited the son of the Chevalier de St. George, usually styled *the Pretender,* a young man of a sanguine and adventurous disposition, to risk an invasion of Great Britain, then almost destitute of troops, and in a state of great apparent dissatisfaction with the government. It is not necessary to enter into a very circumstantial narrative of this bold but abortive attempt. Prince Charles,

Charles, as he was called by his adherents, landed in the Western Islands of Scotland in the month of August, the King of England being then at Hanover. The Lords of the Regency treated the first intelligence of his arrival as an idle tale; but, on receiving farther and undoubted information that he had collected a considerable force, and was advancing southward, they issued a proclamation, offering a reward of thirty thousand pounds for his apprehension, and dispatched a messenger to the Continent to hasten the return of his Majesty, making, at the same time a requisition of six thousand auxiliaries, which the Dutch were by treaty under obligation to furnish; and several British regiments were also recalled from the Netherlands. Instructions were sent to the Lords Lieutenants throughout the kingdom to array the militia in their several counties, and commissions were issued to levy new regiments for the speedy and effectual suppression of this rebellion. Many different corps of volunteers were incorporated; addresses were presented from all parts, testifying the utmost abhorrence of this attempt to subvert the government; and, notwithstanding the previous symptoms of discontent, the whole kingdom seemed united as one man in the moment of danger, in support of the national religion, laws, and constitution. Sir John Cope, commander in chief of the forces in North Britain, advanced at the head of what troops he could collect to Inverness, in order to oppose the farther progress of this adventurer, who, in the mean time, marched by another route to the capital, which surrendering to him without resistance September 16, 1745, he caused his father to be proclaimed King of Great Britain at the high cross of Edinburgh, declaring himself, at the same time, regent of his dominions, and fixing his head-quarters at the palace of Holyrood-house, the royal residence of his ancestors. On receiving this intelligence, Sir John Cope hastened back to Edinburgh; and, on the twentieth of September, he encamped with his army, consisting fisting of about three thousand regular troops, near the village of Preston-pans, in the environs of the capital. Early the next morning, he was attacked, sword in hand, by the Prince Regent, at the head of about an equal number of Highlanders, who, in less than ten minutes, entirely broke the King's troops, unaccustomed to their ferocious and terrific mode of fighting. Sir John Cope was heavily censured for his presumption and ignorance on this occasion. Colonel Gardiner, an officer of distinguished merit, and himself a native of Scotland, remonstrating with him on the impropriety of the disposition he had made, was treated with neglect and rudeness, and predicted a total defeat, which, however, he disdained to survive, falling gloriously, covered with wounds, in the midst of the enemy, and in sight of his own mansion. In consequence of this victory, the pretended Prince Regent saw himself absolute master of Scotland, a few fortresses excepted. He received large supplies from France, and was joined by the Lords Kilmarnock, Cromarty, Balmerino, and many other persons of rank and distinction; and the enterprise, romantic as it originally appeared, began to wear a serious aspect. The Campbells, the Monroes, the Macdonalds, and other loyal clans, assembled, however, in arms, in defence of the government, under the Earl of Loudon. An army was collected in England under General Wade, who received orders to march to the north, and proceeded as far as Newcastle. The Prince Pretender, however, resolving to try his fortune in the south, took the route of Carlisle, which surrendered to him in November. Another army, under Sir John Ligonier, was now forming in Staffordshire; notwithstanding which, the Prince determined to proceed, hoping for a co-operation from a body of French forces on the southern coast, and not doubting but he should be joined by great numbers of the English malcontents in his progress through the kingdom. In this expectation, however, he was grievously disappointed; at Manchester,

chester, only, he was received with any demonstrations of joy. Crossing the Mersey at Stockport, he advanced through Macclesfield and Congleton to Derby, which was the extreme point of his progress; for, understanding that the King had determined to take the field in person, and to set up the standard of England on Finchley Common—the Earl of Stair, Field-Marefchal of Great Britain, being, at this momentous crisis, again received into favor and confidence, and appointed General of the royal army—he took a sudden resolution, though he had actually advanced within a few days march of the metropolis, to provide for his safety by a retreat. This amounted plainly to a virtual relinquishment of his object, which, indeed, could only be accomplished by a series of desperate efforts, crowned with continual and decisive success. A single disaster must, in his situation, be fatal. No sooner was the resolution formed for retreating to the north, than it was carried into effect with almost incredible diligence and celerity. Abandoning Derby December 6, their vanguard entered Manchester on the ninth, and on the nineteenth they reached Carlisle; and, after reinforcing the garrison at that place, the rebel army crossed the rivers Eden and Solway into Scotland, with all their artillery and military stores, eluding the attempts of both the adverse armies to intercept them on this memorable march, in which no violence was offered, no outrage or rapine committed, in a country abounding with plunder, and presenting every temptation to the unrestrained indulgence of military rapacity. On the twenty-first of December Carlisle was invested by the Duke of Cumberland, who had now assumed the chief command, and surrendered on the thirtieth at discretion. In the mean time, the Prince Regent proceeded to Glasgow, from which place he exacted heavy contributions, in revenge for the loyalty they had displayed in the course of the rebellion; after which he invested the castle of Stirling, though with little prospect of success. General Hawley,

Hawley, now at the head of the King's forces in North Britain, marched to Falkirk, in order to relieve this fortress by an attack upon the rebels. On the seventeenth of January, 1746, however, the General was himself unexpectedly attacked by them, and after sustaining for some time a disorderly and irregular fight, was compelled by a precipitate retreat, not, indeed, suffering so much loss as disgrace, it having been customary for him to boast that, with two regiments of dragoons, he would drive the rebel army from one end of the kingdom to the other. The Duke of Cumberland in person being now arrived at Edinburgh with large reinforcements, took upon him the command, and moving towards Linlithgow, the rebels not only abandoned the siege of Stirling castle, but passed the Forth with evident symptoms of consternation ; and the Prince Pretender still continuing to advance northward, the Duke of Cumberland, after securing the important passes of Stirling and Perth, advanced to Aberdeen. This changeful drama now drew towards a termination. In the beginning of April (1746) the Duke began his march from Aberdeen, and, on the twelfth, passed the deep and rapid river Spey, in sight of the advanced posts of the enemy, without opposition. At Nairne, his Royal Highness received intelligence that the Prince Pretender had advanced from Inverness to Culloden, in order to give him battle. On the sixteenth the Duke decamped from Nairne early in the morning, and, after a march of nine miles, perceived the rebel army drawn up in battalia in thirteen divisions. About one in the afternoon the engagement began, and the Highlanders attempted, as formerly at Preston-pans, to break the royal troops, by rushing down with their broadswords and Lochaber axes ; but being now prepared for this mode of fighting, they received the enemy with fixed bayonets, and kept up a continual firing by platoons, which did prodigious execution. Being thrown into visible disorder, the cavalry of the royal army attacked them in flank, and, in less than thirty minutes, the battle was converted into a general rout; and, orders being issued to give no quarter, vast numbers were slain in the pursuit. It is even affirmed, that unnecessary and wanton barbarities were committed on the persons and families of the rebels long after the cessation of resistance; and that the Duke of Cumberland sullied the glory of his victory, by displaying a savage thirst of revenge, and a courage untinctured with the feelings of humanity. As, nevertheless, the temper and conduct of this Prince were upon no other occasion tainted with this imputation, it is reasonable to believe, either that he was transported into these temporary excesses by that rage which is so frequent and horrid a concomitant and characteristic of civil discord; or that he really conceived these severities to be necessary for the prevention of farther resistance on the part of the rebels. The Pretender escaped with great difficulty from the field of battle; and after wandering for many months a wretched and solitary fugitive among woods and lakes and mountains, and passing through a series of the most extraordinary and romantic adventures, to be paralleled only by those of King Charles II. after the battle of Worcester, he found means, on the twentieth of September, to embark on board a small vessel, which conveyed him to Morlaix, in Bretagne. The executions which ensued on the suppression of this rebellion seemed much more numerous than the necessity of the case required; and the Lords Balmerino, Lovat *, and Kilmarnock, suffered the sentence of decapitation on Tower Hill, as did also the Earl of Derwentwater, without any form of trial, being arraigned on the sentence passed against him in 1716. The Earl of Cromarty only received a pardon. Both Houses of Par-

---

* Lord Lovat, who was of a character infamously profligate, suffered with great dignity and resolution : " So much easier is it," says Sir Dudley Carleton on a similar occasion, " for a man to die well than to live well."

liament presented addresses of congratulation to his Majesty, and of thanks to his Royal Highness the Duke, on this auspicious occasion. The sum of twenty-five thousand pounds *per annum* was added, by the House of Commons, to the revenue of the Duke, now become the idol of the nation, and extolled as equal to the most illustrious of its heroes.

During these transactions in England, the triumphs of Mareschal Saxe in Flanders still continued. The King of France again taking the field in person, invested the city of Antwerp, which surrendered after a very slight resistance. Mons made a better defence, but was compelled to capitulate before the end of June: and St. Guiflain and Charleroy shared the fate of Mons and Antwerp. On the second of December (1746) the trenches were opened before Namur, and, on the twenty-third, that strong and important fortress, after an unavailing effort previously made by the Prince of Lorraine, who now commanded the confederate army, for its relief, surrendered to the arms of France. On the thirtieth of September, Mareschal Saxe crossed the Jaar, behind which river the Allies were posted, near the village of Roucoux, in order to force them to a battle. After an obstinate conflict, in which the Prince of Waldeck displayed heroic bravery, the Allies were obliged to abandon their posts with the loss of five thousand men and thirty pieces of artillery, and retire to Maestricht; and this action terminated the campaign. A singular instance of presence of mind is recorded on this occasion of the Earl of Crawford, who, being attended by his aid-du-camp and a few dragoons, had rode out the morning preceding the battle to reconnoitre the situation of the enemy, and fell in unexpectedly with one of their advanced guards. The serjeant who commanded it immediately ordered his men to present their pieces; but the Earl, without the slightest emotion, told him there was no occasion for that ceremony, and enquired if he had seen any of the enemy's parties;

parties; and, being anfwered in the negative, replied, "Très bien—tenez vous fur vos gardes—et fi vous etiez attaqué, j'aurai foin que vous foyéz foutenu*." This incident coming to the knowledge of Marefchal Saxe, that Commander difmiffed an officer on his parole with a complimentary meffage to the Earl, affuring him " that he could not pardon the fergeant for not procuring him the honor of his Lordfhip's company to dinner." The States of Holland began now to be ferioufly alarmed at the progrefs of the French, and declared themfelves determined to carry on the war with increafe of vigor.

In March 1747, the allied forces took the field under the command of the Duke of Cumberland; the Prince of Waldeck and the Marefchal Bathiani conducting the Dutch and Auftrian troops under him. The whole army amounted to more than one hundred thoufand men. But, on account of the unufual inclemency of the weather, Marefchal Saxe remained in his cantonments, contenting himfelf with obftructing the fupplies of the allied army, and publicly declaring he would teach the Duke of Cumberland, when his forces were fufficiently diminifhed by hunger and ficknefs, that it is the firft duty of a General to provide for the health and prefervation of his troops. In April, the French Commander detached Count Lowendahl, at the head of thirty thoufand men, to invade Dutch Flanders; and Sluys, Sas-van-Ghent, and Hulft, were quickly reduced. The French General now prepared for a defcent on Zealand; and the whole Dutch nation being feized with extreme confternation, violent popular commotions took place throughout all the provinces. The people at large, ever attached to the Houfe of Orange, and mindful of the important fervices rendered to the republic by that illuftrious family, infifted upon the Prince of

---

* Very well—be upon your guard; and, if you are attacked, I will take care that you fhall be fupported.

Orange's being immediately invested with the dignity of Stadtholder; and the States General not choosing, or not daring, to oppose the general sense of the nation, the Prince was on the second day of May (1747) declared Stadtholder, and Captain-General and Admiral of the United Provinces; and, in the course of the ensuing year, the dignity was made hereditary in the House of Orange. Upon this change in affairs, many spirited resolutions passed in the Assembly of the States. An augmentation of the army was decreed, the peasants were armed and exercised, inquiries were instituted into the conduct of the Governors who had surrendered the towns on the frontier, and hostilities were denounced against France both by sea and land. Mareschal Saxe, regardless of these internal changes and commotions, advanced with the grand army to Louvaine; and the Duke of Cumberland took post at Laffeldt, near Val, in order to cover the city of Maestricht. The Mareschal determined upon a general attack, in order to dislodge the enemy, and open the way to Maestricht. The Allies defended themselves with great resolution and perseverance: The French were repeatedly broken and dispersed; but fresh brigades continually succeeded to those which retired, and the village was three times lost and recovered. At length, the line being dangerously disordered by an impetuous assault of the French cavalry, the Duke ordered a retreat, which was effected with inconsiderable loss, chiefly through the extraordinary intrepidity and presence of mind of Sir John Ligonier, who, at the head of a few British regiments of dragoons and squadrons of Imperial horse, arrested the pursuit of the whole French army. He was himself, his horse being killed under him, made prisoner; but the regiments he commanded retired unbroken from the field. When this officer was introduced to the presence of his most Christian Majesty, that Monarch exclaimed, " When, Sir, will the King your master deign to grant us peace?"

And

And he was soon released on his parole, intrusted with certain general propositions of a pacific tendency, for the consideration of the English Court.

The military arrangements of the Commander in chief were the subject of much censure on this occasion. When the French first appeared on the heights of Herdeeren, the Mareschal Bathiani urged the necessity of an immediate attack, but his advice was received with coolness and neglect; and the Commander in chief asking the Mareschal where he might be found in case of need, the Austrian haughtily replied, that he should always be found at the head of his troops *. The Allies however, notwithstanding their late defeat, were still able to cover Maestricht from attack; and Mareschal Saxe, perceiving his original project disconcerted, detached Count Lowendahl, with about fifty thousand men, to lay siege to Bergen-op-Zoom, the strongest fortification of Dutch Brabant, and accounted almost impregnable, being the *chef-d'œuvre* of the famous engineer Coehorn. The enemy appeared before the walls on the twelfth of July, and from this time to the middle of September, a tremendous scene of carnage was exhibited. The roar of bombs, mortars, and cannon, was incessantly heard, and all the dreadful apparatus of war displayed. Baron Cronstrom, a gallant old veteran, being appointed to the command of the fortress, repeated and desperate sallies were made by the garrison, and mines sprung with horrible success. It was generally believed that Count Lowendahl would be obliged to abandon his enterprise; but some inconsiderable breaches being made in a ravelin and two adjoining bastions, the Count deter-

---

* We are told, that a French officer remarking to an English private, who had been made prisoner after displaying extraordinary remarks of valor, that if there had been fifty thousand such men as he in the allied army, they should have found it very difficult to conquer them; the Englishman replied, There were men enough like me, but we wanted one like Mareschal Saxe."

mined

mined upon an assault. The Governor, not imagining the breaches practicable, had taken no precautions to guard against the attack, which was made with astonishing intrepidity on the night of the sixteenth of September. The success of the attempt justified the apparent rashness of it. The French gained the ramparts, and formed, before the garrison could assemble. The Baron being awaked from his sleep, was informed that the French were in possession of the town, and with difficulty effected his own escape. Thus the enemy became entire masters of the navigation of the Scheldt. Lowendahl was promoted, in consequence of this success, to the rank of Mareschal of France, and the King of France returned once more in triumph to Versailles. Notwithstanding the successes of the French in Flanders, they began to feel the continuation of the war extremely burthensome; they had suffered great losses at sea; their navy had sustained repeated shocks; their commerce was ruined; their finances were exhausted; the war in Italy had proved disastrous; the views of the French Monarch in Germany were entirely frustrated; the election of a Stadtholder had armed against him the whole power of Holland; and he knew that the Courts of London and Vienna were in treaty with the Czarina, who had actually issued orders for the march of forty thousand Russians from the banks of the Wolga to the borders of the Rhine. Moved by these considerations, his Most Christian Majesty made direct and repeated advances of accommodation to the Courts of London and of the Hague; and though they were at first received with coldness, it was finally agreed that a congress should be opened at Aix la Chapelle, and which accordingly met early in the ensuing spring, March 1748, the Earl of Sandwich and Sir Thomas Robinson acting as Ambassadors Plenipotentiary from the King of Great Britain. After the conferences commenced, Mareschal Saxe, notwithstanding the utmost efforts of the Allies, invested the city of Maestricht;

tricht; but the preliminaries of peace being signed in the space of a few weeks, hostilities were suspended, and the city, which had been defended by the Governor, Baron d'Alva, with such skill and gallantry that the besiegers had made little progress, was happily preserved.

We are now to resume the narration of the domestic and political transactions of Great Britain, which has suffered great interruption through this long, but necessary, detail of foreign military operations. After the resignation of Sir Robert Walpole, Lord Carteret succeeded to all the plenitude of ministerial power, and he even seemed to enjoy the favor and confidence of the Sovereign in a degree superior to his predecessor. The nation, however, heavily complained that the war with Spain was become a secondary object, or, rather, was wholly neglected, while the affairs of the Continent only engrossed the attention of the Court, and of the Minister, who had entirely forgotten his former eloquent declamations and invectives against standing armies, votes of credit, foreign subsidies, Continental connexions; and whose speeches *now* breathed only glory, conquest, and defiance to France.

A very courtly address being moved in the House of Peers, December 1743, in reply to his Majesty's speech from the throne, " recommending *measures of vigor*, and demanding supplies to enable him to enter into such engagements with other powers as might be necessary for the support of his allies, and the restoration of the balance of Europe;" the Earl of Chesterfield rose, and expressed his hope that by *vigorous measures* were not intended such wild attempts and romantic expeditions as might hazard the national honor and safety, without the possibility of advantage; that we were not called upon to squander millions, and stain the fields of the Continent with the blood of our countrymen, without being fully informed concerning the end and object of the war; that we were not to stand alone against the united power of the House

of

of Bourbon, and sacrifice our lives and fortunes for those who will not endeavor to defend themselves. " The true interest of England, my Lords, said this Nobleman, is to be at peace with its neighbors; for peace is the parent of prosperity; and, when I find the Governors of a nation inclined to war, I am always ready to ask them, by what mode of calculation they can compute the costs, or ascertain the consequences; and I think it my duty to warn them against such counsels as may precipitate their country into an abyss of poverty and ruin. When I hear a proposal for declaring war, I figure to myself a suspension of commerce, a decay of wealth, an increase of taxes, a state of impatience, anxiety, and discontent. Should the war prove unsuccessful, the acrimony of revenge will strongly incite us to the continuance of it. If it be prosperous, we shall be easily deluded into the imagination that the empty glitter of military glory is preferable to the plenty and tranquility of peace; and that we flourish as a nation when we adorn our public halls with the standards and ensigns of Spain and France. To these general maxims, however, the conduct of the present Ministers, said his Lordship, may perhaps be cited as an exception; for, though the war with Spain is the only war desired by the people, and the only war which it is their interest to prosecute, they who have assumed the management of our affairs appeared neither fired by revenge, nor irritated by disgrace, at the losses and disappointments we have sustained in the progress of it. This war, so important to our commercial interests, only has been neglected—this alone has been forgotten. We have been told of the danger which may arise to the State from the boldness of political discussion—'*flagrante bello*;' but, my Lords, who does not see that the expression is inapplicable, and that the noble Secretary should have said *languente bello?* Spain, weak and defenceless as she is, laughs at our armaments, and perceives no other consequence from our declaration of war

war than a greater licenfe of plunder, and a more eafy diftribution of prizes."

The Minifter, in a fpeech of great ability and eloquence, attempted to defend the meafures of his adminiftration. " He called the attention of the Houfe to the ftate of affairs on the Continent a few fummers paft, when the Empire was over-run by the arms of France; when the Queen of Hungary was attacked by Pruffia on the one fide, and Bavaria on the other; when, to fecure her perfon from captivity, fhe was compelled to abandon her capital, and her condition was confidered as hopelefs and irretrievable. To the powerful affiftance of Great Britain alone is it owing, faid he, that the armies of France have been obliged, with difgraceful precipitation, to evacuate the Empire; that her ally, the Emperor, is left, without fuccour, a helplefs fpectator of the conqueft of his hereditary dominions; and that Pruffia is converted from a dangerous enemy into a firm friend and ally. Such had been the fuccefs, and fuch the confequences, of the meafures which he had recommended, and of which he now with confidence demanded the approbation and *vigorous fupport* of that illuftrious Affembly. Armies are only to be repelled by armies, and they who engage in war muft refolve to fuftain the calamities infeparable from it. In the prefent conjuncture, no meafures can be called wife or prudent which are not vigorous. By vigor only can the Houfe of Auftria be reftored, and by the reftoration of the Houfe of Auftria only can the balance of power be preferved. That the war againft Spain had been either negligently or unfuccefsfully profecuted the Minifter pofitively denied: at this moment we blockaded up both her fleets and her armies. It was known to all Europe that the Spanifh Generals in Italy were continually embarraffed and impeded in all their enterprifes by the operations of the Britifh fleet. And it is not, perhaps, eafy to conceive a more deftructive method of carrying on war than that of fhutting up an army

in

in an enemy's country, where it cannot be succored, and from which it cannot be recalled; no prospect remaining but that of perishing by hardships and famine. But Spain is not the adversary against which our force ought chiefly to be directed. There is an enemy nearer and more formidable—an enemy which, equally in war and peace, endeavors our destruction—an enemy so insidious, that the utmost friendship which can subsist between us is only an intermission of hostilities—an enemy whose perpetual object it is in all her designs and transactions, whether she ratifies or violates treaties, whether she offers mediation or foments discord, whether she courts or insults her neighbors, to weaken and depress all other powers, and to exalt herself to universal dominion. The ambition and pride of France, infatuated as that nation is with the glory of their monarch and the desire of aggrandizing their empire, are permanent and hereditary. If one King dies, another succeeds to the same views; and if a Minister be removed, it is because they hope the grand design of enslaving the world will be more actively carried on by another. Against such an enemy if it be necessary to make war, it is surely necessary to prosecute it with our utmost force; because war is a calamity to which a desirable and secure termination can be put only by success, and success is only to be obtained by vigor. It is yet, my Lords, happily in our power to check them in their career, and fix, it may be hoped, more lasting barriers of empire, which shall for ever destroy that thirst of boundless dominion which has given so much disturbance to mankind." Such were the glowing colors with which this eloquent Statesman had the art to varnish over the rashness and absurdity of his measures; and such the arguments by which the House was induced to give its sanction to the proposed address.

A motion being made in the House of Commons for the discharge of the Hanoverian mercenaries,—Mr. Pitt contended, with much warmth, " that there existed no necessity of hiring auxiliary troops, since it had never been shewn that either justice or policy required us to engage in the quarrels of the Continent. The Minister, he said, affected to speak of the balance of power, the Pragmatic Sanction, the preservation of the Queen of Hungary, as if England only were concerned in re-establishing the House of Austria in its former grandeur, and that the power of France were formidable to Great Britain alone. The King of England, no less in his electoral than his regal capacity, had guaranteed the Pragmatic Sanction, and the troops hired by England were, no less than ourselves, allies of the Queen of Hungary. Supposing the assistance granted to the Queen of Hungary a matter of right and justice, due by solemn treaty, Hanover is equally bound with us to observe the terms of this treaty. Or, if it be an act of mere generosity, why should the Elector of Hanover display his generosity at the expence of the people of England? But the transactions of every year exhibited proofs of this *perfidious partiality*. Few of the Members of that House, it might be presumed, had forgotten the ever-memorable treaty, of which the tendency was discovered in the name—the treaty of Hanover; by which we disunited ourselves from Austria, destroyed that building which we may now endeavor in vain to raise again, and weakened the only power which it was our interest to strengthen. He declared, in animadverting on that paragraph of the King's speech which called the attention of Parliament to the late change of affairs in Europe, that we had indeed felt a remarkable change; from one extreme we had run to the utmost verge of another. Our former Minister betrayed the interest of his country by his pusillanimity; our present Minister sacrificed it by his Quixotism. Instead of acceding to every treaty however dishonorable, we now refuse to listen to any, however reasonable. In other respects, the nation had experienced no change, notwithstanding the change of a few individuals in the administration;

tion; for the same prodigal, corrupt, adulatory spirit, still pervaded all the departments of government. He affirmed, that we ought to have advised the Queen of Hungary to have accepted the terms of the King of Prussia, when he first invaded Silesia: nay, we ought to have insisted on it, as the condition of our assisting her against any of the other claimants. Had we done this, the Court of Vienna must have acceded to it; the Queen of Hungary would have retained, in all human probability, firm possession of her other dominions; and the Duke of Lorraine would have been elevated to the imperial throne. Instead of this, we encouraged the Court of Vienna in its obstinacy, and gave the Queen of Hungary reason to believe that we would support her against all the world, though, when Hanover appeared to be in danger, we immediately abandoned the interests of Austria, and co-operated with France to exalt the Elector of Bavaria to the dignity of Emperor. The accommodation between Austria and Prussia, and the subsequent successes of the Queen of Hungary, afforded us a fair opportunity of concluding the war. Peace was proposed by the Emperor and France upon the moderate terms of *uti possidetis*; but we were so far from advising the Queen of Hungary to accept, that there is good reason to believe we advised her not to accept, of the terms offered. Nothing now would satisfy us but the conquest of Alsace and Lorraine, to serve as an equivalent for Silesia; though a general jealousy now prevailed of the ambitious designs of Austria, which would effectually preclude any effort on the part of the Princes of Germany in the prosecution of that romantic scheme. Deceived as the Queen of Hungary had before been, she trusted, strange as it may seem, a second time to our delusive promises; though I will venture to prophesy that, whenever Hanover shall be a second time endangered, she will find herself a second time deceived. The temerity of our counsels was equalled only by the timidity and feebleness of our operations. The whole campaign would have passed in supine inactivity, had not the French found an opportunity, through the misconduct of our Generals, to attack us in a situation which exposed our whole army, and the person of his Majesty, to the most imminent hazard of captivity or destruction. Thank GOD! the courage of some of the French Generals so far exceeded the limits of discretion, as to cause them voluntarily to relinquish the advantage they possessed; and the whole French army, after suffering a severe repulse, were compelled to retire with precipitation over the Maine: But, instead of pursuing a flying enemy, we hastened our own retreat to Hanau, leaving our slain unburied on the field, and our wounded to the mercy of the enemy. This action may therefore, on our side, be called a *lucky escape*; but I shall never give my consent to honor it with the name of a victory. When the French at length repassed the Rhine at the approach of Prince Charles of Lorraine, was any thing done by the allied army? I know of nothing but the exploit of sending a party of hussars into Lorraine with a manifesto, though the Dutch auxiliaries had then joined our army. But had we been seconded by the whole power of Holland, instead of a small detachment of their forces, the vast schemes we have formed would have been equally impracticable, and I should only have lamented that this wise republic had become insane through our example. I could wish erased from the annals and records of our history all mention of the famous treaty of Worms. By that destructive and ridiculous measure we have taken upon ourselves a burden which it is impossible to support; and we have involved ourselves in the guilt of such an act of injustice towards Genoa as must alarm all Europe, and give the French a signal advantage. From thence all Europe will see what regard we have to equity when we think we have power, and have shewn how much it is the general interest to prevent its increase. I hope, therefore,

we

we shall now see the necessity of putting a stop to the farther prosecution of these dangerous and ruinous projects. If we put a negative upon this question, it may awaken Ministers out of their delusive dream; if we agree to it, they will dream on until they have dreamed Europe and their country, as well as themselves, into perdition*."

The same question which had been agitated with equal or greater warmth in the House of Peers, was, in the course of the session, renewed with a slight variation in point of form. And the Lords in opposition indulged themselves in vehement, although historic impartiality must pronounce them for the most part captious and groundless, invectives against the conduct of these mercenaries, and the gross partiality pretended to be shewn them on all occasions. They were declared to be a burthen on the nation, equally hateful and ignominious, and more the objects of political detestation than the enemies against whom they were employed; and the whole system of Continental and Hanoverian politics became again the theme of the severest animadversion. The Earl of Halifax, a young Nobleman distinguished by his political and personal accomplishments, expressed, in warm and eloquent language, "his indignation that England should be condemned to waste the treasure and the lives of its inhabitants in quarrels which either did not at all regard its interests, or regarded them only remotely and consequenti-

---

* The characters of the two Ministers, Walpole and Carteret, were contrasted by a political writer of this period with extraordinary felicity, in the following passage from Cicero, originally applied to Cæsar and Antony with his associates:

"An vos estis ulla re cum eo comparandi? Fuit in illo ingenium, ratio, memoria, literæ, cura, cogitatio, diligentia. Multos annos regnare meditatus, magno labore quod cogitarat, effecerat: Muneribus, monumentis, congiariis, multitudinem imperatam delenierat, suos præmiis, adversarios clementiæ specie devinxerat—quid multa? attuleret jam liberæ civitati partim metu, partim patientia, consuetudinem serviendi. Cum illo ego vos dominandi cupidine comparare possum, cæteris vero rebus nullo modo estis comparandi."

ally.

ally. He declared himself unable to discover for what reason we, who were not principals in the war, and have no separate interest to promote, should hire mercenaries to carry it on, at an immense and intolerable expence. We are now contending, said this Nobleman, not for our rights and privileges—not for our persons, our liberty, or our property. We are attempting by force of arms to fix what the course of events is ever tending to unfix—the balance of Europe. The balance of Europe has a powerful and fascinating sound, which has been frequently employed to subject this nation to the oppressive exactions of foreign powers. When the people complain of the load of taxes, and the perpetual increase of burdens, of which they were never able to perceive any effect, or derive any advantage, they are stilled with the necessity of supporting the balance of Europe. When they cry aloud for justice against their domestic oppressors—when they demand that the deceivers and flatterers of the Prince should be brought to punishment—and the proper interests of the nation alone diligently and faithfully pursued—they are censured and stigmatized as wretches ignorant of the true interests of policy, and who have no regard to the balance of Europe. The folly and guilt of this conduct were not unknown during the last administration to the noble Lord who now assumes the direction of foreign affairs, and were reprobated by him with generous warmth and all the appearance of honest detestation. But we have often seen that opinions are variable with other human things. The system of the noble Lord is now entirely changed, and, to use the language of the medical *charlatan*, the heart is removed to the other side."

Lord Carteret, with his accustomed energy of language and plausibility of argument, entered into an elaborate defence of his ministerial conduct. He declared, " that a proposition to withdraw all our forces from the Continent, and, instead of courting danger in foreign countries, to sleep

sleep in security till we are awakened by an alarm upon our own coasts, would be far less unreasonable than the motion actually before the House; for, doubtless, it is better to enjoy peace, however precarious, than to carry on a war with certainty of defeat, and to rush into the field of battle only to be overcome by the number of our enemies. Is it seriously meant that we are to neglect all the rules of war and all the maxims of policy, and to set our enemies at defiance, expecting assistance from causes invisible or præternatural? The Lords who support the motion must know, that a compliance with it would be virtually to yield up all for which WILLIAM and MARLBOROUGH fought—all which can secure our own independence or the liberties of the Continent. The topics enlarged upon by the noble Lords, of numerous armies and burthensome expences, are such as will always raise a declaimer high in the esteem of the people, whose sufferings he appears to compassionate, and whose cause he professes to defend; and measures, however necessary and however just, *must* be unpopular for a time, of which the expence is immediate and the advantage distant. It is the opinion of some, that, from the nature of our situation, we may bid defiance to the rest of mankind, and, from our rocks and floating castles, look with unconcern and tranquility upon all the commotions of the European kingdoms; but if any one monarchy has, by any means, arisen to such an height of grandeur as to make it justly formidable to the rest of Europe, threatening the eventual subversion of all the kingdoms on the Continent, surely Great Britain has more cogent reasons than any other nation to endeavor the suppression of such a power, because of all nations she has most to lose; and being farthest exalted above slavery, must feel proportionate pain from political depression. But this purpose can be effected only by supporting on the Continent some power capable of opposing the ambitious projects of France; and it is universally admitted,

mitted, that the House of Austria alone can be deemed of weight to be placed in the balance against the House of Bourbon. If the House of Austria is to be supported, we must submit to the expence necessary for its support. Nothing, therefore, can be more improper than this motion, unless it were intended that the cause of general liberty should be instantly and totally abandoned, and that we should submissively consign to France the fate of ourselves and our posterity. By the disseminations of falsehood and malignity the nation has been irritated, and discontent has, indeed, too generally prevailed: but, by the same arts, the same odium might and would have attended any other scheme; and the present clamor will, in a short time, give way to the force of reason and truth. Upon a former occasion, in which the neutrality of Hanover was the subject of discussion, I observed that, if England were to be steered by that Electorate, it were necessary that the rudder should be separated from the ship. This was then my opinion; for then, my Lords, England was subservient to Hanover: but Hanover is now subservient to England, and regulated by our measures; for who can doubt but a neutrality might have been easily obtained for that Electorate? But his Majesty scorned to exempt himself from hazard, by countenancing the claims of ambition, and would not forbear to assist his ally only because her distress was urgent, and her danger imminent. It is evident, upon the whole, then, my Lords, that the war has been conducted with wisdom and success—that the troops of Hanover were not retained but by the counsel and authority of the legislature—that they have been eminently useful in contributing to the expulsion of the armies of France—that, though objections more worthy of notice could be produced, those troops cannot, at this juncture, be dismissed, because other troops cannot be obtained so soon as the exigencies of the war require."

The

The question was at length put, and the motion rejected by a majority of eighty-six Peers against forty-six: but a very strong protest was signed by the minority, and the measure was manifestly carried in both Houses by the influence of the Court, against the unanimous voice of the nation, which loudly exclaimed against the interested ambition and political apostacy of the Minister, who had now involved himself and his country too deeply in the quarrels of the Continent to be able to recede either with honor or with safety.

In the course of this important and interesting session, the House of Commons, apprised of the recent machinations of the Court of St. Germains, sent up to the Lords a bill, making it high treason to correspond with the sons of the Pretender. On the commitment of this bill, the Lord Chancellor Hardwicke moved, that the committee be instructed to receive a clause for continuing the penalties and forfeitures legally incurred by the descendants of traitors, to the death of the sons of the Pretender, and which, by the operation of an act passed in the reign of Queen Anne, expired with the Pretender himself. On which the Duke of Bedford arose, and, in a very able manner, stated his reasons for refusing his assent to the motion. "His Grace declared his zeal for the security of the Constitution, and of the settlement of the Crown in the present family, to be in no degree inferior to that of any of their Lordships: and he expressed his conviction that a Prince forced upon us by the armies and fleets of France would be only the viceroy of the Monarch to whom he owed his exaltation. Nevertheless, said this Nobleman, your Lordships will not be surprised that I am alarmed at the prospect of a law like this. I, whose family has suffered so lately the deprivation of its rank and fortune by the tyranny of a court—whose grand father was cut off by an unjust prosecution—and whose father was condemned for many years to see himself divested of the rights of his birth, which were at length

length restored to him by more equitable judges;—it is surely reasonable, my Lords, that I should oppose the extension of penalties to the descendants of offenders, who have scarce myself escaped the blast of an attainder*. Whatever may be the malice of our enemies, the ill success of past attempts is a convincing proof that government can have no just cause of fear; that recourse, therefore, need not be had to new degrees of severity, or the enacting penal laws of an extraordinary kind, to prevent that which experience has shewn impossible to be accomplished. On the present occasion, my Lords, the people have demonstrated their loyalty by innumerable addresses from all parts, drawn up in terms expressive of the firmest fidelity and the warmest affection—professions which surely deserve far other return than the severity of a penal law, by which one person is condemned to suffer for the crime of another. If it be necessary, my Lords, that subjects should obey their governors, it is no less necessary that governors should not harass their subjects by causeless suspicion; for this will certainly tend to weaken their affections—it may incite them to violate their duties. The multiplicity of penal laws, the establishment of armies, the distribution of pensions, are transitory and uncertain supports of govern-

---

* In the illustrious roll of martyrs to the cause of liberty, no name stands more conspicuously distinguished, or is written in fairer characters, than that of Lord RUSSEL, whose patriotism appears unsullied with any base alloy of personal resentment or interest. In reply to those sophistical reasons by which Burnet, afterwards Bishop of Sarum, attempted to draw from this Nobleman an inglorious acknowledgment of culpability in meditating resistance to tyranny, he made this excellent and memorable declaration—" That he could form no conception of a limited monarchy which had no right to defend its own limitations." So long as sensibility and gratitude are numbered amongst the affections of the human heart, so long shall we honor with a supreme reverence those who have dared to die for their country; and, with an almost superstitious devotion,

" Kiss with joy the sacred earth
That gave a HAMPDEN or a RUSSEL birth."

ment, which the first blast of discontent may drive before it, and which have a tendency to produce that rage which they cannot furnish the means of resisting. Ten thousand penal laws cannot so much contribute to the establishment of the present royal family as one act of confidence, condescension, or bounty, by which the affections of the people may be conciliated. We are not, my Lords, to appease the suspicions of the throne by sacrificing the safety or happiness of the people : we are, indeed, to support our Sovereign, but not by such means as to destroy the ends for which sovereignty was established—the public welfare and common security. How, then, can we assent to a measure which may involve thousands in undeserved misery, by punishing them for crimes which they did not commit, and which it was not in their power to prevent—and inflicting penalties in order to enrich by forfeitures the minions of a court? But exclusive of these considerations, and to advert to an objection of a different nature, what evidence exists by which it can be ascertained that there never will come a time, in which a superstitious, ambitious, or tyrannical Prince may once more attempt the subversion of the rights and liberties of the kingdom? If, then a time so fatal shall ever arrive, and another revolution be necessary, how must a law like this damp the ardor of that patriotism by which all revolutions have been accomplished! Who will be found hardy enough to oppose the Crown, when not only himself but his whole posterity are involved in the danger and ruin of a failure? We are to reflect, that the King may not only be in danger from his people, but that the people may be in danger from their King; and as, on the one hand, no privilege should be conferred tending to the encouragement of popular sedition; on the other, no prerogative ought to be endured which may incite to acts of royal oppression. The dependence of the monarch and the subject ought to be on reciprocal affection and mutual assistance ; and if I am desirous

rous

rous of securing the throne, it is not by disarming the people, but by placing them as guards before it." The clause in question was also vigorously and eloquently opposed by the Lords Talbot, Chesterfield, and others—and defended by the Lords Carteret and Hardwicke, and Secker, Bishop of Oxford, though a measure flagrantly incompatible with the mild and benevolent spirit of Christianity. The question being put, it passed in the affirmative; but it was accompanied by a strong and animated protest.

The bill, when returned to the Commons with this new and unexpected clause, occasioned great dissatisfaction and opposition. Mr. Fazakerley, the original mover of the bill, expressed, in warm and indignant language, his detestation of the clause added by the Lords. " Forfeitures and confiscations, he said, he had always regarded as unjust, cruel, and of dangerous consequences to the liberties of a free people. As to the authority of Grotius and Puffendorf—which had been adduced in the course of an elaborate speech in defence of the amendment by the Attorney General, Sir Dudley Ryder—he said, they wrote in countries where forfeitures for treason had been established for ages, at a period far less enlightened than the present, when it would have been not only unusual but dangerous absolutely and explicitly to have condemned them, and an *indirect disapprobation* is easily discernible. At any rate, we are not blindly to resign our judgments either to the learned Grotius, or the learned Puffendorf. Still less satisfactory was the appeal made to the divine than to human authority in vindication of this law. It is certain that we find no such punishment inflicted by the law of Moses: and if David seized, as the learned Gentleman has affirmed to the House, upon the estate of Saul, this was certainly the *commission*, and not the *penalty*, of treason. As to the case of Mephibosheth, he was not so much as accused of treason, but of ingratitude; and the punishment inflicted upon him was the mere act of arbitrary power. But

But admitting that the Kings of the Jews acted upon the principle of this iniquitous law, their example can be no authority; for Samuel had before warned the Jews of the oppressions they were to expect from Kings: he had told them that the King would take their fields, their vineyards, and their olive-trees, and give the best of them to his servants. The charge of treason was no doubt made use of to furnish a pretext for these enormous injuries; and the experience of our own government may convince us what tyranny might be exercised under a veil so specious. It will be alleged, perhaps, that this law, however inconsistent with humanity and justice, is necessary to the preservation of the government; but is this the fact in the eastern countries, where punishments still more horrid and barbarous are inflicted in cases of this nature? These unjust and odious penalties only serve to lull a government into a fatal security, and to embolden arbitrary Ministers to tyrannize over the people, till, inflamed by repeated acts of oppression, the train is set fire to, and the Ministers, with their Master, are blown up by the combustibles which they had so assiduously prepared for the destruction of others." The House, however, agreed to the amendment, by a majority of eighty voices; and a new proof was exhibited to the world of how little estimation, in the view of Princes, are all considerations of moral and political justice, when deemed incompatible with their interest or security.

This year, 1743, the Swedes terminated an unsuccessful war with Russia, by a peace signed at Abo, by which they were totally detached from their political connection with France. This event, so intimately affecting the general state of politics in Europe, requires a distinct elucidation. At the death of the last Monarch of Sweden, the celebrated Charles XII. (A. D. 1718), who had governed with a sway the most arbitrary and imperious, and whose rash and romantic enterprises had reduced his country to the

verge

verge of ruin, Sweden found itself in a situation the most favorable for finally abolishing despotism, and establishing a free and equal government on a solid and permanent basis. A Diet being immediately convoked, the throne of Sweden was declared VACANT—Charles having died without issue, and the claim of his sisters to the succession being barred, conformably to a fundamental law of the kingdom, by their previous marriage. The States, therefore, determined to make an offer of the crown to Ulrica Eleanora, consort of Frederic, hereditary Prince of Hesse Cassel, subsequently associated in the government, to the exclusion of the Duke of Holstein, son of the elder sister, on the express condition that this Princess should declare her readiness to hold the crown in virtue of a FREE ELECTION; and should take an oath to adhere to the new *formula* or model of government, now, by the authority of the nation, solemnly instituted. "The Counsellors and States of the kingdom assembled, having, as they express themselves, experienced the sad consequences of that arbitrary power which has so much weakened and injured the kingdom, to the almost irreparable ruin of us all, have seriously and unanimously resolved to abolish entirely a power which has proved so prejudicial." It is to be remarked that the Diet, or States General of the kingdom of Sweden, consists of four distinct chambers or houses—the Nobles, the Clergy, the Burghers, the Peasants. These, agreeably to the constitution now established, were to be convoked every three years, or more frequently if occasion required. And should the King, or Senate in his absence, neglect to assemble them at the expiration of this term, or even should they not convoke them on the very day the States had, the last time they were assembled, chosen to appoint for their next meeting, these should then have a right to assemble of themselves. And whatever the King or Senate should have done in the mean time, was to be considered as void. The time specified for the shortest legal duration of the

Diet

Diet was three months; but the power of dissolution was vested in themselves alone. While the States were assembled, they were in fact possessed of the whole supreme power; the authority of the King and Senate was then suspended—they became mere cyphers, having little or no share in the public transactions but what consisted simply in affixing their seals and signatures to whatever the Diet should think proper to resolve. The legislative power the States reserved at all times wholly to themselves, the King and the Senate not even possessing a negative on those resolutions which directly attacked the regal and senatorial rights. "For the preservation of these, it is remarked with just derision*, they were to depend on the MODERATION OF A POPULAR ASSEMBLY." The following powers were likewise vested in the States alone: Those of declaring war or making peace—that of altering the standard of the coin—whenever a vacancy happened in the Senate, that of presenting to the King three persons, one of whom his Majesty was bound to make choice of to fill the vacant office—lastly, that of dismissing any member of the Senate whose conduct they disapproved. During the session of the Diet, a standing secret committee was chosen, selected from the three orders of Nobles, Clergy, and Burghers, of which one half were Nobles—the order of Peasants being too mean and insignificant to be associated in this commission—by which the ordinary functions of the Senate were almost entirely superseded, and the executive powers of the government exclusively exercised. With regard to the judicial power the States assumed to themselves a right of exercising that also, whenever they thought proper, by taking at pleasure causes out of the high courts of justice established by law, to try them before a temporary tribunal erected by themselves, and composed of their own members. Nothing, therefore, could be more formidable than

* Vide History of the Swedish Revolution, A. D. 1772, by Charles F. Sheridan, Esq.

the

the power of this assembly, or more subversive of liberty; as, in reality, it united within itself the legislative, judicial, and executive powers—and as the province and jurisdiction of the occasional tribunal comprehended all cases of treason, sedition, and public libel, it was evidently, at the same time, both judge and party. Even during the intervals of the Diets, the King was little more than a cypher of state, and was distinguished from the other Senators, consisting of fourteen in number, only by the privilege of a double voice in the first instance, and of a casting vote in case of an equality of voices. The Senate were empowered to assemble themselves whenever they thought proper, and to transact the national business whether the King were present or not; and to their resolutions his Majesty was obliged to affix his signature. The great employments of the State were conferred by a majority of voices in the Senate; and to others of inferior importance three persons were nominated by the Senate, one of whom the King was obliged to appoint. Thus the outward pomp and decorations of Majesty were almost all that remained of a prerogative lately so formidable: but a more recent experience soon taught the Swedes that political oppression might exist under a variety of forms, and that the liberty of the people was not necessarily increased in proportion as the power of the Monarch was diminished; and the scenes of corruption, distraction, and anarchy, which ensued, were the most decisive proofs of the numerous and radical defects of the new *formula* of government. When compared with the British constitution, the prodigious superiority of the latter is manifest in almost every point of view in which they can be placed—their whole structure, genius, and spirit forming a most instructive and striking contrast. In England, the Crown is vested by the constitution with the whole active power of government, subject to the authoritative inspection and control of Parliament; and it is also possessed, by means of its extensive patronage, of that

degree

degree of influence over the legiflative body which muft not only preclude the idea of foreign intrigue and interference; but of that fpecies of oppofition which arifes from the natural and inceffant defire of aggrandizement, the interefts of the individual members being oppofed to the aggregate intereft of the body—the negative of the King and the power of diffolution coming likewife in aid of that prerogative which is at once fo open to the attack, and fo unequal to the encounter. On the other hand, the conftitutional powers of Parliament, and its component principles, are fuch as eminently to qualify it for its province of legiflation and control. The Houfe of Commons is invefted with the fole difpofal of the national revenue, which, of itfelf, gives it a decided preponderance over the other, and, with refpect to rank, the higher branch of the legiflature. The Commons of England are not, like the Commons of Sweden, divided into diftinct chambers, by which their collective force is fenfibly enfeebled. The Englifh Houfe of Commons likewife contains a much greater combination of interefts than, in confequence of the abfurd reftraints on the freedom of election, can take place in Sweden; where the burghers and peafants muft be actually of the feveral claffes of the community which they reprefent. Alfo, in Sweden all the privileges of the Nobility, that of fitting in the Diet excepted, extending to all the defcendants of Nobles, a vaft proportion of the landed property of the kingdom, and almoft all the military and civil offices, are confined to that privileged clafs: the ariftocratic branch of the legiflature, fupported by this immenfe chain of connections and dependencies, rifing far above all competition: whereas, in England, the defcendants of the Nobility, the heirs of the title only excepted, are immediately blended with the general mafs of the community, and their political interefts ftand confequently in unavoidable and direct oppofition to thofe of their neareft relatives, as compofing a diftinct and privileged order. Thus the Nobles of England

land are placed in that precife rank which properly belongs to the moft illuftrious order of citizens in a free and well-governed community. Invefted with the higheft dignity, though not the higheft power, of the State, they compofe an hereditary Senate, peculiarly qualified, from that diffimilarity of views and interefts by which, as a diftinct branch of the legiflature, they muft be neceffarily actuated, for the province of revifion, and refiftance to ambitious or infidious innovation—ftanding as a perpetual barrier againft all attempts to encroach upon the conftitutional prerogative of the Crown, upon which they depend as the firmeft bafis of their own authority. For the weight of the democracy in the Englifh conftitution is fuch, as to preclude the ariftocracy from the fainteft hope of fuccefs in any conteft for pre-eminence which might fucceed the eventual reduction or annihilation of the regal power. It cannot certainly be pretended, that the progreffive improvement of former ages, or even the important and beneficial changes which took place at the Revolution, were the refult of any comprehenfive abftract fpeculation; they were fuch as the emergency of the occafion rendered obvious and neceffary; and we fpeak of the wifdom of the conftitution, not with a reference to the fpeculative fagacity of individuals, but to the practical advantages and firm contexture of a form of government finifhed, undoubtedly, more through happinefs than pains. It is true, indeed, that, through the grofs inequality of the prefent fyftem of reprefentation, deftined doubtlefs, if Liberty furvive, to undergo a radical reform, a degree of influence is exerted by the executive power over the legiflative, inconfiftent with the true fpirit of the conftitution, and productive of the moft injurious effects. Under fuch a government as that eftablifhed in Sweden, it can excite no aftonifhment that the intrigues of foreign courts fhould very powerfully and fenfibly operate. In fact, from the æra of that eftablifhment, all the apparently weak and capricious

transactions

transactions of this kingdom were guided solely by the predominance of the different political factions, the violent and malignant conflicts of which were excited and perpetuated by the most shameful corruption, universally practised, and almost openly avowed. The whole power of the State virtually resting in the hands of the Nobles, no advance was made, or design entertained, to extend to the nation at large the blessings of civil liberty. And the people feeling themselves in no degree relieved from the oppression of the ancient government, notwithstanding the system of political liberty recently established—of the excellence of which they heard indeed much, but comprehended little—were loud in their complaints of the misconduct and tyranny of their rulers. The fixed policy of the leading men originally concerned in framing the new form of government*, who were persons of virtue and probity, and, in all probability, far from being sensible of its imperfections, was, to renounce all ambition of foreign conquests, and assiduously to cultivate the friendship of Russia, the superiority of whose power they had so fatally experienced. And the influence of Russia continued, with little interruption, to predominate in their councils till the meeting of the Diet in 1738, when, through the profusion of French gold previously distributed amongst its members, a great majority appeared determined to abandon the alliance of Russia, and to enter into a strict connection with the Court of Versailles ; which flattered them with the chimerical hope of recovering, by a rupture with the Court of St. Petersburgh, their long-lost provinces. And, at the instance of the French Minister, war was actually declared by Sweden against Russia, without any just reasons, or even plausible pretences ; the real motive on the

---

* Count Horne is said to have been the person principally concerned in the establishment of this constitution—a Nobleman of unquestionable abilities and integrity.

part of France being, as the Queen of Hungary obferved in her manifefto, to prevent the Czarina from interpofing in the affairs of the Empire. This unjuft and impolitic war was undertaken by Sweden at a time when the armies of Ruffia were returning triumphant from the Turkifh campaigns; and the fuccefs was fuch as might be reafonably expected. The Swedifh army in Finland was deftroyed, and the whole of that country loft. The Generals Lewenhaupt and Buddenbroek were facrificed to the fury of a faction. The government of Sweden, alarmed at the rapid progrefs of the Ruffians, were compelled to folicit a peace, which was granted upon very moderate terms, Ruffia reftoring the whole of her conquefts, a fmall diftrict to the eaftward of the Kymen only excepted. And, in return, the Swedes renewed their alliance with Ruffia, and agreed to appoint Adolphus Frederic, Bifhop of Lubec, a Prince of the Houfe of Holftein, nearly related to the Emprefs Elizabeth, fucceffor to the prefent King; the young Duke of Holftein, grandfon of the elder fifter of Ulrica, being deftined to the fucceffion of Ruffia, as nephew to the Emprefs, on his previous and formal renunciation of all claim to the Crown of Sweden. In allufion to this tranfaction, as likewife to the late difpofition of the Crown of Poland, the Imperial Ambaffador at Peterfburg obferved to the Emprefs, " that he wifhed his Court had found it as eafy to keep poffeffion of kingdoms as it was to Ruffia to give them away."

Though France had thus, by the perfidy of her own policy, loft one ufeful ally, fhe made vigorous efforts to indemnify herfelf by the acquifition of another—the contiguous kingdom of Denmark. From the memorable æra in which the Danes made a voluntary furrender of their ancient liberties to the Monarch, the Kings of Denmark had been poffeffed of authority not inferior to that of any Sovereigns in Chriftendom; and the want of ability, rather than of inclination, had fince prevented them from making more conspicuous figure in the general history of Europe; as they never appeared reluctant or scrupulous in embracing any favorable opportunity of aggrandizement. Christiern V. who acceded to the throne A. D. 1670, waged unsuccefsful war with the Swedes, in the vain hope of recovering the beautiful provinces of Halland, Schonen, and Bleking, loft by his father Frederic III. and ceded to Sweden by the treaty of Rofchild, 1658. Christiern dying in 1699 was succeeded by his son Frederic IV. who joined the confederacy against Charles XII. was besieged by that Monarch in his capital, and compelled to submit to the terms dictated by Sweden, under the mediation of England and Holland, at the treaty of Travendahl. After the decline of that Monarch's fortunes, Frederic renewed the war, and seized upon the Duchies of Bremen, Verden, and Slefwic, the latter of which was guaranteed to Denmark by King George I. in return for the ceffion of the two former to Hanover. This Monarch dying A. D. 1730 was succeeded by Christiern VI. a sagacious and pacific Prince, who afpired, nevertheless, when the succefsion to the throne of Sweden was vacant, to revive the ancient and celebrated union of Calmar; and to combine, by an indissoluble federation, the three Scandinavian kingdoms into one empire, under one head, in the person of his son. Flattered with the aid and affiftance of France in the accomplifhment of this great object of his ambition, he relinquifhed, at this period, the alliance, and refufed the subfidies, of Great Britain, in order to connect himself with that rival power. But notwithftanding that the idea of this union was very popular in Sweden, and was supported by a very ftrong party in the Diet, the oppofing politics of Ruffia proved finally succefsful; and the King of Denmark had the good fense to defift from the farther profecution of a project which was become too hazardous to attempt to enforce, although great military preparations had been made for that purpose. But the Czarina declared,

that,

that, if the Swedes were attacked, she would assist them with the whole force of her empire. The good understanding between Denmark and Great Britain was, immediately on the relinquishment of this visionary scheme, restored and cemented by the marriage of Frederic, Prince Royal of Denmark, with Louisa, youngest daughter of his Britannic Majesty, which took place towards the conclusion of the present year. The King of Denmark survived this alliance, which was productive of general satisfaction to the inhabitants of both kingdoms, little more than two years. The Princess Mary, third daughter to the King of England, had, at a period somewhat anterior to the events now related, been married to Frederic, Prince of Hesse Cassel, nephew to the King of Sweden, and presumptive heir to the Landgraviate.

At this time Admiral Matthews commanded with high reputation the British Naval force in the Mediterranean. The Corsicans having revolted from the dominion of Genoa, and elected a German adventurer as their Sovereign, by the name of King Theodore, were supported and encouraged by this Commander, in revenge for the partiality shewn by the Genoese to the French and Spanish arms in Italy; though these brave islanders were, in the sequel, forgotten and abandoned to their fate. Stores having been landed at Civita Vecchia for the use of the Spanish army under the Count de Gages, the British Admiral declared it to be a violation of the neutrality professed by his Holiness the POPE, and threatened a bombardment of that city; but desisted in consequence of the interposition of his Sardinian Majesty. The commerce of France and Spain was interrupted, many prizes made, their coasts kept in continual alarm, and the combined squadrons of the two powers were blocked up for several successive months in the harbor of Toulon. On the ninth of February 1744, they were at last perceived standing out of the road, to the number of four-and-thirty sail of the line. The British Admiral

miral immediately weighed, and an engagement enfued, which notwithftanding the great fuperiority of the Britifh fleet, proved extremely indecifive ; and which was afterwards the fubject of much and vehement debate and difcuffion. It is admitted that Matthews behaved with heroic gallantry ; but he was very ill feconded by fome of his officers, particularly by Admiral Leftock, who with his whole divifion, remained at a great diftance aftern. It is not pretended that this officer was really deficient in courage ; but he had long been upon very ill terms with his Commander, whom he affected to defpife, and whofe fignals on the day of battle he affirmed to be unintelligible and inconfiftent—fheltering himfelf behind thofe rigid rules of difcipline, againft which, in the crifis of danger, it is often the higheft merit glorioufly to offend. Admiral Matthews, on his arrival at Minorca, fufpended Leftock for difobedience, and fent him as a prifoner to England, where he, in return, accufed, and recriminated upon his fuperior. Thefe proceedings became the fubject of parliamentary inveftigation ; and a court-martial was appointed to try the delinquents. It appears that the object of De Court, the French Commander, whofe fhips greatly outfailed thofe of the Britifh fquadron, being to avoid an engagement, the Englifh Commander was compelled to commence the attack before the line was completely formed ; and he directed his principal effort againft the Spanifh divifion, which failing in the rear of the French, and at fome diftance, he endeavored to cut off—being himfelf, in the Namur, clofely engaged with the Spanifh Admiral Don Navarro, in the Royal Philip, an immenfe fhip of one hundred and fourteen guns. Admiral Leftock was, at this time, five miles aftern, fuffering by an obftinate adherence to the fignal for the line of battle, then flying at the fame time with the fignal for a clofe engagement, the rearmoft fhips of the Spanifh fquadron to pafs him : on which Admiral Matthews, though bravely feconded by Captain Cornewall,

Cornewall, in the Marlborough, who gloriously fell in the action, and other ships of his own division, was obliged to relinquish his prey at a moment when he flattered himself that she could not have escaped him, being, as he affirms in his public letter, " within musket shot of the Royal Philip, then lying a mere wreck, when the sternmost ships of the enemy came up and tore him to pieces." In the result, Admiral Lestock, to the general surprise and indignation, was honorably acquitted, and Admiral Matthews declared incapable of serving for the future in his Majesty's navy. The King himself, who was personally brave, and a lover of the brave, is said to have expressed, in warm terms, his disapprobation of this decision. And, when an elaborate technical vindication of the sentence of the court-martial was offered, he indignantly replied, " that he knew but little of naval phraseology ; but this, said his Majesty, I know, that Matthews did fight, and that Lestock did not."

In July, Sir John Balchen, an officer of great merit, sailed from Spithead with a strong squadron, in quest of a French fleet expected to depart about this time from the harbor of Brest. In the Bay of Biscay he encountered a violent storm, by which the fleet was entirely scattered, and the Admiral's own ship, the Victory, a new and beautiful first-rate, with eleven hundred men on board, foundered at sea, near the rocks of Alderney ; and the whole crew, with all the officers and their commander, most unfortunately perished.

Another revolution about this period (November 1744) took place in the British cabinet. Lord Carteret, now become Earl of Granville, had insinuated himself so far into the good graces of his Sovereign as to excite, in a very high degree, the apprehension and dislike of the Duke of Newcastle and his brother, Mr. Pelham, who secretly intrigued with the popular leaders in Parliament to effect the downfall of this ambitious and haughty Minister,

ter, whose power they envied, and whose talents they feared. The Earl, comprehending the nature and extent of the combination against him, and sensible of his own unpopularity, heightened by the ill success of the war, avoided the conflict by a voluntary resignation of his employments, in which he was followed by Mr. Sandys, created Lord Sandys, and various others. Mr. Pelham, who, on the death of Lord Wilmington, had succeeded to the direction of the Board of Treasury, was now nominated Chancellor of the Exchequer, and may be considered from this period as first Minister. The Earl of Chesterfield was appointed to the government of Ireland, the Duke of Bedford placed at the head of the Admiralty, the Lords Gower and Cobham reinstated in their former posts, and, after an interval of delay and reluctance on the part of the Court, Mr. Pitt constituted Paymaster of the Forces, and sworn a member of the Privy Council. Several of the Tories were admitted to offices in consequence of this coalition of parties; and Sir John Hynde Cotton and Sir John Philips, those morose and turbulent patriots, were—for a time of short duration indeed, " a little month"—transformed into courtiers and placemen. The Parliament met in December (1744), and it soon appeared that the result of the late changes was by no means unfavorable to the views of the Court; for the same system was pursued with less difficulty and interruption: and the patriots still in opposition, wearied with long and useless exertion, seemed at length to acquiesce in measures which the nation at large, now roused into passionate resentment against France, and admiration of the courage and fortitude of the Queen of Hungary, began to regard with partiality and approbation. And the unremitted efforts of thirty years, efforts which had produced such signal displays of knowledge, virtue, and eloquence, ingloriously terminated in the ancient maxim—" Si populus vult decipi, decipiatur." As the last struggle of expiring patriotism, however, the House

was

was moved, January 1745, that an act made in the fourth year of Edward III. entitled—" a parliament shall be holden once every year," and also that an act made in thirty-sixth year of the reign of King Edward III. entitled—" A parliament shall be holden once every year," shall be read; and the acts being read accordingly, Mr. Carew* arose, and declared his determination to bring to a DECISIVE TEST the sincerity of those professions which the Ministers of the Crown recently appointed to their offices had, for so many successive years, accustomed themselves to repeat within the walls of that House; and, from the fate of the question he was about to propose, a judgment might be formed whether the present Ministers themselves merited those severe appellations which they had so lavishly bestowed upon their predecessors. It was not enough, he said, for the satisfaction of the impartial and intelligent

---

* This member, in a subsequent session of the present Parliament, moved an address to the King, that he would be pleased to order a monument to be erected in Westminster Abbey to the memory of the gallant Captain Cornewall, who lost his life in the engagement off Toulon; which being unanimously carried, Velters Cornewall, brother to the deceased, rose " to express the pride and satisfaction he felt on this occasion; more particularly as the motion originated with one of the most able, upright, and disinterested patriots who had ever sat in that House." We may, therefore, fairly presume, that the speech of Mr. Carew does not contain words of empty sound, intended for the mere purpose of embarrassing the administration, but that it exhibits the real sentiments of his understanding, and the genuine feelings of his heart. And it may be remarked, that the value and utility of exertions of this nature are not to be estimated by the advantage they *immediately* produce. Mr. Carew and Mr. Sydenham yet speak in history; nor will it ultimately be found that such men speak in vain. In our own times, the orations of Mr. Fox in support of his several motions for the repeal of the test and penal statutes, were negatived by great majorities; but are these generous efforts in the cause of truth and liberty therefore lost? No—doubtless they will produce their effect at the destined period on minds more susceptible of improvement, and less under the dominion of prejudice——

" When Statesmen, Heroes, Kings, in dust repose,
Whose sons shall blush their fathers were his foes."

public, that the new Minifters fhould give a fimple affent to the motion he had in contemplation; for, if they had coalefced with perfons whofe influence was, upon trial, found fufficiently powerful to defeat all efforts of political reform, it was incumbent upon them immediately to relinquifh thofe offices which they had fo precipitately accepted, without any ftipulations in favor of the public; and unrefervedly to declare againft thofe with whom they had fo rafhly united. Amongft the topics moft frequently infifted upon by the prefent Minifters, when in oppofition to the Court, was the neceffity of counteracting the baleful effects of minifterial corruption, which they then feemed to think, and he hoped they ftill thought, could by no means fo effectually be done as by a reftoration of the ancient conftitution of Parliament, agreeably to which, the Houfe would perceive, by the acts now read, that Parliaments were to be holden once every year. And as long prorogations and adjournments were not then introduced or thought of, the meaning of this famous law muft be, that a Parliament fhould be every year chofen as well as held. And this is a conftitution not only fanctioned by ancient practice, but by the unalterable dictates of reafon. In order that the reprefentation of a great nation may be perfectly acquainted with the ftate of its wifhes, wants, and grievances, it is neceffary that there fhould be an intimate and habitual communication between them and their conftituents. But, when Gentlemen are chofen for a term of years, they too frequently, on their election, appear at once to relinquifh the character and feelings of delegates; they fix their abode in the metropolis, and vifit their conftituents only when it becomes neceffary to folicit their votes at the eve of a new election. Nay, fuch was the degraded and corrupt ftate into which the national reprefentation had fallen fince the eftablifhment of Septennial Parliaments, that there were Gentlemen in that Houfe who never faw the borough which fent them thither;

who.

who, perhaps, would be at a loss even to recollect its name; and who were obliged to have recourse to the Court Calendar to inform them of whom they were the representatives. It was the peculiar and proper province of the House of Commons, he said, to convey to the Sovereign the sentiments of the nation, both with respect to the measures he adopts, and the Ministers he employs. But could this duty be justly or faithfully executed, when there is no proper intercourse established between those who represent and those who are represented? The interests of the Prince and of the People cannot really and truly differ; he can only be great in their greatness, and prosperous in their prosperity. But the general interest of the People, and the personal interest of the Ministers, may very essentially differ; they may have no other ends in view than to impoverish and enslave the People, in order to enrich and aggrandize themselves: and during a long term of delegation, how easy will it ever be for artful and designing men to misrepresent the sentiments of the People to the Sovereign, and to pervert, by sinister and corrupt practices, the integrity of those persons whose duty it is, and who are expressly appointed, to guard the liberties, and protect the rights of the community? Properly speaking, Mr. Carew said, the House of Commons were no more than the attornies of the People: and is it reasonable that any man should be entrusted with a power of attorney irrevocable for a long term of years? Shall a whole People do that which would be the height of foolishness in every individual?" Who can depend upon the continuance of any man's integrity? But the Septennial Bill was passed for the purpose of compelling the people to give an irrevocable power of attorney for that term. The practice of long Parliaments was first introduced in the reign of Richard II. when the interests of the country were sacrificed by wicked Ministers, to gratify the violent passions of the Monarch. But what was the result? The discontents and

murmurs

murmurs of the People, so carefully concealed from the knowledge of the King, at last produced an universal convulsion, which terminated in his ruin, and in the advancement of the Duke of Lancaster to the throne, without any other title than that of having rescued the People from slavery. This was the fate of the Prince who first introduced long Parliaments; but so long as a corrupt majority may be more easily obtained in a long than a short Parliament, so long will it be the interest of Ministers to oppose any limitation of the duration of Parliaments, though the interests both of the Monarch and the People ever so manifestly require it. If Septennial Parliaments be continued in this country, the Minister's letters of recommendation may, in time, be as implicitly obeyed in our counties, cities, and boroughs, as the King's *congé d'élire* is now in the chapters of our episcopal cathedrals. But will any one assert, that we should then have the slightest pretence to the character of a free nation? No—we should be slaves; God knows to whom—not, it may be hoped, to a Minister from HANOVER; though it is hard to say what a corrupt Parliament may not attempt, or to what a corrupt nation may not submit. To prevent however, as far as my exertions can contribute to the prevention of such a catastrophe, I shall conclude with moving for leave to bring in a Bill to enforce the calling of a new Parliament every year after the expiration of this present Parliament."

This motion was very ably seconded by Mr. Sydenham, in an interesting speech, of which a concise epitome only must suffice. This Gentleman began by observing, " that he must take it for granted that every member of that House must be conscious of the necessity of adopting measures of some kind for preventing, or, at least, diminishing the extent and effect of ministerial corruption. And, of all the measures that could be devised, none would be found so effectual as the restoration of annual

nual Parliaments. To the fatal introduction of long Parliaments, and their concomitant evils, he ascribed, in a great measure, that remarkable change in the manners and morals of the people at large, which had of late years taken place in this country. Formerly the higher classes among us were distinguished for generosity and hospitality, and those of inferior rank for honesty, frugality, and industry. But these virtues are in danger of being utterly extinguished by the prevalence of political corruption. No sooner did Ministers begin to solicit the votes, instead of convincing the understandings of the Members of Parliament—no sooner were rewards lavished on those who complied with those solicitations, than the public order was disturbed by violent competitions at elections. Voters began to claim a merit with those to whom they gave their vote: the regular channel through which honors and preferments flowed was perverted,, and the interest of the country was sacrificed for the sake of promoting those who had the chief interests in elections. Even in our army and navy, of late years, this has appeared to be the best qualification for entitling a man to preferment. We must, therefore, demolish from the foundation this fabric of corruption; we must render it impossible for a Minister to expect to gain a majority in Parliament, or at elections, either by bribery, or by a partial distribution of places and preferments. I say, we must do this, if we intend to restore that spirit by which our ancestors preserved their liberties, and gained so much glory to their country. And, for this purpose, nothing can be so effectual as the restoration of annual Parliaments. Then may we hope to see that simplicity, generosity, and hospitality of manners revived, which is now no more. For I hope it will not be called generosity to give a voter, by express bargain, five or ten guineas for his vote; or hospitality, to make a county or borough drunk once in seven years, by way of preparation for an

ensuing

ensuing election. When a Gentleman perceives that the favor of his countrymen muſt be purchaſed, not won, he contracts his domeſtic to provide for his election expences ; and, if he ſucceeds, he retires with his family to London, certain of his ſeat for ſeven years, and reſolving ſo to regulate his conduct in Parliament as may ſecure his future indemnification. This change of a country life into a town life has been attended with unſpeakable inconveniencies. A man of fortune who reſides in London may, in operas, routs, aſſemblies, French wines, and Italian muſicians, expend as much yearly as may ſuffice to maintain his rank in the moſt hoſpitable ſtyle of ancient liberality at his ſeat in the country. But will it be pretended that the money ſo expended is of equal advantage to the community ? that the ſame charity is extended to the indigent, the ſame employment to the induſtrious ? Annual Parliaments would undoubtedly produce a mighty alteration of national manners in this reſpect. They would make conſtant reſidence and a conſtant inter-communication of kind offices neceſſary ; they would preſerve the honeſty of our people, by removing the means of temptation ; for no candidate would then be at the expence of corrupting, eſpecially as he could not expect to be repaid, by being himſelf corrupted by the Miniſter after he is choſen. Annual Parliaments will demoliſh the market of corruption. Miniſters will not corrupt when corruption can be of no avail ; and, though conteſts may occaſionally take place, the magnitude of the object will not be ſuch as to occaſion either venality or violence. If, therefore, we cheriſh a laudable ambition to reſtore the practice of thoſe virtues for which our anceſtors were ſo conſpicuous, and by which they handed down to us riches, renown, and liberty, we muſt reſtore the conſtitution of having Parliaments not only annually held, but annually choſen. It was a regulation *reſtored* and eſtabliſhed by one of the greateſt and wiſeſt Princes that ever ſwayed the ſceptre of

this

this kingdom. The Bill passed in the fourth year of the reign of this Monarch (Edward III.) was indeed evaded by the *ingenuity* of the lawyers. The words of the act were these—' A Parliament shall be holden once a-year, and oftener if need be.' The lawyers maintained that the words ' if need be' related to the first part of the law as well as the second ; *i. e.* that a Parliament shall be held once a-year if need be, or oftener if need be ; a construction which rendered the act itself wholly nugatory. In the thirty-sixth year of the reign of the same Monarch, therefore, a new law was passed, by which it was enacted, without any reserve or limitation, ' that a parliament shall be holden every year.' This set the invention of the lawyers again at work, in order to find a new evasion ; and, in the next reign, the practice of prorogation was introduced. Every session of Parliament was declared to be a Parliament, and the liberties of the nation were sacrificed by a Parliament corruptly chosen and illegally continued. Should this now be attempted, it will be found very difficult, if not impossible, to rescue them by force of arms, as was done in the reign of Richard II. ; for the crown has now a regular disciplined army to support its encroachments, and the People have neither arms nor discipline to oppose to such a King and such a Parliament. This consideration alone would make me sanguine in the support of the measure now proposed ; and for this reason, among many others, I conclude with seconding the motion." The speeches of these able and virtuous senators have been thus distinctly recited, because they discover just and noble sentiments of government, and disclose a glorious prospect of political reformation, which it is left to a happier and more enlightened age to realize*. The motion was fee-

* In the writings of SWIFT, a man naturally of a sound and excellent judgment, though unhappily too much under the dominion of violent and malignant passions, is somewhere to be found this remarkable acknowledgement : " I adore the wisdom of that Gothic constitution which made Parliaments annual."

bly opposed in a diffusive and labored speech by Sir William Yonge, Secretary at War, by arguments which, if they proved any thing, would prove that Parliaments ought to be perpetual. But the principal Ministers of the Crown observed a profound silence, not being able to endure the *test* of this *experimentum crucis*. It is, however, extremely remarkable, that, on the division, the question was negatived by a majority of thirty-two voices only, in a house of two hundred and sixty-three members. No attempt at parliamentary reform, in any shape, after this, was made for fourteen years, when a motion for shortening the duration of Parliaments was negatived almost without the formality of a debate. Very recently, indeed, the question has been revived with great lustre and advantage under the auspices of men of the highest talents, and bids fair to excite the serious and continued attention of the public, especially as it is at last combined, as it ever ought to have been, with the kindred question of an equalization of the representation[*]. So long as this grand reform of Parliament itself remains unaccomplished, no essential reform in other respects is to be expected.

Previous to the departure of the Earl of Chesterfield for the government of Ireland, he was invested with the character of Ambassador Extraordinary and Plenipotentiary to the States General, in order to prevail upon their High Mightinesses to take a more active and decisive part in that war, which it could not fail to be remarked that his Lordship had repeatedly inveighed against in Parlia-

---

[*] It will easily be supposed, that an allusion is here intended to the association lately instituted in the metropolis, for obtaining a reform in Parliament; which, exclusive of the avowed approbation of the great rival-statesmen, Mr. PITT and Mr. Fox, respecting its objects, boasts the distinguished names of GREY, FRANCIS, LAMBTON, WHITEBREAD, ERSKINE, SMITH, and many others, which would reflect honor on any cause; and this is certainly a cause which would reflect honor upon any names.

ment as romantic, abfurd, and contrary to the interefts of both countries. Neverthelefs, as the nation had determined upon war, his Lordfhip might deem it no violation of moral or political obligation to exert his utmoft efforts, as a public man, to render it fuccefsful; and it is certain, that he never ceafed to ufe his influence in the cabinet to accomplifh the reftoration of peace; and, in confequence of his difappointment and diffatisfaction in not being able to attain that favorite object of his wifhes, he refigned the Seals of Secretary of State, which were configned to him after his return from Ireland. " Every thing," fays the Earl, fpeaking confidentially of the ftate of affairs at this period, " which does not tend to a peace, is abfurd, and will, in the end, prove fatal." And it is but impartial juftice to declare, that no man entertained more juft or comprehenfive ideas refpecting the national intereft and happinefs than this nobleman, and that few, if any, of his cotemporaries, can be named, who purfued them more refolutely and fteadily. Inceffantly urged and incited by the whole power and influence of the Orange faction, the States at length acceded to the fubftance of the Ambaffador's propofals, and engaged to maintain an army of fifty thoufand men in the field, exclufive of garrifons. But, torn by inteftine divifion and animofity, the terms of the treaty were, after the conclufion of it, little attended to; and, though the proportion of expence to be borne by Holland was mitigated from two-fifths to one-third, the danger to which the republic was expofed was neither fufficiently urgent, nor obvious, to excite a fpirit of national ardor or unanimity*.

* When Metrodorus was fent by Mithridates to folicit the aid of the King of Armenia againft the Romans, Tigranes faid, " What would you, Metrodorus, advife me to do in this cafe?" To which Metrodorus replied, " As an Ambaffador I fhould exhort you to it; but, as your Counfellor, I fhould advife you againft it." Had Lord Chefterfield been afked the fame queftion, doubtlefs he muft, if equally ingenuous, have returned a fimilar anfwer.

In

In the speech made by the Ambassador in the assembly of the States, at his audience of leave, are to be found the following animated expressions: "The love of liberty, which first laid the foundation of this republic, and has since so often signalized her, this so noble and generous love still unites your strength and your counsels to those of the King my master. Actuated by the same spirit, and pursuing the same end, the sole object of your endeavors is to restore and secure the public liberty and tranquillity. What design can be more laudable? what work more worthy of a just and magnanimous zeal? Pursue, High and Mighty Lords, that design with your wonted steadiness and wisdom: continue those efforts without suffering yourselves to be discouraged, and may Heaven crown your undertakings with the success they so well deserve!" Exclusive, however, of the influence of French political intrigues, the majority of considerate persons in the commonwealth could not but regard the neutrality offered by France as infinitely more eligible than the war urged by England; nor could it be reasonably doubted, if the restoration of the peace of Europe were the real object in view, that Holland, who could propose to herself no prospect or possibility of advantage by the continuance of hostilities, might act with much greater effect and dignity as a mediator than as a party.

On the return of the Earl of Chesterfield from his embassy, he repaired to his government; and, during his continuance in that high office, he executed the duties of it with a vigilance, attention, and fidelity, which gave the most perfect satisfaction to the Irish nation; and have deservedly endeared his memory to that generous and grateful people. The violent measures which were proposed to him at the breaking out of the rebellion, respecting the Roman Catholics, he rejected with indignation. On the contrary, he treated them with a mildness and moderation which engaged their affection and confidence. A profound tranquility prevailed throughout the kingdom; and it was observed, that the pastoral letters of the Irish priests, in their public discourses, and more private admonitions, were equally and invariably directed for the service of the government. In his Excellency's speech from the throne, at the opening of the session, October 1745, after expressing his ardent wishes to co-operate with Parliament in whatever might tend to establish or promote the true interest of the kingdom, he tells them, "that their own reflections will best suggest to them the advantages they have enjoyed under the just and legal authority of the present race of Princes; and their own history will best paint the miseries and calamities of a people scourged, rather than governed, by blind zeal and lawless power; that these considerations must necessarily excite their highest indignation at the attempt now carrying on in Scotland, to disturb his Majesty's government by a pretender to his crown—one nursed up in civil and religious error, formed to persecution and oppression in the seat of superstition and tyranny; whose groundless claim is as contrary to the natural rights of mankind, as to the particular laws and constitutions of these kingdoms; whose only hopes of support are placed in the enemies of the liberties of Europe in general, and whose success would consequently destroy our liberty, our property, and our religion." So well assured was this Nobleman of the peaceable and loyal disposition of the nation at large, that he treated with pleasant ridicule the information brought to him by a Gentleman high in office, who, with marks of evident consternation, told his Excellency that the people in Connaught were certainly *rising*. The Earl, with perfect calmness and composure, replied, "It is now nine o'clock, and time for them to rise; I therefore incline to believe your intelligence true."

This

This year, March 1745, died Robert, Earl of Orford, in circumstances by no means affluent, although he had for twenty years the revenues of Great Britain at his disposal. His death was occasioned by the violent operation of a medicine which he took as a solvent for the stone; and he declared that he died a victim to the neglect of his own maxim—not to disturb that which is at rest.

The naval operations of this summer were spirited and successful. A great number of rich prizes were captured from the enemy both in the East and West Indies. But the achievement by which it was chiefly distinguished was the conquest of the island of Cape Breton, in North America. This enterprise originated with the inhabitants of the province of New England; and the plan proposed by them being approved by the government, Admiral Warren, now commanding the British fleet in those seas, was commanded to co-operate with them. Six thousand colonial troops were embarked from Boston, which, with eight hundred marines from on board the fleet, constituted the whole of the land force. But with such courage and vigor did these raw and undisciplined troops, under the conduct of the British engineers, carry on their approaches, and with such skill and judgment were their operations seconded by the Admiral, that, in about eight weeks after the commencement of the siege, the fortress and city of Louisburg, and the whole island of Cape Breton, surrendered to the arms of his Britannic Majesty. The Americans, who were freed by this conquest from a dangerous neighbor, acquired great and deserved applause on the occasion. The rising importance of the Colonies became the subject of public attention and acknowledgment; and, by a generous excess of partiality, the magnitude of their services, and the beneficial consequences of this new conquest, were extolled and appreciated somewhat, perhaps, beyond their real and intrinsic value.

At

At the meeting of Parliament, January 1746, the King declared his regret at being obliged to have recourse to his people for farther aids; and, at the same time, his confidence in their zeal and unanimity in support of the public credit and safety. A new convulsion in the Ministry, however, retarded the progress of the supplies. A recent effort to introduce once more the Earl of Granville into the administration, had been made by the Sovereign, over whom that Nobleman had acquired a surprising ascendency: but the Duke of Newcastle, and all who adhered to the widely-extended connection of the Pelhams, immediately on being acquainted with the King's determination, delivered in their resignations. Lord Granville was, notwithstanding, actually appointed to the office of Principal Secretary of State; but, relying on the greatness of his talents, he had ever disdained to court the support and assistance of friends; and, after a very short trial, he was compelled reluctantly once more to render back the Seals. The Pelhams again resumed their stations; and Lord Granville, relinquishing for ever the contest for superiority, was, after an interval of political obscurity, made President of the Council, which station he occupied many years, rather dignifying the office than dignified by it*. The supplies were now granted by the Commons with more than ordinary profusion. About one hundred and twenty thousand men, land forces, seamen, and marines, were provided for by Parliament. The sum of three hundred thousand pounds was voted to the King of Sar-

---

* February 10, 1746, the Duke of Newcastle and Lord Harrington resigned the Seals, and the Earl of Granville was appointed Principal Secretary. The next day, Mr. Pelham resigned the Treasury, the Earl of Pembroke his gold key, and Mr. Legge and Mr. George Grenville their seats at the Board of Admiralty. The Lord Chancellor, the Duke of Bedford First Lord of the Admiralty, the Earl of Chesterfield (Lord Lieutenant of Ireland,) and almost all the great Officers of State, were expected to follow, when on Friday, February 14, the Earl of Granville returned the Seals into his Majesty's hands, which were immediately re-delivered to the Duke of Newcastle.

dinia;

dinia; four hundred thousand pounds to the Queen of Hungary, although the Princess had now fully surmounted her political embarrassments. Subsidies also were granted with an unsparing hand to the Dutch, the Hessians, the Saxons, the Hanoverians, the Electors of Mentz and Cologne; and the whole was crowned with a vote of credit and confidence for the sum of five hundred thousand pounds to his Majesty*. Notwithstanding this unheard-of prodigality of expenditure, no sensible effect was produced in the general system of affairs. An unsuccessful attempt was made in the course of this year, by Admiral Lestock and General St. Clair, on Port L'Orient, an opulent maritime town on the southern coast of Bretagne, and the grand depository of the vessels and stores belonging to the French East India Company. The fleet, with six battalions of regular forces on board, arrived, on the twentieth of September, in Quimperly Bay, ten miles distant from the city, which was immediately summoned to surrender. In the first emotions of surprise and consternation, a capitulation was agreed to,

---

* It was boldly and shrewdly remarked by a political writer of these times, that, according to the historian Matthew Paris, when King Henry III. demanded money of his Parliament to defray the expences of a foreign expedition, which concerned not the interest of England, the Parliament told him flatly, that this was a most audacious requisition: " Talia effrons *impudenter* postularet.—Contradixerunt Regi in faciem, nolentes amplius pecunia sua spoliari." And upon his remonstrating, that his royal faith was pledged, and pleading the absolute necessity in which he stood of a supply, they expressed their astonishment that the immense sums of money already granted could be so soon dissipated: " Admiramur in quam abyssum submersæ sunt innumerabiles pecuniæ, quas, Domine Rex, immulxisti, quæ nunquam Regno vel modicum contulerunt incrementum."—M. Paris, p. 561, 26 Henry III.

It is said that Mr. Mitchel, the English Resident at Berlin, during the second Silesian war, in communicating to the King of Prussia the intelligence of some advantage obtained over the enemy, made use of the following expression—" By the help of GOD we have gained a victory over the French." " What, said the King, is GOD one of your allies?" " Yes certainly, Sire, replied the Ambassador, and the only one who demands no subsidies of us."

on condition that the magazines of the Company, upon the payment of forty thoufand pounds by way of ranfom, fhould remain untouched, and the inhabitants be protected from pillage. Thefe terms the Britifh Commanders inftigated by the predominating avidity of plunder, haughtily and rafhly rejected; and the inhabitants, driven to extremity, prepared to defend themfelves with refolution. The invaders were utterly deftitute of the artillery and implements neceffary for a fiege. A fingle battery, raifed with difficulty and mounted only with a few fieldpieces, played upon the fortifications without any effect. At length the troops ftationed in the environs, with the militia of the province, collecting in great force; the General was compelled to abandon the enterprife, embarking his troops September 29, and after fome ufelefs bravadoes on the French coaft, the whole armament returned to Portfmouth. The French accounts affert, that the place, if attacked immediately on the landing of the troops, might have been eafily taken by fcalade; but the operations of the Englifh General indicated as little of vigor as of judgment; and the Admiral did nothing to retrieve the reputation which, notwithftanding the acquittal of the court-martial, he had, by his conduct at Toulon, loft in the eftimation, of the public. In the month of September, the important fettlement of Madras, on the coaft of Coromandel, furrendered to the French arms in India; which difafter the Englifh, in the courfe of the next year, attempted in vain to avenge by the unfuccefsful fiege of Pondicherry.

In November 1746, the Parliament was again convened, and the fupplies again voted with the fame lavifh profufion—four hundred and thirty thoufand pounds to the Queen of Hungary; three hundred thoufand pounds to King of Sardinia; five hundred and feventy thoufand pounds for the maintenance of the Hanoverian and Heffian auxiliaries; fubfidies to the Electors of Saxony, Mentz,

Mentz, Cologne, and Bavaria; five hundred thousand pounds as a vote of credit; and it was remarked, that the entire aggregate of the supplies exceeded by two millions and a half the greatest annual sum raised during the reign of Queen Anne, when Great Britain filled the world with the renown of her victories, though her riches were now exhausted to purchase only disgrace and misfortune. It must be acknowledged indeed, that at this period the King exhibited a laudable proof of his desire to diminish the public expence, by ordering the third and fourth troops of his life-guards to be disbanded, and reducing three regiments of horse to the quality of dragoons, But these reductions were, at the same time, invidious and ineffectual, and the dignity of the nation seemed even in some sort affected by them. That the Monarch was well satisfied with the rectitude of his own policy, and even willing to make considerable personal sacrifices, in order to fix that ideal balance of power which he deemed so necessary to the happiness and tranquillity of Europe, it would seem ungenerous to doubt. Happy! had the wisdom of his measures borne any proportion to the integrity of his intentions.

An Act of Parliament of a very important nature passed this session, for the abolition of the heretable jurisdictions in Scotland—that distinguishing feature of the feudal system; since which period the peculiarities which seemed to stamp upon the Highland clans the cast and character of a separate nation have been gradually softening, and, at this time, seem rapidly hastening to their final and utter extinction.

This year died Philip V. King of Spain, to whom succeeded, without any visible or immediate effect upon the general political system, Don Ferdinand, Prince of Asturias.

In April 1747, a squadron sailed from Brest Water, commanded by M. de la Jonquiere, bound for America, and had made little progress in their voyage when they were encountered by a superior English fleet, under the Admirals Anson and Warren. The enemy fought with courage, but were compelled to yield to superior force, and, towards evening, six ships of the line struck their colors, and a great part of their convoy, with several frigates, were also taken. For this service Admiral Anson was ennobled, and Admiral Warren created a Knight of the Bath. In the month of October, Admiral Hawke, with a force much superior, fell in with a fleet of nine line of battle ships, seven of which, after an obstinate engagement, were captured by the English. The nation failed not to remark, that, in both these instances, the English fleet bore down upon the enemy; regardless of the preservation of the line of battle; while the brave Admiral Matthews still continued in a state of disgraceful suspension for the same contempt of the established punctilios of discipline.

The Parliament having been dissolved in June, a new Parliament was convened in November 1747, highly favourable to the interest of the present Ministery. The minds of all were visibly animated by the late naval successes; the ablest men in Parliament were engaged in the different posts and offices of government; the Minister, Mr. Pelham, had acquired much of the public confidence; and the popularity of the King himself had very sensibly increased since the suppression of the late rebellion. He declared, that the attachment of his people on that occasion had impressed his heart with indelible sensations of gratitude, and that he felicitated himself upon an event, without which he had never known how much he was the object of their regard and affection. Opposition now seemed to languish, and, for the first time since the accession of the House of Hanover, England might be

said

said to be governed by a popular administration*. The King signified, in his speech to the Parliament, that a

* About this time a very excellent performance, deservedly honored with a large share of the public approbation, appeared under the title of "Free and Candid Disquisitions" respecting the necessity of a reform in the national Church. The celebrated Warburton, in a letter to his friend Dr. Doddridge, a dissenting teacher of great eminence, writes—" As to the 'Disquisitions,' I will only say, that the temper, candor, and charity, with which they are wrote, are very edifying and exemplary. I wish success to them as much as you can do. But I can tell you, of certain science, that not the least alteration will be made in the ecclesiastical system." Dr. Chandler, another non-conformist divine of distinguished reputation and ability, making an occasional visit at this period to Dr. Gooch, Bishop of Norwich, met with Dr. Sherlock, then Bishop of Salisbury. The discourse happened to fall on the propriety and utility of a *comprehension*. Dr. Sherlock said, " Our church, Mr. Chandler, consists of three parts, doctrine, discipline, and ceremonies. As to ceremonies, they are in themselves indifferent, and ought to be left so; and the discipline of our church is ****; but what have you to object to the doctrines of it?" Mr. Chandler replied, " Your Articles, my Lord, must be expressed in Scriptural words, and the Athanasian Creed must be discarded." Both the Bishops answered—they wished they were rid of that Creed, and had no objection to altering the Articles into Scriptural words. The two Bishops, at the conclusion of the visit, requested Mr. Chandler to wait on the Archbishop, Dr. Herring, which he did, and met the Bishop of Norwich. The Archbishop being informed by Dr. Gooch of the conversation that had taken place on the subject of a comprehension, replied, " A very good thing —he wished it with all his heart; and the rather, because this was a time which called upon all good men to unite against infidelity and immorality, which threatened universal ruin: and added, he was encouraged to hope, from the piety, learning, and moderation, of many dissenters, that this was the proper time to make the attempt." " But, said Dr. Gooch, Mr. Chandler says the Articles must be altered into the words of Scripture." " And why not? rejoined the Archbishop. " It is the impertinencies of men thrusting their own words into Articles, instead of the words of God, which have occasioned most of the divisions in the Christian Church from the beginning to this day." The Archbishop added, that the Bench of Bishops seemed to be of his mind, and that he should be glad to see Mr. Chandler again, but was then OBLIGED TO GO TO COURT. The good Archbishop, it may be presumed, according to the prediction of Dr. Warburton, met with little encouragement at COURT to persevere in his benevolent design; for, during the remainder of this reign, we hear no more of ecclesiastical REFORM or COMPREHENSION.

congress would speedily be opened at Aix-la-Chapelle, for concerting the means of a general pacification. As the event, however, was uncertain, the former supplies and subsidies were renewed, and a new demand made for an additional subsidy to the Empress of Russia, whom England had, by this means, the honor to class with the Empress-Queen of Hungary, the Kings of Denmark, Sweden, Poland, and Sardinia, and a multitude of Germanic Sovereigns, in her imperial, royal, and princely band of mercenaries. But, previous to the termination of the session, in May 1748, the King informed the two Houses that preliminaries of peace were actually signed, and that the basis of the accommodation was a general restitution of conquests. If we take into consideration the relative situation of the belligerent powers, the treaty of Aix-la-Chapelle must undoubtedly, upon the whole, be considered as very favorable and advantageous to the Allies. The King of France was now in actual possession of almost the whole of the Austrian Netherlands, and had even penetrated into Dutch Brabant and Flanders. Except the fortune of the war, had, contrary to all reasonable expectation, entirely changed, the Allies must soon have been driven beyond the Rhine, and the United States might have once more seen the *Oriflamme* of France dispayed at the gates of Amsterdam. The history of Europe in modern times exhibits, perhaps, no instance of a disparity of talents between opposing Commanders so great and manifest, as that which subsisted between the Duke of Cumberland and the Mareschal Saxe. Yet it is very remarkable, that the States-General seemed to think it unnecessary to impose those restraints upon his Royal Highness by which, in consequence of the *tribunitian negative* vested in the field deputies, the Duke of Marlborough had been formerly fettered. A vast army was assembled in the Netherlands at a ruinous expence to England, without the slightest necessity, as it was not pretended

tended that the French had threatened the Dutch barrier
—and which, when affembled, acted merely upon the
defenfive—which attempted no fiege—which relieved no
fortrefs—and which gained no battle. And the nation
had reafon to recollect the coarfe but fagacious political
adage of Hyde, Earl of Rochefter, " that to attack
France in Flanders was to take a bull by the horns."
For the facrifice of all her conquefts no other compenfation was required by France than the ceffion of the Duchy of Parma, with its appendages, to the Infant Don
Philip, and of which territories that Prince was already
in actual poffeffion. Thus, in the fpace of little more
than ten years, the Houfe of Auftria was deprived of the
Sicilies and Parma by Spain, of the rich and extenfive
provice of Silefia by Pruffia, and of Servia and Belgrade,
the bulwark of her empire on the fide of Hungary, by
the Turks; yet, by the wife and excellent adminiftration
of the Emprefs-Queen, whofe councils were, from this
period, chiefly directed by that great Statefman who, to a
very recent period, prefided at the helm of affairs in the
Imperial Court*, Auftria appeared, in a fhort time, more
potent and formidable than it had ever done under the imperious but feeble government of her father, the Emperor
Charles VI. By this treaty England was compelled
reluctantly to refign her favorite conqueft of Cape
Breton, in order to obtain the reftitution of Madras.
With Spain England had little occafion to negotiate.
In the whole courfe of a war which had continued
nine years, nothing had been loft, and nothing gained,
Porto Bello excepted, which had been immediately
evacuated. The original caufe of the war feemed, in
the progrefs of it, to be entirely forgotten, and, at the
conclufion of the peace, not a fyllable was mentioned refpecting the pretended *right of fearch*, which had formerly

---

* The Count, afterwards created Prince de Kaunitz.

occafioned

occasioned such loud and indignant clamours. As the same complaints have never been revived, it appears, however, that Spain has virtually, though silently, relinquished her claims. The settlement of the boundaries of the French and British empires in America, a question in the highest degree doubtful and disputatious, was referred to the decision of commissaries; and France retained no mark of superiority in this treaty, with relation to England, excepting the requisition of hostages to reside in France till the reciprocal restitution of conquests should be actually made; and the Earls of Sussex and Cathcart were nominated for that purpose. This afforded the Patriots a pretence to exclaim against the peace as disgraceful to the nation. But the nation, who were with reason wearied with the expences and disasters of the war, were well satisfied with the terms of peace, and it was celebrated with great and universal rejoicings. The Opposition in Parliament, nevertheless, still retained some degree of importance, from the countenance and patronage of the Prince of Wales, who, from recent causes, had become more than ever alienated from the Court. And, at this period, his Royal Highness distinguished by peculiar marks of his favor and confidence the famous Viscount Bolingbroke, who having, many years since, received a full pardon from Government, without however being restored to his seat in Parliament, now resided at the rustic mansion of Dawley, in Middlesex; and was visited in this beautiful and sequestered retreat, to make use of the expression of a contemporary historian, " as a sainted shrine, by all the distinguished votaries of wit, eloquence, and political ambition." Matured and mellowed by experience, reflection, and age, this all-accomplished Nobleman, " framed in the prodigality of nature," and no less conspicuous in the lofty fanes of science, than the rosy bowers of pleasure, or the gorgeous palaces of ambition, shone forth in the evening of life with a mild

and

and subdued, but rich and resplendent lustre. And, in his political writings, he exhibited to an admiring world that IDEA of a PATRIOT KING, which the heir of the British Monarchy was supposed ambitious to form himself upon, as a complete and perfect model*. The hopes of the

---

* It will be, perhaps, not unacceptable to select a few extracts from this celebrated performance, in composing which, Lord Bolingbroke seems to have determined to lay aside all prejudice and party attachment, and to pourtray the lineaments of Truth, as she appeared to his imagination, in her own heavenly and radiant form; and which derives an high additional value from its proceeding from a writer who possessed an intimate practical knowledge of his subject, and who has, therefore, steered perfectly clear of those visionary ideas of government which have unhappily blended themselves with the theories of many philosophical statists. " In all cases of great concernment, the noble writer tell us, that the shortest and surest method of arriving at real knowledge is to remount to first principles; for it is about them that almost all the juggling and legerdemain employed by men, whose trade it is to deceive, are set to work. And he who does so on the subject of government, will discover soon that the notions concerning the divine institution and right of Kings, as well as the absolute power belonging to their office, have no foundation in fact or reason; but have risen from an OLD ALLIANCE between ecclesiastical and civil policy. Reverence for government obliges us to reverence governors, who, for the sake of it, are raised above the level of other men. But reverence for governors independently of government, any farther than reverence would be due to their virtues if they were private men, is preposterous, and repugnant to common sense. As well might we say, that a ship is built, and loaded, and manned, for the sake of any particular pilot, instead of acknowledging that the pilot is made for the sake of the ship, her lading, and her crew, who are always the OWNERS in the *political vessel*, as to say that Kingdoms were instituted for Kings, not Kings for Kingdoms. All this is as true of hereditary as of elective Monarchy; though the SCRIBBLERS for tyranny, under the name of Monarchy, would have us believe that there is something more august and more sacred in the one than the other. They are sacred alike, and this attribute is to be ascribed, or not ascribed, to them, as they answer, or do not answer, the ends of their institution.— Enough has been said to establish the first and true principles of monarchical, and indeed of every other kind of government; and I will say with confidence, that no principles but these, and such as these, can be advanced, which deserve to be treated seriously; though Mr. Locke *condescended* to examine those of Filmer, more out of regard to the prejudices of the time than the

the nation were, however, fatally blasted by the unfortunate and untimely death of the Prince, who, after a short illness

the importance of the work. The good of the People is the ultimate and true end of government; governors are therefore appointed for this end; and the civil constitution which appoints them with their power, is determined to do so, by that law of nature and reason which has determined the end of government, and which admits this *form* of government as the proper means of arriving at it. Now, the greatest good of a People is their liberty; without liberty no happiness can be enjoyed by society. The obligation therefore, to defend and maintain the freedom of such constitutions, will appear most sacred to a PATRIOT KING. The constitution will be considered by him as one law, consisting of two tables—or as one system composed of different parts and powers, but all duly proportioned to one another, and conspiring, by their harmony, to the perfection of the whole. He will make one, and but one, distinction between his rights and those of his people,—he will look on his to be a trust, and theirs a property; he will discern that he can have a right to no more than is entrusted to him by the constitution; and that the People alone, who had an original right to the whole by the law of nature, can have the sole indefeasible right to any part, and really have such a right to that part which they have reserved to themselves. Thus he will think, and on these principles he will act, whether he come to the throne by immediate or remote election. For in hereditary Monarchies, where *men* are not elected, *families* are: and therefore *some authors* would have it believed, that, when a family has been once admitted, and an hereditary right to the Crown recognised in it, that right cannot be forfeited. How much more agreeable to truth and to common sense would these authors have written, if they had maintained that every Prince who comes to a Crown in the course of succession, were he the last of five hundred, comes to it under the same conditions under which the first took it, whether expressed or implied! I mention this the rather because I have an imperfect *remembrance* that some SCRIBBLER was employed, or employed himself, to assert the *hereditary right of the present family*; a task so unnecessary to any good purpose, that I believe a suspicion arose of its having been designed for a bad one. A PATRIOT KING will never countenance such impertinent fallacies, nor deign to lean on broken reeds."—Was this *recollection* in Lord Bolingbroke, or *prophetic anticipation?* or is it necessary to say, that whoever defends the absurd and pernicious tenets here reprobated is a SCRIBBLER, however *sublime* and *beautiful* his language? A Nobleman yet living, who was in habits of strict intimacy with Lord Bolingbroke, relates of him, that he was accustomed to express, in high and enthusiastic language, his admiration of the genius and talents of ALCIBIADES,

illness, expired, March 20, 1751, leaving the education of his numerous offspring to the care of a Princess, amiable, indeed, for her maternal and domestic virtues, but who had brought from the Court of Saxe-Gotha principles and maxims of government ill according with those which form the basis of the English constitution. Soon after the death of his Royal Highness, his eldest son, Prince George, was committed to the care of the Earl Harcourt as governor, and the Bishop of Norwich as preceptor—men whose principles and characters deservedly stood high in the esteem of the nation. But it was soon discovered that the Earl of Bute, who had been introduced into the Prince's household as a Lord of the Bedchamber, had acquired so high a degree of influence at the Court of Leicester House, as to make the situation of those who possessed responsible offices very uneasy. It was confidently asserted, that books had been repeatedly found in the hands of the Prince of a most dangerous political tendency. On a remarkable motion made in the House of Peers, March 1753, by the Duke of Bedford, for the production of certain papers and documents relative to this subject, Lord Harcourt declared that he found he had no authority over the Prince's education, nor could he be of any service unless the sub-governor and others were dismissed, whom he had strong reasons to believe tainted with Jacobite principles. Impressed with this idea, his Lordship and his co-adjutor, the Bishop, resigned their offices, and to them Lord Waldegrave and the Bishop of Lincoln succeeded. But the baleful influence of the Earl of Bute was too plainly

---

ADES, not unconscious, perhaps, that to the character of this celebrated Athenian his own bore a striking analogy. And Lord Orrery assures us, that the conversation of Lord Bolingbroke united the wisdom of Socrates, the dignity and ease of Pliny, and the wit of Horace.

discerned to be still all-prevalent, affording, notwithstanding the private and personal virtues of the Prince, just and serious ground of national solicitude and apprehension*.

Next to the Minister himself, two of the most distinguished personages at this period in the British Parliament were Mr. Murray, Solicitor General, and Mr. Pitt, Paymaster of the Forces—both, indeed, possessing an extent of genius and splendor of eloquence superior to Mr. Pelham, who, founding his power on the firm and solid foundation of public esteem and public virtue, suffered no mean or corroding political jealousies to enter his breast. The first of these, promoted, in the progress of his fortunes, to the Chief Justiceship of England,

---

* In the Diary of Lord Melcombe, which exhibits an amusing picture of the interior of a Court, delineated by a vain, obsequious, temporising courtier, are contained many characteristic and interesting anecdotes. With respect to this memorable resignation, his Lordship informs us, that Lord Harcourt complained strongly to the King of dangerous notions and arbitrary principles being instilled into the Prince; and that he could be of no use unless Stone, Cresset, and Scot, were dismissed: that, as he named no particulars, the King had sent the Archbishop of Canterbury and the Lord Chancellor to confer with his Lordship upon the subject; but Lord Harcourt declared, that the particulars were fit only to be communicated to the King, and that he would wait on his Majesty with them: that he did so, and the satisfaction he required not being given, the King appearing to yield a slow and reluctant credit to these allegations, the Earl and Bishop immediately resigned their offices. It is a curious circumstance, that, in a conversation which Lord Melcombe held with the Duke of Dorset on the subject of these resignations, *it was agreed*—" that there must be a *counter-story* on the court side, or the resigners would run away with the public opinion." It is superfluous to say, that this *counter-story* never appeared. The original appointment of Stone, who was the intimate friend of Murray, the Solicitor General, was extremely disagreeable to the late Prince of Wales, who was accustomed, as the Princess related to Lord Melcombe, when affairs went ill, passionately to exclaim— " How could better be expected when such a Jacobite as Stone was trusted!"

and

K. GEORGE II.

and the title of Earl of Mansfield, was educated in sentiments by no means favorable to his political advancement; but, from his first entrance into public life, he suffered no symptoms of his original attachments to appear, excepting a certain bias always discernible, throughout all the variations and vicissitudes of his political career, in favour of prerogative. His person was graceful, the tones of his voice exquisitely melodious, and his style of oratory clear, dignified, calm, and persuasive*. To this historical portrait that of Mr. Pitt may be exhibited as a just and striking contrast. This celebrated Statesman was introduced early in life into the House of Commons, where he soon distinguished himself by the animation of his eloquence and the superiority of his talents. His reply to the political veteran Horace Walpole, who had on some occasion affected to mention him with contempt, as an unpractised and youthful orator, is not yet forgotten: " Whether youth could be justly imputed to any man as a reproach, Mr. Pitt said, he should not determine; but he would affirm, that the wretch, who, after having seen the consequences of repeated errors, continues still to blunder, and whose age has only added obstinacy to stupidity, deserves not that his grey hairs should secure him from insult; and much more is he to be abhorred who, as he has advanced in age, has receded from virtue, who deliberately devotes the remnant of his life to the ruin of his country." As a public speaker, he possessed such commanding force and energy of language, as struck his hearers with astonishment and admiration.

---

* The æra so feelingly anticipated by the Poet is, almost in the moment of writing, at length arrived. This Nobleman's career of life and honor is closed—
  And Murray, long enough his country's pride,
  Is now no more than Tully or than Hyde.

The power and effect of his oratory have been compared to " the lightening which flashed from heaven, blasting where it smote, and withering the nerves of opposition." His ambition was open and undisguised; but he disdained to seek the gratification of it by any mean or degrading compliance. On the contrary, he was pertinacious in his opinions, imperious in his deportment, fearless and resolute in his conduct. All attention to pecuniary considerations he seemed to think beneath the dignity of his character, ever maintaining an inviolable integrity in the midst of temptation*. And in that theatre of political corruption in which it was the shameless boast of the Minister, that *every man had his price*, the public virtue of Mr. Pitt was universally acknowledged to be " pure as the icicle pendent from Dian's temple."

In the foremost rank of Statesmen at this period, likewise, must be classed the Secretary of War, Mr. Fox, afterwards advanced to the Peerage by the title of Lord Holland. His talents appear, indeed, less brilliant than solid. Long and intimately attached to the connection of the Pelhams, he had, on all occasions, distinguished himself as a most able advocate of the measures of the

---

* Two signal proofs of the disinterested integrity of Mr. Pitt in the discharge of his office, are distinctly specified. On his accession to the post of Paymaster, he refused the customary perquisites of half per cent. on the subsidies voted by Parliament to the Queen of Hungary, the King of Sardinia, &c. amounting to an immense sum. The King of Sardinia, struck with admiration at this conduct, ordered his Ambassador to offer the same as a royal present to Mr. Pitt; but this Mr. Pitt peremptorily, though respectfully, refused, saying, that he did no more than his duty in paying it entire. The other fact, equally to the honor of this great man, is, that he would never appropriate any of the balances of the public money in his hands to any purposes of private emolument, paying them invariably into the Bank of England, and satisfying himself with the common legal appointments annexed to his office.

present

prefent adminiftration. In common with the other adherents of that powerful party, he efpoufed with zeal the antient principles of whiggifm eftablifhed at the Revolution—blended as they were with the courtly bias in favor of the new fyftem of policy introduced at the acceffion of the prefent family. His underftanding was vigorous, and his knowledge extenfive; and he commanded the attention of the Houfe not by the fplendor of his eloquence, but the fuperior weight and force of his obfervations. Though far from harboring the idea of a political competition with Mr. Pelham, whom he fupported with the cordiality rather of friendfhip than of intereft, he regarded himfelf, and was univerfally regarded, as fecond only in political importance to the Minifter; nor, in cafe of a vacancy in the higheft department of government, did there appear any probability of a conteft for the pre-eminence—Mr. Pitt at this period, not to mention his inferior ftanding in office, boafting little advantage over Mr. Fox in the eftimation of the public, and poffeffing much lefs of the confidence of the Court.

The moft confiderable controverfy which took place in the Houfe of Commons, during the feffion immediately fucceeding the conclufion of the peace, was occafioned by fome important innovations in the annual mutiny bill, particularly the final claufe, by which martial law was extended to all officers on half pay, and which, by extending in the fame proportion the influence of the Crown, might in its confequences, as the oppofition affirmed, prove very dangerous to the Conftitution. But Mr. Pitt defended the claufe, which was ultimately carried by a confiderable majority, as a neceffary extenfion of military difcipline—urging, in order to obviate the alarm of danger, "that the very exiftence of Englifh liberty muft, and did, actually depend upon the moderation of the Sovereign, and the virtue of the army. To that

that virtue, said he, we trust even at this hour, small as our army is—to that virtue we must have trusted in whatever manner this bill had been modelled; and without this virtue, should the Lords, the Commons, and the people of England, entrench themselves behind parchment up to the teeth, the sword will find a passage to the vitals of the Constitution." Certainly a more forcible argument could not be found to demonstrate the necessity of reducing that army, and of diminishing that influence, which the clause in question was calculated to confirm and increase.——At this period, a plan was formed and carried into execution, chiefly under the patronage and direction of the Earl of Halifax, First Lord of Trade and Plantations, for the establishment of a colony on the peninsula of Acadie. By the treaty of Utrecht this peninsula, originally settled by the French, was ceded, with the entire provice of Nova Scotia, to the English. But the small town and fortress of Annapolis, situated in the midst of the French settlers, excepted, no trace appeared of its being an English possession. By the plan now adopted, it was determined to found a city on the opposite or eastern side of the peninsula, to which the name of Halifax was given, on a spot commodiously situated, and with the advantage of a secure and excellent harbour. This colony, though viewed by the French with jealous eyes, being primarily designed for a military station, and subjected, by an unpardonable error in the original plan, to a military and despotic form of government, did not answer the high expectations excited by it: but of late years, in consequence of many judicious regulations and unexpected changes, it has risen rapidly in commercial and political importance.

From the firm establishment of peace, the extension of commerce, and the accumulation of wealth, the public funds, all or the far greater part of which bore the

same

same interest of *four per cent.* now rose so much above par, as to make it practicable for the Minister to bring forward a grand measure of finance, which, however daring in appearance, was attended with no difficulty in the execution. This was no other than an improvement of the scheme formerly offered to Parliament by Sir John Barnard, to liquidate all the redeemable annuities, comprehending almost the whole of the public debts, by an immediate payment of the principal. This proposal was, however, attended with an alternative which the Minister well knew it was the interest of the stock-holder to accept. An option was allowed by the act, either to receive the entire amount of the debt, at *par, i. e.* at a discount of more than thirty *per cent.* below the actual transfer price, or to consent to a reduction of the interest from four to three and a half *per cent.* for seven years, and afterwards to remain at three *per cent.* This had all the effect and operation of a tax of twenty-five *per cent.* upon the public funds, and it was a blow most severely felt by very many families in the middle classes of life, whose property was confided to the faith of government. Yet no violation of the public faith could be pretended; for, in conformity to the original terms of the agreement, the perpetual annuities were at all times redeemable by the government at *par*. A very great proportion, therefore, of the public creditors assented, however reluctantly, to the terms of the Minister. The three great chartered Companies, nevertheless, and various individual proprietors of stock, to the amount of eight or ten millions, refused to subscribe. But Mr. Pelham, encouraged by the general success of his project, now assumed an higher tone; and he declared that, as they had suffered the time prescribed by the act to elapse, they should no longer be admitted to take advantage of the terms originally offered. But, that their obstinacy and igno-

rance

rance might not be too rigorously punished, he would now propose a second subscription, in which the reduction of the interest from three and a half to three *per cent.* should take place at the end of five years. Upon reconsideration, the Bank, the East India Company, and South Sea Company, and the individual proprietors who had concurred with them, and were probably influenced by their authority to reject with disdain the former proposition, unanimously thought proper to accept of the favor and indulgence now offered; and the plan of the Minister was carried into complete execution, not only with reputation but triumph. But it is remarkable, that no effort was at any time made by Mr. Pelham for the re-establishment of the sinking fund, as originally proposed by Sir Robert Walpole, a measure of much greater efficacy, though of less *eclat,* than this boasted scheme of reduction.

About this time, an Act of Parliament also passed for the encouragement of the British Fisheries, by which a company was incorporated, in order to carry into effect the purposes of the act. But as the vessels designed to rendezvous at the sound of Brassa were, according to this project, to be fitted out at the port of London, to mention no other of its numerous defects, it was clearly foreseen, and peremptorily foretold, that the scheme would prove abortive. Various efforts have since been made, at different times, to revive the public attention to this national concern, but with little success. And it yet remains for some future able and patriotic Minister to adopt a grand and comprehensive plan, for the accomplishment of this most important and laudable object. Had a tenth part of the immense sums dissipated and squandered in Italian and German subsidies been employed in erecting towns, forming canals, building vessels, and procuring implements, in order to carry on the fisheries to advantage

tage upon the spot, the Highlands of Scotland might, at this day, have exhibited a smiling scene of industry and plenty, instead of presenting to our view the cheerless aspect of poverty and wretchedness, or rather the hideous picture of solitude and desolation.

Philip V. of Spain, whose partiality to France seemed to increase with increasing years, being now deceased, and his son and successor Ferdinand cherishing a sincere desire to maintain a perfect amity with Great Britain, a treaty or convention was this year concluded at Madrid, between Don Joseph de Carvajal, the Spanish Minister, and Mr Keene, the English Envoy, by which the points referred to the decision of Commissaries, by the peace of Aix-la-Chapelle, were finally determined, and the commercial privileges of the English nation fully restored. No mention, however, and much less any direct renunciation, was made of the right of search claimed by the Spaniards, and which was the original cause of the war. And when this omission was strongly urged by the opposition in Parliament, as inconsistent with the positive declaration of the two Houses at the commencement of the war, who concurred in the address to the Throne, that no treaty of peace with Spain should be admitted unless such renunciation should be first obtained as a preliminary, Mr. Pitt, who had been a strenuous advocate for this address, offered an apology for his conduct, as a Minister of the Crown concurring in the measures now the subject of censure, somewhat novel and singular. " He acknowledged that he had contended strongly for the address alluded to, because at that time, being young and sanguine, he thought it right and reasonable. But he was now ten years older, had considered matters more coolly, and was convinced that the privilege of *no search* with respect to British vessels sailing near the American shore, would never be obtained unless Spain should be brought so low as to acquiesce in any terms we, as victors

victors might propose." This was a virtual vindication of the conduct and principles of the late Minister, Sir Robert Walpole, in his negociations with Spain, against which Mr. Pitt had so often and so eloquently declaimed; and such an avowal could only be regarded as an involuntary species of homage paid to the memory of that sagacious and able Statesman.

In the course of the present summer, 1750, died Don Juan V. King of Portugal; a Prince not destitute of ability, but tainted with a wretched spirit of bigotry and persecution. He was succeeded by his son Don Joseph, at whose accession the Infanta Isabella became heiress of the crown. And, in order to preserve the sceptre of Portugal in the House of Braganza, this Princess, by virtue of a Papal dispensation, was married to her uncle the Infant Don Pedro, brother to the King; the first issue of which nuptials, Joseph Xavier, Prince of Brazil, while of an age yet immature, was, by a similar alliance —an alliance at which nature and custom equally revolt —married to his aunt Donna Maria, sister to Isabella, the present Queen.

In consequence of the death of his Royal Highness the Princess of Wales, a Bill was presented by the Duke of Newcastle to the House of Peers (May 1741), to provide for the administration of government, in case the crown should descend to a minor: and the Princess Dowager of Wales was appointed Regent of Great Britain and Ireland, assisted by a council composed of the Great Officers of State, the Duke of Cumberland presiding at the head. This was a hazardous and dangerous plan, which, had it been carried into effect, would have laid the foundation of a divided and distracted government. Happily, however, the King lived till his successor attained to the age of majority, and the regency bill, which was justly and strongly opposed in Parliament, sunk unnoticed into silence and oblivion.

Amongst

Amongst the most remarkable bill of the present session was that introduced by the Earl of Chesterfield for the reformation of the Calendar, notwithstanding the previous and avowed disapprobation of the Duke of Newcastle, who declared himself "averse to disturb that which was at rest; adding, that he did not love new-fangled things." The bill, however, was received with general applause, and was supported in the House of Peers by the Earl of Macclesfield, with a display of profound and scientific knowledge which reflected upon that Nobleman the highest honor, as the successor to the chair of NEWTON, and President of the most learned society in Europe. The Julian computation of time, either from ignorance or negligence, supposing a complete solar revolution to be effected in the precise period of three hundred and sixty-five days and six hours, made no provision for the apparently trifling deficiency of eleven minutes, which however, in the lapse of eighteen centuries, amounted to a difference of eleven days. A reformation of the Calendar had been accomplished in the sixteenth century, under the auspices of Pope Gregory XIII; but the authority of the Roman Pontiff extending over the Catholic countries only, the antient computation still continued in use in England and other northern kingdoms. But by the bill now introduced, it was decreed that the new year should begin, in conformity to the Gregorian reform, on the first of January, and that eleven intermediate nominal days, between the second and fourteenth of September 1752, should be omitted, so that the day succeeding the second should be denominated the fourteenth of that month—an alteration not less favorable to commercial than to astronomical accuracy and precision.

Frederic, King of Sweden, and Landgrave of Hesse Cassel, dying at this period, was succeeded, agreeably to the convention formerly made with Russia, by Adolphus Frederic, Duke of Holstein Eutin, Bishop of Lubec—married

married to the sister of his Prussian Majesty. This Prince, on his accession to the throne, took a voluntary oath in full senate that he would never attempt to introduce a despotic authority, but would maintain their liberties with his blood, and govern his subjects in all respects according to the laws and form of government established in Sweden. This declaration was peculiarly acceptable to the Court of St. Petersburg, which had entertained jealous apprehensions that the intrigues of the French and Prussian factions, for changing the form of government, were countenanced and supported by the successor—and had actually assembled an army on the frontiers of Finland, which menaced Sweden with invasion; declaring, at the same time, her firm resolution to maintain inviolate that constitution of which she was the guarantee. By this complaisant, or rather submissive conduct, the harmony between the two countries appeared firmly consolidated. The political depression of Sweden, which was the necessary consequence of the radical defects of her government, was in the highest degree favorable to the ambitious designs of Russia; and, in conformity to the same insidious and interested policy, the Court of St. Petersburgh will suffer no improvement of the anarchic constitution of Poland. A violent misunderstanding between the Courts of Petersburg and Berlin was the result of their opposing politics relative to the affairs of Sweden—his Prussian Majesty declaring his determination to defend that kingdom with his whole force, in case of an attack from Russia; and the Ambassadors on each side were recalled. This misunderstanding, heightened by mutual criminations and reproaches into the most bitter animosity, after an interval of some years, terminated in open rupture: and the King of Prussia was taught, by fatal experience, to repent the gross and wanton provocations by which he ventured to excite the resentment of the Czarina. It is worthy of remark, that

the

the subsidies received, during the course of his reign, from England, by the late King of Sweden, in the mere capacity of Landgrave of Hesse Cassel, on an accurate computation, amounted to the astonishing sum of one million two hundred and forty-nine thousand six hundred and ninety-nine pounds sterling*. In the course of this year, 1751, also died Louisa, Queen of Denmark, youngest daughter of his Britannic Majesty, a Princess endowed with every graceful and amiable accomplishment, and deservedly dear to the Danish monarch and nation. Nearly at the same time, the United Provinces sustained a public loss by the death of his Serene Highness the Prince of Orange, who leaving only an infant son, the administration of the government devolved upon the Princess of Orange, as governante, during the minority, in which station she conducted affairs with much prudence and ability. When the Parliament met in November (1751), the King informed them that he had, in conjunction with the States General, whose intimate union and friendship with England had been in no degree impaired by the unfortunate death of the Stadtholder, concluded treaties with the Electors of Bavaria and Saxony, in addition to those subsisting with the Electors of Mentz and Cologne; and another was soon afterwards happily adjusted with the Elector Palatine; and the vast sums which these Princes demanded as the purchase of their friendship were cheerfully and loyally voted at the requisition of the Court. The immediate object of these alliances was to secure a majority of the voices of the Electoral College, in the view of an approaching election of a King of the Ro-

---

* Soon after the death of the King of Sweden, Prince Frederic of Hesse Cassel, who had, in 1740, espoused the Princess Mary, third daughter of the King of England, thought fit to renounce his religion, and declare himself a Roman Catholic, to the great injury of the Protestant interest in the Empire, and the general regret of the English nation and the Protestants throughout Europe.

mans in the person of the Archduke Joseph, eldest son of the Emperor: for this Prince having yet scarcely passed the years of infancy, it was reasonably to be apprehended, that this favorite project might in the execution, be attended with embarrassment and difficulty. A vigorous, however, if not a formidable resistance was made in the House of Commons to the ratification of these treaties by Parliament. For some years past Lord Egmont had been regarded as the head of the anti-courtiers—a Nobleman whose knowledge and talents were considerably above mediocrity, but whose opposition was too palpably indiscriminate and personal; and the voice of the minority in the House of Commons was no longer the voice of the majority of the people. This was an occasion, however, which furnished his Lordship with a wide scope for argument as well as invective. " He declared himself an enemy to all subsidy-treaties in time of peace. The views and circumstances of Princes and States were perpetually changing, and their decisions would ever be influenced by present interests, and not past obligations, of which, he said, we had full proof during the last war in the conduct of the Danes and Hessians, the former of whom deserted us, and the latter had actually engaged against us. By entering into treaties of this nature, without the previous authority of Parliament, he acknowledged the House was indeed reduced to a disagreeable dilemma— they must either expose their Sovereign to the contempt of foreign powers, or they must sacrifice the interests of their constituents by imposing unnecessary burdens upon the country. But of two evils he would choose the least, by refusing the subsidies, and endeavor to vindicate the honor of the Sovereign by punishing those Ministers who advised such pernicious measures." Sir John Hynde Cotton forcibly remarked, that France was one of the guarantees of the treaty of Westphalia, and consequently of the liberties and constitution

of

of the German Empire; and our thus granting subsidies to the Electors will furnish her with a plausible pretext for asserting that the liberties of the Empire are invaded by means of bribery and corruption; and may incite her to assume the character of the defender of the Germanic Constitution against such scandalous attempts. With regard, therefore, to the election of a King of the Romans, he was of opinion that the German Princes ought to be left entirely to themselves; and that the wisest course England could take was, by the establishment of an œconomical system and the effectual reduction of the national debt, to prepare for a future war whenever a real and national necessity to engage in a war should be proved to exist." It was also urged, in the course of the debate, that motives of policy no less than of œconomy militated against the granting of these subsidies; for, when we have taken the whole Electoral College into pay, they will certainly, for the sake of having the subsidies renewed and continued, put off from time to time, on such pleas as can never be wanting, the election until the death of the present Emperor; for, should the election be once made, the subsidies will of course cease. By the officious and invidious interposition of Great Britain, it was affirmed to be too probable that an intestine war in the Empire might be not *prevented*, as was alleged by the partisans of the Court, but *excited:* for the other two Colleges of the Diet would certainly join with France in protesting against the validity of an election so circumstanced; in which case, it might be reasonably expected that some of the Electors themselves, who now so readily accepted our bribes, might be bribed to act against us. The goodness of his Majesty's *intentions* no one presumed to doubt; but to compliment, in the mode now proposed, the depth of his wisdom, or the extent of his penetration, would be ridiculous. As to that " union with his allies," on which such stress seemed to be laid in

his

his Majesty's speech from the throne, it was certainly very desirable if it could be effected without sacrificing the true interests of the nation: but there could be no sufficient reason for purchasing their friendship by extravagant subsidies, at a time when we had so little money to spare, since this union must always be a matter of much more importance to them than to us. England should at all times be flow and cautious of intermeddling in the affairs of the Continent, if we wished to avoid exciting resentments and jealousies. Were the liberties of Europe at this or any other crisis really endangered, the powers of the Continent would no doubt solicit with eagerness our assistance; whereas, we were now giving them bribes for permission to interpose when there was no reason to believe that the Empire at large were desirous of our interference, or would be benefited by it." The system of policy adopted by the English Court was not, however, to be shaken by such frivolous arguments; and after an inextricable tissue of negotiations and intrigues, most assiduously carried on with the different German Princes, the Elector of Mentz, Chancellor of the Empire, at length convoked an Electoral Diet. But the King of Prussia, Elector of Brandenburg, who had, on the first indication of this design, manifested his dislike and disapprobation, now publicly opposed it with the utmost vehemence and pertinacity. " He declared the election in contemplation to be contrary to the laws and constitution of the Empire, as promulgated in the *Golden Bull*, and confirmed by the treaty of Westphalia, from which the Electoral College had no right to depart. In the cases only of long absence, continued indisposition, or accidental emergency, which could not now be pretended to exist, did the Imperial capitulations admit the lawfulness of proceeding to the election of a King of the Romans during the lifetime of the Emperor.

And,

And, should the imperial crown devolve to a minor, he affirmed, that many mischiefs and disorders must necessarily ensue, as the constitutions of the empire had established no regency for the government of it in a case unknown to all preceding times, but had only appointed vicars during an actual vacancy of the imperial throne. That an election in these circumstances would be incompatible with the Germanic liberties, and with the fundamental privileges of the princes and states of the empire —that the imperial dignity would be virtually changed from an elective to an hereditary succession, perpetuated in one family, which must thus be aggrandized to the prejudice of its co-estates, and the manifest subversion of the constitution of the empire." In consequence of these spirited remonstrances of the Prussian monarch, several of the electors seemed to waver in their opinion; the king of France also solemnly protesting, " that although, for the sake of peace, he would not oppose this election, contrary as it was to the *golden bull*, provided it should be confirmed by the unanimous consent of the electoral college; yet should ANY ONE of the members signify his dissent, and claim the protection of France, he could not refuse granting his assistance, as guarantee of the treaty of Westphalia." Attempts having been in vain made to soften the king of Prussia, the courts of Vienna and London were at length compelled to desist from the prosecution of their design, though their imperial majesties could not refrain from displaying marks of the bitterest resentment at the conduct of the Prussian monarch; and were evidently watching, with eager anxiety, for a favorable opportunity of revenge. The determined and resolute opposition of the king of Prussia to this measure, which he passes over, in the history of his times, in deep and mysterious silence, seems best accounted for by the prevalent suspicion that, in case of the demise of the emperor, he harbored a secret design of offering himself as a candidate for the imperial throne. And it is probable, that a knowledge or persuasion of the aspiring views of the Prussian monarch principally incited the court of Vienna to urge with such persevering ardor a project so irregular and invidious. At this period, the courts of Berlin and London were scarcely less at variance than those of Vienna and Berlin; and the king of Prussia openly expressed his resentment of the conduct of the king of England, " who had, by the influence of English subsidies, embarrassed and embroiled the affairs of Germany, in which he had no right to interfere."

A profound tranquillity at this time prevailed throughout the island of Great Britain; and the attention of the minister seemed, by a perfect novelty in politics, to be wholly engrossed in devising and bringing forward, for the discussion and approbation of parliament, plans and proposals for the public good. Amongst other laudable and liberal projects, a bill, of a nature not very important indeed, was introduced and passed in the session of 1753, permitting the naturalization, under certain restrictions, of persons born out of the realm, professing the jewish religion *, it being supposed, or at least hoped, that such a measure would operate as an inducement to opulent foreigners of that persuasion to remove with their effects to Great Britain, to the obvious increase of the national commerce, credit, and prosperity. A most absurd and unexpected alarm, however, was taken by the public at this just and beneficial measure; and it was asserted, that this adoption of *vagrant jews* into the community, and investing them with the rights of denizens, would rob

---

* This famous bill of naturalization gave no greater privileges to those who might be desirous of taking the advantage of it, than to Jews who were born in England, which are much inferior to those which they enjoy in many other countries.

the

the natives of their birth-right—would tend to deprive them, by setting up a rivalship of interest and industry, of the means of employment—would endanger the constitution in church and state, and would be an indelible reproach to the legislature of a christian nation. It was even affirmed, by some heated enthusiasts, that this act was an impious attempt to invalidate the scriptural prophecies, which declare that the jews shall be a scattered people, possessing no fixed or settled habitation until their conversion to christianity, and their consequent restoration to the promised land; though it certainly could not be pretended, that the nations of the earth are enjoined, by any precept of christianity, to treat the jews with injustice or inhumanity, in order to ensure the accomplishment of this prophecy. In the ensuing session, however, the clamor continuing, and even increasing, the bill was repealed, as one of those necessary sacrifices which wisdom is occasionally compelled to offer at the altar of prejudice and folly. This was one of the last acts of Mr. Pelham's administration—that minister dying, March 1754, in the meridian of his life, reputation, and usefulness. Rectitude of understanding and disposition seems to have constituted his leading characteristic. Whatever appears erroneous in his conduct proceeded chiefly from the imperfection and absurdity of that general system of politics, which he found too firmly established to be, without an effort too mighty, susceptible of any material alteration *. But the many excellent acts

---

* In a confidential conversation with Mr. Pelham, lord Melcombe tells us that this minister opened to him the bottom of his politics—" that he had a great regard for all Europe, but did not trouble himself much about it; that his concern was to keep things on a right foot at home; that he was at this period chiefly solicitous to have a thorough whig parliament chosen, which would make the remainder of his majesty's

acts passed under his influence and patronage, plainly indicate an unremitted attention to the interest, and a sincere and earnest desire to promote the happiness of his country. His genius was not of an enterprising cast, and, when occasionally urged to adopt more bold and vigorous measures of political reform, he was accustomed to answer, "that things would last his time." And the general tenor of his conduct shewed, that he was less anxious to avoid the censure of timidity than of rashness. He lived and died esteemed and lamented, both by the sovereign and the nation *. Mr. Legge, a man of honor and capacity, after a short interval, succeeded Mr. Pelham as chancellor of the exchequer. The seals being consigned to Sir Thomas Robinson, formerly ambassador at the court of Vienna, a minister of very moderate political attainments, and little conversant in parliamentary intrigues and conflicts, the post of first lord of the trea-

---

jesty's life easy, and would settle the young prince upon the throne so as to secure him the prospect of a prosperous reign. If they would let him do this, he was at their service; if not, he could be contented to be a private man as well as another. Touching upon the subsidies attending the election of a king of the Romans, *Mr. Pelham's face fell*, and he grew very uneasy upon it; and expressed much dislike of the way it was conducted. He said he was always against those subsidies; that his idea was, that, if the dissentient electors would give in the *ultimatum* of their demands, and perform the conditions before they received the reward; then, indeed, when we were sure of our bargain, it might be worth considering *whether it were prudent to pay the price*; but to be buying one elector after another was what he ABHORRED: it must have an end, and he declared so in parliament.

* To the mild and amiable character of this justly valued minister, Mr. Pope has paid an elegant tribute of applause in one of his poetic epistles:

"Pleas'd let me own in Esher's peaceful grove,
Where Kent and Nature vie for Pelham's love,
The scene, the master, opening to my view,
I sit and dream I see my Craggs anew."

fury

fury was occupied by the duke of Newcastle. But it soon appeared how unequal were the talents of this nobleman to the task of government, when deprived of the assistance of the counsellor and coadjutor with whom he had been ever united in the strictest bands of political and fraternal amity. And the first remarkable incident of his administration too plainly shewed that public measures were no longer actuated by the wise and beneficent counsels of Mr. Pelham. Dr. Cameron, brother to the celebrated Cameron of Lochiel, had been engaged in the rebellion of 1745, and, after the decisive victory of Culloden, had effected his escape to the continent. Notwithstanding his being attainted by act of parliament, he ventured, after an interval of nine years, to return *incognito* to Scotland, in order to transact certain affairs of great consequence, but of a nature entirely private and personal—relying, in case of exigence, with fatal indiscretion, on the mildness and equity of the British government, now raised far above the apprehension of danger, on the temper of the times, and the general respectability of his own character. Being, however, by some means discovered, he was apprehended and brought to his trial at the Old Baily; and his person being legally identified, he was convicted, and suffered the death of a traitor with admirable firmness and resignation. It is remarkable, that even the populace were melted into tears at the melancholy spectacle of his execution; generously lamenting the excessive rigor of his fate; which can never be justified upon any public principles of necessity or utility, and which bears the odious aspect of an act of obdurate and sanguinary revenge. A far more conspicuous proof, however, of the rashness and incapacity of the present administration, appeared in the haughty tenor of their conduct respecting the parliament of Ireland, in an affair of great delicacy and importance—

unmindful

unmindful that the harp, emblematic of this kingdom, produces by means of soft and gentle touches only its genuine harmony. In the year 1749, a considerable surplus remaining in the Irish exchequer, the house of commons in that country, conceiving that they had an undoubted right to appropriate such surplus to national purposes, prepared heads of a bill with that design, to which was affixed the following preamble: " Whereas, on the 25th of March last, a considerable balance remained in the hands of the vice-treasurers, or receivers-general, of the kingdom, or their deputy or deputies, unapplied: and it will be for your majesty's service, and for the ease of your faithful subjects in this kingdom, that so much thereof as can be conveniently spared should be paid, agreeably to your majesty's most gracious intention, in discharge of part of the national debt," &c. &c. On the transmission of this bill to England, it was affirmed, by the warm partisans of prerogative in the council, that the commons of Ireland had no right to apply any part of the unappropriated revenue, nor even to take into consideration the propriety of such appropriation, without the previous consent of the crown, formally and explicitly declared. In the ensuing session of parliament therefore, A. D. 1751, the duke of Dorset, lord lieutenant of Ireland, informed the two houses of parliament, in his speech from the throne, that he was commanded by the king to acquaint them, that his majesty, ever attentive to the ease and happiness of his subjects, would graciously *consent*, and recommended it to them, that such a part of the money then remaining in his treasury as should be thought consistent with the public services, be applied towards the farther reduction of the national debt. The commons of Ireland, astonished at this procedure of the court, and tremblingly alive in a case which so nearly concerned their privileges, omitted, in their address of thanks, all mention of his majesty's *consent*, and only acknowledged his
gracious

gracious attention to their ease and happiness in *recommending* to them the application of the surplus. And in the subsequent bill framed for this purpose, in which one hundred and twenty thousand pounds were appropriated to the discharge of the public debt, the same omission was observable. The ministers in England, highly offended with this contumacious conduct, returned the bill with an alteration in the preamble, signifying his majesty's *consent* as well as approbation. And the Irish house of commons, unwilling to risk the consequences of a serious rupture, passed the bill without farther notice. So far had the misunderstanding between the crown and parliament of Ireland proceeded previous to the death of Mr. Pelham, and thus might it have for ever rested, had not the evil genius of the present minister suggested the necessity of supporting the *honor of government*, by positive directions to the duke of Dorset, in opening the session of the present year, to repeat the expression of his majesty's gracious *consent*, in mentioning the surplus of the public money. The house, in their address, not only again omitted the obnoxious word *consent*, but the former expressions of grateful acknowledgement: and the bill of appropriation was transmitted to England, entirely divested of the usual complimentary preamble, which the ministers of the crown in England, in their great wisdom, thought fit thus to supply—" And your majesty, ever attentive to the ease and happiness of your faithful subjects, has been graciously pleased to signify that you would *consent*, and to recommend it to us that so much of the money remaining in your majesty's treasury as should be necessary, be applied to the discharge of the national debt, or such part thereof as should be thought expedient by parliament." On the return of the bill, the whole nation seemed animated by the spirit of resistance, and, notwithstanding the utmost efforts of the court, the bill, thus amended, was thrown out by a majority of five voices,

and

and the victory of the oppofition was celebrated by univerfal rejoicings. In revenge, all thofe who voted againſt the bill holding public employments were immediately difmiſſed. But the rejection of the bill occafioning a great ſtagnation in the ufual courfe of circulation, and the clamor of the public rifing high againſt the government, it was thought proper and neceſſary, by an humiliating conceſſion, to devote the furplus to the difcharge of the debt in virtue of a royal letter. Thus was the dignity of government, which ought never to be lightly or capriciouſly committed, moſt ſenfibly wounded. Ireland was taught to know her own ſtrength and importance, and the firſt fymptoms of that high and haughty fpirit of independence were now difcernible, which have fince produced fuch mighty effects.

If England, at this period, exhibited, by the clamorous oppofition of almoſt all ranks of people to the Jew bill, plain indications that the fpirit of fanaticifm was by no means extinguiſhed in the nation, the fame fpirit operated, at the fame time, in France, in a manner much more ferious and alarming. Under a delufive veil of feſtivity, pomp, and fplendor, the court of Verfailles, during the whole of the reign of Louis XIV. and particularly the latter years of it, concealed a moſt unrelenting and fanguinary fpirit of bigotry and perfecution. This fpirit difplayed itſelf not merely in the favage folly of that policy by which he attempted the extirpation of the proteſtants, but alfo in his treatment of fuch of the Catholics themfelves as prefumed, in any refpect, to deviate from the eſtabliſhed dogmas of the Romiſh church. About the middle of the laſt century, a very celebrated treatife, under the title of *Auguſtinus*, had been written by Cornelius Janfen, biſhop of Ypres, on the abſtrufe theological topics of grace, predeſtination, and free will, in which he explains thofe tenets in a mode different from that ufually adopted and maintained

tained in the schools, but perfectly consonant, as this reverend and learned prelate alleged, to the divine and apostolic doctrine of the great St. Austin. As this novel, and therefore rash explication, however, very nearly accorded with that of Calvin and the other leading reformers of the protestant churches, it excited great alarm and indignation; and the book was repeatedly censured, at different and distant intervals of time, by the intervention and authority of the Papal chair. Nevertheless, the partisans and admirers of this famous treatise, who were now distinguished by the name of Jansenists, seemed continually to increase; and it was at length thought necessary, by a bull issued by pope Clement XI. at the beginning of the present century, with all the terrific accompaniments of pontifical authority, solemnly to declare, " that all the faithful ought to condemn as heretical, not only with their mouths, but in their hearts," certain specified propositions, in number no less than one hundred, extracted from the book of Jansenius. This constitution was received by the Gallican church, and promulgated by the king's command and authority. But this bull, far from terminating, only aggravated and inflamed the dispute; and converted it from a theological to a political controversy. The clergy in general, and more especially the Jesuits, were eager and zealous in their efforts to support the dignity of the Romish See, and to enforce the acceptance of the Papal bull. On the other hand, the parliaments of the kingdom, and particularly the parliament of Paris, embraced every opportunity to express their contempt and hatred of the bull and its partisans. The archbishop of Paris, a haughty and turbulent prelate, stood forth at this period as the champion of the church, and encouraged and commanded the clergy to deny the sacraments *in articulo mortis* to all persons refusing

fusing to subscribe the bull Unigenitus *. Divers ecclesiastics adhering to this injunction, were apprehended by authority of the parliament, for their contumacious and illegal conduct. Severe censures were passed upon the archbishop, and a prosecution actually commenced against the bishop of Orleans; when a mandate from the court was issued, prohibiting all farther proceedings in these matters. The parliament, in return, presented a spirited remonstrance to the throne, declaring it to be their indispensable duty and privilege to denounce and execute judgment on all delinquents. And, on the renewal of the royal command, they framed new remonstrances, to which the king refused to reply, referring them to his former peremptory declaration. Upon which the parliament resolved " that the different chambers should remain assembled, but that all business should be suspended while, by the practices of evil-minded persons, truth was prevented from reaching the throne." Another mandate was now issued, ordering the parliament to revoke this resolution, on pain of the king's high displeasure; instead of which, a second resolution passed, that they could not comply with this injunction without violating their duty and their oath. Upon which, *lettres de cachet* were immediately issued, and the members of the parliament banished to distant parts of the kingdom: and a royal chamber was instituted for the intermediate administration of public justice. The letters patent for the establishment of this court were, however, according to the laws and customs of the kingdom, not valid till they were judicially enregistered; and the parliament of Paris being now no more, application was made to the inferior court of

---

* By this appellation the bull was universally known, the term *Unigenitus* being the first word contained in it.

the Chatelet, which declared its absolute incompetency for that purpose: and the *lieutenant Civile* appearing in the court in order to enforce the regiftery, all the counfellors rofe up and retired, leaving on the table an *arrêt*, containing their proteft againft thefe proceedings: in confequence of which, feveral of the moft refpectable and fpirited members of this court were committed to the Baftile. The nation at large was now in the higheft degree inflamed and exafperated at the defpotic conduct of the court. The provincial parliaments prefented bold remonftrances to the throne, juftificatory of the parliament of Paris. The profecutions of the contumacious priefts were every-where continued, and things feemed evidently tending to open and general revolt, when the court thought proper to avert the ftorm by a recal of the parliament, who publicly re-entered Paris amidft the loudeft acclamations of the people. And the archbifhop perfifting in his former exhortations and directions to the clergy, was fent as an exile to Conflans-fous-Charenton. But the wound occafioned by this diffenfion between the court and parliament was never radically healed; and the king, after the lapfe of about two years, not only recalled the archbifhop, but received, with decided marks of royal approbation, a bull from the Roman Pontiff, in which thofe who rejected the bull *Unigenitus* were pioufly configned to everlafting damnation, and the reiterated refufal of the facraments confirmed by the authoritative fanction of the Holy See. The parliament of Paris, regarding this bull as a direct attack upon the rights of the Gallican church and nation, iffued an *arrêt* for its fuppreffion; upon which frefh contefts arofe, but the parliament remained firm, and the court was finally compelled to defift from thofe claims and pretenfions, which it had fo unwifely and unfeafonably agitated. This memorable ftruggle made a mighty and lafting impreffion upon the minds

of

of the people. The popularity of the monarch, formerly distinguished by the flattering appellation of *Le bien aimé*, was for ever departed. New and interesting ideas began to revolve in the public mind. The origin of the controversy was, in the progress of it, forgotten; and the recal of the parliament was not the triumph of Jansenism, but of liberty. The despotic acts of the court were regarded by the nation with emotions of horror. Various publications, by writers of the highest talents, successively appeared, in which the principles of just and equitable government were explained and illustrated with irresistible force and energy; the boldest speculations were indulged; prejudices, the most deeply rooted, were successfully assailed; an eager and ardent spirit of research was excited; touched by the wand of philosophy, the mighty talisman by which the nation had been fast bound in the sleep of a thousand years, was suddenly dissolved; reason began to resume her empire, and an internal revolution now commenced —a revolution of the mind, which was pre-ordained, in the gradual and regular progression of events, to produce an external revolution unparalleled for the magnitude of its object, and the extent of its consequences, in the annals of mankind. But, alas! no unmixed good has ever yet been the lot of mortals; and experience too clearly evinces that truths of the highest moral and political importance, when first suggested to men long bowed down by the iron hand of oppression, and newly awakened to a sense of their own rights, are as flashes of lightning which irradiate the gloom with a pale, terrific, and dangerous lustre.

The political contentions, however, which at this period arose between the kingdoms of Great Britain and France, and which terminated in a long and bloody war, seemed for some years, to absorb all internal and domestic

domestic commotion; and the resources of both nations were exhausted in a contest which a very small portion of wisdom, had they been really and mutually disposed to conciliation, might have sufficed to accommodate.— After the cession of Nova Scotia by the treaty of Utrecht, the British colonies in North America extended along the western shore of the Atlantic for near a thousand miles, and, according to the tenor of the charters granted to the original settlers, the dominion of the soil was bounded only by the Pacific ocean on the opposite side of the Continent. Spain, in whom were vested the rights attached to the first discovery, advanced claims no less extravagant, and regarded as unwarrantable usurpations the successive settlements of the English nation. France, which held in contempt the pretensions both of England and Spain, established, at a more recent period, colonies on the river St. Laurence to the north, and on the Mississippi to the south, of the English settlements: and a systematic and artfully concerted plan was formed to connect these widely-distant establishments by the gradual erection of a chain of fortresses from the lakes Erie and Ontario, along and beyond the Ohio to the *embouchure* of the Mississippi. To the rich and immense plains extending on both sides of that vast river they gave the appellation of Louisiana; and they contended, that the English colonies were of right bounded by the range of high lands which ran parallel to the coast, at the distance of one hundred and fifty, or two hundred miles, under the different names of the Apalachian, Alleghaheny, or Blue Mountains. The province of Nova Scotia being ceded to England, according to the *ancient limits* of that territory, fruitless and endless altercations arose, as to the import of this expression, between the commissaries of the two nations, to whom the right of fixing the boundaries of the rival empires was assigned; the English claiming the whole territory as far as the southern bank of the river St. Laurence, and the French admitting their right only to the peninsula of Acadie. Another very serious cause of dispute originated in a royal charter inconsiderately and injuriously granted to certain merchants and adventurers of the city of London, who assumed the title of the Ohio company, of a large tract of ground situated on the banks of the Ohio, with an exclusive privilege of commerce with the Indian tribes inhabiting those regions. This extraordinary grant excited extreme disgust in the minds of the Virginian and Pennsylvanian traders, who saw themselves deprived of a lucrative branch of traffic, and the highest alarm amongst the Indian nations, who perceived with astonishment their lands measured and parcelled out by English surveyors, as if they, who were the actual occupants, had neither interest nor property in them. And M. du Quesne, governor of Canada, declared that he would suffer no encroachments or depredations to be made on the Indian tribes under the protection of the crown of France. Towards the latter end of the year 1753, major Washington, since so famous under the name of general Washington, was deputed by the government of Virginia to the French commandant on the Ohio, to demand by what authority fortresses were erected, and settlements made, on the territories of the king of Great Britain; and to require him immediately to desist from the prosecution of designs carried on in open violation of the treaties subsisting between the two crowns, and totally subversive of the harmony and good understanding which his Britannic majesty was desirous to maintain and cultivate with the most christian king. To this peremptory requisition, which almost assumed the air and tone of a menace, the French officer replied with equal spirit, that it was not his province to specify the evidence, and

demonstrate

demonstrate the right of the king his sovereign to the lands situated on the river Ohio; but that he would transmit his message to the marquis du Quesne, his immediate superior. In the mean time, he declared his total disregard of the summons of the English governor, and holding his command by virtue of a commission from his general, he was prepared and determined to maintain the rights, and to fulfil the duties, of his station. A far more serious remonstrance was, about the same time, presented by the earl of Albemarle, the English ambassador at Paris, to the court of Versailles, in which the various causes of complaint on the part of England were stated in very strong language. It was declared that, while the commissaries of the two nations were engaged in adjusting the limits of the two empires, the French had taken actual possession of the territories in dispute; that they had incited the Indians of Nova Scotia and the French inhabitants of Acadie to rise in arms against the English government, and had assisted them with vessels and military stores; that acts of violence had been repeatedly exercised by the authority or countenance of the French governors against the subjects of Great Britain; and numerous fortresses erected with a view to defend their continual and manifest encroachments on the territories of his Britannic majesty: and his excellency concluded with demanding the erasure of the forts, the restitution of the persons and properties of all those who had been captured, an unequivocal assurance that effectual care should be taken, by the most positive instructions to the French commandants in America, to prevent any similar causes of complaint in future. The French court not being yet prepared, or not having yet resolved to risk an open rupture with Great Britain, replied to this memorial in terms civilly evasive, and engaged that inquiries should be made, and instructions transmitted to America to

obviate

obviate all misunderstanding; and several British subjects, traders and others, seized by the French on various pretences, were actually dismissed.

On the last day of May 1754, the parliament, newly elected, was opened by commission, and, in the speech delivered by the lord chancellor, the two houses were informed, that his majesty did not at that time think it necessary to call their attention to the general state of the nation, reserving all discussions of this nature to the usual time of their assembling in the winter; and, on the fifth of June, the lords commissioners prorogued the parliament. Notwithstanding this apparent indifference, the court of London, confiding little in the specious and artful professions of the court of Versailles, issued orders to the English governors in America to repel force by force, and to take effectual measures to dislodge the French from their settlements on the Ohio, where they still continued their hostilities and encroachments. A congress being appointed at Albany, consisting of commissioners from the different colonies, to which the chieftains of the Indian nations bordering on the Ohio were invited, it soon appeared, though they refused not to accept the offered and customary presents, that they were entirely attached to the French interests—a predilection indeed easy to be accounted for by the superior humanity and justice displayed in every part of the conduct of the French nation in their transactions with the ancient inhabitants of the Continent, compared with the violent and imperious deportment of the English. At this meeting, it was determined that major Washington, who had already distinguished himself by his gallantry and spirit, should be detached with a corps of four hundred men, in order to occupy a post on the Ohio, where he threw up works, and began the erection of a fort, in expectation of speedy and effectual reinforcements; but before the intended succours

cours could arrive, this officer was suddenly attacked by a much superior force of French and Indians, commanded by M. de Viller, who, after in vain summoning major Washington to surrender, marched to the attack of the fort, yet incomplete, and ill prepared for an assault, which was nevertheless sustained with great vigor; but the English garrison were at length compelled to a capitulation, and they were allowed to retreat, not unmolested indeed by the irregular attacks of the savages, to the province of Virginia. This event, as soon as the intelligence arrived in Europe, was stated, in a memorial of the earl of Albemarle, as an open violation of the peace. But the court of Versailles, no longer solicitous to keep any measures with England, treated all remonstrances with disregard; and sent large reinforcements of men, and supplies of military stores, to Quebec, with a manifest determination to pursue and defend her ambitious projects.

The parliament of England met in November, but a profound silence respecting the present critical situation of affairs was observed on the part of the crown, till, in the month of March (1755), a message was delivered from the king to the parliament by Sir Thomas Robinson, secretary of state, importing that " his majesty having, at the commencement of the session, declared it to be the principal object of his solicitude to preserve the public tranquillity, and to protect those possessions which constitute a primary source of the public prosperity, now found it necessary to acquaint the house of commons, that the present state of affairs made it requisite to augment his forces by sea and land, and to take such other measures as might best tend to preserve the peace of Europe, and to secure the just rights of his crown in America." This message produced a warm and affectionate address, and the sum of one million was instantly voted for the purposes specified by his majesty. While M. de Mirepoix, the French ambassador in London, still continued to amuse the British ministry with empty professions of peace and amity, certain intelligence was received that a powerful armament was preparing in the ports of Rochefort and Brest, destined for America; and admiral Boscawen was immediately appointed to the command of an equal force, fitted out for the avowed purpose of intercepting them. On which M. de Mirepoix declared, that the king his master would consider the first gun fired at sea as a declaration of war. The British admiral, hoping to obstruct the passage of the French fleet into the gulf of St. Laurence, took his station off the banks of Newfoundland; but, under cover of the thick fogs which so commonly prevail in those northern latitudes, the French commander eluded his vigilance; two ships of the line only, the Alcide and Lys, being by some accident separated from the rest, fell into the hands of the English. Upon the arrival of this intelligence at Paris, the Duc de Mirepoix was immediately recalled from London, and M. de Bussy from Hanover—the king of England being now resident in that city. Letters of general reprisal were issued by the English court at this period, as well in Europe as America, and three hundred merchant ships, for the most part unsuspicious of danger, fell, in the course of the year, into the hands of the English, with not less than eight thousand sailors on board. The French vehemently exclaimed against the conduct of the English government as inconsistent with the law of nations, war not having been as yet formally proclaimed; but the English insisted that the French themselves being clearly the aggressors, it was just and lawful to repel force by force, and that the omission of a form was wholly immaterial.

Early in the year 1755, general Braddock had sailed from Cork with a considerable body of regular troops, and,

and, on his arrival in Virginia, took upon him the command of the forces destined to act against the French on the Ohio. This officer was a man of approved bravery, completely versed in all points of military discipline, but opinionated and positive in his temper, and in his deportment austere and imperious. Wholly unacquainted with the country in which he was appointed to the chief command, and entertaining a sovereign contempt for the colonial militia, of whom his army was in a great measure composed, he heard with silent disdain all that information which the provincial officers were desirous to offer respecting the mode of conducting an American expedition through woods, deserts, and morasses, and the precautions which were necessary to guard against surprise, particularly as the Indian nations were for the most part in alliance with France. Having advanced with the most fearless security to less than ten miles of Fort Du Quesne, and without condescending, though earnestly pressed, to employ the irregulars in the service as an advanced guard, or to send out any parties to reconnoitre the country, about noon on the ninth of July, in his march through a pathless swamp, entangled amid brakes and rushes, he was on the sudden saluted with the horrid sound of the Indian war-whoop, accompanied by a general fire both on his front and flank from a concealed and invisible enemy. The van-guard immediately fell back, and terror and confusion soon spread throughout all the ranks of the army. The general, far from making any efforts to discover and disperse this dangerous ambuscade, exerted himself only to re-form and rally his troops, as if engaged with a regular army in an open plain. But the exactest discipline was, in this situation, of little avail; for, though no enemy appeared, the havoc and slaughter still continued, and the general himself being at length killed by a musquet shot, the regular troops fled from the field with the utmost precipitation—the provincials, so much despised, forming in the rear, and covering their retreat; major Washington their commander acquiring on this occasion, in the midst of defeat, the honors and laurels of victory. All the artillery, ammunition, and baggage of the army were left in the hands of the enemy, and even the general's own cabinet, with all his letters and instructions; and the whole conduct of this expedition plainly proved that personal courage, though an indispensable requisite, is only a secondary qualification in the character of a military commander. Very indifferent success also attended the operations carried on in the more northerly parts of the Continent. On the death of general Braddock, the chief command devolved upon general Shirley, who formed a plan for the reduction of the important fortresses of Crown Point and Niagara, erected by the French on the banks of the lakes Champlain and Ontario. The expedition against the former was conducted by general, afterwards Sir William Johnson, a native of Ireland, but long resident in America, where he had acquired great and deserved popularity. From various causes of delay, the troops destined for this service arrived at the place of rendezvous late in the summer; and were, soon after the commencement of their march, attacked in their camp by baron Dieskau, the French commander, with great bravery, who was, notwithstanding, repulsed with great loss—the baron himself being made a prisoner. General Johnson, however, found himself, after this bloody encounter, too much weakened to proceed in his expedition; and, after some deliberation, he determined upon a retreat to Albany. General Shirley himself undertook the conduct of the enterprise against Niagara, which, from its position, commands the communication between the lakes Erie and Ontario. But on his arrival

arrival at Ofwego, a fort belonging to the Englifh on the fouth-eaftern fhore of lake Ontario, he deemed it neceffary to leave a very large proportion of the troops under his command for the defence of this poft; and, after waiting till the end of September for his expected reinforcements and fupplies of provifions and ftores, he was informed that it would be attended with danger to crofs the lake at this advanced feafon of the year. He therefore determined to defer the fiege of Niagara to the next campaign; and fet out in October on his return to Albany. The earl of Loudon, an officer of reputation and merit, was now appointed commander in chief of the Britifh forces in America, and vefted with very extenfive powers. But this nobleman, from caufes not eafy to develop, did not embark from England till the latter end of May; and, on reaching the head-quarters at Albany June the 29 (1756), he found all military operations in a manner fufpended, in the expectation of his arrival; after which, a confiderable time elapfed in debates and confultations refpecting the plan moft proper to be adopted, and whether the efforts of the army now affembled fhould be directed againft Crown Point and Ticonderago, fituated at the fouthern extremity of lake Champlain; whether a fecond attempt fhould be made againft Niagara; or whether an expedition fhould be undertaken againft Fort Du Quefne on the Ohio. In the midft of thefe deliberations, intelligence arrived that the French, under M. de Montcalm, had made themfelves mafters of Ofwego, although ftrongly garrifoned, plentifully provided with all kinds of warlike ftores, and defended by one hundred and twenty pieces of artillery. Apparently difcouraged and difconcerted by this unfortunate event, it was determined not to rifk any offenfive operation during the remainder of the prefent feafon, but to employ

ploy the autumnal and winter months in making preparations for an early and vigorous campaign the enfuing year. Notwithftanding the former difappointments, high and fanguine hopes were entertained from the great military force collected in the fpring of 1757, and the avowed purpofe of the commander in chief to employ his whole ftrength in fome grand and decifive operation. Admiral Holborne arrived at Halifax with a powerful fquadron, and large reinforcements of troops, in the beginning of July; and the earl of Loudon directing his march northward, an invafion of Canada with their united forces was reafonably to be expected. At length, however, Louifburg, in the ifland of Cape Breton, was declared to be the object in contemplation—a fcheme very favorable to the views and interefts of France at this period, as it left M. de Montcalm entirely at liberty to profecute his plans of conqueft, and Louifburg was fo ftrongly defended, that little apprehenfion was entertained for its fafety. And the Britifh commanders receiving certain intelligence, after the whole of the military and naval force deftined for this expedition had rendezvoufed at Halifax, that the garrifon of Louifburg confifted of fix thoufand regular troops, exclufive of provincials, and that feventeen line-of-battle fhips were moored in the harbor; it was refolved, according to the cuftom of this war, to poftpone the expedition to a more convenient opportunity. In the mean time, the marquis de Montcalm had taken an advantage of the abfence of the earl of Loudon to lay fiege, with an army of ten thoufand men, to the important poft of Fort William Henry, fituated on the fouthern fhore of lake George. The garrifon confifted of three thoufand men; the fortifications were ftrong and in good condition; and general Webb, with about four thoufand men, was pofted in the vicinity,

nity, in order to maintain a communication with it. Notwithstanding which, so vigorously were the approaches of the French commander urged, that articles of capitulation were signed in six days, not only importing the entire surrender of the fort, artillery, and stores, but restraining the garrison from serving against his most christian majesty, or her allies, for the space of eighteen months. By this conquest, the French acquired the entire command of the extensive and magnificent chain of lakes which connects the two great rivers St. Laurence and Mississippi, and which forms a grand line both of communication and division between the northern and southern parts of this vast continent. And thus disgracefully terminated the third campaign of the American war, in which the French, with a very inferior force, had maintained an uniform superiority, and in the course of which no advantage had been gained by the English, excepting, indeed, the expulsion of the French from Nova Scotia, by the vigorous exertions of colonel Monckton, assisted by a body of provincials, expressly voted and detached by the assembly of Massachusetts for this important purpose. Nor were the operations of the war at this period more skilfully or prosperously conducted by the English nation in Europe than in America. The court of Versailles, finding a rupture with England inevitable, had employed earnest solicitations with the court of Madrid to take an active part in her favor. Her efforts, however, were in vain, though supported by all the influence of the queen mother and the marquis de la Ensenada, the prime minister. The king of Spain himself was not disposed to interrupt the harmony which subsisted between Spain and Great Britain; and Don Ricardo Wall, a Spaniard of British extraction, and formerly resident at the British court, and who possessed great credit with the king, took all imaginable pains to confirm

his

his majesty in these favorable sentiments: and the intrigues of the minister with the court of Versailles being discovered, he was divested of his offices, which were immediately conferred upon his competitor Don Ricardo. The court of Madrid, however, offered her *mediation* to compose the differences between England and France; but France insisting upon a suspension of arms in America as the preliminary condition of a negotiation, and England refusing to assent to any such preliminary, nothing could be effected. And the courts of London and Versailles, foreseeing a violent and long protracted conflict, were assiduously engaged in forming and cultivating alliances in the different courts of Europe, in order to strengthen their respective interests. A treaty was signed by the king of England, when at Hanover, June 25 (1755), with the Landgrave of Hesse Cassel, by which his serene highness engaged to hold in readiness for his majesty's service a body of twelve thousand men. But Saxony and Bavaria, notwithstanding the subsidies which they had regularly received during the years of peace, in contemplation and as the earnest of future services, now entered into opposite connections—laughing, no doubt, at the credulity of the English nation, in supposing honor and gratitude to be ties obligatory upon princes. In September, a treaty was signed at the palace of Kensington between his Britannic majesty and the empress of Russia, by which that princess stipulated to maintain, on the frontiers of Livonia, an army of forty thousand infantry, and fifteen thousand cavalry, and a naval force of fifty gallies, to be in immediate readiness to act at the requisition of the king of England, should the electoral dominions of that monarch be invaded in consequence of the connection of Hanover with Great Britain; for which an annual subsidy of five hundred thousand pounds was to be advanced to the Czarina. The court of Berlin was, at this crisis, strongly assailed by the courts of London and

and Versailles, each flattering itself with a decision in its favor. But the Prussian monarch, knowing the engagements already contracted between England and Russia, and the strict amity subsisting between the imperial courts of Vienna and Petersburg, would not venture to draw upon himself the resentment of these three formidable powers, by a renewal of the alliance with France; and, in January 1756, a treaty was signed at London between the kings of Great Britain and Prussia, by which they engaged to oppose the introduction of any foreign troops into the empire. This article, though immediately pointed against France, amounted to a virtual renunciation of the alliance with Russia; and the Czarina resenting the conduct of the king of Great Britain, and exasperated, from causes of a personal as well as political nature, against the king of Prussia, began to listen with attention, or rather with eagerness, to the overtures of France, hitherto so much the object of her jealousy and aversion.— " The empress Elizabeth, says the king of Prussia, who had ever been at enmity with France, rather chose to enter into a league with her, than to preserve the shadow of union with a power which had Prussia for an ally." The court of Versailles, astonished and alarmed at the defection of Prussia, which, as the king himself tells us, seemed to be considered in France almost in the light of a revolt *, now directed its attention to the court of Vienna; which since the termination of the late war had given clear and repeated intimations of a desire to enter

---

* " La Cour de Versailles paroissoit croire que le Roi de Prusse étoit à l'égard de la France ce qui est un despote de Valachie à l'égard de la Porte, c'est-à-dire, un Prince subordonné et obligé de faire la guerre dès qu'on lui envoie l'ordre. La nouvelle de cette alliance causa une vive sensation à Versailles dans l'esprit de Louis XV. et de son Conseil; peu s'en fallut qu'ils ne disent que le Roi de Prusse s'étoit revolté contre la France."—*Hist. de la Guerre de Sept Ans.*

into bonds of permanent amity with France: and, to the amazement of Europe, a treaty of mutual guarantee and support was concluded and signed at Verſailles, May 1756, by theſe two great rival powers; and the inveterate hereditary animoſity ſubſiſting for ages between the houſes of Bourbon and Auſtria, in conſequence of which oceans of blood had been ſhed, and the faireſt countries of Chriſtendom deſolated, was at length, if the profeſſions of princes could merit any ſerious regard, for ever terminated. Theſe profeſſions were indeed, in this inſtance, unuſually ſincere. The ruling paſſion of France was, at this period, the depreſſion of the power of England—and of Auſtria, the ſubverſion of that of Pruſſia, which had ſo recently aſpired to a ſtation in the firſt rank of European powers, and preſumptuouſly eſtabliſhed an unheard of rivalſhip in the boſom of the empire itſelf to the imperial family. When an union between England and Pruſſia therefore took place, that repulſive force by which the houſes of Bourbon and Auſtria had been ſo long ſundered, was inſtantly changed to a political attraction, naturally leading to a ſtrict and intimate adheſion. The general conduct of France left ſcarcely a doubt of her intention to take advantage of the political relation of Hanover to Great Britain, by the invaſion of that electorate; although it muſt be acknowledged, that terms of neutrality were offered to the king of England as elector of Hanover, which he did not deem it conſiſtent with his honor and dignity to accept. Mighty preparations being made by the French court, with the avowed deſign of forming a powerful army in Weſtphalia, an army of obſervation, conſiſting of about forty thouſand Heſſians, Hanoverians, and Brunſwickers, was aſſembled for the protection of the electorate: and requiſitions were made by the court of London, both at Vienna and the Hague, for the
aſſiſtance

assistance stipulated by treaties. The empress-queen at first alledged that, as the contest between England and France related to America only, it was not a *casus fœderis*, and that Hanover might be secured by a treaty of neutrality. When the war became general, and the application was renewed, she professed that troops could not be spared with safety to her own dominions, which were in danger from the enmity of Prussia. And being again urged after the alliance between England and Prussia was concluded, she declared in plain terms, that, being abandoned by England, she was reduced to the necessity of securing herself by an alliance with France. As to the provinces of the Belgic union, they had scarcely recovered from the terrors of the former war; the public finances were exhausted, and the people in general extremely averse to engage in hostilities. The court of Versailles, moreover, by a counter-memorial, declared, that, " should the states grant the succors in question, the king of France would consider their compliance as an act of hostility against himself." The application of the English court, therefore, being perceived, from the operation of these causes, useless and unavailing, colonel Yorke, the English ambassador, was directed to inform their high mightinesses, that the king of England would not insist on the requisition ; and the states expressed, in grateful terms, their acknowledgments to his Britannic majesty for thus generously relieving them from their embarrassment.

The parliament of England assembled in November 1755; and, in the opening speech, his majesty informed the two houses " that he had adopted what appeared to him the most proper and effectual measures for the protection of the national possessions in America, no reasonable terms of accommodation having been proposed by France; and also to disappoint such designs as, from various appearances and preparations, there was ground to believe had been formed against his kingdoms and dominions; that he had greatly augmented his forces by land and sea; and that he had concluded treaties with Russia and Hesse Cassel, copies of which should be laid before them." In the address moved in both houses, in answer to this speech, were the following words: "That they looked upon themselves as obliged by the strongest ties of duty, gratitude, and honor, to stand by and support his majesty in all such wise and necessary measures and engagements, as his majesty might have taken in vindication of the rights of his crown, or to defeat any attempts which might be made by France in resentment for such measures, and to assist his majesty in disappointing or repelling all such enterprises as might be formed not only against his kingdoms, but also against any other of his dominions *though not belonging to the crown of Great Britain*, in case the king should be attacked on account of the part which his majesty had taken for maintaining the essential interests of his kingdoms." The declaration contained in this clause met with a most vehement and formidable opposition in the house of commons, not from the powerless party usually voting in opposition, but from Mr. Pitt and Mr. Legge, the most popular members of the present administration, and a very considerable number of other gentlemen possessing posts under the government. Mr. Pitt declared "the whole system and scheme of politics now adopted, to be flagrantly absurd and desperate. It was no other than to gather and combine the powers of the continent into an alliance of magnitude sufficient to withstand the efforts of France and her adherents against the electorate of Hanover, at the single expence of Great Britain. The three last wars with France had cost Britain above one hundred and twenty millions of money; the present exhibits a prospect of treasure still more enormous: and, when we consider that such immense issues of money are to be supplied by

new

new loans, heaped upon a debt of eighty millions, who will anſwer for the conſequence, or venture to enſure us from a national bankruptcy? Mr. Pitt contended, that a naval war we could and ought to ſupport, but a continental war, upon this ſyſtem, we could not. We have ſuffered ourſelves to be deceived by names and ſounds; the general cauſe, the balance of power, the liberty of Europe; and have exhauſted our wealth without any rational object. Should Hanover be actually attacked on account of her connection with England, he acknowledged that we ought not to make peace without procuring for its inhabitants ample ſatisfaction and indemnity. But the idea of defending Hanover by an army of mercenaries, he ridiculed as prepoſterous and impracticable, this ſyſtem, he ſaid, would, in a few years, coſt us more money than the fee-ſimple of the electorate was worth; for it was a place ſo inconſiderable, that its name was ſcarcely to be found in the map. He ardently wiſhed to break thoſe fetters which chained us, like Prometheus, to that barren rock." The clauſe was, however, carried on a diviſion; and the king, in his reply to the addreſs, thanked the two houſes in the ſtrongeſt terms for this ſignal proof of their affection to his perſon and regard for his honor. This tranſaction was followed by the immediate diſmiſſion of Mr. Pitt and Mr. Legge from their reſpective employments.

It muſt be remarked that, three days before the meeting of parliament, Sir Thomas Robinſon, ſecretary of ſtate, from an honeſt and ſincere conſciouſneſs of his own incapacity to conduct the buſineſs of government in the houſe of commons, had reſigned the ſeals, which were directly transferred to Mr. Fox, ſecretary at war, who unqueſtionably, in reſpect of political ability, had at this time no rival in the houſe of commons, Mr. Pitt only excepted. Though engaged for ſeveral years paſt in the support of the same administration, they were actuated by a very visible jealousy on almost all occasions. And it was observed, that they agreed in nothing so well as in those sentiments of contempt for the late minister, which they were at little pains to conceal. It may easily be supposed, therefore, that Mr. Pitt, who could endure no superior, was very little delighted with the advancement of his competitor, who seemed as firmly resolved to admit no equal: and Mr. Legge entering entirely into the views of Mr. Pitt, it was imagined that the new minister would not long be able to maintain his ground against an opposition strengthened by so powerful a secession, founded on professions so popular and patriotic. Mr. Fox however, supported by the favor of the king, the patronage of the duke of Cumberland, and the undivided interest of the Pelhams, was able to secure a triumphant majority: and the treaties with Russia and Hesse Cassel, though strongly and obstinately opposed, were ratified in a house consisting of four hundred and forty-eight members, by three hundred and twenty against one hundred and twenty eight. This great majority could not, however, disguise the impolicy and imbecility of the conduct of the premier, who, perplexed by all the fears and jealousies incident to a weak yet aspiring mind, had neither dared, at the demise of Mr. Pelham, to enter into a confidential connection with Mr. Pitt and Mr. Fox, the only men in the house of commons by whom he could be effectually supported, nor entirely to break with them. On his assuming, therefore, the direction of the treasury, the seals of his department as secretary were indeed offered to Mr. Fox, but in a mode and under conditions which Mr. Fox thought too degrading to accept—Mr. Pitt being, at the same time, amused with artificial professions and assurances of regard *signifying nothing*. On the resignation of Sir Thomas Robinson, whose utter inability to elevate himself

self into the rank of a rival to the duke was his grand recommendation to the high office he held, the seals were given to Mr. Fox on his own terms, and his grace was reduced to the necessity of *soliciting* a favor, when he had it in his power to have *conferred* one*. In the midst

---

* In an official conference between the duke of Newcastle and Mr. Pitt, his grace mentioning the American expedition on the Ohio, Mr. Pitt said, " Your grace knows that I have no capacity for these things ; and I do therefore desire to be informed about them." In the summer of 1755, changes being in contemplation, advances were made to Mr. Pitt ; and the lord chancellor, on the part of the duke of Newcastle, told him, that although the king had taken disagreeable prejudices, and was very fond of lord Holderness and Sir Thomas Robinson; in case any accident should take place, if he would assist them cordially, it might perhaps happen, that they might procure the seals for him, *which he so much desired*." Mr. Pitt repeating the last words of the chancellor, asked, " Of whom ? He did not remember he had ever applied to his lordship for them ; he was sure he never had to the duke of Newcastle ; and he assured the chancellor that, if they could prevail upon his majesty to give them to him under present circumstances, all the use he would make of them would be to lay them at his majesty's feet. If he asked for any favor, it would be that they should inform his majesty better. To enable him, or any one else, to conduct the business of the nation in the house of commons, they must give him proper distinction and powers ; he said the duke's system would not do, and, while he had life and breath to utter, he would oppose it. There must be men of efficiency and authority in the house, who should have access to the crown, habitual, frequent, familiar access, that they might be able to speak and act with effect, to do themselves and their friends JUSTICE, and not be the victims of a WHISPER."

Lord Melcombe.

Some years previous to this period, on occasion of a petition presented to the house of commons, relative to a contested election for the borough of Seaford, in which the duke of Newcastle had too grossly and publicly interfered, Mr. Potter, son of Abp. Potter, the successor of Dr. Wake in the metropolitan see of Canterbury, a young man whose talents and accomplishments would have rendered him, could he have relinquished the monstrous ambition " to shine a TULLY and a WILMOT too," the ornament of his country—declared, in the debate which arose,

midst of these political contentions, intelligence arrived of a disaster which excited the most vivid emotions of grief and compassion amongst all ranks and orders of persons throughout the nation. This was no other than the almost total destruction of the city of Lisbon by a tremendous earthquake, on the first of November *. The two principal shocks, which were not of the *horizontal*, but *vorticose* species, continued near a quarter of an hour, and they were immediately followed by a most extraordinary rise and inundation of the Tagus. A vast number of churches, monasteries, and other public buildings, and many thousand private houses, were, in the space of a few minutes, thrown down—the earth heaving, rocking, and, in many parts, rending asunder, with incredible noise and violence, vast volumes of mingled smoke and flame issuing from the apertures. And this superb city, after the final cessation of the concussions, presented to the view of the astonished spectator only an heap of ruins. The royal

arose, " that, if ever the annals of those times were delivered down to posterity by a faithful historian, he would have a new portrait to draw—of a minister the most incapable though the most ambitious, the weakest though the most insolent, the most pusillanimous though the most presumptuous." Mr. Pelham, upon this, rose up to call to order, saying, " that, though no person had been as yet actually named, this character must be intended for somebody; and cautioning this youthful speaker, if he thought proper to mention any name, to be prepared to prove what he should assert." Mr. Potter replied, " that he was happy to find he had as yet been guilty of no irregularity, and that even the apprehension of it was groundless; for it was not within his intention to mention any individual. He did not think himself so ill a painter as to make it necessary for him to write the names of those to whom his portraits belonged." It would, however, be injustice not to allow the duke of Newcastle the merit of disinterestedness as to the emoluments of office, and of zeal for the general interests of his country.

* 1755.

family were compelled to leave the palace with precipitation, and to retire into the neighboring fields for safety; and ten thousand of the inhabitants, as it was computed, were killed by the fall of the buildings, or swallowed up in the chasms formed by the numerous and horrid dispartings of the earth. A message from the throne informed the two houses of this dreadful calamity; and, by an act of generosity and humanity which conferred the highest honor on the parliament and nation, the sum of one hundred thousand pounds was instantly and unanimously voted for the use of the distressed inhabitants of that metropolis; and supplies to this amount in corn, flour, rice, and other necessaries, were shipped without delay for Portugal, and proved a most welcome and seasonable relief. And his most faithful majesty expressed on this occasion, in terms of the warmest emotion, his grateful acknowledgements to the British crown and nation. Amidst the millions and millions expended for the purposes of devastation and destruction, a vote of this description seems as a paradise blooming in the wild.

Early in the year 1756, Mr. Fox, the new minister, received a letter from Mr. Rouillé, secretary of state for foreign affairs in France, expostulating, in the name of his sovereign, " upon the hostile instructions given by the king of England to general Braddock and admiral Boscawen, in direct contradiction to the amicable professions of the British court. He complained of the insult offered to the French flag in the capture of two ships of war, and of the depredations on the French commerce, without any previous declaration of war, in contempt of the law of nations. He demanded therefore, in the name of the king his master, full and entire satisfaction for this atrocious violation of the dignity of his crown, as well as a complete reparation for the injuries sustained by his people." To this peremptory requisition Mr. Fox replied

replied with firmness and spirit, "that the king of England would willingly consent to an equitable accommodation of differences, but would not comply with the demand of restitution as a preliminary condition, his Britannic majesty having taken no steps but such as the hostilities previously committed by the French, and a regard to his own honour, and the rights of his crown and people, rendered just and indispensable." War being now considered on both sides as virtually, though not actually declared, the French court issued an order to seize all British vessels in the French harbors, and began with great assiduity to repair the fortifications of Dunkirk. The naval preparations at Brest were prosecuted with unremitting diligence; a vast number of transports were collected in the different ports in the channel, and numerous bodies of land forces were seen moving from all parts towards the coasts of Normandy, Picardy, and Bretagne. About the close of March, the king sent a message to parliament, stating, "that he had received repeated and authentic advices that a design was actually formed by the French court for the invasion of Great Britain; that he had taken the proper precautions for putting the kingdom in a posture of defence; that, in order farther to strengthen himself, he had made a requisition of the Hessian troops which the Landgrave had, by the late treaty, agreed to furnish."— An address was immediately presented, thanking his majesty in warm terms for this seasonable and prudent requisition. And, in a few days, Mr. Fox, encouraged by the prevailing unanimity of the house, moved a second address, "beseeching his majesty that, for the more effectual defence of his kingdoms, and for the better security of the religion and liberties of his subjects, he would be graciously pleased to order twelve battalions of his electoral troops to be forthwith embarked for England." This also was carried by a very great majority, and, in the

the course of the ensuing month, these troops actually arrived. Such was the consternation excited throughout the kingdom by the idea of an invasion, that these measures of the minister were received with great and general applause; though it appeared, in the view of Europe at large, not less unaccountable than disgraceful, that England should, at the commencement of a foreign war, deem herself unequal to provide for her own internal safety; and should have recourse to the aid of foreign mercenaries for the protection of her laws and liberties, when none of the natural means of defence were wanting, when her naval force was confessedly far superior to that of the enemy, and her armies were not engaged, as formerly, in fighting Quixotic battles on the continent*. At the close of the session, the Speaker, Mr. Onslow, on presenting the money-bills for the royal assent, addressed the king in a speech replete with sentiments so just and constitutional, expressed in language so bold and animated, as to merit the most distinguished regard.— After specifying the extent, and remarking the liberality of the grants, exceeding those of any former period, he declared, "that the COMMONS of ENGLAND hoped the sword, so bravely drawn and so effectually supported, would be intrusted only in capable and honest hands: and that the naval strength of Great Britain will do service as much greater as it is exalted higher than ever before.— His majesty's faithful commons apprehended that the pre-

---

* Les François annoncèrent avec ostentation qu'ils se preparoient à faire de leur côté une descente en Angleterre. Ils répandirent des troupes le long des côtes de la Bretagne et de la Normandie: ils firent construire des bateaux plats pour transporter ces troupes, et assemblèrent quelques vaisseaux à Brest. Ces démonstrations épouvantèrent les Anglois; il y eut des momens où cette nation, qui passe pour si sage, se crut perdue. Le Roi George afin de la rassurer eut recours à des troupes Hanovriennes et Hessoises. *Oeuvres de Frederic II. tom. 2.*

sent

sent critical juncture convinces that alliances on the continent, as they are unnatural, so they must ever be prejudicial to the true interest of England; that there is no gratitude to be expected from, no dependence to be placed on such allies, who, supported as they have been by the blood and treasure of this kingdom, have taken the opportunity of the first prospect of present profit to break through every tie. Not discouraged, however, by the ingratitude of allies, or the ambition of enemies, they have with pleasure beheld the sword drawn to vindicate the national honor and interest—proud to let all the world see that England is able to fight her own battles, and to stand by her own natural strength. Though ever attached to his majesty's person, he declared, nevertheless, that there were circumstances existing at which nothing but their confidence in his majesty's justice, and love to his people, could hinder them from being most seriously alarmed. Subsidies to foreign princes, when already burdened with a debt scarce to be borne, cannot but be severely felt—an army of foreign troops, a thing UNPRECEDENTED, UNHEARD-OF, UNKNOWN, brought into England, cannot but alarm. Still they had reliance upon his majesty, and hoped that their burdens might be lightened, their fears removed, as soon as possible; and, in the mean time, that the sword of these FOREIGNERS should not be intrusted a MOMENT out of his own hand to any other person whatsoever." The unanimous approval of the principles and sentiments inculcated in this spirited address reflects certainly great honor on the house, and it is much to be regretted that they should ever have been induced, *in practice*, to deviate from them. This speech, however, discovers symptoms of democratic resolution, which, had the liberties of the country been openly invaded, would have displayed itself in a manner fatal to ministers, terrible to kings!

Whether

Whether the French ever seriously meditated a descent upon the English coast, remains, after all, extremely doubtful; and it appears highly probable, that the preparations which occasioned this universal alarm were designed chiefly, or solely, as a veil to disguise their real design of an attack upon the island of Minorca. And, while the attention of the English ministry and nation was superfluously occupied with the armaments of Brest and Dunkirk, it seemed entirely to escape their notice, that a formidable fleet was, at the very same time, equipping at Toulon; till at length its destination becoming notorious, a squadron very incompetent to the purposes of the expedition was detached to the mediterranean, under admiral Byng, an officer of whom the public knew little more than that he was the son of the gallant and heroic viscount Torrington. This armament, consisting of ten ships of the line, afterwards joined by two or three others, sailed from Spithead April 7, 1756, and, on the second of May, the admiral arrived at Gibraltar, where he was informed that the French fleet under M. de la Galissoniere, consisting of thirteen ships of the line and transports, on board of which were embarked fifteen thousand land forces, had sailed from Toulon on the tenth of April, with a view to a descent on the island of Minorca, and were now actually engaged in the siege of Fort St. Philip. On this intelligence, the admiral transmitted dispatches to England, written in a style of great apparent dejection, "lamenting that he was not sent out in time to prevent the landing of the French; complaining of the bad condition of the ships, and of the total deficiency which he found at Gibraltar of all the necessary requisites for careening and refitting. He signified his opinion of the impracticability of throwing any supply of troops into the fortress, and of the impolicy of attempting it, if feasible, as the siege could not be raised without the co-operation of a land-force,

and

and any reinforcement of men would confequently only increafe the number of prifoners, which muft ultimately fall into the hands of the enemy." This extraordinary letter being confidered by the miniftry as a virtual accufation of their negligence or incapacity, and as plainly ominous of the lofs of the place, they determined to convince the admiral that fuch language was not to be held with impunity. On approaching Minorca, the admiral defcried the Britifh colors ftill flying at the caftle of St. Philip's: and, at the fame time, the French fleet appearing to the fouth-eaft, he formed the line of battle, and, about two o'clock, threw out fignals to bear away two points from the wind and engage. Admiral Weft, who commanded the van divifion, perceiving the inconfiftency of the two orders, chofe to comply with the laft, and bore away with his divifion feven points from the wind, as abfolutely neceffary to bring the enemy to a clofe and regular engagement. Finding himfelf, however, not fuftained by his commander, he could not purfue the advantage he had gained without imminent danger of having his communication with the remainder of the fleet entirely cut off. When the commander was exhorted by his captain to bear down upon the enemy, in order to fupport the fhips of the van, admiral Byng coolly replied, that it was his determination to keep the line of battle entire; and that he would avoid the error of Admiral Matthews, who, in his engagement with the combined fleets of France and Spain off Toulon, had broke the line by his precipitation, and had expofed himfelf by his rafhnefs to a fire which he could not fuftain. Under color, therefore, of preferving the line of battle entire, in order to fight with the more advantage, it could fcarcely be affirmed that he fought at all—the diftance at which he engaged being fo great that he received only fome few fhots in his hull, and not a fingle man was killed or wounded on board the admiral's own fhip,

a noble

a noble second-rate of ninety guns. M. de la Galissoniere was well pleased to perceive the British commander so little in earnest, and, having no urgent reasons on his part to wish for a continuance of the fight, he bore away under an easy sail towards evening; and, though the British admiral made the signal for chasing, it so happened that the French were not overtaken, and, next morning, they were entirely out of sight. On inquiry into the condition of the fleet after this engagement, it was found, that three of the principal ships were so much damaged in their masts, that they could not keep the sea with safety, that about two hundred men were killed and wounded in the engagement, and many others disabled by sickness. The admiral represented to a council of war, held on the occasion, that his squadron was much inferior to the enemy in weight of metal and number of men; and that they had also the advantage of sending their sick and wounded to Minorca, from whence they received continual supplies and reinforcements; that, in his opinion, it was impracticable to relieve the castle of St. Philip; and that they ought, therefore, to make the best of their way back to Gibraltar, to refit and wait for farther orders from England. The despondency of a commander is ever contagious; and, though no effort whatever had been made to accomplish the object of their destination, the council concurred unanimously in these sentiments, and the fleet immediately set sail for Gibraltar, the French returning to their former station off Mahon.

When the official dispatches of the admiral arrived in England, the ministry, fully prepared for intelligence of this nature, and presuming that the sequel of the history would correspond with the prelude, commissioned, without delay, admirals Hawke and Saunders to take the command in the Mediterranean; and, at the same time, orders were given to send home admiral Byng in arrest;

arreſt; and, on his arrival in England, he was committed cloſe priſoner to Greenwich hoſpital.

Notwithſtanding that the garriſon of St Philip had reaſon to conſider themſelves as abandoned to their fate, a very gallant defence was made by general Blakeney, the Governor, from the middle of April to the beginning of July; when no intelligence being received from England, and no proſpect of relief diſcernible, the works, and even the body of the caſtle being much ſhattered, the embraſures and parapets demoliſhed, many cannon diſmounted, and a lodgment actually made by the enemy on one of the principal redoubts, the garriſon alſo being exhauſted with hard and inceſſant duty, it was reſolved to beat the *chamade*, and a very favorable capitulation was granted by the Duc de Richelieu, the French commander, the garriſon being permitted to march out with all the honors of war, and with the liberty of a free and unmoleſted conveyance to Gibraltar. In a few days after the ſurrender of the iſland, admiral Hawke appeared in view, with a fleet much ſuperior to that of the French; but M. de la Galiſſoniere had ſeaſonably retired: and the Engliſh admiral ſeeing the French colors flying on the caſtle of St. Philip, this gallant officer found every effort precluded; and indeed, had he arrived previous to the ſurrender, there was little probability of his being able even by an abſolute defeat of the French ſquadron, to effect its relief.

This conqueſt was celebrated in France with great triumph and rejoicings; while, in England, it produced a degree of depreſſion much more than proportionate to the real magnitude and importance of the loſs ſuſtained. This depreſſion was accompanied with a prevailing emotion of reſentment, and even of rage, againſt the unfortunate admiral Byng, which could ſcarcely have been exceeded had he, by his criminal miſconduct, ſacrificed

crificed half the navy of Great Britain. In the enfuing feffion of parliament, an inquiry was inftituted in the houfe of commons into the caufes of the lofs of the ifland of Minorca; and the houfe having addreffed his majefty for copies of all letters and inftructions relative to this fubject, fuch a prodigious mafs of papers was produced as feemed rather calculated to overwhelm and ftifle, than to explain and elucidate the object of this inveftigation. After a loofe and curfory examination of thefe *documents*, which it would have been the bufinefs of a feffion to methodife and digeft, the houfe refolved, " 1. That from the intelligence repeatedly received by his majefty's minifters, there was juft reafon to believe that an invafion of Great Britain or Ireland was actually intended by the French king; and, 2. That no greater number of fhips of war could, with fafety to his majefty's dominions and the intereft of his fubjects, be fent to the Mediterranean than were actually fent thither under the command of admiral Byng." Thefe refolutions were evidently dictated by the fpirit of refentment or prejudice, and feemed conftructed folely for the exculpation of the minifters: though it ftill appeared abfolutely incomprehenfible to all impartial cenfors that, with more than one hundred and fifty fhips of war in commiffion, fo fmall a force only could be fpared for fo great a fervice. It is certain that Mr. Fox was defirous to have detached a ftrong fquadron to the Mediterranean the firft week in March, but could not prevail over the fears of the duke of Newcaftle, and the prefumption of lord Anfon, who affured him that Byng's fquadron would beat any thing that the French had or could have in the Mediterranean. After the lofs of the ifland, the duke of Newcaftle eagerly affirmed to Mr. Fox, " that no blame could reft, or be thought to reft, upon him; that the fea was not his province; and that the nation and the houfe of commons

mons were well satisfied with his conduct." Mr. Fox replied, that those who had the chief direction in an administration would bear the greatest share of the blame; and that those people deceived him who told him it was otherwise *now*. He had, indeed, defended his grace in the house of commons in every thing where he could defend him, but in one thing he never could, which was in his not believing it must be war, and in not arming sooner *."

The clamors of the people for justice still continuing, the trial of admiral Byng commenced December 28, 1756, before a court-martial held on board the ship St. George, in the harbor of Portsmouth. And, after a long investigation of evidence, the court determined that the admiral, during the engagement on the 20th of May last, did not do his utmost endeavor to take, seize, and destroy the ships of the French king; and that he did not exert his utmost power for the relief of the castle of St. Philip—they, therefore, unanimously agreed, " that he fell under the letter of the twelfth article of the Naval Code, which, for this offence, positively prescribes *death*, without any alternative left to the discretion of the court. But, believing his misconduct to arise neither from cowardice nor disaffection, they earnestly recommended him as a proper object of mercy." The admiral heard his doom pronounced without the least alteration of countenance or feature; and, with a low obeisance to the court, retired in dignified silence. Great interest was made from various quarters to obtain a remission of the sentence, but without effect; and a warrant was issued by the lords of the admiralty for the execution of the admiral on the fourteenth of March 1757. During this interval he re-

---

* Lord Melcombe.

mained

mained on board the Monarque in cuftody of the marfhal of the admiralty, and was at no time perceived to lofe his compofure or cheerfulnefs. About noon on the day appointed, the admiral, having taken the laft farewel of his friends, advanced with a firm ftep and ferene afpect from the great cabin to the quarter-deck, where a guard of marines awaited to execute the fentence; and kneeling, without any paufe or delay, on a cufhion provided for the purpofe, he tied with his own hands a white handkerchief over his eyes, and immediately dropped another as a fignal for the executioners, and five balls paffed inftantly through his body—the whole of this ftriking fcene, from his leaving the cabin, being over, and the admiral depofited on his bier, in the fpace of about three minutes. On a general review of this melancholy cataftrophe, and of the caufes by which it was produced, the fate of admiral Byng muft be pronounced beyond all example fevere and rigorous. Deftined to execute a commiffion hopelefs and impracticable, or at leaft not to be effected without the moft defperate efforts of courage, he fuffered his mind to be too ftrongly impreffed with the difficulties of his fituation; and though poffeffed, probably, of a degree of calm refolution which would have fecured his character from imputation upon occafions which required no extraordinary exertion, he was doubtlefs totally and conftitutionally incapable of that heroic and ardent enthufiafm which kindles at the view of danger, which is inflamed with the thirft of glory, and which, if it cannot command fuccefs, is at leaft ambitious to convince the world that it has left nothing uneffayed in order to deferve it. Firmly perfuaded that the object of his enterprife was unattainable, this officer appears to have funk under his accumulated embarraffments, and appeared to his friends perhaps, on a retrofpective view of this tranfaction, to

fall

fall as much below the usual level of his character, as it was necessary, in such circumstances, to rise above it. The fortitude of his conduct during the trial, and previous to the execution, sufficiently rescue his memory from the vile and indelible taint of cowardice: and, in a paper which he delivered immediately before his death to the marshal of the admiralty, he declares the satisfaction he felt in the consciousness of having faithfully discharged his duty to the utmost of his judgment and ability; and he styles himself, not without some appearance of reason, "a victim destined to divert the indignation and resentment of an injured and deluded people."

Notwithstanding the sacrifice of this victim, the nation exhibited symptoms of the highest dissatisfaction at the conduct of the administration under whose guidance and government nothing but disgraces and disasters had happened. The prospect of a German war for the protection of Hanover was odious to the majority of the people; the defeat of Braddock, and the subsequent losses in America, were the subject of equal astonishment and indignation; and the recent capture of Minorca threw the kingdom into a paroxysm of rage, as the apprehension of an invasion had before done into that of terror. And though the ministry, in calling in the assistance of the Hessian and Hanoverian auxiliaries, had acted with the general approbation, and even applause, their conduct, now the danger had passed over, was stigmatized as the effect of a ridiculous and reproachful timidity, if not rather of absolute treachery. It was suggested that the kingdom had been left purposely unprovided, and that the natives of south Britain had been formerly subdued by auxiliaries of the same country, hired, like these, for their defence and protection. And the public suspicion and hatred of these foreign mercenaries rose to such an height, that the modest, orderly, and

and inoffenſive behaviour only, by which they were diſtinguiſhed, could, we are aſſured, have ſecured them from acts of outrage. War had been declared in form by Great Britain againſt France in May 1756, and, in the following month, by France againſt Great Britain: and much pains were taken in the manifeſto publiſhed by the latter, to contraſt the moderation and equity of the court of Verſailles with the intemperate violence of the court of London, and particularly ſtigmatizing the ſeizures of the French ſhips of war and commerce, before a declaration of war, as piracy and perfidy. And it muſt be acknowledged, that no very ſolid or ſatisfactory reaſon has been aſſigned for delaying the declaration on the part of England, when hoſtilities were not only reſolved upon but actually commenced. The duke of Newcaſtle and Mr. Fox, now at the head of the adminiſtration, finding the tide of popularity and opinion ſet ſtrongly againſt them, dreaded with reaſon the approaching meeting of parliament, and determined, by a timely reſignation, to avert the diſgrace and danger attending a compulſive diſmiſſion. In November 1756, Mr. Pitt was appointed principal ſecretary of ſtate; Mr. Legge reinſtated in his poſt of chancellor of the Exchequer, which had been occupied during his ſeceſſion by Sir George, afterwards lord Lyttelton; and the duke of Devonſhire was nominated to the high office of firſt lord commiſſioner of the treaſury. On the ſecond of December the ſeſſion was opened by a very animated ſpeech from the throne, in which his majeſty expreſſed his confidence " that the union, fortitude, and affection of his people would, under the guidance of the divine providence, enable him to ſurmount every difficulty, and vindicate the dignity of his crown againſt the ancient enemy of Great Britain. He declared, that the recent loſſes in America demanded reſolutions of vigor and diſpatch; and that he had nothing ſo much at heart to remove all grounds of diffatisfaction from his people: for this end, he had remanded the foreign troops which had been brought hither at the defire of parliament; and recommended the framing of a national militia, relying with pleafure on the fpirit and zeal of his people in defence of his perfon and realm. He took notice of the unnatural union of counfels abroad, threatening the fubverfion of the empire, and of the *proteftant intereft* on the Continent; concluding with profeffions of his unwearied care and unceafing endeavors to promote the glory and happinefs of his people." Soon after the commencement of the feffion, Mr. Pitt, now regarded as firft minifter, delivered to the houfe a meffage from the king, importing, that as the formidable preparations and vindictive defigns of France were evidently bent againft his majefty's electoral dominions, and the territories of his *good ally* the king of Pruffia, his majefty confided in the zeal and affection of his faithful commons to affift him in forming and maintaining an army of obfervation for the juft and neceffary defence of the fame, and to enable him to fulfil his engagements with his Pruffian majefty, for the fecurity of the empire, and the fupport of their common interefts." Notwithftanding the great popularity of the prefent adminiftration, fuftained by the fuperior talents and general integrity of the minifters, there were not wanting thofe in the houfe of commons who forcibly urged the contraft between this recommendation, and the former eloquent reafonings and invectives of the minifter againft the whole fatal fyftem of Continental connection; the inexpreffible folly and madnefs of which appeared in the moft ftriking point of view at the prefent crifis, when, after all the millions expended, and the legions facrificed to the prefervation of a chimerical balance of power, with which the fafety of England

England was supposed, or pretended, to be connected, we were left destitute of an ally, excepting a prince so embarrassed in his own affairs, that, far from being able to grant assistance to us, he would certainly need to be supported by us. England, they asserted, was under no obligation, either of interest or duty, to exhaust her treasure and her blood in the defence of Hanover. That electorate was sufficiently secured in common with the other electorates, principalities, and co-estates, of the Germanic body, by the constitutions of the empire. It was not imagined, that the princes of the empire, or even that Austria itself, notwithstanding her recent and forced alliance with France, would suffer so formidable a power to acquire a permanent establishment in Germany; that, if any reluctance appeared to engage in the defence of a cause in which they had an immediate and common interest, it arose entirely from the firmness of their persuasion, that the interposition of England would render all interference on their part superfluous. It was boldly affirmed, that the whole of the public debt contracted since the accession of the house of Hanover, was incurred in pursuance of measures totally foreign to the interests of these kingdoms: and that if Hanover must at all events become the object of the solicitude of Great Britain, it would be infinitely better that France should be allowed to acquire and retain peaceable possession of the electorate during the continuance of the war, and to indemnify the inhabitants for the losses and sufferings which they might incur at the conclusion of it, than to maintain vast armies at an immense expence for its defence and security, of which, after all, it remained extremely problematic whether we were equal to the accomplishment." The message, nevertheless, was received by the house with loyal approbation, and the supplies granted to the utmost extent demanded by the minister. It was, however,

strongly

strongly suspected, that the measure thus coldly recommended, or rather stated to the house, had been previously objected against in the cabinet; and, in a short time, it could no longer be concealed that the new administration was agitated by a great internal convulsion; and that the favorite project of the king for strengthening the army in Germany with large reinforcements of troops from England was not assented to by the patriot ministers Mr. Pitt and Mr. Legge. His majesty, irritated by the pertinacity of their opposition, at length resolved upon an effort to relieve himself from this unwelcome and imperious control; and, in April 1757, Mr. Pitt and Mr. Legge were suddenly dismissed from their offices; the chancellorship of the Exchequer being consigned, *pro tempore*, to the chief justice of England. And Mr. Fox, again destined to take the lead in affairs, and invested with full and unlimited powers, had made proposals to his former coadjutor, the duke of Newcastle, to resume his station at the head of the treasury. But his grace, doubting the stability of the new arrangement, thought it expedient to demur; and, in the mean time, commenced a secret negotiation with the ex-ministers, and, after an interregnum of some weeks agitated by the violence of political conflict and cabal, joined them openly with all his powerful connections. The alarm of the nation at the dismission of Mr. Pitt and Mr. Legge is scarcely conceivable. Numberless addresses from all parts were presented to his majesty, beseeching him to reinstate these ministers in their employments. The principal cities and corporations in the kingdom presented them with the freedom of their respective guilds in golden boxes. Party spirit seemed to be extinguished; for all voices, without one dissonant murmur, were now united in their praise. Mr. Fox, perceiving it impossible to stem the torrent, wisely counselled the monarch to yield, without resistance, to

the

the wishes of the people. And, in June, Mr. Pitt resumed the seals of secretary of state; Mr. Legge and the duke of Newcastle their former stations at the board of treasury; lord Anson was placed at the head of the admiralty; Sir Robert Henley appointed keeper of the Great Seal in the room of lord Hardwicke; and Mr. Fox himself, acceding to the new order of things, was gratified with the lucrative office of paymaster-general of the army *. In consequence of this general coalition of parties, all opposition in parliament seemed annihilated, and Mr. Pitt, to whom the entire direction of the war was now entrusted, had free and full scope to exert his utmost ability in the service of his country. The events, however, which marked the commencement of his administration were by no means fortunate. A formidable armament, equipped with incredible diligence, sailed from the harbor of Portsmouth the beginning of September, consisting of eighteen ships of the line, and a large

---

* "Public matters, says lord Chesterfield in a letter to his friend Mr. Dayrolles, February 1757, have been, and are still, too undecypherable for me to understand, consequently to relate Fox, out of place, taking the lead in the house of commons; Pitt, secretary of state, declares that he is no minister, and has no ministerial influence. The duke of Newcastle and lord Hardwicke lie by and declare themselves for neither party.—April 1757, Our public situation is now perhaps, more ridiculous and unaccountable than ever. Two posts which were once thought considerable ones, which used to be solicited by many, and wished for by more, I mean those of secretary of state and chancellor of the Exchequer, have been proffered about to a degree of profusion, and yet refused. The late possessors of them were most imprudently turned out before the end of the session, and are thereby become not only the most, but, perhaps, the only two, popular men now in this kingdom.—July 1757, after many negotiations, breakings off, and recommencements, things are at last fixed. About three weeks ago, Fox was in a manner declared minister, to the exclusion

a large body of land forces, under the command of Sir Edward Hawke and Sir John Mordaunt. When Mr. Pitt ordered the fleet to be equipped, and appointed the period for its being at the place of rendezvous, lord Anson said it was impossible to comply with the requisition: but Mr. Pitt, with great warmth, replied, "That it might be done; and, if the ships were not ready at the time specified, he should signify his neglect to the king, and *impeach* his lordship in the house of commons." The menace produced its effect, and on the twenty-third of the same month, the fleet anchored off the river Charente with a view to attempt the reduction of the city of Rochefort. Many days passed in sounding the river, in reconnoitring the coasts, in removing the troops from the transports to the boats, and the boats to the transports; and in deliberations upon the intent and practicability of the instructions under which they were to act. At length it was concluded to *risque an attack* upon the isle of Aix, situated in the mouth of the Charente, and defended by a small fort and garrison; and this service, equal in importance to that of picking up shells on the shore, being performed, and the works demolished, a council of war was held, in which it was resolved, agreeably to that spirit of *quietism* by which it

sion of the duke of Newcastle and Pitt, and the seals of the chancellorship of the Exchequer were to have been given to him the next day. Upon this Holderness resigned; the duke of Rutland, and some others, declared their intentions of following his example, and many refused the places that were offered them by Fox as the first minister for those two or three days. Upon these discouragements, Fox went to the king, and told him, that it was impossible for him, in such a situation, to undertake the management of affairs. The king hereupon, though very unwillingly, sent for the duke of Newcastle again; and at last, after a thousand difficulties, things are as you have seen in the papers."
— *Lord Chesterfield's Miscellaneous Works.*

has been obferved that councils of war are in general diftinguifhed*, to return without delay to England. Great expectations having been entertained of the event of this expedition, the nation was proportionably difappointed, and enraged at its failure: and the public cenfure was directed chiefly, if not folely, againft the general, it being admitted that the minifter had left nothing undone to enfure the fuccefs of it, and that the admiral had acted in no refpect inconfiftently with his high character for judgment and fpirit. It was faid that the inactivity and timidity of Sir John Mordaunt were lefs pardonable than the rafhnefs and prefumption of general Braddock, who, if he failed to attain his object, had at leaft fuftained the national reputation by his courage; and fo high did the clamor arife, that it was thought neceffary to inftitute a court-martial for the trial of this commander, by whom he was, to the amazement of the public, unanimoufly acquitted: and the fentence was univerfally contrafted with that of the former court, which had condemned an admiral to death for not doing his *utmoft*; whereas a general was now acquitted, though it was univerfally acknowledged that he had done *nothing*. But the failure of the enterprife againft Rochefort, however it might excite the chagrin of the public, was of little eftimation or importance in the view of the court, when compared with the difafters which had befallen the army of obfervation in Germany. Early in the fpring (1757) his royal highnefs the duke of Cumberland had embarked for Hanover, in or-

---

* Lord Clive declared to the parliamentary committee of enquiry, inftituted A. D. 1773, " that he never called a council of war but once, which was previous to his paffing the Ganges on his famous expedition to Moorfhedabad; and, if he had then followed the decifion of the council, the company had been undone."

der to take upon him the command of the confederate troops, now, in consequence of the recent junction of the Prussians, amounting to about fifty thousand men. Marefchal d'Etrees, the French commander, an officer of great ability, advancing from the banks of the Rhine, the passage of which the king of Prussia in vain urged the duke to defend, the confederate army was compelled to retire beyond the Wefer: and the French general having passed this river also without opposition, attacked the duke in his camp at Haftenbeck, July 25; and, while the battle was yet doubtful, the English commander, from a defect, not of courage, but of military skill and judgment, is charged with giving orders for founding a retreat. A redoubt in centre of the allied army having been carried by the French, it was instantly retaken, sword in hand, by the hereditary prince of Brunswick, " who by this *coup d'essai* discovered, says the king of Prussia, that nature had destined him for a hero." The duke being still pressed by the French army, retreated first to Nienburg, then to Verden, and at length to Stade. The marefchal d'Etrees, regarding with a watchful and penetrating eye the motions of the duke, when urged to embrace a favorable moment of attack, replied that there was no occasion for fighting. And, in fact, his royal highness was quickly reduced, as the marefchal foresaw, to a most distressing dilemma. In front his farther march was arrested by the German ocean; on the right and left he was inclosed by the rivers Elbe and Wefer; and the French having taken possession of the passes as the confederate army receded, the duke had no option remaining but to submit to terms of capitulation, which were signed, under the mediation of Denmark, in the month of September (1757), at Cloifter-Seven, by which the electorate of Hanover was left in the hands of the French; and the whole confederate army, amounting to about forty thousand

Hessians,

Hessians, Hanoverians, and Brunswickers, were disarmed and disbanded—the king of Prussia having previously withdrawn his troops, from the apprehension of this catastrophe. On his return to England, the duke of Cumberland not receiving those marks of gratitude and acknowledgment which he thought due to his eminent services, resigned all his military employments in high disgust, and henceforth took no farther public part in any civil or military transaction. The inglorious convention of Cloister-Seven seemed as it were the crisis of the war; and England was now reduced to that extreme point of depression from which she was destined, in gradual retrocession, to attain to a height of elevation unknown to the most brilliant æras of her former history.

After the unsuccessful campaign of 1757 in America, the earl of Loudon returned to England, leaving the chief command in the hands of general Abercrombie, from whom it quickly devolved to major-general, now lord Amherst, who, on the arrival of admiral Boscawen from England, early in the year 1758, with very powerful reinforcements, concerted with general Abercrombie a plan of spirited and active operations for the ensuing campaign. The troops now assembled, both regulars and provincials, amounted to no less than fifty thousand men, a military force to which the new world had seen nothing comparable; and much too great to be employed on any single object. The garrison of Louisburg being greatly reduced in consequence of the perfect security it was supposed to enjoy after the abandonment of the expedition of the last summer, it was resolved to renew the attempt. And general Amherst, with twelve thousand men, being convoyed by the fleet under admiral Boscawen, anchored June 2, in sight of the fortress, which in a few days was formally invested. The approaches were made with great skill and circumspection;

tion; and the Chevalier Drucourt, the governor, seeing no prospect of relief, assented to a capitulation on the twenty-seventh of July. Exclusive of the city of Louisburg and the whole island of Cape Breton, six ships of the line and five frigates, which were stationed in the harbor for the protection of the place, were either destroyed or taken by the English. General Abercrombie himself undertook, at the head of a still greater force, to reduce the French forts on the lakes George and Champlain. The first attempted was Ticonderago; a fortress which commands the communication between the two lakes, surrounded on three sides with water, and, in front, secured by a morass, and farther defended, upon this emergency, with a breast-work, entrenchments, and *abbatis*. The general, however, determined upon an assault; but met with a severe repulse, and was compelled to retreat with the loss of one thousand eight hundred men; with which disaster he was so much dispirited, that he immediately reimbarked his troops, though still much superior in force to the enemy, and returned to the camp at Lake George, from whence he had taken his departure.

An event still the subject of tender recollection and regret in America, took place on this occasion in the death of lord Howe, a young nobleman who combined the most amiable manners with the most shining talents and the most heroic courage. His memory was honored by a vote of the assembly of Massachusetts for the erection of a superb cenotaph, at the expence of the province, amongst the heroes and patriots of Britain, in the collegiate church of Westminster.

A considerable corps, however, detached by general Abercrombie, under colonel Bradstreet, against Fort Frontenac, situated on the northern bank of the river St. Laurence, at the precise point of its departure from Lake Ontario, reduced this important post with little loss.

loss. And Brigadier Forbes, who was destined to command the expedition against Fort du Quesne, on the Ohio, finding it, on his arrival, dismantled and abandoned, immediately repaired and garrisoned the fort, changing its name, in compliment to the minister, to Pittsburgh. And, in October, peace was established by a formal treaty between Great Britain and the Indian nations inhabiting the rich and fertile plains between the Lakes and the Ohio. At the grand conference which preceded this treaty, the following oration, not unworthy of historic notice, was addressed to the English commissioners by one of the Sachems, delegated to conduct this negotiation on the part of the Indians:

"Brethren—I have raised my voice, and all the Indians have heard me as far as the Twightwees, and have regarded my voice, and are now come to this place. Brethren, the cause why the Indians of Ohio left you was owing to yourselves. The governor of Virginia settled in our lands, and disregarded our messages: but, when the French came to us, they traded with our people, used them kindly, and gained their affections. Our cousins the Minisinks tell us, they were wronged of a great deal of land, and pushed back by the English, settling so fast upon them as not to know whether they have any lands remaining in surety. You deal hardly with us; you claim all the wild animals of the forests, and will not let us come on your lands so much as to hunt after them; you will not let us peel the bark of a single tree to cover our cabins—surely this is hard! Our fathers, when they sold the land, did not purpose to deprive themselves of hunting the wild deer, or using a branch of wood. Brethren, we have already acquainted you with our grievances; and we have referred our cause to the great king. I desire to know if king GEORGE has yet decided this matter, and whether justice will be done to the Minisinks?"

Governor

Governor Bernard, in return, assured them that full satisfaction should be given to the Minisinks; and governor Denny, delivering to the chief a belt and string of *wampum*, declared " the ancient union of the British and Indian nations to be renewed and confirmed, and that fresh earth was put to the roots of the tree of peace, in order that it may bear up against every storm, and flourish as long as the sun shines, and the rivers continue to flow."

These events sufficiently indicated that the fortune of the war had at length changed, and the French, who had been hitherto the assailants, now saw the necessity of concentrating their force, in order to defend themselves from future attack and invasion. General Amherst, who possessed in an high degree the spirit of military enterprise, had, on assuming the chief command, formed a project, which would doubtless have appeared romantic and impracticable to his predecessors, for the entire conquest of Canada in one campaign.

For the accomplishment of this grand scheme, Brigadier-general Wolfe, an officer who had distinguished himself, in a very remarkable manner, at the late siege of Louisburg, was directed, as soon as the navigation of the St. Laurence should be clear of ice, to proceed with a strong squadron of ships of war, and a large body of land forces, to undertake the siege of Quebec, the capital of French America. General Amherst, in person, proposed, with the principal army, to reduce the forts of Ticonderago and Crown Point; to cross the lake Champlain, and, marching along the river Richelieu, and the southern banks of the St. Laurence, to join general Wolfe under the walls of Quebec. Lastly, Brigadier-general Prideaux, with another separate corps, reinforced by a numerous body of Indians, assembled and conducted by the influence and authority of Sir William

William Johnson, was deſtined to inveſt the important poſt and fortreſs of Niagara, which commanded the navigation of the lakes, and the communication of the rivers St. Laurence and Miſſiſippi. After the reduction of Niagara, the forces were ordered to be embarked on the Lake Ontario, and, proceeding down the river St. Laurence, to undertake the ſiege of Montreal, the ſecond city of Canada, and then to join the grand army before Quebec. It is ſcarcely to be imagined that ſo magnificent and daring a project ſhould, in the execution, prove completely ſuccefsful in all its parts. It was however doubtleſs the conception of a great military genius; and the final reſult of this plan forms the higheſt eulogium which can be beſtowed upon it.

General Amherſt, in the month of July, arrived at Ticonderago, which at firſt the enemy ſeemed preparing reſolutely to defend: but, in the night of the 27th, they ſuddenly and unaccountably abandoned this ſtrong and hitherto impregnable poſt, and retired to Crown Point. The general, after giving the neceſſary orders for the ſecurity of the fortreſs, embarked with the army, and reached Crown Point on the 4th of Auguſt; but by this time Crown Point alſo was evacuated, and the Engliſh commander was informed that the French had retired to the Iſle aux Noix, at the northern extremity of the lake Champlain, where they were reported to be encamped in force. The general, after making the moſt vigorous and indefatigable exertions to ſecure a naval ſuperiority on the lake, again embarked his troops, in order to proceed to the attack of Iſle aux Noix: but a continued ſucceſſion of ſtorms and tempeſts compelled him to deſiſt from the proſecution of his deſign, and he returned to Crown Point, in the vicinity of which he took up his winter-quarters, in order to facilitate the early commencement of the enſuing campaign. Here he had the ſatisfaction to learn that the expedition againſt Niagara had terminated happily; for though General Prideaux was unfortunately ſlain by the burſting of a ſhell in viſiting the trenches, general Johnſon, who ſucceeded to the command, after defeating a body of forces which attempted the relief of the fort, had become maſter of it by capitulation, July 25; the projected deſign againſt Montreal, in conſequence of various combining obſtacles, nevertheleſs remaining for the preſent ſuſpended.

But by far the moſt difficult and dangerous branch of the plan originally concerted, was allotted to general Wolfe, whoſe riſing talents and reputation now began to excite univerſal attention. On the 26th of June, the armament deſtined for the invaſion of Canada arrived at the iſland of Orleans, formed by the branches of the river St. Laurence, and extending to the baſon of Quebec. This metropolis is ſituated at the confluence of the rivers St. Laurence and St. Charles. The fortifications are ſtrong, and the city elegant and extenſive. It conſiſts of an upper and a lower town; the lower town is built upon the ſtrand, which ſtretches along the baſe of the lofty rock on which the upper town is ſituated. This rock continues with a bold and ſteep front far to the weſtward, parallel to the river St. Laurence. On this ſide, therefore, the city might well be deemed abſolutely inacceſſible. On the other, it was protected by the river St. Charles, the channel of which is rough and broken, and its borders interſected with ravines. On the left bank of this river the French army, amounting to about 10,000 men, under the command of M. de Montcalm, were poſted; the encampment extending to the river of Montmorenci to the eaſt, and their rear was covered with impenetrable woods.

The Engliſh general, perfectly ſenſible that unleſs the enemy could be brought to a deciſive engagement, his enterpriſe muſt prove abortive, reſolved,

after

after some feints, in vain made to induce his able and cautious antagonist to relinquish this advantageous post, to attack the French in their entrenchments, near the falls of Montmorenci. On the last day of July, dispositions being made for a general assault, the troops were landed under the cover of the cannon of the ships of war; but, notwithstanding the express orders given, not to march forward till the whole army was formed, the English grenadiers, rushing to the attack with irregular impetuosity, were soon thrown into confusion by the enemy's fire, and suffered very severely in their retreat. The general advancing in person with the remaining brigades, the fugitives formed again in the rear of the army; but the plan of attack was effectually disconcerted; and the English commander was compelled to give orders for repassing the river to the island of Orleans, which was effected not without considerable loss.

At this period the general transmitted dispatches to England, penned with remarkable perspicuity and elegance, but in a tone of depression which demonstrated a perfect sense of the embarrassments of his situation. " We have, said he, almost the whole force of Canada to oppose. In such a choice of difficulties I own myself at a loss how to determine. The affairs of Great Britain, I know, require the most vigorous measures; but the courage of a handful of brave men should be exerted only where there is some hope of a favorable event *."

* Though the *disappointment* of general Wolfe must have been inexpressibly great, at the failure of the concerted plan of co-operation on the part of general Amherst; yet it is highly pleasing to observe, that throughout this celebrated letter not a symptom is to be found of *dissatisfaction* at the conduct of that commander, whose utmost exertions general Wolfe was well assured would not be wanting to its accomplishment. The whole exhibits a picture of gloomy grandeur, of a mind revolving and meditating designs, of the temerity of which it is perfectly conscious.

The

The disaster of Montmorenci made a deep impression on the lofty and susceptible mind of the English general. He was observed often to sigh; and, to his intimate friends, he declared his determination to die rather than endure the censure and reproach which invariably attend the want of success. An effort transcendently bold, and approaching in other circumstances to rashness and desperation, yet remained to be tried. A plan was formed, in concert with the naval commander admiral Saunders, for landing the troops on the northern bank of the river, above the city, and, by scaling the heights hitherto supposed inaccessible, to gain possession of the grounds at the back of the town, where it was but slightly fortified. The admiral, in order to deceive the enemy, moved up the river several leagues beyond the spot fixed upon for the landing; but, during the night, he fell down with the stream, in order to protect the disembarkment of the troops, which was happily accomplished in secrecy and silence. The precipice now remained to be ascended; and, with infinite labor and difficulty, the troops sustaining themselves by the rugged projections of the rock, and the branches of the trees and plants which sprang from the innumerable clefts into which it was every-where broken, they at last attained the summit, and immediately formed in order of battle. The intelligence being quickly conveyed to M. de Montcalm that the English army was in actual possession of the heights of Abraham, that commander declared himself unable to express his astonishment, and immediately comprehended the necessity of risquing an engagement, in order to save the city.

Abandoning, therefore, his strong camp of Montmorenci, he passed the river St. Charles, and advanced to the attack of the English army, with great intrepidity. A very warm engagement ensued; and general Wolfe, who stood conspicuous in the front of the line, received

a shot

a shot in the wrist, which, wrapping a handkerchief around it, he seemed not to notice, and continued giving orders without the least emotion. But advancing at the head of the grenadiers, another ball pierced his breast, and compelled him to retire to a spot a little distant from the field of action, where he expressed the most eager anxiety to learn the fate of the battle. He was, after an interval of suspense, told that the enemy were visibly broken: and reclining, from extreme faintness, his head on the arm of an officer standing near him, he was in a short time aroused with the distant sound of They fly! they fly!—" Who fly?" exclaimed the dying hero— On being told "The French,"—" Then, said he, I depart content," and almost immediately expired in the arms of victory. A death more glorious, and attended with circumstances more picturesque and interesting, is no-where to be found in the annals of history. The death of Epaminondas only, to which that of Wolfe has frequently been compared, seems to dispute the præ-eminence *.

> * Sic certus hostes terga dare in fugam
> Thebanus Heros " extrahe telum" ait:
> Vultuque subridens amœno
> Magnam animam exhilaratus efflat.
>
> Ambo beati! Plaudite, milites,
> Morte invidendâ plaudite nobilem!
> Te rura, fortunate, et urbes,
> Te recinet nemus omne, WOLFI.

Vide CANADIA, an ode published in the year 1760, and fraught with all the beauties of elegant and classic composition. The glorious deaths of other heroes press at the same time upon the imagination—of a Bayard; a Sydney; a Gaston de Foix;—of a Gustavus Adolphus; and of Constantine the last emperor of the Greeks, which, though not adorned by the purple coloring of success, is perhaps beyond all others intrinsically illustrious.

The generals Monckton and Townshend, after the loss of their commander, continued the fight with unabating ardor; and M. de Montcalm, the French commander, receiving a mortal wound, the French gave way on all sides, and a most complete victory was gained, at a comparatively inconsiderable expence. The city of Quebec, struck with consternation at this event, almost immediately capitulated, though still provided with the means of a vigorous defence; and the shattered remains of the French army retired with precipitation to Montreal.

In England this intelligence, which very closely followed the former doubtful dispatches of the general, excited that delirium of joy which the return of national prosperity, after a long series of national disasters, is alone adequate to inspire. This was damped only by the death of the hero who had achieved the conquest; but so fascinating were the glories with which it was invironed, that in fact it rather heightened than diminished the exultation of the triumph.

General Murray, who had been appointed to the government of Quebec, took every precaution that prudence could suggest to secure and maintain this important possession. Nor were they found superfluous; for, early in the spring of the year 1760, the chevalier de Levis, who succeeded M. de Montcalm as commander of the French forces, assembled with great diligence, from all quarters, the troops remaining in Canada, and began his march from Montreal, in the month of April, hoping to recapture Quebec before the garrison could receive the expected succors from England. General Murray, though much inferior in numbers, took possession of an advantageous post in the vicinity of Quebec, and determined to risque an engagement, which, if it proved unsuccessful, would not prevent his retiring within the walls of the city, which he determined to defend to the last extremity.—

The

The great disparity of force soon decided the conflict in favor of the French, and the general retreated to Quebec, which was immediately invested by the French army. But on the intelligence that an English fleet destined for its relief was already in the gulph of St. Laurence, they raised the siege with great precipitation, leaving their provisions, stores, and artillery, in the hands of general Murray. And the marquis de Vandreuil, governor-general of Canada, now centered all his hopes in the defence of Montreal, which, in the expectation of an attack from general Amherst, he had strengthened with new fortifications, had recruited his army with new levies of troops, and had collected large magazines of military stores. The English commander, after detaching colonel Haviland with a strong force to besiege the post occupied by the French at Isle aux Noix, proceeded himself to the banks of the lake Ontario, where he embarked his troops, and crossing the lakes reduced the *Isle Royale*, commanding the entrance of the great river St. Laurence, the navigation of which, to the island of Montreal, is rendered extremely dangerous, by the number of rapids and falls. The general, however, arrived with his army at Montreal, the beginning of September, with inconsiderable loss; and in a short time he was joined by general Murray, who had received orders to co-operate with him on the side of Quebec. And colonel Haviland also, after the reduction of Isle aux Noix, had advanced with the forces under his command, to the south side of the river, opposite to Montreal. The marquis de Vandreuil perceiving himself completely invested, and despairing of relief, demanded a capitulation, which was granted upon very favorable terms. And thus the conquest of the province of Canada was finally completed—a conquest the most glorious and the most important ever achieved by the arms of Great Britain.

Uninterrupted

Uninterrupted prosperity also, during the same period, attended the operations of the war, on the part of England, in the other quarters of the globe. Early in the year 1758, a plan had been presented to the minister, by one Cumming, an African merchant, of the pacific sect of quakers, for the reduction of Fort Louis, on the river Senegal; which being examined and approved, a small squadron was equipped, under the command of captain Marsh, hoisting a broad pennant; Mr. Cumming embarking also on board the commodore's ship, as a promoter and director of the expedition. After dispersing some armed vessels, which opposed their entrance into the river, the fort and adjoining factory surrendered without a blow to the commodore; and Mr. Cumming defended his recommendation as perfectly consonant to his religious principles, affirming himself to have been previously persuaded that it would prove a bloodless conquest.

And in the latter end of this year, a successful attempt was made, under the conduct of commodore Keppel, with a more considerable force, upon the island of Goree, situated to the south of the Senegal. The island was defended by two small forts, and several batteries, mounted with more than one hundred pieces of cannon; but they were soon silenced by a furious cannonade from the ships of war. During the attack, the opposite shores were covered with multitudes of the natives, who expressed with loud clamor and uncouth gesticulations their astonishment at the terrible execution performed by the British squadron.

Nearly at the same time, a very powerful armament, with six regiments of infantry on board under the command of generals Hopson and Barrington, sailed from St. Helens, and being joined on their arrival in Carlisle Bay, in the island of Barbadoes, by a considerable additional force under commodore Moore, the united squadrons
proceeded

proceeded to Martinique; but finding this important island better prepared for its defence than was expected, they directed their course to Gaudaloupe, of which, after a long and obstinate resistance, they made themselves masters—the neighboring isles of Defeada and Marigalante surrendering also on capitulation. Notwithstanding the ill success of the expedition against Rochefort, the minister determined upon another attempt of the same nature; the execution of which was entrusted to commodore, now lord Howe, an officer of approved judgment and gallantry, who disembarking the troops, agreeably to his instructions, on the coast of Normandy, took possession of the town of Cherburg without opposition: and, after destroying the harbor and bason of that place, upon which much labor and much money had been expended, the fleet set sail for England; but, in a short time, it again weighed and stood to the southward; and the land forces, under general Bligh, disembarked under the cannon of the shipping, two leagues to the westward of St. Maloes, which they found, however, too strongly fortified to be carried by a *coup de main*. The general, therefore, determined to penetrate into the open country, and advanced, for what purpose is not easy to divine, to a considerable distance beyond the possibility of protection from the fleet. The unimportant operations of this predatory war soon received an alarming interruption from the intelligence that the Duc d'Aguillon, governor of Bretagne, was in full march, at the head of eighteen regular battalions and squadrons, to intercept their retreat. The general immediately began his march for the bay of St. Cas, where the English fleet lay at anchor: but, before he could complete the reimbarkation of his troops, the rear-guard, consisting of fifteen hundred men, was attacked by the French, and the far greater part of them killed or taken. The utility of expeditions of this nature, even when moſt ſucceſsful, ſeems very liable to queſtion; and the expence attending the preſent unfortunate attempt, in particular, was ſo great, and the damage ſuſtained by the enemy ſo trivial, that it was by ſome perſons inſolently ſtyled " a ſcheme to break windows with guineas."

In the enſuing ſummer (1759), admiral Rodney was detached with a ſquadron, under pretext of impeding the rendezvous of the tranſports collecting in its vicinity, to bombard the town of Havre de Grace, which was, at the firſt alarm, deſerted by the inhabitants, in great conſternation. Nineteen hundred ſhells, and eleven hundred carcaſes, were, it is ſaid, expended in this direful act of unavailing vengeance.

In the ſucceeding month of Auguſt, admiral Boſcawen, who now commanded in the Mediterranean, had, however, an opportunity of aſſerting the honor of the Britiſh flag in a manner much more effectual. M. de la Clue, endeavoring to paſs the ſtrait of Gibraltar with a conſiderable ſquadron, was intercepted by the Engliſh admiral off Cape Lagos; and, after a fierce conflict, the French admiral's own ſhip, the Ocean of eighty guns, and three other capital ſhips, ſtruck their colors to the Engliſh. This victory was ſoon ſucceeded by another of yet greater importance. Vaſt preparations had been, for ſome time paſt, making in the French ports in the channel, with a view, as was imagined, to a deſcent in ſome part of Great Britain or Ireland. And a powerful fleet was actually equipped in the harbor of Breſt, which was long prevented from putting to ſea by the vigilance of Sir Edward Hawke, who had, with a ſuperior force, blockaded that port during the greater part of the ſummer. At length, being driven from this ſtation by ſtreſs of weather, M. de Conflans, the French admiral, embraced the opportunity of weighing anchor from Breſt Water with an

armament

armament of twenty-one ships of the line. On the first intelligence of their departure, Sir Edward Hawke sailed in pursuit of them. As soon as the French admiral perceived the English fleet off Quiberon Bay, he retired close in shore, in order to avoid an engagement. The English commander, however, was not deterred by his knowledge of the coast, which is in this part rendered extremely dangerous by rocks, shoals, and quickfands, from following and attacking the enemy with the most undaunted resolution; the weather also was uncommonly tempestuous, the days much diminished in length, and the English admiral had to encounter the additional disadvantage of a lee shore. About three o'clock on the twentieth of November 1759 the battle began, and continued till the fleets were enveloped in darkness, which seasonably intervened to save the French fleet from total destruction. Two capital ships, the Superbe and Thesee, were sunk during the action; the Hero struck her colors, but no boat could be sent with safety to take possession; the Soleil Royal, the flag-ship of the French commander, was next day burnt by her own crew, to prevent her falling into the hands of the English; and two other ships of the line were also stranded and destroyed. The rest of the fleet, with much difficulty, sheltered themselves in the river Vilaine, where they were long blockaded, but at length found means to escape to Rochefort. This was a fatal blow to the French marine; and, after this defeat, the French court attempted no further naval expedition of moment. Very important advantages also were obtained in the latter years of the war by the British arms on the coast of India, of which it will now be necessary to offer a concise but distinct narration.

HINDOSTAN, that vast country, extending two thousand miles in length from the mountains of Tartary and Thibet on the north, to Cape Comorin, divided only by a narrow strait from the beautiful island of Ceylon, on the south, presents, among the various regions of the earth, a most conspicuous and interesting object of political and philosophical contemplation. The civilization of this immense peninsula may be traced back to an æra of the most remote antiquity. Learning and the arts, which have descended to the modern nations of Europe from the Romans and the Greeks, were indubitably transmitted or transferred to them from the Phœnicians and Egyptians; who, as there is great reason to believe, derived the radical principles of the knowledge which they possessed from the sages of Hindostan, with whom science and the arts seem to have originated. And it is very remarkable, that such as the inhabitants of Hindostan are described to have been two thousand years ago, such they still remain; and the established laws, institutions, customs, manners, and religion of India, have, in this long succession of ages, suffered neither any essential addition or diminution. Nothing, indeed, can be imagined more strongly calculated to perpetuate the system originally formed than the singular and remarkable division of this people into tribes, professions, or CASTES, separated by a superstition so rigorous, as to render it unlawful and profane even to eat or drink out of the same vessel, excepting on their solemn festivals in the same temple or pagoda, when joining in the same religious sacrifice. All the different tribes, the military *caste* only excepted, are required, under certain exemptions or indulgencies, to abstain from animal food; and the high and venerable *caste* of the Brahmans in particular, from whom more rigid examples of virtue are expected, touch nothing that has life, but subsist entirely upon milk, fruit, and vege-

vegetables *. The principles of their philofophy, as well as the myfteries of their religion, are contained in certain records of the moft obfcure and recondite antiquity, ftyled the *Veds* or *Vedams*, fuppofed to be of divinely-infpired origin, and written in the Sanfcrit language, which has long ceafed to be a living tongue, and is now underftood only by the learned Brahmans, whofe peculiar province and privilege it is to read and meditate thefe facred volumes. The Khatries, who rank next in dignity, are permitted to hear them read; but the inferior

---

* The principal *caftes* of India are, the Brahmans, or men of fcience, including the priefthood; the Khatries, or the military, and proprietors of land; the Bhyfe or Banian, comprehending the merchants and cultivators of the foil; and the Sooderahs, or mechanics and laborers, including the bulk of the people. But thefe are fubdivided into many others, all of which are kept religioufly diftinct. In the myftic language of the Vedams, the Brahmans are faid to be created from the mouth of Brimha, the Khatries from his arms, the Bhyfe from his body, and the Sooderahs from his feet. The Hallachores, ftyled, in the Sanfcrit, Chandalas, are the refufe and *outcafts* of all the different tribes; but the number of them is happily inconfiderable, as they are held in a kind of religious abhorrence; their very touch, or the flighteft accidental intercourfe with them, being accounted, even by the loweft Sooderah, an almoft indelible pollution. Alfo, fcattered throughout the immenfe regions of Hindoftan, are to be found multitudes of wandering devotees, or afcetics, known under the various appellations of Yoghees, Sonaffees, Faquiers, &c. &c. Deeply impreffed with the doctrine taught by the Brahman philofophy, that man's fupreme felicity confifts in a kind of intellectual apathy or abforption, thefe enthufiafts, with deplorable folly, inflict upon themfelves the moft rigorous and almoft incredible corporeal penances, vainly hoping, by this means, to affimilate and exalt their minds more nearly to the perfection of the divine nature, and to detach themfelves more effectually from that fyftem of matter which they are taught to contemn as bafe and vile. And fuch is the veneration in which this fpecies of voluntary martyrdom is held, that the profane and abject Chandala is not admitted to the enviable privilege of devoting himfelf to this facred profeffion.

tribes are restrained to the knowledge of the *Shastahs*, which are commentaries of high and established authority upon the Vedams, adapted to popular use. The grand and fundamental article of their religious creed is, that there is one supreme GOD, whose essence is infinitely removed from human comprehension, eternal, omnipotent, invisible, who ordains and accepts the various religious rites of various nations, and that he is best pleased and propitiated by charity and good works. They teach that this GOD is to be worshipped by SYMBOLS, representing his various attributes—a most pernicious and fatal error, with admirable wisdom guarded against in the Jewish decalogue—which, from a system of pure and refined theism, has converted, by a natural and irresistible gradation, the popular religion of the Hindoos into gross idolatry *. The philosophers of Hindostan admit, without

---

* When BRAHM determined to create the universe, the Vedams teach that he first commanded into existence the GODS Vishnoo, Brimha, and Shivah, to whom he delegated the task of forming, preserving, and governing all things which it contains. This mythological account, however, is understood to be entirely allegorical; and this TRIAD or TRINITY of divine emanations, expressed in the Sanscrit language by the mystic word OUM, are unquestionably nothing more than symbols of the different energies of the divine nature, or of the power, wisdom, and goodness, of the Supreme Being. This is the *Trinity* with which the mind of PLATO was so deeply impressed and enraptured, and which, in consequence of the wide diffusion of the Platonic system of philosophy, blended itself so intimately with the learned theories of the early heathen converts to christianity. Such was the scientific ardor of this celebrated Grecian, and such his admiration of the Indian philosophy, that, we are told, " he once entertained a purpose—emulous, perhaps, of the fame of Pythagoras—of visiting Hindostan in person: " Ad Indos," says Apuleius, " et Magos intendisset animum, nisi eum bella tunc vetuissent Asiatica." In the famous dialogues, preserved in the Sanscrit language, between Vishnoo and Arjoon, Vishnoo says, " All things proceed from me, and there is not any thing, animate or inanimate'

without hesitation, the doctrine of the immortality of
the soul, which they conceive to be an emanation from
the divine essence; and capable of an accidental and
temporary conjunction with, and transmigration to, any
organical system of matter; and into the same infinite
essence from which it originally sprang, after completing
its destined series of transmigrations, it will be ultimately
absorbed. The general characteristics of this people are
mildness, simplicity, and indolence. They delight to repose
under the romantic shade of their vast forests; or to re-
fresh

inanimate, without me. In me all things are reposited. I am in the
incense, in the fire, and in the victim. He who believeth in UNITY,
and worshippeth me present in all things, dwelleth in me. They who,
delighting in the welfare of all nature, serve me in my incorruptible,
ineffable, and invisible form, omnipotent, incomprehensible, exalted,
fixed, and immoveable, with subdued passions, and who are the same
in all things, shall come unto me." Arjoon says, in reply, " Reverence be unto thee, again and again reverence, O thou who art all in
all! Great is thy power, and great thy glory. By thee the universe
was spread abroad. Thou art Vayoo the God of the winds, Agnee the
God of fire, Varoon the God of the ocean, &c. Worthy to be adored,
bear with me as a friend with a friend, a lover with the beloved."—
Vishnoo answers—" He is dear to me who is free from enmity, merciful,
and exempt from pride and selfishness, who is the same in pain and in
pleasure, patient of wrongs, contented, and whose mind is fixed on me
alone. He is my beloved, of whom mankind is not afraid, and who is
not afraid of mankind, who is unsolicitous about events, to whom praise
and blame are as one, who has no particular home, and is of a steady
mind. The man who, performing the duties of life and quitting all
interest in them, placeth his affections upon BRAHM the supreme, is not
tainted with sin, but remaineth, like the leaf of the lotos, unaf-
fected by the waters." KRISHEN, or Krishna, is the God Vishnoo in
one of his various incarnations; in which capacity he is represented as
a blooming and beautiful youth, with the characteristic appendage of a
flute or lyre, resembling the Apollo of the Greeks; and, amongst many
other striking analogies between the Indian and Grecian mythologies,
described as encircled by the same number of graceful nymphs endowed
with

fresh and purify themselves with frequent bathings and ablutions in their majestic and salubrious streams; especially coveting to immerge in the sacred waters of the Ganges, for which celebrated river they universally entertain a superstitious and enthusiastic reverence. The famous expedition of Alexander into India was rather a discovery than a conquest. But the more recent invasion of Tamerlane was attended with serious and lasting consequences. That illustrious oriental victor, after subduing the more considerable northern provinces of

the

with the same divine accomplishments, styled the GOPIA, who are said to have fixed their residence in the delightful groves of Matra. In a hymn addressed to Kama-diva, or the God of love, in the Hindoo system, son of Maya, the power of attraction, we read, in the elegant translation of Sir William Jones—

> Can men resist thy power when Krishen yields?
> Krishen, who still in Matra's holy fields
> Tunes harps immortal, and to strains divine
> Dances by moonlight with *the Gopia nine.*

In the temples of Vishnoo this God is worshipped under the symbol of an human figure, having a circle of heads and a multiplicity of hands, to denote the universality of his knowledge, presence, and power. The most celebrated of these temples or pagodas is situated on the banks of the Coleroon, near the western extremity of the island of Seringham. It consists of seven square inclosures, standing at three hundred and fifty feet asunder. In the inmost inclosure are the altars and the image of the Deity. The grand entrance is richly ornamented with pillars of granite of prodigious size. When the wars in the Carnatic between the French and English commenced, these rude invaders scrupled not to profane, by the entrance of their troops, the first courts of this hallowed edifice. And we are told that, on their approach, a Brahman, standing on the summit of the lofty portico of the temple, cried to them with a loud voice to desist from this impiety; but finding his menaces and supplications equally disregarded, he threw himself down with violence upon the pavement below, and was instantly

dashed

the Peninsula, fixed his imperial throne at Dehli, where the great Moguls his descendants, now reduced to the mere phantoms and shadows of royalty, still continue to reside. For several ages, however, they retained great power and authority, and the empire of Hindostan was divided into extensive kingdoms or provinces, which were governed by viceroys, styled Subahs, and

subordi-

dashed to pieces. It is a singularity of the Hindoo system, that it refuses to admit proselytes; for the Hindoo philosophers maintain that the different modes of faith and worship established in different countries, when practised with a pure mind, are equally acceptable to the SUPREME, to whom they give the appellations of " the Principle of Truth," the " Spirit of Wisdom," the " Universal Soul," whose essence pervades all things, who fills all space, and who cannot therefore be justly pourtrayed under any visible and distinct form. A celebrated Danish missionary, M. Ziegenbalg, tells us " that the Brahmans uniformly affirmed to him that GOD was a Being wholly spiritual and incomprehensible; but that the adoration before idols being ordained by their religion, GOD would receive and consider it as adoration offered to himself—in the multitude of images they professed to adore One Divine Essence." M. Bernier, a French traveller in the last century, who passed some time at the city of Benares, the sacred seat of Indian science, affirms, that he was told, in a conference which he held with the chief of the Pundits, " that though they had, in their temples, numerous images or idols to fix the attention of the worshipper— " *afin qu'il y ait quelque chose devant les yeux qui arrête l'esprit;*" yet the honors paid to them were entirely to be referred to the Being whose attributes they represented." And St. Francis Xavier, the great apostle of India, at a still earlier period, informs us, that a Brahman on the coast of Malabar revealed to him in confidence, " that one of the mysteries of the Hindoo doctrine consisted in believing that there was only one God, creator of the heavens, and of the earth; and that this God alone was worthy to be adored." The learned Brahmans, employed by Mr. Hastings—in his laudable attention, amidst the complicated cares of government, to scientific researches—for the purpose of translating from the Sanscrit to the Persian language, the authentic records of their laws and customs, say, in the preliminary discourse affixed to their work, " From men of enlightened understanding, and

found

subordinate governors, under the appellation of Nabobs and Rajahs, tributary to, and removable at, the pleasure of, the emperor.

At so recent a period as the commencement of the present century, Aurengzebe swayed the sceptre of the Moguls with unabated majesty and splendor. But the power of this house received a tremendous shock from the invasion of the Persians, under the famous Shah Nadir, or Kouli Khan: and the governors of the provinces, seizing with eagerness the favorable moment, threw

sound judgment, who in their researches after truth, have swept away from their hearts malice and opposition, it is not concealed that the diversities of belief which are causes of enmity and envy to the ignorant, are in fact a demonstration of the power of the Supreme Being. The truly intelligent well know, that the difference and variety of created things, and the contrarieties of constitutions, are types of his wonderful attributes, whose complete power formed all things in the animal, vegetable, and material world; whose benevolence selected man to have dominion and authority over the rest, who having bestowed on him judgment and understanding, gave him supremacy over the regions of the world, who having put into his hands the control and disposal of all things, appointed to each nation its own religion, and who constituted a variety of tribes, and multiplicity of customs; but views, with pleasure, in every place, the mode of worship particularly appointed to it. He is with the attendants upon the mosque, in counting the sacred beads; and he is at the temple with the Hindoos, at the adoration of the idols." The grand dogmas of Indian theology are exhibited with the blended energies of philosophy and poetry, in an ancient hymn, or divine ode, addressed to NARAYANA, or the *Divine Intellect*, as it appears in the animated translation of Sir William Jones, from which these stanzas are transcribed.

> SPIRIT of spirits, who thro' every part
> Of space expanded, and of endless time
> Beyond the stretch of laboring thought sublime,
> Bad'st uproar into beauteous order start;
>   Before heav'n was, THOU art!

Ere

threw off their dependency upon the emperor, and almost universally established their authority as sovereign princes of the empire, of which the Mogul is at present regarded only as the nominal head. Tamerlane, the founder of the Mogul empire, and the Mogul and other Tartar tribes, who acquired, in virtue of his conquests, permanent establishments in India, being zealous pro-

    Ere spheres beneath us roll'd, or spheres above,
      Ere earth in firmamental ether hung,
    Thou sat'st alone; till thro' thy mystic love
      Things unexisting to existence sprung.——

          * * *

    ——Wrapt in eternal solitary shade,
    Th' impenetrable gloom of light intense,
    Impervious, inaccessible, immense,
    Ere spirits were infus'd, or forms display'd,
    BRAHM his own mind survey'd.——

          * * *

    ——Mountains whose radiant spires
    Presumptuous rear their summits to the skies,
    And blend their emerald hue with sapphire light,
    Smooth meads and lawns, that glow with varying dyes
    Of dew-bespangled leaves, and blossoms bright,
      Hence! vanish from my sight.

          * * *

    Delusive pictures! unsubstantial shows!
    My soul absorb'd, ONE only Being knows
    Of all perceptions, one abundant source,
    Whence every object, every moment flows;
      Suns hence derive their force,
      Hence planets learn their course;
    But suns and fading worlds I view no more,
    GOD only I perceive, GOD only I adore.

fessors of the religion of Mahomed, the viceroys of the provinces, the viziers, and other great officers of state, were from that period invariably selected from the number of the faithful; but few or no innovations were attempted in the internal government or constitution of the empire. And the wisdom of Tamerlane, which is no less the subject of oriental panegyric than his valor, appears in no respect more conspicuous than in his cautious avoidance of those measures of political violence, which would probably have converted his newly-acquired dominions into one vast scene of desolation and anarchy *.

In consequence of the important discovery made by the celebrated Portuguese navigator, Vasco de Gama,

of

---

* The Subahs and Nabobs are universally Mahommedans—the Rajahs, Mirzahs, Omrahs, and other subordinate governors or princes, are chiefly Hindoos. In a remarkable petition or remonstrance, presented by the Rajah Jusswont Sing to the celebrated Aurengzebe, in consequence of an oppressive capitation recently and arbitrarily imposed throughout all the provinces and kingdoms of Hindostan, by that imperious and warlike emperor, we find the following passages, which exhibit a striking picture of the ancient and accustomed tenor of the Mogul administration in India.—" May it please your majesty, your royal ancestor, Mahomed-Jelaul ul-Deen-Akbar, whose throne is now in heaven, conducted the affairs of this empire in equity and firm security, for the space of fifty-two years, preserving every tribe of men in case and happiness; whether they were followers of Jesus, or of Moses, or of Mahommed. Were they Brahmans, were they of the sect of the Dharians, which denies the eternity of matter, or of that which ascribes the existence of the world to chance, they all equally enjoyed his countenance and favor—insomuch that he was distinguished by his people, in gratitude, by the appellation of " Guardian of mankind." His majesty, Mahomed Noor-ul-Deen-Jehangheer, whose dwelling is now in Paradise, extended, for a period of twenty-two years, the shadow of his protection over the heads of his people. Nor less did the illustrious Shah Jehân, by a propitious reign

of

of a passage in India by the Cape of Good Hope, the
attention of the European nations was powerfully attracted by the immense riches of Hindostan, now placed
as it were within the general reach, particularly that of
the Portuguese themselves, who established, by extraordinary exertions of valor, a commercial and political
empire in India, of which the city of Goa was the emporium and metropolis. When Portugal was annexed
by the arms of Philip II. to the crown of Spain, Holland successfully contended with that power for pre-
eminence in India. And England and France were at
length induced, from an increasing attention to their
commercial interests, and without any ambition of do-

of thirty-two years, acquire to himself immortal reputation, the glorious reward of clemency and virtue. Such were the benevolent inclinations of your ancestors: wheresoever they directed their steps,
conquest and prosperity went before them. How can the dignity of
the sovereign be preserved, who employs his power in exacting heavy
tributes from his people? At this juncture, it is told from east to west,
that the emperor of Hindostan, regardless of the illustrious honor of
his Timurean descent, will exercise his power over Brahmans, Sono-
rahs, Sonassees—that he will condescend to oppress the poor Indian de-
votee, the solitary inoffensive anchoret. If your majesty places any
faith in those books, by distinction called divine, you will there be instructed that God is the God of all mankind, and not the God of Mahommedans alone. This Pagan and Mussulman are equal in his presence.—In the mosque his name is invoked—in the pagoda he is the
object of adoration. To vilify the religion of other men is to set at
nought the pleasure of the Almighty. In fine, the tribute you demand
from the Hindoos is repugnant to justice—it is equally foreign to good
policy; and moreover it is an innovation, and an infringement of the
laws of Hindostan. It is wonderful, that the ministers of your government should have neglected to instruct your majesty in the rules
of rectitude and honor." If any credit be due to the doctrine of the
metempsychosis, surely the soul of this illustrious Rajah must have
transmigrated into the body of a Montesquieu, a Locke, or a Tur-
got!

minion, to form settlements both on the eastern and western coasts of the peninsula. During the violent and frequent contests between these rival nations, destined to carry their rivalship into every part of the globe, no transactions of sufficient moment to demand a place in general history are to be found relative to India for a long succession of years.

At the period of the *accession* of the house of Brunswick, England was, on the western or Malabar coast, in possession of the island of Bombay and the factory of Surat: on the opposite, or Coromandel coast, of Fort St. David, and, farther to the northward, of Fort St. George, usually styled Madras, from its contiguity to that city, which, with several villages in the vicinity, was purchased in the last century, by the East India company, of the king of Golconda: still farther to the north, at the mouth of the Ganges, was Fort William, closely adjoining the town of Calcutta, a vast and populous commercial mart, situated in the kingdom of Bengal.

The commerce of the French chiefly centred in the city of Pondicherry, a large and beautiful town on the Coromandel coast, between the forts St. David and St. George. Chandernagore, on the Ganges, ranked next in importance to Pondicherry, and they had also established factories at Rajapore, Calicut, and Surat, on the western side of the Continent. During the course of the war which commenced in the year 1740, Fort St. George, or Madras, the residence of the governor-general, and the seat of the civil administration, extending over all the English settlements in India, was conquered by the French; but restored in exchange for Cape Breton, at the ensuing pacification of Aix-la-Chapelle.

Some years previous to that period, M. Dupleix had been appointed to the governor-generalship of the French

French settlements in India—a man of singular ability and daring ambition, who seized with avidity every opportunity to extend and establish the empire of France in Hindostan. Nizam-al-Muluc, the Subah or Viceroy of the Decan, in the year 1745, had constituted, in virtue of his office, Anaverdi Khan, Nabob of the province of Arcot, a dependency upon his government. The Subah not long surviving this appointment, was succeeded by his son, Nazir-Zing, whose claim to the succession was strongly opposed by his own kinsman Muzapher-Zing—for by these uncouth names, to our ears of barbarous sound, must the page of history, in recording the transactions of the European nations in India, be darkened and disfigured. Muzapher-Zing had recourse to the assistance of M. Dupleix, who readily granted him powerful succors, in consideration and prospect of great future advantages. Thus reinforced, and joined by Chunda-Saib, a man of high rank and influence in the Subahdary, he took the field against Nazir-Zing, who was strongly supported by the English, from motives similar to those which actuated M. Dupleix. In a short time Muzapher-Zing was reduced to absolute submission, and Nazir-Zing, in clemency, spared his life; but detained him as a state prisoner. In this situation Muzapher-Zing found means to carry on dark and dangerous intrigues with Dupleix and Chunda-Saib, who had taken refuge in Pondicherry, and even with the ministers of Nazir-Zing; and a deep and traitorous conspiracy was formed, in consequence of which Nazir-Zing was murdered in his camp, and Muzapher-Zing proclaimed Subah of the Decan. Chunda-Saib was, in consequence of this revolution, appointed Nabob of Arcot, Anaverdi-Khan, the late Nabob, having been previously defeated and slain, and his son Mahomed-Ali-Khan reduced to the necessity of putting

himself

himself under the protection of the English government at Madras. Muzapher-Zing did not long enjoy the fruits of his crimes; for, by a conspiracy similar to that by which he had himself risen to the throne, he was suddenly hurled from it: and the chiefs of the conspiracy, after putting this faithless usurper to death, proclaimed Sallabat-Zing, brother to Nazir-Zing, Subah of the DECAN.

On the other hand, the MOGUL, by an Imperial *phirmaund*, appointed Gawzedi Khan, the elder brother of Sallabat-Zing, to the viceroyalty; at the same time declaring Chunda-Saib a traitor, and confirming Mahomed-Ali-Khan in the government of Arcot. But the mandate of the emperor would have been of little avail without the support and assistance of the English company, who determined upon sending a confiderable military force, at the head of which was placed captain Clive, in the sequel so famous under the title of lord Clive, into the province of Arcot, who, conducting all his operations with a vigor and dispatch which at once established his reputation as a military commander, took possession of the city of Arcot in the summer of 1751. Chunda-Saib having assembled a considerable army, with the aid of M. Dupleix, invested the city of Arcot, but was compelled to raise the siege with great precipitation; and was afterwards, in repeated engagements, defeated and foiled by the English commander. In the spring of 1752, major-general Lawrence, commander in chief of the company's troops, took the field in person, and attacking the grand army of the enemy, headed by the Nabob Chunda-Saib, he gained a complete victory. Chunda-Saib, being taken prisoner, had his head struck off by order of the Rajah of Tanjore, a neighboring prince of India, in alliance with the company. M. Dupleix now proclaimed Rajah Saib, son

of

of Chunda-Saib, Nabob of Arcot. And Salabat-Zing, in return for the powerful support he had received from the French in the Decan, and having devised means to rid himself of his competitor Gawzedi Khan by poison, made a grant to M. Dupleix of all the English possessions to the northward of Pondicherry. But the French governor being recalled before this grant could be carried into effect, and the Sieur Godeheu, the new governor, professing the most pacific intentions, a provisional treaty was quickly agreed upon on the footing of *uti possidetis*, till fresh instructions should arrive from their respective courts or principals in Europe. This interval of quiet, however, was of short duration; for no sooner was the inimical disposition of the two courts ascertained, than hostilities recommenced in the Carnatic, and were carried on with various success, but, upon the whole, with considerable advantage by general Lawrence on the part of the English, when the attention of that commander was, by a series of extraordinary and interesting events, diverted to another part of the Continent, the peace of which had hitherto remained undisturbed by European ambition. Ali-Verdi-Khan, Subah of Bengal, with the contiguous provinces of Bahar and Orissa, a prince who had forced his way to the throne by great crimes, and had maintained possession of it by great talents, dying in April 1756, was succeeded by his adopted son Sou-Rajah-Dowla, the grandson of his brother Hadjee Hamet, a young man immersed in debauchery, weak in his understanding, violent in his passions, and profligate in his morals. Ali-Verdi-Khan, notwithstanding his early and continued partiality for this unhappy youth, with reason dreaded the consequences of his elevation to the *Musnud*. In his last illness, he obliged Sou-Rajah-Dowla to swear upon the Koran never more to touch any intoxicating liquor, a vow which he observed with surprising and undeviating fidelity. The Subah, feeling the near and rapid approach of death, addressed his adopted son and heir in the following words: " My life has been a life of war and stratagem. For what have I fought, to what have my counsels tended but to secure, my son, to you a quiet succession to my Subahdary! My fears for you have rendered my nights sleepless. I consider who had power to give you trouble after I am gone hence. Hussein-Cooley-Khan, by his reputation, wisdom, courage, and affection to Shah Amet-Jung and his house, I feared would obstruct your government; but his power is no more. Monichund Dewan, who might have been your dangerous enemy, I have taken into favor. But, my son, keep in view the power of the European nations in this country. This I would have freed you from, if God had lengthened my days. The work must now be yours. Their wars and perfidious politics should keep you waking. The power of the English is great; reduce them first; the others will then give you little trouble. Suffer them not, my son, to have forts or soldiers; if you do, the country is not yours." Strongly impressed with these ideas, the new Subah viewed with the highest alarm and apprehension the additional fortifications carrying on at Fort William, in consequence of the war now declared against France, and from the prosecution of which he repeatedly required the governor to desist. But his orders being neglected or evaded, he appeared suddenly before Calcutta, in the month of June, with a large body of troops, and summoned the fort and city to surrender. Mr. Holwell, who acted as governor, made a resolute defence, but was at length compelled to submit to superior force. The Subah, notwithstanding his assurances of protection from personal injury, instantly ordered the English garrison,

amount-

amounting to one humdred and forty-six persons, into confinement. And there being, at a small distance, a strong stone prison, forming within the walls a cube of about eighteen feet, open only to the westward by two windows, strongly barred with iron, they were conveyed for immediate security to this dungeon. Mr. Holwell, on entering the place, immediately conceived all the horrors which must ensue, if they failed in obtaining a speedy release; and accosting the Jemmautdaur or officer of the Indian guard, promised to gratify him with a thousand rupees if he would remove one half of them to a separate apartment. The Jemmautdaur, allured by the prospect of this reward, assured him he would use his utmost endeavor to procure for them this indulgence, and retired for that purpose; but returning in a short time, he told the governor that the Subah, by whose order alone such a step could be taken, was asleep, and no person durst disturb his repose. Mr. Holwell, in his pathetic narration of this unexampled scene of distress, compares their situation, in this dark and sultry cell, to that of so many miserable animals in an exhausted receiver—no circulation of fresh air sufficient to continue life, and not enough divested of its vivifying particles to put a speedy period to it. A most profuse perspiration, accompanied with a raging thirst, soon took place, which, becoming each moment more insupportable, gradually changed into phrensy and delirium. The prison now resounded with the ravings of despair, and, nature being at length reduced to extremity, with the groans and broken accents of the dying. In the morning twenty-three only were found alive, and in these scarcely were there any perceptible remains of sensation or sensibility. Their sufferings, however, appeared to make little impression upon the ferocious and obdurate heart of the Subah, who visibly exulted in the

success

success of his enterprise—not having the least conception that the English would return in force to Calcutta; and contemptuously declaring, that he did not believe there were ten thousand fighting men in all *Frenghistan* *. The wretched remains of the factory were now embarked on board a few trading vessels lying at the mouth of the Ganges; and these the Subah did not offer to molest. He even expressed his wishes that the English merchants would return to Calcutta, if they could be satisfied to live under his government, without laws or fortifications of their own, and carry on their traffic like the Armenians and his own native subjects. And happy for mankind assuredly would it have been, had Europe never extended her views farther than this in India. No sooner, however, was the intelligence of this calamity conveyed to Madras, than vigorous preparations were made by the English government to revenge the injury, and obliterate the disgrace. A formidable armament under the command of admiral Watson and colonel Clive, to the great astonishment of the Subah, anchored in the Ganges in December; and immediately commencing their operations, Calcutta was invested and reduced in the month of January (1757), and also the city of Hughley on the Ganges, where the principal magazines of the Subah were deposited. Soon after which, the Subah himself, who had assembled a vast army in order to repel the invaders, was attacked by colonel Clive, and obliged to retreat in confusion, and with considerable loss. Intimidated by the successes of the English, he consented to sign articles of peace, February 9, 1757, by which it was stipulated that the fac-

---

* *i. e.* The country of Franks—the appellation universally given to the Europeans throughout the East.

tories and poffeffions belonging to the Englifh company fhould be reftored, and full compenfation made for their loffes; and, in general, that whatever rights and privileges had been at any time granted to the company by virtue of the *phirmaunds* of the emperor fhould be confirmed and ratified. After the conclufion of this treaty, the Englifh commanders proceeded to the attack of the French fortrefs and factory of Chandernagore; the reduction of which filled the Nabob with new apprehenfions and alarms. And he remonftrated in ftrong terms to admiral Watfon againft thefe acts of violence: " It is, faid the Subah, contrary to all rule and cuftom that you fhould bring your animofities' and differences into my country: it has never been known fince the days of Timur that the Europeans made war upon one another within the emperor's dominions. If you are determined to befiege the French factories I fhall be neceffitated in honor and duty to my fovereign, to affift them with my troops." But admiral Watfon, regardlefs of his remonftrances, and jealous of his defigns, declared to him, " that, if he protected the king's enemies, he would light up a flame in his country that all the waters of the Ganges would not be able to extinguifh." Such, indeed, was the capricious and tyrannic conduct of Sou-Rajah-Dowla, that thofe who were originally moft attached to his interefts began to be weary of his government. Amongft other men of high rank in the Subahdary of whom he entertained juft fufpicion, was Meer-Jaffier-Ali-Khan, nearly allied to the Subah by his marriage with the fifter of Ali-Verdi-Khan. In the vehemence of his paffion he had been heard to declare that he would have the head of Meer-Jaffier: and Meer-Jaffier, fenfible of the imminent dangers of his fituation, made fecret propofals to the Englifh refident at the court of Moorfhedabad the capital

tal of Bengal, which were eagerly embraced by the English council and commandants at Calcutta, for the deposition of Sou-Rajah-Dowla, and the advancement of Meer-Jaffier to the *Musnud*. The jealousies of the Subah continuing to increase, Meer-Jaffier retired from court to his residence in the country, from whence he transmitted dispatches to colonel Clive, urging him to begin his march to Moorshedabad. The colonel seeing that the die was cast, and that they had already gone much too far unless they proceeded still farther, immediately put the whole army in motion, and with a just, though daring reliance on his own talents, and the valor of his troops, crossing the Ganges, he advanced to Plassey, within one day's march of the capital, where he found the Subah encamped with a force of seventy thousand men, in all the "*pomp, pride, and circumstance*" of oriental magnificence. The number of elephants with their scarlet housings, the rich variegated embroidery of their tents and standards, and the martial splendor of the cava'ry parading over the field with their drawn swords glittering in the sun, made a grand and striking appearance. The Subah, feeble of mind and infirm of purpose, on the first intelligence of the march of the English army, had eagerly courted the support and assistance of Meer-Jaffier, whom he had, beyond all possibility of forgiveness, previously offended. A full and free pardon was granted to Meer-Jaffier, who, being introduced into the presence of the Subah, took a solemn oath upon the Koran that he would be his faithful soldier; and in return, the Subah swore that he would never attempt the life of Meer-Jaffier. Though the army of the Subah was advantageously posted upon an eminence, colonel Clive advanced at the head of his troops, consisting of little more than three thousand men, with great intrepidity to the attack. Such, on the other hand, was the distrust and secret despondency

spondency prevailing ... out the A... ny, that resistance seemed to ... With the trifling loss of about ... victory was gained—the artillery, and stores of the enemy falling into the hands of the victors. Doubtful, perhaps, of the final event, and perplexed in the mazes of his own policy, Meer-Jaffier, who commanded the left wing of the Subah's army, took no part whatever in the action. But the English commander, far from discovering any impolitic symptoms of resentment at his ambiguity of conduct, saluted him, with apparent complacency, Subah of the three provinces, and exhorted him to pursue his march to Moorshedabad at the head of his troops—engaging, without delay, to follow and support him with his whole force. Sou-Rajah-Dowla, who had fled with the foremost from the field of action, abandoned himself to despair; and on his arrival at Moorshedabad, after some tumultuous consultations and inconsistent resolutions, he disguised himself in the habit of a faquier, and left his palace in the dead of night, in order to seek for safety in obscurity. Meer-Jaffier, all obstacles to his advancement being now surmounted, was seated, with all the accustomed ceremonies of state, upon the *Musnud*; and acknowledged as Subah of Bengal by all the Rajahs and Omrahs of the kingdom: and the unhappy Sou-Rajah-Dowla, being discovered in his flight, was put to death, imploring in vain for mercy, after a reign of fifteen months, by the express command of the son of the new Subah. In conformity to the treaty previously concluded with the English, this prince paid into the treasury of the company a crore of rupees *, as an indemnification

---

* A crore is an hundred lacks of rupees, considerably exceeding one million sterling. Upon the whole, and on various pretences, not less than

nification for their losses at Calcutta, and ceded to them a considerable territory in the vicinity of that city. And thus was a revolution accomplished very marvellous in the eyes of the inhabitants of Bengal, who could not comprehend how the throne of Ali-Verdi-Khan could be subverted by an handful of foreign mercantile adventurers. The affairs of the company being thus triumphantly re-established in the northern provinces of India, the watchful attention of the supreme council and of the military commandants was again turned to the coast of Coromandel, where the French had taken advantage of the temporary diminution of force on the part of the English, to make themselves masters of Ingeram, Vizagapatam, and other subordinate settlements in that quarter: and being now strengthened with large reinforcements from Europe conducted by M. Lally, under convoy of a powerful squadron commanded by M. d'Aché, they threatened the entire conquest of all the English possessions on that coast. Fort St. David's was first invested, which surrendered after a very short and feeble defence. The Rajah of Tanjore having distinguished himself as a zealous and faithful ally of the English, M. Lally marched into his dominions; and on the Rajah's refusal to advance the enormous sum of seventy-two lacks of rupees, demanded by the French general, he invested the city of Tanjore, which was so resolutely defended by the native troops of the Rajah, assisted by some European engineers, that M. Lally was compelled to raise the siege with considerable loss. He took possession however, in

than one million eight hundred thousand pound sterling, exclusive of presents to individuals to an immense amount, was exacted from the new Subah on this occasion. A lack of rupees is estimated at about 11,500l.

his

his retreat from Tanjore, of the city of Arcot, the refidence of the Nabob Mahomed-Ali-Khan, without oppofition; and, in the beginning of December 1758, he advanced with his whole force to Madras, to which he laid clofe fiege. But the place being ftrongly fortified and plentifully provided, the garrifon made an obftinate defence; and, on the arrival of a confiderable reinforcement of troops and military ftores, under the conduct of captain Kempenfelt, in February (1759), M. Lally abandoned the attempt, and retired with precipitation to Arcot, extremely chagrined at the ill fuccefs of this enterprife. "I reckon (fays he, in an intercepted confidential letter to his friend M. le Gret) that we fhall, on our arrival at Pondicherry, endeavour to learn fome other trade—this of war requires too much patience; were I judge of the point of honor of the company's officers, I would break fome of them like glafs." This commander was a man of impetuous courage, but capricious, paffionate, proud, and opinionated. Vizagapatam and Mafulipatam were, about this time, recovered from the French by a detachment under Colonel Ford. And Salabat-Zing, Subah of the Decan, perceiving the fortune of the war now vifibly inclining to the Englifh, made eager advances to the government of Madras; and a treaty was concluded with the Subah, by which he renounced his former alliance with France, and ceded the entire *Circar* of Mafulipatam to the company; and the Englifh, on their part, engaged not to affift or protect the Subah's enemies. Colonel Cooote, who now commanded in chief the company's forces in the Carnatic, gained feveral advantages over M. Lally; and a general engagement taking place between the two armies near Wandewafh, at the beginning of the year (1760), the French were defeated with the lofs of their camp and cannon. Colonel Coote immediately undertook the fiege, and effected the reduction of Arcot. Several bloody but indecisive naval encounters intervened also, since the commencement of the preceding year, between M. d'Aché and admiral Pocucke, the successor of admiral Watson, who had died soon after the re-capture of Calcutta, universally lamented and esteemed as a man of great professional skill, of firm integrity, and of untarnished honor.

After the defeat of Wandewash, M. Lally retreated to Pondicherry, where he was pursued with unremitting diligence by colonel Coote, who, with the assistance of the British squadron, soon formed the complete blockade of that important city. As soon as the periodical rains abated, and the season for active operations recommenced, the blockade was converted into a regular siege; and the place, though defended with great vigor by M. Lally, was reduced to extremity before the end of January (1761), not so much from the damage sustained from the assaults of the besiegers, as from the excessive scarcity of provisions, which the temporary but critical absence of M. d'Aché, now repairing and careening his ships at Mauritius, left M. Lally wholly destitute of the means to remedy. The English squadron, however, being driven from their station by a violent tempest, he dispatched a letter to the French resident at Pulicat, fortunately intercepted by the English, urging him, in the strongest terms, to exert himself in the procurement of supplies: Lose not an instant, says he, in sending chelingoes upon chelingoes laden with rice. We are no longer blockaded by sea. The salvation of Pondicherry hath been once in your power already—Risque all—attempt all—force all!" The English admiral, however, soon resuming his station, he lost all hope, and demanded a capitulation, which colonel Coote would grant upon no other terms, than that of the garrison surrendering prisoners of war; to which M. Lally at length indignantly assented. Thus the proud

and

and opulent capital of the French settlements in the East fell, by the fortune of war, into the hands of the enemy, nearly at the same time that the conquest of Canada was completed in the West; and the genius of England triumphed over that of France, at this propitious period, on both sides of the globe.

There yet remains to be investigated, another grand and essential branch of the memorable contest now under contemplation; that is to say, the war in Germany, resumed with fresh vigor after a short interval, subsequent to the convention of Cloister-Seven. No sooner was the alliance concluded between the courts of Vienna and Versailles, than it was communicated to the court of Petersburgh, and the empress of Russia acceded to it without hesitation. Sweden also speedily became a party in the confederacy; though extremely opposite to the views and inclinations of the monarch, who by the constitution of government, established after the death of Charles XII. possessed little more than the shadow of regal authority: the king of Poland, elector of Saxony, was deterred from following the example of Sweden, only by his vicinity to Prussia, and the bitter recollection of his former losses and sufferings.

Great military preparations, however, being made in all parts of the Austrian dominions, and the king of Prussia having received undoubted intelligence of negotiations which had been long secretly depending between the courts of Vienna, Petersburg, and Dresden, extremely to his prejudice, and of which the dismemberment of his dominions was understood to be the ultimate object, ordered M. Klingraffe, his minister at the imperial court, to demand of the empress queen a positive and explicit declaration of her intentions. Count Kaunitz, by command of the empress, replied in general terms, "that her imperial majesty had found it necessary, in the present juncture,

juncture, to arm for her own defence, and that of her allies; but that her armaments did not tend to the prejudice of any person or state whatever."—On the transmission of this answer, M. Klingraffe received fresh orders from the court of Berlin, to represent to the empress, " that his Prussian majesty was well acquainted with the secret hostile projects of the imperial courts; that he constituted the empress arbiter of peace or war; that he would be satisfied with nothing less than an express assurance of peace; and that he would regard an ambiguous answer as a declaration of war." The empress, in return, signified, in indignant terms, her astonishment at the memorial now presented. She said, that she had, in common with all other sovereigns, a right to take such measures as she deemed necessary for her safety, and that it belonged to none but herself to estimate her own danger; that no treaty of offensive alliance did exist, or had ever existed, between her and the empress of the Russias; and that the positive assurance required of her, in terms so unusually peremptory, could not be more binding than the solemn treaty actually subsisting, and which she had no intention to violate."

The Prussian monarch, firmly persuaded by evidence, transmitted through secret channels * of intelligence, of the

---

* Le Roi avoit un canal par lequel il tiroit des avis certains sur les projets de ses ennemis qui étoient près d'éclater. C'étoit un commis de la Chancellerie Secrète de Dresde, qui remettoit toutes les semaines au Ministre Prussien les dépêches que sa Cour recevoit de Petersbourg et de Vienne, ainsi que la copie de tous les traités qu'il avoit trouvés dans les archives. Il parut par ses écrits que la Cour de Russie s'excusoit de ne pouvoir entreprendre la guerre cette année, à cause que sa flotte n'étoit pas en état d entrer en mer.——La réponse du Comte Kaunitz se trouva conçue en termes équivoques et ambigus; mais il s'expliqua plus ouvertement avec le Comte de Flemming, Ministre du Roi de
Pologne

the infincerity of the court of Vienna, and that Saxony waited only a favorable occafion openly to join the confederacy againft him, entered that electorate with a numerous army, and took poffeffion of the city of Drefden on the 8th of September 1756, declaring, however, that he did not mean to violate the neutrality profeffed by his Polifh majefty, and requiring only that monarch to feparate his army into cantonments, as a proof and pledge of his amity and good faith. The king of Poland, aftonifhed and exafperated at this unexpected intrufion, feemed neither to know how to comply or to refift. Relying, however, upon the ftrength of the inacceffible camp of Pirna, fingularly and romantically fituated, on the fummit of a lofty range of rocks, extending along the banks of the Elbe, to which the Saxon army had retreated, he ventured to declare his refolution to keep his troops affembled for the defence and protection of his perfon and dominions. This, with an antagonift fuch as the king of Pruffia, was equivalent to a declaration of war; and the Pruffian general, finding it impoffible to attack the Saxons, took immediate poffeffion, by order of the king, of all the paffes leading to this impregnable poft; and the whole Saxon army, reduced to extremity by famine, was on the 14th October, compelled to fur-

---

Pologne à Vienne, lequel rendit compte de cet entretien dans une relation à fa Cour: La copie de cette dépêche fut envoyée incontinent de Drefde à Berlin; le Comte Flemming y dit, " Le Comte Kaunitz fe propofe a'inquiéter le Roi par fes réponfes, et de le pouffer à commettre les premieres hoftilités." *Hift. de la Guerre de Sept Ans.*—Count Hertzberg, however, in his Hiftoric Memoir of the Reign of Frederic the Great, prefumes to fuggeft a doubt whether that Monarch might not rely too confidently on this fecret intelligence, and whether it was, or is, perfectly clear that the two Empreffes had nearly formed a fixed and ferious defign for the fubverfion of the Electoral Houfe of Brandenburg.

render

render prisoners of war. The king of Poland now retired for personal security to Warsaw, and the king of Prussia took possession, as a conquered country, of the whole electorate. During the blockade of Pirna, that monarch had made an attempt to penetrate into Bohemia; but finding the Austrian army, under count Browne, strongly posted at Lowoschutz, on the Egra, a bloody engagement ensued, which terminated with nearly equal loss; but the advantage remained with the Austrians, as the king of Prussia was compelled to measure back his steps to Saxony, where he took up his winter-quarters.

The king of Prussia, on re-entering Dresden, commanded the royal cabinet to be forced, in defiance of the personal opposition of the queen of Poland. In it was found deposited an authentic copy of a *defensive treaty* of alliance between the courts of Vienna, Petersburg, and Dresden, which had been some years concluded, and which contained six secret articles. The fourth of these articles, for the sake of which the whole treaty seemed to be formed, imported that if the king of Prussia should depart from the peace of Dresden, which the contracting powers declare their intention religiously to observe, by attacking either of the contracting powers, or even the republic of Poland, the rights of the empress-queen to Silesia, &c. shall again revive and be considered as in full force; and the eventual partition of the Prussian dominions should take place as stipulated in the treaty.

In consequence of these daring acts of violence, the king was, at the subsequent meeting of the Diet at Ratisbon, in his quality of elector of Brandenburg, put under the *ban* of the empire, divested of his privileges and prerogatives, his fiefs escheated, and the circles ordered to furnish their respective contingencies for carrying this sentence into execution. Not in the least intimidated

midated by this formidable denunciation, that monarch, early in the enfuing fpring (1757), entered Bohemia, at the head of a vaft army, aflifted by the Marefchals Keith and Schwerin, and advancing towards Prague, found the Auftrians, who were at leaft equally numerous, entrenched on the banks of the Moldaw, commanded by prince Charles of Lorraine and count Browne, whom he attacked without hefitation or delay—forcing the entrenchments with refiftlefs intrepidity and complete fuccefs, though with the lofs of the gallant Marefchal Schwerin, who, after furviving the dangers of fifty campaigns, was flain, fighting at the head of his troops, covered with laurels, in the moment of victory. The fhattered remains of the Auftrian army took refuge in the city of Prague, where Marefchal Browne foon after died of the wounds which he received in the battle, or rather of the chagrin occafioned by the lofs of it. The Pruffians immediately formed the inveftment of that city, which, in confequence of the vaft number inclofed within the walls, was quickly reduced, by famine, to the laft extremity of diftrefs.

At this critical period, the famous Leopold count Daun, originally a fubaltern officer ferving in the fchool of the great Khevenhuller, who with the penetrating eye of military fagacity marked his extraordinary talents, and predicted his future eminence, was appointed to the chief command of the imperial armies. This general immediately prepared for the relief of Prague, by collecting troops from all quarters; and reinforcing them by numerous levies, he encamped with this new army in an almoft impregnable fituation at Kolin, near Prague, in order to harafs and retard the operations of the fiege. The king of Pruffia, impatient of moleftation, and elated with fuccefs, formed the rafh refolution of attacking Marefchal Daun in his camp; but, after repeated efforts, he was finally repulfed with prodigious flaughter. The

fiege

siege of Prague was immediately raised in consequence of this disaster, and Bohemia evacuated.

The king of Prussia now found his prospects darkening on every side. The French army, under the duc de Richelieu, who, with merit very inferior, had superseded Mareschal D'Estrées in the command, had penetrated into the electorate of Brandenburg, taken Halberstadt, and laid a great extent of territory under contribution. Mareschal Apraxin, at the head of one hundred thousand Russians, had entered ducal Prussia, where they committed the most enormous excesses. Pomerania was menaced with a powerful invasion from Sweden. The army of the empire, reinforced by a strong body of troops under the prince of Soubize, had entered Lusatia. The victorious Austrians, after laying close siege to Schweidnitz, the key of Silesia, ravaged the whole country; general Haddick, at the head of a numerous detachment, carrying terror even to the gates of Berlin. It was at this period that the king of Prussia thus expressed himself, in a letter to his friend the celebrated earl Mareschal: " What say you of this league, which has only the marquis of Brandenburg for its object? the great elector would be surprised to see his grandson at war with the Russians, the Swedes, the Austrians, almost all Germany, and a hundred thousand French auxiliaries. I know not whether it will be disgrace in me to submit; but I am sure there will be no glory in vanquishing me."

The Russian army, after reducing Memel, and leaving the country behind them a perfect waste, reached the frontiers of Germany in August; but were soon after unexpectedly attacked in their camp at Norkitten, by Mareschal Lehwald, who commanded on that side: and, though that general was finally obliged to desist, the Russians sustained immense loss, and they soon afterwards made a precipitate retreat from the Prussian territories. In the mean time the king of Prussia, and Mareschal Keith,

Keith, engaging the combined forces of France and the empire, at Rofbach, Nov. 5 (1757), commanded by Soubize, gained a complete victory, with inconfiderable lofs. But this victory by no means extricated him from his difficulties. The Auftrians, headed by Marefchal Daun, had taken Schweidnitz, and laid fiege to Breflau, and, on the 22d November, forced, after an obftinate refiftance, the entrenchments of the army under the prince of Bevern, pofted near that place. Breflaw immediately furrendered on capitulation. The king of Pruffia, on the news of this misfortune, inftantly marched to the relief of Silefia; and, coming up with the Auftrians at Liffa, the two armies joined battle with inconceivable fury. Notwithftanding the military conduct and perfonal bravery difplayed by count Daun, on this occafion, the Auftrians were totally defeated with the lofs of twenty thoufand men. Breflaw opened its gates to the victors; and the whole province, excepting Schweidnitz, fell once more into the hands of the Pruffians.

The fudden retreat of the Ruffians, which was better to be accounted for from political than military caufes, left Marefchal Lehwald at liberty to act againft the Swedes, who had advanced into Pruffian Pomerania, and were preparing to lay fiege to Stetin; but on the appearance of the Pruffian army, they not only evacuated the towns they had captured, but retreated with precipitation into Swedifh Pomerania, where they were followed by Lehwald, who drove them from one poft to another, till nothing remained to them at the end of the campaign but the city of Stralfund. Such was the fituation of the king of Pruffia, when it was determined by the Englifh minifter, that the army of obfervation, fcattered and difperfed by the convention of Clofter-Seven, fhould refume their arms; for which the exceffes committed by the

the French troops in the electorate gave them a very fair and plausible pretext.

Mr. Pitt was not ignorant or insensible to the charge of inconsistency, which he well knew would be advanced against him with all the force of truth, if not of eloquence, on this occasion: but very powerful reasons now influenced this minister to act in contradiction to that general system of policy which he had uniformly avowed and defended. The king of England, retaining all his partiality for German politics, and yielding only to the necessity of the times, had Mr. Pitt continued inflexible, would doubtless have embraced the first favorable opportunity of again dismissing a minister, who might not again be able to reinstate himself with the same eclat. But a consideration of still greater weight, it may be presumed, with Mr. Pitt, was, the visible change of sentiment in the nation at large, on this subject. The king of Prussia, since the dissolution of his political connection with France, and his consequent alliance with England, had become a very popular character in that country; and this national predilection, after the victory of Rosbach, rose to enthusiasm. That monarch artfully affected to consider the union of the two great Catholic powers, as a combination to oppress and subvert the protestant interest in the empire; and the people of England, to whom the name of popery was still formidable, delighted to applaud and extol this sceptred infidel, as THE PROTESTANT HERO. Their feelings and principles were, at this crisis, equally interested. The national honor was concerned to efface the stain of the ignominious convention of Cloister-Seven, by which an army had been annihilated.

The ingratitude of the queen of Hungary, whose obligations to England were of a nature and magnitude never to be forgotten, was the favorite theme of indignant

nant declamation: whilst the courage, the talents, the
successes of the king of Prussia excited an involuntary
admiration and partiality in the breast even of those
whose better judgment led them to condemn the
whole tenor of his political conduct, as proceeding
from a spirit of lawless and unprincipled ambition.
It was not possible for Mr. Pitt to act with feebleness
and indecision; and, if he resolved to engage in a Germanic war, which, after the alliance concluded with
Prussia, seemed a sort of necessary appendage to the general system *, he would at the same time resolve to
prosecute it with vigor and effect. This minister dif-
cerned also the advantage which might eventually arise
to the distant and multifarious operations of Great Britain, from fixing the chief attention of France upon an
object, which, from local circumstances, must be at all
times more interesting and important to that kingdom
than to England. And he scrupled not, at a distant and
subsequent period, to affirm, that " AMERICA had been
conquered in GERMANY." And, upon the whole, it
must perhaps be admitted, that the vast superiority of
force maintained by France in Germany, and which
was attended with no real or permanent advantage, was

---

* " Is it possible, said his Prussian majesty, in an expostulatory letter addressed at this crisis to the king of England, that your majesty
can have so little fortitude and constancy, as to be dispirited by a small
reverse of fortune? Are affairs so ruinous that they cannot be repaired? I hope your majesty will consider the step you have made me hazard, and remember you are the sole cause of those misfortunes that
now impend over my head. I should never have abandoned the alliance with France, but for your flattering assurances. I do not now repent of the treaty I have concluded with your majesty; but I expect
you will not ingloriously leave me at the mercy of my enemies, after
having brought upon me all the force of Europe."

the principal cause of her invariable inferiority in almost all other parts.

The disbanded army being actually re-assembled at Stade, in November 1757, the command of it was conferred upon prince Ferdinand of Brunswick, brother to the reigning duke. This able general immediately put his troops in motion, and, though the season was so far advanced, he obtained several advantages over the enemy. Two considerable detachments from the French army were entirely defeated by generals Schuylenburg and Zastrow, the town and castle of Harbourg reduced, and the cities of Lunenburg and Zell recovered; after which the two armies went into winter-quarters. In the course of the ensuing spring, the famous subsidy treaty was concluded between Great Britain and Prussia, by which the king of England engaged to pay into the hands of his Prussian majesty the annual sum of 670,000l. or four millions of German crowns, to be employed at his discretion for the good of the common cause. This great supply enabled that monarch to take the field with redoubled force. In April 1758, he opened the trenches before Schweidnitz, and kept a continual fire upon the town, with a prodigious train of artillery, consisting of three hundred pieces of cannon and eighty mortars. The garrison were obliged to surrender upon capitulation, before the end of the month. The Austrian army, after the battle of Lissa, having retired into Bohemia, the king of Prussia levied immense contributions in Saxony, Pomerania, and Mecklenburg.

About the middle of February 1758, prince Ferdinand put himself at the head of the allies, and advancing towards the French army, which retired at his approach, took possession of Bremen without opposition. The Duc de Richelieu was now succeeded in the command

mand by the count de Clermont, who found his troops reduced by the accidents of war, and a variety of hardships, to a moſt deplorable condition. Under theſe circumſtances he determined to march back to the Rhine with all expedition. In conſequence of this reſolution, Hanover was evacuated, after having been in the poſſeſſion of the French about ſix months. The Duc de Randan, governor of that city, for his moſt chriſtian majeſty, gained the higheſt honor by the generoſity, rectitude, and humanity of his conduct, for which he received the formal and grateful acknowledgements of the regency of the electorate. Such was the precipitation of the enemy's retreat, and ſo great was their confuſion and embarraſſment, that they were obliged to abandon their ſick and wounded to the mercy of the allies, who alſo took many priſoners, with ſeveral entire magazines of proviſion and forage, which they had not time to deſtroy.

The count de Clermont, having at length reached the farther borders of the Rhine, was ſtill cloſely purſued by prince Ferdinand, who paſſed the river in the beginning of June; and, on the 23d of that month, attacked the French army poſted at Crevelt, the left wing of which, after a warm engagement, was defeated with the loſs of ſix thouſand men; but the right and centre made a ſkilful and regular retreat. The count de Giſors, only ſon of the mareſchal Duc de Belleiſle, and one of the moſt accompliſhed noblemen of the French court, fell in this action. Prince Ferdinand immediately inveſted Duſſeldorp, which ſoon ſurrendered on capitulation. At this period the count de Clermont was ſucceeded by mareſchal de Contades, who being joined by powerful re-inforcements, menaced an attack upon the prince in his turn; and the prince of Yſemburg, who commanded a ſeparate corps on the other ſide the Rhine,

Rhine, being about this time defeated by marefchal Broglio, his ferene highnefs thought it neceffary to repafs that river, as well in order to fupport the vanquifhed army, as to meet the reinforcements from England, commanded by the duke of Marlborough, which were now landed at Embden. Accordingly a bridge was thrown over the river at Griethuyfen, and the allies paffed it on the tenth of Auguft without lofs. The feafon was fo far advanced previous to the junction with the Britifh forces, that no military operations of importance enfued during the remainder of the campaign between the two grand armies on the Rhine. On the Wefer, the prince of Yfemburg was again worfted by Soubize and Broglio. Prince Ferdinand now entered into winter-quarters at Munfter, and the French again eftablifhed themfelves in Weftphalia.

During thefe tranfactions the king of Pruffia had his hands fully employed in Saxony and Bohemia. After the reduction of Schweidnitz, he began his march at the head of fifty thoufand men into Moravia, and laid fiege to Olmutz, the capital of that Marquifate. Marefchal Daun immediately advanced to its relief, and, though he did not think proper to hazard a battle, he pofted himfelf in fo judicious a fituation, that the Pruffians found it extremely difficult to carry on their operations, being themfelves kept in perpetual alarm. The garrifon alfo made feveral fuccefsful fallies, and the Auftrian general having at length intercepted a great convoy of provifions and ammunition, the king of Pruffia found himfelf under an abfolute neceffity of raifing the fiege, which he effected with fuch fecrefy and expedition as to have penetrated far into Bohemia, before it was known in the Auftrian camp that he had loft fight of the walls of Olmutz. Marefchal Daun immediately followed the Pruffian monarch into Bohemia, but

but found himself without an antagonist, his majesty having evacuated that kingdom at the approach of the Russians, who had now entered Brandenburg in two large bodies, commanded by generals Fermor and Browne, and spread terror and devastation wherever they appeared. A detail of the outrages perpetrated by these northern barbarians cannot be read, or related, without horror. In the course of this campaign, they plundered and destroyed fourteen large towns, and more than one hundred villages. The Prussians came up with them at Zorndorf, August 25 *, when a desperate engagement ensued. The battle began about noon, and lasted till night, when the Russians gave way in great confusion. As the Prussians gave no quarter, the slaughter was terrible. Notwithstanding this defeat, the Russians continued extremely formidable. Upon the retreat of the king of Prussia from Bohemia, mareschal Daun had advanced towards the Elbe, and, being joined by the prince of Deux Ponts at the head of the army of the empire, threatened to surround prince Henry of Prussia, who commanded with much reputation and ability for the king his brother in Saxony: but his force was too weak to stop the progress of the Austrians, who took Konigstein, and established themselves in the strong camp at Pirna. Immediately after the battle of Zorndorf, the king began his march to join the prince; but, upon his arrival, found the imperialists so strongly entrenched, that they could not be attacked with any prospect of success. However, he gained some trifling advantages, and dislodged a corps of troops posted in the village of Hochkirchen, which was immediately occupied by the Prussian army. But, in the middle of the

* A. D. 1758.

night of the 14th of October, he was suddenly surprised in his camp by marefchal Daun; and, after a severe and bloody conflict, maintained amidst all the horrors of darkness and confusion, he was obliged to leave the Austrians in possession of the field and camp. Marefchal Keith gloriously fell in the action. The Prussian monarch, on this misfortune, retiring into Silesia, the Austrians invested Dresden. On their appearance, the Prussian governor Schmettau set fire to the beautiful suburbs of that city. The king of Prussia, in his answer to the Saxon memorial presented to the Diet on this subject, affected to feel the utmost distress and compassion at the situation of the inhabitants; and lamented, in the most pathetic terms, that the necessities of war rendered unavoidable a measure so repugnant to those principles of philanthropy which glowed in his royal breast. His Prussian majesty, after putting a stop to the progress of the Austrian arms in Silesia, and raising the sieges of Neisse and Cosel, returned to the relief of Dresden more formidable than ever, being joined by a strong body of troops, under the generals Dohna and Wedel, the former of whom had been engaged in obferving the motions of the Ruffians, who had by this time, after attempting the siege of Colberg without success, retired beyond the Vistula. The latter had opposed the Swedes in Pomerania. The campaign in that province greatly refembled that of the last year; for the Prussian monarch being obliged to withdraw all his forces, excepting those in garrison, the enemy not only recovered every thing they had lost, but made bold incursions into the Prussian territories, and even levied contributions within twenty miles of Berlin; but, at the approach of general Wedel, they evacuated their conquests with great precipitation, and their possessions in Pomerania at the end of the campaign were once more

more reduced to the city of Stralfund. The Pruffian general being now at liberty to co-operate with the king, marched into Saxony, and raifed the fiege of Torgau; and, being afterwards joined by general Dohna, proceeded to the relief of Leipfic, which was clofely invefted by the army of the empire; and this defign being happily completed, they effected a junction with the king, and advanced towards Drefden; but, at their approach, marefchal Daun thought proper to draw off his forces, and, on the 20th of November, his Pruffian majefty entered that city in triumph: and thus ended the campaign of 1758.

The French began the next year with an act of fingular perfidy, in feizing the imperial city of Francfort, which, indeed, was productive of the moft important advantages, as it commanded the navigation both of the Maine and the Rhine; and here the prince of Soubize eftablifhed his head-quarters.

Early in the fpring, feveral officers of rank in the allied army diftinguifhed themfelves by their activity and courage in beating up the enemy's quarters, deftroying their magazines, and defeating various detached corps; particulary the hereditary prince, who, in an action at Meinungen, made three entire battalions prifoners of war: but the general of the allies was difappointed in his grand defign of driving the French army from Francfort before the arrival of their expected reinforcements. With this intention, he made, on the 13th of April, an attack on marefchal Broglio at Bergen; but, being repulfed in three different affaults, he was obliged at length to retreat with lofs—the brave but unfortunate prince of Yfemburg fell in the action. In confequence of this check, prince Ferdinand returning to his former cantonments in Munfter, the French army, now under the command of marefchal Contades, advanced
northwards

northwards and took poffeffion of Caffel and Gottingen, Lipftadt, Munfter, and Minden. The regency of Hanover, alarmed at the rapidity of their progrefs, fent off the archives of the electorate, and the moft valuable effects, to Stade, in order to be fhipped for England; and his ferene highnefs, finding himfelf unable to oppofe them in the field, encamped with his troops in a ftrong fituation near Minden, where, on the firft of Auguft, the French general refolved to attack them. This refolution produced the famous battle of Minden. The French charged with great impetuofity, but met with fo warm a reception, that, after a conflict which lafted from dawn of day till noon, they were broken and routed on all fides, and gave way in extreme diforder and confufion. At this critical moment, the prince fent orders to lord George Sackville, who commanded the cavalry of the right wing, which formed a corps de referve, to advance with all poffible expedition to the attack; and, had thefe orders been properly executed, the diforderly retreat of the French army muft have been converted into a precipitate flight; but his lordfhip unfortunately not deeming his highnefs's orders fufficiently explicit, chofe to apply to the prince in perfon for an explanation; by which means, as well as by repeated orders to halt after the march was begun, fo much time was loft that the cavalry did not arrive foon enough to be of the leaft fervice. The grand allied army, however, without his lordfhip's affiftance, obtained a glorious victory. The Englifh infantry, in particular, commanded by generals Waldegrave and Kingfley, acquired immortal honor. They not only fuftained, with the utmoft intrepidity, the repeated attacks made upon them, but, charging the enemy in their turn, totally broke and routed the gendarmerie, carabineers, and the choiceft veterans of the French army. In this action
M. Contades

M. Contades loſt ten thouſand men, together with forty-three pieces of large cannon, a great number of colors and ſtandards, and his own equipage and cabinet, containing papers of the utmoſt conſequence. The garriſon of Minden immediately ſurrendered at diſcretion. The very ſame day, a ſeparate corps, under the Duc de Briſſac, was totally defeated at Coveldt by the hereditary prince. The French army now began its retreat to Caſſel, which they ſoon abandoned, and fell back to Gieſſen, being exceedingly haraſſed during their march, and ſuffering much damage. The city of Munſter was now the only place in Weſtphalia which remained in the hands of the French. After in vain attempting to reduce it by a bombardment and cannonade, the allies inveſted it in form about the beginning of November, when it ſurrendered upon capitulation.

The Duc de Broglio had by this time aſſumed the command of the French army, M. Contades being recalled with ſome marks of diſgrace. The military talents of the new general had, in the courſe of the war, appeared very conſpicuous; but all his efforts to retrieve the ſuperiority loſt by the defeat of his predeceſſor at Minden proved ineffectual, and he would, in all probability, have been driven beyond the Rhine, had not the exigency of the king of Pruſſia's ſituation made it neceſſary to detach the hereditary prince into Saxony with a large body of troops to his aſſiſtance. That heroic monarch had experienced the uſual inconſtancy of fortune in this campaign, though it was opened with great *eclat* by prince Henry, who, forcing a paſſage into Bohemia by way of Peterſwald, deſtroyed the Auſtrian magazines at Leutmeritz, and from thence penetrating into Franconia, drove the army of the empire before him to Nuremberg, laid the country under contribution, and captured upwards of fifteen-hundred priſoners. In the

the mean time, general Wedel had been sent into Poland to oppose the progress of the Russians, who had begun their march from the banks of the Vistula; but, in an obstinate engagement which took place at Kaye near Zullichau, the Prussians were defeated with great loss. The enemy immediately advanced into Brandenburg, and made themselves masters of the important city of Francfort upon the Oder. The king of Prussia, extremely alarmed at their success, ordered a detachment of ten thousand men from the grand camp in Silesia to join the army under general Wedel, who had been also reinforced by about the same number under general Finck; and the king took upon himself the command of the whole, amounting to fifty thousand men. The Russians, to the number of eighty thousand, were strongly entrenched at Cunersdorf; but the king's affairs requiring a desperate effort, he determined to attack them in their camp, and, about eleven in the morning of the twelfth of August [*], the action was begun with an heavy cannonade; after which the Prussians charged the left wing of the Russian army with so much vigor, that, after a furious contest of six hours, they forced the entrenchments with great slaughter, and seventy pieces of cannon fell into their hands. The battle was now looked upon as decided, and the king, in the first transports of his joy, dispatched the following billet to the queen at Berlin: " Madam, we have driven the Russians from their entrenchments—in two hours more expect to hear of a glorious victory." But he soon found himself fatally mistaken. The Russian general Soltikoff, exerting all his powers, rallied his troops upon an eminence under cover of a redoubt;

[*] 1759.

and his artillery, which was still greatly superior to that of the Prussians, was planted so judiciously as to render his situation almost impregnable. However, the king was resolved to hazard a fresh attack, though against the advice of all his generals. His infantry being repulsed in repeated assaults, the cavalry were ordered to succeed to the charge, but with no better success. At length the Russian cavalry, and a body of twelve thousand Austrian horse, under M. Laudohn, who had joined Soltikoff just before the engagement, and had hitherto remained inactive, seeing the Prussians discouraged and exhausted, fell in amongst them sword in hand with such fury, that, in a short time, the Prussians were totally routed and dispersed, notwithstanding the extraordinary efforts of the king, who exposed his life in the hottest parts of the engagement, had two horses shot under him, and his clothes shattered with musket balls. Nothing but the approach of night could have saved him from total ruin. On leaving the field of battle, he dispatched a second billet to the queen, expressed in these terms: " Remove from Berlin with the royal family. Let the archives be carried to Potzdam. The town may make conditions with the enemy." This was by far the most bloody action that had happened since the commencement of hostilities. Thirty thousand men were left dead on the field, of whom two-thirds were Prussians. No less than twelve generals were killed or wounded in this engagement, and the king of Prussia left his whole train of artillery in the hands of the Russians. This, however, was soon replaced from the arsenal at Berlin; and by his indefatigable diligence in recruiting his army, which was farther strengthened by the recall of general Kleist from Pomerania, he soon retrieved his importance.

During

During these transactions, prince Henry had gained several advantages over the army of the empire, which, again entering Saxony, had taken possession of the city of Dresden; and also over the Austrian army co-operating with them under general Haddick. The prince being at length joined by his Prussian majesty, general Finck was detached with a strong body of forces to cut off the retreat of the Austrians into Bohemia. But this measure proved a most unfortunate one; for mareschal Daun receiving intelligence of general Finck's remote and isolated position, immediately resolved upon an assault: and dividing his fortes into four columns, he conducted his march with such secrecy and expedition, that the Prussians found themselves entirely surrounded before they had entertained the least suspicion of being attacked. In this emergency, they fought with great bravery; but at length, overpowered by numbers and destitute of the possibility of relief, they were compelled to surrender prisoners of war to the amount of 19 battalions and 35 squadrons. It was at this critical period that the Prussian monarch was joined by the hereditary prince, without whose assistance it was feared he would have found himself unable any longer to cope with such numerous and powerful adversaries. The approach of winter at last freed him from any apprehensions from the Russians, who retired into their old quarters in Poland. As to the Swedes, they had fortunately been extremely inactive during the whole campaign, and, after some idle and fruitless excursions, had retreated as usual into the neighbourhood of Stralsund.

In spite of all his losses, the king of Prussia still kept his ground in Saxony; and even his enemies could not help expressing their admiration of that heroic fortitude and invincible perseverance which supported him amidst all the dangers and difficulties of a situation, by universal acknowledgment, unparalleled in the annals of Europe.

The court of Versailles had made great preparations for a vigorous campaign in Westphalia the ensuing summer[*]. The grand army, under Mareschal Broglio, was reinforced to the number of one hundred thousand men; and the count de St. Germaine commanded a separate corps of about thirty thousand. The hereditary prince, who had rejoined the allied army early in the spring (1760), met with a mortifying repulse at Corbach, in a too adventurous assault upon the count de St. Germaine; but he had soon an opportunity of retrieving his honor at Exdorf, where, on the sixteenth of July, he attacked a numerous body of the enemy under general Glaubitz, who were totally defeated after a very warm action, five whole battalions being taken prisoners, including the commander, with their arms, baggage, and artillery.— Elliot's regiment of light-horse appeared, for the first time, in the field upon this occasion; and, to the astonishment of the veteran troops, charged five different times, and broke through the enemy at every charge. This advantage was succeeded by another of still greater consequence; for the chevalier Muy, who commanded the reserve of the French army, amounting to thirty-five thousand men, being ordered to pass the Dymel, with a view to cut off the communication of the allied army, then posted near Cassel, with Westphalia, prince Ferdinand immediately decamped and followed him; and, on the 31st of July, made so masterly a disposition of his forces, that M. de Muy, who then lay encamped near the village of Warbourg, found himself at once attacked in flank, front, and rear. The French retreated to

[*] 1760.

precipitately, that the English infantry could not arrive in time to have any share in the action; but the cavalry, with the marquis of Granby at their head, distinguished themselves in the most honorable manner. The general of the allies, however, being obliged, in consequence of this movement, to leave the Landgraviate of Hesse exposed to the enemy's attack, Mareschal Broglio made himself master of Cassel, and even reduced Munden, Gottingen, and Eimbeck, in the electorate of Hanover. Notwithstanding the capture of these towns, the superiority acquired by the late victory enabled the English general to detach the hereditary prince on an expedition to the Lower Rhine, which was by no means productive of the advantages expected from it. The city of Cleves, being weakly garrisoned, made little resistance; but at Wesel, which place he next invested, he met with a much warmer reception than he looked for; and his operations also being much retarded by heavy rains, he found it impracticable to carry the place before the arrival of a very superior force, detached from the French army, under M. de Castries, for its relief. The siege being raised, an engagement ensued near Campen, in which the prince sustained considerable loss; notwithstanding which he repassed the river in the face of the enemy without molestation, and rejoined the main army, which had been ineffectually employed in the blockade of Gottingen; soon after which, prince Ferdinand retired into winter-quarters, leaving the enemy in possession of the whole country eastward of the Weser.

The king of Prussia, on his part, had made surprising exertions during the whole of this campaign. Whilst the two grand hostile armies remained strongly entrenched in the neighborhood of Dresden, general Laudohn made great progress in the reduction of Silesia, by defeating a strong body of troops under general Fouquet, and taking

taking the important town of Glatz, which contained an immenfe magazine of military ftores; after which he invefted Breflau. But count Tavenftein the governor, by making a moft refolute defence, gave opportunity to prince Henry of marching to its relief. Such was the expedition of the Pruffian general, that he marched one hundred and thirty Englifh miles in five days, and at his approach Laudohn abandoned his enterprife, after laying the city in afhes by a furious cannonade and bombardment, by which he hoped to intimidate the governor to a furrender. The king of Pruffia himfelf, after befieging in vain the city of Drefden, marched into Silefia, whither he was followed by count Daun; and advancing to Lignitz, with a view to effect a junction with the prince, who ftill remained at Breflau, he found himfelf in imminent danger of being furrounded, Marefchal Daun being pofted in front, general Laudohn on his left, and general Lafcy on his right; the grand army of the Ruffians, under Marefchal Soltikoff, being alfo on their march to co-operate with the Auftrians. In this emergency he determined rather to give battle than wait the attack; and, after taking the neceffary precautions for the fafety of his camp, he made a movement to the left with the greater part of his forces, in the evening of the 14th of Auguft*, with an intention of furprifing general Laudohn, who, in confequence of a plan formed by Marefchal Daun, of which his Pruffian majefty had obtained previous intimation, was at the very fame time on his march to furprife the king. The two armies met about two o'clock in the morning, between the villages of Pfaffendorff and Lignitz, and after a very fharp action, which lafted till fix, the Auftrians gave ground, and were purfued to a confiderable diftance: but Marefchal Daun,

* 1760.

who, in the execution of his part of the plan, had marched to the right of the Pruſſian camp, finding the tents apparently deſerted, and hearing the remote reverberation of cannon, inſtantly conjectured the nature of the king's manœuvre, and haſtened, but in vain, to the relief of Laudohn, the Auſtrians being previouſly and totally routed.

By this victory the king opening himſelf a paſſage to Breſlau, joined his brother prince Henry at Neumarcke, and they immediately began their march to Schweidnitz, now cloſely blockaded by the Auſtrians, who retired at their approach with ſome precipitation to the mountains of Landſhut. But while the king and prince triumphed in Sileſia, general Hulſen, who had been left in Saxony, found great difficulty in maintaining his ground againſt the imperial army, under the prince of Deux-Ponts. And the Swedes, who had ſurpriſed and killed general Manteuffle in the beginning of the year, now ravaged all Pomerania, without meeting any oppoſition. But the ſufferings of the Pomeranians were inconſiderable in comparison of thoſe the electorate of Brandenburg, and even the city of Berlin itſelf, experienced: for a grand detachment of the Ruſſian army, under count Czernicheff, penetrating into the marche on one ſide, and a numerous body of Auſtrians, under the generals Laſcy and Brentano, on the other, joined their forces in the neighborhood of that capital, which being of great extent, and imperfectly fortified, could make but a very feeble reſiſtance; the garriſon, to the amount of twelve hundred men, being compelled to ſurrender themſelves priſoners of war. The Ruſſian and Auſtrian troops no ſooner entered the place than they demanded the immediate payment of eight hundred thouſand guilders, and afterwards exacted a contribution of one million nine hundred thouſand German crowns.

Theſe

These exorbitant impositions the inhabitants were obliged to comply with, in order to save the city from total destruction. However, neither their compliance, nor the united efforts of the Austrian and Russian generals, could prevent the Cossacks, Croats, and other irregular troops, from being guilty of the most atrocious excesses. Not contented with demolishing the public magazines, arsenals, founderies, and hospitals, many hundred private houses were broke into and plundered, during the few days they remained there; for, upon hearing that the king was in full march to the relief of his capital, they abandoned the city, and, taking different routes, laid the whole country desolate in their retreat. The havoc made by them in the royal castle of Charlottenburg would have disgraced an army of Goths and Vandals. The rich and costly furniture of that splendid palace was totally destroyed; and even the celebrated collection of paintings and statues, made by the cardinal de Polignac, and deposited in this place, was miserably despoiled and disfigured. The king was followed by Marefchal Daun, at the head of one hundred thousand men. The Prussian army, after the junction with general Hulsen, amounted to eighty thousand. Notwithstanding this inferiority, the king determined to risque a battle; and indeed the situation of his affairs seemed to render some desperate effort necessary: for at this time general Laudohn was at the head of a numerous army in Silesia, and the Russians, who still threatened Breslau, had actually laid siege to Colberg, whilst the prince of Deux-Ponts, at the head of the army of the empire, being joined by general Lascy, had made himself master of Saxony, and the Swedes continued their ravages, uncontrolled, in Pomerania.

On the 3d day of November*, the whole Prussian army advanced towards the Austrians, advantageously posted at Torgau, upon the banks of the Elbe, their front being fortified with two hundred pieces of cannon; but the king giving his troops to understand that they had no alternative but to conquer or die, they charged the enemy with the most desperate intrepidity. The victory, however, remained in suspense, till general Zeithen, who had taken a circuit with part of the right wing of the Prussians, fell upon the rear of the Austrian army, which then began to give way, in some disorder; but Marefchal Daun receiving a dangerous wound, which obliged him to quit the field, the confusion became general. The darkness of the night, however, favored the retreat of the Austrians across the Elbe, over which they had previously thrown three bridges of boats, leaving the field of battle dearly purchased in the hands of the enemy. In consequence of this defeat, Marefchal Daun being under the necessity of recalling his detachments, general Laudohn abandoned Landshut, and his other acquisitions in Silesia. The Russians also, at the approach of winter, which the king styled his best auxiliary, raised the siege of Colberg, and retired to their cantonments in Poland, the Swedes into their old quarters near Stralsund, and the imperialists into Franconia; so that the king of Prussia found himself nearly in the same situation as at the beginning of the campaign.— That monarch was deservedly regarded, both by friends and foes, as a prodigy of fortitude, genius, and courage: but his uncommon abilities only served to prolong the war; and the inhabitants of the empire at large, who would have been happy had any decisive advantage been gained on either side, could now see no prospect of an end to their calamities.

Early in the spring of 1761, prince Ferdinand opened the campaign with the sieges of Ziegenhayn and Caſſel, hoping to reduce them before Mareſchal Broglio ſhould receive his reinforcements; but the garriſons making a vigorous reſiſtance, and part of the allied army under the hereditary prince being defeated near Heimbach, his ſerene highneſs found himſelf obliged to withdraw his troops and ſtand upon the defenſive. The army under Mareſchal Broglio being at length recruited, and in a condition to take the field, prince Ferdinand retired behind the Dymel, and eſtabliſhed his head-quarters at Paderborn. The Duc de Broglio having paſſed that river in June, drove general Sporcken from the poſt he occupied on the left ſide, and made himſelf maſter of Warbourg and Paderborn, and compelled prince Ferdinand to retire behind the Lippe. On the 15th July, in the evening, the French army made a furious attack upon the left wing of the allies poſted at Fellinghauſen, commanded by the marquis of Granby; and being repulſed with conſiderable loſs, they renewed the attack at dawn of day with redoubled vigour; but finding that no impreſſion could be made by their repeated efforts, their ardor began to abate: and at length, upon being charged by the marquis, in his turn, with great ſpirit, they abandoned the field in confuſion, leaving behind them four thouſand men dead on the ſpot.

Immediately after this action, the French generals divided their forces; the prince de Soubize retreating to Dortmund, and Mareſchal Broglio marching back to Caſſel. In a ſhort time that general paſſed the Weſer, with an intention of penetrating into the electorate of Hanover; but on the approach of prince Ferdinand he repaſſed that river with the greater part of his army: however, a detachment, under the command of the

count

count de Broglio his brother, by a forced march, took possession of Wolfenbuttle, and invested Brunswick; but the hereditary prince, flying to the relief of his father's capital, obliged the besiegers to relinquish this enterprise. For the rest of the campaign Mareschal Broglio remained inactive in his camp; and prince Ferdinand, not being able to force him to a battle, retired into winter cantonments in the vicinity of Munster and Osnaburg.

The spring * was far advanced before hostilities commenced in Saxony and Silesia. Warineſs and caution seemed to succeed to that spirit of enterprise and activity which had so long prevailed. The grand armies, on each side, were so strongly posted that neither chose to risque the attack. The imperialists, attempting to enter Saxony, were repulsed by general Seydlitz; but a numerous body of Russians, commanded by general Romanzoff, could not be prevented from penetrating into Pomerania, in July, and investing Colberg by land, whilst it was blocked up by a powerful squadron at sea. Their main army was soon after put in motion, and all the efforts of his Prussian majesty could not prevent its junction with Laudohn; and now the ruin of that monarch was again confidently predicted. If any event could make his affairs apparently more desperate, it was the loſs of Schweidnitz, which general (now Mareschal) Laudohn surprised about this time, by a very brilliant *coup de main*. Prince Henry of Prussia, who commanded in Saxony, by an uncommon display of military skill, prevented Mareschal Daun, who was at the head of a much superior army, from obtaining any advantage; that general was even obliged, in an attempt to storm the Prussian camp, to retreat with considerable loſs, soon

* 1761.

after which both armies were diftributed into quarters of cantonment.

The fatal confequences which had been apprehended from the fo much dreaded junction of the Auftrian and Ruffian armies did not, however, take place; and the Ruffian general foon perceived, or at leaft afferted, the neceffity of feparating, in order to cover his magazines in Poland, which were vigoroufly attacked by a large detachment from the Pruffian army under general Platen. But the fiege of Colberg ftill continued with unabating ardor. General Romanzoff feemed even to fet the winter at defiance, and, in the profecution of his defign, gave early proofs of thofe great talents which have fince rendered his name fo illuftrious. At length the place furrendered, Dec. 17, 1761: a conqueft of fingular importance, as it enabled the court of St. Peterfburg, at all times, to fend fupplies and reinforcements to their armies in Germany by fea; and the Ruffian general eftablifhed his head quarters in Pomerania, during the winter, with a view of taking the field early in the enfuing fpring.

The French court, refolving to exert their utmoft efforts in Weftphalia, affembled a vaft army upon the banks of the Wefer (A. D. 1762), under the prince de Soubize and the count d'Eftrées. Prince Ferdinand lay encamped behind the Dymel, watching their motions and waiting the favorable moment for an attack. At length, on the 24th of June, the enemy being then pofted at Grabenftein, a difpofition was made for that purpofe; the Prince himfelf croffing the river to charge in front, and generals Luckner and Sporcken being feverally detached to fall upon them at the fame time in flank and rear. This plan was executed with fuch fuccefs, that the French army was thrown into the utmoft confufion; and the French generals, after a fhort refiftance,

ance, gave orders for striking the tents, and sounding a retreat; but such was the impetuosity of the assailants, that in all probability a total defeat would have ensued, had not Monsf. de Stainville, with the most heroic gallantry and presence of mind, collected some regiments, consisting of the flower of the French infantry, with which he made so resolute a stand at the pass of Wilhelmsthal, that he effectually covered the retreat of the two Mareschals, who retired without much loss under the cannon of Cassel; but the corps under his command was either cut to pieces, or taken prisoners. The marquis of Granby, who commanded the reserve of the allied army, and was closely engaged with Stainville, distinguished himself in a remarkable manner. In consequence of this defeat, the French generals abandoned Gottingen, after demolishing the fortifications, which they had erected at an immense expence, and retired to Melsungen, in order to preserve the communication with Francfort; but on the approach of the prince they thought proper to pass the Fulda rather than hazard another battle, and the post of Melsungen was occupied by the allies.

In the month of July, Monsf. de Stainville, at the head of several regiments of dragoons fell into an ambuscade at Merschen, and his whole corps was totally routed and dispersed. But the joy occasioned by those various successes was somewhat damped by an unfortunate enterprise of the hereditary prince, who, prompted by youthful impetuosity, attacking with very inferior force the prince of Condé on his march from the Lower Rhine to join Soubize, was not only defeated, but so dangerously wounded that he was rendered incapable of taking any active part in the operations of the remaining part of the campaign. Prince Ferdinand now determined to lay siege to Cassel, and the French generals perceiving

his

his intentions, made repeated efforts to throw supplies into the place: but were effectually prevented by the vigilance and activity of that able commander. The trenches were opened on the 16th of October, and the operations carried on with such vigor, that, notwithstanding the place was defended with great bravery by the baron de Diesbach, the governor, he found himself obliged to sign a capitulation on the 1st of November, when the garrison marched out with all the honors of war.

His serene highness intended to have closed the campaign with the siege of Ziegenhayn, which was the only fortress in Hesse now possessed by the French; but his preparations were interrupted by the cessation of arms which took place at this period, immediately on signing the preliminaries of peace between Great Britain and France. Thus ended the military career of that celebrated commander, after he had, in the course of six successive and prosperous campaigns, exhibited to the world the most convincing proofs of his consummate knowledge of the art of war.

On the 2d of January 1762, died Elizabeth empress of Russia, by which fortunate event the most formidable and inveterate of all the enemies of the Prussian monarch were converted into friends and allies; for her successor Peter III.—a prince of the house of Holstein, and a descendant of the eldest daughter of Peter the great—entertained so enthusiastic an attachment to that hero, that he not only concluded a treaty of peace, but sent express orders to the Russian commanders to co-operate with him; and a body of troops under count Czernicheff actually joined the Prussian army. The Swedes also, by his example, were induced to accede to terms of accommodation.

In

In the beginning of May, prince Henry, unexpectedly passing the Muldaw, surprised the left wing of the Austrian camp; on which occasion general Zetzwitz was taken prisoner, with fifteen hundred men: after which the prince made himself master of Freyburg; and in the beginning of June repulsed the Austrians, who made a sudden attack upon his camp, with great loss. In Silesia, the king, now strengthened by the accession of the Russians, as well as by the troops he had withdrawn from Pomerania, advanced towards count Daun, who retired at his approach, and left a free passage for the Prussians, who invested Schweidnitz on the 8th of August, notwithstanding the secession of the Russians, who, in consequence of a surprising revolution that had taken place at the court of St. Petersburg, were no longer at liberty to co-operate with him. This was no other than the deposition of the reigning emperor, by his own consort Catherine of Anhalt, a woman of great talents, courage, and ambition, whose just resentment he had fatally provoked. This enterprise was conducted with wonderful secrecy, resolution, and dispatch. The emperor was indulging himself in the most perfect ease and security, at his country palace of Oranjebaum, when the empress suddenly appearing before it, at the head of ten thousand men, summoned him to surrender. With this demand he instantly complied with the most abject pusillanimity, though he was accompanied with his Holstein guards, and in a condition to have made a vigorous defence. He was immediately sent, under a strong escort, to the castle of Petershoff, where, in a few days, he was carried off by *a sudden illness*. This revolution was not productive of the least discontent or disorder, in any part of that vast empire; the follies and vices of the late Czar having rendered him the object of the public contempt and detestation. The empress Catherine,

therine, though she would not grant any assistance to the Prussian monarch, was by no means inclined to recommence the war, and the Russian armies immediately began their march to their own country.

The siege of Schweidnitz was now carried on with great vigor; and a mine being sprung by the besiegers on the 8th of October, in consequence of which great part of the wall was thrown into the fosse, and preparations made for a general assault, count de Guasco, the governor, thought proper to beat the *chamade*, and he, with the whole garrison, were made prisoners of war. The Imperial and Austrian armies in Saxony had, during the progress of the siege, defeated a body of troops under general Belling, and retaken Freyburg; but prince Henry, receiving a strong reinforcement from Silesia, attacked the combined forces under the command of the prince of Stolberg, at break of day, on the 29th of October (1762). The action lasted till two o'clock in the afternoon, when the enemy being entirely routed, abandoned the field of battle, and the town of Freyburg, with the loss of five thousand men.

A suspension of arms between the courts of Vienna and Berlin taking place soon afterwards, this was the last service performed in the field by prince Henry, in the course of this war, in which he had repeatedly displayed all the qualities of an accomplished general. And if the monarch was celebrated for his spirit of enterprise, for a genius fertile in resources, for his wonderful activity, and for a valor almost approaching to desperation, the prince was not less remarkable for his cool intrepidity, his sagacity, his firmness, and vigilance. The suspension of arms was quickly followed by the treaty of Hubertsburg, the most material article of which imported, that all conquests on each side should be evacuated, and peace re-established on the footing of

former

former treaties. Such was the iffue of a war in which two hundred and fifty thoufand lives were facrificed, an immenfity of treafure expended, and the faireft provinces of the empire reduced to a ftate of ruin and defolation.

We are now at liberty to advert to the civil and political tranfactions by which the adminiftration of Mr. Pitt was diftinguifhed. Amongft the firft and moft remarkable of which we may reckon the eftablifhment of a national militia: a meafure highly popular and patriotic; though the plan itfelf, which was calculated for the emergency of the occafion, and which has never fuffered any effential alteration, muft be acknowledged extremely crude, imperfect, and defective. Nor is it to be imagined that a comprehenfive and effectual fyftem of national defence is to be fupported at fo fmall an expence as the infignificant fum allotted for this moft important purpofe, and which is fcarcely equal to the ufual amount of a retaining fee to a German elector. The number of men was originally fixed by the houfe of commons at fixty-four thoufand, but by the houfe of lords reduced to thirty-two thoufand. The grand and radical defect of this plan is, that a fervice which ought to be fought as a privilege is impofed as an obligation. This national army is abfurdly and arbitrarily felected from the general mafs of the community, by lot, or, in other words, by a blind and indifcriminate compulfion; fo that it neceffarily exhibits a bizarre and fortuitous combination of alacrity and fullennefs, of imbecility and vigor. Were regular and reafonable pay allowed to each man, in the intervals of actual fervice, thofe who are beft qualified to ferve would voluntarily and cheerfully enrol themfelves, and the kingdom would be defended not by the refufe, but by the choice and flower of the nation. And with proper attention to difcipline, thefe troops

troops might soon be raised nearly or entirely to a level with the regulars of the service. In fact, the standing army of Prussia is at this day no other than a well-regulated national militia, adapted to the circumstances of that country. And were a national militia corresponding to the circumstances of this kingdom once established, the far greater part of the present formidable and unconstitutional standing army might be safely disbanded. And though it is remote from the province of history to descend to specific or minute calculation, it might be easily demonstrated, that the expence of such an establishment would not equal the amount of the sums annually voted by parliament, for maintaining possession of the barren rock of Gibraltar, the unjust retention of which, notwithstanding the plain dictates of common sense, and the dear-bought experience of Calais, Dunkirk, Port Mahon, and Tangier, we still continue with credulous enthusiasm to believe essential to the national prosperity and welfare.

In the summer of 1757, the empress-Queen recalled her minister, count Coloredo, from London; and at the same time notified to Mr. Keith, the English minister at Vienna, her determination to break off all correspondence with the king of England, declaring that she could not see with indifference his Britannic majesty enter into an alliance with her enemy the king of Prussia, instead of assisting her with the succors due by the most solemn treaties.

The French interest in Holland prevailing at this time in an alarming degree, Sir Joseph Yorke, the English ambassador at the Hague, was ordered to represent to the states-general the astonishment of the king of England at the permission given by their high mightinesses for the free passage of a large train of warlike imple-
nent

ments and stores through Namur and Maestricht, for the use of the French army; and still more at their tame acquiescence in the surrender of Ostend and Nieuport, by the empress-queen, to the French, in direct contravention of the barrier treaty, and of the treaty of Utrecht, which expressly declare, that no fortress, town, or territory of the Austrian Low Countries shall be ceded or transferred to the crown of France, upon any pretext whatever. The states, however, were not inclined to deviate from their professed system of neutrality; and they alleged, without reserve or hesitation, their inability to prevent these infractions of former treaties, as sufficiently excusing, or rather justifying their connivance at them.

At the meeting of parliament, December 1757, the king, in his speech from the throne, mentioned the late happy successes in Germany, and recommended " that his good brother and ally, the king of Prussia, might be assisted in such a manner as his magnanimity and zeal for the common cause appeared to deserve; expressing his firm reliance on the zeal of his faithful commons for the support of the *Protestant religion,* and of the liberties of Europe." The answer of the commons was in the highest degree dutiful and loyal; and the supplies, amounting to considerably more than ten millions, voted almost without the formality of a debate—Sir Francis Dashwood only venturing to express his total dissent from, and disapprobation of, the measure now adopted*. How the protestant religion was concerned in the disputes

---

* In a debate of the house of commons several years subsequent to this period, Mr Pitt declared, that every session during his administration he called out, " Has any body any objection to the German war? Nobody would object to it, one gentleman only excepted, since removed

putes of the present belligerent powers, it seemed, in particular, far beyond the reach of men of *common understandings* to comprehend. It was notorious that Saxony, long accounted the first protestant power in Germany, was ruined and desolated by the *Protestant Hero*; that the Swedes, who have ever distinguished themselves by their zeal in defence of the protestant faith, were themselves parties in this pretended confederacy against protestantism; that Denmark and Holland discovered no particular symptoms of alarm on this occasion, though as little inclined to advance the interests, or extend the power, of popery, as Great Britain itself.

The resentment of Holland was, at this period, inflamed in a very high degree against England, in consequence of the numerous seizures made by the English of Dutch vessels, employed in carrying naval stores and transporting merchandize, the produce of the French islands, to Europe. A memorial, to which was affixed a prodigious number of commercial signatures of the first consequence, was presented to the states general, in which their high mightinesses are strongly urged to protect the commerce and navigation of the republic by an armed force. The king of England, on the other hand, declared, by his ambassador, that he would not

---

moved to the upper house by succession to an ancient barony (Sir Francis Dashwood, now lord Le Despencer); he told me he did not like a German war; I honored the man for it, and was sorry when he was turned out of his post." On another occasion, he affirmed, " that it was impossible, after the treaties made with the king of Prussia, to leave that monarch to the mercy of his enemies; and that he entered into office with the German war tied like a mill-stone about his neck."

suffer

suffer an illicit and injurious trade to be carried on under the specious pretext of neutrality. And the wisdom and moderation of the princess Governante scarcely sufficed to prevent an open rupture. The death of that princess, which took place at the beginning of the ensuing year, was the subject of real and equal regret to both nations.

In the month of August 1758, a decree of the aulic council was published, enjoining all directories of circles, imperial cities, &c. to transmit to Vienna an exact account of those who had disobeyed the *avocatoria* of the empire, and adhered to the REBELLION raised by the elector of Brandenburg, that their revenues might be sequestered, and themselves punished in their honors, persons, and effects. The king of England, knowing himself to be chiefly aimed at in this decree, presented by his minister baron Gemmingen, a spirited memorial to the diet of the empire, enumerating the important services which he had rendered to the house of Austria, for which he had even exposed his life in the field of battle; in return for which the empress-queen had formed an alliance with France for the invasion of his electorate: and the duke of Cumberland, who had been wounded at Dettingen in the cause of her imperial majesty, was compelled to fight at Hastenbeck against the troops of that princess, in defence of his father's dominions; that the king of England was threatened with the ban of the empire for not complying with the resolutions of the Diet for assembling an army, although the conduct of the imperial court rendered it indispensable to his safety to retain his troops for the protection of his subjects. He acknowledged that, in quality of king of England, and for just reasons, he had sent over English troops to Germany, and had taken possession of Embden; for which he was accountable to

no

no power upon earth. And he expressed his hope that the Diet would, upon deliberate advice, not only exhort the emperor to recall or annul his recent mandates, but institute such proceedings against the empress-queen, in the quality of arch-duchess of Austria, as she wished to enforce against the king of England, as elector of Hanover." The original aggression of the laws of the empire rested, after all, solely and plainly with the king of Prussia, who was as clearly supported and defended in his contumacy by the king of England; and if these two monarchs, as members of the Germanic body, were at liberty to disobey and contemn the decrees of the Diet, the Germanic constitution was no more; no common centre of union remained, by which that vast body could exercise its sovereign authority, or even demonstrate its political existence. The Diet, however, wisely chose to refrain, in present circumstances, from the assumption of a prerogative which they were in no condition to enforce; and the numberless memorials, and counter memorials, published in the course of this war, served to little other purpose than to shew the extraordinary degree of animosity and rancor by which the belligerent powers were universally actuated.

In the course of this year died the celebrated Prosper Lambertini, who, on his elevation to the Papal chair, A. D. 1740, assumed the name of Benedict XIV. The good sense, candor, and moderation of this amiable Pontiff made him scarcely less the subject of esteem and veneration in the protestant than the catholic states of Europe. But, unfortunately, his political influence was too weak to enable him to compose those differences by which Christendom had been so long disgraced and desolated. He was succeeded in the Papacy by Cardinal Rezzonico, bishop of Padua, who took the name of

Clement

Clement XIII. And the new Pope found an early opportunity of displaying his weakness and bigotry, by sending a consecrated banner, accompanied with his apostolic benediction, to the Austrian general count Daun. A recent attempt, scarcely worthy of historic notice, as neither arising from any political cause, nor producing any political effect, had been made on the life of the king of France, by an insane fanatic of the name of Damien, who, in consequence of this crime, expired in torments; the national sufferance, and much more the national approval, of which, in the view of reason and humanity, degraded the character of the most polished and civilized country on the globe to a temporary level with that of the Onondagas and Cherokees. In the autumn of the present year, a royal assassination in all its circumstances much more extraordinary and interesting, the full extent and mysterious nature of which have never been perfectly developed, was attempted on the person of his most faithful majesty, who passing, September 3, in his carriage over a solitary spot near the palace of Belem, was fired at and dangerously wounded by two villains on horseback, one of whom made his escape; the other being put to the question, impeached the Duc d'Aveiro, president of the palace, the marquis and marchioness of Tavora, the count d'Atouguia, and several other persons of the highest rank, as parties in this conspiracy, who were accordingly tried, convicted, and suffered death on the scaffold. It appearing from undoubted evidence, that the Jesuits, who had been for some time past in disgrace at court, were the principal instigators to this wicked attempt, the effects and property of the whole order were sequestered, and a decree of banishment finally issued against them.

The parliament of England being convened in November (1758), the lord keeper Henley made a speech to both houses, by command of his majesty, in which the successes of the year were ostentatiously enumerated; and the commons were anew exhorted vigorously to support the king of Prussia, and the rest of his majesty's allies. The expence incurred by England at this time for the payment of subsidies, and the maintenance of armies in Germany alone, exceeded three millions sterling; which immense sum, as well as all the other supplies demanded by the minister, were now voted almost as a matter of course. Towards the termination of the session, May 1759, the king informed the two houses, by messages delivered by lord Holderness and Mr. Pitt, the two secretaries of state, that he had received authentic advice of preparations making by the French court with a design to invade Great Britain: and both houses, in return, assured his majesty of their determination to support, with their lives and fortunes, his person and government against all attempts whatever. Directions also were issued to the lords lieutenants of the respective counties of the kingdom to use their utmost diligence and attention in executing the several acts of parliament made for the better ordering the militia. This alarm, however, after the defeat of the French fleet by admiral Hawke, entirely subsided.

In the month of August, an event of great political importance took place in the death of Ferdinand, king of Spain, who, in consequence of the loss of the queen his consort, had for many months, renounced all company, neglected all business, and indulged in the utmost excesses of sorrow, under the weight of which he languished, without relief or intermission, to the final termination of his life. He was succeeded by his brother Don Carlos, king of the Sicilies—a prince by no means so favorably difposed as his predeceffor to the Englifh nation; and who ftill harbored a deep refentment of the infult offered to his crown and dignity in the former war, by the threatened bombardment of his capital, and the humiliating treaty of neutrality to which he was compelled to accede. This monarch, previous to his departure from Naples, by a folemn edict, refigned the kingdoms of Naples and Sicily to his younger fon, Don Ferdinand, in contravention and contempt of the treaty of Aix-la-Chapelle, which exprefsly declares, that, if the infant Don Carlos fhall fucceed to the throne of Spain, the duchies of Parma, Placentia, and Guaftalla fhall revert to the houfe of Auftria, and the infant Don Philip fhall fucceed to the throne of the Sicilies. But to this article Don Carlos had never acceded; and the court of Vienna was not at this time in a fituation to enforce the obfervance of it.

In November 1759, the parliament was again opened by commiffion, and the lord keeper again enlarged on the fignal fucceffes of his majefty's arms by fea and land; particularly diftinguifhing the reduction of Quebec and the victory of Minden—declaring, however, by the command of his fovereign, " that, as his majefty entered not into this war from views of ambition, he did not wifh to continue it from motives of refentment; that the defire of his majefty's heart was to fee a ftop put to the effufion of Chriftian blood, whenever juft and honorable terms of peace could be obtained." It was confolatory to the humane and difpaffionate part of the nation, after the facrifice of fuch countlefs hecatombs of human victims, and the expenditure of fo many millions of treafure, at length to hear the found of peace. But the majority, intoxicated with ideas of conqueft, were far from wifhing the fpeedy termination of the war; and from the enormous fupplies granted by
parliament,

parliament, amounting this year to no less than fifteen millions, it seemed as if the nation, eager for its own impoverishment and ruin, was willing to purchase glory with bread.

In the course of this session, an effort was made to render efficient the famous parliamentary qualification act of queen Anne, by the introduction of a bill, which, with some modifications, eventually passed into a law. By virtue of the new act, it became necessary for every person elected a member of the house of commons, to deliver in a paper or schedule to the speaker of the house, specifying the lands, tenements, and hereditaments, whereby he makes out his qualification. But this regulation served only to increase in some degree the trouble, and not at all to diminish the frequency of evasion. The truth is, that the act, which was originally designed to promote the interests of a faction, is so contrary to the sense and to the interest of the nation, that it neither can nor ought to be enforced. Perfect freedom of choice on the part of the people is the only rational security for the integrity of the representative body; and to impose any arbitrary restrictions of this nature, by which they might be eventually deprived of the services of some of the most honest and able members of the community, is an unconstitutional violation of their just and imprescriptible rights *.

The

---

* This act of queen Anne, originally framed to strengthen the interest of the Tory faction, can be justified on no principle of reason or equity; for there is no ground to suppose that integrity bears any determinate *ratio* to property. Men in higher walks of life are far from being, on that account, the most independent. Having a specific rank to support, and dreading the least degradation from it, they have al-

The subject which at this time chiefly engrossed the public attention, was the court-martial held upon lord George Sackville, commander of the British forces in Germany, in consequence of the charge brought against him of disobeying the repeated orders of Prince Ferdinand, to advance with the cavalry, in order to sustain the infantry, and to attack the enemy, already broken, at the memorable battle of Minden. From this charge his lordship was not able to clear himself to the satisfaction of the public. For, though it appeared that there were

ways much for themselves and families to ask—admitting that they cherish no ambitious ideas of advancement—at least to maintain their accustomed level in society. Whereas, persons in less elevated stations, of inferior fortune, and different habits, more easily learn to moderate their desires, and not unfrequently entertain a real indifference for those honors and riches which it is the lot of so few to possess——

> " And which to leave's a thousand fold more bitter
> Than sweet at first t' acquire."

It is true, that absolute indigence is apparently incompatible with independence: but there is little danger that persons of this description should be returned members to parliament, except the virtue of the individual should in some rare instance be deemed proof against all temptation, as in the case of the famous Andrew Marvel, who is said, after refusing a treasury warrant for a thousand pounds, to have been under the necessity of applying to a friend for the loan of a guinea.

> " Gemmas, marmor, ebur, Tyrrhena sigilla, tabellas,
> Argentum, vestes Gaetulo murice tinctas
> Sunt qui non habeant; est qui non curat habere."
>
> Hor.

> " Gold, silver, ivory, vases, sculptur'd high,
> Paint, marble, gems, and robes of Tyrian dye,
> There are who have not—and thank Heaven there are,
> Who, if they have not, think not worth their care."
>
> Pope.

were in the orders transmitted by the different Aides-du-camp some degree of variation, perhaps of inconsistency, it was universally acknowledged that the necessity of bringing the cavalry into *immediate action* was strongly and repeatedly urged to his lordship. Colonel Fitzroy [*], in particular, after stating the circumstances which occasioned the order, added, with great gallantry, " that it was a glorious opportunity for the English to distinguish themselves, and that his lordship, by leading them on, would gain immortal honor." Admitting, then, the commands of his serene highness to be in any respect doubtful, his lordship might surely have been guided in the interpretation of them by his own discretion; and nothing could be more absurd or unpardonable than to waste those irreparable moments in coldly seeking an explanation of orders, which ought to have been occupied in the vigorous execution of them. In conclusion, the court-martial adjudged that lord George Sackville was guilty of disobeying the orders of prince Ferdinand of Brunswick, his commander—declaring him, for this offence, incapable of serving his majesty in any military capacity whatsoever. This sentence was confirmed by the king, who, as a farther mark of his resentment, called in council for the council-book, and ordered the name of lord George Sackville to be struck out of the list of privy counsellors. Such was the last public act of this monarch's reign and life: for, on Saturday the 25th of October 1760, being at the palace of Kensington, where he commonly resided, he was suddenly seized with an apoplectic fit, soon after his rising in usual health in the morning, Recovering his senses after a short interval, he desired, with a faint voice, that his daughter the princess Amelia might be

---

[*] Now lord Southampton.

sent

sent for; but, before her arrival, he expired, in the seventy-seventh year of his age, and the thirty-fourth of his reign. During this long period, he had experienced many vicissitudes of fortune; but he lived to see himself the most successful of all the English monarchs. And, after the dark and lowering aspect which his political horizon occasionally exhibited, his sun set at last in a golden cloud.

The character of this monarch it is not easy either to mistake or to misrepresent. Endowed by nature with an understanding by no means comprehensive, he had taken little pains to improve and expand his original powers by intellectual cultivation. Equally a stranger to learning and the arts, he saw the rapid increase of both under his reign, without contributing in the remotest degree to accelerate that progression by any mode of encouragement, or even bestowing, probably, a single thought on the means of their advancement. Inheriting all the political prejudices of his father—prejudices originating in a partiality natural and pardonable—he was never able to extend his views beyond the adjustment of the Germanic balance of power; and resting with unsuspicious satisfaction in that system, into which he had been early initiated, he never rose even to the conception of that simple, dignified, and impartial conduct, which it is equally the honor and interest of Great Britain to maintain in all the complicated contests of the continental states. It is curious to remark, that the grand objects of the two continental wars of this reign were diametrically opposite: in the first, England fought the aggrandizement—in the second, the abasement of the house of Austria. And in what mode the consequent advancement of Prussia, at an expence to England so enormous, to the rank of a primary power in Europe, has contributed to the establishment or preservation of that political

cal balance upon the accurate poize of which many have affirmed, and perhaps some have believed, that the salvation of England depends, yet remains to be explained. In the internal government of his kingdoms, this monarch appears, however, to much greater advantage than in the contemplation of his system of foreign politics. Though many improper concessions were made by the parliament to the crown during the course of this reign, it must be acknowledged, that no violation of the established laws or liberties of the kingdom can be imputed to the monarch. The general principles of his administration, both civil and religious, were liberal and just. Those penal statutes which form the disgrace of our judicial code, were, in his reign, meliorated, and virtually suspended, by the superior mildness and equity of the executive power. And it was a well-known and memorable declaration of this beneficent monarch, "that, during his reign, there should be no persecution for conscience sake." Though subject to occasional sallies of passion, his disposition was naturally generous and easily placable. On various occasions, he had given signal demonstrations of personal bravery; nor did the general tenor of his conduct exhibit proofs less striking of his rectitude and integrity: and, if he cannot be ranked amongst the greatest, he is at least entitled to be classed with the most respectable princes of the age in which he lived, and his memory is deservedly held in national esteem and veneration.

The general state of literature and the arts during this reign, it may be thought improper to pass over without a specific, however transient, mention. In the early part of it, a shadow of royal protection and encouragement displayed itself in the countenance given by queen Caroline—a princess of an excellent understanding and much liberality of sentiment—to several learned men,

men, with whom she loved freely to converse; particularly with Dr. Samuel Clarke, so famous for his theological and metaphysical writings; and whose speculative opinions, in their full extent, the queen was believed to have deeply imbibed. Hoadley, the friend of this illustrious philosopher, was advanced, through a long series of promotions, to the bishopric of Winchester; and Dr. Clarke himself was, it is said, destined, had not his death prematurely and unexpectedly intervened, to the archbishopric of Canterbury. These great and celebrated ecclesiastics, the brightest ornaments and luminaries of the English church, were anxiously solicitous to advance its true interest, as well as honor, by effecting a farther reform, both of its discipline and doctrine, on the genuine principles of protestantism. But the political caution, and not the religious bigotry, of the governing powers unhappily precluded the attempt.

The prince of Wales also, at a subsequent period, shewed a disposition, though restrained in the ability, to become a munificent patron of literature: and Mallet, Thomson, and Young, are said to have been particularly distinguished by his bounty. The *Seasons*, and the *Night Thoughts*, are poems of high and deserved celebrity. But the most truly poetical genius of this reign was unquestionably Gray, had his powers been fully expanded by the sunshine of popular and courtly encouragement. The *Bard* and *Church-yard Elegy* are master-pieces of sublime enthusiasm, and plaintive elegance. In the drama no tragedies appeared which could stand even a momentary competition with the admired and pathetic productions of Otway, or even the elegant though less impassioned performances of Rowe. In comedy, Congreve, Vanburgh, and Farquhar *yet* remained unrivalled. And of the far greater part of the numerous dramatic pieces of this period, it may be affirmed in the words of

Dryden,

Dryden, "that the tragic muse gave smiles, the comic sleep."

In one species of literary composition, however, and that of the highest importance, the reign of George II. may boast, a decided and indisputable superiority; and in the province of history, the names of Hume and Robertson will ever claim the highest rank of eminence. Taking it for all in all, Hume's history of England may perhaps be justly regarded as the greatest effort of historic genius which the world ever saw. His philosophic impartiality, approaching indeed occasionally the confines of indifference, his profound sagacity, his diligence of research, his felicity of selection and arrangement, the dignified elegance of his style, which yet rarely aspires to elevation or energy—all combine to stamp upon this work the characteristics of high and indisputable excellence. With such happiness, and with touches so masterly, are the principal personages of his history delineated, that a more clear and perfect idea is frequently conveyed by Mr. Hume, in a few lines, than we are able to derive from the elaborate amplifications of lord Clarendon, whose historical portraits, though drawn certainly with great accuracy and closeness of observation, are finished rather in the style of the Flemish than the Roman school. With respect to the Historian of Charles V. it is sufficient to say, that he has been often highly, but never too highly praised. From a rude and indigested chaos of matter he has selected those facts which are truly and permanently interesting, and which alone it imports posterity to know, connecting them with exquisite skill, and adorning his narration with all the graces of a simple, pure, and luminous diction, wholly free from those meretricious ornaments, that tumid pomp, and gaudy display of eloquence, by which later writers have

have been unfortunately ambitious to acquire reputation.

In metaphyfics, Hartley eftablifhed a fyftem admirable for its fimplicity, for the extent and importance of its practical application, and its perfect correfpondence with all the actual phænomena of human nature, upon the firm and immovable foundation of Locke. This fyftem, now rifing into general regard and eftimation, has been violently attacked by fome ingenious writers, whofe darts have " faintly tinkled on the brazen fhield" of this great philofopher, the theory of whom has been moft ably vindicated by the pen of the celebrated Prieftley, whofe name, at once the glory and the reproach of the Englifh nation, is revered in every part of the globe where the light of fcience has penetrated; and whofe peculiar praife and honor it is, long to have been the object of the malignant animofity, and, as far as the fpirit of the times would permit of the perfecution of the " holy Vandals" of the age.

In philology, morals, and criticifm, Bentley, Warburton, and more recently Johnfon, fhone with diftinguifhed luftre.

In theology, amidft an hoft of great and refpectable names, it cannot be deemed invidious to beftow the higheft applaufe on that of Lardner, who, unaffifted by the advantages, and unadorned by the honors of our national feminaries of education, compofed a ftupendous work on the credibility of chriftianity, no lefs to be admired for its candor, impartiality, and fagacious fpirit of refearch, than its amazing extent and depth of erudition; and it is not without reafon that he has been ftyled, by a juftly celebrated writer, who cannot be fufpected of partiality either to the caufe or the advocate, " the prince of modern divines." Fofter, Leland, Chandler, Abernethy, Duchal, and many other eminent names, not of

the

the eſtabliſhed church, maintained alſo, with diſtinguiſhed honor to themſelves, by their various learned theological and philoſophical writings, at once the reputation of their ſeparate communion, and the authority of that common faith which all denominations of chriſtians are equally concerned to ſupport. In the pale of the eſtabliſhment, the venerable Lowth diſtinguiſhed himſelf above all his cotemporaries, by adorning the profoundeſt diſquiſitions in ſacred literature with all the charms of claſſic elegance. And the excellent Jortin, in the juſtneſs and comprehenſion of his views, the clearneſs and accuracy of his reaſonings attained to high, perhaps unrivalled pre-eminence. His *remarks on eccleſiaſtical hiſtory* abound with the moſt candid and liberal ſentiments; and his *life of Eraſmus* diſcovers a mind perfectly congenial with that of the illuſtrious ſcholar whoſe portrait he has delineated—the ſame ingenuous ſimplicity, the ſame urbanity, wit, and poliſhed keenneſs of ſatire—in rectitude equal, in fortitude ſuperior. Had Eraſmus flouriſhed in our days, Jortin would ſurely have been his favorite and choſen friend; for we know that his admired and beloved Colet was but the Jortin of a former age. For the famous and incomparable preface prefixed to his *remarks*, he is ſaid to have been menaced by the high church bigots of his time with a legal proſecution; but this threat was rendered ineffectual by the moderation of the governors of the church at that period, and particularly of Herring, archbiſhop of Canterbury—a prelate eminent for diſcernment, candor, and benignity, and who had declared to Dr. Jortin that he would be to him what Warham had been to Eraſmus. It was, however, late in life before the extraordinary merits of Jortin attracted that attention to which they were ſo well intitled: and he himſelf truly and feelingly ſpeaks of the patronage ſaid to be afforded to literature by men of rank

rank and fortune, as " a Milesian fable and a fairy tale."

Before the conclusion of this reign, Reynolds in painting, in sculpture Wilton, began to rise into fame: and the exquisite musical compositions of Handel were vigorously emulated by Arne and Boyce. But to whatever degree of perfection science, literature, and the arts, arose, during even its last splendid and memorable period, the sole and exclusive honor of patronage appertains—not to the court—nor to any Mæcenas or Dorset of the age—not to the encouragement derived from academical honors or premiums—but to the taste, discernment, and generosity of the NATION.

INDEX.

A

ABERCROMBIE, general, appointed to the chief command in America, vol. ii. 193.—His unsuccessful attempt on Ticonderago, ii. 194.—Superseded by general Amherst, 196.

Abo, peace of, between Russia and Sweden, ii. 89.

Achmet III. Emperor of the Turks, his extraordinary deposition, i. 210.—213.

Addison, Mr. advanced to the post of secretary of state, i. 128; but resigns, ibid.—His literary character, 198.

Adolphus-Frederick, king of Sweden, his accession to the throne, ii. 135.—His voluntary oath, 136.

Aix-la-Chapelle, Convention of, i. 196.—General peace of, ii. 120.—

Alberoni, Cardinal, his character and romantic projects, i. 106.—118.

Albemarle, earl of, his spirited memorial to the French court, ii. 155.

Amherst, general, assumes the command in America, ii. 193.—Captures the city of Louisburg, 194.—Reduces the forts of Ticonderago and Crown-Point, 197.—Takes the city of Montreal, and completes the conquest of Canada, 203.

Anne, queen of Great Britain, succeeds to the throne on the death of king William, i. 7.—Declares war against France, 8.—Her prejudices, political and religious, 41.—Dismisses the Whig ministry, 50.——Orders the attorney general to commence a prosecution against the duke of Marlborough, 52.——Her death and character, 62, 63.

Anne Iwanowna, empress of Russia, her accession, i. 210.—Her conquests over the Ottomans, 279.—Her death, ii. 13.

Anson,

INDEX.

Anson, commodore, detached with a squadron into the south-sea, ii. 12.—Returns to England after a circumnavigation of the globe, 13.—Engages and defeats a French squadron, 118.—Ennobled, ibid.——Placed at the head of the admiralty, 189.

Argyle, duke of, defeats the rebels at Sheriff Moor, i. 81.—His character drawn, 202.—Opposes the bill for inflicting penalties on the city of Edinburgh, 276.—Accepts the master-generalship of the Ordnance, which he quickly resigns, ii. 39.

Ashby and *White*, case of, i. 12.

Atterbury bishop of Rochester, refuses to sign the protestation against the Pretender, i. 122.—Opposes the petition of the Quakers, 156.—Engages in a conspiracy against the government, and banished, 159. Remarkable declaration of lord Harcourt respecting him, 163.—His character and death, 164.

Augustus I. King of Poland, his death, and its political consequences, i. 249.

Augustus II. King of Poland, joins the confederacy against the queen of Hungary, ii. 15.—Concludes a treaty of peace, 18.—Joins the queen of Hungary against Prussia, 55.—His troops defeated at Keffeldorff, and the city of Dresden compelled to surrender, 60.—Concludes a treaty of peace with Prussia, ibid.—Engages in a subsidy treaty with England, 137; whom he abandons, 164.—Enters into secret intrigues to the prejudice of the king of Prussia, 231.—His dominions invaded by the king of Prussia, who takes possession of Dresden, 233.—His army compelled to capitulate, 234.

B

Balchen, admiral Sir John, lost, with his whole crew, in the Victory, ii. 100.

Barnard, Sir John, his opposition to the foreign loan bill, i. 215.—His speech against the acquisition of an unlimited vote of credit, 265.—His plan for reducing the public debt, 284.

Bedford, duke of, declares his disapprobation of the Hanoverian system, ii. 44.——His speech against the bill for extending the forfeitures of treason, 85.—Appointed first lord of the admiralty, 101. His remarkable motion in the house of peers, 125.

Belhaven, earl of, his eloquent speech against the treaty of union, i. 26.

Benedict, Pope, XIII. his accession to the papacy, i. 155.—His death, 210.

Benedict, Pope, XIV. his death and character, ii. 269.

Berwick, duke of, gains the battle of Almanza, i. 34.—Captures Fontarabia and St. Sebastian, 119.—Reduces fort Kehl and Traerbach, 250.—Killed by a cannon-ball at the siege of Philipsburg, 251.

Braddock, general, his disastrous expedition to the Ohio, ii. 159.

Bligh, general, his unfortunate retreat to St. Cas, ii. 205.

Bolingbroke, viscount, appointed secretary of state, i. 51.—Repairs to Paris to negotiate the peace, 56.—His character, 58.—Brings in a bill against the Pretender, 61.—Removed from his office, 72; and

impeached

I N D D X.

impeached of high treason, 75.—Withdraws to the Continent, ibid.—Engages in the service of the Pretender, 77.—Bill of attainder passed against him, 79.—His character of the Pretender, 83.—Act of attainder reversed, 162.—Joins the opposition, instigated by chagrin and ambition, 163. Acquires the favor and confidence of the prince of Wales, ii. 122.—His character in the concluding years of his life, ibid.

Boscawen, admiral, captures the Alcide and the Lys, ii. 158—Defeats the French fleet off Cape Lagos, 206.

Bourbon, duke of, succeeds the duke of Orleans as regent of France, i. 172.

Breslau, treaty of, ii. 18.

British Fishery, act passed for its encouragement, ii. 132.

Bute, earl of, introduced into the household of the prince of Wales, ii. 125.—His baleful influence, 126.

Byng, Sir George, defeats a French armament from Dunkirk, i. 32.—Engages and destroys the Spanish fleet off Messina, 111.—Created viscount Torrington, 112.

Byng, admiral, dispatched to the relief of Minorca, ii. 177.—His indecisive engagement with Monf. Galissioniere, 178.—His pusillanimous retreat to Gibraltar, 179.—His trial and execution, 182, 183.

C

Cambray, congress of, i. 119.

Cameron, Dr. his trial and barbarous execution, ii. 145.

Cape Breton, island of, taken by admiral Warren, ii. 113.—Restored by the peace of Aix-la-Chapelle, ii. 121.—Captured by general Amherst, 194.

Carew, Mr. his motion for restoring annual parliaments, ii. 102.

Carteret, lord, his character, i. 202.—Appointed to the government of Ireland, 209.—His wise administration, ibid.—He resigns his offices, and joins the opposition, 224.—Supports the pension bill, ibid.—Declares against votes of credit, 288.—Appointed principal secretary of state, ii. 35.—Votes against the pension bill, 36.—Insinuates himself into the favour of the king, 42.—Appointed ambassador extraordinary to the states general, ibid.—His insidious policy, 9.—Engrossed by continental politics, 74.—His speech in vindication of the continental war, 76.—Against dismissing the Hanoverian mercenaries, 82.—Compelled to resign his office, 101.—Becomes earl of Granville, is re-appointed to the office of secretary of state, and again resigns, 114.—Made president of the council, ibid.

Carlos, Don, succeeds to the duchies of Parma, &c. i. 224.—Conquers Naples and Sicily, 252.—Succeeds to the crown of Spain, ii. 171.

Caroline, queen of Great Britain, dies, i. 278.—Her liberality of sentiment, ii. 277.

INDEX.

Catherine I. empress of Russia, her accession to the throne, i. 182.—Offended at the measures of the English court, ibid.—Accedes to the treaty of Vienna, 183.—Death of the empress, 195.

Catherine II. empress of Russia, her accession and character, ii. 262.

Charles XII. king of Sweden, offended at the purchase of Bremen and Verden, i. 98.—Projects the invasion of Great Britain, 99.—His death and character, 104.

Charles VI. Emperor of Germany, concludes a peace with France, at Al-Rastadt, i. 57—Engages as a party in the quadruple alliance, 108.—Refuses to the king of England the investitures of Bremen and Verden, 120.—Grants a protectorial commission for Mecklenburg, 121.—His jealousy of the king of England, 171.—Establishes an imperial East India company at Ostend, ibid.—Concludes an alliance with Spain, 173.—Agrees to preliminaries of accommodation with England, 196.—Offended at the treaty of Sevile, 210—224.—His unsuccessful war with Turkey, 279.—His death, ii. 13.

Charles VII. emperor of Germany, elector of Bavaria, his claim upon the Austrian succession, ii. 15.—Invades the archduchy of Austria, and threatens Vienna, 16.—Crowned king of Bohemia at Prague, 17.—Elected emperor at Francfort, ibid —Reduced to great difficulty and distress, 19.—His decree against the queen of Hungary, 20.—In danger of being made a prisoner, 45.—Signs a treaty at Francfort, with Prussia, Sweden, and the elector Palatine, 55.—Recovers possession of Munich, his capital, and dies, 57.

Charles-Emmanuel, king of Sardinia, succeeds to the crown on the resignation of his father, i. 210—Orders the person of the late king to be seized, 244.—Declares war against the emperor, in conjunction with France and Spain, 260.—Joins the house of Austria against Spain and France, ii. 20.—In danger of losing his dominions 23.—He is remunerated for his services, 26.

Charles, prince of Lorraine, opposes the king of Prussia in Silesia, ii. 18.—Advances into Bohemia, and invests the city of Prague, 19.—Crosses the Rhine, and invades the kingdom of France, 54.—Compels the king of Prussia to evacuate Bohemia, 55.—Defeated by Mareschal Saxe, at Roucoux, 69—Defeated by the king of Prussia at Prague, 235.—Superseded in the command by Marshal Daun, 236.

Cherbourg, city of, taken by lord Howe, who destroys its bason and harbour, ii. 205.

Chesterfield, earl of, his character, i. 201.—His speech against the bill for licensing the stage, 281.—Inveighs against a continental war, ii. 43.—His speech on moving the address, 74.—Appointed to the government of Ireland, 101.—Goes as ambassador-extraordinary to Holland, 109.—The wisdom and popularity of his government, 111.—Presents a bill for the reform of the calendar, 135.

Christiern VI. king of Denmark, endeavours to revive the union of Calmar, ii. 97—Refuses the subsidies of Great Britain, ibid.—Renews the alliance with Great Britain, 98.—His death, ibid.

Clement XI. Pope, dies—his character, i. 153.

Clement XII. Pope, his accession, i. 210.—Fills the papal chair ten years, ibid.

Clive

INDEX.

Clive, colonel, takes the city of Arcot, ii. 220.—Captures, in conjunction with admiral Watson, the city of Calcutta, 224.—Defeats Sou Rajah Doula, 225.—Takes Chandernagore, ibid.—His march to Moorshedabad, 226.—Gains a complete victory at Plassey, ibid.

Cloister-Seven, convention of, ii. 192.

Coote, colonel, defeats M. Lally at Wandewash, ii. 229.—Takes the city of Pondicherry, 230.

Cope, Sir John, defeated by the rebels at Preston-Pans, ii. 65.

Cotton, Sir John Hynde, his description of a genuine Whig, i. 280.—Accepts a place at court, which he soon resigns, ii. 101.—His opposition to the subsidizing system, 138.

Cowper, lord, removed from his office of lord chancellor, i. 51.—Reinstated, 73.—Opposes the repeal of the test laws, 132; and the bill for banishing the bishop of Rochester, 161.

Crawford, earl of, his extraordinary presence of mind, ii. 69.

Cumberland, duke of, wounded at Dettingen, ii. 47.—Assumes the command of the allied army against Marefchal Saxe, 53.—Defeated at Fontenoy, 63.—Gains a complete victory over the rebels at Culloden, 68.—Defeated by Marefchal Saxe, at Laffeldt, 71.—His military character, 120.—Appointed to the command of the army of observation in Germany, 191.—Defeated at Haftenbeck by Marefchal D'Etrées, 191.—His injudicious retreat to Stade, ibid.—Obliged to capitulate with his whole army, ibid.—Resigns his employments, 193.

D

Daun, Marefchal, defeats the king of Prussia at Kolin, and relieves Prague, ii. 235.—Captures Schweidnitz, 237.—Defeats the Prussians under the prince of Bevern, and takes Breslau, ibid.—Defeated by the king of Prussia at Lissa, ibid.—Relieves Olmutz, and pursues the king into Bohemia, 242.—Defeats the king at Hochkirchen, 244.—Captures general Finck and his whole army, 248.—Defeated by the king at Torgau, 256.

Derwentwater, earl of, appears in arms against the government, i. 80.—Surrenders himself prisoner, 81.—Beheaded on Tower-hill, 84.

Devonshire, duke of, appointed first commissioner of the treasury, ii. 185.

Dorset, duke of, his declaration to the parliament of Ireland, ii. 146.

Dupleix, M. his abilities and ambition, ii. 219.

E

Egmont, lord, his opposition to German subsidies, ii. 138.

Elizabeth, empress of Russia, her accession, ii. 13.—Orders the march of 40,000 men to the Rhine, 73.—Carries on a successful war with the Swedes, 96.—Her infidious and interefted policy, 120.—Concludes a fubfidy treaty with England, 165.—Enters into engagements with France, 166.—Joins the confederacy againft Pruffia, 231—236.—Her death, 261.

Eugene, prince, his interview with the duke of Marlborough, i. 17.—Co-operates with the Englifh general in gaining the victories of Schellenburg and Blenheim, 18.—Gains a complete victory at Turin, and relieves the city, 22.—Lays fiege to Toulon, 34 —Joins the duke of Marlborough in Flanders, 35.—Commands the army on the Rhine, 39.—Arrives in England, 54. Repulfed at Denain, and compelled to raife the fiege of Landreci, 56.—Triumphs over the Ottomans, 107.—Oppofes the duke of Berwick on the Rhine, 251.

F

Fazakerly, Mr. his fpeech againft the extenfion of forfeitures for high treafon, ii. 88.

Ferdinand, prince, reaffembles the allied army at Stade, ii. 240.—Recovers Hanover, and compels the French to repafs the Rhine, 241.—Defeats the French army at Crevelt, 24.—Repulfed by Marefchal Broglio at Bergen, 245.—Gains a complete victory at Minden, 246.—Defeats the French at Warbourg, 251 —Defeats the French at Grabenftein, 259.—Takes the city of Caffel, 160

Ferdinand II. king of Spain, his acceffion, ii, 117 —Reftores to the Englifh their commercial privileges, 186.—Determined to maintain his neutrality, 163 —Offers his mediation to the courts of Verfailles and London, 164.—His exceffive grief at the lofs of the queen, and death, 271.

Finale, marquifate of, belonging to Genoa, fraudulently ceded to the king of Sardinia, ii. 48.

Fleury, cardinal, gains the reverfion of Lorraine for France, i. 253.—Offers the mediation of France to accommodate the differences between Spain and England, ii 10.— His death, 52.

Fox, right honourable Henry, his character, ii. 128.—Appointed principal fecretary of ftate, 169.—His fpirited reply to M. Rouille, 173. His motion for the introduction of foreign troops, 175.—Refigns his office, 185.—Appointed paymafter to the forces, 189.

Francis I. emperor of Germany, duke of Lorraine, elected emperor at Francfort, ii. 59.

Frederick V. king of Denmark, his acceffion, ii. 98.—Lofes his queen, daughter to the king of England, 137.

Frederick, king of Sweden, landgrave of Heffe Caffel, accedes to the crown on the refignation of his queen Ulrica, ii. 90.—His political fituation and deficient authority, 90—95.—Forced into a war with Ruffia, 96.—Dies—the amount of his fubfidies from England, 137.

Frederick

INDEX.

Frederick II. king of Pruſſia, ſucceeds to the crown on the demiſe of his father, ii. 14.—His unexpected invaſion of Sileſia, ibid.—Gains the battles of Molwitz and Czaſlaw, 18.—The entire province of Sileſia ceded to him by the treaty of Breſlau, ibid.—Invades Bohemia, and concludes a treaty with the emperor, 54.—Compelled to evacuate Bohemia with loſs, 55.—Opens the campaign in Sileſia, and defeats the Auſtrians at Friedburg, 59; and at Sohr, 60; and the Saxons at Keſſeldorff, ibid.—Signs a treaty of peace at Dreſden, ibid Oppoſes the election of a king of the Romans, 140. Signs a treaty of alliance with the king of Great Britain, 165.—Enters the electorate of Saxony, and compels the whole Saxon army to capitulate, 233.—Fights an indeciſive battle with the Auſtrians at Lowofchutz, 234.—Put under the ban of the empire, ibid.—Gains a complete victory over the prince of Lorraine at Prague, 235.—Defeated by Mareſchal Daun, at Kolin, 236 —Gains a complete victory the French at Roſbach, 237; and over the Auſtrians at Liſſa, ibid —— Becomes extremely popular in England, 239.—Subſidy treaty ſigned, 240.—Compelled to raiſe the ſiege of Olmutz, 242.—Defeats the Ruſſians at Zorndorf, 243.—Defeated by Mareſchal Daun at Hochkirchen, 244 —Relieves ſix cities beſieged by the enemy, ibid. Defeated with great loſs by the Ruſſians at Cunerſdorff, 248.——In imminent danger of being ſurrounded, 253.——Defeats general Laudohn at Lignitz, 254.——Defeats Mareſchal Daun at Torgau, 256.—Concludes a ſeparate peace with Ruſſia, 261 —Captures the fortreſs of Schweidnitz, 263 —Concludes a peace with the queen of Hungary at Hubertſburg, ibid.

Frederick, prince of Wales, arrives in England, i. 207.——Married to Auguſta Princeſs of Saxe Gotha, 277 —— Motion in the houſe of commons for ſettling one hundred thouſand pounds per annum on the prince, 277.—Divides in perſon againſt the Convention with Spain, ii. 9 —His reply to the king's meſſage, 34.—Again alienated from the court, 122.—His death, 124.

G

Gages, Count, de, ſucceeds the Duc de Montemar in the command of the Spaniſh army in Italy, ii 20,—Defeated by M. Traun, Campo Santo, 21 —His march acroſs the Appennines, 23 —Defeated by the Auſtrians at San Lazaro, 24; and Tortona, ibid.—Retires to Provence, 25.

Genoa, republic of, treated with flagrant injuſtice by the courts of Vienna and London, ii. 49.——Joins the confederacy againſt the queen of Hungary, 23, 49.——City of Genoa taken by the Auſtrians, 25.——Recovered by the heroic bravery of the Genoeſe, ibid.

George, prince of Denmark, his death and character, i. 33.

George I. his acceſſion and deſcent, i 65.—State of parties, 66.—His predilection for the Whigs and Diſſenters, 71.—Diſmiſſes the Tory miniſters, 72.—His remarkable proclamation for convening a parliament, 74.——Purchaſes of the king of Denmark the duchies of Bremen

INDEX.

Bremen and Verden, 98.—His aillance with France, ibid.—Causes the Swedish ambassador to be arrested, 99.——Quarrels with the Czar, 104.——Joins in the Quadruple alliance, 108.—Consequent war with Spain, 112.—Concludes a treaty of alliance with Sweden against the Czar, 120.——Sends a fleet into the Baltic, 122.—Restrains the violent proceedings of the Convocation, 131.—Recommends the limitation of the peerage, in a speech from the throne, 13 ; and the repeal of the test laws to the parliament of Ireland, 140.—Concludes a treaty of peace with Spain, 155.—Informs the parliament of a dangerous conspiracy, 157.——Declines to mediate between Spain and the Emperor, 173.—Treaty of Hanover, 174.—Sends a fleet into the Baltic, 182; to the Mediterranean, 184; to the West Indies, ibid——Revives the order of knights of the Bath, 186.—His letter to the king of Spain, 189.—Orders the imperial ambassador to depart the kingdom, 193—Preparations for war, 194.—Articles of accommodation signed at Aix-la-Chapelle, 196.—The king's death and character, 196, 197.

George II. his accession, 200—Concludes a treaty with Spain at Seville, 210—His angry mention of incendiaries, 216.—His remarkable speech from the throne, ibid.—Concludes a treaty of peace with the Emperor, 224.—Guarantees the Pragmatic sanction, 226.—Receives the investitures of Bremen and Verden, 243.—Extraordinary message to the house of commons, 259—Sends a fleet to the Tagus for the protection of Portugal, 271.——Declares war against Spain, ii. 11; and France, 51.—Signs a treaty of neutrality for Hanover, 16.—Takes the field in person, 46.—His fortunate escape at Dettingen, 47.—Concludes a treaty at Worms with the king of Sardinia, 48. His personal sacrifices for the public advantage, 117.—Signs a general treaty of peace at Aix-la-Chapelle, 120.——Sends hostages to France, 122.—Concludes subsidy-treaties with the electors of Mentz, Bavaria, Saxony, Cologne, and the elector Palatine, 137; and with the Landgrave of Hesse-Cassel, 164; and Russia, ibid.—Declares war against France, 185.—Concludes a subsidy treaty with Prussia, 240.—His spirited memorial to the Diet of the empire, 268.—His death and character, and review of his reign, 275.

Georgia, colony of, settled i. 224.

Goertz, baron, his machinations against England, i. 99—Arrested by order of the states-general, ibid. Vindicates his conduct, and is set at liberty, 100.- His death, 104.

Godolphin, earl of, created Lord High Treasurer, i. 8.—Connects himself with the Whigs, 10.—His exertions to accomplish the treaty of union, 25, 31.—Scurrilously attacked by Dr. Sacheverel, under the name of Volpone, 45.—Removed from his office, 51.—Unjust vote of censure passed on him, 52.

Goree, island of, reduced by commodore Keppel, ii. 204.

Guadaloupe, island of, conquered by the English, ii. 205.

H

Halifax, earl of, impeached by the commons, i. 4.—Made First Lord Commissioner of the Treasury, 72.- His death and character, 125.

Halifax,

INDEX.

Hallifax, earl of, his speech againſt the Hanoverian mercenaries, ii. 81.
—Town of Halifax founded under his patronage, 130.
Hanover, treaty of, i. 174.
Harcourt, lord, ſucceeds lord Cowper as lord chancellor, i. 51.——
Removed, 73 ——His propoſition reſpecting the earl of Oxford,
129.
Harcourt, earl of, reſigns his office as governor of the prince of Wales,
ii. 125.
Hardwick, earl of, created Lord High Chancellor, i. 186.—Removed
from his office, ii. 189.
Hawke, admiral defeats a French ſquadron commanded by M. Le
Tendeur, ii. 118.——Superſedes admiral Byng in the mediterranean,
179.—Makes an unſucceſsful attack on Rochefort, 190.—Defeats the
French fleet off Breſt, 207.
Hawley, general, defeated by the rebels at Falkirk, ii. 67.
Henley, Sir Robert, appointed lord keeper of the great ſeal, ii.
189.
Herring, archbiſhop of Canterbury, his character, i. 287.—His candor
and catholicism, ii. 119.
Heritable Juriſdictions, in Scotland, aboliſhed, ii. 117.
Hindoſtan, the country and its inhabitants deſcribed, ii. 207—216.
Hoadley, biſhop, his famous ſermon, i. 129.—His ſpeech againſt the
teſt laws, 133.
Hoſier, admiral, his diſaſtrous expedition to the Weſt Indies, i.
184.
Holt, lord chief juſtice, his ſpirited and upright conduct in oppoſition
to the houſe of commons, i. 12.
Howe, lord, his unfortunate death and amiable character, ii. 194.
Hungary, queen of, ſucceeds to the hereditary dominions of the houſe
of Auſtria, ii. 13.—Her diſtreſſes, 17.—Receives immenſe ſubſidies
from England, 32. 41. 115. 116. &c.—Forms an alliance with
France, 166.—Recalls her ambaſſador from England, 265.

I

Ireland, act declaratory of its dependence on England paſſed, i.
140.
Jekyl, Sir Joseph, his ſpeech at the trial of Sacheverel, i. 48.—He
oppoſes the ſyſtem of ſubſidies, 205.
Jenkins, his inhuman treatment by the captain of a Spaniſh guarda-
coſta, ii. 2.
Juan V. king of Portugal, his difference with the court of Spain, i.
270.—His death and character, ii. 134.
Johnſon, Sir William, defeats a body of French troops, ii. 160.—Gains
a ſecond victory, and becomes maſter of Niagara, 197.

K

Kennet, bishop of Peterborough, his speech against the test laws, i. 134.—Declaration against the bill for suppressing heresy, 152.

Khevenhuller, field-marcschal, his military character and achievements, ii. 18.

King, Sir Peter, one of the managers at the trial of Sacheverel, i. 46. —Created lord King, and lord high chancellor, 105.

L

Lally, M. takes Fort St. David's, ii. 228.—Compelled to raise the siege of Tanjore, ibid.—Captures the city of Arcot, 229.—Ineffectually besieges the city of Madras, ibid —Defeated by colonel Coote at Wandewash, ibid.—Surrenders Pondicherry, 231.

Lansdowne, lord, committed to the tower, i. 80.—His speech against the bill for repealing the test laws, 135.

Laudohn, Mareschal, decides the victory of Cunersdorff, ii. 249.— Defeats general Fouquet, and takes Glatz, 252.—Lays Breslau in ashes by a bombardment, ibid.—Defeated by the king of Prussia at Lignitz, 253.——Captures Schweidnitz by a *coup-de main*, 258.

Lawrence, general, his operations in India, ii. 221.

Legge, Right Hon. Henry Bilson, appointed chancellor of the Exchequer, ii. 145.——Dismissed from his office, 169.——Reinstated, 185.—A second time dismissed, 188 ; and again reinstated, 189.

Lestock, admiral, his misconduct off Toulon, ii. 99.—His miscarriage at Port l'Orient, 116.

Leopold, emperor dies, i. 20.

Lisbon, city of, destroyed by an earthquake, ii. 172.

Loudon, earl of, assembles the loyal clans in Scotland, ii. 65.—Appointed to the chief command in America, 161.—His dilatoriness and inactivity, ibid.—His unsuccessful expedition against Louisburg, 164. —Superseded in the command by general Abercrombie, 193.

Louis XIV. his advances for peace rejected, i. 44.—Death and character, 95.

Lutwyche, Mr. his excellent speech against the Roman Catholic bill, i. 165.

M

Macclesfield, earl of, succeeds lord Cowper as lord chancellor, i. 85.——Impeached and convicted of misdemeanors in office, ibid.

Madras

INDEX.

Madras, city of, taken by the French, ii. 116.—Restored by the peace of Aix-la-Chapelle, 121.

Mahmout V. emperor of the Turks, his unexpected elevation to the throne, i. 211.——Attempts to mediate a peace in Christendom, ii. 57.

Mansfield, earl of, his character, ii. 127.

Mathews, admiral, compels the king of Naples to sign a treaty of neutrality, ii. 20.—Supports the Corsicans, 98.——Threatens the bombardment of Civita Vecchia, ibid.—Engages the combined fleets off Toulon, 99.—His trial and unjust sentence, 100.

Mar, earl of, proclaims the Pretender in Scotland, i. 80.—Escapes to the continent, 82.——Makes application in vain for pardon, 109.

Marlborough, duke of, made captain-general of the forces of Great Britain, i. 8; and ambassador-extraordinary to the states-general, ibid.——Captures the cities of Venlo, Ruremond, Stevenswart, and Liege, 9.—Takes the city of Bonne, 10.—His march to the Danube, 17.—Victory of Schellenburg, ibid.—and of Blenheim, 18.—His march to the Moselle, and retreat, 20.—Attacks Mareschal Villeroy, and forces the French lines, ibid.—Victory at Ramilies, and conquest of the Spanish Netherlands, 21.—Battle of Oudenard, and capture of Lisle, 35; and of Tournay, 36.—Battle of Malplaquet, and capture of Mons, 37.—Towns of Douay, St. Venant, &c taken, ibid.—Appears for the last time at the head of the grand army, 39.—Penetrates the French lines at Arleux, 40.—Takes Bouchaine, ibid. Divested of his civil and military employments, ibid.—Inquiry instituted by the house of commons into his conduct, 52.—Censured, ibid.—Prosecuted, ibid.—Reinstated in his offices, and command of the army, by king George, 73.—His death and character, 147.

Mecklenburg, affairs of, i. 121.

Meer-Jaffier-Ali-Khan, his conspiracy against Surajah Doula, ii. 225.—His advancement to the Musnud, 227.

Methodism, rise of, i. 273

Methuen, Sir Paul, appointed secretary of State, but resigns in disgust, i. 102.—Opposes the excise bill, 247.

Militia bill, ii. 264.

Minorca, island of, invaded and captured by the French, ii. 179.

Molesworth, lord, his speech against the alliance with Sweden, i. 154.—His memorable observation repeated, 217.

Monckton, colonel, his successful exertions in Nova Scotia, ii. 163.—Gallantry at Quebec, 201.

Montcalm, Monsieur de, makes himself master of Oswego, ii. 161; of Fort William Henry, 163.——Repulses the English at Montmorenci, 199.——Defeated and slain at the battle of Quebec, 202.

Mordaunt, Sir John, his unfortunate expedition to Rochefort, ii. 190.—His trial and unexpected acquittal, 191.

Murray, general, appointed to the government of Quebec, ii. 202.—His gallant defence of that city, ibid.—He co-operates with general Amherst in the reduction of Montreal, 203.

VOL. II.   U   *Newcastle*

N

Newcastle, duke of, secretary of state, his character, i. 201.—His impenetrable secrecy, 287.—Resigns and is reinstated, ii. 114.—Presents a regency bill to parliament, 134.—His dislike to "new-fangled things," 135.—Advanced to the office of first commissioner of the treasury, 145.—His incapacity for government, ibid.—Permits the barbarous execution of Dr. Cameron, 146.—His weak and haughty treatment of the Parliament of Ireland, ibid.—His empty and artificial professions, 170.—His political portrait, 172.—His eager vindication of his own indiscretion and misconduct, 181.—Resigns, 185.—Reinstated in consequence of a coalition of parties, 189.

Nottingham, earl of, opposes the peace of Utrecht, i. 54.—Revives the occasional conformity bill, 55.—Constituted president of the council, 73.—Resigns, and opposes the septennial bill, 87.—Defends the doctrine of the Trinity against professor Whiston, 150.—Brings in a bill for the suppression of heresy and blasphemy, 151.—Ridiculed by Swift, 153.

O

Occasional Conformity Bill passed by the commons, and rejected by the lords, i. 9.——Again passed and rejected, 10.—Passes into a law, 54.—Repealed, 135.

Onslow, Arthur, Esq chosen speaker of the house of commons, i. 204.—His animated address to the king, ii. 176.

Orange. prince of, marries the princess-royal of England, i. 267.——His character, ibid.——Declared hereditary Stadtholder, ii. 71.——His death, 137.

Orleans, duke of, appointed regent of France, i. 97.—Enters into an alliance with the king of England, ibid.——Dies——his character, 172.

Ormond, duke of, fails in his attempt on Cadiz, but takes Vigo, i. 9.—Succeeds the duke of Marlborough in the command of the army, 51.—Co-operates with prince Eugene in the siege of Quesnoy, 55.—Proclaims an armistice with France, ibid.—Departs for England, ibid.—Impeached of high treason, 76.—Withdraws to the continent, ibid.—Enters into the service of the Pretender, 77.—Appointed to the command of an armament for the invasion of Great Britain, 118.

Oxford, Robert Harley, earl of, dismissed from his office of secretary of state, i. 43.—Appointed Chancellor of the Exchequer, 51; and Lord High Treasurer, 5.—His character, 57.—Removed from his office, 62.—Impeached of high treason, 75.—His defence and commitment, 78.—His acquittal, 120.

P

Palms, M. his insolent memorial, i. 191.—Ordered to depart the kingdom, 193.

Peerage Bill introduced, i. 137; and rejected, 138.

Pelham, right hon. Henry, secretary at war, his character, i. 201.—— appointed first commissioner of the treasury, and chancellor of the exchequer, ii 101.—Reduces the interest of the public funds, 131.—Patronizes the Jew-naturalization bill, 142; which is repealed, 143. —His death, ibid.—Review of his administration, 144.

Peter the Great, his resentment against the king of England, i. 103, 120.—His death and character, 181.

Peter II. emperor of Russia, his accession and death, i. 210.

Peter III. emperor of Russia, his deposition and death, ii, 261, 262.

Peterborough, earl of, conquers the kingdom of Valencia, i. 22.—Resigns his commission in anger, 23.—Opposes the bill for religious persecution, 152.

Philip V. king of Spain, resigns and resumes his crown, i. 169, 170.— His death, ii. 117.

Philip, infant of Spain, enters Savoy, and takes Chamberri, ii. 20.— Parma and Placentia ceded to him, 121.

Pitt, right hon. William, his speech in support of the motion of enquiry into the conduct of sir Robert Walpole, ii. 37.—His speech in support of the motion for discharging the Hanoverian mercenaries, 77.—Appointed paymaster of the forces, 121.—His political character, 127.—His observations on the Mutiny bill, 129.—On the right of search, 133.—Vehemently opposes a war on the continent, and is dismissed from his office, 169.—Appointed secretary of state, 185.— Delivers a royal message, which he does not support, 186.—A second time dismissed, 188; and again reinstated, 189.—His vigorous exertions, 190.—Engages with ardor in the German war, 238.—His reasons, 239.

Porteous, captain, his remarkable execution, i. 276.

Pragmatic Sanction, edict so called, i. 173.

Pulteney, right hon. William, resigns his office as secretary at war, i. 127.—Openly declares against the political system of the court, ibid. —Opposes the alienation of the sinking fund, 194.—Inveighs against grants for secret service, 206.——Exposes the inconsistent politics of the court, 235.—His name struck out of the list of privy counsellors, 239.——His retrospective view of the conduct of sir Robert Walpole, ii. 28.—Created earl of Bath, and loses the public confidence, 35.—Opposes the repeal of the septennial act. 36.

Q

Quadruple alliance concluded, i. 108.

Quakers, act passed in their favor, i. 156.

INDEX.

Qualification-act, of queen Anne, remarks upon it, ii. 273.
Quebec, city of, surrenders to the English, ii. 202.

R

Raymond, Sir Robert, his speech against the septennial bill, i. 92.
Riot act passed, i. 125.
Ripperda, duke of, his character and political projects, i. 178.
Robinson, Sir Thomas, appointed secretary of state, ii. 144.—Delivers a message from the king, 157.—Resigns his office, 169.
Rodney, admiral sir George, bombards the town of Havre-de-Grace, ii. 206.
Rooke, admiral sir George, captures the Spanish flota in the port of Vigo, i. 9.—Surprizes the fortress of Gibraltar, 19.

S

Sacheverel, Dr. his impeachment and its consequences, i. 45. 50.
Sandys, Mr. revives the place bill, i. 258.——His motion for the removal of sir Robert Walpole, ii. 28.—Appointed chancellor of the Exchequer, 35.—Opposes the repeal of the septennial act, 36.—Opposes the place bill, ibid.—Resigns his office, and is created a peer, 101.
Sardinia, island of, conquered by admiral sir John Leake, i. 36.——Ceded to the Emperor by the treaty of Al-Rastadt, 57.—Conquered by Spain, 106.——Re-conquered by the Imperialists and English, 118.——Transferred to the house of Savoy in exchange for Sicily, 108, 119.
Saxe, Marefchal, appointed commander in chief of the French army in Flanders, ii. 52.—Captures Menin, Ypres, and Furnes, ibid.—Invests Tournay, 62.—Defeats the allies at Fontenoy, and reduces the greater part of Flanders, 63.—Captures Antwerp and Mons, &c. 69.—Defeats the allies at Roucoux, ibid.—Invades Dutch Flanders, 70.——Defeats the allies at Laffeldt, 71.——Detaches Count Lowendahl. who takes Bergen-op-Zoom, 72.—Invests the city of Maestricht, 73.
Scarborough, earl of, opposes a dangerous motion of the duke of Marlborough, i. 257.—His character ibid.
Seaton, Mr. of Pitmeden, his speech in favor of the Union, i. 28.
Security, act of, passed by the Scottish parliament, i. 25.
Senegal, settlement of, reduced by commodore Marsh, ii. 204.
Septennial act passed, i. 95.—Attempt to repeal it, 253.
Seville, treaty of, i. 210.

Sherlock

INDEX.

Sherlock, bishop of Bangor, his remarkable declaration respecting regal influence, i. 223.

Shippen, William, his speech against the septennial bill, i. 88.—Against standing armies, 113.—Committed to the Tower, 115.——His unbroken spirit, 117.—Opposes the increase of the civil list revenue, 204.—Opposes the farther continuance of the standing army, 245.—His speech against unlimited votes of credit, 260.—His opposition to continental subsidies and connections, ii. 32, 33.

Sleswick, duchy of, guaranteed by Hanover to Denmark, i. 98 ——by Great Britain, 121.—By the emperor and Russia, with remarkable attendant circumstances, 229.

South Sea bill introduced and passed, i. 142.—Its fatal consequences, 144.

Su-rajah-Doula, his character and barbarous conduct, ii. 227.—His defeat and death, ibid.

Stair, earl of, appointed ambassador to France, i. 97.—Recalled, 141. —His spirited vindication of his conduct, ibid.—Appointed generalissimo of the continental army, ii. 42.—Gains the battle of Dettingen, 47.—Resigns, 50.—His character, 51.——Reinstated in his offices, ibid.

Stanislaus, king of Poland, besieged in Dantzic, i. 250.

Stanhope, general, conquers the island of Minorca, i. 36.—Routs the Spanish cavalry at Almanara, 38.—Surrounded and compelled to capitulate at Brihuega, 39.—Appointed manager at the impeachment of Sacheverel, 47.—Advanced to the post of secretary of state, 73. —Impeaches the duke of Ormond of high treason, 75.—Delivers a remarkable message from the king, 101.——Made first lord of the treasury, which he soon resigns, and is created an earl, 128.—Introduces a bill for the repeal of the occasional conformity, test, and schism acts, 131.—Another for the limitation of the peerage, 137. —His death, 145.

Steinhorst, lordship of, difference between Denmark and Hanover respecting it, i. 287.

Strafford, earl of, demands of the states the performance of their guarantee, i. 62.—His impeachment, 75.

Sunderland, earl of, removed from his office of secretary of state, i. 51.—Appointed to the government of Ireland, 73.—Succeeds Mr. Methuen as secretary of state, 128.—Appointed first lord of the treasury, ibid.—Compelled to a precipitate and disgraceful resignation, 144.—His death and character, 147.

Swift, dean of St. Patrick's, his insolence, i. 209.—His declaration concerning annual parliaments, ii. 108.

Sydenham, Mr. his speech in support of the motion for restoring annual parliaments, ii. 105.

T

Talbot, lord, appointed lord high chancellor, i. 186.—His death and character, ibid.

Tallard

INDEX.

Tallard, Marefchal, defeated and taken prifoner at Blenheim, i. 18.

Townshend, Vifcount, made fecretary of ftate, i. 73.—Appointed lord lieutenant of Ireland, but difmiffed from his office, 102.—Appointed a fecond time fecretary of ftate, 145.—His character, 146.

Traun, Marefchal, gains the battle of Campo Santo, ii. 21.—His able conduct in Alface, 53; and Bohemia, 55.

U

Unigenitus, bull fo called, its origin and confequences, ii. 150.

V

Vendome, Duc de, oppofes with reputation the duke of Marlborough in Flanders, i. 35.—Defeated at Oudenarde, 36.—Appointed to the chief command in Spain, and recovers Catalonia and Arragon, 38.

Vernon, admiral, takes Porto Bello with fix fhips only, ii. 11.—Fails in his attempt on Carthagena, 12.

Victor Amadeus, king of Sardinia, exchanges Sicily for Sardinia, i. 108. Refigns his crown, 210.—He attempts in vain to refume it, 244.

Villars, Marefchal, defeated at Malplaquet, i. 37.—His lines penetrated by the allied army, 40.—Defeats the allies at Denain, 55.—Takes Marchiennes, Douay, &c. ibid.—Affumes the command of the army in Lombardy, 252.——Expels the imperialifts from the Milanefe, ibid.—Dies, ibid.

Villeroy, Marefchal, defeated at Ramilies, i. 21.

W

Wake, Archbifhop of Canterbury, his declaration at the trial of Sacheverel, i. 48.—His oppofition to the repeal of the teft laws, &c. 132.—Moves for the commitment of the bill againft herefy, 151.—His death and character, 286.

Walpole, Sir Robert, appointed manager at the trial of Sacheverel, i. 47.—Chofen chairman of the fecret committee, 75.—Impeaches lord Bolingbroke of high treafon, ibid.—Succeeds the earl of Halifax as firft commiffioner of the treafury, but refigns in difguft, 96, 100. Declaims againft ftanding armies, 113.——Againft the continental politics of the court, 115.—Frames the project of the finking fund, 126.—Oppofes the bill for limiting the peerage, 168.—Declares againft the fouth fea bill, 143.——Reinftated in his office, 145.——Moves for a fubfidy to Sweden, 154.——Difclofes to the houfe of commons the particulars of a confpiracy againft the government, 158. —Introduces a penal bill againft the Roman Catholics, 164—His favor with the new king, 201.——Propofes an addition to the civil lift, 203.—Prefents a bill to parliament againft foreign loans, 215. —His extraordinary defence of the meafures recommended from the throne, 221.—His political character delineated, 240, 241.—His bill for the revival of the falt duties, 241.—His direct alienation of

the

INDEX.

the sinking fund, 246.—His excise bill, 248.—Opposes with singular sagacity, the dangerous motion of lord Morpeth, 256.—Delivers a message from the king, requiring an extraordinary vote of credit, 259.—Opposes the repeal of the test, 272.—His motives, ibid.——His reluctance to enter into a war with Spain, ii. 3.—His masterly vindication of the convention signed at the Pardo, 5.——Acts with vigor on the commencement of the war, 11.—His spirited reply to the motion for his removal from office, 30.—Is left in a minority in the new parliament, and in danger of impeachment, 34.—Resigns his office, and is created earl of Orford, ibid —Parliamentary inquiry into his conduct, 36.——Review of his administration, 38.——His death, 113.

Walpole, Horace, his speech in defence of the treaty of Hanover, i. 174.—Defends the treaty of Vienna, 235.—His singular assertion respecting the army, 245.—His speech in defence of votes of credit, 265.—Moves for a subsidy to Denmark, 269.—Known under the appellation of Balance-master, ibid.

Washington, major, his spirited message to the French governor on the Ohio, ii. 156.—Defends with vigor a post on the Ohio, 157.

Watson, admiral, his naval operations, death and character, ii. 225, 230.

Wharton, duke of, his malicious reflection on lord Stanhope, 145.—Opposes the heresy bill, 151.—Death and character, 152.

William, king, concludes with France the first and second treaties of partition, i. 3.—Revives the grand alliance, 5.—Summons a parliament, ibid.—His speech, ibid.—His death and character, 6.

Wolfe, general, distinguishes himself at the siege of Louisburg, ii. 190. Commands the expedition against Quebec, 198.—Lands his forces on the isle of Orleans, ibid.—Attacks the enemy at the falls of Montmorenci, and is repulsed, 199.—His apparently insurmountable embarrassments, 200.—His daring and successful attempt to gain the heights of Abraham, ibid.—Forces M. de Montcalm to a general engagement, ibid.—His heroic death in the moment of victory, 201.

Worms, treaty of, ii. 48.—Its abominable injustice, ibid.

Wyndham, Sir William, reprimanded by the Speaker, i. 74.—Committed to the Tower, 80.—His observations on the state of affairs, 188.—He opposes the alienation of the sinking fund, 246.—His memorable speech on the motion for repealing the septennial act, 254.—His remarks on the convention of Madrid, ii. 8.—His death and character, 9.

END OF THE SECOND VOLUME.

www.ingramcontent.com/pod-product-compliance
Lightning Source LLC
Chambersburg PA
CBHW031933290426
44108CB00011B/534